Psychodiagnostic Assessment of Children

Dimensional and Categorical Approaches

Edited by

Randy W. Kamphaus
Jonathan M. Campbell

JOHN WILEY & SONS, INC.

Copyright © 2006 by John Wiley & Sons, Inc. All rights reserved.

Published by John Wiley & Sons, Inc., Hoboken, New Jersey.
Published simultaneously in Canada.

This publication is designed to provide accurate and authoritative information in regard to the subject matter covered. It is sold with the understanding that the publisher is not engaged in rendering professional services. If legal, accounting, medical, psychological or any other expert assistance is required, the services of a competent professional person should be sought.

Designations used by companies to distinguish their products are often claimed as trademarks. In all instances where John Wiley & Sons, Inc. is aware of a claim, the product names appear in initial capital or all capital letters. Readers, however, should contact the appropriate companies for more complete information regarding trademarks and registration.

For general information on our other products and services or for technical support, please contact our Customer Care Department within the United States at (800) 762-2974, outside the United States at (317) 572-3993 or fax (317) 572-4002.

Wiley also publishes its books in a variety of electronic formats. Some content that appears in print may not be available in electronic books. For more information about Wiley products, visit our web site at www.wiley.com.

Library of Congress Cataloging-in-Publication Data:

Kamphaus, Randy W.
    Psychodiagnostic assessment of children : dimensional and categorical approaches / by Randy W. Kamphaus, Jonathan Campbell.
        p.   cm.
    Includes bibliographical references and index.
    ISBN-13: 978-0-471-21219-5 (cloth)
    ISBN-10: 0-471-21219-9 (cloth)
  1. Behavioral assessment of children. 2. Child psychopathology—Diagnosis. 3. Psychodiagnostics. I. Campbell, Jonathan. II. Title.
    RJ503.5.K38
    618.92′89—dc22

                                                                                2005044869

Printed in the United States of America.

10 9 8 7 6 5 4 3 2 1

To Norma, Ashley, and Natalie

—RWK

In memory of my grandparents,
Clay and Belva Campbell, Marcus and Alsie Carr,
Jerry and Gustava Martin

To my beautiful wife,
Joy Campbell, my daughter, Cassidy Greer,
and my son, John Hampton

—JMC

CONTENTS

Chapter 6

Depressive Disorders   **169**
Jonathan M. Campbell

Chapter 7

Anxiety Disorders   **211**
Jonathan M. Campbell

Chapter 8

Chapter 9 _____

Eating and Feeding Disorders   **283**

Kathryn F. Moon and Jonathan M. Campbell

Chapter 10_____

Chapter 11_____

Chapter 12 _____

Assessment and Diagnosis of Substance Use in Childhood and Adolescence   391
 Meghan C. VanDeventer and Randy W. Kamphaus

Chapter 13

Clusters of Child Adjustment 437

Erin T. Dowdy, Cheryl N. Hendry, and Randy W. Kamphaus

The process of making a diagnosis of a mental disorder is one of the principal duties of psychologists and psychiatrists, a duty and right preserved in numerous statutes governing the practice of medical and allied health professions. Psychologists, however, face the process of diagnosis conflicted, due to a chasm between two diagnostic traditions; the psychiatric and the psychometric. This text is intended to help psychologists, and psychiatric physicians, bridge this chasm in order to make diagnoses that are theoretically and empirically defensible and ultimately more useful for treating patients and conducting research.

The psychiatric and psychometric traditions differ in their most basic assumptions beginning at the level of definition. Diagnosis, for example, may be defined as, "The process of determining the nature of a disease etc.; the identification of a disease from a patient's symptoms etc.; a formal statement of this" (Simpson & Weiner, 1989). The psychometrician, on the other hand, often refers to the similar process of classification, where to classify may be defined as, "Arrange in classes; assign to a class" (Simpson & Weiner, 1989). Note that one crucial difference between the classification and diagnostic processes is the assumption of the presence of a disease state in the former. Still other differences are explicated in subsequent chapters but these definitions make clear that these traditions are, in some important ways, nearly orthogonal, making it difficult for clinicians to use them jointly as they are often called upon to do. It is hoped that this text will ease this process.

Although distinct, considerable evidence exists to suggest that these two assessment traditions each possess some evidence of empirical support. Subsequent chapters identify and discuss these two approaches to form a basis for diagnostic practice that capitalizes on the strengths of both.

Ultimately, however, a logical melding of these traditions is inadequate for the needs of science and practice. Modern measurement science has provided some statistical methodologies for combining these approaches that maximizes their reliability and validity. Specifically, latent profile and class analyses, taxometrics, and cluster analysis are gaining acceptance as more rigorous methods for "carving nature at its joints" for identifying distinct groups of individuals in a population with similar behavior, emotions, functional impairment, or mental health status. These newer ways of grouping individuals are discussed as appropriate because they, more than other scientific approaches, portend change and improvement in diagnostic practice for the future.

In addition to the more theoretical aspects of measurement and classification, the text is designed to illustrate how several current psychiatric, psychological, and educational diagnostic systems work in practice. To achieve this goal, we review theoretical constructs thought to be important in the classification of child and adolescent psychopathology and link the constructs to both current diagnostic systems and available measures. With this goal in mind, specific measures are identified and reviewed, albeit briefly, that were created for psychodiagnostic use with children and youth. A variety of tests are referred to in this book including some instruments that have been authored or coauthored by RWK. RWK, therefore, wishes to acknowledge that his coauthorship of the Behavior Assessment System for Children with Cecil R. Reynolds and other assessment instruments may represent a potential conflict of interest.

For the purpose of illustrating links between constructs, diagnostic criteria, and measurement, many chapters focus on a general class or group of disorders, such as depressive disorders, and include brief overviews of criteria necessary for formal diagnosis. Disorder-focused chapters also include case study material to illustrate how constructs are measured by traditional psychometric data and how such data may inform categorical diagnosis. Following each case study, the text includes a brief discussion regarding diagnostic decision making and outlines recommendations for psychological and educational intervention. General issues that affect psychodiagnosis, such as developmental aspects of psychopathology and comorbidity, are embedded within each chapter and discussed as related to the specific group of disorders.

RANDY W. KAMPHAUS, PhD
JONATHAN M. CAMPBELL, PhD

University of Georgia

The authors wish to acknowledge the efforts of the following students and coauthors: Dr. Juliana S. Bloom, Dr. Morris J. Cohen, Dr. Erin T. Dowdy, Mauricio A. García-Barrera, M.Ed., Dr. Cheryl N. Hendry, Carrah L. James, M.Ed., Dr. Anna P. Kroncke, Kathryn F. Moon, M.Ed., Dr. Matthew Quirk, Dr. Ellen W. Rowe, and Meghan C. VanDeventer, M.Ed, and appreciate their willingness to be mentored by us throughout this process.

RWK acknowledges his colleagues, students, and administrators at the University of Georgia, College of Education, and Department of Educational Psychology and Instructional Technology for their long-term support of his professional development.

JMC acknowledges the efforts of his parents, Marvin Campbell, Sarah Martin, and Dr. Marc Carr, in instilling a desire to pursue his goals and aspirations with passion. And, more important, to value and honor hard work, whatever form this might take. He also acknowledges the efforts of his academic and professional mentors, Dr. David M. McCord and Dr. Sam B. Morgan. Both have been instrumental in fostering creative and critical thought throughout his career and continue to offer sage advice. Finally, JMC acknowledges the encouragement of his wife, Joy. In addition to her unwavering support, he is indebted to for her willingness to serve as a sounding board and her critical proofreading eye. He also acknowledges the love and support of his children, Cassidy and Hampton. He is thankful for their energy, curiosity, creativity, empathy, and sense of humor, both are daily reminders of the utility and limitations of various theories of child development.

Randy W. Kamphaus, PhD
University of Georgia
Athens, Georgia

Jonathan M. Campbell, PhD
University of Georgia
Athens, Georgia

Juliana S. Bloom, PhD
Children's Hospital of Philadelphia
Philadelphia, Pennsylvania

Morris J. Cohen, EdD
Medical College of Georgia
Augusta, Georgia

Erin T. Dowdy, PhD
Children's Hospital Los Angeles
Los Angeles, California

Mauricio A. García-Barrera, MEd
University of Georgia
Athens, Georgia

Cheryl N. Hendry, PhD
Athens-Clarke County
  Public Schools
Athens, Georgia

Carrah L. James, MEd
University of Georgia
Athens, Georgia

Anna P. Kroncke, PhD
Atlanta City Schools
Atlanta, Georgia

Kathryn F. Moon, MEd
University of Georgia
Athens, Georgia

Matthew Quirk, PhD
California State University
Long Beach, California

Ellen W. Rowe, PhD
George Mason University
Fairfax, Virginia

Meghan C. VanDeventer, MEd
University of Georgia
Athens, Georgia

Classification and Diagnosis Concepts

**Randy W. Kamphaus, Ellen W. Rowe,
Erin T. Dowdy, and Cheryl N. Hendry**

1

Chapter

Defining Classification and Diagnosis

Psychological constructs are more enduring than diagnostic systems. This premise serves as an organizing principle underlying this text about the process of identifying children and adolescents who need a service: educational, health, mental health, prevention, monitoring, or any other type of service that promotes children's adjustment to their context of development.

Prerequisite to the process of service delivery is classification, a fundamental, continuously unfolding task that is relevant to all sciences, including the applied clinical process of making a mental health diagnosis. Biological taxonomies exist for classifying various animals and plants according to both common and distinct characteristics. Classification, due to its overarching nature, is a more important activity for a clinician to master than diagnosis—a far more restrictive term. Classification, for example, may lead to the provision of a variety of services, whereas diagnosis is designed to lead to identification and treatment of a disorder—in this text, a mental illness. Classification, the broader term, serves many purposes, diagnostic or

Portions of this chapter are adapted from the dissertation studies of Drs. Ellen W. Rowe, Erin T. Dowdy, and Cheryl N. Hendry.

otherwise, not the least of which is allowing for natural phenomena, be they disorders or theoretical constructs, to be better defined and measured to enhance our understanding of them.

Diagnosis, the type of classification that is the focus of this text, may be considered a specialized type of classification, one concerned with the categorization of diseases. Although psychiatric diagnostic processes were initiated long ago (Kamphaus, 2001), modern psychiatric diagnosis began with the work of Emil Kraepelin who proposed that a system be created for classifying mental illnesses according to their symptoms, causes (or etiologies), and course (progression of symptomatology). As in the medical sciences where conditions such as heart disease and high blood pressure are classified as separate diseases in psychiatric classification, disorders such as borderline personality disorder are classified separately from schizophrenia or panic disorder.

In spite of various objections and its imperfect nature (Kamphaus & Frick, 2002), the majority of mental health professionals concur that the basic purposes and inherent advantages of classification support its use and further development (Cantwell, 1996). Related to this assumption, Blashfield (1998) described five primary purposes for classification in psychopathology that also serve to illustrate its utilitarian properties:

1. Creation of a common professional nomenclature
2. Organization of information
3. Clinical description
4. Prediction of outcomes and treatment utility
5. The development of concepts upon which theories may be based

These goals, although sound and pragmatic, have yet to be achieved by any one classification system. The predominant diagnostic classification schemes do attempt to provide a common nomenclature, organize information, and clinically describe syndromes or patterns of behavior. Nevertheless, the reliability and validity of prevailing models have not been demonstrated adequately, nor has a clear line of research established expediency with regard to treatment and theory development (Kamphaus & Frick, 2002).

Categorical and Dimensional Methods

Two primary models of diagnostic classification have been presented in the psychopathology literature, categorical and dimensional. Categorical models are dichotomous, inferential in nature, involving the identification of qualitative differences in behavior that are based on clinical observations and careful history taking. The dichotomous nature of categorical approaches deems that an individual either has or does not have a disorder as long as predetermined criteria for that disorder are met. To date, categorical approaches such as the *Diagnostic and Statistical Manual of Mental Disorders, fourth edition, text revision* (*DSM-IV-TR;* American Psychiatric Association, 2000) and the Individuals with Disabilities Education Act (IDEA) are used most frequently in health and education, perhaps due in part to tradition and relative ease of application.

In comparison, dimensional classification methods are quantitative and empirical in nature, adopting the assumption that there are a number of behavior traits that all individuals possess in varying degrees that exist along a continuum. These traits or dimensions of behavior are typically derived from measures (e.g., behavior rating scales) through the use of multivariate statistical procedures such as cluster analysis, latent profile or class analysis, or factor analysis (Kamphaus & Frick, 2002). It has not been clearly demonstrated that either of these classification approaches optimally meets the criteria for the five purposes of diagnostic classification as outlined by Blashfield (1998).

The relative value of categorical or clinical-inferential, for example, the *DSM-IV-TR* (American Psychiatric Association, 2000) and dimensional or empirical, for example, Edelbrock and Achenbach (1980), classification methods has been frequently debated (Fletcher, 1985). However, an increasing body of literature has described the advantages of dimensional models (LaCombe, Kline, Lachar, Butkus, & Hillman, 1991). For example, Achenbach and McConaughy (1992) noted that the yes/no nature of categorical methods does not necessarily account for children whose problems vary in degree or severity. As a result, the shift between "normalcy" and psychopathology cannot be well understood with categorical methods since most high prevalence problem behaviors in children, such as inattention and hyperactivity, are not classifiable when below diagnostic threshold levels. Substantial evidence is emerging to suggest that child behavior problems such as inattention, hyperactivity, depression, and conduct problems, in fact, fall along continua in the population. Therefore, the continuous nature of these child behaviors is more appropriately measured with dimensional scales (Hudziak et al., 1998) rather than with categorical systems (Scahill et al., 1999).

Although not fully incorporated in popular diagnostic schemes, empirically based dimensional classification approaches have demonstrated their usefulness in the study of psychopathology. For example, dimensional approaches have demonstrated more predictive validity than categorical approaches (Fergusson & Horwood, 1995), as well as statistical reliability (Cantwell, 1996). Such methods also minimize the need for clinical judgment and inference (Haynes & O'Brien, 1988), provide greater sensitivity to the presence of comorbid conditions (Caron & Rutter, 1991), and have the ability to depict multiple symptom patterns in a given individual simultaneously (Cantwell, 1996). Further, and perhaps most importantly, the use of dimensional, person-oriented approaches to identify subtypes or clusters of individuals can lead to more efficient, streamlined subtype-specific intervention and prevention services (Achenbach, 1995; Bergman & Magnusson, 1997).

In one sense, a dimensional approach to classification can be viewed simply as another means of translating underlying latent traits into categories (e.g., internalizing/externalizing behaviors), thereby offering only a communicative alternative to existing classification schemes such as the *DSM-IV*. This point of view suggests that the ultimate goal of classification or diagnosis, the categorization of individuals into homogeneous groups with similarities, is shared by proponents of both categorical and dimensional methods, and arguments that these approaches are entirely distinct are simplistic.

Psychiatric Diagnostic Classification

Psychiatric classification models seek to place disorders into discrete categories as is characteristic of the *DSM-IV-TR*. The *DSM-IV* was published in 1994 and is currently the most widely used method of psychiatric classification in the United States (Beutler & Malik, 2002). The first *DSM* was published in 1952 by the American Psychiatric Association and included three main categories of psychopathology: mental deficiency, functional disorders, and organic brain symptoms. In 1968, the *DSM* was revised to include 11 major diagnostic categories (*DSM-II*) and in 1980 the third edition introduced a multiaxial system, the inclusion of explicit criteria, and many unsubstantiated theoretical inferences were removed. The *DSM-III-R* (American Psychiatric Association, 1987) emphasized empirical literature and the *DSM-IV* continued with this emphasis on empirical findings (Scotti & Morris, 2000). The *DSM-IV* reportedly made modest improvements in the reliability and validity of several diagnostic categories, but reliability estimates for many disorders of childhood and adolescence remain inadequate (Nathan & Langenbucher, 1999). The *DSM-IV* is recognized to be a categorical or taxonomic system of classification (Arend, Lavigne, Rosenbaum, Binns, & Christoffel, 1996) and is concerned with classifying mental disorders—significant distress, functional impairment, and/or special risk (House, 1999). This approach uses rules to determine membership in a category. Using these decision rules, disorders are seen as being either present or absent (Blashfield, 1998). While it appears that improvements have been made in the *DSM,* some have asserted that the categorical nature of this system has been shown to impede progress toward a more accurate system of classification (Jensen et al., 1993).

Characteristics of Psychiatric (Categorical) Diagnosis

First, diagnosis is made based on the presence of marker symptoms or deviant signs that define a syndrome (*DSM-IV-TR,* American Psychiatric Association, 2000). Each diagnostic category has a characteristic and unique set of symptoms or signs that are qualitatively different from "normal." Cancer cells, for example, are cells that differ qualitatively from healthy ones. Similarly, paranoia differs from caution, conducts disorder from mischief, anxiety disorder from occasional worry, clinical depression from normal bereavement, and social phobia from shyness, in quality. Qualitative differences are assessed via structured diagnostic and unstructured patient interviews, and history taking. An adolescent patient may be seen by a clinician for tearfulness and crying, loneliness, inability to sleep, and poor appetite accompanied by weight loss. These are all potential symptoms of depression but through historical interview it could be determined that their duration has been about 10 days and their onset was abrupt. Upon still further questioning, the clinician may discover that the patient broke off a long-term romantic relationship that apparently precipitated these problems. Although the patient experiences waves of sadness, she or he continues to enjoy the company of friends and has a generally optimistic outlook. In fact, the patient may state that she or he desires some medication just until the feelings of sadness pass. She or he is mostly concerned now about getting some sleep in order to be able to function better at work or school. This patient's expectations for improvement belie the presence of "negative affectivity" that is commonly associated with depression (Kamphaus & Frick, 2002). As the patient's history unfolds, it becomes increasingly clear that the quality of this individual's symptomatology differs from that of depression in duration and intensity, thus causing the clinician to be unwilling to classify or diagnose this symptom pattern as a case of depression.

Formal psychometric tests are less valuable for identifying qualitative differences in symptomatology necessary for making a *DSM* diagnosis leading to dependence in psychiatric diagnosis on interview methods of assessment. The mental status examination (see Kamphaus & Frick, 2002) is characteristic of psychiatric diagnosis and is used as a means for identifying qualitative differences in symptomatology. It is not "scored" or submitted to any type of quantitative analysis; not even the mathematical process of addition of symptoms. The method uses questions to clarify the nature of symptomatology. A child patient, for example, may report that he or she "hears things." The child might remark that, "I hear someone telling me to do bad things." After further questioning the clinician may learn that the child often worries about the bully in his classroom who threatens him in an effort to convince him to be disruptive in class. This child's explanation for "hearing voices" is not unlikely given that psychotic disorders are relatively rare in the population. This "innocent" response is therefore qualitatively different than a case of hearing voices that would suggest the presence of psychotic symptomatology in childhood. Such a response would be something like, "I hear terrorists telling me to kill my friends. I'm scared because they will not stop. I hear this all day long most days. I can't get it out of my head. I am afraid I will hurt someone because I think that if I do this then maybe they won't talk to me any more." Interview methods are ideal for clarifying the meaning of, and qualitative differences in, symptomatology.

Psychiatric syndromes are also mutually exclusive (e.g., mental retardation and autism, versus Asperger's syndrome) but potentially comorbid or co-occurring (e.g., diabetes and heart disease, Attention-Deficit/Hyperactivity Disorder and Tourette's syndrome, Conduct Disorder and depression). The assumption of distinctness is consistent with another assumption of psychiatric diagnosis—syndromes are presumed to be pathogenically distinct as well (i.e., to have differing etiologies). Not only do syndromes have presumed differing etiologies, they also have differing outcomes (e.g., morbidity differs significantly for stomach ulcers versus stomach cancer), and prognoses (e.g., schizophrenia is more debilitating versus dyslexia). Depression has a higher morbidity rate than dyslexia due to the higher risk of suicide associated with the former. In the case of psychiatric diagnosis, other outcomes may substitute for the rare occurrence of death. School drop out, criminality, substance abuse, and elevated risk for developing a more severe psychiatric disorder may serve as proxies for morbidity. Prognoses may differentiate mental health disorders on the basis of chronicity and intensity of services needed. Mental retardation and autism are examples of disorders with greater chronicity and continuing impairment, whereas phobias and separation anxiety disorder may not be chronic, nor are they as likely to require residential care or other more invasive services.

Psychiatric diagnosis, like general physical diagnosis, is categorical or dichotomous in that one either has the disorder or not (e.g., Attention-Deficit/Hyperactivity Disorder [ADHD], irritable bowel syndrome, clinical depression). One cannot be mildly, moderately, or severely pregnant, for example. Severity of symptoms along a continuum is not directly measured although it is "estimated" by the clinician. An exception is that the global assessment of functioning (GAF) code of the *DSM* system is used by the psychiatric clinician to rate severity of functional impairment. More commonly, however, *DSM* criteria do not exist to differentiate "severe" from "mild" ADHD, Conduct Disorder, generalized anxiety disorder, and so on.

Severity is not easily determined when interview methods are used as the primary method for diagnosis because they are not as amenable to quantitative analysis, an essential characteristic of a severity scale. Some aspects of physical diagnosis are amenable to quantitative measurement and the disorder can be rated by severity. Vision, disorders of height, and obesity are some examples. Generally, however, the *DSM* and IDEA classification systems do not apply diagnoses that are either based on or present classifications for severity.

Severity of psychiatric disorder is established readily when psychometric tests are incorporated into the diagnostic criteria. Mental retardation, for example, is not diagnosed based on qualitative criteria or via interview methods (Kamphaus, 2001). The presence of intelligence and adaptive behavior test scores are adequate to the task, and progressively lower test scores are associated with different comorbidities, outcomes, prognoses, and needs for care (American Association on Mental Retardation [AAMR], 2002). Mental retardation diagnosis provides an example of the progress of the development of the *DSM* criteria, toward incorporation of psychometric tests and other well-documented scientific improvements in classification.

Subtyping is common in psychiatric diagnosis. For example, there are numerous types of cancer, three types of ADHD, subtypes of depression, and early versus late onset conduct disorder. Diagnosis then sometimes resembles a decision tree where one must decide on the condition and within that, the subtype that best describes the individual's symptom cluster, age of onset, or other distinctive characteristics.

The extent to which subtyping of mental health diagnoses is of value is still open to debate. There is, for example, a large literature on subtypes of learning disabilities based on methods that have formed subgroups of individuals with different types of academic disabilities (Kamphaus, 2001). Controversy remains regarding the differentiation of ADHD subtypes as well (Kamphaus & Frick, 2002), although Scahill et al. (1999) have shown differences in functional impairment and comorbidity for children beneath and beyond the *DSM* diagnostic threshold for ADHD. Given that subtypes are at their essence new "types" or diagnoses that lie within diagnostic categories, their validity will likely always be more difficult to establish with clarity, especially in light of any lack of evidence of validity for the overall diagnostic category of which the subtype is likely to be a member. If, for example, the learning disability diagnostic category remains ill-defined (Dombrowski, Kamphaus, & Reynolds, 2004), then nonverbal, written expression, and other subtypes will of necessity be difficult to validate adequately.

Differential diagnosis is emphasized in psychiatric classification, thus, there is an emphasis on "rule outs," or determining whether or not there are alternative causes for the symptom presentation of a disorder. Inattention or hyperactivity symptoms of ADHD, for example, may be caused by a variety of disorders, inattention by clinical depression and hyperactivity by mania are just some examples (C. R. Reynolds & Kamphaus, 2004). The clinician must then decide, often using a very high level of inference, the primary "cause" of the symptoms in order to make the proper diagnosis.

History taking via interview is useful for this purpose because the method is particularly well-suited to the identification of qualitative variables such as age of onset of symptomatology, and developmental course of symptomatology. Through careful history taking, the onset and course of symptoms of various disorders may be identified in order to rule out alternative causes. A case of "sudden" onset of ADHD at age 16 illustrates the value of history taking. A referred adolescent could very well display the core symptoms of the disorder, hyperactivity/impulsivity and inattention, and nevertheless not have ADHD. History taking may reveal that the adolescent had a history of high academic achievement and placement in a program for gifted and talented children until the age of 12, was popular and well-liked up to this age, and was exposed to numerous stressors at about age 12 including the death of a favorite aunt, parental divorce, change of schools, association with a new substance abusing peer group, and removal from the gifted and talented program due to sudden poor achievement and motivation that resulted in low school marks. The sudden onset of the symptoms gathered via interview in this case and the presence of multiple stressors that coincided with the onset of symptoms of ADHD, suggest that ADHD may be effectively ruled out.

An associated practice in medical and psychiatric diagnostic assessment is that diagnosis of high frequency disorders should typically take place before the diagnosis of those with a low base rate of occurrence in the population (Kamphaus & Frick, 2002). A physician, for example, is more likely to label upper respiratory symptoms as either a common cold or influenza unless there are compelling symptoms of lung cancer such as clear laboratory findings. In the ADHD example, it may have been found that this 16-year-old is in fact experiencing symptoms of depression including suicidal ideation, anergy, anhedonia, and symptoms of conduct disorder such as lying, stealing, and insolence at school. Diagnosis of depression and conduct disorder may be warranted in this case more than bipolar disorder since the latter is of lower base rate with less prevalency among 16-year-olds in the population than is the case for adults. Bipolar disorder may eventually be diagnosed but more clinical findings will be necessary to confirm the diagnosis. Specifically, when torn between diagnostic decisions, clinicians are often advised to at least provisionally make the diagnosis of the higher frequency condition (e.g., depression) over a low frequency one (e.g., schizophrenia) to increase diagnostic accuracy.

Reliability and validity of *DSM* diagnoses tends to be lower than is characteristic of psychological tests (Sroufe, 1997; Widiger, 1992), a fact that is well known to clinicians. While interdiagnostician agreement of ADHD is very good with obtained correlations ranging from .60 to .80, this reliability is far inferior to composite scores on psychometric measures of intelligence tests that yield reliability coefficients of .95 and higher. Even child behavior rating scales completed by parents and teachers commonly have clinical scale reliabilities of .80 and higher with some scales (e.g., attention problems) having reliabilities as high as .90 (C. R. Reynolds & Kamphaus, 2004).

Overall, there are several strengths to using a categorical system, such as the *DSM*. The impact of operational diagnostic criteria in the *DSM-IV* has made it possible to increase diagnostic agreement;

improve the reporting on comorbidity, services, treatment, and outcomes; introduce rigorous diagnostic standards in research; provide an international reference system; and improve communication with consumers, health providers, and the public (Jablensky, 1999). Parsimony is another key strength of the *DSM*. This system of diagnosis provides a clear, concise description of disorders and the widespread use and familiarity with the *DSM* allows for ease of communication among professionals for consistent research and treatment development (Blashfield, 1998).

Disadvantages of a Categorical Method: According to the *DSM-IV-TR* (American Psychiatric Association, 1994), categorical classification is most appropriate when all members of a diagnostic disorder (i.e., class) are homogeneous, when the different diagnoses (i.e., classes) are mutually exclusive, and when the boundaries between diagnoses are clear. Typically, these criteria are not met when using the *DSM* as a classification tool. Individuals with the same diagnosis are likely to be heterogeneous, the boundaries between classes might be imperceptible, and different diagnoses are not completely exclusive (American Psychiatric Association, 1994). There seems to be a lack of "goodness of fit" between current categorical classification systems and "clinical reality" (Jablensky, 1999), as verified by empirical findings.

First, comorbidity is not well accounted for in categorical classification systems. There are a large number of individuals, at least one-third of current cases in the general population, who meet diagnostic criteria for more than one disorder (Wittchen, 1996). In fact, epidemiological surveys indicate that more than half of the individuals with one *DSM* diagnosis have at least one additional disorder (L. A. Clark, Watson, & Reynolds, 1995). This finding suggests that psychiatric illness is typically characterized by comorbidity, or that this current classification system fails to discriminate between disorders (Jablensky, 1999). In the anxiety and depression literature, for example, the high rate of comorbidity (up to 65%; *DSM-IV*) between the two disorders gives rise to the theory that they emanate from a "common nosological stream" (Chorpita, Plummer, & Moffit, 2000). Comorbidity seems to be the rule, rather than an exception

(Sroufe, 1997) and psychiatric systems of classification are not designed for adequate description of this co-occurrence of disorders.

Second, categorical classification systems fail to account for severity of symptoms, or quantitative differences among individuals with the same core symptoms (Kamphaus & Frick, 2002). Research suggests that there are quantitative differences in symptomatology for numerous behavioral and emotional disorders of childhood. Specifically, evidence demonstrates quantitative differences in symptoms of hyperactivity/impulsivity, attention problems, conduct problems, depression, and anxiety (Deater-Deckard, Reiss, Hetherington, & Plomin, 1997; Fergusson & Horwood, 1995; Hudziak et al., 1998; Hudziak, Wadsworth, Heath, & Achenbach, 1999; Nease, Volk, & Cass, 1999; Scahill et al., 1999). For example, Hudziak et al. (1999) tested whether attention problems in 2,100 children were continuously distributed in the population or categorically discrete and found that symptoms of inattention should be considered as continuously distributed. A similar study by Hudziak et al. (1998) found continuously distributed symptoms of inattention, hyperactivity, and the combination of the two in a sample of adolescent female twins.

Quantitative differences have also been found in symptoms of mood and anxiety disorders. A study by Nease et al. (1999) investigated the symptom severity of mood and anxiety symptoms and compared the degree of congruence with current *DSM* classification. This study suggested that individuals grouped by symptom severity, rather than type of symptom (as is done in the *DSM*) significantly explained differences in quality of life, independent of *DSM* diagnosis. The authors suggested that severity should be accounted for in classification models.

Third, this lack of attention to matters of severity indicates that categorical systems of classification are also not appropriate for classifying subsyndromal psychopathology (Cantwell, 1996). Scahill et al. (1999) studied the psychosocial and clinical correlates of ADHD in a community sample of 449 children and found that symptom severity was associated with higher levels of psychosocial severity. Additionally, they found that children beneath the diagnostic threshold for ADHD still possessed evidence of functional impairment in school; impairment nearly identical to children above the diagnostic threshold (Scahill et al., 1999). Furthermore, results from a study by Hudziak et al. (1999) indicate that imposing the structure of the *DSM*, or a categorical system, on symptoms that are quantitatively distributed might not identify children with significant problems. These results point to the limitations of purely categorical systems of classification that could fail to classify, or diagnose, children who will nevertheless experience functional impairment due to the use of essentially arbitrary diagnostic thresholds, because they are not grounded sufficiently in a strong program of research.

Fourth, psychiatric classification systems do not account for normally functioning or marginally functional behavioral systems. This lapse leads to difficulty in investigating phenomena such as healthy behavioral adjustment (Jensen, Watanabe, Richters, & Roper, 1996), variations in normality, the transitions between health and disease, and the endogenous and exogenous variables that affect these transitions (Rutter & Sroufe, 2000). The study of adaptive behavior or behavioral competency, and range of behaviors are also precluded by use of a categorical classification system.

Fifth, atypical disorders, such as those frequently diagnosed as "not otherwise specified" or "other," point to the shortcomings of current psychiatric classification systems (Jablensky, 1999). The discrete nature of categorical classification does not account for individuals who do not meet specific diagnostic criteria or meet criteria for "not otherwise specified" disorders. Heterogeneity within diagnostic categories and within individuals that display mixed symptom patterns leads clinicians to question the utility and validity of the categorical approach to classification (L. A. Clark et al., 1995). Clinical trials of classifications suggest that there is an unsatisfactory match between the diagnostic criteria and the actual symptom features of patients in 18% to 22% of cases (Regier, Kaelber, Roper, Rae, & Sartorius, 1994).

A final limitation of psychiatric classification systems is their excessive reliance on clinical judgment to make complex diagnostic decisions. Most all *DSM-IV* diagnoses rely entirely or primarily on the clinician's ability to elicit, integrate, and apply complex decision rules to information in an entirely unbiased or objective manner (Jablensky, 1999). Considerable research indicates that reliance on clinical judgment for classification purposes is inferior to purely actuarial methods (Achenbach, 1995; Dawes, Faust, & Meehl, 1989; Grove & Meehl, 1996). Clinicians are subjected to numerous biases when they engage in diagnostic decision making including: a tendency to refute disconfirming evidence, determining diagnoses before collecting all relevant data, and assigning a diagnosis with which they are most familiar (Lewczky, Garland, Hurlburt, Gearity, & Hough, 2003).

These studies highlight the growing concern that categorical classification methods, while convenient and parsimonious, inadequately represent current empirical knowledge and are insufficient to serve new research needs (Helzer & Hudziak, 2000). The categorical model of classification is based on the assumption that disorders form discrete categories. This premise contributes to a "fallacious belief that psychopathological processes constitute discrete entities, even medical diseases, when in fact they are merely concepts that help focus and coordinate our observations" (Millon, 1991). Such overarching problems with categorical classification have been cited as a major factor in hindering research in psychopathology (Arend et al., 1996).

Individuals with Disabilities Education Act

The Individuals with Disabilities Education Act (IDEA) legislation that mandates a free and appropriate public education for children with disabilities is not a diagnostic system per se, but the implementation regulations of IDEA have created a de facto diagnostic system because it is used routinely to "classify" individuals as eligible for special education or related services, or ineligible (see Table 1.1). The IDEA regulations provide definitions of a variety of disorders evident early in childhood including learning disabilities, mental retardation, and "emotional disturbance." The diagnoses of mental retardation, speech/language, ADHD, and other disorders are not well explicated in the regulations likely because these syndromes and their diagnosis are fully described in the *DSM*, American Association on Mental Retardation manual *Mental Retardation; Definition, Diagno-*

Table 1.1   **"Diagnostic" Criteria for Emotional Disturbance from the Individuals with Disabilities Education Act (1999)**

(i) The term means a condition exhibiting one or more of the following characteristics over a long period of time and to a marked degree that adversely affects a child's educational performance:

    (A) An inability to learn that cannot be explained by intellectual, sensory, or health factors.

    (B) An inability to build or maintain satisfactory interpersonal relationships with peers and teachers.

    (C) Inappropriate types of behavior or feelings under normal circumstances.

    (D) A general pervasive mood of unhappiness or depression.

    (E) A tendency to develop physical symptoms or fears associated with personal or school problems.

(ii) The term includes schizophrenia. The term does not apply to children who are socially maladjusted, unless it is determined that they have an emotional disturbance. (Federal Register, March 12, 1999, Section 300.7, p. 12423)

---

sis, and Systems of Care (AAMR, 2002). The IDEA regulations, however, have proved influential for the diagnosis of "Specific Learning Disabilities," and have generated considerable controversy in this regard (Dombrowski et al., 2004). The category of "Emotional Disturbance" was essentially created by these regulations. Therein lay the controversy regarding eligibility for special education and related services; the school-based equivalent of obtaining a *DSM* diagnosis that makes a person eligible for mental health treatment and reimbursement from an insurance carrier.

The "diagnostic" criteria for emotional disturbance were inspired by a 1968 study by Eli Bower of the University of California at Berkeley. In this investigation, he took teacher ratings of child behavior in an effort to form subgroups of children who exhibited behaviors so deviant from their peers that they were likely to need specialized instruction and management at school. These subgroups are basically described in the regulations quoted in Table 1.1. Dr. Bower may not have anticipated, however, that his work would be incorporated into the original version of Public Law 94-142 some years later.

The IDEA criteria for emotional disturbance have thus been controversial since their origin, due to the fact that they do not align themselves in any significant way with the *DSM* or other criteria. As displayed in Table 1.1, they are also not particularly well developed leaving considerable room for interpretation, particularly subgroup one "an inability to learn that cannot be explained by intellectual, sensory, or health factors." This category of "disability by rule out" is particularly difficult to apply in everyday diagnostic practice in schools. Although classifications such as this one appear nearly impossible to apply, they are nevertheless applied daily by school-based multidisciplinary special education eligibility teams of psychologists, special educators, school administrators, counselors, social workers, and others. Thus, the question must be asked as to how these professionals are to apply such nebulous and unvalidated "diagnoses." The answer probably lies in substituting diagnoses or dimensions with some evidence of validity for those offered by IDEA as emotional disturbance.

The regulations do refer to the existence of a "condition exhibiting one or more of the following characteristics" suggesting that impairments or problems that do result in the application of diagnoses by some other system such as the *DSM* would be harder to justify as meeting the criteria. In addition, the condition must exist "over a long period of time and to a marked degree," suggesting that transient problems due to bereavement, and a mental health disorder of a known mild symptomatology such as adjustment to parental divorce, would not be sufficient to warrant an IDEA "diagnosis." Finally, the condition must be one that "adversely affects a child's educational performance," which may indicate that a child with clinical depression or ADHD, who is in the gifted education program and receiving marks of A would be difficult to classify under IDEA.

With these prescriptions in mind, the remaining five categories of emotional disturbance become somewhat easier to apply. Even the ill-defined first criterion is not met in the absence of a condition that is not diagnosable by any other diagnostic system such as the *DSM*, and is associated with significant behavioral or emotional impairment, that is long standing and accompanied by substandard educational performance.

The second and third areas of eligibility involve an "inability to build or maintain satisfactory interpersonal relationships with peers and teachers," or "inappropriate types of behavior or feelings under normal circumstances." Conditions that may be associated with such impairment may include schizophrenia and autism spectrum disorders. The fourth area of eligibility requires "a general pervasive mood of unhappiness or depression," and the fifth area, "a tendency to develop physical symptoms or fears associated with personal or school problems." *DSM* diagnoses of major depression, bipolar disorder, and somatiform disorders may meet these requirements. The IDEA criteria do specifically acknowledge that schizophrenia is a qualified disorder, however, the relationship of other *DSM* diagnoses to IDEA has to be inferred. The lack of prescription is negative in the sense that clinicians do not have the specific guidance that they desire to ensure compliance with IDEA. Alternatively, little specificity provides the flexibility to utilize new diagnostic categories as they are identified or old ones that are significantly modified by research.

The IDEA explicitly states an important exclusionary criterion as well by stating that "social maladjustment" in the absence of an emotional disturbance, does not constitute an emotional disturbance that makes a child eligible for special education and related services. Social maladjustment introduces yet another term and classification that does not have an agreed on definition. The lack of specificity of this construct further compromises the ability of the school-based clinician to make a correct classification. The introduction of this term has caused some to question whether or not *DSM* diagnoses of Conduct Disorder or Oppositional Defiant Disorder constitute cases of social maladjustment, emotional disturbance, or both. The inclusion of these "disruptive" behavior disorders in the *DSM* suggests that they are clinical syndromes and not forms of social maladjustment; a social rather than mental health condition.

In effect, the IDEA system is another categorical classification system that requires diagnoses from another categorical system, the *DSM*, to classify an individual as having an emotional disturbance. In this sense, the IDEA and *DSM* systems are hierarchically related to one another.

Dimensional Methods of Classification

The dimensional approach to classification assumes that behavior does not occur dichotomously, but rather along a continuum. Descriptive variables such as symptoms, behaviors, and/or scales from a rating scale are collected and combined with other correlated variables to form a dimension. Thus, the dimension summarizes information about the descriptive variables into an abstract, higher order variable (Blashfield, 1998). There are a smaller number of dimensions than descriptive variables that should account for much of the systematic reliable variance that would be present if using the larger number of variables (Blashfield, 1998). A major assumption of this dimensional model is that individuals can exist anywhere along these dimensions (Scotti & Morris, 2000). Dimensional models classify individuals based on quantification of attributes and best describe behaviors that do not have clear boundaries and are distributed continuously (American Psychiatric Association, 1994).

Dimensional classification stands in direct contrast to categorical classification systems. Dimensional methods are also not widely used or sanctioned for use to diagnose mental disorders, because they have not been fully incorporated into either the *DSM* or IDEA classification systems. These latter classification systems have dominated diagnostic practice in the United States and elsewhere.

The unit of measurement in dimensional systems is the scale not the symptom or item level of measurement. Dimensional systems that have their roots in psychometric assessment and the attempt to measure "latent traits" or "latent constructs" made up of multiple indicators (i.e., items) or behaviors (Kamphaus, 2001; Kamphaus & Frick, 2002). These traits in turn are thought to be distributed dimensionally in the population as continua, thus making it possible to assess "severity" or the amount of the latent trait possessed by an individual. In this way of thinking, depression, anxiety, hyperactivity, and social withdrawal are not considered disorders but latent constructs that are more or less characteristic of individuals. Children may have less depression than average, modal depression, or considerably more of the depression construct than average; enough to cause functional impairment in an important developmental context such as school.

Norm referencing is used to define deviance or the level of a construct assessed in psychometric assessment. In other words, the standard for deviance is not set a priori by theory, but rather it is set a posteriori by comparing an individual to a population of interest. Norm referencing is powerful in that it allows a clinician to state with considerable accuracy the level of the construct possessed by a child. In comparison to saying the child has clinical depression as defined by the *DSM,* dimensional classification allows the clinician to say that the child's depression is equal to our worse that 70%, 80%, 98%, or 99% of children of the same age. These percentile ranks provide definitive answers to parents' or others' questions about the severity of a child's depression.

Dimensional assessment methods such as child behavior rating scales also typically assess adaptive traits or competencies as part of the classification process (C. R. Reynolds & Kamphaus, 2004). A child's classification depends not only on the presence of psychopathology but also on the absence of important competencies. In this way dimensional assessment is similar to some aspects of physical assessment. A child, for example, may be diagnosed as having a growth disorder if his or height is insufficient in comparison to same age peers, or hearing is inadequately developed.

The collection of evidence of reliability and validity is emphasized to a greater extent in dimensional assessment. Dimensional assessment scales such as the MMPI-A have known evidence of reliability and validity allowing clinicians to estimate the amount of error associated with a classification. If, for example, a depression scale has an internal consistency coefficient of .90, the clinician knows that the classification of depression at or above the 98th percentile rank has a 10% error rate associated with it and 90% reliable variance. The specification of error for *DSM* or IDEA diagnoses by contrast is not as readily obtained or included in written or oral communication by clinicians.

Overall, dimensional measures require less inference on the part of the diagnostician. If a child scores highly on a dimensional scale the construct is possessed in abundance unless there are clear contraindications. Using height as an example again, there is little reason to suspect problems with the ruler unless the child was standing on her or his toes or slouching considerably.

Advantages of Dimensional Methods of Classification

Dimensional methods account for many of the shortcomings of categorical methods of classification. First, dimensional methods more adequately portray the agreement among many research findings supporting the notion that symptomatology for children and adolescents is dimensionally distributed. Research suggests that children who qualify for diagnoses are quantitatively different (Sroufe, 1997) and that these quantitative differences are of greater import than qualitative differences for classification purposes (Deater-Deckard et al., 1997). Furthermore, it has been argued that knowing the exact nature of disorder may be less important than assessing for the severity of dysfunction (L. A. Clark et al., 1995). Dimensional classification models are in accordance with research regarding quantitative differences and take severity into account by calculating the individual's deviance from the norm.

Second, the use of dimensional classification methods minimizes many of the problems associated with the diagnosis of comorbidity and atypical, mixed, and not otherwise specified categories (Westen, Heim, Morrison, Patterson, & Campbell, 2002). Dimensional methods report clinical symptom presentations that might be subthreshold, comorbid, or atypical in a categorical system of classification, thus communicating a wider range of information.

Third, dimensional systems increase the reliability and validity of diagnosis (American Psychiatric Association, 1994). Evidence suggests that there are not true, or clinically meaningful, qualitative points where individuals should be categorically separated, or "diagnosed" (Sroufe, 1997; Widiger, 1992), supporting the need for dimensional methods. When quantitative symptoms are artificially converted to a dichotomous, categorical scale, reliable and valid information is lost (Widiger, 1992). Therefore, reliability and validity are increased by using a set of scores examined through factor analysis and other statistical approaches (Arend et al., 1996), and by not arbitrarily forming dichotomous variables from continuous variables (Westen et al., 2002).

Disadvantages of Dimensional Methods of Classification

Limitations of dimensional models of classification are also apparent. These limitations include descriptors that are less concise and familiar to researchers and clinicians, thus limiting the ease of communication afforded by categorical systems. However, the description offered by psychiatric categorical systems might be misleading because they will not always recognize the complexity that exists within individuals (Widiger, 1992). Another limitation of dimensional methods is that agreement has not been reached as to the optimal dimensions that should be used for classification purposes (American Psychiatric Association, 1994). Furthermore, dimensional methods that require inferential statistics and computational methods might prove cumbersome and more difficult to understand than a categorical name. To date, dimensional methods have been rejected as an alternative to categorical methods due to issues such as clinical utility and lack of consensus (L. A. Clark et al., 1995).

There continues to be an inadequate number of studies that directly examine the relationship between categorical and dimensional classification systems (Arend et al., 1996). It has been suggested that categorical methods might be more useful for some syndromes, while dimensional methods might better explain others (Meehl, 1995). A study by Arend et al. (1996) compared categorical and dimensional approaches to classification in preschool children and failed to provide sufficient evidence to suggest one approach over the other. As there are significant advantages and disadvantages of both categorical and dimensional approaches to classification, and superiority among the systems has not yet been unequivocally established, it has been recommended that the systems be used in combination to learn the strengths and weaknesses of each system (Mattison & Spitznagel, 1999; Widiger, 1992). However, issues such as comorbidity continue to produce complicated results when the two systems are used together, and neither classification method may adequately deal with the issue of comorbidity (Nathan & Langenbucher, 1999).

Combining Categorical and Dimensional Diagnostic Methods

The forgoing discussion of categorical and dimensional approaches to classification is necessarily oversimplified in order to draw conceptual distinctions between research traditions. The *DSM* system, for example, has increasingly adopted dimensional assessment practices with each new edition. The *DSM-IV-TR* provides lists of symptoms with "cut scores" beyond which diagnoses of ADHD or several other disorders are made. In fact, in the case of ADHD, the diagnosis is almost purely quantitative and dimensional, in that the nature of the specific symptoms of hyperactivity/impulsivity and inattention is not as important for making the diagnosis as the number of symptoms acknowledged by the parent or child reporter. This methodology of symptom counting and derivation of cut scores associated with the presence of functional impairment, with more emphasis on the number than type of symptoms represents the influence of dimensional, quantitative, and psychometric methods on the popular psychiatric nosology.

This rapprochement between methods has been a long time in the making, having its roots in "composite" models of classification espoused by Skinner (1981) and others. According to Skinner,

> *The more complex structures offer considerable potential for the integration of seemingly disparate theories of abnormal behavior. For instance, the debate over dimensions versus categories has generated a heated controversy throughout the history of psychiatry. . . . Hybrid models, such as the class-quantitative structure, may prove fruitful for integrating the distinctive merits of each approach. . . . Perhaps a real breakthrough in our understanding of psychiatric disorders awaits the skillful use of composite models. (p. 72)*

Although the focus of this book is on the practical enterprises of classification and diagnosis, the clinician would be disserved by merely offering yet another manual for using the *DSM* or IDEA. Given the eventual changes in diagnostic systems, and their history of significant change from version to version, the clinician is best served by developing a deeper understanding of how the process of diagnosis relates to the overarching process of classification, and the need to continually improve both processes. For these reasons, the clinician is advised to begin to anticipate changes in diagnostic systems based on current and previous trends, the most promising one being the development of composite models of classification that have been advised for decades, are partially incorporated in the *DSM*, and capitalize on diverse views of classification science.

There is a continuing desire to take the process of diagnosis beyond the realm of description, to the point of understanding, by integrating theory with classification research (Skinner, 1981). This point of view was echoed in the opening sentence of this book where it was suggested that constructs such as anxiety, depression, hyperactivity, and so on, are more enduring than versions of the *DSM* or other classification systems. Theories of these constructs should inform classification research which, in turn inform theory in a continuing interplay that pushes the boundaries of the fields of psychopathology and classification science forward in productive directions (Skinner, 1981).

With humility about the current state of diagnostic system development and knowledge of psychopathology, the reader is advised to begin the diagnostic process by developing an understanding of both construct theory and classification. Each chapter in this volume aims to integrate the two. In addition, each succeeding chapter recommends currently accepted categorical and dimensional methods for diagnosing each disorder or class of disorders under consideration.

A Composite Diagnostic Model

First, the construct, diagnosis, or pathologies under consideration should first be defined based on theory because theories influence the choice of assessment methods, and the relative importance of various methodologies for making a diagnosis or classification. The diagnostic process represents a case of concept mapping where the clinician determines the fit between their theory of a disorder, the assessment results collected, and a diagnostic system template for disorder.

If, for example, one adopts the theory that ADHD is comprised of two core sets of symptoms that are continuously distributed in the population (Kamphaus & Frick, 2002), then an assessment of these dimensions takes on importance for assessment design. The inattention and hyperactivity/impulsivity core symptoms of ADHD, like several other important constructs, are clearly more amenable to dimensional assessment than some other symptoms.

Childhood disorders that are related to the well documented dimensions of externalizing and internalizing disorders are differentiated well by dimensional methods and measures of these constructs (Achenbach & Edelbrock, 1978). The disorders related to these constructs, with symptoms that are known to be distributed as continua in the population are:

- Inattention (Hudziak et al., 1999; Scahill et al., 1999)
- Hyperactivity/impulsivity (Barkley, 1996; Deater-Deckard et al., 1997)
- Conduct problems, defiance, and oppositional behaviors (Fergusson & Horwood, 1995; Hinshaw & Anderson, 1996)
- Anxiety and somatization (*DSM-IV*; American Psychiatric Association, 1994)
- Depression (Hammen & Rudolph, 1996)
- Learning disability (Dombrowski et al., 2004)
- Mental retardation (Kamphaus, 2001)

Disorders associated with these constructs or combinations of them should emphasize assessment via methods designed to assess quantitative differences such as the ubiquitous and practical behavior rating scales (Hart & Lahey, 1999).

Still other disorders differ qualitatively from normality like schizotypy and schizophrenia (Beauchaine, 2003). These disorders require the assessment of individual deviant signs (symptoms) rather than aggregating symptoms into dimensions in order to produce a score. Similarly, substance abuse disorders are best assessed by collecting specific information about the type and frequency of inappropriate use of substances, and eating disorders by collecting information about deviant eating behaviors. A theory of schizophrenia may posit that patients with this disorder display qualitative differences in social interactions, thinking, and affect that influence adjustment. This theoretical conceptualization dictates that interview and other methods of assessment be used to document the existence of deviant signs indicative of the disorder.

Second, assessment methods are selected based on theory and current scientific understanding of the syndrome under consideration. Disorders that are better represented quantitatively would benefit from dimensional or psychometric assessment methods such as:

- Behavior rating scales completed by teachers and parents
- Self-report inventories of constructs of interest such as depression, anxiety, hyperactivity, inattention, and conduct problems
- Formal cognitive tests of intelligence and academic achievement
- Tests of adaptive behavior and related behavior competencies and skills

Measures of individual symptoms and qualitative factors associated with a diagnosis could include:

- Structured diagnostic interview schedules
- Unstructured or semi-structured interviews and mental status examinations
- Collection of symptom, medical, educational, cultural/linguistic, and other history
- Classroom observations, structured observation schedules, responses to projective stimuli, and clinical observations
- Laboratory assessment such as serum alcohol content and body weight

Third, data are compared to the known dimensional and symptom characteristics of a disorder to determine match or mismatch to the a priori theory of the disorder or to a template offered in a diagnostic system. These processes are not identical, although they often are considered the same in everyday practice. One may make a diagnosis consistent with theory that is inconsistent with a diagnostic system if theory and science has outpaced the diagnostic system. This scenario is likely given that science and theory development continue while a diagnostic system remains stagnant while waiting to be updated. It is therefore a certainty that clinicians may make diagnoses that are either not included in the *DSM* or inconsistent with the *DSM* criteria since the *DSM* was last fully revised in 1994. Making the diagnosis of auditory processing disorder or bipolar disorder for a 5-year-old is not unlike "off-label" prescribing of medications. Hence, there is a constant tension between the pace of theory development based on scientific findings and the classifications offered by diagnostic systems.

These three processes of theory specification, assessment method selection, and data collection based on theory, and matching of findings to the a priori theory or to a diagnostic system, are demonstrated in the chapters that follow for a variety of disorders of childhood.

Conclusion

Diagnosis is a specialized type of classification with the latter taking on increased importance for the work of mental health service providers of all professions but particularly for psychiatrists and psychologists who have done much of the "diagnosing" historically. There is far more interest today in classifying children as "healthy," "resilient," "at-risk," and "subsyndromal," than was the case previously.

Related to the increased focus on the broader purpose of classification is the improved appreciation for the fact that much of children's behavior patterns and emotional tendencies are continuously distributed in the population, not unlike the constructs of intelligence and academic achievement. Granted, some of these distributions are quite skewed (e.g., conduct problems) but there are nevertheless meaningful differences in severity and degree of health along the distribution of these constructs. Accompanying this knowledge is an increased dependence on the use of behavior rating scales and related technologies for the classification and diagnosis of children (Hart & Lahey, 1999).

Although nascent there is an increased interest in using theory to guide the assessment, classification, and diagnostic processes. Whether formally acknowledged or not, all clinicians enter into the assessment process with a guiding theory. Clinicians, for example, do not emphasize the use of laboratory measures (e.g., blood tests) for the assessment of conduct disorder because the biological locus of such problems is not yet well established.

The chapters in this volume reflect all three of these trends. Each chapter discusses relevant theories of each disorder or class of disorders, uses theory to map an assessment strategy, defines the constructs or dimensions of interest, and guides the practitioner through the processes of diagnosis and a variety of other classification decisions depending on the syndrome.

Interpretation of Findings

Randy W. Kamphaus

2
Chapter

The process of deriving meaning from assessment results and communicating those findings effectively is the central and sometimes most challenging aspect of the diagnostic process. This work is made even more nuanced by the mixture of methods, qualitative versus quantitative, and diagnostic paradigms, categorical versus dimensional. This chapter presents a hybrid methodology that attempts to bridge these seemingly opposing views. Borrowing from an interpretation rubric offered by Kamphaus and Frick (2002), a 4-step interpretation method is offered:

1. Assess core constructs/symptoms and severity of same.
2. Assess onset and developmental course.
3. Rule out alternative causes.
4. Rule in comorbidities.

This framework, though straightforward at first glance, requires consideration of the tensions cited at the outset of this chapter and an additional consideration, of actuarial versus clinical methods. Our approach leans more toward the actuarial and evidence-based interpretation, as is clear from the notable absence of projective methods. With this premise in mind, the remainder of this chapter attempts to navigate among these tensions to foster interpretation that uses sound principles of measurement science as tempered by the fallible nature of diagnostic systems, clinical judgment, and imperfect data.

Assessing Core Constructs/Symptoms

The *DSM* approach to assessing symptoms involves a tally of the presence or absence of symptoms based on stated criteria. History taking is the method of choice for making this tally and determining if the number and, in some cases, quality of the symptoms meet the criteria stated. Dimensional measures, on the other hand, focus on the assessment of constructs with the goal of measuring a latent trait rather than specific symptoms of disorder. We propose that it is simultaneously important to assess the core latent constructs associated with a child's problems because constructs are more long-lived than the specific diagnostic criteria. Informant rating scales are ideal for this purpose in that they are often not linked to current diagnostic criteria, have detailed information on their reliability and validity available, and are norm-referenced (Kamphaus & Frick, 2002). We advise that clinicians use both methods to provide adequate understanding of both the constructs and symptoms that may be impairing daily functioning.

From a dimensional assessment perspective the five latent constructs that are well-documented as existing along continua should be assessed in all cases, namely, hyperactivity/impulsivity, attention problems, conduct problems, depression, and anxiety (see Chapter 1). Similarly, structured diagnostic interviews may be used to assess for the various symptoms of disorders that are consistent with referral questions. Dimensional assessment and categorical assessment are complimentary at this first stage of assessment in that while full symptom coverage is not necessary to assess the presence and severity of a construct it is nevertheless necessary to assess all symptoms of a categorically-defined disorder. In fact, Kamphaus and Frick observed that most rating scales did not assess all *DSM* symptoms of depression, typically vegetative symptoms such as weight gain/loss or sleep disturbance, necessitating some diagnostic interview assessment to ensure full coverage of symptoms.

The assessment of severity of symptoms or problem constructs varies substantially as noted in Chapter 1. It is necessary for the number of symptoms to meet or exceed *DSM* symptom counts (e.g., for ADHD diagnosis) in order to make a diagnosis. Once this threshold is achieved the severity of symptoms remains an important question, one that is best answered via norm-referenced dimensional assessment of relevant constructs.

The use of ratings scales to assess latent constructs raises additional questions about the definition of deviance. In the case of rating scales, deviance is assessed empirically via norm referencing with the addition of diagnostic convention. A common convention is that *T*-scores of about 70 (the term "about" is specifically used to encourage clinicians to use the standard error of measurement of obtained scores as a consideration) are considered "deviant" or "clinically significant." This cut criterion is probably the result of the precedent set by the Minnesota Multiphasic Personality Inventory literature, set by intelligence and academic and achievement testing, and the fact that such a score is about 2 standard deviations above the mean. In the case of intelligence and adaptive behavior testing for the purposes of mental retardation diagnosis, the cut score is also about 2 standard deviations above and below the mean, respectively. Such a cut score criterion may not be unreasonable if the goal is to ensure a fairly small base rate for deviance in the population, and an additional goal is to ensure that psychopathology is indeed associated with functional impairment (Bird, 1999).

This norm referencing then begs the question of the normative standard to use for assessing the deviance of the core constructs associated with a disorder. Behavior problem assessment via rating scale is unusual in that separate sex-based subgroup norms are commonly used for deriving *T*-scores. In direct contrast, this practice is rare in the assessment of constructs such as intelligence, academic achievement, and adaptive behavior, although sex differences occur for these constructs as well. Breast cancer provides a potential metaphor for thinking about this practice in that the sex differences in diagnostic rates of the disorder are huge, and yet a separate sex-based diagnostic standard, men's symptoms are compared only to those of other men to make the diagnosis of breast cancer for a male, is not used. In other words, for the most part, diagnostic systems such as the *DSM* are sex blind as is the case for the diagnosis of many medical conditions like breast cancer, heart disease, and diabetes in spite of the fact that large differences exist in prevalence of the disorders by sex group.

If separate sex-based norms are used; the sex differences for conduct problems, somatic complaints, and other problems that have been commonly identified to be at higher rates for either boys or girls would be erased or delimited. Given the well-established differences between the sexes on constructs such as aggression and somatic complaints (Kamphaus & Frick, 2002), more girls would be classified as having aggression problems and boys more somatization difficulties. The use of a combined sex norm group retains the sex differences in the population. Said another way, general combined-sex norms are desirable for making a diagnosis of a construct that is problematic, although separate sex-based norms may provide additional insights regarding treatment or other questions of interest. A general normative comparison using combined sex-group norms answers the question, "How severe is Miguel's hyperactivity in comparison to other children his age," whereas a sex-based comparison asks the question, "How severe is Martha's inattention in comparison to other girls her age?" With these considerations in mind we suggest that the process of assessing the severity of core constructs associated with a disorder begin with the use of a combined-sex general national normative sample norm-referenced comparison.

Another emerging convention is for the establishment of an at-risk range for the diagnosis of problem constructs, characterized by *T*-scores between about 60 and 70, this range is associated with functional impairment. For example, Ostrander and colleagues (1998) found that scores in this range (the low 60s) were associated with significant academic functional impairment in school due to attention problems.

Generally speaking, all disorders that nearly meet or exceed *DSM* criteria or *T*-scores of 60 and above on dimensional measures warrant consideration as important areas of possible diagnosis. The assessment of core symptoms and constructs is influenced to some extent by choice of informants or is it?

Variance between informants depends on the informants' extent of knowledge about the symptoms in question. For example, if the disorder is characterized by observable symptoms that are causing impairment in one setting in particular, as is the case for suspected Attention-Deficit/Hyperactivity Disorder (ADHD) in young school-age children. In this scenario the child's teacher may be the informant of choice for the history taking or diagnostic interview. Teachers are also particularly adept at assessing problems of inattention, a key temperamental variable that is associated with numerous social and psychopathological outcomes (Molina & Pelham, 2003).

Alternatively, the issue of interinformant agreement may be less problematic than conventional wisdom would dictate and may not have a routinely dramatic impact on child diagnosis or assessment. In a comprehensive review of available studies Johnston and Murray (2003) concluded that individual informants are generally as useful for making diagnostic classifications as aggregating information from multiple raters. This outcome, however, could be due in part to the possibility that clinicians generally tend to select able and knowledgeable informants.

Research has also shown that, in the case of rating scale-based dimensional assessment of children and adolescents, all raters possess some evidence of criterion-related and predictive validity (Kamphaus & Frick, 2002). Although there are certainly flaws and gaps in the research base, and recognizing the desirability of erring in the direction of more false positives than false negatives, we suggest that any symptom count, informant rating, observation, or other indicator of the presence of psychopathology is more likely to be valid than invalid, and warrant careful consideration as possible disorders warranting diagnosis.

Onset and Developmental Course

Historical data collection, both qualitative and quantitative, is necessary to assess these variables of central importance. History may also be used to clarify formal test results and determine when these results may suggest false positives, malingering, or false negatives. For example, an adolescent could have been referred for "sudden-and late-onset" ADHD, with evidence of hyperactivity/impulsivity and attention problems being obtained on rating scales, continuous performance tests (CPTs), and diagnostic interviews with parents. These clinical or laboratory findings of symptoms and constructs, however, could be interpreted quite differently depending on history. If history and school records suggest that these problems were evident to at least some degree beginning in early elementary school, a case of ADHD may be present. In direct contrast, if behavioral development was normal and academic progress was excellent up until 2 years ago, with an onset at age 18, then ADHD is highly unlikely based on history alone, and the formal assessment results are likely false positives, much like a blood pressure reading taken after climbing several flights of stairs prior to arrival at the physician's office.

Asperger's syndrome is an example of a disorder characterized by an early onset of symptoms and chronic course. This information may be helpful for differentiating Asperger's from an alternative cause for similar symptoms. The onset of interpersonal difficulties, regressed language, fixations with inanimate objects, social isolation, and similar problems at age 16 or 17 would indicate that Asperger's is not a likely explanation for these symptoms and that Schizophrenia should be explored instead. In like fashion, a less than chronic course for these problems would indicate that clinical depression, dysthymia, or Bipolar Disorder may better explain this adolescent's behavior.

Most disorders have a typical age of onset and developmental course that allow one to use history to clarify assessment findings. Examples of disorders with chronic course and gradual and/or early onset include autism spectrum disorders, mental retardation, reading or other learning disability, ADHD, and Bipolar Disorder. Disorders that are typified by either more abrupt and/or later onset include clinical depression, Schizophrenia, and specific phobias. Tests, observations, rating scales, and diagnostic interviews are generally of little value for identifying issues of onset (rapid, gradual, and age) and developmental course (chronic versus episodic), making history taking central to the diagnostic process.

Alternative Causes and Etiologies

We suggest using broadband interviews and/or rating scales to begin the diagnostic assessment process, as opposed to using disorder-specific screening scales to direct further assessment. The former gives the clinician the opportunity to consider possible alternative forms of psychopathology that may be causing the symptoms observed, whereas the latter provide information about only one disorder, thus providing limited opportunity to consider other forms of psychopathology. Our approach is akin to beginning diagnostic assessment at the broad end of a funnel and working toward the narrow end. It is only by beginning with broadband assessment that we can entertain all possible causes for the symptoms presented. An ADHD-specific scale, for example, will not direct the evaluator to the possibility that the child is suffering from clinical depression. It is particularly important to begin at the wide end of the funnel given that most referral questions and suspicions are either poorly articulated, not databased, or simply wrong (Tallent, 1999). Most clinicians can site cases where the referral concern was X (e.g., hyperactivity), but the problem turned out to be Y (e.g., inattention).

The Achenbach System of Empirically Based Assessment, Behavior Assessment System for Children (BASC), and other rating scales are particularly well suited to this purpose because their parent, teacher, and self-report rating scales are more time- and cost-efficient than diagnostic interviews (Hart & Lahey, 1999). These broadband measures assess the most common forms of internalizing and externalizing psychopathology, and the BASC provides a more in-depth assessment of adaptive skills deficits. A child referred for suspected ADHD, for example, may obtain a Child Behavior Checklist rating of 72 for the Internalizing composite. This information is useful for guiding the next steps in the diagnostic process because it requires the psychologist to eliminate clinical depression, a somatoform disorder, or Generalized Anxiety Disorder as alternative diagnoses that may explain the referral concerns about inattention and poor academic attainment. This finding may indicate the presence of a comorbid condition (e.g., ADHD and depression) as well, as is discussed in the final diagnostic step.

In effect, the rating scales in this rubric are serving as "routing tests" in that they direct the psychologist to the most important constructs and conditions to assess. Diagnostic interviews are also suitable for this process; however, they are more time-consuming and costly in terms of professional time. Eventually, the clinician is directed, in a databased way, toward the narrow end of the funnel and diagnoses that are most plausible for guiding professional communication and treatment.

History taking may also be used to link psychopathology to specific etiological agents. Depression and symptoms of ADHD are examples of disorders that may be "caused" or secondary to treatments for medical conditions. Similarly, symptoms of ADHD may be secondary to clinical depression. Among the variety of etiologies associated with clinical depression are traumatic brain injury, some chemotherapies for child cancer, and complicated bereavement. History taking is particularly useful for documenting the chronology of symptom onset in the interest of establishing which symptoms or constructs may be secondary or manifestations of another disorder or specific etiology.

To assess chronology, history should cover many potential domains, including the following:

- Family (parental, sibling, and caregiver) psychological, social, medical, educational, and occupational history
- Child psychological, social, medical, and educational history
- Early child developmental history
- Child social, educational, community, recreational, artistic, and peer history, activities, and interests
- Child behavioral and emotional history

Rule in Comorbidities

Just as it is important to diagnose comorbidity in medicine (e.g., heart disease plus cancer), it is equally important to diagnose it in psychiatry and psychology because the presence of co-occurring disorders may suggest a poorer prognosis and the need for a greater variety and/or intensity of treatments. If diagnosis is to guide treatment, then proper diagnosis of comorbidities is a central goal of the diagnostic process. The somatic treatment of a case of "uncomplicated" ADHD Combined type would be very different from a case of ADHD that is comorbid with clinical depression and Generalized Anxiety Disorder. Psychosocial or educational therapies are also influenced by knowledge of comorbidities as would be the case for a child with both mental retardation and ADHD.

A variety of assessment methods are necessary for documenting the presence of multiple disorders, all of which, however, need to be linked to the *DSM* system. Alternatively, the comorbidity may be defined as the coexistence of multiple constructs of concern as assessed by formal psychological tests or dimensional rating scales. For example, a child may have reading achievement test scores that are far below average, deviant enough to warrant the diagnosis of a reading disability. This child may be treated quite differently, in an educational intervention sense, if she or he also has below normative average scores in mathematics, writing, science, and social studies.

In fact, the problem of assessment for comorbidity provides the best argument for the use of person-oriented methods of assessment using dimensional assessment measures (Caron & Rutter, 1991). The purpose of a person-oriented paradigm, as noted at other points in this text, is to describe the child's adjustment idiographically. In addition, a presumption of these methods is that the classification system created as a result is ecologically valid, or represents a case of "carving nature at its joints," or defines psychopathology as it occurs. Person-oriented research clearly shows that few children's behavioral or emotional problems fit neatly into a single *DSM* "box." Instead, person-oriented methods suggest that comorbidity is the rule rather than the exception in child psychopathology (DiStefano et al., 2003;

Huberty et al., 1997; Kamphaus & DiStefano, 2001; Kamphaus et al., 1997, 1999).

In this sense, psychological or psychiatric assessment may be similar to medical assessment. Psychological systems such as the temperamental, executive functioning, arousal, emotional control, and cognitive may, in fact, be more interrelated than the analogous pulmonary, cardiac, circulatory, and other systems that are the focus of medical diagnosis.

CASE STUDY

Daniel is a 10-year-old fifth grader who has had increasing problems with behavior and academics in school that began in kindergarten. He has been monitored by psychology staff since school entry for problems with poor work organization, work incompletion, resistance to teacher direction, anger outbursts, and low frustration tolerance and poor emotional self-control. All of these problems have worsened in the face of interventions delivered both inside and outside school, thus precipitating a referral for consideration for special education class placement.

Family history indicates chronic problems, including criminality on his father's side and major mental disorders, including problems with depression and Bipolar Disorder, on his mother's side. The family is marked by numerous disruptions, including a death of an aunt who served as Daniel's primary caregiver for 3 years, parental separation and reconciliation, frequent moves between different households, chronic verbal fighting among caregivers, financial problems, and school absences ranging from 10 to 30 days per year.

Daniel was diagnosed with ADHD at age 5 and placed on psychostimulant therapy, with no benefit noted. He has received counseling at school and his teachers have received classroom consultation to assist them in dealing with him. Both of these interventions have proved to be minimally effective.

Daniel's symptoms were considered chronic, with early onset and deteriorating course. His behavioral and emotional problems date to toddlerhood, whereas his academic difficulties were not present at the outset of school but have worsened gradually.

Results from the Wechsler Intelligence Scale for Children—Fourth Edition were consistently in the below average range, with composites ranging from 93 to 109. Academic achievement scores were similarly in the average range, with the exception of written expression composite standard scores of 75 and 81 and two separate measures.

Behavior, personality, and emotional assessment results are given in Tables 2.1 (self-report assessment), 2.2 (teacher ratings), and 2.3 (parental ratings). Significant problems were noted by all informants. Daniel's self-report indicates considerable distress in a variety of domains, including the core symptoms of ADHD, depression, impaired relations with peers and adults, and poor adaptive skills. Both teacher and parent ratings agree in that externalizing, internalizing, and adaptive skills problems are noted.

From a psychiatric nosology standpoint, the diagnoses of depression, ADHD, Conduct Disorder, Oppositional Defiant Disorder, Bipolar Disorder, and learning disability in written expression were considered. A learning disability was the first disorder ruled out, due to the gradual onset of symptoms, decreased learning opportunities due to worsening behavior and emotions at school, decreased learning opportunities due to poor work completion, and decreased learning opportunities due to absence from school. His relative

Table 2.1   **BASC Self-Report of Personality— Child *T*-Score Results for Daniel**

Attention Problems	68
Attitude toward School	64
Attitude toward Teachers	84
Atypicality	48
Hyperactivity	80
Locus of Control	68
Social Stress	60
Anxiety	55
Depression	68
Sense of Inadequacy	78
Relationship with Parents	10
Interpersonal Relationships	31
Self-Esteem	34
Self-Reliance	36
Critical item: "Sometimes I want to hurt myself."	

Table 2.2   **BASC Teacher Rating Scales—Child *T*-Score Results for Daniel**

Scale	Teacher A	Teacher B
Hyperactivity	67	69
Aggression	73	73
Conduct Problems	79	79
Anxiety	62	65
Depression	77	66
Somatization	46	64
Atypicality	71	61
Learning Problems	63	63
Withdrawal	71	61
Attention Problems	76	75
Adaptability	27	27
Functional Communication	40	43
Social Skills	33	34
Leadership	35	35
Study Skills	27	31

weakness in written expression was to become the target of more focused academic intervention.

Assessment of the core symptoms revealed a complex clinical picture for Daniel that suggested the presence of either a severe disorder with multiple symptoms or substantial comorbidity or both internalizing and externalizing disorders. The early onset and chronicity of his problems, the deteriorating nature of his behavior, and their poor response to earlier treatments with known effectiveness suggests that a severe disorder is present. The treatment team concluded that his condition was best described currently as Bipolar Disorder given the similarity of his clinical picture to new research findings and conceptualizations of the condition by the National Institute of Mental Health as indicated in the following text from the NIMH web site (2006, www.nimh .nih.gov/publicat/bipolarupdate.cfm):

Symptoms of mania and depression in children and adolescents may manifest themselves through a variety of different behaviors. When manic, children and adolescents, in contrast to adults, are more likely to be irritable and

Table 2.3 **BASC Parent Rating Scales—Child *T*-Score Results for Daniel**

Scale	Mother	Father
Hyperactivity	65	71
Aggression	76	67
Conduct Problems	75	91
Anxiety	59	59
Depression	74	72
Somatization	73	53
Atypicality	76	50
Withdrawal	57	47
Attention Problems	73	73
Adaptability	25	27
Activities of Daily Living	34	33
Functional Communication	40	47
Social Skills	35	37
Leadership	35	37

prone to destructive outbursts than to be elated or euphoric. When depressed, there may be many physical complaints such as headaches, muscle aches, stomachaches or tiredness, frequent absences from school or poor performance in school, talk of or efforts to run away from home, irritability, complaining, unexplained crying, social isolation, poor communication, and extreme sensitivity to rejection or failure. Other manifestations of manic and depressive states may include alcohol or substance abuse and difficulty with relationships.

Existing evidence indicates that bipolar disorder beginning in childhood or early adolescence may be a different, possibly more severe form of the illness than older adolescent- and adult-onset bipolar disorder. When the illness begins before or soon after puberty, it is often characterized by a continuous, rapid-cycling, irritable, and mixed symptom state that may co-occur with disruptive behavior disorders, particularly attention deficit hyperactivity disorder (ADHD) or conduct disorder (CD), or may have features of these disorders as initial symptoms. In contrast, later adolescent- or adult-onset bipolar disorder tends to begin suddenly, often with a classic manic episode, and to have a more episodic pattern with relatively stable periods between episodes. There is also less co-occurring ADHD or CD among those with later onset illness.

A child or adolescent who appears to be depressed and exhibits ADHD-like symptoms that are very severe, with excessive temper outbursts and mood changes, should be evaluated by a psychiatrist or psychologist with experience in bipolar disorder, particularly if there is a family history of the illness. This evaluation is especially important since psychostimulant medications, often prescribed for ADHD, may worsen manic symptoms. There is also limited evidence suggesting that some of the symptoms of ADHD may be a forerunner of full-blown mania.

Findings from an NIMH-supported study suggest that the illness may be at least as common among youth as among adults. In this study, one percent of adolescents ages 14 to 18 were found to have met criteria for bipolar disorder or cyclothymia, a similar but milder illness, in their lifetime.

Although comorbidities were not indicated, the breadth of Daniel's problems as noted by dimensional rating scales suggested that multimodal interventions were warranted, especially in light of the ineffectiveness of prior interventions. Such interventions may include parent training, family therapy, tutoring, special class placement at school, somatic therapies, psychotherapy to build coping skills and emotional self-control, social skills training at school, and mentoring to improve relationships with teachers and other authority figures.

Conclusion

Short of an exhaustive treatment of a topic that could easily be of book length, this chapter provides a 4-step process of integrating information from a variety of assessment methods to make diagnostic decisions. We proposed an interpretation rubric designed to meld the categorical and dimensional approaches to child diagnostic classification. As is noted in the sample case, both approaches provide unique information that is more powerful than using either method in isolation. The categorical diagnostic approach provides a link to an existing body of scientific literature that is useful for guiding further research, communication among professionals, treatment selection, and determination of prognosis. The dimensional method provides an assessment of core constructs with greater reliability and validity, defines a more substantial universe of constructs/symptoms that need treatment, is useful for the assessment of treatment effectiveness, and allows clinicians to make exacting statements about severity of the problems identified.

We fully expect interpretive and diagnostic practice to become increasingly empirical and to meld the categorical and dimensional methods. Specifically, we think that the next goal of mental health diagnostic assessment will be to engage in template or profile matching, using the most valid measures available to match a child's constructs/symptoms of concern to empirically derived profiles.

Mental Retardation/ Intellectual Disability

Jonathan M. Campbell

3

Chapter

Characteristics

Mental retardation is associated with a large number of conditions, including genetic disorders (e.g., Down syndrome, fragile X syndrome), prenatal or early environmental insults (e.g., fetal alcohol syndrome, lead poisoning) health-related conditions (e.g., tuberous sclerosis), and pervasive developmental disorders (e.g., autism, Rett's disorder; C. C. Murphy, Boyle, Schendel, Decoufle, & Yeargin-Allsopp, 1998). Over 500 genetic disorders have been identified that are associated with mental retardation, with Down syndrome and fragile X syndrome often reported as the two most frequent genetic causes (Flint & Wilkie, 1996; Moldavsky, Lev, & Lerman-Sagie, 2001). Outside of the realm of congenital causes, fetal alcohol syndrome is considered to be one of the leading causes of mental retardation in the United States, occurring in about 1 per 1,000 births (C. C. Murphy et al., 1998). In approximately 30% to 40% of all individuals diagnosed with mental retardation, no etiology can be determined (American Psychiatric Association, 2000). In individuals with IQ scores of less than 50, approximately 40% to 70% of the time an etiology is identified; however, in individuals with IQ scores in the mild range of mental retardation (50 to 70), a cause is identified in only about 20% to 24% of cases (Flint & Wilkie, 1996; C. C. Murphy et al., 1998). In cases where no clear etiology exists, mental retardation is typically thought to be the result of multiple causal factors, such as polygenic inheritance and environmental risks (e.g., Flint & Wilkie, 1996; Roeveld, Zielhuis, & Gabreëls, 1997).

Despite sharing common deficits in intellectual functioning and adaptive skills, individuals with mental retardation exhibit a wide range of cognitive and behavioral features. As evidenced by the diagnostic criteria described later in this chapter, individuals with mental retardation vary according to the severity of intellectual impairments as well as unique strengths and liabilities within the realm of adaptive skills (Luckasson et al., 1992). For example, one individual with mild mental retardation may exhibit impaired adaptive skills in the areas of functional academics and self-care while another individual with severe mental retardation may show impairments across the entire range of adaptive areas.

Prevalence rates of mental retardation are frequently reported to range from 1% to 3% for school-age children, although rates fluctuate considerably depending on definitions of mental retardation, methods used to detect individuals with mental retardation, and the size of the study population. In a recent review, the average reported prevalence rate for severe mental retardation, that is, IQ < 50, was 3.8 per 1,000 and the average reported prevalence rate for mild mental retardation, that is, IQ from 50 to 70, was 29.8 per 1,000 or roughly 3% (Roelveld et al., 1997). Males are more frequently diagnosed with mental retardation than females at a rate of approximately 1.2:1 in the severe range of mental retardation and 1.4:1 in the mild range of mental retardation (C. C. Murphy et al., 1998; Roelveld et al., 1997).

Constructs of Interest

At the core of defining mental retardation is the complex and theoretical task of identifying those constructs or areas that are thought to be essential to an individual's self-sufficiency, competence, and adaptation. Attempts to define what constitutes a competent individual have given rise to a host of theories that have emphasized broad constructs such as intelligence, social competence, personal competence, and adaptive functioning. Over time, definitions of mental retardation have changed and provided greater or lesser emphasis on different constructs, particularly the construct of intelligence. For example, prior to the development of intelligence tests, early notions of mental retardation emphasized practical, functional, and social limitations (i.e., adaptive behavior) residing in the individual that were essential for classification (Nihira, 1999). Beginning with the American Association on Mental Deficiency's (AAMD) definition of mental retardation in 1959, the construct of adaptive behavior was included as a construct associated with mental retardation, which was defined as subaverage intellectual functioning. Beginning in 1973, formal definitions of mental retardation included limitations in both intelligence and adaptive behavior as essential criteria for the purposes of classifying an individual with mental retardation (Luckasson et al., 2002).

Despite the inclusion of both intelligence and adaptive behavior as necessary criteria for diagnosing mental retardation, debates continue about the nature and relationship of these constructs. As evidenced by recent definitions and models of mental retardation, adaptive behavior and intelligence have given rise to a host of constructs hypothesized to exist in hierarchical structures and associated groups. Initially defined with one (i.e., intelligence) and two constructs (i.e., intelligence and adaptive behavior), models of mental retardation have evolved into increasingly sophisticated theoretical and statistical models of multiple intelligences, competencies, and domains of adaptive behavior (e.g., Luckasson et al., 2002; J. R. Thompson, McGrew, & Bruininks, 1999). Such an explosion in the numbers of constructs has yielded definitions of mental retardation that are more complex and difficult to define operationally and apply clinically than before.

Intellectual Functioning

Definitions of mental retardation are tied closely to the long-standing controversy regarding the definition of intelligence, particularly the debate regarding the unidimensionality versus multidimensionality of intelligence (Luckasson et al., 2002; Nihira, 1999). Theorists and researchers have generated definitions of intelligence for years with considerable variety existing between ideas and constructs (e.g., Spruill & Black, 2001). Arguably the most dominant ideas about the nature of intelligence are those that identify a hierarchical structure, with a general factor of intelligence (i.e., *g*) atop the hierarchy and multiple specific intellectual functions existing below. Among theorists that define intelligence as a hierarchical construct, variations of the hierarchy exist. For example, Carroll's (1993) three-stratum theory of intelligence identifies *g* as a general construct that subsumes broader abilities, identified as stratum II level constructs (e.g., Fluid Intelligence, Broad Visual Perception). Also identified in Carroll's model are 69 narrow (stratum I) abilities, such as Induction and General Sequential (Deductive) Reasoning, which contribute to stratum II constructs, such as Fluid Intelligence. Although quite similar, Cattell-Horn's contemporary fluid and crystallized intelligence theory varies slightly from Carroll's (1993) model as evidenced by no specified general *g* factor of general intelligence and slightly different broad cognitive abilities identified in the model (e.g., a reading-writing ability factor, *Grw*). However, Cattell-Horn's theory identifies multiple primary abilities as opposed to stratum I abilities that contribute to the broad cognitive factors. Carroll's theory and contemporary fluid-crystallized intelligence theory have been combined to yield what is known as Cattell-Horn-Carroll (CHC theory), which identifies a general *g* factor of intelligence, broad abilities, and numerous narrow cognitive abilities (McGrew & Woodcock, 2001).

Outside of the hierarchical models of intelligence, such as CHC theory, other conceptualizations of intelligence exist, such as H. Gardner's (1993) theory of multiple intelligences, Sternberg's (1988) triarchic theory of intelligence, and Das, Naglieri, and Kirby's (1994) PASS model of human cognition (i.e., *P*lanning, *A*ttention, *S*imultaneous processing, and *S*equential processing). Gardner's model asserts that intelligence exists as a multidimensional construct, involving problem-solving capacities across multiple contexts. Gardner has identified eight "intelligences" to date: logical-mathematical, linguistic, spatial, musical, kinesthetic, interpersonal, intrapersonal, and naturalistic. Traditional intelligence tests tap logical-mathematical, linguistic, and spatial abilities as identified by Gardner.

Sternberg's (1988) theory asserts that intelligence involves an interaction and interplay between (a) the individual, (b) his or her experiences, and (c) his or her larger interpersonal contexts. Within the individual, internal cognitive processes, called "components," such as metacognition, knowledge-acquisition and performance, are applied to experiential tasks of varying familiarity. When tasks are familiar, components are applied in more of an automatic fashion than when tasks are unfamiliar, and components are applied in newer and more novel ways. The first two aspects of intelligence (i.e., componential and experiential) are applied to one's contexts to meet demands of the environment. Sternberg's (1988) triarchic theory is frequently associated with three types of intelligence: analytical abilities, creativity, and practical intelligence (Luckasson et al., 2002). According to Sternberg, traditional intelligence tests tap analytical abilities, with little or no measurement of creativity or practical intelligence.

The PASS theory is an information-processing model of cognitive ability that is grounded in Luria's theories of brain structures and functions. Luria identified three functional units of human cognition: arousal/attention; simultaneous/sequential processing; and planning/self-monitoring (Das, 2004). These information-processing units are thought to be tied to brain structures; attentional functions are thought to be associated with the brain stem and the reticular activating system. Simultaneous (e.g., gestalt-like reasoning) and sequential (e.g., serial reasoning) information processing involve occipital-parietal and fronto-temporal areas in the cerebral cortex. Finally, planning and self-monitoring abilities are thought to be associated with frontal and prefrontal areas in the cerebral cortex. Within a larger information-processing framework, PASS processing occurs between sensory input and motor output (see Das, 2004 for an overview of the PASS theory).

Adaptive Behavior

Like the construct of intelligence, ideas and definitions of adaptive behavior vary. For example, Grossman's (1983) frequently cited definition of adaptive behavior identifies the construct as "the effectiveness and degree with which the individual meets the standard of personal independence and social responsibility expected of his age and cultural group" (p. 1). Bruininks, Thurlow, and Gilman (1987) defined adaptive behavior as the "achievement of skills needed for successful adaptation and often the reduction or elimination of behaviors that interfere with effective adjustment in typical environments" (p. 73). Despite the variety of definitions as suggested earlier, several core assumptions about the nature of adaptive behavior have been proposed. Definitions of adaptive behavior typically emphasize *independent functioning* within the community, the maintenance of *socially responsible relationships,* and meeting *cultural standards* of behavior (J. R. Thompson et al., 1999).

Structure of Adaptive Behavior: J. R. Thompson et al. (1999) reviewed several previously published reviews of factor analytic studies targeting the structural properties of adaptive behavior. The review summarized evidence relevant to conceptualizing adaptive behavior as either a unidimensional or multidimensional construct, as well as the number of adaptive behavior factors that emerged consistently across analyses. First, J. R. Thompson et al.'s review strongly suggests that adaptive behavior is best conceptualized as a multidimensional construct. Second, the review suggests that the dimensions of personal independence (e.g., self-sufficiency), social responsibility (e.g., functioning appropriately within social contexts), and cognitive/academic are the three factors most clearly supported by factor analyses. Although still considered robust findings, somewhat less empirical support emerged for two other areas of adaptive functioning across measures: physical/developmental functioning and vocational functioning.

J. R. Thompson et al. (1999) noted that adaptive behavior may be best understood in terms of a hierarchical structure, similar to the contemporary Gf-Gc theories of intelligence that identifies layers or "strata" of cognitive abilities, with a general factor atop the hierarchy and broad band and narrow abilities existing in lower levels of cognitive skills (see previous section for additional discussion of hierarchical theory of intelligence). In terms of adaptive behavior, J. R. Thompson et al. outline a possible model of adaptive behavior that exists in similar terms, with the construct of personal competence sitting atop the hierarchy of practical competence/adaptive behavior and smaller domains of adaptive functioning existing within the domain of practical competence. To date, however, narrow domains of adaptive behavior have not been established reliably to include as narrow band skills within the hypothetical model.

A Comprehensive Model of Personal Competence

In an effort to identify and organize constructs essential for effective adaptation, functioning, and well-being, Greenspan (1981, 1999) outlined a theoretical model of personal competence that proposes a hierarchical structure consisting of four domains: physical competence, affective competence, everyday competence (also defined as adaptive behavior), and academic competence. Within Greenspan's model of personal competence, intelligence and adaptive behavior are defined within a larger model of constructs thought to be important for effective adaptation and functioning. Each area of competence is further defined by two subdomains. *Physical competence* consists of organ and motor functioning, *affective competence* consists of temperament and character, *everyday competence* consists of social and practical intelligence, and *academic competence* consists of conceptual intelligence (i.e., IQ) and language (Greenspan, 1999).

Aspects of Greenspan's model of personal competence have received empirical support via factor analysis and hierarchical linear modeling (e.g., Ittenbach, Spiegel, McGrew, & Bruininks, 1992; McGrew & Bruininks, 1990). In general, McGrew and Bruininks's findings support the conceptual distinction of physical competence, emotional competence, conceptual intelligence, operationalized as IQ, and practical intelligence, defined as adaptive behavior. Ittenbach et al.'s (1992) findings provide additional support for the distinction between physical competence, conceptual intelligence, and practical intelligence within Greenspan's model of personal competence. Neither nonhierarchical nor hierarchical linear modeling solutions statistically distinguished between physical competence and practical intelligence in 2- to 6-year-old children in the McGrew and Bruininks's study; however, the findings of Ittenbach et al. did not agree with the earlier results. Therefore, it is unclear if or how developmental factors influence the structure of personal and social competence according to Greenspan's model. Although the results reviewed provide some evidence to support aspects of the personal competence model, additional validation is necessary for support of the model in its entirety.

Considerations of Maladaptive Behavior with a Model of Personal Competence: Individuals with mental retardation often exhibit maladaptive behavior, creating barriers to achieving adaptation and optimal functioning. Recently, theorists have begun to consider how the construct of maladaptive behavior might exist within a model of personal competence. From a structural perspective, J. R. Thompson et al. (1999) proposed that maladaptive behavior may fit within Greenspan's theory of personal competence, existing as broad-level constructs under the general level of emotional competence. In their review of factor analysis evidence, J. R. Thompson et al. identified two main factors of maladaptive behavior, personal (intrapunitive; e.g., self-injurious behavior) or social (extrapunitive; e.g., destructive or socially disruptive behavior). By extending Greenspan's model of personal competence, J. R. Thompson et al. offer a reasonable rendering of how maladaptive behavior might be understood as a separate construct. It is important to note that the model is speculative and also structural in nature. That is, the construct of maladaptive behavior is organized and located within the model, but no hypotheses are made regarding how maladaptive behavior may impede optimal functioning.

Psychopathology

Children and adolescents diagnosed with mental retardation suffer from rates of psychopathology and behavioral problems that are higher than typically developing peers (Dykens, 2000; Luckasson et al., 2002; Wallander, Dekker, & Koot, 2003). Rates of comorbid psychopathology range widely across studies, from as low as 10% to as high as 70% (Borthwick-Duffy, 1994; Dykens, 2000; Dykens & Hodapp, 2001; Wallander et al., 2003). Differences in reported rates of psychopathology are attributable to a variety of factors, such as level of intellectual functioning, inpatient versus outpatient samples, categorical versus empirically defined presence of psychopathology, and changing diagnostic systems over time (Dykens, 2000; Wallander et al., 2003). For example, children and adolescents with lower intellectual functioning are usually more at risk for co-existing problems with self-injurious behavior, motor stereotypies, or other severely disruptive behavior problem. Children with milder delays, however, appear to be more at risk for conventional psychiatric diagnoses of mood and anxiety disorders (Dykens, 2000).

Theories of Psychopathology and Mental Retardation: Multiple theories have been proposed to account for the increased risk of individuals diagnosed with mental retardation to be also diagnosed with mental health problems. Theories include biological, behavioral, developmental and sociocultural models (see Matson & Sevin, 1994 for review). Biological theories account for the increased risk of psychopathology by linking mental retardation with increased biological vulnerabilities. Many biological factors have been associated with increased risk for psychopathology in individuals with mental retardation, such as genetic abnormalities, presence of seizure disorders, and sensory impairments (Matson & Sevin, 1994). For example, children with mental retardation are at increased risk for epilepsy, which is also associated with behavioral problems and psychosis (Dykens, 2000). As described later in the chapter, individuals with mental retardation caused by genetic abnormalities are at risk for showing symptoms of anxiety, depression, and socially disruptive behaviors. Children with mental retardation are also at risk for visual and hearing impairments, which are associated with greater risk for behavioral and psychiatric problems, such as anxiety, conduct disorders, and hyperactivity (Dykens, 2000).

Behavioral theories account for the increased risk of psycho-pathology in individuals with mental retardation by invoking the idea that all behavior, including deviant and maladaptive behavior, is learned via behavioral principles, particularly operant condition-ing. From the operant conditioning perspective, several possibilities exist to explain the increase in deviant behavior: (a) insufficient re-inforcement of appropriate behavior, (b) inappropriate punishment, and (c) inadvertent reinforcement of deviant behavior (Matson & Sevin, 1994). Deviant behavior may arise due to too little reinforce-ment being present in the environment, such as limited opportuni-ties for positive socialization experiences due to custodial care and exclusive special education placements. For example, lack of positive socialization opportunities may contribute to feelings of de-pression in individuals with mental retardation. Inappropriate pun-ishment may contribute to the presence of psychopathology as understood by models of learned helplessness. In this case, greater rates of depression are explained by noncontingent punishment, that is, punishing stimuli presented regardless of the individual's be-havior. Social and biological factors have been identified as possible sources of noncontingent punishment, such as reprimands from staff members in custodial settings or the unpredictable occurrence of seizures (Matson & Sevin, 1994).

Concepts of positive and negative reinforcement have also been identified as contributing to the establishment and maintenance of deviant behavior. For example, an anxiety response may be initially established via associative (classical) conditioning and maintained through avoidance. In other instances, deviant behavior may be in-advertently reinforced by environmental contingencies. For exam-ple, self-injurious or oppositional behavior may be reinforced through social attention (i.e., positive reinforcement) or removal of difficult task demands, such as academic work (i.e., negative rein-forcement). Theories of reinforcement have given rise to a variety of functional assessment methods that attempt to establish links be-tween deviant behavior and environmental contingencies, such as experimental functional analysis (EFA) procedures (e.g., Iwata, Dorsey, Slifer, Bauman, & Richman, 1994).

Familial and sociocultural models acknowledge the potential contribution of family functioning and larger social and cultural factors in contributing to increased rates of psychopathology in individuals with mental retardation. The presence of a child with mental retardation is frequently associated with family stress, which, in turn, has been associated with psychopathology in children. Although links between family stress and psychopathology exist, the direction of cause is not clear. Findings have documented that child psychopathology predict family stress, while others have shown that children's maladaptive behavior is predicted by marital problems and parental psychopathology (Dykens, 2000). Outside of the family, individuals with mental retardation are at greater risk of victimization as well as exposure to chronic social disadvantage. Children with mental retardation are at greater risk for exploitation as well as physical and sexual abuse (Dykens, 2000). Outside of overt traumatic events, children and adolescents with mental retardation are subject to subtle and not so subtle sociocultural stigma and prejudices. For example, children with mental retardation are at greater risk for peer rejection than typically developing peers, and peer rejection has been linked to greater risks for psychopathology in typically developing children (Parker & Asher, 1987).

Phenotypic "Profiling"

With recent technological advances in molecular genetics, research has focused on linking physical, cognitive, and behavioral phenotypes to genetic causes of mental retardation, that is, linking a specific presentation with a specific genetic abnormality (Dykens, 2000). In this regard, research has begun to yield phenotypic presentations associated with known genetic causes of mental retardation, such as Down syndrome, fragile X syndrome, Prader-Willi syndrome, and Williams syndrome. Outside of genetic disorders, there is also growing evidence for a phenotypic profile for children with fetal alcohol syndrome and related disabilities. Phenotypes associated with three of the most common causes of mental retardation are briefly reviewed: Down syndrome, fragile X syndrome, and fetal alcohol syndrome.

Down Syndrome: Down syndrome is caused by the presence of extra genetic material from the 21st chromosome. Approximately 95% of individuals with Down syndrome have an extra 21st chromosome and are identified as having the "trisomy 21" subtype (Ramirez & Morgan, 1998). Distinct from the trisomy 21 subtype, approximately 3% to 4% of individuals with Down syndrome are classified as "translocation" subtypes, due to a portion of chromosome 21 being attached to other chromosomes. The "mosaicism" subtype of Down syndrome refers to the presence of normal and trisomic cells within the individual and occurs in about 1% to 2% of cases. Among others, common physical characteristics associated with Down syndrome include muscle hypotonia, flat facial profile, an upward slant to the eyes (i.e., oblique palpebral fissures), and hyperflexibility (Moldavsky et al., 2001; Ramirez & Morgan, 1998). Individuals with Down syndrome frequently show moderate to severe cognitive delays, often show expressive language delays with relative strengths in pragmatical versus grammatical language abilities, and exhibit relative strengths in visual versus auditory/verbal memory (Chapman & Hesketh, 2000). Down syndrome is associated with a greater risk of developing a range of serious health problems, such as hearing deficits, heart defects, leukemia, hypothyroidism, and gastrointestinal disorders (Ramirez & Morgan, 1998). Down syndrome is also associated with an increased risk of developing Alzheimer's-type dementia. In the general population, Alzheimer's disease typically develops after the age of 50 with the largest prevalence rate of 5% to 10% in individuals over the age of 65 (Ramirez & Morgan, 1998). In contrast, up to 25% of individuals with Down syndrome develop Alzheimer's-type dementia by the age of 35, and over 50% of individuals with Down syndrome over the age of 50 develop dementia (Chapman & Hesketh, 2000; Ramirez & Morgan, 1998). Postmortem brain studies have documented consistently the presence of the characteristic senile plaques and tangles associated with Alzheimer's-type dementia in individuals with Down syndrome over the age of 40. The stereotypic representation of individuals with Down syndrome is an affectionate child with an easy temperament. In general, individuals with Down syndrome show lower levels of maladaptive behaviors and psychiatric disorders when compared to peers with mental retardation (Chapman & Heseketh, 2000). However, parents and teachers have reported higher rates of depression when compared to peers with mental retardation, and more behavioral problems when compared to the general population (Chapman & Heseketh, 2000; Ramirez & Morgan, 1998).

Fragile X Syndrome: Fragile X syndrome is considered the most common form of inherited mental retardation caused by an expanded repetition of the normally occurring CGG (cytosine/guanine/guanine) genetic sequence on the long arm of the X chromosome (Mazzocco, 2000). The abnormal genetic repetition inhibits the fragile X MR-1 (FMR-1) gene from producing a protein that results in cognitive, affective, physical, and behavioral difficulties observed in fragile X syndrome (Moldavsky et al., 2001). Full mutation (CGG repetitions of greater than 200) and premutation (CGG repetitions of about 50 to about 200) subtypes have been identified with the premutation subtype generally resulting in less severe symptoms. Although significant phenotypic variability exists within each group, in general, females are less affected than males (Mazzocco, 2000). The majority of males with fragile X syndrome show cognitive delays compared to only 50% of females with the full mutation (Klaiman & Phelps, 1998). Characteristic physical features in boys with fragile X include hyperextensible finger joints, flat feet, large ears, narrow face, and macroorchidism (i.e., enlarged testicles; Moldavsky et al., 2001). In general, the presence of physical characteristics is less prevalent in girls with fragile X (Klaiman & Phelps, 1998). Males with fragile X syndrome frequently exhibit social deficits ranging from autistic-like features (such as poor eye contact, stereotyped behavior, and perseverative speech), pragmatic language deficits, and social anxiety. Approximately 7% to 25% of children with fragile X syndrome also meet criteria for autistic disorder (Mazzocco, 2000; Moldavsky et al., 2001). Similar to children with autistic disorder, boys with fragile X syndrome frequently show sensory hypersensitivity across tactile, visual, and auditory channels. In contrast to males with autism, however, males with fragile X syndrome tend to use more repetitive speech and tangential language, possibly due to increased difficulties with social anxiety, hypersensitivity, and behavioral inhibition (Belser & Sudhalter, 2001; Sudhalter & Belser, 2001). Hyperactivity and distractibility are also common with up to 70% of boys meeting full criteria for attention-deficit hyperactivity disorder (Moldavsky et al., 2001). Females with fragile X syndrome often show a pattern of shyness, social anxiety, poor eye contact, and social avoidance. Hyperactivity, inattention, and distractibility are frequently present in girls with fragile X syndrome (Klaiman & Phelps, 1998).

Fetal Alcohol Syndromes: Prenatal exposure to alcohol can result in the presence of fetal alcohol syndrome or other disorders of less severity, such as partial fetal alcohol syndrome and alcohol-related neurodevelopmental disorder (Hagerman, 1999). Fetal alcohol syndrome is characterized by the presence of prenatal and/or postnatal growth delay, abnormalities of the face and head (e.g., microcephaly), and central nervous system dysfunction (Astley & Clarren, 2001). The characteristic facial phenotype includes small eyes, smooth philtrum (i.e., indistinct groove between upper lip and nose), and a thin upper lip. In addition to these physical features, children with fetal alcohol syndrome are more likely to suffer from chronic otitis media, visual problems (e.g., strabismus), cardiac problems, skeletal malformations, and immune system deficits (Smith & Graden, 1998). In addition to cognitive delays, children with fetal alcohol syndrome often exhibit problems with sustained attention, overactivity, and deficient social skills. Their conversational style has been characterized as active, overinquisitive, and intrusive (Smith & Graden, 1998). Adults with fetal alcohol syndrome show an increased risk for psychopathology and social problems, such as incarceration, attention deficit disorders, depression, alcohol and drug dependence, and suicide (Hagerman, 1999). It is unclear what contribution social factors play in these outcomes, as children with fetal alcohol syndrome may continue to reside with parents who continue to abuse alcohol.

Diagnostic Standards

Two classification systems are used widely in the classification of mental retardation: (1) guidelines published by the American Association on Mental Retardation (AAMR) and (2) diagnostic criteria outlined by the American Psychiatric Association's *Diagnostic and Statistical Manual of Mental Disorders, Fourth Edition, Text Revision* (*DSM-IV-TR*). In addition, the Individuals with Disabilities Act (IDEA) guidelines established by the U.S. Office of Special Education and Rehabilitative Services and U.S. Department of Education are also used to classify children with mental retardation for the purposes of providing special education services. Each classification system is briefly introduced next.

American Association on Mental Retardation

In its 10th edition of the definition of mental retardation, the American Association on Mental Retardation (AAMR) defined mental retardation as "a disability characterized by significant limitations both in intellectual functioning and in adaptive behavior as expressed in conceptual, social, and practical adaptive skills" (Luckasson et al., 2002, p. 1). The AAMR definition also specifies that the disability must be present prior to the age of 18. The two most recently published AAMR guidelines (Luckasson et al., 1992, 2002) do not include specific subcategories to describe functioning. Emphasizing the ecological interplay between the person, environments and supports necessary for an individual with mental retardation, the 1992 guidelines delineated four categories (i.e., Intermittent, Limited, Extensive, and Pervasive) to describe an individual's need for intervention services within areas of delay. The 2002 AAMR guidelines continue to adhere to this general theoretical position but define supports as mediators between a person's capabilities and resultant functioning. However, the 2002 AAMR definition allows for classification based on support intensity, IQ range, limitations in adaptive behavior, or etiology, among others. The 1992 and 2002 AAMR guidelines were proposed in order to reduce reliance on IQ for classifying disability level, as well as to emphasize the ecological interdependency of an individual's needs, supports in the environment, and level of functioning.

Assumptions Associated with the 2002 AAMR Definition: The 2002 AAMR definition of mental retardation is accompanied by a set of five assumptions identified as essential when applying the definition of mental retardation (Lukasson et al., 2002). First, an individual's functional limitations are to be understood within larger contextual considerations of typical age and cultural expectations. Second, valid assessment and diagnosis considers diversity in terms of language, culture, sensory/motor/communication limitations, and behavioral features of the individual. Third, the AAMR definition asserts that individual strengths often exist alongside weaknesses or limitations, which are essential to document for the purposes of classification. Fourth, one of the most important purposes of documenting the presence of mental retardation is to yield information about supports and interventions that are needed to improve an individual's functioning. Finally, the definition assumes that an individual's functioning will typically improve over time if appropriate supports are provided over an adequate time period.

Operational Definitions of Constructs: The 2002 AAMR guidelines define *intelligence* as "a general mental capability" that includes a variety of cognitive processes, such as abstract thinking, planning, and experiential learning (Luckasson et al., 2002, p. 14). For the purpose of diagnosing mental retardation, the guidelines assert that IQ scores continue to represent the most viable means to represent intelligence and that the intelligence criterion is met when IQ scores fall approximately two standard deviations below the normative mean. Adaptive behavior is defined within a triad of skills, identified as "conceptual, social and practical skills that have been learned by people in order to function in their everyday lives" (Luckasson et al., p 14). For the purpose of diagnosing mental retardation, the 2002 guidelines define significant limitations as performance that falls at least two standard deviations below the normative mean in one of the areas of adaptive skills (i.e., conceptual, social or practical) or an overall composite score that represents functioning across these three adaptive skill areas. The 2002 operational definition for adaptive skills represents a departure from the 1992 AAMR definition that identified 10 adaptive skill areas including domains such as self-direction, health and safety, leisure, and work (Luckasson et al., 1992). The identification of such a relatively large number of adaptive skill domains created practical problems in terms of measurement.

Diagnostic and Statistical Manual of Mental Disorders, Fourth Edition, Text Revision

Within the *DSM-IV-TR*, mental retardation "is characterized by significantly subaverage intellectual functioning (an IQ of approximately 70 or below) with onset before age 18 years and concurrent deficits or impairments in adaptive functioning" (American Psychiatric Association, 2000, p. 39). In contrast to the 2002 AAMR definition, the *DSM-IV-TR* includes subcategories of mental retardation used to describe an individual's level of impairment based on current level of intellectual functioning: Mild (IQ of 50 to 55 to about 70), Moderate (IQ of 35 to 40 to 50 to 55), Severe (IQ of 20 to 25 to 35 to 40), and Profound (IQ < 20 to 25) (American Psychiatric Association, 2000). As with the AAMR definition, *DSM-IV-TR* guidelines define mental retardation as the combination of limitations in the domains of intellectual functioning and adaptive behavior as necessary for diagnosis. Adaptive functioning is defined as the degree to which individuals cope with life demands and personal independence when compared to someone of similar age, sociocultural background and community setting (American Psychiatric Association, 2000).

Operational Definitions of Constructs: The *DSM-IV-TR* defines general intellectual functioning as equivalent to an IQ score obtained from assessment with an individually administered measure of intelligence. Similar to the 2002 AAMR definition, subaverage intellectual functioning is operationally defined as an IQ score that falls approximately two standard deviations below the normative mean for a particular measure. For the *DSM-IV-TR*, limitations in adaptive functioning can be established through independent sources, such as through teacher reports or via educational or medical history. The *DSM-IV-TR* also includes a brief discussion of the usefulness of psychometric scales of adaptive behavior and directs the clinician to use individual cut-off scores included for measures of adaptive behavior, such as the Vineland.

The *DSM-IV-TR* guidelines differ from the 10th AAMR definition with respect to two points regarding the adaptive functioning diagnostic criterion. First, mental retardation is diagnosed when an individual shows two or more deficits or impairments among 11 areas of adaptive functioning, defined as "communication, self-care, home living, social/interpersonal skills, use of community resources, self-direction, functional academic skills, work, leisure, health, and safety" (American Psychiatric Association, 2000, p. 41). This is in contrast to the AAMR guidelines that require adaptive functioning deficits within one of three areas. Second, the *DSM-IV-TR* provides less operational specificity for establishing a diagnosis of mental retardation than those found in the 10th AAMR definition. For example, the 10th AAMR adaptive behavior criterion for diagnosing mental retardation is operationally defined as "performance that is at least two standard deviations below the mean" (Luckasson et al., 2002, p. 14) in an area of conceptual, social, or practical adaptive behavior skills or an overall score on a measure in one of these three areas. In contrast, the *DSM-IV-TR* does not provide a clear operational definition for identifying adaptive behavior deficits, but directs the clinician to gather evidence from independent sources (e.g., medical history) *or* use cutoff scores included on standardized measures of adaptive behavior.

Individuals with Disabilities Education Act Guidelines

For the purposes of educating children with mental retardation, the IDEA defines mental retardation in more general terms than either the AAMR (2002) guidelines or the *DSM-TR-IV.* The IDEA defines mental retardation as "significantly subaverage general intellectual functioning, existing concurrently with deficits in adaptive behavior and manifested during the developmental period, that adversely affects a child's educational performance" (Federal Register, 1999; p. 12422). When compared to the AAMR and *DSM-TR-IV* operational definitions of mental retardation, IDEA provides much less precision in defining deficits in intellectual functioning and adaptive behavior required for classification.

Assessment Methods and Procedures

As outlined in the definitions of mental retardation, diagnosis requires documentation of significant subaverage performance on an individually administered test of intellectual ability, such as the Wechsler Intelligence Scale for Children—Fourth Edition (WISC-IV; Wechsler, 2003a). Significant delays in adaptive behavior must also be documented across one or more domains, depending on diagnostic definition. The 2002 AAMR guidelines describe diagnosis of mental retardation as the first step in a three-step process of appropriate assessment of an individual with mental retardation. In addition to measuring intellectual functioning and adaptive skills across several areas, the AAMR recommends assessment of the individual's psychological functioning, physical health, and current environmental placement in order to provide the most appropriate level of support and intervention (Luckasson et al., 2002).

Intellectual Functioning

For the purpose of diagnosing mental retardation, guidelines concur that intellectual delays exist for an individual, as reflected in that individual's performance on an appropriate assessment instrument, typically an individually administered measure of intelligence. In the next section, we present brief introductions to three commonly used measures of cognitive functioning, the Stanford-Binet, the Wechsler scales, and the Woodcock-Johnson III Tests of Cognitive Abilities including a short summary of the theoretical underpinnings of each measure and brief review of relevant psychometric properties. Of particular interest for the diagnosis of mental retardation are: (a) the reliability of measurement, (b) adequate full scale or composite IQ score test floors to detect significantly subaverage intellectual functioning across age groups, and (c) criterion validity relevant to the performance of individuals with mental retardation on the test. Information relevant to these psychometric issues is highlighted in each summary. For the purposes of evaluating the adequacy of test floors, we calculated FSIQs or other appropriate summary scores for hypothetical individuals who responded incorrectly to *all* test items at the youngest ages for the test's normative sample. Regardless of the test, we realize that the validity and usefulness of the resulting IQ scores in such cases are questionable; test manuals and software scoring programs appropriately describe the questionable validity of resulting scores if an individual earns a certain number of raw scores of zero (e.g., Wechsler, 2002a). However, the hypothetical case of an individual of a young age earning raw scores of zero is used for illustrative purposes only and allows for consistent comparison across tests.

Stanford-Binet Intelligence Scale—Fifth Edition (SB-V; Roid, 2003a, 2003b): The SB-V is an individually administered assessment of intelligence designed for individuals ages 2 through 89 years 11 months. The SB-V represents the most recent revision of the Stanford-Binet scales originally published in 1916 by Terman. Consistent with its most recent predecessor, the Stanford-Binet—Fourth Edition (SB-IV; Thorndike, Hagen, & Sattler, 1986), the SB-V is built on a hierarchical model of intelligence consisting of a global factor, "*g*," and five second-level factors of intelligence: Fluid Reasoning, Knowledge, Quantitative Reasoning, Visual-Spatial Processing, and Working Memory (Roid, 2003a). The SB-V consists of 10 subtests that yield a full scale IQ (FSIQ), a verbal IQ (VIQ), a nonverbal IQ (NVIQ), and five-factor index scores as identified earlier with a mean of 100 and standard deviation of 15, a slight departure from SB-IV scaling that used a mean of 100 and standard deviation of 16.

Standardization procedures, reliability data, and validity evidence are presented in detail in the SB-V Technical Manual (Roid, 2003b). The SB-V was normed using a sample of 4,800 individuals matched across a range of stratification variables to 2001 U.S. census data. Internal consistency reliability for the SB-V meets or exceeds .93 for all IQ scores for all age groups; average internal consistency reliability for index scores meets or exceeds .90 for all five factors. Internal consistency reliability of index scores appears to be most robust for ages 14 and higher. The SB-V also shows adequate temporal stability as evidenced by FSIQ, VIQ, and PIQ test-retest correlations that meet or exceed .90 for all ages except for NVIQ scores for ages 21 to 59. Also relevant to the diagnosis of mental retardation in young children, the SB-V shows adequate floor for the four youngest age groups (i.e., 2 years 0 months to 2 years 7 months). For example, a child earning a raw score of 0 for all subtests at 2 years, 0 months would earn a FSIQ score of 53, which falls over three *SD*s below the normative mean for his or her age group. A variety of content, construct, and criterion validity evidence is also presented in the SB-V Technical Manual and the interested reader is referred to the manual for complete information in this regard.

Among other purposes, the SB-V is identified as appropriate for the diagnosis of mental retardation and other developmental disabilities. A sample of 119 individuals with documented mental retardation was included in the initial validation of the SB-V and yielded FSIQ, NVIQ, VIQ, and index scores that fell greater than two *SD* below the normative mean. Mean scores ranged from 64.2 (*SD* = 11.9) for Quantitative Reasoning to 56.5 (*SD* = 12.7) for FSIQ scores (Roid, 2003b). Initial evidence presented in the technical manual and briefly reviewed here suggests that the SB-V is appropriate for use in diagnosing mental retardation.

Wechsler Scales of Intelligence: Based on David Wechsler's ideas about intelligence and its measurement, beginning with Form I of the Wechsler-Bellevue Intelligence Scale (Wechsler, 1939), a group of intelligence tests now carry Wechsler's name. Wechsler's notions of intelligence were those of a multifaceted and multidetermined construct reflected in an "overall competency or global capacity, which in one way or another enables a sentient individual to comprehend the world and to deal effectively with its challenges" (Wechsler, 1981; p. 8). This definition is clearly supportive of a *g* conceptualization of intelligence, that of global capacity, general competence, or global entity. However, the multiplicity of cognitive domains included in Wechsler's instruments also reflects his belief that intelligence can (and should) be sampled through distinct tasks, such as those involving abstract reasoning, processing speed, and quantitative reasoning (e.g., Spruill & Black, 2001; Wechsler, 2002b). For example, Wechsler (1958) stated that the grouping of verbal (Verbal scale) and nonverbal (Performance scales) subtests did not reflect measurement of different *types* of intelligence but rather different *measures* of intelligence. At present, three comprehensive versions of the Wechsler scales exist organized around age: (a) the Wechsler Preschool and Primary Scale of Intelligence—Third Edition (WPPSI-III; Wechsler, 2002a, 2002b), appropriate for 2 years 6 months to 7 years 3 months; (b) the Wechsler Intelligence Scale for Children—Fourth Edition (WISC-IV; Wechsler, 2003a, 2003b), appropriate for 6 years 0 months to 16 years 11 months; and (c) the Wechsler Adult Intelligence Scale—Third Edition (WAIS-III; Wechsler, 1997a, 1997b), appropriate for individuals ages 16 through 89. An abbreviated version of the Wechsler scales also exists, the Wechsler Abbreviated Scale of Intelligence (WASI; Wechsler, 1999), which is appropriate for individuals ages 6 through 89. Each measure contains traditional summary FSIQ scores, in addition to Verbal (VIQ)/Verbal Comprehension Index (VCI) and Performance IQ (PIQ)/Perceptual Reasoning Index (PRI) scores.

The set of Wechsler scales are identified as the most commonly used measures to assess intelligence and appear to have become regarded as the "gold standard" for evaluating intelligence across age ranges (e.g., Spruill & Black, 2001). From standardization and psychometric standpoints, there are good reasons to hold the Wechsler scales in high regard as these tests are traditionally among the strongest available. Standardization samples routinely match U.S. census data quite well, regardless of the timing of the revision. Indices of various types of reliability, such as internal consistency reliability (e.g., split-half; Cronbach's alpha coefficient) and temporal stability (i.e., test-retest reliability), are also quite strong across versions and revisions. For example, internal consistency reliability for VIQ/VCI and FSIQ scores meets or exceeds .91 for all age groups across all current versions of the Wechsler scales (Wechsler, 1997b, 1999, 2002b, 2003b). For PIQ/PRI scores, internal consistency reliability falls below .90 only for the WPPSI-III and only for children between the ages of 2 years, 6 months and 3 years, 5 months (Wechsler, 2002b). The comprehensive Wechsler scales (i.e., all except the WAIS) show adequate floors for FSIQ scores. For example, the WPPSI-III yields a FSIQ of 48 for the youngest age groups (2 years 6 months to 2 years 8 months) when earning all subtest raw scores of zero (Wechsler, 2002a). Similarly, the youngest WISC-IV age groups (6 years 0 months to 6 years 11 months) earn a FSIQ of 40 when all subtest raw score are zero (Wechsler, 2003a). The WASI yields a FSIQ of 68 for the youngest age group (6 years 0 months— 6 years 3 months) when all subtest raw scores of zero, reflecting a test floor that is too high for the purposes of diagnosing mental retardation with this age group (Wechsler, 1999).

Across the board, the most recent versions of the Wechsler scales are backed by content, criterion, and construct validation as presented in the relevant technical manuals for the scales. Relevant to criterion validity for mental retardation, all recent Wechsler revisions have included clinical samples of individuals diagnosed with mental retardation. Across age ranges, each clinical contrast group has earned FSIQ scores that fall within the range of mental retardation. For example, a sample of 40 children with mild mental retardation earned an average FSIQ of 62 on the WPPSI-III while a sample of 19 children with moderate mental retardation earned an average FSIQ score of 53 (Wechsler, 2002b). Similarly, a sample of 63 children with mild mental retardation earned an average FSIQ of 60 on the WISC-IV while a sample of 57 children with moderate mental retardation earned an average FSIQ score of 46 on the WISC-IV (Wechsler, 2003b).

Woodcock-Johnson III Tests of Cognitive Abilities (WJ III COG; Woodcock, McGrew, & Mather, 2001):   The WJ III COG represents the most recent revision of the Woodcock-Johnson psychoeducational battery (Mather & Woodcock, 2001a, 2001b). The WJ III COG is built from the "blueprint" of CHC theory, which guided the measurement of cognitive abilities and organizing of summary scores. Similar to its predecessor, the WJ III COG is designed to be used with individuals between the ages of 24 months to ages 90 or older. The WJ III COG consists of 20 subtests which yield three scores representing overall cognitive functioning: the General Intellectual Ability, Standard Scale (GIA-Std), the General Intellectual Ability, Extended Scale (GIA-Ext), and a Brief Intellectual Ability (BIA) scale. The GIA-Std and GIA-Ext scores represent the first principal component factor (or *g* factor) for the relevant tests used in the first 17 subtests. Each GIA score is comprised of either one (GIA-Std) or two (GIA-Ext) measures of each of the seven broad ability scores proposed in the theoretical model. The GIA-Std consists of the first seven subtests of the WJ III COG battery, while the GIA-Ext consists of 14 subtests, tests 1 to 7 and 11 to 17.

Standardization procedures, reliability data, and validity evidence are presented in detail in the WJ III COG Technical Manual (McGrew & Woodcock, 2001). The WJ III COG was normed using a sample of 8,818 individuals matched across a range of stratification variables to 2000 U.S. census data. Internal consistency reliability for the GIA-Ext and GIA-Std scores (i.e., measures of *g*) meets or exceeds .96 for all age groups; median internal consistency reliability for the seven broad ability scores (e.g., *Gf* and *Gc*) meets or exceeds .81. The Visual-Spatial Thinking (*Gv*) broad ability score was an outlier at .81, with Long-Term Retrieval (*Glr*) and Short-Term Memory (*Gsm*) scores also falling below .90.

The Technical Manual does not include norms tables; therefore, we used the WJ III COG Compuscore and Profiles Program (Schrank & Woodcock, 2001) to calculate GIA-Std scores for total raw scores of 0 and 1 for ages 2 years, 0 months (2-0); 3-0, 4-0, and 5-0. The scoring program did not produce a GIA-Std score for any of the ages when all raw scores were entered as zero. For a 2-0 child earning a raw score of 1 on the Verbal Comprehension, Spatial Relations, *or* Concept Formation subtests, the GIA-Std score ranged from 119 to 120. For a 3-0 child earning a raw score of 1 for *any* one of the first six subtests, the GIA-Std score ranged from 85 to 86. For a 4-0 child earning a raw score of 1 for *any* one of the first six subtests, the GIA-Std score ranged from 65 to 67. For a 5-0 child earning a raw score of 1 for *any* one of the first seven subtests, the GIA-Std score ranged from 51 to 52.

A variety of construct and concurrent validity evidence is presented in the WJ III COG Technical Manual. For example, concurrent validity of the WJ III COG was examined in typically developing preschoolers and elementary school children by showing strong correlations with other measures of intelligence, such as the WPPSI-R and SB-IV. Relevant to the criterion validity of the WJ III

COG for use with individuals with mental retardation, the Technical Manual does not include a clinical group of individuals with cognitive delays. Samples of individuals with attention-deficit hyperactivity disorder and learning disability were included in the validation of the WJ III COG. The interested reader is referred to the Technical Manual for complete information (McGrew & Woodcock, 2001). Overall, the high floors for preschool children under the age of 5-0 and lack of validation with individuals with mental retardation make the WJ III COG unsuitable for diagnosing cognitive delays in very young children.

Adaptive Functioning

Delays or deficits in adaptive functioning are required for formal diagnosis of mental retardation. For example, the 2002 AAMR guidelines require that an individual must perform two standard deviations below average on a standardized measure of adaptive behavior in either a single area of adaptive behavior (i.e., conceptual, social, and practical) or an overall score on a standard measure of adaptive behavior, such as the Adaptive Behavior Composite of the Vineland Adaptive Behavior Scales (Vineland; Sparrow, Balla, & Cicchetti, 1984). In addition to the Vineland, the 2002 AAMR guidelines identify four measures that show appropriate content coverage as well as demonstrate adequate psychometric properties for the purpose of diagnosing mental retardation, including: the AAMR Adaptive Behavior Scales (ABS; Nihira, Leland, & Lambert, 1993), the Scales of Independent Behavior—Revised (SIB-R; Bruininks, Woodcock, Weatherman, & Hill, 1996), and the Comprehensive Test of Adaptive Behavior—Revised (CTAB-R; G. L. Adams, 1999).

Psychological and Behavioral Assessment

As noted earlier in the chapter, children with mental retardation can suffer from the full range of psychopathology, typically at rates higher than reported in the general population; therefore, assessment of emotional functioning has been defined as essential to comprehensive understanding of an individual with mental retardation (Luckasson et al., 1992). Historically, psychological disorders appear to have been underdiagnosed in individuals with mental retardation due to the phenomenon known as *diagnostic overshadowing,* that is, the tendency to attribute behavioral disturbances associated with psychopathology to the presence of mental retardation (Jopp & Keys, 2001; Luckasson et al., 2002). Diagnostic overshadowing has been shown to exist regardless of type or severity of mental disorder (e.g., schizophrenia, depression, or anxiety) and is present in practicing clinical, school, and counseling psychologists as well as rehabilitation counselors (Jopp & Keys, 2001). Psychological and emotional assessment of individuals with mental retardation is problematic due to cognitive limitations and associated language delays; therefore, a focus on behavioral signs of mental illness as opposed to verbally reported symptoms is typically most useful. As with typically developing children, assessment of psychological functioning includes a parent or caregiver interview, interview with the individual with mental retardation, and behavioral rating scales (Szymanski & King, 1999).

Third-Party Ratings Specific to Mental Retardation: In light of the cognitive delays present in individuals with mental retardation, third-party rating scales are frequently used to assess psychological functioning. In a recent review of rating instruments specifically designed to assess psychopathology in individuals with mental retardation, Wallander et al. (2003) found the Aberrant Behavior Checklist (ABC; Aman, Singh, Stewart, & Field, 1985; Freund & Reiss, 1991), Developmental Behavior Checklist (DBC; Einfeld & Tonge, 1995), and Nisonger Children Behavior Rating Form (NCBRF; Aman, Tassé, Rojahn, & Hammer, 1996) to show acceptable psychometric evidence for use with children with mental retardation. The ABC was originally developed as a rating scale to assess effects of interventions for individuals with mental retardation within residential or institutional settings (Aman et al., 1985; E. C. Brown, Aman, & Havercamp, 2002). The original ABC (now titled the ABC-Residential; E. C. Brown et al., 2002) was modified by Freund and Reiss (1991) and Aman and Singh (1994) for use as a rating scale by parents and teachers outside of residential settings. The modified ABC (titled the ABC-Community) consists of 58 items that can be completed by parents or teachers measuring behaviors such as irritability, stereotypic behavior and inappropriate speech (E. C. Brown et al., 2002; Freund & Reiss, 1991). Across clinical samples, the ABC has reliably yielded either a four-factor structure (i.e., Irritable/Uncooperative; Lethargy/Withdrawal; Hyperactivity; Stereotypy/Self-injury; E. C. Brown et al., 2002) or five-factor structure that includes the four-factor solution plus an Inappropriate Speech factor.

The DBC (Einfeld & Tonge, 1995) exists in two forms, a 96-item parent version and a 94-item teacher version. Six clinical scales for the DBC were empirically derived from an initial sample of 1,093 children and adolescents as follows: Disruptive; Self-absorbed; Communication Disturbance; Anxiety; Social Relating; and Antisocial (Einfeld & Tonge, 1995). Further validation (e.g., Hastings, Brown, Mount, & Cormack, 2001) and revision (Dekker, Nunn, Einfeld, Tonge, & Koot, 2002) of the DBC has yielded a revised factor structure that consists of five clinical subscales with the Disruptive/Antisocial subscales combining to form a scale and the other scales remaining intact (e.g., Self-absorbed; Communication Disturbance).

Representing a revision of the original Child Behavior Rating Form (CBRF; Edelbrock, 1985), the NCBRF is a psychopathology rating scale that consists of 71 problem behavior items and a 10-item social competence scale that is appropriate for both parents and teachers (Aman et al., 1996). For the parent version, the NCBRF problem behavior items yielded six problem behavior factors as follows: Conduct Problems; Insecure/Anxious; Hyperactive; Self-injury/Stereotypic; Self-isolated/Ritualistic; and Overly Sensitive. Factor analysis for the teacher version yielded a similar factor structure when compared to the parent version, with five of six factors almost identical across versions. The teacher version yielded a sixth factor identified as an "Irritable" problem area consisting of content such as tearful, frustrated, and prone to tantrums. Similar to other multi-informant rating scales, the parent and teacher versions of the NCBRF show only modest interrater agreement for the five factors yielded in the initial factor analyses, ranging from .54 to

.37. Concurrent validity for the NCBRF has been established with the ABC as similar scales shared strong relationships (e.g., for Teacher-rated ABC Irritability subscale and NCBRF Irritability, r = .85). Overall, the NCBRF has shown good internal consistency reliability for subscales and total scores; however, additional validation is needed for the NCBRF.

General Behavioral Rating Scales: The factor structure of the Child Behavior Checklist (CBCL; Achenbach, 1991a, 1991b), a widely used parent (or caregiver) report of behavioral problems in children and adolescents, has been examined with children with mental retardation. The higher order CBCL factors of Internalizing and Externalizing problems emerged in a sample of 67 children and adolescents, while narrow-band factors, such as somatic problems, anxious/depressed, and delinquent behavior, were not replicated (Borthwick-Duffy, Lane, & Widaman, 1997). The findings suggest that the syndrome-based taxonomy of the CBCL that emerged from the standardization sample and has been validated with clinic-referred samples does not necessarily hold for individuals with mental retardation. It does appear, however, that the broader Internalizing/Externalizing factor structure of the CBCL is found with individuals with mental retardation. Embregts (2000) raised questions about the reliability of the CBCL for use with individuals with mental retardation. Embregts found that interrater and test-retest reliability for CBCL items and syndromes is lower for adolescents with mental retardation when compared to the standardization sample.

The Behavior Assessment System for Children (BASC; C. R. Reynolds & Kamphaus, 1998) a frequently used measure of children's behavioral adjustment, has been examined with children and adolescents with mental retardation. In a sample of 112 children and adolescents with mental retardation, teachers reported problems with learning, atypical behaviors, and social withdrawal that were greater than one *SD* above the mean of the standardization sample. Teachers' ratings of adaptive skills for the group yielded adaptive skills scores that were greater than one *SD* below the mean of the standardization sample. In a sample of 89 children and adolescents with mental retardation, parents reported problems with atypical behaviors and attention that were greater than one *SD* above the mean of the standardization sample, while adaptive skills fell below the standardization mean. Unlike the CBCL, the factor structure and reliability of the BASC rating scales have not been examined specifically for individuals with mental retardation.

Self-Report Instruments: In light of the cognitive limitations that, in part, define mental retardation, self-report measures have been used less frequently than third-party ratings when evaluating the psychological and emotional functioning of individuals with mental retardation. In a few instances, however, self-report has been used to assess the psychological adjustment of individuals with mental retardation, typically through altering the response format of the scale. For example, a 173-item abbreviated form of the Minnesota Multiphasic Personality Inventory, the MMPI-168(L), was administered in interview format to evaluate the presence of psychopathology in individuals diagnosed with mild to moderate mental retardation, including adolescents as young as 17 (McDaniel, Passmore, & Sewell, 2003). Individuals' MMPI-168(L) responses yielded clinically significant elevations (i.e., *T*-scores ≥ 70) on scales measuring thought disorder, anxiety, and somatic complaints (McDaniel et al., 2003). As another example of self-report use with individuals with mental retardation, the BASC self-report form was completed by 37 children and adolescents with mental retardation whose ratings produced no significant elevations across 14 behavior problem scales (C. R. Reynolds & Kamphaus, 1998).

Behavioral Assessment: Up to 15% of individuals diagnosed with mental retardation engage in problem behaviors, such as aggression and self-injury (Emerson et al., 2001), which often requires behavioral assessment to guide appropriate intervention. Functional behavioral assessment (FBA) techniques are frequently recommended to understand variables that serve to maintain and reinforce problem behaviors exhibited by an individual.

Functional behavioral assessment can take a variety of forms, including a correlational analysis, such as behavior checklists or antecedent-behavior-consequence (A-B-C) charting, and experimental manipulation, such as experimental functional analysis (EFA; Iwata et al., 1994). Experimental functional analysis procedures involve systematic manipulation of the environment typically within highly controlled settings in order to identify potentially reinforcing conditions for problem behaviors. Through EFA, problem behaviors for individuals with mental retardation have been identified as being maintained by: (a) *positive reinforcement,* such as inadvertent provision of social attention or tangible rewards when problem behavior is exhibited, (b) *negative reinforcement,* such as the removal of task demands when problem behavior occurs, or (c) *automatic reinforcement,* such as problem behavior that is not reinforced by social variables. For example, rocking behavior might be automatically reinforced through vestibular stimulation. Experimental functional analyses have also shown that problem behavior may be reinforced by multiple environmental variables that require multiple behavioral modifications to reduce the behavior. Regardless of the particular method used in FBA, the underlying goal is shared; that is, to identify and alter circumstances that contribute to the display of problem behavior.

Health, Physical, and Etiological Considerations

Assessment of physical health is important for making recommendations to improve adaptation. As mentioned earlier in the chapter, individuals with mental retardation are at greater risk for developing a host of physical problems when contrasted with the general population, such as epilepsy, cerebral palsy, and cardiac abnormalities. The 1992 and 2002 AAMR guidelines also assert that the assessment of physical health is important to establish the etiology of mental retardation, if possible (Luckasson et al., 2002). Etiological information is important because it: (a) increases professionals' awareness of associated health problems, (b) may lead to prescriptive intervention (e.g., dietary restriction for phenylketonuria

[PKU]), (c) helps to guide prevention efforts, and, (d) allows for individuals to be grouped together for research, administrative, and clinical purposes (Luckasson et al., 1992). Establishing etiological factors is also important in light of the growing number of behavioral phenotypes being defined through cognitive profiles, behavioral presentation, and long-term outcome (Dykens & Hodapp, 2001).

Environmental Considerations

Aspects of the environment significantly influence behavioral adaptation in terms of facilitating or hindering independence, community integration, and overall well-being. For example, providing access to medical services improves an individual's physical health, and allowing an individual control of possessions improves independence and self-efficacy. As noted earlier, operant conditioning theories have also identified environmental variables as potentially important in understanding the increased rates of psychopathology in individuals with mental retardation. For these reasons, the AAMR provides recommendations for the analysis of environments across educational programs, living environments, and employment settings (Luckasson et al., 1992). The purpose of the analysis is to identify factors within each environment that facilitate or inhibit adaptation. Incorporated within the context of other information, analysis of an individual's environment allows for the most appropriate recommendations for support systems and intervention.

CASE STUDY

The following case study is presented in the form of a psychological report. Identifying information, such as child and family name, child sex, and other particulars has been removed, altered, or fictionalized to protect confidentiality. A short interpretive description follows the report.

Identifying Information and Reason for Referral

Cass Green, a 7-year-old girl, was referred by her mother to determine if she showed symptoms indicative of an autism spectrum disorder. Mrs. Green identified several concerns regarding Cass's development, particularly in the areas of delayed speech, lack of academic progress, and socially inappropriate behaviors at home. Cass lives with her parents and two older brothers. Cass is currently enrolled in regular and special education programming and served as a child with Moderate Intellectual Disability (MOD).

Evaluation Procedures

Autism Diagnostic Observation Schedule, Module 1 (ADOS)

Beery-Buktenica Developmental Test of Visual-Motor Integration (VMI)

Behavior Assessment System for Children (BASC)

   Parent Rating Scales

   Teacher Rating Scales

Bracken Basic Concept Scale—Revised (BBCS-R)

Childhood Autism Rating Scale (CARS)

Parent Interview

Peabody Picture Vocabulary Test—Third Edition, Form A (PPVT-III)

Review of Medical Records, Prior Psychological Reports, and Current Individualized Education Program (IEP)

Vineland Adaptive Behavior Scales—Interview Edition—Survey Form (Vineland)

Wechsler Intelligence Scale for Children—Third Edition (WISC-III)

Background Information

According to Mrs. Green, Cass was the product of a normal pregnancy and delivery. She was born at 37 weeks gestation via Caesarean section without complication, weighing 5 pounds, 11 ounces. Cass has met several developmental milestones with mild to moderate delay with language delays more apparent than motor delays. For example, Cass did not crawl, but walked alone at age 17 to 18 months. She spoke her first word at around 12 months and has rarely spoken in complete sentences. Cass has received appropriate pediatric care and does not suffer from any major illnesses. Family history is significant for learning problems and ADHD.

With respect to the referral question, Mrs. Green reported concerns about Cass's limited academic progress, inappropriate behaviors, tantrumming behaviors, and mild self-injury. According to Mrs. Green, Cass has shown little motivation to learn academic concepts and demonstrates variable mastery of academic tasks. For example, some days Cass recognizes a letter but will not the next. Mrs. Green also reported a history of inappropriate and sometimes aggressive behavior, such as pulling others' hair, kicking at babysitters and family friends, and inappropriate touching of others' faces. Mrs. Green also noted that Cass has tantrummed when taken to school, and she has engaged in mild self-injurious behaviors, such as pulling her hair and scratching herself.

Due to concerns with Cass's overall developmental delays, she was evaluated at age two and received occupational and speech therapy. A genetic evaluation was conducted and resulted in several positive findings in terms of physical features, such as flat nasal bridge, however, genetic testing was negative. Due to concerns about staring episodes, an EEG test was conducted, which was also negative.

GENERAL BEHAVIORAL OBSERVATIONS

Cass presented as a socially engaging and compliant girl who separated easily from her mother for the purposes of formal testing. She worked diligently on testing tasks and seemed to enjoy time spent with the examiners across different contexts, including formal testing, informal play, and snack breaks. Cass's articulation was poor and her language was restricted to one- and two-word utterances. Additional behavioral observations are presented later in the report pertaining to Cass's social and communication functioning. In general, Cass was alert, compliant, and interested in the testing materials; therefore, this assessment is viewed as an adequate estimate of her current intellectual, academic, and social-emotional functioning.

COGNITIVE AND LANGUAGE FUNCTIONING

The WISC-III was used to evaluate Cass's overall cognitive development including verbal and nonverbal reasoning abilities. Cass earned the following WISC-III composite scores:

Scale/Index	Standard Score	Percentile Rank
Verbal IQ	52	0.1
Performance IQ	47	<0.1
Full Scale IQ	46	<0.1
Verbal Comprehension	56	0.2
Perceptual Organization	50	<0.1
Freedom from Distractibility	50	<0.1
Processing Speed	50	<0.1

Cass is functioning in the Intellectually Deficient range of general intelligence with equally developed verbal and nonverbal reasoning skills. Cass's performance is consistent with prior evaluations that document her cognitive impairments as falling within the moderate range of mental retardation. Cass's WISC-III subtest scores are as follows:

Verbal Subtests	Scaled Score	Performance Subtests	Scaled Score
Information	4	Picture Completion	1
Similarities	1	Coding	1
Arithmetic	1	Picture Arrangement	1
Vocabulary	1	Block Design	1
Comprehension	1	Object Assembly	2
Digit Span	1	Symbol Search	1

Note: Subtest scores have a mean of 10, a standard deviation of 3, and can range from 1 to 19. Subtest scores that fall between 8 and 12 are considered Average.

To assess Cass's receptive language abilities, she completed the PPVT-III and earned a standard score of 40 (< .01st percentile), which falls within the Intellectually Deficient range. Visual-motor integration skills were assessed using the VMI. Cass earned a standard score of 45 (0.01st percentile), which is roughly equivalent to a child around the age of 2 years, 11 months. Overall, Cass's performance indicates consistent and significant delays across all areas of cognitive, language, and visual-motor functioning.

Bracken Basic Concept Skills—Revised (BBCS-R)

Cass's mastery of preacademic concepts was assessed using the BBCS-R. The BBCS-R assesses children's mastery of numbers, letters, colors, shapes, sizes, direction/position, self-awareness, textures, quantity, and time. Cass earned a School Readiness Composite score of 52 (0.1st percentile) and Total Test score of 51 (<0.1st percentile) indicating significant delays in mastery of basic concepts across all content areas.

SOCIAL-EMOTIONAL AND BEHAVIORAL FUNCTIONING

Behavior Assessment System for Children—Preschool Form (BASC-P)

The Behavior Assessment System for Children (BASC) was used as a global, comprehensive assessment of Cass's behavior in a variety of domains. Mrs. Green and Cass's special education resource teacher completed BASC rating forms. At home, Mrs. Green endorsed significant problems with Cass: (a) *atypical behaviors,* such as repetitive behaviors and picking at her skin, (b) *attention problems,* such distractibility and fatigue during learning, and (c) *social withdrawal,* such as being shy, avoiding other children, and being clingy in unfamiliar surroundings. Mrs. Green also endorsed significant problems with Cass's adaptive behavior within the domains of social skills and adaptability to change. Within the school setting, the special education resource teacher reported significant problems with: (a) *attention problems,* such as being distractible, having a short attention span, and forgetfulness, and (b) *learning problems,* such as making careless errors, having reading problems, and difficulties with following instructions. In general, behavioral reports highlight Cass's difficulties with attention across different settings, while she shows more social difficulties and disruptive behaviors in the home environment versus the school setting.

Vineland Adaptive Behavior Scales—Interview Edition,
Survey Form (Vineland)

Cass's mother provided information necessary for the completion of the Vineland Adaptive Behavior Scales—Interview Edition, Survey Form. The Vineland provides a measure of a child's self-help skills in four areas: Communication, or the skills involved in receptive and expressive language acquisition; Daily Living, including skills involved in self-care; Socialization, or the skills needed for relating to others, playing, and coping with environmental demands; and Motor, movement and control of the large muscles and hands and fingers. Cass's scores on the four general Vineland domains and subdomains were:

Area	Standard Score (Mean = 100)	Age Equivalent (Years,Months)	Adaptive Level
Communication	46	2,4	Low
Receptive	—	3,11	Mod Low
Expressive	—	2,2	Low
Written	—	1,6	Low
Daily Living Skills	34	2,5	Low
Personal	—	2,7	Low
Domestic	—	2,0	Low
Community	—	2,5	Low
Socialization	59	2,10	Low
Interpersonal Relationships	—	2,9	Low
Play and Leisure Time	—	2,1	Low
Coping Skills	—	3,10	Low
Motor Skills (Estimated)	73	4,3	Mod Low
Gross	—	4,0	Mod Low
Fine	—	4,5	Mod Low
Adaptive Behavior Composite	43	2,6	Low

Cass's repertoire of adaptive skills is generally commensurate with her cognitive development, as measured by the WISC-III. In the Communication area, Cass points accurately to all body parts, says at least 100 recognizable words, and follows instructions in "if-then" form. She does not yet use the words "a," "the," "behind," "between" in sentences or ask "Wh" questions. In the area of Daily

Living Skills, Cass bathes herself with help and sets the table with assistance. She is not yet toilet trained through the night and does not dress herself independently. In the area of Socialization, Cass addresses familiar adults by name, imitates others' phrases and movements, and engages in make-believe play activities. She does not share toys independently, follow rules of games independently, or have a best friend. Although the Motor Skills scale was not normed with children under six, we administered these items due to Cass's documented delays in this area. Her scores in this area should be considered estimates as she is being compared to children between 5 years, 10 months and 5 years, 11 months of age. In the area of Motor Skills, Cass catches a small ball, cuts out items with scissors, and draws some recognizable forms with a writing instrument. She does not yet hop forward with ease, unlock key locks, or ride a bicycle without training wheels. The Adaptive Behavior Composite score indicates that Cass's overall adaptive skill level is approximately at the 2-year, 6-month-old level. Overall, Cass shows significant delays across many areas of intellectual and adaptive functioning.

Autism Diagnostic Observation Schedule (Module 1)

Relevant to the referral question, Cass was administered the Autism Diagnostic Observation Schedule, Module 1 (ADOS). The ADOS is a standardized observation of social behavior and communication in a variety of structured and unstructured situations designed to elicit social and communicative symptoms indicative of autism spectrum disorders. Module 1 is appropriate for use with children with expressive language that typically involves phrase speech or expressive language skills that fall below an age-equivalent of 30 months, such as Cass's. By sampling a range of nonverbal social behaviors, the ADOS is particularly useful in discriminating between children with autism spectrum disorders and those with mental retardation and/or language delays.

During ADOS administration, Cass communicated with single word and two-word utterances, such as "bear," "Ma-ma," "Help me," and "My turn." Cass exhibited an array of appropriate verbal and nonverbal social behaviors that did not indicate the presence of an autism spectrum disorder. In terms of "receptive" social behaviors, Cass was responsive to her name being called, was responsive to bids for shared attention, responded appropriately with social smiling, and participated appropriately in two play activities, a make-believe birthday party and game of peek-a-boo. Cass appropriately initiated and coordinated social behaviors as well. She turned to show her mother items of interest and paired her showing behavior with appropriate gesture or speech, such as smiling at the examiner during a bubble blowing activity. Cass also demonstrated appropriate imaginative and imitative play activities with a variety of objects, such as pretending a block was an airplane and comb. Overall, Cass's ADOS Communication, Social Interaction, and Total scores were not indicative of an autism spectrum disorder.

Childhood Autism Rating Scale

Based on observational data and parent interview, the Childhood Autism Rating Scale (CARS) was completed by the examiners. The CARS is a rating form used to assist in the diagnosis of autism and autistic-like disorders. Cass's Total CARS score of 22 fell within the Non-Autistic range.

SUMMARY AND RECOMMENDATIONS

Cass is a 7-year-old girl who shows cognitive impairments and delays in adaptive behavior that meet formal diagnostic criteria for Moderate Mental Retardation (*DSM-IV-TR* 318.0). In our opinion, Cass does not meet diagnostic criteria for an autism spectrum disorder. Cass demonstrated a repertoire of appropriate social behaviors, such as initiating and responding to joint attention, engaging in imitative and pretend play, combining nonverbal gestures with limited expressive language, reciprocating social smiles, and sharing in enjoyable activities. Despite varied and seemingly comprehensive attempts, no etiological cause has been identified to explain Cass's cognitive and developmental delays. Like other professionals who have evaluated Cass, we noticed several unusual physical features in her presentation which resembled Down syndrome, such as a flat nasal bridge and protruding tongue.

Based on the test results the following are recommended:

1. Mr. and Mrs. Green are encouraged to share the results of our evaluation with educators and medical professionals who work with Cass.
2. In our opinion, school professionals should consider identifying Cass as a child who is eligible for special education services, most appropriately under the category of Intellectually Disabled.
3. Cass would benefit from special education programming appropriate for a child diagnosed with Moderate Mental Retardation. In our opinion, one beneficial teaching approach to use with Cass would involve discrete trial training using applied behavior analysis (ABA) to teach social behaviors, increase expressive speech, and increase adaptive skills. Applied behavior analysis training of this sort should be provided in a small and structured educational setting within the context of an explicit and regular routine. Special education services should include the following additional components for Cass:
    a. Enrollment in extended school year activities,
    b. Ongoing access to speech and language therapy services, and
    c. Occupational and physical therapy to target Cass's development in the areas of fine and gross motor skills.
4. Within the school setting, Cass should interact with typically developing peers throughout the instructional day. She should also participate in social programming that involves structured social situations, such as well-defined play activities with a peer "buddy." Social programming of this sort should be facilitated by a school professional (e.g., counselor) and might take the form of structured social interactions with an older typical peer who demonstrates appropriate social behaviors.
5. Cass would also benefit from ABA intervention provided within the home to target reduction of self-injurious behavior, increase compliance, and improve adaptive behavior skills. In our opinion, Cass's self-injurious behavior should be evaluated through functional behavioral assessment methods to learn if environmental variables are serving to reinforce this behavior. Mrs. Green has made contact with a local parent support

agency that assists families in the recruitment and appropriate training and supervision of behavioral interventionists. The examiners offered to assist Mrs. Green in her efforts to recruit therapists for Cass.

6. The family would also benefit from behaviorally based parent training services targeting the improvement of Cass's adaptive skills as well as management of problem behaviors she exhibits within the home. Mrs. Green reported a high level of parenting stress and the family would benefit from intervention services that involve both parents.

7. Mr. and Mrs. Green may also benefit from accessing services, referrals, and advocacy through contact with the local chapter of the Association for Retarded Citizens (ARC).

Discussion of Case Study

Cass's evaluation illustrates many of the concepts and assessment methods relevant to the assessment of suspected or documented mental retardation. Given that the initial referral question was posed as a suspected diagnosis of autistic disorder in addition to mental retardation, the reader is referred to Chapter 5 of the present volume for a discussion of Autism Spectrum Disorders. Cass is formally diagnosed with Moderate Mental Retardation according to *DSM-IV-TR* criteria. This is so because she demonstrates delays in cognition and adaptive behavior that are present prior to the age of 18 years, as set forth in the *DSM-IV-TR* criteria. We did not find sufficient evidence to warrant an additional diagnosis of an autism spectrum disorder.

Cass shows a rather characteristic profile of cognitive and adaptive functioning for a child with mental retardation with consistent delays across cognitive, language, academic, social, adaptive, and motor functioning. Her profile stands in contrast to the fairly characteristic profile of functioning observed for children with autism, with impairments in social functioning often beyond what is predicted by cognitive delays. Cass also exhibits mild self-injurious behavior and tantrumming, concerning behaviors sometimes seen in children with mental retardation. Relevant to the possible functional aspects of these behaviors, school teachers did not report self-injurious behavior or tantrumming in the classroom; therefore, environmental reinforcement seemed to occur only at home, particularly in the presence of the mother.

Conclusion

The chapter presented an overview of important constructs of interest when faced with a diagnostic decision about the presence of mental retardation. Conceptualizations and definitions of mental retardation have moved away from sole reliance on cognitive functioning for diagnosis to include considerations of adaptive functioning and day-to-day behavioral adjustment. Most recently, classification of individuals with mental retardation have relied less on cognitive functioning (e.g., mild, moderate, severe, profound) and focused on multiple domains of functioning and the provision of necessary supports to maximize an individual's functioning.

Different classification systems for mental retardation converge on two essential domains that must be assessed for the purposes of diagnosis: cognitive functioning and adaptive behavior. Outside of the purposes of classification, other areas are important for assessment, particularly an individual's psychological and emotional functioning, as individuals with mental retardation frequently demonstrate comorbid psychiatric and behavioral impairments, such as depression and self-injury. In addition, individuals with mental retardation often experience associated physical problems; therefore, involvement of medical professionals in comprehensive assessment is necessary.

Recent trends in understanding mental retardation have focused on the identification of an increasing number of genetic and environmental causes. For some causes of mental retardation, such as Down syndrome, fetal alcohol syndrome, and fragile X, cognitive and behavioral phenotypes have been identified that can assist with outlining appropriate intervention and improving prognostic accuracy. At present, however, most causes of mental retardation are not known, particularly for those individuals functioning in the mild range of cognitive impairment.

Learning Disabilities

Randy W. Kamphaus, Matthew Quirk, and Anna P. Kroncke

4

Chapter

Learning disability (LD) remains one of the most controversial diagnoses currently in use (Kamphaus, 2001). The validity of the diagnosis per se has been called into question by leaders in the field such as Stanovich (2005), who has suggested that the use of the traditional ability/achievement discrepancy criteria for LD diagnosis is so flawed that it threatens to make the entire LD field irrelevant and relegated to the status of "pseudoscience." Consequently, definition of the relevant constructs to assess remains as a central challenge that has not yet been settled by any semblance of a consensus in the field.

Constructs of Interest

This controversy is, therefore, first presented as a backdrop for defining the constructs of interest. Because reading disability has been the focus of most of the research and controversy, the following section introduces developmental dyslexia, or reading disability, and presents the various diagnostic criteria for this disorder as well as a proposal for criteria for diagnosis.

The most well-known learning disability is developmental dyslexia (now referred to as reading disability), which is characterized by extraordinary difficulty acquiring basic reading skills. Developmental dyslexia was first described as a separate disorder in the late 1800s. This disorder is often characterized as being neurologically based despite the fact that there is limited research to support such an assertion (Stanovich, 1999), although newer imaging technologies portend a breakthrough.

Before these recent technological advances in neuropsychological research methods, the primary source of evidence supporting the existence of a neurological abnormality in children with learning disabilities came from noninvasive diagnostic procedures such as crude imaging procedures or the rare autopsy study. Technology has now allowed for new methods of detection including functional neuroimaging including the use of position emission tomography (PET), functional magnetic resonance imaging (fMRI), magnetic source imaging (MSI), and magnetic resonance spectroscopy (MRS; Vellutino, Fletcher, Snowling, & Scanlon, 2004). Although the methods used in each of these procedures is beyond the scope of this chapter, new methods such as these are allowing for more detailed examination of the biology behind dyslexia and specific reading disabilities. There is evidence emerging from recent studies that some of the neurological structures of children with reading disabilities may be different from those of normal readers (Kamphaus, 2001).

While widespread agreement on the specific neurological structures that are impacted in students with learning disabilities have not yet been reached, there is considerable evidence that the core psychological processing deficit lies in phonological coding (Siegel, 1999; Stanovich, 1999; Vellutino et al., 2004).

Berringer (2001) characterizes dyslexia as an uneven development between word reading and higher level processes within the functional reading system, such as those involved in reading comprehension. Therefore, reading difficulty is due to phonological processing deficits, orthographic-phonological connections, or limitations of fluency, including automaticity and reading rate.

Siegel (1999) offered the following definition of dyslexia:

Dyslexia involves difficulties with phonological processing, including knowing the relationship between letters and sounds. Over the years, a consensus has emerged that one core deficit in dyslexia is a severe difficulty with phonological processing. (p. 306)

Siegel also proposes that establishing a specific spelling or written expression disability is difficult due to the intertwined nature of reading disabilities with problems in written expression. The commingling of reading and other problems is represented in a definition of dyslexia offered by Padget, Knight, and Sawyer (1996, cited in Siegel, 1999, p. 306) who proposed the following definition:

Dyslexia is a language-based learning disorder that is biological in origin and primarily interferes with the acquisition of print literacy (reading, writing, and spelling). Dyslexia is characterized by poor decoding and spelling abilities as well as deficit in phonological manipulation. These primary characteristics may co-occur with spoken language difficulties and deficits in short-term memory. Secondary characteristic may include poor reading comprehension (due to the decoding and memory difficulties) and poor written expression, as well as difficulty organizing information for study and retrieval. (p. 55)

Siegel (1999) proposed further that there is a second type of learning disability referred to as "writing-arithmetic" or "output failure" disability, which is defined as:

difficulty with computational arithmetic and written language, typically in the absence of reading difficulties, although, this disability can co-occur with dyslexia. They often have difficulties with spelling, fine-motor coordination, visual-spatial processing, and short-term and long-term memory (e.g., multiplication tables), but usually have good oral language skills . . . (p. 306)

Subtypes of either reading disability or writing-arithmetic disability have not been found consistently in the literature (Siegel, 1999).

Based on these consistent findings of core deficits in phonics, there is an emerging consensus that reading disabilities may be diagnosed reliably by using basic word reading scores, and/or tests of phonics knowledge and processing. This consensus has implications for diagnosticians in that it suggests that the use of intelligence tests to identify ability/achievement discrepancies is of little value for making the diagnosis. Many researchers have agreed that the evidence supporting the use of IQ-achievement discrepancies for identifying reading disabilities is quite limited (Fletcher et al., 2002; Hoskyn & Swanson, 2000; Lyon et al., 2001, 2002; Stuebing et al., 2002; Vellutino et al., 2000). Vellutino et al. (2004), for example, concluded, "regardless of level of intelligence, the ability to learn to decode print is determined primarily by phonological skills such as phonological awareness, facility in alphabetic mapping, name encoding and retrieval, and verbal memory" (p. 29). If we agree that intelligence does not play a prominent role in determining whether a person can learn to decode text, the use of IQ tests in determining whether a person has a reading disability becomes invalidated.

In the 1980s, Siegel (1990) concluded that intelligence tests were unnecessary for making an LD diagnosis and advised the use of reading-like processing tests in isolation. In a subsequent 1992 investigation, Siegel found that "both these groups [reading disabled (dyslexic) and poor readers] deserve the label of reading disabled and have similar problems in reading and spelling and significant problems in phonological processing, memory, and language" (p. 627). Similarly, Fletcher, Francis, Rourke, Shaywitz, and Shaywitz (1992) tested the validity of discrepancy-based definitions of reading disabilities by comparing the performances of four groups of children classified as reading disabled according to four different methods, with one group of nondisabled children on a battery of neuropsychological tests. They found no significant differences among the "disabled" groups of children, thus calling into question the "validity of segregating children with reading deficiencies according to discrepancies with IQ scores" (p. 555). Stanovich and Siegel (1994) subsequently tested Stanovich's phonological-core variable-difference model of reading disability, again finding that "garden variety" poor readers did not differ from children with reading disabilities on measures of phonological, word recognition, and language skills. They concluded:

If there is a special group of children with reading disabilities who are be-
haviorally, cognitively, genetically, or neurologically different, it is becoming
increasingly unlikely that they can be easily identified by using IQ discrep-
ancy as a proxy for the genetic and neurological differences themselves. Thus,
the basic assumption that underlies decades of classification in research and
educational practice regarding reading disabilities is becoming increasingly
untenable. (Stanovich & Siegel, 1994, p. 48)

Additional evidence against using intelligence test scores to diagnose learning disabilities in children is provided based on reading
intervention studies. Vellutino, Scanlon, and Lyon (2000) found
that IQ-achievement discrepancy did not reliably distinguish poor
from normal readers or poor readers who were difficult to remediate
from those who were more susceptible to improvement. Researchers
administered extensive literacy skill assessments as well as assessments of reading related cognitive abilities to 1,284 middle- to
upper-class kindergarteners in Albany, New York. The following
year, 118 children identified as poor readers and 64 children identified as normal readers were selected from the sample. Seventy-six of
the impaired readers were randomly assigned to receive daily tutoring for one to two semesters, with progress assessed over time. No
statistically significant differences were found to exist between the
normal subjects and the tutored subjects on intelligence measures,
and IQ did not differentially predict response to reading intervention or level of reading ability in any subjects (Vellutino et al., 2000).

It is also important to note that intelligence test and academic
achievement tests are interrelated. A disorder that causes a low
achievement score may also have an effect on an intelligence test
score (Stanovich, 1999).

Another consensus emerging is that reading and related test
scores used to make the diagnosis should be below population av-
erages. Stanovich (1999) offered that the reading disability cut
score should be set at about a standard score of 85 with some flexibility built in to account for measurement error. This methodology
requires that each individual considered as LD show functional impairment (see Gordon, Lewandowski, & Keiser, 1999). By aban-
doning the notion of severe discrepancy, individuals with average

or better reading scores could no longer be considered LD just because they had the high intelligence test results necessary to produce an ability/achievement discrepancy. Vellutino and colleagues (1996) have also suggested using reading achievement scores alone to identify children struggling with reading. For the current Individuals with Disabilities Education Act reauthorization, proponents of this position propose eligibility criteria that include this "significantly low achievement" and "insufficient response to intervention." When children are identified as low achieving, a type of remediation would be applied and a child's progress would be evaluated. Children who made significant improvements with remediation would not be classified as disabled, while children who do not improve would qualify for further evaluation. Some response to intervention models include three levels of intervention: first in the general classroom, next in intensive small-group instruction, and third in a one-on-one tutoring model. When students fail to respond to these levels of intervention, they will be placed in special education. Presumably, this response to intervention model would reduce the number of children served in special education, and it would be more humane in that it would not require children to fail before receiving intervention.

Based on current evidence, Dombrowski, Kamphaus, and Reynolds (2004) concluded that intelligence tests are most appropriately used in a learning disability evaluation to identify cognitive rule outs or comorbidities that may affect educational achievement. Some intelligence tests may be well suited to identifying the short- and long-term memory, spatial/visualization, or other cognitive problems that are not core deficits of LD but, rather, affect prognosis and response to remediation (Dombrowski et al., 2004).

Diagnostic Standards

Learning disability, due to its nature as an educational disorder, has increasingly become differentiated from medicine where it was first discovered by physicians. The "gold standard" for LD diagnosis, therefore, is not promulgated by the American Psychiatric Association and the *DSM* but rather by U.S. federal legislation in the form of the Individuals with Disabilities Education Act (IDEA). The diagnostic criteria outlined in the HR1350, Individuals with Disabilities Education Improvement Act of 2004 (IDEIA) are:

> *(30) Specific Learning Disability*
>
> *(A) In General—The term "specific learning disability" means a disorder in 1 or more of the basic psychological processes involved in understanding or in using language, spoken or written, which disorder may manifest itself in the imperfect ability to listen, think, speak, read, write, spell, or do mathematical calculations.*
>
> *(B) Disorders Included—Such term includes such conditions as perceptual disabilities, brain injury, minimal brain dysfunction, dyslexia, and developmental aphasia.*
>
> *(C) Disorders Not Included—Such term does not include a learning problem that is primarily the result of visual, hearing, or motor disabilities, of mental retardation, of emotional disturbance, or of environmental, cultural, or economic disadvantage. (HR 1350, Sec 604)*

It is noteworthy that the ability/achievement discrepancy concept is not part of this latest definition (see Table 4.1). In fact, the practice is discouraged in the law, stating:

> *(A) In General—Notwithstanding section 607(b), when determining whether a child has a specific learning disability as defined in section 602, a local educational agency shall not be required to take into consideration whether a child has a severe discrepancy between achievement and intellectual ability in oral expression, listening comprehension, written expression, basic reading skill, reading comprehension, mathematical calculation, or mathematical reasoning.*

This proscription represents a significant change from prior versions of the law that reflects the growing evidence of the conceptual problems involved in comparing intelligence and achievement tests. The law goes even further with the statement (as shown in Table 4.1):

> *(B) Additional Authority—In determining whether a child has a specific learning disability, a local educational agency may use a process that*

Table 4.1   **Assessment Regulations from IDEA Legislation (HR 1350)**

Section 614. Evaluations, Eligibility Determinations, Individualized Education Programs, and Educational Placements.

(b) *Evaluation procedures*

   (1) *Notice:* The local educational agency shall provide notice to the parents of a child with a disability, in accordance with subsections (b)(3), (b)(4), and (c) of section 615, that describes any evaluation procedures such agency proposes to conduct.

   (2) *Conduct of evaluation:* In conducting the evaluation, the local educational agency shall—

   (A) use a variety of assessment tools and strategies to gather relevant functional, developmental, and academic information, including information provided by the parent, that may assist in determining—

   (i) whether the child is a child with a disability; and

   (ii) the content of the child's individualized education program, including information related to enabling the child to be involved in and progress in the general education curriculum, or, for preschool children, to participate in appropriate activities;

   (B) not use any single measure or assessment as the sole criterion for determining whether a child is a child with a disability or determining an appropriate educational program for the child; and

   (C) use technically sound instruments that may assess the relative contribution of cognitive and behavioral factors, in addition to physical or developmental factors.

   (3) *Additional requirements:* Each local educational agency shall ensure that—

   (A) assessments and other evaluation materials used to assess a child under this section—

   (i) are selected and administered so as not to be discriminatory on a racial or cultural basis;

   (ii) are provided and administered in the language and form most likely to yield accurate information on what the child knows and can do academically, developmentally, and functionally, unless it is not feasible to so provide or administer;

   (iii) are used for purposes for which the assessments or measures are valid and reliable;

   (iv) are administered by trained and knowledgeable personnel; and

   (v) are administered in accordance with any instructions provided by the producer of such assessments;

   (B) the child is assessed in all areas of suspected disability;

   (C) assessment tools and strategies that provide relevant information that directly assists persons in determining the educational needs of the child are provided; and

   (D) assessments of children with disabilities who transfer from 1 school district to another school district in the same academic year are

Table 4.1 *Continued*

coordinated with such children's prior and subsequent schools, as necessary and as expeditiously as possible, to ensure prompt completion of full evaluations.

(4) *Determination of eligibility and educational need:* Upon completion of the administration of assessments and other evaluation measures—

    (A) the determination of whether the child is a child with a disability as defined in section 602(3) and the educational needs of the child shall be made by a team of qualified professionals and the parent of the child in accordance with paragraph (5); and

    (B) a copy of the evaluation report and the documentation of determination of eligibility shall be given to the parent.

(5) *Special rule for eligibility determination:* In making a determination of eligibility under paragraph (4)(A), a child shall not be determined to be a child with a disability if the determinant factor for such determination is—

    (A) lack of appropriate instruction in reading, including in the essential components of reading instruction (as defined in section 1208(3) of the Elementary and Secondary Education Act of 1965);

    (B) lack of instruction in math; or

    (C) limited English proficiency.

(6) *Specific learning disabilities*

    (A) *In general:* Notwithstanding section 607(b), when determining whether a child has a specific learning disability as defined in section 602, a local educational agency shall not be required to take into consideration whether a child has a severe discrepancy between achievement and intellectual ability in oral expression, listening comprehension, written expression, basic reading skill, reading comprehension, mathematical calculation, or mathematical reasoning.

    (B) *Additional authority:* In determining whether a child has a specific learning disability, a local educational agency may use a process that determines if the child responds to scientific, research-based intervention as a part of the evaluation procedures described in paragraphs (2) and (3).

    (C) *Additional requirements for evaluation and reevaluations:*

(1) *Review of existing evaluation data:* As part of an initial evaluation (if appropriate) and as part of any reevaluation under this section, the IEP Team and other qualified professionals, as appropriate, shall—

    (A) review existing evaluation data on the child, including—

        (i) evaluations and information provided by the parents of the child;

        (ii) current classroom-based, local, or State assessments, and classroom-based observations; and

        (iii) observations by teachers and related services providers; and

(continued)

95

Table 4.1   *Continued*

    (B) on the basis of that review, and input from the child's parents, identify what additional data, if any, are needed to determine—

          (i) whether the child is a child with a disability as defined in section 602(3), and the educational needs of the child, or, in case of a reevaluation of a child, whether the child continues to have such a disability and such educational needs;

        (ii) the present levels of academic achievement and related developmental needs of the child;

      (iii) whether the child needs special education and related services, or in the case of a reevaluation of a child, whether the child continues to need special education and related services; and

      (iv) whether any additions or modifications to the special education and related services are needed to enable the child to meet the measurable annual goals set out in the individualized education program of the child and to participate, as appropriate, in the general education curriculum.

---

determines if the child responds to scientific, research-based intervention as a part of the evaluation procedures described in paragraphs (2) and (3).

This paragraph refers to the emerging practice of some researchers and school systems to use a so-called response to intervention (RTI) approach to diagnose the disorder. This model calls for schools to begin a series of targeted interventions using research-based instruction as soon as a student shows signs of struggling to learn. The student's response to these interventions would be closely monitored. Those who fail to show progress despite intense, targeted interventions delivered by general education teachers would be considered candidates for further evaluation and special education eligibility.

The discrepancy or low achievement indicating the disability cannot be caused primarily by any of the following: environmental, cultural, or economic disadvantage; limited school experience; vision, hearing, or motor impairment; mental retardation; emotional disturbance; unfamiliarity with the English language; or lack of instruction in reading and math. The identified learning disability must be negatively affecting classroom performance.

Diagnostic and Statistical Manual of Mental Disorders **Criteria**

According to the *DSM-IV* learning disabilities are referred to as Learning Disorders and reading disability is classified as Reading Disorder. The essential feature of a reading disorder is reading achievement in accuracy, speed, or comprehension that falls substantially below what is expected taking into consideration an individual's age, intelligence, and age-appropriate education. The disturbance must significantly interfere with academic achievement or daily living skills requiring reading. Finally, if the individual in concern has a sensory deficit, reading problems must be in excess of what one would expect to occur with that sensory deficit. The *DSM-IV* further stipulates that in the case of a reading disorder, oral reading is characterized by distortions, substitutions, or omissions, and, in general, reading is plagued with slowness and errors in comprehension.

The *DSM-IV* does not specify an exact score or condition associated with "substantially below what is expected." The interpretation and final judgment on whether a disorder is present is left to the clinician. The manual states that "substantially below" usually refers to a discrepancy of more than two standard deviations, but a smaller discrepancy between one and two standard deviations is sometimes used in typical diagnostic practice (Kamphaus, 2001). The *DSM* warns that an intelligence test result may be compromised by a deficit in cognitive processing, a comorbid mental disorder, a general medical condition, or an individual's ethnic or cultural background. In these situations, a clinician may consider a smaller discrepancy between achievement and measured intelligence. Prior federal criteria for a learning disability required a deficit in cognitive processing (the current law also includes the phrase "psychological processes" in the definition), which according to the *DSM* may compromise an intelligence test score and make identification of a discrepancy particularly difficult. Some associated features of a reading, mathematics, or written expression disorder are identified by the *DSM,* including demoralization, low self-esteem, and social skills deficits (*DSM-IV-TR*).

Emerging Diagnostic Criteria

There are at least three possibilities for current and future diagnostic practice for LD. One option is to maintain the past practice of using some sort of discrepancy model to diagnose LD. Given that the empirical and conceptual underpinnings of this approach are increasing apparent, this practice will be a legacy that will gradually fall into disuse (Stanovich, 2005). A second option is the response to intervention or instruction model that has the key advantage of emphasizing the prevention of academic disabilities by offering additional intensive educational experiences to all children, particularly those identified as at risk. For the current IDEA reauthorization, proponents of this position propose eligibility criteria that include this "significantly low achievement" and "insufficient response to intervention." When children are identified as low achieving, a type of remediation would be applied and a child's progress would be evaluated. Children who made significant improvements with remediation would not be classified as disabled, while children who do not improve would qualify for further evaluation. Some response to intervention models include three levels of intervention: first in the general classroom, second in intensive small group instruction, and third in a one-on-one tutoring model. When students fail to respond to these levels of intervention they will be placed in special education. Presumably, this methodology will reduce the number of children served in special education. Although some consider RTI unnecessary and others prefer to continue with the use of intellectual assessment in the diagnosis of LD, a change in the method of assessment is inevitable.

This methodology holds great promise for improving the academic achievement of many children but not for fostering the definition of LD and fostering research on the etiology of LD that may lead to prevention methods that are even more effective, or deliverable in preschool years. The response to instruction method requires considerably more research to assess its practicality (e.g., cost versus benefits), and its effectiveness as assessed by randomized controlled trials conducted longitudinally. The question of control of the quality of intervention in such a model is likely to elude consensus. A third option to address the problems of the ability/achievement discrepancy model and questions about using instruction to make a diagnosis simultaneously is by proposing a third model. For psychological practitioners another possibility is to document an academic deficit and then ensure that there are not alternative causes for the deficit other than LD. As stated by Shepard (1989): "If LD is an inexplicable inability to learn, an effective assessment strategy is to start with the evidence of inadequate learning and test for other explanations for the problem" (p. 559).

Shepard's (1989) straightforward approach has been operationalized recently by Dombrowski et al. (2004). This method first determines whether functional impairment in academic achievement is present using norm-referenced tests of mathematics, reading, and written expression at a minimum. The advised level of specific academic functional impairment must be at or below the 80 to 85 (9th to 16th percentile) standard score range, a level deemed significant enough to denote inadequate learning. This assessment could easily be conducted after an intervention or prevention program has occurred using pre-referral intervention or a response to instruction paradigm. This level of functional impairment is key for making the diagnosis because it ensures that achievement is deviant from that of other classmates, not merely relatively lower. Of particular concern are those students that are labeled "gifted" LD or "high-functioning" LD, who score well above average on IQ measures and show discrepancies with measures of achievement, yet their achievement levels are still at an average level in comparison with the general population of students. Douglas Fuchs, co-director of the National Research Center on Learning Disabilities and a professor of special education at Vanderbilt University, describes why such a broad definition, which includes these students may be problematic: "What that means is that not only are more kids being identified as learning disabled and more kids being served in special education, but that a greater percentage of local and state dollars are being redirected from general education to special education" (cited in Bailey, 2003). Stanovich (1999) argues strongly that the integrity of the LD diagnosis would always be questionable if it allowed individuals to be effectively "normal" (i.e., average or above academic achievement) and yet considered deviant enough to carry the LD diagnosis. The requirement of functional impairment would a priori limit LD diagnosis by eliminating some children who previously carried it but had only a "relative discrepancy" between intelligence and achievement (Gordon, Lewandowski, & Keiser, 1999).

The second part of the process is to rule out alternative causes for the functional impairment in academic achievement including speech, language, or hearing disorders; motor disability; impaired vision; Attention-Deficit/Hyperactivity Disorder (ADHD); mental retardation; Bipolar disorder; and so on (Dombrowski et al., 2004). It is at this stage that a test of general intelligence is warranted to rule out the presence of mental retardation. Dombrowski et al. (2004) advise that intelligence test scores should be at or above the same 80 to 85 (9th to16th percentile) standard score range to ensure the absence of mental retardation. This effort to rule out alternative causes is consistent with the current IDEIA, which stipulates that "the relative contribution of cognitive and behavioral factors, in addition to physical or developmental factors" should be assessed (see Table 4.1). The conceptual underpinnings and diagnostic rubric of the approach espoused by Dombrowski et al. (2004) is shown in Table 4.2.

Table 4.2   **Decision-Making Rubric for the Diagnosis of Learning Disabilities**

Test Scores	LD	No LD	LD	No LD	LD
Word Read	80	80	85	90	75
IQ	85	70	120	120	90

Source: "After the Demise of the Discrepancy: Proposed Learning Disability Diagnostic Criteria," by S. C. Dombrowski, R. W. Kamphaus, and C. R. Reynolds, 2004, *Professional Psychology: Research and Practice, 35,* pp. 364–372.

Assessment Methods

Specific guidance for the use of assessment methods for diagnosis is provided by IDEIA. These prescriptions are consistent with and expand on the requirements for technical adequacy of tests espoused by the Standards for Educational and Psychological Tests (American Educational Research Association, American Psychological Association, & National Council on Measurement in Education [AERA, APA, & NCME], 1999). Assessment methods (see Table 4.1) are required to be:

1. Multifaceted or not dependent on a single measure to make the diagnosis (e.g., a mathematics test would not be adequate to the task of diagnosing a learning disability because it would not provide information adequate to rule out mental retardation or a reading disability).
2. "Technically sound instruments" in that they meet the requirements of relevant standards (AERA, APA, & NCME, 1999).
3. Assessments of comorbidities such as ADHD or alternative causes such as mental retardation.
4. "Selected and administered so as not to be discriminatory on a racial or cultural basis."
5. Administered in a language that is most likely to produce accurate test findings that are measuring the constructs of interest and not language facility per se.
6. Used only for purposes for which the tests have been validation. Intelligences tests, for example, have been validated for the purposes of assessing cognitive development but not for the diagnosis of ADHD (Kamphaus & Frick, 2002).
7. Administered, scored, and interpreted by qualified personnel, and in accordance with instructions for use given in the test manual.

Standardized measures of academic achievement are advised for complying with these requirements for several reasons. First, such measures are likely to be nationally normed, yielding percentile ranks as indicators of functional academic impairment that foster consistent LD diagnosis across school districts and states. Second, nationally normed measures are more likely to have collected the large samples of diverse children necessary to rule out item bias by sex, race, or ethnicity. Third, nationally normed and developed measures are likely to have conducted more studies of reliability and validity than can be independently corroborated by other researchers. Examples of measures that are popular for use in schools include:

- Kaufman Test of Educational Achievement II (www.agsnet .com/group.asp?nGroupInfoID=a32215), which measures:
  —Reading
  —Reading-related (Phonics and fluency-related tests)
  —Mathematics
  —Written Language
  —Oral Language
- Woodcock-Johnson III Tests of Achievement (www.riverpub .com/products/clinical/wj3/achievement.html), which measures:
  —Oral Expression
  —Listening Comprehension
  —Written Expression
  —Basic Reading Skills
  —Reading Comprehension
  —Math Calculation Skills
  —Math Reasoning
- Wechsler Individual Achievement Test II (harcourtassessment .com/haiweb/Cultures/en-U.S./dotCom/WIAT-II.com.htm), which measures:
  —Oral Language
  —Listening Comprehension
  —Written Expression
  —Spelling
  —Pseudoword Decoding
  —Word Reading
  —Reading Comprehension
  —Numerical Operations
  —Mathematics Reasoning

Not surprisingly, these measures assess constructs as defined in part by the areas of LD defined by IDEIA in Table 4.1. They use national normative data to assess functional impairment, and issues of culture and fairness have been assessed for all measures. There are numerous additional measures of academic achievement with similar characteristics available. The Buros Institute of Mental Measurements (www.unl.edu/buros), for example, currently has reviews of over 160 reading tests and over 90 mathematics tests (as of 6 August, 2005).

Interpretation of Findings

Given that LD is a developmental disability its sign and symptoms should appear early in childhood and persist throughout life. Therefore, the academic impairment central to the disorder should not vary significantly from age to age, nor show periods of remission. Similarly, the onset of LD should not be sudden and should occur in elementary school for the vast majority of cases. Therefore, the developmental course of the impairment and onset should be documented carefully through history. Fortunately, in the case of LD the developmental course of academic problems are well documented in school grades and academic achievement scores that are typically included in children's school files. Achievement tests, for example, are available for most U.S. school children on at least a biannual basis, thus providing documentation of developmental course and severity based on measures with known reliability and validity.

A response to instruction paradigm, as well as the assumption that LD is a developmental disability, would dictate that a child is not LD if her or his score becomes average or better subsequent to tutoring or other academic interventions and remains in this range long term. This developmental course is an example of one that would be atypical for a case of LD. A case of sudden onset LD, where a child in middle school develops severe academic problems that were not present in elementary school, would suggest the presence of alternative causes, perhaps a behavioral or emotional disorder in this case.

Learning disability is a disorder that lends itself best to dimensional diagnosis given that the core constructs of reading, mathematics, and written language among others are normally distributed in the population of school children and readily assessed with formal educational tests. Signs and symptoms, therefore, are secondary and in many cases not relevant to the diagnosis. Symptoms, such as letter or word reversals or poor academic self-esteem, may be related to other disorders or problems unrelated to the diagnosis of LD. Because of the dimensionality of academic achievement areas, the diagnosis of LD is based on measures with better reliability and validity indices than most personality or behavioral measures for example.

Historically, the "cognitive processes" cited in most definitions of LD have been presumed to be those often assessed by intelligence tests and related cognitive measures (e.g., auditory short-term memory, spatial ability, and sequencing). Although present in the current IDEIA legislation, the assessment of such processes has been heavily criticized as irrelevant to the diagnosis (Stanovich, 2005). One way of reframing the issue of assessment of cognitive processes is to focus on the assessment of those that are directly related to poor academic achievement. Phonological awareness would be an example of such a process in the reading domain. This "cognitive process" is highly relevant to the diagnosis in that it is considered the core symptom of reading disability making it an important process to assess. Clinicians may be well advised to change the assessment of cognitive processes to focus on the assessment of those closely linked to the area of academic disability. Some of these rubrics for interpretation are applied in the following case.

CASE STUDY

Identifying information, such as child and family name, child sex, and other particulars, has been removed, altered, or fictionalized to protect confidentiality.

Psychological Evaluation

NAME: Jeff Ross	SCHOOL: Sherwood Forest Elementary
GRADE: 5th Grade	EXAMINER: Anna King
AGE: 10 years, 11 months	SUPERVISOR: Mathew Pierce

ASSESSMENT PROCEDURES

Achenbach Child Behavior Checklist—(CBCL)

Beery-Buktenica Developmental Test of Visual-Motor Integration (VMI)

Behavior Assessment System for Children—PRS (BASC)

Child Interview

Comprehensive Test of Phonological Processing (C-TOPP)

Gray Oral Reading Tests—Fourth Edition (GORT-4)

KeyMath—Revised (KeyMath-R)

Oral and Written Language Scales (OWLS)

Parent Interview

Peabody Picture Vocabulary Test—Third Edition (PPVT-III)

Review of Records

Teacher Interview

Test of Written Language—Third Edition (TOWL-III)

Wechsler Intelligence Scale for Children—Fourth Edition (WISC-IV)

Woodcock-Johnson III Tests of Achievement (WJ III ACH)

Woodcock-Johnson III Tests of Cognitive Abilities (WJ III COG)

REASON FOR REFERRAL

Jeff is a 10-year, 11-month-old male who was referred by his parents for a psychoeducational evaluation. The purpose of the evaluation was to address concerns about his learning abilities in the areas of reading and mathematics. Mrs. Ross reported that Jeff had been previously diagnosed with a reading disability. Mr. and Mrs. Ross wanted to know more about processing difficulties that Jeff exhibits. In addition, Jeff currently struggles with mathematics in school and Mr. and Mrs. Ross were concerned that he might have an additional learning disability in mathematics.

BACKGROUND AND DEVELOPMENTAL INFORMATION

Review of Jeff's developmental and medical history indicates that Jeff is the product of a full-term pregnancy. Developmental milestones such as crawling, walking, and talking were within normal limits. Mrs. Ross described Jeff as being active socially. She reported that he has several friends and will frequently take a leadership role when with others. She reported that other children respond well to Jeff and appear to enjoy his company. She reported that Jeff has never had difficulty behaviorally. Mrs. Ross stated that Jeff, at times, can be "perfectionistic" and that he sometimes worries excessively. She did not feel that his "worrying" interferes with his current functioning; however, she commented that he has always had difficulty sleeping. Mrs. Ross reported that Jeff currently sleeps in the bed with his sister because he does not like to sleep alone. Mrs. Ross reported that at school Jeff's teachers comment that they enjoy teaching him.

REVIEW OF SCHOOL RECORDS AND EDUCATIONAL HISTORY

Jeff is currently enrolled in the fifth grade at Sherwood Forest Elementary School. Mrs. Ross reported that Jeff had great difficulty in Kindergarten. She reported that despite the fact that he spoke frequently at home, Jeff spoke rarely in his kindergarten class. In addition, Mrs. Ross reported that Jeff had difficulty learning his letters and numbers. She reported that the school considered retaining Jeff in kindergarten, but that he passed a state-mandated competency test for kindergarten and advanced to the first grade. Mrs. Ross reported that Jeff had unclear speech as he entered elementary school, pronouncing "/w/" instead of "/l/." Mrs. Ross reported that Jeff was in a special class for speech for approximately 1 year and that this treatment seemed to work well. In addition, he started tutoring outside school. She stated that, in the first grade, he improved but still needed a great deal of individual attention from his teacher and needed directions repeated for him frequently.

In the second grade, Jeff was diagnosed with a Reading Disability by his school. Mrs. Ross reported that at this time, Jeff began receiving special education services for reading. Jeff currently receives daily instruction in Language Arts. Mrs. Ross reported that Social Studies and Science are currently Jeff's favorite subjects. She reported that he continues to have difficulty reading and is beginning to show a weakness in mathematics.

Interviews with Jeff's teachers supported Mrs. Ross's reports. Jeff's mathematics teacher reported that Jeff has gained many of the basic skills required for mathematics, but has difficulty with problems requiring multiple steps. She said that Jeff also has difficulty with word problems that require fluent reading. This teacher also reported that she is concerned about Jeff's ability to organize his assignments when he progresses to middle school and changes classes several times a day. Jeff's language arts/special education teacher reported that Jeff has difficulty processing the steps required for reading. In addition, Jeff displays difficulties with phonics. She stated that she has spent time in instruction on the segmentation of word parts and on learning phonics skills. In addition, Jeff continues to struggle with spelling but, despite Jeff's difficulty reading, he displays good reading comprehension skills.

BEHAVIORAL OBSERVATIONS

Jeff was neat in appearance, polite, and cooperative throughout the session. Jeff demonstrated no hearing or vision difficulties during testing. Jeff frequently initiated conversation throughout the day and never appeared to become discouraged with testing.

TEST RESULTS AND INTERPRETATION

COGNITIVE DEVELOPMENT

Jeff's cognitive functioning was measured using the Wechsler Intelligence Scale for Children—Fourth Edition (WISC-IV). The WISC-IV yields three scores: Verbal, Performance, and Full Scale. The Verbal Scale includes subtests such as orally defining words and describing how two things are similar. The Performance Scale includes subtests such as using blocks to copy designs and identifying missing parts within a picture. Jeff earned a Verbal IQ Score of 101 (53rd percentile) and a Performance IQ Score of 111

(77th percentile). These scores combine to produce a Full Scale IQ Score of 106 (66th percentile), which suggests average development of Jeff's cognitive abilities.

ACADEMIC ACHIEVEMENT

Jeff was administered a substantial test battery including the Woodcock-Johnson III Tests of Achievement (WJ III ACH), the Oral and Written Language Scales (OWLS), the Comprehensive Test of Phonological Processing (CTOPP), and the Peabody Picture Vocabulary Test—Third Edition (PPVT-III), the Gray Oral Reading Tests—Fourth Edition (GORT-4), the Test of Written Language—Third Edition (TOWL-III), and the KeyMath Diagnostic Arithmetic Test—Revised.

The WJ III ACH is a comprehensive school achievement test, which evaluates reading, mathematics, and writing. The OWLS is a test of language skills in areas of listening and speaking. The CTOPP is a test used to identify strengths and weaknesses among developed phonological processes, such as phonological awareness, phonological memory, and rapid naming. The PPVT-III is a test of receptive vocabulary and a screening test of verbal ability. The GORT-3 is a measure of reading skills and oral reading comprehension. The TOWL-III provides a spontaneous writing test in which a student tells a story about a picture presented. The KeyMath-R is a diagnostic inventory of mathematic abilities including basic concepts, operations, and applications.

READING

On the WJ III, Jeff's Broad Reading Composite was an 83 (13th percentile). Specifically, Jeff demonstrated below average skills in the identification of words, correctly identifying many single syllable words such as "they" but incorrectly identified more complicated multisyllable words such as "distance." Jeff was below average in reading fluency, indicating that his rate and accuracy of reading is below average compared to his peers. On the GORT-4, Jeff achieved scaled scores of 4 for Rate (2nd percentile) and 4 for Accuracy (2nd percentile) demonstrating that he is Significantly below average compared to his peers in these areas. However, Jeff's reading comprehension was found to be in the Average range consistent with teacher report. On the WJ III ACH, he achieved a standard score of 94 (33rd percentile) for Passage Comprehension and on the GORT-4 he achieved a scaled score of 12 (75th percentile) for Comprehension.

The Comprehensive Test of Phonological Processing (C-TOPP) and the Woodcock-Johnson III Tests of Cognitive Abilities (WJ III COG) were used to identify strengths and weaknesses in Jeff's phonological processing skills. For the Phonological Memory Composite, Jeff's standard score was an 88 (21st percentile), indicating that Jeff is low average in his ability to code information phonetically for temporary storage in working and short-term memory. For the Rapid Naming composite, Jeff's standard score was an 85 (16th percentile) indicating low average ability to efficiently retrieve phonological information from long-term memory. Together, these composites indicate that Jeff is low average in Phonological Memory and Rapid Naming. In an assessment of Phonological Awareness on the C-TOPP, Jeff's standard score was an 88 (21st percentile), demonstrating a weakness in Jeff's awareness of and access to the sound structure of his oral language.

On the WJ III COG, Jeff's Phonological awareness skills were assessed using the Sound Blending and Incomplete Words subtests. Taken together, these tests create a phonological awareness composite on the WJ III COG of 107 (69th percentile). When examining Jeff's performance on the C-TOPP and WJ III COG measures of Phonological Processing, it was determined that the two tests provide slightly different requirements in phonological awareness skills. On the C-TOPP test for phonological awareness, sounds are presented in small chunks for the examinee to decode and make one word, for example, "/s/—/t/—/a/—/m/—/p/." On the WJ III, however, sounds are presented in larger chunks, such as "/num/—/ber/." Jeff performed much better at phonological processing when phonological information was presented in larger and more meaningful units, such as consonant blends and consonant-vowel blends versus single consonant or single vowel sounds. Jeff's processing weaknesses exhibited on the C-TOPP indicate difficulties with mastery of basic phonological awareness skills necessary for fluent reading.

MATHEMATICS

On the WJ III ACH, Jeff demonstrated average mathematics abilities with a Broad Mathematics score of 101 (52nd percentile) and a mathematics Calculation Skills score of 103 (59th percentile). Jeff's mathematics abilities were more thoroughly examined using the KeyMath-R. On the KeyMath-R, Jeff's skills for Basic Concepts using tests for numbers, rational numbers, and geometry were assessed. Jeff demonstrated abilities in the average range with a score of 108 (70th percentile). Jeff's skills for Operations were also assessed using tests for addition, subtraction, multiplication, division, and mental computation. Jeff demonstrated average abilities for Operations achieving a standard score of 107 (68th percentile). Finally, Jeff's Applications skills were assessed using tests for abilities such as measurement, time and money, and problem solving. Jeff demonstrated average abilities for Applications achieving a standard score of 93 (32nd percentile). When assessing individual items missed within these subtests, Jeff demonstrated difficulty with multistep problems. While it appears that Jeff has mastered basic mathematics skills, such as multiplication facts and borrowing, problems involving multiple steps were difficult for Jeff. Jeff's scores on the WJ III ACH and KeyMath-R indicate average range mathematics abilities and no indication of functional impairment associated with a learning disability in mathematics.

WRITING

Jeff's standard score for the Broad Written Language Composite of the WJ III ACH was 89, indicating low average abilities in writing. This low average score can be largely attributed to the inclusion of the spelling subtests on which Jeff achieved a score of 82 (12th percentile). On this test, Jeff's spelling mistakes included phonological inaccuracies such as "avengher" for "adventure." This is consistent with Jeff's observed difficulties with phonological processing. Jeff's Written Expression Composite score on the WJ III ACH was a 96 (39th percentile), indicating average abilities compared to his peers in written expression. On the TOWL-III, Jeff was asked to write a story about a picture that was presented. Jeff demonstrated average to high average abilities in writing ability. Jeff achieved a standard score of 9 (39th percentile) for Contextual Conventions, a 13 (84th percentile) for Contextual Language, and 15 (95th percentile) for Story Construction.

EXPRESSIVE AND RECEPTIVE LANGUAGE

Jeff's standard score on the Listening Comprehension subtest of the OWLS was 85 (16th percentile). This indicates that Jeff has low average abilities in his receptive language skills. On the PPVT-III, a test of receptive vocabulary, Jeff's standard score was a 98 (32nd percentile). This difference in scores is likely due to the fact that while the OWLS provides an assessment of receptive language, the PPVT-III is a test of only receptive vocabulary without requiring the use of full language skills. Jeff appears to possess average vocabulary ability compared to his peers. Jeff's expressive language skills are also in the average range. On the Oral Expression subtest of the OWLS, Jeff achieved a score of 94 (34th percentile). Together, these scores indicate that Jeff has a relative weakness in receptive language abilities; however, his understanding of single words and expressive language do not indicate the presence of functional impairment because they were average compared to his same age peers.

SOCIAL AND EMOTIONAL FUNCTIONING

In an interview, Jeff reported that Social Studies is his favorite subject in school, namely that he enjoys studying war histories and inventions. Jeff reported that mathematics is his least favorite subject. He said that he gets along with his teachers well and that his parents think he is doing "okay" in school. Jeff reported that occasionally he has difficulty concentrating on his work when there are other kids around that are distracting. Jeff reported that he has several friends and that he sometimes gets along with them while other times not. He reported that other kids sometimes come over to his house to play and that sometimes he visits them. When asked about any anxious feelings he might have, Jeff reported that he usually does not like to spend the night at friend's houses because he has difficulty sleeping. Jeff reported that he often has nervous and jumpy feelings and that many times he does not know why he has them. Jeff said that he sometimes gets nervous right before a friend comes to play or when he has to stand in front of a large group of people at school.

Mr. and Mrs. Ross both rated Jeff as average overall with Mr. Ross indicating mild concerns pertaining to attention problems. Mrs. Ross reported that Jeff has a great attitude and is a joy to be around. She reported that Jeff easily initiates friendships and has several friends. In addition, she reported that, while Jeff frequently receives tutoring, special education services, and additional academic help at home, he works diligently on assignments and rarely becomes frustrated. She reported that she has no concerns about him behaviorally or socially. In teacher interviews, neither of Jeff's teachers expressed concerns for him socially or behaviorally. Given Jeff's teacher's positive behavioral reports, no teacher rating scales of behavior were used to further assess Jeff's behavioral functioning within the classroom.

SUMMARY

Jeff is a 10-year-old male who was referred by his parents for a psychoeducational evaluation. The purpose of the evaluation was to assess Jeff's parents' concerns about his learning abilities in the areas of reading and mathematics. He has received special education services for a Learning Disability in Reading. Specifically, Jeff's parents wanted a psychological evaluation conducted in order to evaluate the possibility of a Mathematics Disability. In addition, Mr. and Mrs. Ross wanted further information on any processing difficulties that Jeff might exhibit and how these difficulties might inform further educational interventions.

Intellectual testing indicated that Jeff's cognitive functioning is in the average range as compared to his peers. Academically, Jeff exhibited functional impairment in basic reading skills with consistently low average scores at about the 16th percentile rank. When examining phonological processing skills that might account for this difficulty in reading, Jeff exhibited a weakness in phonological memory and rapid naming. On two different tests of phonological awareness in which Jeff was required to put sounds together to create a word, Jeff achieved scores both in the average and below average range. This difference could be attributed to the difference in presentation of the sounds. On the test in which Jeff achieved an average score, phonetic information was presented in larger "chunks" such as "/num/—/ber/" than during a test presenting individual phonemes such as "/c/—/a/—/t/." In contrast to his reading performance, Jeff's scores in mathematics and written language were in the average range. On tests of expressive and receptive language, Jeff demonstrated a relative weakness in receptive language with low average scores. Jeff's expressive language skills and receptive vocabulary were average.

No significant emotional and behavioral problems were noted. As reported by Jeff's parents and teachers, Jeff easily initiates friendships and has several friends. In addition, Jeff's parents and teachers reported that Jeff works diligently on assignments and rarely becomes frustrated completing academic assignments or when receiving assistance from teachers or tutors.

Jeff's basic reading abilities, including his difficulties in phonological processing, have not responded to intervention, and remain areas of functional academic impairment. Jeff's previous diagnosis of a Learning Disability in reading is confirmed and alternative causes such as emotional or behavioral problems are effectively ruled out by this evaluation. When assessing Jeff's abilities in mathematics, scores consistently indicated that he is in the average range, consistent with his cognitive abilities. Therefore, these scores do not indicate the presence of a Learning Disability in mathematics at this time (see Table 4.3).

Conclusion

The field of LD diagnosis is about to undergo rapid change subsequent to the passage of IDEIA. The hastening of change is necessary due to a lack of progress over the last several decades of stagnation (Stanovich, 2005). Although the ability/achievement discrepancy model is not viable long term, it is not clear that a response to

Table 4.3 **Diagnostic Impressions and Psychometric Summary for Jeff**

DIAGNOSTIC IMPRESSION

Axis I   315.00   Reading Disorder
Axis II   None
Psychometric Summary

WECHSLER INTELLIGENCE SCALE FOR CHILDREN— FOURTH EDITION (WISC-IV)

Verbal Subtests	Scaled Scores	Performance Subtests	Scaled Scores
Information	11	Picture Completion	10
Similarities	10	Coding	3
Arithmetic	10	Picture Arrangement	11
Vocabulary	10	Block Design	13
Comprehension	10	Object Assembly	10
(Digit Span)	9	(Symbol Search)	13

Composite Scores	Standard Scores	90% Confidence Intervals
Verbal	101	96–106
Performance	110	102–116
Full Scale	106	101–110
Verbal Comprehension	102	96–108
Perceptual/Organizational	107	99–113
FD (Third Factor)	98	91–106
Processing Speed	90	84–99

WOODCOCK-JOHNSON III TESTS OF ACHIEVEMENT (WJ III ACH)

Subtests	Standard Scores	90% Confidence Intervals
Letter-Word Identification	82	78–86
Reading Fluency	82	79–86
Passage Comprehension	94	88–99
Word Attack	83	79–88
Story Recall	110	99–120
Understanding Directions	93	85–100
Calculation	109	100–118
Applied Problems	98	93–103

Table 4.3   *Continued*

Subtests	Standard Scores	90% Confidence Intervals
Math Fluency	92	86–97
Spelling	82	76–88
Writing Fluency	98	90–107
Writing Sample	93	82–104
Composites		
Broad Reading	83	80–86
Broad Mathematics	101	96–106
Math Calculation Skills	103	97–110
Broad Written Language	89	83–94
Written Expression	96	88–103
Academic Skills	89	86–92
Academic Fluency	88	84–91
Academic Applications	95	91–99
Total Achievement	87	84–89

WOODCOCK-JOHNSON III TESTS OF COGNITIVE ABILITIES (WJ III COG)

Subtests	Standard Scores	90% Confidence Intervals
Sound Blending (Ga)	112	103–121
Visual Matching (Gs)	98	91–106
Incomplete Words	96	84–107
Phonemic Awareness	107	98–116

REVISED CHILDREN'S MANIFEST ANXIETY SCALE (RCMAS)

	Scaled Scores	*T*-Score	Percentiles
Physiological Anxiety	9		44
Worry/Oversensitivity	12		79
Social Concerns/Concentration	11		73
Lie	14		94
Total Anxiety Score		55	70

(continued)

Table 4.3 *Continued*

BEHAVIOR ASSESSMENT SYSTEM FOR CHILDREN—PARENT RATING SCALES (BASC-PRS)

	T-Scores	
	Mother	**Father**
Hyperactivity	41	38
Aggression	32	32
Conduct Problems	37	37
Externalizing Problems Composite	34	33
Anxiety	44	40
Depression	36	36
Somatization	36	36
Internalizing Problems Composite	35	34
Atypicality	42	38
Withdrawal	35	35
Attention Problems	58	63
Behavior Symptoms Index	39	37
Adaptability	67	64
Social Skills	51	47
Leadership	39	37
Adaptive Skills Composite	53	49

BEERY-BUKTENICA DEVELOPMENTAL TEST OF VISUAL-MOTOR INTEGRATION (VMI)

Standard Score   99
Percentile   47

ORAL AND WRITTEN LANGUAGE SCALES (OWLS)

	Standard Scores	**90% Confidence Intervals**
Listening Comprehension	85	75–95
Oral Expression	94	84–104

Table 4.3   *Continued*

COMPREHENSIVE TEST OF PHONOLOGICAL PROCESSING (C-TOPP)

Subtests	Scaled Scores
Core	
Elision	9
Blending Words	7
Memory for Digits	9
Rapid Digit Naming	8
Nonword Repetition	7
Rapid Letter Naming	7

Subtests	Standard Scores	Percentiles
Composites		
Phonological Awareness	88	21
Phonological Memory	88	21
Rapid Naming	85	16

GRAY ORAL READING TESTS—FOURTH EDITION (GORT-4)

	Scaled/ Standard Scores	Percentiles
Rate	4	2
Accuracy	4	2
Passage score	4	2
Comprehension Score	11	63
Oral Reading Quotient	85	16

PEABODY PICTURE VOCABULARY TEST—THIRD EDITION (PPVT-III)

Standard Score	99
Percentile	47

(continued)

Table 4.3   *Continued*

KEYMATH—REVISED

	Scaled	Standard Score
Numeration	9	
Rational Numbers	11	
Geometry	13	
Basic Concepts Area		108
Addition	11	
Subtraction	12	
Multiplication	11	
Division	13	
Mental Computation	10	
Operations Area		107
Measurement	10	
Time and Money	9	
Estimation	8	
Interpreting Data	9	
Problem Solving	9	
Applications Area		93
Total Test		99

instruction model will be adequate to the task of LD diagnosis that retains the integrity of the diagnosis for research and clinical purposes. A breakthrough in diagnosis is still necessary and some researchers are pursuing additional alternatives.

However, LD may be said to be relatively easily diagnosed because the core constructs of academic difficulty are easily, reliably, and validly assessed by the ubiquitous academic achievement tests administered with regularity in U.S. schools. Until the process of diagnosis is settled, the presence of academic functional impairment can be readily established, and alternative causes for such problems should be ruled out with intelligence tests, behavior rating scales, and other widely used measures.

Autism Spectrum Disorders

Jonathan M. Campbell

5

Chapter

The core features of autism were first described in Leo Kanner's (1943) remarkable description of 11 children who showed a cluster of social, communicative, and behavioral features unique from other diagnostic entities such as mental retardation or childhood schizophrenia. One year after Leo Kanner, Austrian physician Hans Asperger's initial report was published describing a group of four children who also showed unusual social and behavioral impairments (Asperger, 1944). Despite their independent descriptions, Asperger and Kanner identified children who showed significant social impairments in the presence of unusually repetitive behaviors, restrictive interests, or both. Like Kanner's group of children with autism, Asperger's disorder was found to be about four times more prevalent in boys than girls. Asperger's sample, however, showed cognitive and language abilities that were generally superior to those children described by Kanner.

Although Asperger's disorder shares considerable symptom overlap with autism, the disorder has only recently become recognized in the United States as a distinct entity (J. M. Campbell & Morgan, 1998). In addition to autism (Autistic Disorder) and Asperger's Disorder, the *Diagnostic and Statistical Manual of Mental*

Disorders, Fourth Edition, Text Revision, describes two further sub-types of Pervasive Developmental Disorders (PDD): Rett's Disorder and Childhood Disintegrative Disorder (CDD). Pervasive developmental disorder, along with Autistic Disorder and Asperger's, are increasingly known as autism spectrum disorders (ASD). Regardless of diagnosis, all children with PDD show severe impairments, typically in communication and social interactions emerging in early childhood and deviating from overall developmental level. Children across the PDD spectrum usually engage in repetitious, stereotyped behaviors, interests, and activities, often similar to those described with autistic children. Most children with PDD, except for those with Asperger's disorder, function in the mentally retarded range. Consistent with Kanner's and Asperger's initial case reports, most children with PDD are boys by a great margin, except for children diagnosed with Rett's Disorder, which is almost exclusively diagnosed in girls.

Constructs of Interest

The functional impairments associated with ASDs are broad based, and in some cases they may be profound, necessitating the assessment of numerous constructs.

Social Functioning

Kanner (1943) stated that the most outstanding and fundamental symptom evident in his group of children with autistic disturbance was an inability to relate to others. Kanner described this impairment as an "extreme autistic aloneness" (p. 242). As is discussed in more detail later in this chapter, Kanner's statement continues to hold true, as impairments in social relatedness and interpersonal functioning continue to represent the core features that most reliably distinguish PDDs from other disabilities, such as mental retardation (e.g., Carpentieri & Morgan, 1994, 1996; Stone & Hogan, 1993; Volkmar, Carter, Sparrow, & Cicchetti, 1993) and developmental language delay (Liss et al., 2001).

Various social impairments in the domains of social cognition and behavior have been documented for children with ASD across development and beginning very early in life. Kanner (1943) first identified this important clinical finding by noting that most parents reported the absence of anticipatory posturing in their children during infancy, which occurs in the first few months of typical infant development. For newborns and infants with autism, lack of orienting to social stimuli, lack of initiation and response to joint attention, and impaired motor imitation also have been identified as indicators of autism in children as young as 12 months of age (e.g., Osterling, Dawson, & Munson, 2002). For example, study of videotapes from 1-year-old birthday parties of children with autism and children with other delays has revealed that infants later diagnosed with autism look at others less and orient to their names with significantly less frequency than infants later diagnosed with mental retardation (Osterling et al., 2002). The absence of these early social behaviors in infants has informed and guided the creation and use of diagnostic measures, including early screeners, such as the Checklist for Autism in Toddlers (CHAT; Baron-Cohen, Allen, & Gillberg, 1992) and diagnostic observations, such as the Autism Diagnostic Observation Schedule (ADOS; Lord, Rutter, DiLavore, & Risi, 2001), which are discussed later in the chapter. Throughout development, social impairments above and beyond developmental expectations, relative to both chronological and mental age, continue to reliably discriminate between PDDs and children with cognitive delays (e.g., Volkmar et al., 1993).

Beginning with very young children and evident throughout development, play is an important aspect of social communication and language use. Play impairments are also frequently observed in children with ASD and are often seen early in development. For example, young children with autism may show difficulties with simple interactive play such as patty-cake or peek-a-boo—deficits that may represent difficulties with social interest and motor imitation. Further difficulties may be noted with imaginative or symbolic play skills early in development, such as pretending that an object represents another object or concept. For example, young children with autism may not be able to pretend that a broom represents a horse or that a wooden block can be used as a car, comb, or cup during play. In older and higher functioning children, play may lack reciprocal involvement and appear to be one-sided in setting the parameters of play and attempting to involve the play partner. For example, play activities may be imaginative or symbolic, such as a child pretending to be a knight or scientist, but inflexible and idiosyncratic thereby excluding others from the play sequence, such as a script where the scientist *always* searches for microscopic life on another planet or the "plot" of the play sequence is difficult for others to follow.

Language Development and Use

Kanner (1943) reported that 3 of 11 children originally described as autistic remained mute several years after initial evaluation, whereas those children who acquired language continued to show significant problems with echolalia, pronoun reversals, and an overly literal interpretation of language. Language delay is frequently present in individuals with autism, usually appearing at an early age and accounting for the most frequent early complaint by parents of autistic children. About 25% of children with autism are mute (Osterling, Dawson, & McPartland, 2001), and about 25% to 40% will not develop communicative language at all during their lifetimes (Mesibov, Adams, & Klinger, 1997; Osterling et al., 2001). Individuals with autism generally perform well below average on language tasks, especially those requiring verbal comprehension. Moreover, language skills are usually well below developmental age estimated from nonverbal ability tests (Carpentieri & Morgan, 1994). Individuals with autism who develop meaningful speech show a range of differences in their ability to communicate. In children, immediate and delayed echolalia may continue to accompany meaningful speech. Even in the presence of appropriate articulation and syntax, significant delays in the social aspects of language use typically persist, such as difficulties with prosody, initiating and sustaining conversation, and understanding nuances of social communication.

Restricted, Repetitive, and Stereotyped Activities, Interests, and Behaviors

Kanner's (1943) initial description of autism also highlighted children's unusually strong desire for the "maintenance of sameness" (p. 245) and the presence of limited spontaneous activity. These difficulties may take many forms across the autism spectrum, including body rocking, adherence to elaborate and nonfunctional rituals, overly repetitive play activities, and highly focused and idiosyncratic interests. The most "classic" stereotyped and repetitive symptoms of autism are motor stereotypies, such as body rocking, hand flapping or hand watching, and repetitive spinning of objects, such as jar lids or metallic toys.

Outside of these classic examples, however, a range of other possible symptoms exists across the autism spectrum. In higher functioning children with autism or children with Asperger's disorder, highly focused or singular interests that are peculiar may be present. For example, a child may be engrossed with the workings of water fountains, deep-fat fryers, or train schedules. For other children, nonfunctional routines or rituals are present, such as carrying around bags of small toys, requiring a good night song to be sung precisely prior to bedtime, or the location of certain objects, such as furniture, in a room in the child's home.

Neurocognitive Functioning

The social, language, and behavioral constructs described thus far are *essential* in diagnosing autism; however, cognitive and adaptive functioning are areas that must also be assessed to complete an adequate evaluation. These areas are important as many children with ASD also function in the range of mental retardation (see Chapter 3 for discussion of mental retardation). Although the level of functional intelligence varies widely in autistic children, the traditional view holds that the vast majority function in the range of mental retardation. For example, typical rates of mental retardation cited are: 60% with IQs below 50, 20% with IQs between 50 and 70, and only 20% have IQs of 70 or higher (Ritvo & Freeman, 1977). As a greater number of children with high functioning autism are being identified, the prevalence of mental retardation may be lower than originally believed. The assessment of cognitive functioning in autistic children is often complicated by the presence of "splinter" skills or, more rarely, savant skills. These isolated abilities, which may be strikingly higher than the child's general level of functioning, include motor and spatial skills, rote memory, artistic skills, and hyperlexia (Treffert, 1988). Savant skills, which only occur in about 10% of autistic persons, may include exceptional talents in music or art but, in most cases, are shown in individuals who are significantly impaired in general intellectual and adaptive functioning.

Intellectual functioning and language development assume even greater importance in light of the finding that they represent the most potent predictors of eventual adjustment. Onset of meaningful speech before age 5 or 6 appears to be crucial to later adjustment (Kanner, Rodriguez, & Ashenden, 1972). The child who develops functional speech by this age has a better chance of attaining marginal or good adjustment when compared to a child with no language. The measured intelligence of the young child with autism also serves as a strong predictor of later adaptation. In general, the higher the IQ, the closer the child will approach normal adaptation. An IQ below 40 is predictive of poor outcome; conversely, an IQ above 60 or 70 greatly increases the chances of educational progress and social adjustment (e.g., DeMyer et al., 1973). Moreover, there is growing evidence that children with higher language skills and IQs show a better response to behavioral treatment programs (S. J. Rogers, 1998).

A wide variety of hypotheses have attempted to delineate the basic cognitive defect in autism such as difficulties with selective attention, auditory processing, executive functioning, and memory. As early as 1971, Lovaas and his colleagues proposed that a basic feature in autism is "stimulus overselectivity," due to an inability to shift attention. Based on findings indicating cerebellar and parietal anomalies in autism, Courchesne (1995) proposed that autistic individuals exhibit deficits in regulation of three attention operations: orienting, shifting, and distributing attention to, between, and across locations of potential importance. According to Courchesne, these functions are needed to apprehend and engage in everyday nonsocial and social situations. Another hypothesis suggests a deficit in executive functioning as mediated by the frontal lobes resulting in deficiencies in self-regulation (e.g., McEvoy, Rogers, & Pennington, 1993). Despite likely differences in underlying neurological anomalies, as suggested by these hypotheses, problems in self-regulation have emerged as basic deficiencies in autism and other forms of PDD.

Individuals with autism and across the autism spectrum do not typically demonstrate deficits in single domains of cognitive functioning, findings that have given rise to hypotheses that autism and related disorders are disorders of complex information processing (Minshew, Goldstein, & Siegel, 1997). For example, Minshew and colleagues (1997) found that individuals with autism showed multiple primary deficits across domains, such as motor skills, complex language, reasoning abilities, and memory. Minshew et al.'s conceptualization of autism as a disorder of complex information processing is not at odds with social impairments present with autism. Current models of social information processing are complex, requiring the coordination of multiple sensory modalities, accurate social cue interpretation, and behavioral decision making that occurs rapidly (Crick & Dodge, 1994). In addition, social contexts are rarely identical; therefore, novel reasoning—a complex cognitive process—is required to guide appropriate social behavior across disparate contexts and changing settings.

Investigators have attempted to document neuropsychological functioning associated with different disorders along the autism spectrum, focused particularly on distinguishing between children with high-functioning autism versus Asperger's disorder. For example, Klin, Volkmar, Sparrow, Cicchetti, and Rourke (1995) documented a pattern of neurocognitive functioning for individuals with Asperger's disorder that was characterized by significantly better developed verbal versus nonverbal reasoning abilities. In contrast, a sample of individuals diagnosed with autism matched on age, gender, and IQ showed no significant differences between verbal and nonverbal reasoning abilities. Furthermore, Klin et al. reported that 11 neuropsychological deficits discriminated between the autism and Asperger's sample, including fine motor skills, visual-motor integration, gross motor skills, and visual memory. The authors suggested that the neuropsychological profile of deficits and assets in the Asperger's sample was consistent with that seen in individuals with nonverbal learning disability (NLD) and concluded that the NLD profile may serve as a neuropsychological marker for Asperger's disorder. Klin et al.'s findings are not universal, however, as others have failed to document a verbal versus nonverbal cognitive advantage in individuals with Asperger's or a neuropsychological profile that discriminates between Asperger's and individuals with high-functioning autism (Barnhill, Hagiwara, Myles, & Simpson, 2000; Manjiviona & Prior, 1999).

Adaptive Functioning

When compared to children with mental retardation, children with autism often demonstrate social responsiveness that is delayed or unusual. For example, children with Down syndrome, often severely impaired in symbolic and conceptual skills, usually form emotional attachments and relate affectionately to the people in their world (Bieberich & Morgan, 1998). The discrepancy between children with autism and those with mental retardation suggests deficits that do not arise from general retardation—deficits that impair not only cognitive functioning but also social and affective responsiveness. Multiple reports have documented that the everyday adaptive functioning of autistic individuals is typically more impaired than intellectual functioning (e.g., Carpentieri & Morgan, 1996; Volkmar et al., 1993). Furthermore, in the specific instance of Autistic Disorder, adaptive social functioning is significantly delayed in children and adults when compared to individuals with mental retardation, language delays, and psychotic disorders.

Diagnostic Standards

For clinical purposes, the most widely used diagnostic criteria for ASD are those contained in the *Diagnostic and Statistical Manual of Mental Disorders, Fourth Edition, Text Revision* (*DSM-IV-TR*, American

Psychiatric Association, 2000), which delineates criteria for the five PDD diagnoses introduced earlier in the chapter (American Psychiatric Association, 2000). The *DSM-IV-TR* classification system assumes a diagnostic hierarchy, whereby certain disorders take precedence over others in differential diagnosis (Lord & Risi, 1998). For example, CDD and Rett's Disorder diagnoses take precedence over Autistic Disorder and Asperger's, which, in turn, are diagnoses that take precedence over Pervasive Developmental Disorder—Not Otherwise Specified (PDD-NOS; American Psychiatric Association, 2000). Furthermore, when an individual meets diagnostic criteria for both Autistic Disorder and Asperger's Disorder, a diagnosis of Autistic Disorder is made. Practice parameters have been published by the American Academy of Child and Adolescent Psychiatry (Volkmar, Cook, Pomeroy, Realmuto, & Tanguay, 1999) and the Quality Standards Subcommittee of the American Academy of Neurology (Filipek et al., 2000) that outline recommended procedures for screening, assessment, and diagnosis for the field of ASD. The Filipek et al. (2000) practice parameters were approved by professional societies from multiple disciplines including audiology, occupational therapy, speech-language-hearing, and developmental pediatrics. The Filipek parameters were also published in the *Journal of Autism and Developmental Disorders* in 1999. Taken together, both documents offer professionally sanctioned recommendations regarding appropriate screening and diagnosis of ASD; the parameters are introduced here as an additional reference for readers. The following section briefly outlines diagnostic criteria for each PDD disorder as well as brief guidelines contained in the *DSM-IV-TR* and practice parameters mentioned above to guide differential diagnosis.

Autistic Disorder

Consistent with many of Kanner's (1943) initial ideas about autism, the *DSM-IV-TR* describes three clusters of symptoms, often known as the "autistic triad," based on Rutter's (1978) diagnostic concepts, which must be present early in development for diagnosis of Autistic Disorder. Autistic Disorder is sometimes referred to as infantile autism, Kanner's autism, and/or early childhood autism.

The *DSM-IV-TR* criteria state that a minimum of six symptoms from three problem areas must be present for diagnosis. At least two symptoms of *qualitative impairment in social interaction* are required for diagnosis, such as impaired use of nonverbal behaviors and failure to develop peer relationships appropriate to developmental level. At least one symptom indicating *qualitative impairment in communication* is required for diagnosis, such as delays in development of spoken language or stereotyped and repetitive use of language. At least one symptom indicating *restricted, repetitive and stereotyped patterns of behavior, interests and/or activities* is also required for diagnosis, such as an all-encompassing preoccupation that is either abnormal in intensity or focus or stereotyped and repetitive motor mannerisms (e.g., body rocking or hand flapping). For diagnosis of Autistic Disorder, the individual must also meet an onset criterion, which states that delays or dysfunction in social interaction, play, or social communication must be present prior to 36 months of age. The individual also cannot be diagnosed if he or she meets diagnostic criteria for either Rett's Disorder or CDD.

Asperger's Disorder

According to *DSM-IV-TR,* the two essential features of Asperger's Disorder are identical to those for autism: (1) *qualitative impairments in social interaction,* such as gaze aversion, failure to develop normal peer relations, and lack of social or emotional reciprocity; and (2) *restricted and stereotyped patterns of behavior,* such as intense, persistent preoccupations with narrow interests or objects, rigid adherence to nonfunctional routines, and/or stereotyped motor mannerisms. For the purpose of *DSM-IV-TR* diagnosis, children with Asperger's Disorder must show *no* significant delays in the following areas: (a) general language functioning, (b) self-help skills, (c) adaptive behavior (with the exception of social interaction), or (d) cognitive development (American Psychiatric Association, 2000). Significant delays are only generally defined in the *DSM-IV-TR,* however. For example, age-appropriate language functioning is defined as the use of single words by the age of 2 years and communicative phrases by age 3 years.

According to the 10th edition of the *International Classification of Diseases* (*ICD-10*), delayed or impaired motor functioning may be associated with Asperger's and motor clumsiness is described as usually present, although not necessary for diagnosis (World Health Organization, 1993). Children with Asperger's do not always demonstrate significant delays in motor functioning, particularly when compared to children with autism of comparable mental and developmental ages (e.g., Manjiviona & Prior, 1995). The *DSM-IV-TR* diagnostic criteria for Asperger's also require that delays in adaptive functioning, such as communication and/or self-help skills, cannot be present. The adaptive behavior criterion is further described in the *ICD-10* criteria, which states that self-help skills, adaptive behavior, and curiosity about the environment *during the first 3 years of development* should be roughly commensurate with typical cognitive development (World Health Organization, 1993). The statement in *ICD-10* is presumably included to allow for diagnosis of Asperger's Disorder when adaptive behavior and self-help skills fall below age-appropriate expectations for older children, which is likely to occur in light of pervasive social impairments. For example, an individual's social impairments may yield difficulties with independent personal hygiene due to lack of social awareness. Relevant to this criterion, Szatmari, Archer, Fisman, Streiner, and Wilson (1995) described a sample of 4- to 6-year-old children diagnosed with Asperger's who showed normative delays in activities of daily living.

The symptoms of Asperger's Disorder are typically less evident when compared with autism and may not become apparent until the child is older. For example, Howlin and Asgharian (1999) reported, on average, parents first became concerned about children with Asperger's Disorder around the age of 30 months as opposed to 18 months of age for children with autism. Final diagnosis for each disorder also varied, with autism being diagnosed around the age of 5.5 years versus 11 years for children with Asperger's Disorder. The long-term prognosis for individuals with Asperger's Disorder appears to be better than the prognosis for most individuals with autism. Most individuals with Asperger's can achieve independent adjustment in adulthood although problems in social interaction often persist (Klin, Volkmar, & Sparrow, 2000).

DSM-IV-TR includes several statements to guide the differential diagnosis of Asperger's versus autism. First, the differential is guided by the absence of early cognitive and language delays for Asperger's in contrast to the criteria set forth for autism. Second, the *restricted and stereotyped patterns of behavior criterion* for Asperger's is described as typically taking the form of an "all-encompassing pursuit" (American Psychiatric Association, 2000, p. 82). This is in contrast to autism, where stereotypic motor mannerisms, preoccupation with parts of objects, and/or distress in the face of changes in routines or rituals are usually present (American Psychiatric Association, 2000). Third, social interaction is described as marked by more self-isolation in autism, whereas individuals with Asperger's are described as interested in initiating social interaction but take a verbose, one-sided, and insensitive approach in the bid to interact. The social description above is consistent with the "little professor" characterization of children with Asperger's—social communication is often pedantic and confined to restricted areas of interest.

Although *DSM-IV-TR* includes Asperger's Disorder as a distinct diagnostic entity and includes statements to guide the differential diagnosis of Asperger's Disorder versus autism, controversy exists as to whether individuals with Asperger's Disorder are different from high-functioning individuals with autism (e.g., Schopler, Mesibov, & Kunce, 1998). Others have questioned the internal validity of the diagnostic definition of Asperger's Disorder in the *DSM-IV* and *DSM-IV-TR*. For example, some have claimed that when strictly using the *DSM-IV* diagnostic definition of Asperger's Disorder, the disorder is almost impossible to diagnose because children regularly meet criteria for both Asperger's and Autistic Disorder and autism takes precedence over Asperger's in the *DSM* diagnostic hierarchy (Mayes, Calhoun, & Crites, 2001).

Childhood Disintegrative Disorder

The essential features of CDD (Heller's syndrome) are a period of at least 2 years of normal development followed by a period of severe regression in development across multiple areas of functioning (American Psychiatric Association, 2000). The 2-year period of normal development must be marked by age-appropriate communication, social relatedness, play and adaptive behavior. After typical development between birth and 24 months, clinically significant losses in acquired skills must take place prior to the age of 10 and must occur in at least two of five areas: (1) expressive or receptive language, (2) social skills or adaptive behavior, (3) bowel or bladder control, (4) play, or (5) motor skills. In addition to developmental regression, diagnosis of CDD also requires abnormal functioning in two of three areas: (1) qualitative impairment in social interaction, (2) qualitative impairment in communication, and (3) restricted, repetitive, and stereotyped patterns of behavior, interests, and activities. The additional criterion cites the identical symptoms present in the autistic triad; however, only the presence of symptoms in two of three areas is required for diagnosis of CDD. The *DSM-IV-TR* criteria also require a rule-out of schizophrenia for diagnosis. Childhood Disintegrative Disorder is reported to be very rare and typically associated with functioning in the range of severe mental retardation.

As reported earlier, in contrast to Autistic Disorder where symptoms are usually noted in the first 12 to 18 months of development, children with CDD must show typical development in the first 2 years of life. The *DSM-IV-TR* specifies that if early developmental history is unavailable to document deterioration, Autistic Disorder should be diagnosed. Childhood Disintegrative Disorder is distinguished from Rett's by the presence of developmental deterioration in the latter by age 5 months (see following diagnostic criteria), as well as characteristic course marked by head growth deceleration and stereotypic hand movements. Childhood Disintegrative Disorder is distinguished from Asperger's by the loss of acquired skills and much greater likelihood of functioning in the range of severe mental retardation.

Rett's Disorder

Similar to CDD, Rett's Disorder is also defined by significant developmental deterioration. In Rett's, a brief period of normal development is observed prior to a significant loss of previously acquired purposeful hand movements, severe psychomotor retardation, and deceleration of head growth (American Psychiatric Association, 2000). Formal diagnostic criteria require normal prenatal and perinatal development, normal psychomotor development through the first 5 months, and normal head circumference at birth. For Rett's Disorder to be formally diagnosed, developmental deterioration must also follow a characteristic course defined as: (a) deceleration of head growth between the ages of 5 and 48 months; (b) loss of acquired purposeful hand skills between the ages of 5 and 30 months, followed by stereotypic hand movements such as hand-wringing; (c) loss of social engagement; (d) appearance of poorly coordinated gait or trunk movements; and (e) severe psychomotor retardation and severely impaired expressive and receptive language development (American Psychiatric Association, 2000). Rett's is included as a PDD due to similar clinical presentation, mainly the loss of social interaction, communication delays, and stereotypic movements. Rett's has been documented almost exclusively in girls and has been associated with severe mental retardation. Differential diagnosis is guided by the sex differences between Rett's, observed primarily in girls, and other PDD, which, as noted, show a preponderance of boys versus girls. Rett's is differentiated from Autistic Disorder by head growth deceleration and somewhat more transient social interaction delays than observed in Autistic Disorder.

Pervasive Developmental Disorder—Not Otherwise Specified

Because many children fail to fully meet the diagnostic criteria for a specific PDD, *DSM-IV-TR* includes the category of PDD-NOS (American Psychiatric Association, 2000; Towbin, 1997). A diagnosis of PDD-NOS is made in the presence of severe and pervasive impairment in reciprocal social interaction and *either* verbal or nonverbal communication *or* stereotyped behavior, interests, or activities (American Psychiatric Association, 2000, p. 84). Children with a PDD-NOS diagnosis do not meet formal diagnostic criteria for any of the previously described PDD diagnoses, schizophrenia, schizotypal personality disorder, or avoidant personality disorder.

Atypical autism is included in the PDD-NOS category to describe children who show symptoms indicative of autism, but fall short of full criteria due to onset after 36 months, subthreshold symptomatology, or unusual symptom presentation that falls outside of established guidelines. The PDD-NOS category is defined on the basis of the judgment of the evaluating clinician (Volkmar et al., 1999).

As might be expected given the expansive diagnostic descriptors, the group of individuals diagnosed with PDD-NOS represents heterogeneity above and beyond that already observed in the other PDD diagnostic groups. Compared to other diagnoses, less is known about individuals diagnosed with PDD-NOS; however, limited data suggests that social and communication deficits are usually less severe and prognosis generally better in this group when compared to individuals with Autistic Disorder (Towbin, 1997).

Individuals with Disabilities Education Act

For the purposes of classification for special education services, the Individuals with Disabilities Act (IDEA; Federal Register, 1999) defines autism as "a developmental disability significantly affecting verbal and nonverbal communication and social interaction, generally evidenced before age 3, that adversely affects a child's educational performance" (p. 12421). The IDEA guidelines allow a larger number of children to be diagnosed with autism for the purposes of special education services by stating that "a child who manifests the characteristics of 'autism' after age 3 could be diagnosed as having 'autism' if the criteria [set forth above] are satisfied" (p. 12421). As described above, the IDEA classification system for Autistic Disorder does not clearly match criteria set forth in the *DSM-IV-TR*, as a child can be diagnosed with autism if symptoms are present after the age of 3. In the *DSM-IV-TR* system, a child who presents with communication and social interaction difficulties after the age of 3 would likely be diagnosed with PDD-NOS. The important qualifier for the purposes of IDEA diagnosis is that the presence of autistic symptoms must negatively affect the child's academic performance, which would presumably be the case in the majority of children identified with autism.

Outside of the formal diagnostic category of autism, children diagnosed with Asperger's, Rett's, CDD, or PDD-NOS might be eligible for special education services under other disability categories, such as other health impairment (OHI—a category that includes attention-deficit disorders), speech and language impairment, specific learning disability, or emotional disturbance. As with autism, IDEA guidelines stipulate that special education services are warranted only if the child's disability impairs educational performance. Recently, however, the Committee on Educational Interventions for Children with Autism recommended that any child identified with an ASD (e.g., Asperger's, PDD-NOS) should be eligible for special education services with the autism eligibility category (National Research Council, 2001).

Assessment Methods and Procedures

Although the *DSM-IV-TR* presents a descriptive set of behavioral criteria for the diagnosis of disorders across the autism spectrum, outside of symptom number and age of onset, the manual provides no quantitative system for assessing the symptoms of PDD. Nor does the *DSM-IV-TR* provide quantitative guidance regarding differential diagnosis for differentiating ASD from related disorders, such as mental retardation. What follows is an overview of assessment methods and procedures currently used to measure the constructs defined earlier in the chapter and evaluate the presence of diagnostic features as set forth in *DSM-IV-TR*.

Introduction to the Comprehensive Developmental Approach

Klin et al. (1997) outline a useful strategy for assessing children and adolescents referred for possible ASD, the comprehensive developmental approach (CDA). In Klin et al.'s approach, assessment of children's functioning across a range of areas and contexts is essential (i.e., the "comprehensive" aspect of the approach). Furthermore, assessment of children's functioning is compared to chronological and mental age expectations (i.e., the "developmental" aspect of the approach). The CDA emphasizes identification of resources and deficits relevant to improving the child's adaptation. The CDA assessment approach is particularly useful in evaluating children with autism due to the variability of their psychological functioning and inconsistency of functioning across multiple settings and contexts. The CDA identifies six principles to assessment, including: (1) assessment of multiple areas of functioning, (2) adopting a developmental perspective, (3) emphasis on variability of skills, (4) emphasis on variability across settings, (5) emphasis on functional adjustment, and (6) need for evaluation of delays and deviance (Klin et al., 1997). Important assumptions of the CDA, which pertain to evaluations for individuals with a suspected or confirmed ASD, are described in the following section.

First, as introduced earlier in the chapter, the CDA emphasizes that a range of constructs and areas of functioning are important in a comprehensive diagnostic evaluation of ASD, such as social communication, cognition, and functional, or adaptive, adjustment. Second, given the frequent co-occurrence of mental retardation with ASD, the CDA frames functioning as not only normative delay but also delays from overall developmental or cognitive level. Third, the CDA acknowledges the variable profile of skills that children with ASD present and cautions against the presentation of overall summary scores or overgeneralization of performance of a "splinter" skill area. Fourth, by acknowledging the variability of performance across settings, the CDA emphasizes the need to alter settings to generate descriptions of situations that induce optimal performance for the individual as well as environments that may impede performance and optimal functioning. Fifth, the CDA emphasizes the importance of documenting functional adjustment across domains and its interplay in the context of impacting the individuals' ongoing adjustment. For example, how might impaired socialization affect academic performance in the classroom? Finally, the CDA emphasizes the assessment of both *delays* in development, such as documenting the individual's performance compared to normative expectations, and deviance in development, such as documenting the presence of behaviors that are not usually observed during any developmental stage. The important conceptual difference between delay and deviance informs practical selection of instrumentation and measures. For example, cognitive delays are documented with the use of an intelligence measure that has been adequately standardized and normed with a representative sample of similar-age children, such as the Wechsler Intelligence Scales for Children—Fourth Edition (WISC-IV; Wechsler, 2003a, 2003b). Assessment of deviant behaviors often observed with autism, such as delayed echolalia, exists at such a low base rate in the general population that measures are not typically normed for such behaviors. Therefore, autism specific instrumentation that is not normed should be used to document behaviorally deviant symptoms.

Additional Guidelines for Assessment

In addition to the principles involved in the CDA model, other guidelines are important when conducting assessments with individuals either diagnosed or suspected ASD. Due to the complexities and pervasiveness of delays across a range of functioning, interdisciplinary evaluations are recommended. Involvement of multiple disciplines, such as psychology and communication sciences, is desirable to document cognitive, developmental, language, communicative, and behavioral functioning in individuals. Ideally, interdisciplinary teams involved in the evaluation will be available for collaboration throughout the evaluation to prevent duplication of interviewing and test procedures. Interdisciplinary collaboration is crucial to compare and reconcile clinical observations, findings, and diagnostic impressions prior to sharing evaluation findings with caregivers (Klin et al., 1997).

As an important member of the interdisciplinary team of evaluators, parents and caregivers should be closely involved in the evaluation for a variety of reasons. First, parents' participation is necessary for the collection of developmental information that may guide differential diagnosis (e.g., presence or absence of developmental deterioration early in child's history and first onset of concerning symptoms). Close involvement of parents throughout the process is also important to demystify the evaluation process by allowing discussion of observations during procedures and offering justification for tests and methods used in the evaluation (Klin et al., 1997). Parent involvement during the evaluation also develops relationship and conceptual groundwork for the parent informing session; therefore, discussion of functioning and diagnosis, if appropriate, will occur with parents' or caregivers having some understanding about the rationale for diagnostic conclusions and recommendations for intervention.

The complex symptom presentation of the child with confirmed or suspected ASD creates unique difficulties during formal and informal assessment procedures. Definitive recommendations about maximizing performance for all children with autism are inappropriate due to the heterogeneity that exists in this group. However, several general principles do apply. Reinforcement strategies that may work well with a larger population of children may not work as well for children with autism. For example, children with autism may be less motivated by social reinforcement (e.g., saying, "Great work!" or patting a child on the back) to attend to and perform at tasks; therefore, tangible reinforcement may work well to elicit the child's best performance, such as the use of edible reinforcers or access to favorite toys or activities. Due to frequent difficulties with attention and processing of sensory information, children with autism may require a setting that is as free as possible from distractions, such as a testing room that is quiet, and perhaps free from windows or pictures hanging on the wall. Evaluators must also be aware of the level of verbal and social response required for testing tasks and consider interspersing social and nonsocial or verbal and nonverbal tasks throughout the evaluation.

Diagnostic Assessment of the Autistic Triad: Social Functioning, Communication, and Repetitive Behavior/Interests/Activities

A variety of procedures and measures exist for documenting the core features of social and communicative dysfunction across the PDD spectrum. Historically, observation by a trained child psychiatrist or psychologist served as the gold standard for diagnosing autism and related disorders, typically in the absence of formal rating scales or other assessment instrumentation. Over time, however, expert opinion has been supplemented by standardized diagnostic observation instruments, including rating checklists, such as the Childhood Autism Rating Scale (CARS; Schopler, Reichler, & Renner, 1988), and semi-structured observation sequences, such as those used in the Autism Diagnostic Observation Schedule—Generic (ADOS-G; Lord et al., 2000) and the Screening Tool for Autism in Two-Year-Olds (STAT; Stone, Coonrod, & Ousley, 2000).

The CARS is a 15-item scale used to document social, communicative, and behavioral symptoms indicative of autism across fourteen areas, such as relating to people, adaptation to change, verbal communication, and nonverbal communication; one item is scored for the observers' general impressions regarding the degree of autism. Each item is rated along a 4-point scale grounded in behavioral descriptors that ranges from 1 (age-appropriate/normal) to 4 (severely abnormal) and summed to produce a CARS Total raw score. The CARS Total raw score may fall into one of three categories: Non-Autistic (15 to 29), Mildly-Moderately Autistic (30 to 36), or Severely Autistic (37 to 60). The CARS has been identified as one of the most reliable and valid observational rating scales for identifying children with autism, including the differentiation between autism and mental retardation (Filipek et al., 2000; S. Morgan, 1988). However, the CARS is not designed for use as a third-party checklist by an untrained parent or teacher observer, such as might be the case for a general behavioral checklist like the Behavior Assessment System for Children (BASC; C. R. Reynolds & Kamphaus, 1998); rather, the CARS manual states that raters should receive at least minimal training in its use (Schopler et al., 1988, p. 6).

The ADOS-G was originally developed as a research instrument and has been recently published as the ADOS for clinical use (Lord et al., 2001). The ADOS is a standardized assessment of an individual's communication, social interaction, and play or imaginative use of toys or other materials. The ADOS is built on the presentation of planned social interactions or "presses," which are likely to elicit behaviors or deficits relevant to PDD. The ADOS consists of four separate modules designed for use with individuals from different developmental levels and expressive language abilities. Module 1 is appropriate for individuals whose expressive language level ranges from no speech to simple phrases, which the authors operationally define as less than an age-equivalent score of 30 months on the expressive communication subdomain of the Vineland. Module 2 is appropriate for individuals whose expressive language ranges from three-word phrases to verbal fluency. Module 3 is appropriate for children and younger adolescents who are verbally fluent, while Module 4 is appropriate for adolescents and adults who are fluent with expressive language.

The ADOS consists of a series of activities that vary according to the age of the child, level of child's expressive language, skills tapped, and degree of structure provided by the examiner. The activities are used to elicit or document behavioral symptoms indicative of autism, such as lack of response to bids at joint attention or repetitive use of toys during free play, which are coded using behavioral descriptors. Codes are converted and summed to yield Communication, Social Interaction, and Communication + Social Interaction Total scores. Scores in each of these domains are compared to ADOS diagnostic algorithm scores that were created by the authors to best discriminate between Autistic Disorder, PDD-NOS, or no ASD (Lord et al., 2001). For an ADOS diagnosis of either autism or ASD, scores must exceed the appropriate cutoff scores for each domain (i.e., Communication, Social Interaction, and Total scores). Although the ADOS yields additional scores of either Play or Imagination/Creativity (depending on module) and Stereotyped Behaviors and Restricted Interests, these codes were not included in the diagnostic algorithm due to lack of utility in classifying individuals into diagnostic groups. Although restricted behaviors and interests are coded if they are observed during ADOS administration, the ADOS does not always offer adequate opportunity to measure stereotyped behaviors and restricted interests. Therefore, assessment of the stereotyped behavior and interest criterion may require documentation outside of ADOS observation, such as through additional observation or interviewing teachers or caregivers. The ADOS also does not provide information regarding onset of symptom presentation, which must also be collected for diagnosis of Autistic Disorder or another ASD.

Presently, two parent interviews are recommended for use in the diagnosis of ASD (Filipek et al., 2000): the Autism Diagnostic Interview—Revised (ADI-R; Lord, Rutter, & Le Couteur, 1994) and Parent Interview for Autism (PIA; Stone & Hogan, 1993). The ADI-R is the complement to the ADOS-G and shares a similar background in terms of being developed primarily for research purposes as well as being linked to *DSM-IV* diagnostic criteria for autism and the larger group of ASDs. The ADI-R is a semi-structured diagnostic interview for use with parents and caregivers of children with suspected autism. The ADI-R samples present behavioral functioning as reported by caregivers across the autistic triad as well as other symptoms frequently observed in autism, such as overactivity and sensory sensitivities. Parent responses to interview questions are coded to indicate absence of behavior (a code of 0) or degree of behavior present (typically a code of 1 or 2 indicating that the behavior is probably present/abnormal or definitely present/abnormal). For some items, a code of 3 is used to indicate that behavior or symptomatology is extreme. Autism Diagnostic Interview—Revised items are grouped to indicate degree of impairment in social interaction, communication, and restrictive behaviors as well as to document the age when abnormalities were first observed by caregivers or judged to be present by the interviewer. For ADI-R diagnosis of autism, scores are required to exceed algorithm cutoff scores in each domain as well as the presence of some abnormality in at least one domain prior to 36 months of age (Lord et al., 1994). The ADI-R has shown high internal consistency reliability for the social and communication domains (Cronbach alpha coefficients >.80) and lower internal consistency for the restricted and repetitive behavior domains (.69; Lord et al., 1994). The ADI-R also shows solid interrater reliability, as evidenced by intraclass correlation coefficients that range from .93 to .97, and concurrent validity as evidenced by 96% of children diagnosed with autism correctly classified by the ADI-R algorithm. Conversely, 92% of children diagnosed with mental retardation or language impairment were correctly identified as not autistic (Lord et al., 1994). The ADI-R requires training for clinical use and extensive training for use as a research instrument (Lord, 1997). The ADI-R or ADOS diagnoses are frequently cited as gold standard diagnoses for research either in combination or independently.

The PIA is a 118-item parent interview developed to assess autistic symptoms in children under the age of 6. The PIA samples the child's functioning in 11 domains that include the autistic triad and associated features: (1) Social Relating, (2) Affective Responses, (3) Motor Imitation, (4) Peer Interactions, (5) Object Play, (6) Imaginative Play, (7) Language Understanding, (8) Nonverbal Communication, (9) Motoric Behaviors, (10) Sensory Responses, and (11) Need for Sameness. Parents respond to items using a 5-point Likert scale that ranges from 1 (Almost never/Less than 10% of the time) to 5 (Almost always/Over 90% of the time). Items are worded positively (e.g., "Does your child understand what you say to him/her?") and negatively (e.g., "Does your child avoid looking at people during interactions?") and reverse scored so that lower scores indicate greater degree of pathology associated with autism. The PIA is not a normed instrument; therefore, parent's responses cannot be compared to the larger population of children with ASD. Although a research measure, the PIA has shown adequate total test reliability (.94) and stability (.93) in a sample of 165 preschoolers. The PIA has demonstrated adequate discriminative validity in detecting autism ($n = 58$) versus mental retardation ($n = 36$) in two groups that were equivalent in chronological age, mental age, and sex distribution. Four PIA subscales best discriminated between diagnostic groups, Social Relating (19 items), Motor Imitation (6 items), Peer Interactions (8 items), and Nonverbal Communication (13 items).

A few third-party rating instruments exist for the evaluation of ASD, such as the Gilliam Autism Rating Scale (GARS; Gilliam, 1995), which includes behavioral items tapping symptoms across the autistic triad. As with any third-party rating scale, the GARS does not yield a diagnosis of autism. Rather, the GARS indicates the degree of likelihood that the rated individual will meet diagnostic criteria for autism. Outside of the test's normative sample, the GARS has yielded sensitivity of only .48 for detecting autism in 119 children diagnosed according to *DSM-IV* criteria using the ADOS and ADI-R (South et al., 2002). In the aforementioned sample, the

GARS yielded an average score of 90, indicating "Average Probability of Autism," 10 points below the test's mean of 100. South et al. (2002) also documented that 20% of the sample diagnosed with autism according to the *DSM-IV* received GARS ratings that fell in the "Very Low" or "Low Probability of Autism" categories.

As diagnosis of ASD in higher functioning children has become more common, several third-party rating scales have been published for the purpose of screening for ASD in general preschool and school-age populations (J. M. Campbell, 2005). Three recently published and commercially available measures include the Asperger Syndrome Diagnostic Scale (ASDS; Myles, Bock, & Simpson, 2001), Gilliam Asperger's Disorder Scale (GADS; Gilliam, 2001), and Krug Asperger's Disorder Index (KADI; Krug & Arick, 2003). Each measure includes behavioral descriptors associated with dysfunction across the autistic triad. These measures should be used with caution as questionable normative procedures were used in test construction and psychometric properties are generally poor (J. M. Campbell, 2005). Two additional third-party screening instruments, the Autism Spectrum Screening Questionnaire (ASSQ; Ehlers, Gillberg, & Wing, 1999) and Childhood Asperger's Screening Test (CAST; Scott, Baron-Cohen, Bolton, & Brayne, 2002) have been used exclusively for research purposes, but demonstrate promising psychometric properties.

Other recently developed scales that appear to be useful aids in the diagnostic assessment of ASD and in the early screening for such disorders include the CHAT (Baron-Cohen et al., 1992), and a Modified version of the CHAT, the M-CHAT (D. L. Robins, Fein, Barton, & Green, 2001). The CHAT is designed to provide an early screening measure for autism in children as young as 18 months (Baron-Cohen et al., 1992). The CHAT consists of a caregiver checklist and short observational checklist designed to evaluate the presence of early indicators of autism, such as lack of response to bids for joint attention. The M-CHAT is a 23-item parent checklist that contains the 9 items from the CHAT, plus 14 additional yes/no statements. Across both measures, behavioral symptoms found to be predictive of a diagnosis of an ASD were lack of imitation, lack of protodeclarative pointing, lack of response to or initiation of joint attention, lack of responsiveness to name being called, and little interest in other children. Early screening measures, such as the CHAT, are likely to be used more frequently in coming years due to the increased emphasis on early detection of autism and other forms of PDD.

Language Functioning

The interplay between social functioning, communication, and repetitive behaviors/interests is complex and particularly complicated when discussing assessment of language functioning in the context of ASD. As discussed earlier in the chapter, diagnostic measures for ASD assess aspects of social communicative functioning, such as the coordination of gesture and speech as well as documentation of language delays as indicated by history or parent report. In addition to evaluating a child's communicative functioning for the purposes of diagnosis and classification, additional domains of language should also be assessed.

A major factor regarding how to assess children's language functioning involves the presence or absence of expressive language. When expressive language is absent due to a child being too young to use words or a child being mute, the focus of language assessment is typically on social, communicative, and play behaviors (Klin et al., 1997). Goals of assessment in the case of preverbal children are to document levels of language comprehension, presence of communicative intent, presence of nonverbal communicative behaviors, such as eye contact, gestures, shifting of gaze, and symbolic play behaviors. Measures used for these purposes might include parent interviews, checklists, or language surveys, including broad developmental assessment instruments, such as the ADI-R or Vineland, or language-specific measures, such as the Language Development Survey (Rescorla, 1989). Play-based assessment might take the form of unstructured play sequences or semi-structured sequences such as the tasks involved in Module 1 of the ADOS (Lord et al., 2001) described in the previous section.

For children and adolescents with expressive language, areas of assessment should include receptive and expressive vocabulary skills, articulation, spontaneous language use, prosody, and pragmatic language skills (Klin et al., 1997; Volkmar et al., 1999). Measures of expressive and receptive vocabulary may sample single-word skills, such as the Peabody Picture Vocabulary Test—Third Edition (PPVT-III; Dunn & Dunn, 1997), a measure of single-word receptive vocabulary, or more comprehensive examination of vocabulary abilities such as semantic, syntactic, and pragmatic skills tapped by the Oral and Written Language Scales, Listening Comprehension and Oral Expression subscales (OWLS/LC, OWLS/OE; Carrow-Woolfolk, 1995). With verbal children and adolescents, measurement of pragmatics, or social use of language, might involve informal observations, such as the ability to initiate and maintain conversation during breaks from formal testing, or formal evaluation, such as the use of the Test of Pragmatic Language (TOPL; Phelps-Terasaki & Phelps-Gunn, 1992). The Children's Communication Checklist (CCC; Bishop & Baird, 2001) is a parent and teacher report of pragmatic language functioning that has been researched with groups of children with autism, Asperger's Disorder, PDD-NOS, Attention-Deficit/Hyperactivity Disorder (ADHD), and specific learning disabilities (SLD). The CCC may be a useful measure to assist with differential diagnosis, as children with autism earned significantly lower pragmatic composite scores when compared with children with SLD, and children with Asperger's Disorder earned lower scores when compared to children with ADHD and SLD on subscales of social relationships and restricted interests.

Cognitive Functioning

To assist in educational programming and potentially *aid* in the differential diagnosis between PDD and non-PDD disorders as well as between disorders within the autism spectrum, many instruments are available to assess intelligence and patterns of neurocognitive abilities and deficits. Traditional intelligence scales can be helpful in estimating the autistic child's current level of intellectual functioning and profile of abilities. In higher functioning children, the Stanford-Binet Intelligence Scales (Thorndike et al., 1986) and the Wechsler Intelligence Scale for Children—Third Revision (WISC-III; Wechsler,

1991) have often been used in assessing intellectual functioning. Due to the language difficulties frequently seen in children with autism, nonverbal tests of intellectual functioning, such as the Leiter International Performance Scale—Revised (Roid & Miller, 1997) may also be used, especially with children who show severe verbal impairments.

With frequently used measures such as the Stanford-Binet and Wechsler scales, researchers have attempted to document characteristic profiles of summary IQ and subtest scores. For example, Carpentieri and Morgan (1994) showed that children with autism performed more poorly on the Stanford-Binet-IV Verbal Reasoning Composite when compared to children with mental retardation of comparable chronological and mental age. Also of interest, in the domain of verbal reasoning, children with autism performed more poorly on subtests thought to tap aspects of social knowledge and reasoning, such as Absurdities and Comprehension. Mayes and Calhoun (2003) reported that 3- to 7-year-old children with autism, both low-functioning (IQ < 80) and high-functioning (IQ $\geq$ 80) performed relatively better on nonverbal versus verbal subtests of the Stanford-Binet-IV. Among the Stanford-Binet-IV subtests, children with autism showed relative strengths on the Quantitative and Bead Memory subtests, suggesting better developed visual spatial skills in comparison to overall cognitive functioning (Mayes & Calhoun, 2003). Across the studies cited, there is some evidence that nonverbal skills are better developed than verbal skills, as measured by the Stanford-Binet-IV, in high- and low-functioning children with Autistic Disorder. In the most recent revision of the Stanford-Binet scales, the Stanford-Binet—Fifth Edition (SB-V; Roid, 2003a, 2003b), a contrast group of 83 children identified as having Autistic Disorder completed the measure. On average, individuals earned a Full Scale IQ (FSIQ) score of 70.4 and showed a minimal 3-point difference with Nonverbal IQ ($M = 73.3$) > Verbal IQ (VIQ: $M = 70.2$). Very little scatter between SB-V domain scores is reported for the group, with scores on measures of Working Memory ($M = 71.6$) seeming to differ slightly from the other indices, range of Fluid Reasoning $M = 76.0$ to Visual-Spatial Processing $M = 75.0$ (Roid, 2003a, 2003b).

Research with the Wechsler scales has produced a large amount of information regarding the utility of an "autism" profile.

Cognitive profiling with Wechsler deviation IQ scores and sub-scales has revealed some differences between children with high-functioning autism and Asperger's or high-functioning autism and attention-deficit disorders (Ehlers et al., 1997; Klin et al., 1995). In terms of Wechsler IQ scores, children with autism tend to perform significantly better on the Performance (i.e., Nonverbal) versus Verbal scale. In terms of subtest performance, children with autism often earn their highest subscale score on the Block Design subtest from the Performance scales and their lowest score on the Comprehension subtest from the Verbal scales (see Barnhill et al., 2000, for a summary of research studies).

Recent revisions to the Wechsler scales, the Wechsler Preschool and Primary Scale of Intelligence—Third Edition (WPPSI-III; Wechsler, 2002b) and the Wechsler Intelligence Scale for Children—Fourth Edition (WISC-IV; Wechsler, 2003b) have included initial evidence that supports the PIQ > VIQ profile for children diagnosed with *DSM-IV-TR* Autistic Disorder. Twenty-one children diagnosed with *DSM-IV-TR* Autistic Disorder were administered the WPPSI-III, earning an average FSIQ of 76.6 with PIQ scores 18 points higher than VIQ, on average. When compared to a control group of children matched on age, sex, ethnicity, parent education level, and geographic region, no mean differences were observed on the Block Design and Object Assembly subtests, the highest mean scores for the group. Conversely, when compared to the control group, the group of children with Autistic Disorder showed the greatest impairment on the Comprehension subtest ($M = 3.7$), lower than the control group by an average of 7 scaled score points (Wechsler, 2002b).

Similar to the WPPSI-III, the WISC-IV Technical Manual also reports on a group of 19 children diagnosed with *DSM-IV-TR* Autistic Disorder who completed the measure (Wechsler, 2003b). The group earned an average FSIQ of 76.4 with Perceptual Reasoning Index scores ($M = 85.7$) about 5.5 points higher than Verbal Comprehension Index scores ($M = 80.2$), on average. When compared to a control group of children matched on age, sex, ethnicity, parent education level, and geographic region, no mean differences were observed on the Arithmetic ($M = 8.2$; Cohen's $d = .16$) and Block Design subtests ($M = 7.9$; Cohen's $d = .64$), the highest mean scores for the group. When compared to the control group, the group of children with Autistic Disorder showed the greatest impairment on the Letter-Number Sequencing ($M = 5.5$; Cohen's $d = 1.83$) and Comprehension ($M = 5.3$; Cohen's $d = 1.72$) subtests (Wechsler, 2003b).

In contrast to individuals diagnosed with autism, Klin et al. (1995) documented the opposite deviation IQ profile for individuals with Asperger's Disorder who showed significantly better performance on the Verbal versus Performance scales (i.e., about a 24 point-difference on average). Similarly, Ehlers et al. (1997) documented Wechsler VIQ scores that were approximately 13 points higher than Performance IQ scores in 40 children and adolescents diagnosed with Asperger's Disorder. In Ehlers et al.'s (1997) sample, children with Asperger's Disorder also scored significantly higher on the Comprehension and Vocabulary subscales of the WISC-R when compared to a sample of children with autism matched on chronological age and FSIQ. On average, the Asperger's sample also showed poor performance on the WISC-R Coding and Object Assembly subtests. Although Barnhill et al. (2000) did not document a significant VIQ versus PIQ split in a sample of children and adolescents with Asperger's Disorder, the sample earned their lowest Wechsler score on Coding. Taken together, the findings suggest that children with Asperger's Disorder tend to perform relatively poorly on Wechsler subtests associated with fine motor coordination, visual spatial perception, and constructive tasks, deficits associated with NLD as suggested by Klin et al. (1995).

The WISC-IV Technical Manual also reports on a sample of 27 individuals diagnosed with *DSM-IV-TR* Asperger's Disorder who completed the measure (Wechsler, 2003b). The group earned an average FSIQ of 99.2 with Verbal Comprehension Index scores ($M = 105.6$) about 4.5 points higher than Perceptual Reasoning Index scores ($M = 101.2$), on average. When compared to a control group of children matched on age, sex, ethnicity, parent education level, and geographic region, no mean differences were observed on most subtests and indices, with the exception of the Processing Speed Index that consists of speeded visual-motor tasks, such as Coding. At the subtest level, the group of children diagnosed with Asperger's Disorder showed greatest impairment on the triad of speeded visual-motor processing tasks—the Coding ($M = 6.7$; Cohen's $d = 1.06$), Symbol Search ($M = 8.2$; Cohen's $d = .60$), and Cancellation ($M = 8.0$; Cohen's $d = .65$) subtests (Wechsler, 2003b). The performance for the WISC-IV Asperger's sample matches the findings of others that suggest visual-motor and fine-motor processing are areas of relatively weak neurocognitive functioning for this group (Barnhill et al., 2000; Ehlers et al., 1997; Klin et al., 1995). Despite the Wechsler data reviewed, it is important to note that these findings are not universally observed and should not be considered equivalent to diagnostic criteria for either Autistic Disorder or Asperger's.

Adaptive Functioning

In assessing the adaptive skills of children with autism, the Vineland Adaptive Behavior Scales (Vineland; Sparrow et al., 1984) have been widely used (Luiselli et al., 2001) and researched. For the Vineland, standard scores based on age are derived in four domains: Communication, Daily Living Skills, Socialization, and Motor Skills. These scores then serve as the basis for an overall standard score, the Adaptive Behavior Composite. The Vineland yields an overall score and specific domain scores; therefore, the child's general adaptive level can be determined as well as a profile of adaptive functioning.

As noted earlier, research has documented that children with autism show a characteristic profile of adaptive behavior skills, with socialization skills typically being the most impaired relative to age, mental age, and other areas of adaptive functioning (e.g., Volkmar et al., 1993). When compared to other non-PDD diagnostic groups, studies have demonstrated that the Vineland Socialization domain score is useful in distinguishing between Autistic Disorder and: (a) mental retardation (Volkmar et al., 1993) and developmental language disorder (DLD) in children (Liss et al., 2001), and (b) severe mental retardation and psychotic disorders in adulthood (Matson, Mayville, Lott, Bielecki, & Logan, 2003). There is also some evidence that suggests the Vineland may be helpful in discriminating between disorders in the PDD spectrum, such as distinguishing between autism and PDD-NOS (Gillham, Carter, Volkmar, & Sparrow, 2000). Gillham et al. (2000) documented that children with autism showed more impairment in the Vineland domains of Communication, Daily

Living, and Socialization when compared to children diagnosed with either PDD-NOS or other developmental delays. Differences between groups were observed after mental age was used as a covariate, and delays in socialization were most strongly related to differential diagnosis between autism and the combined group of children diagnosed with either PDD-NOS or developmental delays.

The extensive use of the Vineland in diagnostic evaluations for individuals with autism has also yielded supplementary norms for individuals with autism, divided into four comparison groups: (1) children under 10 years of age who are mute, (2) children under 10 years of age with the presence of some verbal skills, (3) individuals 10 years of age or older who are mute, and (4) individuals 10 years of age or older with the presence of some verbal skills (A. S. Carter et al., 1998). The creation of a supplementary norm group for individuals with autism is useful by providing another reference group for comparison than either the national normative sample, which is required to diagnose mental retardation, or the special population norms that exist for individuals with mental retardation (Sparrow et al., 1984). Comparison to other individuals with autism allows for more detailed description of adaptive skills as well as increased sensitivity to monitor progress toward treatment goals. In addition to the solid psychometric properties of the Vineland and its extensive research base for individuals with autism, the existence of supplementary norms for individuals with autism make the interview a valuable tool for diagnostic assessments.

Assessment of Problem Behaviors

Problem behaviors, such as self-injury, aggression, and motor stereotypies, are not uncommon in individuals with ASD. In addition to traditional psychological assessment procedures described thus far, descriptive behavioral assessment may also occur in a comprehensive evaluation. Behavioral observations should take place during formal, semi-structured, and unstructured sequences during the evaluation, such as during seated cognitive testing, play sequences, transitions across different evaluative tasks, and unstructured breaks. To supplement behavioral observations during the assessment, behavioral checklists exist to document the presence and initial description of the topography of problem behaviors, such as behavioral items included in the Maladaptive Behavior domain of the Vineland or other instruments designed for children with autism and other developmental delays, such as the Aberrant Behavior Checklist (Aman & Singh, 1986). To date, behavior checklists used with larger populations of children, such as the BASC, have not been subjected to rigorous research with the population of children with ASD. Therefore, it is not known if general behavioral rating scales would be useful in the diagnosis or treatment planning for autism or related disorders.

In the context of a comprehensive developmental assessment, behavioral observations may provide a starting point for identifying circumstances associated with the occurrence of problem behaviors both prior and subsequent to its display. For example, self-injury or rocking behavior may be observed during formal cognitive testing only when an utterance is required or observed in the presence of one parent or sibling versus other family members. Although observations such as these are correlational versus experimental in nature, descriptive behavioral observations might generate initial testable and practical hypotheses about environmental contingencies that serve to reinforce problem behaviors. For example, self-injury may occur during language-based tasks due to a learning history marked by negative reinforcement—task removal occurs in the presence of such behavior. Similarly, problem behavior may occur due to positive reinforcement by one family member or another, for example, providing social attention in the presence of the problem behavior when attention was previously absent.

At this point, it is important to note that descriptive behavioral assessments, such as the examples described earlier in the chapter, have been found to be less effective than the use of experimental functional analysis in the treatment of problem behaviors for individuals with autism. In a comprehensive literature review of single-subject treatment outcomes for behavioral therapy, J. M. Campbell (2003) documented that the presence versus absence of an experimental functional analysis resulted in significantly greater reduction of self-injury, aggression, stereotyped behavior, and property destruction. In the traditional assessment setting, experimental functional analysis does not usually occur, as these procedures are typically time intensive and require specialized training. If the frequency, duration, or intensity of problem behaviors emerge as significant in the clinical picture, recommendations regarding the use of behavioral analysis in treating problem behavior should be shared with parents and educators in the diagnostic informing session as well as the final written report.

Emotional Functioning

Children with ASD, particularly those who are high-functioning, appear to be at-risk for comorbid diagnoses of depression and anxiety (e.g., Kim, Szatmari, Bryson, Streiner, & Wilson, 2000). Depression is reportedly more frequent in children and adolescents with autism than the general population and reportedly "very common" in adolescents with Asperger's Disorder (Gillberg & Billstedt, 2000). Using a modified version of the Child Behavior Checklist (Achenbach, 1991a), a widely used parent report of behavioral adjustment in children, Kim et al. (2000) documented clinically significant symptoms of depression in 17% of children diagnosed with autism and Asperger's Disorder. In the same report, almost 14% of children showed clinically significant symptoms of anxiety. Due to the comorbidity of anxiety and depression in children with ASD, these symptoms should be assessed in the context of a comprehensive evaluation. To date, however, there appears to be little consensus regarding how to approach assessment of emotional functioning of children and adolescents with ASD.

For younger children and individuals with impaired cognitive functioning, emotional assessment must take place through observation, such as during unstructured play, parent interview, and third-party behavioral reports. Individuals with significant cognitive and language impairments will be limited in providing a report of their internal emotional states, which may restrict the detection of affective dysfunction in these individuals. For the BASC Teacher and Parent Report Forms, small groups of individuals diagnosed with either Autistic Disorder or PDD-NOS were included in Clinical Norm groups: $n = 19$ for the Teacher Report Form and $n = 16$ for the Parent Report Form (C. R. Reynolds & Kamphaus, 1998). Therefore, parent and teacher ratings for children with ASD can be compared to these small clinical samples in addition to the General Norm group.

In contrast to younger children and children with cognitive delays, older and more able individuals with ASD can respond to interview questions regarding various aspects of emotional functioning, such as feelings of sadness, anger, social stress, loneliness, worries, or other affective states. Interview questions addressing social stress and loneliness are included in Modules 3 and 4 of the ADOS (Lord et al., 2001). In addition to the use of interview, broad-band self-report measures of emotional and behavioral functioning, such as the Self-Report Form of the BASC (C. R. Reynolds & Kamphaus, 1998), might be used for older and higher functioning children and adolescents. If specific concerns about depression or anxiety arise, narrow-band measures, such as the Children's Depression Inventory (CDI; Kovacs, 1992), or Revised Children's Manifest Anxiety Scale (RCMAS; C. R. Reynolds & Richmond, 2000) might also be used during the evaluation. However, no children with an ASD were included in the normative sample of the BASC Self-Report Form or CDI. The RCMAS included approximately 600 children enrolled in special education classes for learning disability, intellectual disability, and intellectually gifted, with no indication if any of these children were diagnosed with an ASD. Findings from self-reports should be interpreted with caution, as children with ASD are absent in either normative or clinical samples for these measures.

Additional Consultations

A variety of medical conditions are more prevalent in children with ASD when compared to the general population; therefore, referrals for appropriate medical evaluation are recommended. Seizure disorders occur in approximately 30% of children diagnosed with autism, whereas neurocutaneous syndromes such as tuberous sclerosis and neurofibromatosis occur in approximately 2% to 9% of children with autism and related disorders (Gillberg & Billstedt, 2000). Chromosomal abnormalities are more frequent in children with autism than the general population, with up to 10% of children with autism also diagnosed with fragile X syndrome (Gillberg & Billstedt, 2000). Given the frequency of the aforementioned medical and genetic disorders, recommendations for neurological and genetic consultations are often warranted. Follow-up evaluations might include an electroencephalogram (EEG) to detect seizure activity or genetic testing to document the presence of chromosomal abnormality.

Interpretation and Communication of Findings

Professionals working in settings where ASDs are diagnosed are responsible for explaining the meaning of the diagnosis as well as communicating clearly the findings of a complex process of evaluation (S. B. Morgan, 1984). Shea (1993) explained that professionals involved in parent informing sessions should strive to meet three important goals: (1) provide information about the child, (2) assist parents with initial emotional responses to this information, and (3) identify plans to meet the child's needs. In terms of the physical setting, disclosure of diagnosis should take place in a private setting with comfortable seating where all parties involved may see and hear one another. In the private setting, professionals may wish to make tissues available during the meeting, which communicates the team's expectation and understanding that some parents will respond with emotion and perhaps cry during the meeting. S. B. Morgan (1984) also recommends that both parents/caregivers be present during the informing session to prevent the difficult situation of one parent communicating complicated findings to another.

Content of Session

At least once during the informing sessions, professionals should provide the names of final diagnoses or labels resulting from the diagnostic process, as well as some description of the severity of the disorder (Shea, 1993). Professionals should also be wary of the use of overly technical language during the informing session and describe the child's functioning with terms understandable to parents without specialized knowledge about ASD, cognitive functioning, and psychometrics. Professionals may describe delayed cognitive or language functioning by referencing the child's chronological age relative to the child's age equivalent on the test, such as "Crissy is about 3.5 years old and her language skills are more like an 18-month-old." Parents may also find that visual aids are useful complements to verbal descriptions, such as locating the child's performance on a measure in a descriptive range, such as Borderline or Impaired. Parents may also find the use of handouts describing the disorder or resource lists helpful.

Shea (1993) also provides useful guidance regarding the professional stance that should accompany the content of the informing session with parents. Professionals should strive to be respectful and sensitive during the meeting and respond honestly and appropriately to difficult questions, which may include responding with "I don't know." Difficult questions posed often involve etiology and long-range expectations for the child. In the case of questions about etiology, most children are diagnosed with autism without known cause, such as a chromosomal abnormality, despite extensive testing to establish etiology. In terms of long-range outcome, two of the strongest predictors of more positive outcomes are the presence of meaningful language by the age of 5 or 6 and level of cognitive functioning. Professionals should also be prepared to respond to the parent's initial reactions toward the diagnosis of an ASD, which might include hopes for a cure or denial of the initial diagnosis. As Shea (1993) observes, parent optimism and hope are rarely harmful and should become concerning only if hope begins to create unrealistic expectations for the child. Denial is impossible to address or "overcome" in the context of a single parent session, and additional sessions or subsequent evaluations over time may be required prior to parents' acceptance of a diagnosis.

Parents' Perspective of the Informing Meeting

Block and Hartsig (2002) provide a set of useful guidelines from the parents' perspective during the initial diagnostic process, including the informing session. As parents of children with autism, the authors offer practical and revealing suggestions for professionals involved in the diagnostic process and informing session. Block and

Hartsig recommend the following guidelines: (a) Engage parents throughout the evaluation process, (b) select an appropriate moment for disclosure of diagnosis (i.e., without other siblings present that may be distracting to parents), (c) provide the family with a short list of resources or packet of information about resources, such as from the Autism Society of America, and (d) avoid guessing at the future although parents may desire such forecasts. Block and Hartsig also point out the importance of follow-up with the family including contact via telephone after the evaluation to help parents and caregivers begin to negotiate different treatment options.

As indicated earlier in this section, one salient index of the effectiveness of the initial informing sessions is parent satisfaction with the process. As outlined by Block and Hartsig (2002), research has illustrated the importance of the quality of interaction between the parents and professionals involved in the initial diagnostic disclosure. For example, Brogan and Knussen (2003) found that only 55% of parents reported that they were satisfied with the initial disclosure of a diagnosis of an ASD. Parents were more likely to report a satisfactory experience if: (a) they viewed positively the professionals involved in the evaluation and disclosure and the quality of information provided; (b) they were provided with written information and allowed the opportunity to ask questions about the diagnosis; and (c) if early suspicions were accepted by professionals involved in the evaluation. Higher parent satisfaction was also associated with a diagnosis of Asperger's Disorder versus Autistic Disorder and if the evaluation resulted in a definitive diagnosis.

CASE STUDY

The following case study is presented in the form of a psychological report. Identifying information, such as child and family name, child sex, and other particulars has been removed, altered, or fictionalized to protect confidentiality. A short interpretive description follows the report.

REASON FOR REFERRAL

Crissy, a 3-year-old girl, was referred by her parents due to concerns about autistic-like behaviors and to determine if she met diagnostic criteria for an autism spectrum disorder, particularly Asperger's Disorder or high-functioning autism. Crissy's parents identified several concerns regarding Crissy's functioning in the areas of social skills, echolalic speech, problem routines, and stereotypic behaviors. Crissy lives with her parents and her older brother, age 8. She is enrolled in a special needs program where she is served as a child with Significant Developmental Delay (SDD) and Speech Impairment. Crissy's psychological evaluation represents part of a multidisciplinary assessment including a formal speech-language evaluation; the reader should refer to the speech-language evaluation in conjunction with this report.

EVALUATION PROCEDURES

Autism Diagnostic Observation Schedule, Module 1 (ADOS)

Beery-Buktenica Developmental Test of Visual-Motor Integration (VMI)

Behavior Assessment System for Children—Preschool Form (BASC-P)

    Parent Rating Scales

    Teacher Rating Scales

Childhood Autism Rating Scale (CARS)

Parent Interview for Autism (PIA)

Review of Records

Vineland Adaptive Behavior Scales—Interview Edition, Survey Form (Vineland)

Wechsler Preschool and Primary Scale of Intelligence—Third Edition (WPPSI-III)

BACKGROUND INFORMATION

According to her mother, Crissy was born on time, head first, and without complication, weighing 8 pounds, 6 ounces. Crissy's condition at birth was good as evidenced by 1- and 5-minute Apgar scores of 8 and 9. Developmental milestones were met within broad normal limits. For example, Crissy walked alone at age 12 months, spoke her first word at 10 months, and spoke in two-word phrases by the age of 30 to 36 months. Crissy has received appropriate pediatric care and does not suffer from any major illnesses. She has not suffered any major injuries to date. Due to concerns about possible seizure activity, Crissy was evaluated by a child neurologist who conducted a complete neurological exam with Crissy that resulted in EEG and MRI findings within normal limits.

Crissy's mother first noticed body rocking when Crissy was 6 months old; tantrum behaviors and decreased interest in socializing with other children were noted to occur around the age of 18 months. Due to ongoing social and behavioral concerns, Crissy was evaluated by her school system. Results of the evaluation revealed Low Average intellectual functioning with significant delays in most areas of adaptive behavior, including social skills, motor skills, daily living skills, and communication. Crissy's mother completed behavior ratings as part of the assessment, resulting in clinically significant problems with hyperactivity, inattention, and atypical social behaviors. Crissy's mother also completed the Childhood Autism Rating Scale (CARS), which resulted in a score indicative of mild to moderate autism. Based on the results of the evaluation, Crissy was deemed eligible to receive special education services appropriate for a child with SDD.

With respect to the referral question, Crissy's mother reported multiple concerns in the areas of social skills, echolalia, unusual routines and focused interests, peculiar sensory experiences, stereotypic behavior, and self-injury. According to her mother, Crissy has shown little interest in interacting with peers, evident since the age of 18 months. Also at approximately 18 months old, Crissy began to engage in immediate and delayed echolalia, which is frequently observed in the home. Crissy frequently uses echolalic speech, both immediate and delayed, such as stating, "You've had enough cream" and "No, Crissy you can't see the cat," when responding to questions or comments made by others. Crissy also uses unusual words (i.e., neologisms) to describe activities, such as "roonting" something while playing or pointing out "steet-sies" to her mother while driving. Crissy's mother also reported a history of routines and restrictive interests for Crissy, including wanting to take the same route to the grocery store, repetitively opening and closing doors in the house, and carrying around a toy

Barney, music box, and small wooden stop sign. Crissy's mother reported that Crissy is overly sensitive to sounds, such as the noise of large groups, and has engaged in unusual sniffing behaviors, such as when first meeting a stranger at the family's house. Crissy has also engaged in repetitive rocking and humming since the age of 6 months and continues to rock and hum to herself when she wakes in the morning. Crissy has also bitten herself, banged her head, and hit herself in the head with open palms in the past; however, the last instance of self-injurious behavior occurred more than 1 year ago at around the age of 2.

GENERAL BEHAVIORAL OBSERVATIONS

Crissy presented as an active preschooler who separated easily from her mother for the purposes of formal testing, seemingly unaffected by her mother's absence. She showed variable response to her name and variable eye contact during initial interactions with examiners; however, her social responsiveness improved over the course of the evaluation. She engaged in immediate and delayed echolalia throughout the evaluation, both during formal testing and informal playtime. She showed unusual sensory interests in several items, such as repeatedly rotating and looking at a small pair of scissors that reflected light. Additional behavioral observations are presented later in the report pertaining to Crissy's social and communication functioning. In general, Crissy was alert, compliant, and interested in the testing materials; therefore, this assessment is viewed as an adequate estimate of her current intellectual, academic, and social-emotional functioning.

COGNITIVE AND LANGUAGE FUNCTIONING

Wechsler Preschool and Primary Scale of Intelligence—Third Edition (WPPSI-III)

The WPPSI-III was used to evaluate Crissy's overall cognitive development including verbal and nonverbal reasoning abilities. Crissy earned the following WPPSI-III composite scores:

Scale	Composite Score	Percentile Rank
Verbal IQ	90	25
Performance IQ	93	32
Full Scale IQ	91	27
General Language Composite	91	27

Crissy's performance indicates equally developed verbal and non-verbal reasoning abilities that consistently fall within the Average range. Crissy's WPPSI-III subtest scores appear below:

Verbal Subtests	Scaled Score	Performance Subtests	Scaled Score
Receptive Vocabulary	9	Block Design	6
Information	8	Object Assembly	12
Picture Naming	8		

Note: Subtest scores have a mean of 10, a standard deviation of 3, and can range from 1 to 19. Subtest scores that fall between 8 and 12 are considered Average.

With respect to receptive vocabulary abilities, Crissy correctly identified pictures of a triangle, basketball, vacuum cleaner, and giraffe, among others. In the area of expressive vocabulary, Crissy correctly named pictures of a fork, turtle, and broom, among others. In the area of nonverbal reasoning abilities, Crissy showed variability in her skills. She copied two- and three-block towers as well as a model using four blocks, but did not successfully complete more complex designs without a model present. However, she successfully completed puzzles with up to seven pieces.

To further assess Crissy's receptive language abilities, she completed the PPVT-III. Consistent with Crissy's performance during the WPPSI-III, she earned a standard score of 95 (37th percentile), which falls within the Average range. Visual-motor integration skills were assessed using the VMI. Crissy earned a standard score of 75 (5th percentile), which is roughly equivalent to a child around the age of 2 years, 9 months. Overall, Crissy's performance indicates age-appropriate reasoning abilities, single-word receptive language, and naming vocabulary. Her visual-motor integration skills fell below cognitive and age expectations.

SOCIAL-EMOTIONAL AND BEHAVIORAL FUNCTIONING

Behavior Assessment System for Children—Preschool Form

The Behavior Assessment System for Children—Preschool Form (BASC-P) was used as a global, comprehensive assessment of Crissy's behavior in a variety of domains. Crissy's parents and her special education preschool teacher completed BASC-P rating forms. At home, Crissy's parents endorsed significant problems with her atypical behaviors, such as repetitive thinking and rocking, quick mood changes, and impaired social skills. Crissy's mother endorsed more behavioral symptoms when compared to Crissy's father, such as overactivity, nervousness, and worry. Within the preschool setting, Crissy's teacher reported similar problems with Crissy's atypical behaviors, such as repetitive thinking and babbling to herself. The preschool teacher noted few difficulties with Crissy's activity level in the classroom. In general, behavioral reports highlight Crissy's unusual behaviors, social difficulties, and overactivity within the home.

Vineland Adaptive Behavior Scales—Interview Edition, Survey Form (Vineland)

Crissy's mother provided information necessary for the completion of the Vineland Adaptive Behavior Scales—Interview Edition, Survey Form. The Vineland provides a measure of a child's self-help skills in four areas: Communication, or the precursor skills involved in receptive and expressive language acquisition; Daily Living, including precursor skills involved in self-care; Socialization, or the skills needed for relating to others, playing, and coping with environmental demands; and Motor, movement and control of the large muscles and hands and fingers. Crissy's scores on the four general Vineland domains, as well as on their subdomains, appear in the following table:

Area	Standard Score (Mean = 100)	Age Equivalent (Years, Months)	Adaptive Level	Percentile*
Communication	82	2,8	Mod Low	SP 50*
Receptive	—	2,6	Mod Low	
Expressive	—	2,4	Mod Low	
Daily Living Skills	74	2,6	Mod Low	SP 35*
Personal	—	2,9	Mod Low	
Domestic	—	2,3	Mod Low	
Community	—	1,9	Low	
Socialization	68	1,9	Low	SP 45*
Interpersonal Relationships	—	2,0	Mod Low	
Play and Leisure Time	—	1,10	Low	
Coping Skills	—	0,11	Low	
Motor Skills	100	3,8	Adequate	SP 80*
Gross	—	2,11	Mod Low	
Fine	—	4,5	Adequate	
Adaptive Behavior Composite	75	2,8	Mod Low	SP 70*

*Supplementary percentile ranks (SP) based on supplementary norms published by A. S. Carter et al. (1998) for individuals younger than 10 years who are diagnosed with autism and show some verbal communication skills.

Crissy's scores indicate that her repertoire of adaptive skills is generally below her cognitive development, as measured by the WPPSI-III. In the Communication area, Crissy points accurately to all body parts, says at least 100 recognizable words, and reads at least 10 words. She does not always listen attentively to instructions, use sentences of four or more words, or ask questions beginning with "Why," and "When." In the area of Daily Living Skills, Crissy dresses herself completely except for tying her shoelaces, she helps with extra chores when asked, and brushes her teeth without assistance from her parents. She does not yet demonstrate an understanding of the function of money, wash and dry her face without help, and is not toilet-trained through the night. In the area of Socialization, Crissy addresses familiar adults by name and imitates others' behavior. She does not share toys without being told to do so, follow rules of games independently, or have a preferred friend. In the Motor Skills domain, Crissy's mother described age-appropriate fine motor skills and somewhat delayed gross motor skills for Crissy. In the area of fine motor skills, Crissy unscrews jar lids, cuts out shapes with scissors, and builds three-dimensional structures with blocks. In the area of gross motor skills, Crissy pedals a tricycle, walks down stairs alternating feet, and hops while holding on to another person; however, she does not yet hop forward at least three times unassisted or catch a small ball.

The Adaptive Behavior Composite score indicates that Crissy's overall adaptive skill level is approximately at the 2-year, 8-month-old level. Taken together, Crissy's WPPSI-III and Vineland scores suggest that her adaptive functioning is mildly to moderately delayed in the areas of daily living and socialization. When compared to her previous evaluation, Crissy has shown improved adaptive functioning, with the notable exception of her socialization skills. When compared to autistic children ages 10 and under who show some language skills, Crissy is functioning in the Average range in all domains.

Autism Diagnostic Observation Schedule (Module 1)

As part of Crissy's evaluation, she was administered the Autism Diagnostic Observation Schedule, Module 1 (ADOS). The ADOS is a standardized observation of social behavior and communication in a variety of structured and unstructured situations designed to elicit social and communicative symptoms indicative of autism spectrum disorders. Module 1 is appropriate for use with children with expressive language that typically involves phrase speech or expressive language skills that fall below an age-equivalent of 30 months, such as Crissy's. During ADOS administration, Crissy showed qualitative impairments in communication as evidenced by her repetitive use of words or phrases and using the examiners' body to communicate her wants. For example, Crissy guided the examiner's hand toward a toy to request that he activate it in the absence of eye contact, verbal request, or other communicative gesture. Crissy also showed impairments in shared social interaction as evidenced by very few facial expressions directed toward others, little initiation of joint attention, and unusual quality of overtures to interact. She showed interest in interacting with examiners throughout the ADOS, but was awkward with her approaches to do so, frequently "bounding" into personal space without eye contact, gesture, or speech. Overall, Crissy's ADOS Communication, Social Interaction, and Total scores were indicative of an autism spectrum disorder.

Parent Interview for Autism and Childhood Autism Rating Scale

Crissy's mother responded to the Parent Interview for Autism (PIA), a structured interview designed to gather diagnostic information about symptoms of autism in children younger than 6 years of age. Crissy's mother reported symptoms that were indicative of autism, particularly regarding Crissy's delayed peer relationships, sensory responses, such as interest in watching spinning objects, and motoric behaviors, such as rocking, spinning, and looking at her hands and fingers. Based on observational data and parent interview, the examiner completed the Childhood Autism Rating Scale (CARS), a rating form used to assist in the diagnosis of autism and autistic-like disorders. Crissy's Total CARS score of 34.5 fell within the Mildly-Moderately Autistic range.

SUMMARY AND RECOMMENDATIONS

Crissy is an active 3-year-old girl who shows impairments in social interaction, unusual social communication and exhibits repetitive motor movements that meet formal diagnostic criteria for Autistic Disorder (*DSM-IV-TR* 299.00). She shows age-appropriate cognitive and language abilities with mild to moderate delays in gross motor skills, daily living skills, and socialization. The reader is referred to the speech-language evaluation that accompanies this report for detailed information about Crissy's language functioning.

Due to Crissy's age-appropriate cognitive abilities, she falls within the minority of children diagnosed with autism, so-called high-functioning children with autism. This is further confirmed by Crissy's average to above average standing among *other children with autism* in adaptive behavior skills. She does not meet formal diagnostic criteria for Asperger's Disorder, due to the presence of delays in adaptive behavior that were documented prior to the age of 36 months. Among the larger group of children diagnosed with autism, Crissy's prognosis is better than most due to her age-appropriate cognitive abilities and meaningful use of language at present. When compared to Crissy's functioning last year, she appears to have made remarkable gains in both cognitive and adaptive areas, which is likely due to her enrollment in special education programming thus far. Further contributing to Crissy's gains are her family members, who are quite vested and involved in her educational and social programming.

Based on the test results, the following are recommended:

1. Crissy's parents are encouraged to share the results of our evaluation with educators and medical professionals who work with Crissy.

2. Crissy would benefit from enrollment in a special education preschool program appropriate for a preschool child diagnosed with Autistic Disorder. In our opinion, the most beneficial teaching approach to use with Crissy is discrete trial training using applied behavior analysis (ABA) to teach social behaviors, spontaneous expressive speech, and adaptive skills. Most of Crissy's special education services (i.e., 20 hours per week) should be provided using ABA intervention. Applied behavior analysis intervention should be provided in a structured educational setting within the context of an explicit and regular routine. Special education services should include the following additional components for Crissy:

   a. Enrollment in extended school year activities, due to her progress in special education services thus far,

   b. Ongoing consultation with occupational and physical therapists to monitor Crissy's development in the areas of fine and gross motor skills, and

   c. Access to a preschool behavioral specialist to assist with managing disruptive behavior (e.g., temper tantrums) that may arise within the classroom environment.

3. Due to autistic children's difficulties with generalizing newly learned skills across settings, discrete trial training should also be provided within Crissy's home environment. Social behavior and adaptive skills should be targeted at home. In order to

maximize Crissy's learning and generalization of new skills Crissy's parents and other family members involved in Crissy's care should receive training by professionals providing discrete trial training services within the home.

4. Within the special education setting, Crissy would benefit from opportunities to interact with typically developing peers in structured social situations, such as well-defined play activities with a peer "buddy." Peers will need guidance regarding how to interact with Crissy during such interactions, such as how to initiate interactions and reinforce appropriate social behaviors. Opportunities to interact with typical peers outside of the special education classroom would also help Crissy. This might take the form of structured "play dates" with a typical peer from her preschool class.

5. Within the home, Crissy's parents described significant problems with overactive behavior, symptoms not observed within the classroom setting. Crissy's parents would benefit from consultation with school professionals or our clinic regarding behavioral intervention to reduce overactive behavior. Behavioral intervention might take the form of creating a tighter schedule of activities within the home and/or reinforcement strategies to increase Crissy's appropriate activity levels in the home.

6. Crissy's parents may wish to purchase and read Michael Powers' book entitled *Children with Autism: A Parent's Guide* (2nd edition). The book is published by Woodbine House and can be ordered by calling 1 (800) 843-7323.

7. Crissy's parents may also wish to purchase Mesibov, Shea, and Adams's (2001) book entitled *Understanding Asperger Syndrome and High Functioning Autism.* The book is published by Kluwer Academic and can be ordered by calling 1 (781) 871-6600. Mesibov et al.'s book provides a practical overview of diagnostic and intervention issues with children with high-functioning autism. The reference also provides an extensive list of additional resources for professionals and family members.

8. Detailed speech and language treatment recommendations are described in the Speech and Hearing Clinic report and should

also be reviewed in conjunction with the recommendations outlined above.

9. Crissy should be re-evaluated by our clinic or school professionals in 1 year to monitor her cognitive, behavioral, and social-emotional progress.

Discussion of Case Study

Crissy's evaluation illustrates many of the concepts and practical assessment methods described in the chapter. Crissy's parents were involved throughout the diagnostic evaluation in terms of providing historical information, describing her current adaptive and behavioral functioning, participating in the ADOS administration, and observing language and cognitive testing from behind a two-way mirror. Although the initial referral question was framed to confirm a suspected diagnosis of Asperger's Disorder, Crissy is formally diagnosed with Autistic Disorder according to *DSM-IV-TR* criteria. This is so because she showed delays and abnormal functioning in the domains of social interaction and communication prior to the age of 36 months, as set forth in the *DSM-IV-TR* criteria and evidenced by her mother's report of her development. Autistic Disorder takes precedence over Asperger's Disorder. To further illustrate Crissy's classification, she is not diagnosed with PDD-NOS due to meeting the appropriate number of symptoms across the autistic triad and the early onset of symptoms. She is not diagnosed with Rett's or CDD due to the absence of significant deterioration of developmental functioning after the age of 5 months and 24 months, respectively.

Crissy shows a characteristic profile of adaptive functioning as documented by the Vineland, showing her greatest impairments in the domain of social functioning. The sample report also illustrates the reporting of the supplementary norms available, which provides more detailed information about Crissy's developmental standing relative to other children with autism. As seen in the report, her adaptive functioning is typical when compared to other children with autism with language skills. The report also illustrates how to *describe* a child's functioning using the Vineland, by giving examples of the child's specific adaptive skills across domains. Such information may prove useful in cases where developmental deterioration is suspected.

In addition to mother's historical and current report of autistic symptoms, she was observed to engage in these behaviors across a range of contexts and situations. For example, communication difficulties, such as echolalic speech, were observed during formal ADOS administration, formal cognitive and language testing, and informal interactions. Difficulties with social communication were also observed across settings, such as Crissy using the examiner's hand to operate a toy during the ADOS and press elevator buttons when leaving the clinic for the day. Crissy did not engage in stereotyped behavior or exhibit evidence of restricted interests during ADOS administration, which illustrates the important of collecting this diagnostic information from parent interview, such as the PIA.

During the parent informing session, faculty from psychology and communication sciences and disorders were present with graduate students to review findings, diagnostic impressions, and recommendations for intervention. Crissy's mother was responsive to the information shared during the parent informing sessions, and shared that she was expecting to receive a "dreaded" diagnosis of PDD-NOS, which she felt was less descriptive or helpful when describing her daughter's difficulty and advocating for her needs. During the session, our team provided Crissy's mother with information about local resources, including contact information for the local chapter of the Autism Society of America as well as several parent guides mentioned in the recommendations of the report.

Conclusion

With the rise in identification of autism and related disorders, psychodiagnosticians working in schools and other settings will be faced with diagnostic questions about the presence of autism. The chapter presented an overview of important constructs of interest when responding to diagnostic questions about autism as well as a framework to guide assessment practice. In our opinion, assessment of children with a suspected or confirmed ASD should include evaluation of multiple domains of functioning that are interpreted in the context of chronological and mental age expectations. A multidisciplinary approach to assessment is also recommended.

In terms of assessment methods and procedures, currently accepted gold standards for diagnosis include the use of semistructured observations and interviews that are coded to correspond closely with *DSM-IV-TR* criteria, such as the ADOS and ADI-R. Other measures are also recommended for detecting and classifying children with autism, such as the PIA and CARS. Outside of the purposes of classification, a variety of areas are also important to assess, including cognitive, language, adaptive, behavioral, and affective functioning. Due to the frequent presence of comorbid medical and visual-motor problems in children with ASD, such as seizures and poor motor coordination, comprehensive evaluation will often include referral to medical professionals and occupational therapists for consultation and perhaps additional evaluation. When communicating findings of the evaluation with parents, professionals should strive to communicate findings effectively, respond sensitively to parents' emotional reactions, and organize a plan for intervention services to begin. Many times, effective evaluation and diagnosis requires additional contact after the initial diagnostic evaluation, such as phone calls with school systems, attendance at school meetings, and follow-up contact with parents.

Depressive Disorders

Jonathan M. Campbell

6

Chapter

Less than 40 years ago, clinicians, theorists, and researchers questioned whether depressive disorders could be experienced by children due to incomplete development of the psychological constructs thought necessary to experience depression, such as understanding emotions, making social comparisons, and developing a coherent concept of self (Weiss & Garber, 2003). In contrast to theoretical suppositions, however, extensive empirical study in the 1970s and 1980s documented the existence of depressive symptoms and formal depressive disorders in youth. Depressive disorders have been reported in roughly 2% to 3% of children and up to 6% of adolescents according to point-prevalence rates from epidemiological studies (see Table 6.1). Children and adolescents report subthreshold or "subsyndromal" depressive symptoms with much greater frequency, with up to 30% of adolescents reporting one of more symptoms of major depression, such as depressed mood and sleeping problems (Roberts, Lewinsohn, & Seeley, 1995). Girls and boys experience similar rates of depressive disorders until adolescence when adolescent females exhibit rates of depression roughly two times greater than males. In community-based and nondiagnosed populations, adolescent girls also report a greater number of

Table 6.1   **Epidemiology, Comorbidity, Course of Depressive Disorders in Children and Adolescents**

Epidemiology Estimates

	Prevalence (in %)	
	3 to 6 Months	Lifetime
Diagnosed depressive disorders		
School-age children	1–3	3–4
Adolescents	5–6	15–20

In childhood, prevalence for all depressive disorders appears equal in boys and girls.

By age 15, girls are affected by depressive disorders more than boys, 2:1 ratio.

Common Comorbidities

	Range for Children and Adolescents (%)	Median Odds Ratio*
Anxiety disorders (all)	30–75	8.2
Conduct Disorder	11–46	6.6
Attention-Deficit Hyperactivity Disorder	20–30	5.5

*Odds ratios reported from Angold et al. (1999); odds ratios are interpreted as the likelihood of comorbid diagnosis (i.e., a diagnosis of a comorbid anxiety disorder is about 8 times more likely when a child is diagnosed with depression versus undiagnosed with depression).

Sources: "Comorbidity," by A. Angold, E. J. Costello, and A. Erkanli, 1999, *Journal of Child Psychology and Psychiatry, 40,* pp. 57–87; "Childhood Mood Disorders" (pp. 233–278), by C. Hammen and K. D. Rudolph, in *Child Psychopathology,* second edition, E. J. Mash and R. A. Barkley (Eds.), 2003, New York: Guilford Press; *Clinical Assessment of Child and Adolescent Personality and Behavior,* second edition, by R. W. Kamphaus and P. J. Frick, 2002, Boston: Allyn & Bacon; "Toward Guidelines for Evidence-Based Assessment of Depression in Children and Adolescents," by D. N. Klein, L. R. Dougherty, and T. M. Olino, 2005, *Journal of Clinical Child and Adolescent Psychology, 34,* pp. 412–432.

depressive symptoms, on average, when compared to adolescent boys (Roberts et al., 1995).

Characteristics

The defining features of depressive disorders include affective, physiological, and cognitive symptoms, such as depressed mood, disruptions with basic physiological processes (e.g., sleeping or slowed motor speed), and difficulty concentrating. Depressive disorders are also associated with a variety of other psychological problems and clinical features, the most significant being suicidal thinking and behavior. Detection and accurate diagnosis of depressive disorders in children is complicated by the "internalized" nature of many of the symptoms, such as subjective feelings of sadness or guilt. Physiological and cognitive symptoms of depressive disorders potentially impair school performance; therefore, children and adolescents experiencing depression may be referred for "learning disabilities" or "attention-deficit problems." Similarly, depressed children and adolescents presenting with symptoms of irritability may also be referred for evaluation due to "behavioral problems."

Phenomenology of Depression in Children and Adolescents

A large and growing amount of empirical evidence supports the position that children, adolescents, and adults exhibit depressive symptoms in fairly consistent ways. Findings do not necessarily refute the impact of development on symptom expression, but suggest that formal diagnostic criteria for adult depression do not require significant modification for children. For example, Roberts et al. (1995), among others, have argued that the diagnostic criteria for Major Depressive Disorder (MDD) are generally appropriate for children and adolescents due to the commonality of depressive symptoms experienced between childhood and adulthood. One large longitudinal study tracking depressive symptoms from adolescence to early adulthood indicated relatively stable symptom expression over time (Lewinsohn, Pettit, Joiner, & Seeley, 2003). Although the symptomatic expression of depression seems consistent over time, some variation in depressive symptomatology has been documented in the research literature. For example, adults report greater rates of insomnia and weight loss when compared to adolescents, and adolescents report less fatigue, agitation, and loss of appetite when compared to adults.

In contrast to the dominant view that depression is isomorphic across development, Weiss and Garber (2003) provide evidence that the phenomenology of depression varies across age groups. In a meta-analysis of studies that examined the impact of development on depressive symptoms, Weiss and Garber found that six depressive symptoms showed significant variability across developmental levels. More developmentally advanced participants experienced five symptoms (i.e., hopelessness, hypersomnia, loss of pleasure, weight gain, and social withdrawal) at higher levels than their younger counterparts. Alternatively, developmentally younger individuals experienced increased levels of energy when compared to older participants. The findings from the review suggest that physiological symptoms of depression are more prevalent for older individuals. Weiss and Garber's review raises important questions regarding the overriding notion that depression is experienced similarly from childhood to adulthood.

Constructs of Interest

Depression is typically defined as a multidimensional construct. Multifaceted definitions of depression have arisen due to broad impairments typically associated with depressive disorders, such as negative affect, physical symptoms, and cognitive processes.

Affective Features and Mood

Depressed mood and anhedonia (i.e., loss of interest or pleasure in activities) represent the core affective features that define depressive disorders. Irritability is also reported for children and adolescents, representing a slightly different expression of negative affect for some depressed individuals. Depressed mood is the most frequently reported symptom for children and adolescents diagnosed with depressive disorders in community samples (Roberts et al., 1995). In a sample of over 500 adolescents with recurrent episodes of major depression, depressed mood was the most stable single symptom over time (Lewinsohn et al., 2003). In community samples, depressed mood was one of the most frequently reported symptoms in individuals not formally diagnosed with a depressive disorder (Roberts et al., 1995).

Physical Manifestations of Depression

For depressive disorders, physiological problems and dysfunction coincide with negative mood. Physical manifestations of depression indicate the presence of dysregulated physical functions, such as an individual experiencing hypersomnia or insomnia. In addition to sleeping problems, physical symptoms include disrupted appetite, weight gain, motor functioning, and lethargy. In Lewinsohn et al.'s (2003) sample of individuals experiencing major depression, over 80% experienced disrupted sleep; furthermore, sleep problems were reported in *all* individuals who experienced four recurrent episodes of depression. Roughly 75% of adolescents with major depression experience weight and appetite changes while 80% to 90% report fatigue and loss of energy. Motor slowing or agitation appears in about 50% to 60% of adolescents diagnosed with major depression. In community samples of nondiagnosed individuals, sleeping problems were the most prevalent physiological symptom of depression (Roberts et al., 1995).

Cognitive Constructs

Depressed individuals often report cognitive symptoms, both in *content* of cognitions and cognitive *processes*. Representing some of the most concerning symptoms associated with depressive disorders, thoughts of death, dying, and suicidal ideation are examples of content-disordered thinking. In addition, individuals who are depressed can also experience difficulty with concentrating and report problems with indecisiveness. Lewinsohn et al.'s (2003) longitudinal study documented recurrent thoughts of death, dying, and suicidal ideation in approximately 40% of individuals with major depression, while 80% to 90% experienced difficulties with concentration and decision making. In nondiagnosed adolescents, thoughts of death and suicide are relatively rare (i.e., less than 2%), while difficulties with concentrating were reported in less than 10% of the sample (Roberts et al., 1995).

Cognitive Triad of Depression: Cognitive distortions and negative attributional styles have been documented in the phenomenological experience of depression, perhaps best captured by Aaron Beck's identification and description of the "cognitive triad" of depressive cognitions (e.g., A. T. Beck & Weishaar, 1989). In the cognitive triad framework, A. T. Beck argues that depressed individuals hold negative view of the *self,* the *world,* and *future.* As such, individuals who are depressed tend to believe that they are worthless, inadequate, and alone; the world is replete with obstacles that prevent access to goals and is absent of pleasure; and the future has more failure in store. From the perspective of cognitive therapy, the triad of distortions is reflexive and automatic and is causally linked to physical symptoms associated with depression, such as fatigue and low energy levels. A. T. Beck's cognitive theory of depression has been fairly well validated with adult populations and has seen variable support with children and adolescents. Indirect support for A. T. Beck's cognitive theory of depression has been reported for child and adolescent psychiatric inpatients (Joiner, Katz, & Lew, 1997). Joiner et al. (1997) found that self-reported depressive symptomatology was strongly related to interest in seeking negative feedback from others. Furthermore, children with depressive disorders reported a greater interest in receiving negative feedback when compared to children with externalizing disorders. In a community sample, Abela and Sullivan (2003) found variable support for the interaction between stress and dysfunctional attitudes in predicting depressive symptoms. For middle school students, dysfunctional attitudes predicted depressive symptoms; however, contrary to theoretical predictions, attitudes predicted depressive symptoms only for students who reported high (versus low) self-esteem and high (versus low) social support.

Negative Attributional Style: A second line of study has examined the role of attributional style in understanding depressive symptomatology. A basic tenet of attribution theory asserts that, as human beings, we strive to understand and interpret events in causally meaningful ways, such as "Why did I fail the math test?" Researchers have examined the cognitive processing styles of depressed adults and documented a tendency toward using a negative attributional style. Overuse of a negative attribution style has been described for depressed individuals whereby *negative* events or outcomes are attributed to internal (self-blaming), global (generalized across situations), and stable (consistent over time) traits, whereas *positive* events or outcomes are attributed to external, specific, and unstable factors (e.g., Hammen & Rudolph, 2003; Gladstone, Kaslow, Seeley, & Lewinsohn, 1997). Consistent with findings with adult samples, Gladstone and Kaslow (1995) found strong support for the association between negative attributional styles and depressive symptoms in children and adolescents in their meta-analytic review of 28 studies. Although a robust relationship between attributions and depressive symptomatology appears to exist for children and adolescents, causal links between attributions and depression have not been established.

Recent conceptualizations, such as transactional models of depression (Hammen & Rudolph, 2003), have hypothesized that the role of cognition, such as a child's self-view or attributional style, is both mediational and bidirectional. Early experiences and biological vulnerability directly and indirectly influence cognitive processing, which, in turn, influences how stress is evaluated and depressive symptoms expressed. Conversely, cognitive processing is influenced by the presence of life stress and depression.

Comorbid Psychopathology

Similar to adults, depression co-occurs with a variety of other psychological disorders in child and adolescent populations, particularly anxiety disorders (Angold, Costello, & Erkanli, 1999). Angold et al. (1999) documented that the presence (versus absence) of depression increased the likelihood of a comorbid anxiety disorder eightfold. Others have documented rates of comorbid anxiety disorders in up to 75% of depressed children and adolescents (see Table 6.1). In addition to anxiety disorders, children with depressive disorders are also frequently diagnosed with Conduct Disorder and Attention-Deficit/Hyperactivity Disorder.

The presence of a co-existing anxiety disorder has been shown to relate to treatment outcome, with additional anxiety resulting in poorer response to treatment. Diagnosis of a comorbid anxiety disorder may also hold important implications for treatment. For example,

Brent et al. (1998) found that children with depression and comorbid anxiety disorders responded equally favorably to cognitive-behavioral therapy, but much less favorably to nondirective supportive therapy. The benefit of cognitive-behavioral therapy for depressed children with anxiety may have been due to altering irrational thinking patterns, which are thought to be important in treating both depressive and anxiety disorders (Brent et al., 1998).

Conceptual Controversies Relevant to Assessment of Depression

The high rate of co-occurrence between anxiety and depression in children and adolescents raises a host of important questions regarding the relationship that exists between the two disorders (see, e.g., Angold et al., 1999; L. A. Clark & Watson, 1991). Numerous possibilities have been outlined in response to the high degree of syndrome overlap: Three are identified here. The first possibility is that depression and anxiety represent two different points that exist on the same continuum, perhaps a general factor of internalized distress (i.e., "internalizing disorder"). Second, depression and anxiety are separable syndromes that are conceptually distinct and independent phenomena. Finally, depression and anxiety are syndromes that share a high degree of overlap, but also demonstrate unique characteristics that serve to discriminate between the two. The overlap between self-reported depression and anxiety in children has been well documented (e.g., Stark & Laurent, 2001), with frequently used measures of both depression and anxiety showing good convergent validity and sensitivity (i.e., detecting depression versus nondepression, or anxiety versus nonanxiety) but poor discriminant validity and specificity (i.e., distinguishing between depression and anxiety).

Tripartite Model of Anxiety and Depression

L. A. Clark and Watson (1991) proposed a tripartite model to account for the similarities among and differences between depressive and anxiety disorders. The model asserts that depressive and anxious syndromes are similar in that both are characterized by general affective distress (i.e., Negative Affect [NA]); however, depressive disorders are further characterized by the absence of Positive Affect (PA), whereas anxious disorders feature specific problems associated with Physiological Hyperarousal (PH; i.e., physical tension). Table 6.2 presents a simplistic representation of the "profiles" for anxiety and depression as predicted by the tripartite model. The model assumes that measurement of general distress (NA) is essential, and "signals the presence of [the] disorders"

Table 6.2 **Hypothesized Differences between Depression and Anxiety According to Clark and Watson's (1991) Tripartite Model of Depression and Anxiety**

Diagnostic Group	Negative Affect (NA) (e.g., fear, sadness, upset)	Physiological Hyperarousal (PH)	Positive Affect (PA) (e.g., active, proud, enthusiastic)
Anxiety	Elevated	Elevated	Okay
Depression	Elevated	Okay	Elevated
Research scale results	High NA Score from PANAS-Child[a]	Physiological Hyperarousal Scale-Child[b]	Low PA Score from PANAS-Child[a]
Possible clinical test results	High CDI or RCMAS total	RCMAS items: (5, 17, 19)[c] (5, 9, 13, 17, 21, 33)[d]	Subset of CDI items: (4, 12, 21, 23)[c] (4, 12, 15, 20, 21, 22)[d]

[a] From "A Measure of Positive and Negative Affect for Children: Scale Development and Preliminary Validation," by J. Laurent, S. J. Catanzaro, T. E. Joiner, K. D. Rudolph, K. I. Potter, S. Lambert, et al., 1999, *Psychological Assessment, 11*, pp. 326–338.

[b] From "Development and Preliminary Validation of the Physiological Hyperarousal Scale for Children," by J. Laurent, S. J. Catanzaro, and T. E. Joiner, 2004, *Psychological Assessment, 16*, pp. 373–380.

[c] From "Tripartite Structure of Positive and Negative Affect, Depression, and Anxiety in Child and Adolescent Psychiatric Inpatients," by T. E. Joiner, S. J. Catanzaro, and J. Laurent, 1996, *Journal of Abnormal Psychology, 105*, pp. 401–409.

[d] From "The Structure of Negative Emotions in a Clinical Sample of Children and Adolescents," by B. F. Chorpita, A. M. Albano, and D. H. Barlow, 1998, *Journal of Abnormal Psychology, 107*, pp. 74–85.

Source: "Tripartite Model of Depression: Psychometric Evidence and Taxonomic Implications," by L. A. Clark and D. Watson, 1991, *Journal of Abnormal Psychology, 100*, pp. 316–336.

(L. A. Clark & Watson, 1991, p. 331) when significantly elevated. For the purposes of differential diagnosis between depression and anxiety, further assessment of PA and PH is also necessary. In this regard, the tripartite model may serve as a useful heuristic and guide organization and interpretation of assessment data.

L. A. Clark and Watson formulated the tripartite model to account for the high degree of comorbidity between depressive and anxiety disorders in adults and based the model on a thorough literature review and summary of psychometric test data. The tripartite model has been subsequently examined and supported in a number of samples of children and adolescents, such as child outpatients (Chorpita, Albano, & Barlow, 1998) and youth psychiatric inpatients (Joiner, Catanzaro, & Laurent, 1996). For example, the combined presence of NA and absence of PA was associated with depressive disorder in psychiatric inpatients; furthermore, the interaction between NA and PA was associated with symptom changes over time for children with depressive but not anxiety disorders (Joiner & Lonigan, 2000). The model has been examined in a sample of 86 children whose mothers were diagnosed with AIDS or were HIV-symptomatic (D. A. Murphy, Marelich, & Hoffman, 2000). D. A. Murphy et al. (2000) found support for a structural model that featured a second-order factor (NA) that was related to the constructs of anxiety and depression. The tripartite model has also been supported in a large community-based sample of urban African American children and adolescents (Lambert, McCreary, Joiner, Schmidt, & Ialongo, 2004). In contrast, the tripartite was not strongly supported in another community sample of elementary and high school students (Jacques & Mash, 2004).

Several studies have attempted validation of the tripartite model using existing clinical measures, such as the Children's Depression Inventory (CDI; Kovacs, 1992); however, adult instruments have been modified and new scales created to provide a direct test of the tripartite model. Laurent et al. (1999) validated an adult version of the Positive and Negative Affect Scale (PANAS) for use with children (PANAS-C), a 27-item scale that provides information necessary to evaluate PA and NA. Additionally, Laurent, Catanzaro, and Joiner (2004) have created and validated the Physiological Hyperarousal Scale for Children, an 18-item measure that assesses the PH construct in the tripartite model (see Table 6.2).

Diagnostic Standards

The *DSM-IV-TR* defines three depressive disorders that are relevant for children and adolescents: (1) Major Depressive Disorder (MDD), (2) Dysthymic Disorder (DD), and (3) Depressive Disorder—Not Otherwise Specified (DD-NOS).

Major Depressive Disorder

For formal diagnosis of MDD as delineated in the *DSM-IV-TR,* a child or adolescent must meet the following criteria:

- Exhibit a minimum of five (out of nine) co-occurring symptoms of depression (e.g., insomnia/hypersomnia; fatigue; thoughts of death; feelings of worthlessness) over a 2-week period; at least one symptom is depressed mood or anhedonia (i.e., loss of interest or pleasure).
- The depressive symptoms are not due to a medical condition, substances, or bereavement, nor are symptoms better explained by other disorders, such as Schizoaffective Disorder or a psychotic disorder.
- The mood symptoms do not meet criteria for a mixed episode (i.e., manic and depressive features co-occur).
- Depressive symptoms cause functional impairment.

Reflecting empirical findings indicating the similar symptomatic presentation of major depression in children, adolescents, and adults, the *DSM-IV-TR* criteria include only two minor variations for diagnosing MDD in children and adolescents. First, the depressed mood criterion (Criterion A.1) can be satisfied for children if irritable mood is present. Second, the weight loss criterion (Criterion A.3) can be satisfied for children if there is a failure to make expected weight gains. Within the *DSM* nosology, specifiers also exist to describe severity, associated problems, course, and onset of MDD. For example, MDD severity can be described as mild, moderate, or severe, and the presence or absence of psychotic features associated with the depressive disorder can be coded.

Dysthymic Disorder

For formal diagnosis of DD as defined in the *DSM-IV-TR*, a child or adolescent must meet the following criteria:

- Depressed mood most days for at least 2 years.
- In the presence of depressed mood at least two (of six) symptoms are present, such as poor appetite, insomnia, fatigue, low self-esteem.
- Depressive symptoms do not remit for a period of longer than 2 months.
- The impairment causes significant impairments in social or academic functioning.
- No MDD is present in the first 2 years of the depressive disorder.
- The depressive symptoms are not due to a medical condition, substance use, or are experienced during a psychotic disorder.

Similar to MDD, the *DSM* describes two modifications that are allowable for DD to be diagnosed in children or adolescents. First, the mood criterion can be met if mood is irritable. Second, as opposed to a 2-year duration of depressive symptoms, children need only exhibit symptoms for a period of 1 year. Within the *DSM* nosology, DD can be further described as exhibiting: (a) an early or late onset, and (b) atypical features such as reactive mood (i.e., presence of euthymia, or the capacity for mood to improve) and extreme sensitivity to interpersonal rejection. For individuals with DD, the *DSM* classification system allows for the coding of superimposed MDD, so-called double depression. The additional MDD diagnosis is allowable when an individual with DD also meets criteria for a major depressive episode.

Depressive Disorder—Not Otherwise Specified

A formal diagnosis of DD-NOS can be rendered if a child or adolescent presents with depressive symptoms that do not meet formal criteria for another depressive disorder or several Adjustment Disorders that feature depressive symptomatology. Depressive symptoms must be associated with functional impairments for a diagnosis of DD-NOS to be rendered. For example, a child might exhibit depressive symptoms for a period of 2 weeks or more; however, less than five criteria are present.

Mixed Anxiety-Depressive Disorder

In light of the literature reviewed regarding the high rate of comorbid anxiety disorders with depressive disorders as well as L. A. Clark and Watson's (1991) tripartite model of anxiety and depression, we thought it useful to describe the research criteria for Mixed Anxiety-Depressive Disorder (MADD). Research criteria for MADD are as follows:

- Persistent or dysphoric mood lasting 1 month or more.
- Presence of at least 4 (of 10) symptoms accompanying dysphoric mood, such as irritability, worry, low self-esteem, or difficulty concentrating.
- Symptoms cause significant distress or social/occupational impairment.
- Symptoms are not due to a general medical condition or substances.
- The individual has never been diagnosed with MDD, DD, Panic Disorder, or Generalized Anxiety Disorder and the symptoms are not better accounted for by another *DSM* diagnosis. The *DSM* diagnostic manual reports preliminary prevalence rates of 1.3% to 2% in primary care settings for MADD and describes the prevalence as "quite common" in mental health settings.

Individuals with Disabilities Education Act

Although the presence of a depressive disorder does not necessarily indicate the presence of an educational or learning problem, children and adolescents diagnosed with a depressive disorder may be eligible for special education eligibility under Individuals with Disabilities Education Act (IDEA; 1997) and Individuals with Disabilities Education

Improvement Act (IDEIA; Public Law 108-446, 2004) federal guidelines. Children with depressive disorders may be served under the disability category of Emotional Disturbance (ED). Emotional Disturbance is defined as a pervasive condition that adversely affects educational performance. Characteristics listed under the definition of ED that are particularly relevant to children with depressive disorders include: presence of pervasive mood of unhappiness or depression, and inability to maintain satisfactory interpersonal relationships with peers and teachers (House, 1999). When a formal diagnosis of depressive disorder is rendered, the clinician should include information about possible eligibility for special education services in light of the depressive symptomatology.

Assessment Methods and Procedures

Assessment of internalizing disorders, in general, and depressive disorders, in particular, should be approached with several caveats in mind. First, children and parents do not typically agree when reporting the presence of depressive symptoms (e.g., Jensen et al., 1999), which raises the question of "who to listen to" and "what counts" toward a diagnosis of a depressive disorder. Solutions for handling disagreement between sources have taken several forms, such as "counting" a symptom toward diagnosis from any source, "counting" a symptom toward diagnosis only if sources agree, and a "best estimate" decision-making approach. The best estimate solution assigns diagnostic decision making to the judgment of the clinician—taking all relevant information into account, the clinician decides whether a symptom is present or not (Klein, Dougherty, & Olino, 2005).

The second major challenge to assessment involves the strong statistical relationships that children's measures of depression and anxiety typically share with one another. For example, Stark and Laurent (2001) found a correlation of $r = .72$ between self-report measures of depression and anxiety in children. Strong relationships between measures are not unexpected given the high frequency of co-occurrence that exists between depressive and anxiety disorders and the similarity of symptoms required for diagnosis. In attempts to improve the discriminative validity of measures of depression, particularly self-report measures, researchers have examined the unique measurement characteristics of certain items that appear on frequently used self-reports, such as the CDI (Kovacs, 1992) and the Revised Children's Manifest Anxiety Scale (RCMAS; C. R. Reynolds & Richmond, 1985). The correlations among newer measures of depression and anxiety are more modest suggesting that these constructs and disorders can be differentiated better than has been the case in the past. The correlation between self-report measures of anxiety and depression on the Behavior Assessment System for Children Self-Report of Personality—Child (BASC SRP-C) was .64, and still lower at .59 on the Self-Report of Personality—Adolescent (SRP-A; C. R. Reynolds & Kamphaus, 2004).

In the following section, information is presented for self-report measures of depression (see Table 6.3), third-party rating instruments, and interviews. The review is selective and the scales are presented in alphabetical order. For comprehensive reviews of self-report measures of depression and additional instrumentation, the reviewer is referred to Myers and Winters (2002) and Klein et al. (2005). Due to the increased risk of suicide in children and adolescents who are depressed, suicide risk assessment is also discussed.

Self-Report Scales

Due to the subjective nature of affective and cognitive aspects of depressive disorders, self-report scales have been developed and studies with children and youth. Several of the most frequently used self-report instruments are discussed in the next section.

Beck Depression Inventory for Youth (J. S. Beck, A. T. Beck, & Jolly, 2001) and Beck Inventories of Social and Emotional Impairment (J. S. Beck et al., 2001): The Beck Depression Inventory for Youth (BDI-Y) is a 20-item self-report measure of depression, which is part of a larger set of inventories collectively referred to as the Beck Inventories of Social and Emotional Impairment (BYI). The BYI consists of five self-report measures designed to assess depressive symptoms (BDI-Y),

Table 6.3   **Description of Selected Self-Report Scales of Depression for Children and Adolescents**

	Clinical Uses	Ages (Years)	Items	Proposed Subscale/Factors
BDI-Y	Identify DEP symptoms	7–14	20	Part of BYI, which includes measures of anxiety, anger, disruptive behavior, and self-concept
CDI	Measure DEP symptoms	7–17	27	Negative mood Screening Interpersonal problems Ineffectiveness Anhedonia Negative self-esteem Total score
RADS-2	Severity of DEP symptoms	11–20	30	Dysphoric mood screening Anhedonia/negative affect Negative self-evaluation Somatic complaints Total score
RCDS	Measure DEP symptoms	8–12	30	Total score screening

Notes: BDI-Y = Beck Depression Inventory for Youth; CDI = Children's Depression Inventory; DEP = Depression; RADS-2 = Reynolds Adolescent Depression Scale—Second Edition; RCDS = Reynolds Child Depression Scale.

symptoms of anxiety (Beck Anxiety Inventory for Youth [BAI-Y]), anger (Beck Anger Inventory for Youth [BANI-Y]), disruptive behavior problems (Beck Disruptive Behavior Inventory for Youth [BDBI-Y]), and self-concept (Beck Self-Concept Inventory for Youth [BSCI-Y]) in children and youth (J. S. Beck et al., 2001). The BYI scales are designed for use with children ages 7 to 14 and were normed with a stratified standardization sample of 800 children representing 1999 U.S. Census data. J. S. Beck et al., (2001) provide support for BYI criterion validity as evidenced by strong relationships between the BYI scales and similar self-report ratings of depression, anxiety, and self-concept. In a thorough review of the BYI scales, Bose-Deakins and Floyd (2004) noted concerns about the lack of validity indices, which may be particularly concerning for the BYI as the items are all grouped according to domains and worded negatively. Therefore, respondents may exhibit a response set that does not necessarily reflect symptomatology. Second, the BYI has not shown the ability to discriminate between children with emotional or behavioral problems and those without. For example, a sample of clinical outpatients did not differ from controls on the BDI (depression) and BAI (anxiety) scales. Finally, no item analysis has been conducted with the BYI to insure that it is culturally unbiased. Given the relatively recent publication of the BYI, future research is necessary to further evaluate the utility of the scales.

Children's Depression Inventory (Kovacs, 1992):   The Children's Depression Inventory (CDI) is widely acknowledged to be the most frequently used self-report of depressive symptomatology for children and adolescents. The CDI is a 27-item self-report measure designed to assess the presence and degree of depressive symptoms in children between the ages of 7 to 17 (Kovacs, 1992). The CDI represents a downward extension of the original Beck Depression Inventory— a self-report measure of depression in adulthood. The CDI manual reports a five-factor structure for the scale measuring affective, cognitive, and social manifestations of depressive symptoms. Subsequent studies examining the factor structure of the CDI with children and adolescents have yielded a range of two to eight factors for the CDI (Cole, Hoffman, Tram, & Maxwell, 2000). For example, Cole et al. (2000) identified a three-factor solution (i.e., Social Self-esteem; Dysphoria-Sadness, Oppositional-Misbehavior) for the CDI in a community-based sample of over 600 sixth graders. Cole et al.'s three-factor solution was found to be robust over time. Stark and Laurent (2001) found evidence that a subset of nine CDI items were relatively independent from general affective distress and self-reported anxiety, as measured by the RCMAS. The nine CDI items tapped anhedonic features (e.g., sadness; crying), self-blame and loathing (e.g., hate self; look ugly), and oppositional/conduct behaviors (e.g., get into fights; disobedient). Although additional study is necessary to document their discriminative utility, the items may hold particular utility in assisting in the differentiation between anxiety and depressive disorders in children and adolescents.

Reynolds Child Depression Scale (W. M. Reynolds, 1989) and Reynolds Adolescent Depression Scale—Second Edition (W. M. Reynolds, 2002): The Reynolds scales are also frequently used measures of self-reported depressive symptomatology in children and adolescents (Myers & Winters, 2002). The Reynolds Child Depression Scale (RCDS) is appropriate for children between the ages of 8 and 12, whereas the Reynolds Adolescent Depression Scale—Second Edition (RADS-2) is appropriate for use with adolescents between the ages of 11 and 20 (W. M. Reynolds, 2002). Both scales consist of 30 items that assess affective, cognitive, and physiological features of depression as described in the *DSM-IV.* The RCDS yields a total symptom score, whereas the RADS-2 features four, 7- to 8-item subscale scores, such as Dysphoric Mood, derived from the standardization sample ($N = 9,052$). The RCDS and RADS-2 feature 6 critical items (e.g., feeling bad), which have demonstrated utility in discriminating between samples of depressed and nondepressed children and adolescents. In reviews of the Reynolds scales, Klein et al. (2005) and Myers and Winters (2002) similarly conclude that the Reynolds scales demonstrate good reliability and concurrent validity, but that discriminant validity has not been well studied.

Third-Party Rating Instruments

In addition to self-report measures of depressive symptoms, third-party rating instruments have also been developed to assist in the detection and diagnosis of depressive disorders in children and youth. In the next section, several broadband rating scales are reviewed in terms of their utility in assessing depression.

Behavior Assessment System for Children—Second Edition (C. R. Reynolds & Kamphaus, 2004) and Achenbach System of Empirically Based Assessment (Achenbach & Rescorla, 2001): The Behavior Assessment System for Children—Second Edition (BASC-2) and Achenbach

System of Empirically Based Assessment (ASEBA) rating scales include measures of depression that exist in the context of a comprehensive behavioral assessment. The BASC-2 features a Depression subscale that appears on both teacher and parent rating scales for individuals between the ages of 2 and 21 (C. R. Reynolds & Kamphaus, 2004). The BASC-2 Depression subscale consists of items measuring a range of depressive symptoms, including affective features (e.g., pouting; crying), social isolation, and verbal reports of suicidality. For children between the ages of 6 to 18, the ASEBA consists of a parent rating form, teacher rating forms, and a self-report form. Across each report form, the ASEBA features two clinical scales relevant to detecting depressive symptomatology, Anxious/Depressed and Withdrawn/Depressed. Item content for the Anxious/Depressed scale consists of crying, fearfulness, worry, and feelings of worthlessness, among others. Item content for the Withdrawn/Depressed scale consists of social withdrawal, sadness, and fatigue. The ASEBA subscales or "syndrome scales" are empirically derived in that no attempt was made a priori to measure the anxiety and depression constructs; therefore, it is not surprising that symptoms of depression and anxiety would co-vary strongly and result in a single syndrome scale.

Children's Depression Rating Scale—Revised (Poznanski & Mokros, 1995):   Fashioned after the Hamilton Rating Scale for Depression, the Children's Depression Rating Scale—Revised (CDRS-R) is a rating scale completed by a clinician who rates depressive symptoms based on semi-structured interviews and behavioral observations of the child (Poznanski & Mokros, 1995). Designed for use with children between the ages of 6 and 12, the CDRS-R samples 17 domains of depressive symptomatology, such as presence and degree of: *anhedonia* (e.g., Difficulty Having Fun domain), *somatic symptoms* (e.g., Sleep Disturbance domain), and *social and academic impairment* (e.g., Impaired Schoolwork domain). Items scored from behavioral observation are: facial affect, listless speech, and hypoactivity. The CDRS-R represents a good example of "best estimate" judgment in practice and incorporates clinical judgment in the scoring system. The CDRS-R generates symptom ratings from child and parent information sources but also includes an additional rating column titled "Best Description of Child," which allows for clinical decision making.

Stovall (2001) reported that the CDRS-R demonstrates temporal stability reliability and interrater reliability as well as various forms of validity. For example, the CDRS-R shows good convergent validity with other clinician-rated depression scales and discriminates between depressed and nondepressed samples. Similar to other measures of depression, however, Klein et al. (2005) identified problems with the discriminant validity of the CDRS-R in distinguishing between children with depressive disorders and anxiety disorders. Stovall also described concerns regarding the standardization sample for the CDRS-R both in terms of being nonrepresentative nationally and not culturally diverse.

Structured Interviews

Structured interviews are available for the assessment of depressive disorders as part of a thorough assessment of a variety of psychiatric disorders. The interview methods to be discussed in the following section are focused only on the diagnosis and assessment of depression or related disorders.

Child and Adolescent Psychiatric Assessment (Angold & Costello, 2000) and Schedule for Affective Disorders and Schizophrenia for School-Age Children (Puig-Antich & Chambers, 1978):   In a review of assessment techniques, Klein et al. (2005) identified the Child and Adolescent Psychiatric Assessment (CAPA) and Schedule for Affective Disorders and Schizophrenia for School-Age Children (K-SADS) as useful structured interviews for diagnosing depressive disorders in children and adolescents. The K-SADS is a well-known and widely used interview that is appropriate for use with children and youth between 6 and 18 years. The CAPA is a structured diagnostic interview that has been developed for use with children and adolescents between the ages of 9 and 17. In addition to assessing depressive symptomatology, the CAPA and K-SADS assess the presence of a range of disorders, such as disruptive behavior disorders and anxiety disorders, both of which are frequently associated with depressive symptomatology. The psychometric properties of the K-SADS have been evaluated extensively and are well established, whereas the CAPA has shown initial evidence of good psychometrics (Angold & Costello, 2000). The major drawbacks of these scales are the length of time required to administer the scales (i.e., up to 2.5 hours), and the requirements for training prior to administering the interviews. For example, CAPA training requires up to 2 weeks of didactic instruction and up to an additional 2 weeks of practice prior to use of the CAPA in clinical settings (Angold & Costello).

Assessment of Suicidal Risk

Approximately 2,000 U.S. adolescents between the ages of 13 and 19 successfully commit suicide each year, with roughly 90% of individuals who commit suicide suffering from a preexisting psychiatric disorder (Shaffer, Pfeffer, & Work Group on Quality Issues, 2001). Suicidal thinking and behavior exists as a spectrum of problems, which are listed in ascending order of lethality: (a) general thoughts about suicide, (b) planning suicide, (c) verbalizing thoughts or plans to suicide, (d) making parasuicidal gestures such as cutting or ingesting a nonlethal dose of a substance, (e) attempting suicide unsuccessfully, and (f) suicide completion. Suicide cannot be predicted; therefore, the most appropriate assessment strategy for assessing suicidality is to document the degree of suicidal risk. Risk factors exist within three broad domains: the individual (e.g., psychological functioning), the social context (e.g., family stress or social support), and the lethality of prior and present suicide attempts and planning (e.g., specific planning or presence of previously lethal attempt).

The primary reason for discussing suicide assessment in this chapter is because mood disorders, particularly MDD, are the most common preexisting psychiatric disorders for completed suicides. For adolescent girls, the most significant risk factor for suicide is the presence of MDD, which increases suicidal risk 20-fold (Shaffer et al., 2001). The two most important risk factors for both boys and girls are: (1) the presence of MDD and (2) a history of prior suicide attempt, which is the strongest predictor of suicide in boys. In addition to MDD and prior attempts, suicidal risk increases in the presence of other factors, such as: male gender, older versus younger age, presence of agitation, presence of psychosocial stress, presence of suicidal plan, absence of social support, and availability of lethal agents such as access to firearms or medications (Shaffer et al., 2001). In general, the risk of suicide increases as a child or adolescent exhibits a greater number of risk factors. If a child or adolescent is exhibiting a significant number of risk factors, the clinician will need to coordinate appropriate intervention services for the child. Intervention might include short-term contracting for safety and initiation of outpatient therapy if the risk is sufficiently low, or immediate contact with medical emergency services or activation of a school's emergency intervention plan if the risk of suicide is sufficiently high.

Mental Status Interview and Caregiver Interview: Suicidal risk should be evaluated through multiple interviews that include an individual interview with the child or adolescent and a caregiver, at a minimum. In the context of both interviews, the clinician is advised to inquire about the risk factors associated with suicidality, particularly the presence of MDD and prior suicidal attempts (Shaffer et al., 2001). Organized around the risk factors linked to successful suicide, interview information should be gathered in three areas: (1) psychological functioning/history of the individual (e.g., history of prior suicidal attempts; presence of depressive disorder), (2) detailed information about the suicide plan per se (e.g., lethality of plan; forethought), and (3) the larger context (e.g., degree of social support or access to lethal weapons; for similar recommendations, see Brent, 1997). Information collected during the child interview should be verified with report from caregivers, due to the child's possible reticence toward reporting suicidal symptoms.

Review of Critical Items on Behavioral Checklists and Self-Reports: Several broad-based measures of general behavioral adjustment feature *critical* items that are relevant in the assessment of suicidal thinking and planning. For example, the teacher and parent forms of the BASC-2 include items that assess suicidal risk, such as the child reporting "I want to die, or I wish I were dead" (C. R. Reynolds & Kamphaus, 2004). Self-report measures of general behavioral functioning, such as the self-report versions of the BASC-2 and Youth Self-Report (YSR; Achenbach & Rescorla, 2001) also include critical items, such as YSR Item 91, which asks about suicidal thoughts. Narrow-band self-report ratings, such as the CDI (Kovacs, 1992) and the RADS-2 (W. M. Reynolds, 2002) also include items asking directly about suicidal risk, such as CDI Item 9 and RADS-2 Item 14. When broad- and narrow-band rating scales are used in the psychodiagnostic evaluation, scanning responses to critical items that assess suicidal potential is strongly recommended. Computer scoring programs are available for most rating scales and highlight responses to critical items. In the absence of computer scoring, the evaluator can easily memorize critical items numbers that are relevant to suicidal risk (e.g., CDI Item 9; RADS-2 Item 14).

Suicide Rating Scales: In addition to clinical interviewing, clinician-administered and self-report rating scales have been developed to assist in assessing suicide risk. N. C. Winters, Myers, and Proud (2002) present detailed psychometric data for 12 scales designed to evaluate suicidal risk in children and adolescents, such as the Suicidal Ideation Questionnaire (SIQ; W. M. Reynolds, 1987). Although a few self-report and clinical rating scales demonstrate acceptable psychometric properties, rating scales should not be used in the absence of detailed interviewing. Rating scales are most appropriately utilized as screening instruments, and as supplements to information gathered by direct clinical interview. Suicide rating scales are limited, in part, due to the low base rate of suicide, which produces problems with predicting who may commit suicide. Due to inherent problems associated with predicting low base rate occurrences, suicide rating scales tend to produce relatively low sensitivity values (i.e., .28 to .87) as well as relatively high number of false positives (N. C. Winters et al., 2002).

CASE STUDY

The following case study is presented in the form of a psychological report. Identifying information, such as child and family name, child sex, and other particulars has been removed, altered, or fictionalized to protect confidentiality. Test data is reported in the form of a psychometric summary presented in the chapter. A short interpretive description follows the report.

ASSESSMENT PROCEDURES

Beck Youth Inventories of Emotional and Social Impairment (BYI)

Behavior Assessment System for Children (BASC)

    Parent Rating Scales (BASC-PRS)

    Teacher Rating Scales (BASC-TRS)

    Self-Report of Personality (BASC-SRP)

Children's Depression Inventory (CDI)

Children's Depression Rating Scale—Revised (CDRS-R)

Clinical Interview

Conners' Parent Rating Scales—Revised: Long Version (CPRS-R:L)

KeyMath—Revised—Normative Update (KeyMath-R-NU)

Parent Interview

Wechsler Intelligence Scale for Children—Fourth Edition (WISC-IV)

Woodcock-Johnson III Tests of Achievement (WJ III ACH)

REFERRAL QUESTION AND BACKGROUND

Joel is a 12-year-old Caucasian male who was referred due to his mother's concerns about his academic difficulties, particularly in mathematics. Mrs. Smith wanted to know if Joel suffered from a learning problem and hoped to gain information about how to help Joel succeed academically. Mrs. Smith also expressed concern over Joel's irritable mood and poor self-esteem.

Physical and Developmental History

Mrs. Smith received regular prenatal care while pregnant with Joel; pregnancy and delivery were unremarkable. Joel was born on time and weighed 7 pounds, 12 ounces. According to Mrs. Smith, Joel met all developmental milestones as expected, including crawling at 5 months, walking at 10 months, and speaking his first words at 12 months. Mrs. Smith noted that she had difficulty getting Joel to eat and sleep when he was an infant and toddler. Joel has worn corrective lenses since fourth grade. He has undergone both vision and hearing exams within the past year, both with normal results. An annual physical exam revealed that Joel's current health is excellent. Joel reported often feeling tired and fatigued, explaining that "it's probably due to staying up too late because I can't sleep."

Family History

Joel lives with his biological mother, Linda Smith, and his 3-year-old brother, Michael. Mr. and Mrs. Smith separated about 8 months ago, and Mr. Smith no longer lives with the family. Mrs. Smith explained that Mr. Smith visits infrequently and never calls. Mrs. Smith reports that the recent separation constitutes a major life change for Joel. Joel's mother is concerned that she and Joel do not share many common interests; however, the family enjoys watching movies and playing with model rockets together. Discipline in the home consists of spanking and time-outs. Mrs. Smith explained that Joel's father and paternal aunt were diagnosed with reading disability as children. According to Mrs. Smith, Joel's father has had one known voluntary psychiatric hospitalization due to suicidal and homicidal threats. Mrs. Smith also reports potential previous alcohol abuse by her father and his brother. No other drug abuse or mental illnesses were reported.

Educational History

Joel attended preschool and kindergarten in a program at Bouschet College. From first through fifth grade, Joel attended Martin Academy (MA). Mrs. Smith reported that Joel needed a change in schools because he was being picked on at MA and was unhappy there. Joel is enrolled as a seventh grade student at Bryan Preparatory School (Bryan), where he started last year. Bryan is a coeducational, private institution at which a college preparatory curriculum and character education are emphasized.

Mrs. Smith reported that math has been a problem for Joel since first grade. Problems became even more apparent in third grade, when Joel began having difficulty learning multiplication. At that time, Mrs. Smith began wondering if Joel had a learning problem, although he continued to earn Bs and Cs in most subjects, including math. Joel's report cards show that he failed math in fifth grade, and passed by only one point last year. This year, Joel is failing Algebra I, English, and Science. His recent overall drop in grades, as well as continuing to fail math despite having a tutor, has provided the catalyst for Mrs. Smith's evaluation request. With regard to Joel's day-to-day academic performance, Mrs. Smith reported that he does not study for tests, his homework grades are better than quiz and test grades, he is disorganized, resistant to being helped in math, distractible, and generally has a poor attitude toward school and teachers. Mrs. Smith reported that Joel is easily bored in the classroom. She also remarked that if Joel becomes frustrated with school work he might rush through it or not do it at all. Additionally, Mrs. Smith notes that Joel does not like asking questions in class. Mrs. Smith's relationship with the school is amicable and she corresponds with Joel's teachers via e-mail.

Joel describes his current performance at school as "fine" except for math. When asked about his other failing grades, Joel shrugged his shoulders. Joel reported that he has "no problems paying attention, except in math." Joel reported that he does not understand the material in algebra and that his teacher goes through it too quickly. Joel also reported that school "is boring" and that many academic topics are irrelevant. Joel indicated that he learns better through practical applications or relating material to daily life. When asked about his plans for the future, Joel reported that he might try to go to college, work with his grandfather in the construction business, or join the Marines.

Social and Emotional History

Mrs. Smith noted that Joel's mood is often negative and irritable. She believes that Joel "tends to keep his feelings bottled up." Mrs. Smith described Joel as having always been somewhat reserved and he preferred to play alone. Mrs. Smith indicated that Joel's mood was somewhat more irritable and withdrawn after his parents' separation. Joel described himself as mischievous with a good sense of humor. He said he tries to look at everything positively, although he also believes he has trouble controlling his temper. When asked what he meant about his temper, Joel responded, "when I get angry, it comes on all of a sudden." Joel participates in Boy Scouts, although Mrs. Smith reports that he does not enjoy it as much as he used to. Joel enjoys playing video games, watching television, and reading. Joel says he is happiest when he is with his friends.

BEHAVIORAL OBSERVATIONS AND IMPRESSIONS

During the evaluation, Joel presented as reserved and quiet, with a somewhat flat and restricted range of affect. He initiated few interactions with the examiners and, overall, seemed indifferent and lethargic. He was soft-spoken and examiners often had to ask him to repeat his answers. Joel was slow to respond throughout testing, irrespective of topic or task. Joel appeared to be giving earnest thought and effort to most items; therefore, the obtained results are considered a valid representation of his current intellectual, academic, and behavioral functioning.

INTELLECTUAL FUNCTIONING

The Wechsler Intelligence Scale for Children—Fourth Edition (WISC-IV) was administered to assess Joel's overall intelligence. Joel's performance revealed age-appropriate overall intellectual functioning with equally developed verbal and nonverbal abilities. Joel's slow response style resulted in a below average Processing Speed Index score; he completed timed measures of psychomotor speed and visual matching accurately but slowly.

ACADEMIC FUNCTIONING

Joel completed two measures of academic achievement to determine his specific strengths and weaknesses within achievement domains. The Woodcock-Johnson III Tests Achievement (WJ III ACH), a test comprised of basic reading, written expression, and mathematical tasks, was administered. Given Mrs. Smith's concerns about Joel's mathematics achievement, the KeyMath—Revised (KeyMath-R) was administered to examine Joel's mathematics skills in detail.

In general, Joel's composite scores indicate that he is performing in the average range of overall academic achievement, which means Joel is performing as would be expected for his age. It should be noted that, however, Joel's academic fluency scores are relatively low. Fluency is the rate at which simple academic tasks are completed accurately. For example, during the Math Fluency subtest, Joel was given three minutes to correctly answer as many basic single digit computations as possible. Although most responses were correct, Joel completed 68 problems in three minutes, whereas other students his age would have answered about 100 problems correctly in the same amount of time.

The KeyMath-R was used to assess Joel's specific mathematics skills in the areas of basic concepts, operations, and applications. Joel's composite scores indicate that he is performing in the average range of functioning in all areas of mathematics. Joel appears to have a relative strength in Applications, which means he performed well on tasks of measurement, calculating time and money, and interpreting data. Mathematical calculations were a relative weakness for Joel, with problems evident in solving fraction problems requiring calculation of a lowest common denominator.

SOCIAL AND EMOTIONAL FUNCTIONING

During the interview, Mrs. Smith shared several concerns about Joel's social and emotional functioning. Her concerns centered around four areas: (1) irritability, (2) negative attitude toward school, (3) social engagement, and (4) self-esteem. These areas of difficulty were confirmed in teacher reports and, to some extent, self-reports. Mrs. Smith reports that Joel is generally argumentative, persistently and pervasively negative about most things, and often impatient. His attitude toward school is described as "very negative" and apathetic. Mrs. Smith reports that Joel believes school is a waste of time and that he acts like he doesn't care. With regard to social engagement, Mrs. Smith worries about the amount of time Joel spends alone and his lack of interest in recreational activities. Mrs. Smith commented that Joel seemed to enjoy extracurricular activities, such as sports, more when in elementary school. Mrs. Smith says that Joel has fun when he spends time with his best friend, but that Joel will rarely initiate such interactions. Joel's self-esteem, especially in relation to academics, is poor according to Mrs. Smith. Joel has commented that he is "not smart enough" to have an office job, or "it's no use" to ask for academic help. Mrs. Smith also reports that it angers Joel to hear positive statements such as "you can do it" or "we'll get it worked out." Mrs. Smith reported that symptoms of irritability, apathy, social withdrawal, and low self-esteem have been present over the past 18 to 24 months.

Joel's mother, math teacher, and English teacher each completed questionnaires to provide information about Joel's adaptive skills, behavior, and emotional functioning compared to others his age. Raters generally agreed that areas of concern for Joel include attention and school problems, social disengagement, and affective or emotional symptoms. With regards to attention and schoolwork, raters indicated that Joel does not complete assignments, often forgets things, is easily distracted, and has a difficult time concentrating. All raters agreed that Joel's adaptive skills are low. This may mean that Joel is less socially engaged and engaging than others his age. Ratings also indicated that Joel may be more prone to negative emotional responses, such as irritability and anger, than other adolescents his age.

It is important to note that Joel's algebra teacher produced more negative ratings than other respondents. The algebra teacher's overly negative report makes it difficult to interpret her ratings. Joel considers algebra his least favorite course and teacher ratings may be reflective of his attitude toward the material. Although the English teacher's ratings were slightly more negative than others', her ratings were in agreement with other data and are viewed as interpretable.

Self-Reports

Interview and self-report questionnaires were also used to evaluate Joel's functioning. During the interview, Joel's affect was blunted and his response style continued to be slow. Several concerning themes emerged which lent support to others' impressions of Joel. Areas of concern included irritability and anger, a negative attitude toward school, a tendency to blame others for problems, and low self-esteem. First, Joel reported having trouble controlling his temper several times. He used the phrase "bad temper" when describing himself and to identify what he liked least about himself and what he would change about himself. When asked what makes him angry, Joel said "things that annoy me . . . over and over" and "when someone asks something they already know the answer to." He also said that when he gets angry "it comes on all of a sudden." Second, Joel's attitudes toward school ranged from indifferent to extremely negative and indicated that he experiences a pervasive discomfort and dissatisfaction with teachers and school. For example, Joel reported that school is a waste of time and that teachers are unfair. Third, Joel tends to blame others for his difficulties with succeeding in school. When asked about his feelings regarding his parents' separation, Joel responded by blaming his mother for the events that led up to the separation. He also indicated that other people often get him in trouble and that life is unfair. Finally, Joel reported feeling that no one understands him, no one listens to him, he is "dumb" compared to friends, he is unimportant in his family, he is lonely even when others are around, and that other children are happier and have more fun than he does. These statements suggest that Joel views himself less favorably than others his age. During formal mental status examination, Joel denied hallucinatory experiences, thoughts of self-harm, and thoughts of harming others.

SUMMARY

Mrs. Smith identified an overall area of concern regarding Joel's academic achievement, with mathematics achievement being of specific interest. Joel's intelligence test scores indicate age-appropriate intellectual functioning with equally developed nonverbal and verbal reasoning abilities and a weakness in processing speed. Joel completed an extensive battery of achievement tests to detect a learning disability. As noted above, Joel's academic achievement is consonant with his intellectual ability, with noted relative weaknesses in timed academic tasks and relative strengths in solving applied mathematics problems. Joel's achievement functioning does not indicate the presence of a learning disability.

Mrs. Smith's second general area of concern centered around Joel's social and emotional functioning. More specifically, Mrs. Smith worried about Joel's poor self-esteem, irritability, negative attitude toward school, and low social engagement. While these issues are to some extent typical for adolescents, they can also be associated with depressive disorders in children and adolescents. The intensity, frequency, and duration of Joel's depressive symptoms are significant enough to impair Joel's day-to-day functioning and are excessive for his age. Taken together, interview data, rating scale reports, self-reports, and behavioral observations of Joel throughout the testing day support a diagnosis of Dysthymic Disorder, which is characterized by chronic depressive symptoms. Joel's depressive symptoms are associated with family stress.

DIAGNOSTIC IMPRESSION

Current evaluation results support the following diagnostic impression:

Axis I	300.4	Dysthymic Disorder, Early Onset
Axis II	V71.09	No Diagnosis
Axis III		None
Axis IV		Separation of parents
Axis V	GAF = 55	(current)

RECOMMENDATIONS

The following recommendations are offered in light of our diagnostic impressions and Joel's current cognitive, academic, and social-emotional functioning.

Depression

1. Joel would benefit from treatment for his anger, irritability, and poor self-esteem. This might take the form of individual cognitive-behavioral therapy (CBT), which typically includes psycho-education about the symptoms of dysthymia, cognitive restructuring, and learning behavioral strategies to reduce symptoms. Within the context of individual therapy, sleeping difficulties should also be targeted for intervention. An additional focus of treatment might be Joel's tendency to blame others for his difficulties. By developing more adaptive coping styles, Joel may feel more empowered. The prognosis for therapy is good provided Joel is receptive and his family is supportive.

2. Family therapy following some progress with Joel in individual therapy is also recommended. Joel is angry toward his mother and blames her for the recent separation of his parents; however, he is not inclined to discuss his feelings with her. Mrs. Smith also expressed some concern about not connecting with Joel, and family therapy could serve as a worthwhile intervention to improve communication, problem-solve, and to improve relationships within the family.

3. Joel should be involved in some type of physical activity every day. Physical activity can take many forms, such as mowing the lawn, roller-skating, participating in P.E. at school, or playing basketball. Exercise may help to improve Joel's irritable mood.

4. Mrs. Smith should continue encouraging Joel to participate in extracurricular and social activities such as Boy Scouts and socializing with peers. Social activities can be reinforcing for people who are depressed, meaning that people feel better after engaging in them. This improvement, in turn, may result in a greater likelihood that the person will engage in the activity again.

5. Consultation with a child psychiatrist is suggested to determine the appropriateness of a trial of medication for Joel's symptoms of dysthymia.

Academic Recommendations

1. Joel has a clear academic strength in mathematical applied problems. Joel seems to learn better through application of

knowledge and concepts as opposed to abstract written or verbal instruction. When possible, it will be important to help Joel make connections between abstract concepts and their application.

2. Joel should receive continued tutoring for math and for other subjects as needed. The tutor should keep in mind Joel's applied problem-solving strengths and use those in instruction. If Joel is to stay at Bryan, increased tutoring may be needed to keep Joel on grade level.

   a. Along with subject content, another focus of tutoring should be to practice timed tasks. By increasing Joel's speed, he should be able to complete work in a more timely fashion. Increased speed may also help with long-term comprehension, as slow processing can interfere with the amount of information that goes from short- to long-term memory.

   b. Joel needs to review the steps involved in establishing lowest common denominators for fractions.

3. Joel needs to complete all of his homework and submit homework assignments to teachers. He can work with his tutor to improve homework habits.

4. Joel's cognitive abilities indicate he is capable of doing all academic work; however, Joel will need to increase his effort and motivation to do well. As Joel's dysthymic symptoms improve, he may be able to improve his efforts to complete homework assignments.

The results of this evaluation were shared with Mrs. Smith and Joel Smith during the feedback session.

Discussion of Case Study

Joel's evaluation illustrates many of the concepts and assessment methods relevant to the assessment of depressive symptoms in children. First, Mrs. Smith primarily characterized Joel's difficulty as a learning problem, particularly in math achievement. She described concerns with Joel's irritability and social-emotional functioning as secondary concerns, almost as afterthoughts. In response to the concerns about mathematics achievement, we organized the assessment battery to evaluate Joel's mathematics achievement thoroughly by including the WJ III ACH and KeyMath—Revised. Joel showed no evidence of a learning disability in any academic area.

In terms of assessment techniques relevant to depressive symptoms, we conducted interviews with Mrs. Smith and Joel and utilized third-party rating scales (i.e., BASC-TRS; BASC-PRS; Conners') and self-reports (i.e., BASC-SRP) of general psychological and behavioral adjustment. We supplemented the rating scales of general adjustment with several scales specific to the assessment of depressive symptomatology in children and adolescents (i.e., BYI, CDI, and CDRS-R). Interestingly, the self-report ratings and clinical rating scale converged consistently, while parent report revealed less severe depressive symptomatology and teacher reports showed discrepancies. Joel's mathematics teacher was particularly negative in her evaluation of his behavior in the classroom. The mathematics teacher's ratings indicated a negative response pattern that produced an elevated validity index score and raised concerns about the usefulness of her ratings. As these ratings were consistently discrepant from other sources of information, we elected to emphasize information obtained from other raters.

We determined that Joel met formal diagnostic criteria for Dysthymic Disorder as delineated in the *DSM-IV-TR*. We also used the specifier, Early Onset, to indicate that onset of the dysthymia occurred prior to 21 years of age. During interview, Mrs. Smith reported a pattern of irritable mood that had existed for at least 12 months (Criterion A), which did not remit for longer than a 2-month period (Criterion C) and was accompanied by symptoms of low energy (Criterion B.3), low self-esteem (Criterion B.4), and poor concentration (Criterion B.5). Depressive symptoms caused difficulties in academic and social domains of functioning (i.e., restricted social relationships and poor relationships with teachers; Criterion H), and were not due to a general medical condition (Criterion G) or psychotic disorder (Criterion F). Joel did not meet criteria for major depressive episode (Criterion D) and did not show evidence of symptoms of mania (Criterion E).

In light of Joel's age, it is important to consider that the mood criterion for depressive disorders can involve irritability in children and adolescents, which was the case for Joel. Joel reported irregular difficulties with sleep that had not been noted by Mrs. Smith, which we did not "count" as insomnia but may have emerged as an area of clinical intervention. Joel appeared to be showing difficulties with psychomotor retardation as evidenced by his slow rate of speech (i.e., behavioral observations), slow cognitive processing speed (i.e., WISC-IV Processing Speed Index), and slower than average academic work speed (i.e., WJ III ACH Academic Fluency). In rendering a formal diagnosis of dysthymia, we ruled out physical causes for depressive symptoms by taking a brief physical history and accepting the results of a recent physical examination that was conducted that indicated the absence of physical problems. Family history was positive for depressive disorder in a first-degree relative, that is, Joel's father. The course of Joel's symptomatology appeared fairly stable and chronic with recent exacerbation due to the separation between his parents (see Table 6.4).

As part of our evaluation, we conducted a mental status examination with Joel and asked directly about the presence of suicidal ideation, prior suicidal behaviors, thoughts of harming others, hallucinatory experiences, and substance use and abuse, among other areas. Joel denied the presence of thoughts of self-harm, which is important to inquire about during any clinical interview, but crucial when detecting depressive symptomatology. Review of parent and teacher BASC reports revealed that no critical items measuring suicidal ideation were endorsed. Joel did not endorse any critical items measuring suicidal ideation for the BYI, BASC, or CDI self-reports. Joel did not show evidence of a comorbid anxiety or conduct disorder; both Mrs. Smith and Joel denied the use of substances.

Recommendations were organized in terms of intervention for depression and academic functioning. We recommended individual psychotherapy for Joel that employed cognitive-behavioral therapy, which has been shown to be an empirically supported treatment for depressive symptoms in children and adolescents. We also outlined the possibility of implementing family based intervention due to the conflict reported between Joel and his mother, particularly due to

Table 6.4   **Psychometric Summary for Joel**

WECHSLER INTELLIGENCE SCALE FOR CHILDREN— FOURTH EDITION (WISC-IV)

Scale/Index	Standard Scores	90% Confidence Interval	Percentile
Verbal Comprehension	108	102–113	70
Perceptual Reasoning	106	99–112	66
Working Memory	99	93–106	47
Processing Speed	78	73–88	7
Full Scale IQ	100	96–104	50

WOODCOCK-JOHNSON III TESTS OF ACHIEVEMENT (WJ III ACH)

Subtests	Standard Scores	90% Confidence Interval	Percentile
Letter-Word Identification	107	100–114	68
Reading Fluency	90	87–92	24
Passage Comprehension	108	99–117	70
Calculation	96	88–104	39
Math Fluency	77	73–81	6
Spelling	83	77–90	13
Writing Fluency	84	77–92	15
Applied Problems	102	97–107	56
Writing Samples	99	83–115	46
Composites			
Broad Reading	98	95–100	43
Broad Mathematics	95	91–99	37
Broad Written Language	85	81–90	17
Math Calculation Skills	88	82–94	22
Written Expression	88	81–95	21
Academic Skills	95	91–99	37
Academic Fluency	85	82–88	16
Academic Applications	105	99–111	62
Total Achievement	92	89–94	29

Table 6.4   Continued

KEYMATH—REVISED: A DIAGNOSTIC INVENTORY OF ESSENTIAL MATHEMATICS (KEYMATH-R)

Test Composites	Standard Scores	Percentile
Basic Concepts Area	106	66
Operations Area	95	38
Applications Area	110	75
Total Test	103	58

CONNERS' PARENT RATING SCALES—REVISED: LONG VERSION (CPRS-R:L)

Scales	T-Scores
Oppositional	61
Cognitive Problems/Inattention	62
Hyperactivity	44
Anxious-Shy	51
Perfectionism	55
Social Problems	57
Psychosomatic	50
Conners' ADHD index	61
Conners' Global Index: Restless-Impulsive	61
Conners' Global Index: Emotional Lability	59
Conners' Global Index: Total	60
DSM-IV Inattentive	60
DSM-IV Hyperactive-Impulsive	45
DSM-IV Total	60

BEHAVIOR ASSESSMENT SYSTEM FOR CHILDREN—PARENT RATING SCALES (BASC-PRS)

Clinical Scales	Mother	
	T-Scores	Percentile
Hyperactivity	43	24
Aggression	47	45
Conduct Problems	55	76
Anxiety	42	21
Depression	60	85
Somatization	38	7
Atypicality	54	75
Withdrawal	47	45
Attention Problems	68	95

(continued)

Table 6.4   *Continued*

Clinical Scales	Mother	
	T-Score	Percentile
Externalizing Problems Composite	48	49
Internalizing Problems Composite	44	27
Behavior Symptoms Index	50	55

Adaptive Scales	Mother	
	T-Score	Percentile
Social Skills	33	4
Leadership	35	8
Adaptive Skills Composite	33	4

BEHAVIOR ASSESSMENT SYSTEM FOR CHILDREN—TEACHER RATING SCALES (BASC-TRS)

Clinical Scales	Math Teacher		English Teacher	
	T-Score	Percentile	*T*-Score	Percentile
Hyperactivity	49	56	48	51
Aggression	60	86	63	89
Conduct Problems	44	25	44	25
Anxiety	48	47	42	22
Depression	73	96	46	45
Somatization	44	30	44	30
Attention Problems	79	99	59	80
Learning Problems	75	98	65	91
Atypicality	76	97	55	80
Withdrawal	79	98	58	83
Externalizing Problems Composite	51	67	52	69
Internalizing Problems Composite	56	78	43	28
School Problems Composite	79	99	63	88
Behavior Symptoms Index	68	94	53	68

Table 6.4   *Continued*

Adaptive Scales	Math Teacher		English Teacher	
	T-Score	Percentile	*T*-Score	Percentile
Social skills	28	1	28	1
Leadership	29	1	29	1
Study skills	30	1	33	4
Adaptive skills Composite	27	1	28	1

BEHAVIOR ASSESSMENT SYSTEM FOR CHILDREN—SELF-REPORT OF PERSONALITY (BASC-SRP)

Clinical Scales	*T*-Scores	Percentiles
Attitude toward School	63	87
Attitude toward Teachers	70	95
Sensation Seeking	63	89
Atypicality	41	19
Locus of Control	62	84
Somatization	39	10
Social Stress	54	69
Anxiety	42	29
Depression	66	94
Sense of Inadequacy	45	39
School Maladjustment Composite	69	95
Clinical Maladjustment Composite	55	69
Emotional Symptoms Index	63	90

Adaptive Scales	*T*-Scores	Percentiles
Relations with parents	52	40
Interpersonal relations	57	83
Self-Esteem	58	77
Self-Reliance	59	84
Personal Adjustment Composite	59	83

BECK YOUTH INVENTORIES OF EMOTIONAL AND SOCIAL IMPAIRMENT (BYI)

Scale	*T*-Score
Beck Self-Concept Inventory for Youth	42
Beck Anxiety Inventory for Youth	52
Beck Depression Inventory for Youth	62
Beck Anger Inventory for Youth	56
Beck Disruptive Behavior Inventory for Youth	55

(continued)

Table 6.4   *Continued*

CHILDREN'S DEPRESSION INVENTORY (CDI)

Scale	*T*-Score
Negative Mood	64
Interpersonal Problems	57
Ineffectiveness	64
Anhedonia	56
Negative Self-Esteem	62
Total CDI Score	64

CHILDREN'S DEPRESSION RATING SCALE—REVISED (CDRS-R)

Scale	Raw Score	*T*-Score	Percentile
CDRS-R Total	44	65	95th

circumstances around the parent's recent separation. In terms of academic recommendations, we identified and described instructional strategies that may serve to accommodate Joel's difficulties with speed of processing information and producing academic work. Due to Joel's enrollment in a private educational setting, we did not include discussion about eligibility for special education services under the IDEA category of Emotional Disturbance. In our opinion, Joel would qualify for such services due to the academic difficulties arising due to his depressive disorder.

Conclusion

Roughly 2% of school-age children and 6% of adolescents suffer from depressive disorders, with depressive disorders more prevalent for girls than boys in adolescence. Depressive disorders are characterized by affective, cognitive, and physiological symptoms that co-occur and cause functional impairments. There is fairly good agreement that symptomatic expression of depressive disorders, particularly MDD, is similar from childhood through adolescence and into adulthood with minor variation in the presence of specific symptoms across development. Dysphoric mood appears to be the single most chronic symptom of depression; however, anhedonia also occurs frequently in children and adolescents. Additional symptoms are required for a formal diagnosis of MDD, with a minimum of four symptoms required beyond depressed mood or anhedonia. In general terms, dysthymia is characterized by less severity but by a more chronic course of depressive symptoms in comparison to MDD.

Comorbid psychopathology exists in the presence of depressive disorders, particularly anxiety disorders, Conduct Disorder, and Attention-Deficit/Hyperactivity Disorder. Similar to adult counterparts, children and adolescents with depressive disorders are at greater risk of suicide than nondepressed peers. The general assessment approach to depression involves collecting information from caregivers and child. A variety of self-report measures, third-party ratings, and interviews exist that assess depressive symptomatology, but all share shortcomings in discriminant validity. Interpretation of assessment data is complicated when evaluating for the presence of depressive disorders due to the lack of concordance that exists between adults and children in reporting their own symptoms. When assessing for depressive disorders, self-reported symptoms should receive more credence due to the subjective nature of experienced symptomatology.

Anxiety Disorders

Jonathan M. Campbell

7
Chapter

Similar to depressive disorders, anxiety disorders are some of the most common psychological disorders diagnosed in children and youth. Epidemiological data indicate that anxiety disorders are prevalent at a rate of between 4% and 30% in community samples, with median rates reported around 10% for all anxiety disorders (Albano, Chorpita, & Barlow, 2003; Costello, Egger, & Angold, 2005; Ford, Goodman, & Meltzer, 2003). Research consistently documents that anxiety disorders are found more frequently in females than in males across all anxiety disorder diagnoses, such as phobias, Panic Disorder, and separation anxiety (Foa et al., 2005). By age 6, roughly twice as many girls suffer from an anxiety disorder when compared to boys, a 2:1 ratio that is fairly stable across development (Lewinsohn, Gotlib, Lewinsohn, Seely, & Allen, 1998). The higher prevalence of anxiety disorders in females over males appears to be robust, as sex differences persist even after multiple confounds are accounted for in the statistical analysis, such as age of onset, duration of anxiety episode, self-esteem, life stressors, and social support (Lewinsohn et al., 1998). There is also evidence to indicate that different types of anxiety are more or less prevalent at different ages. For example, young children are at greater risk than adolescents for

211

problems with anxiety associated with separation from parents (American Psychiatric Association, 2000). Older children and adolescents appear to be at greater risk for panic disorders and agoraphobia; however, for some anxiety disorders, such as generalized anxiety and specific phobias, there does not appear to be a differential risk according to age (Foa et al., 2005).

Constructs of Interest

Prior to defining anxiety as a construct and disorder, one must remain aware that anxiety is part of everyday human experience and part of typical development. There is good reason to accept the notion that anxiety has served an adaptive function for human beings. Anxiety responses signal the presence of danger and serve to organize the response of the individual to act to reduce threats of danger. For children and adolescents, the presence and foci of anxiety follow a fairly typical developmental sequence involving areas such as anxiety toward strangers, separation from parents, and varied fears and phobias. As children progress from preschool to adolescence, there appears to be a fairly stable number of sources of anxiety or fears, but greater differentiation and abstraction associated with increased cognitive development (T. J. Huberty, 1997). Anxiety has also been identified, in part, as an adaptive response to situational threat, perhaps best exemplified by the sympathetic response of the autonomic nervous system. When human beings are threatened, there is a typical "fight or flight" sympathetic response activated by the presence of threat. The visceral response is characterized by accelerated heartbeat, increased secretion of sweat, inhibition of salivation production, and constriction of blood vessels, among other indicators (Purves et al., 1997).

Multidimensional Definition of Anxiety

Broadly defined, anxiety is characterized as a multifaceted construct that consists of cognitive/subjective, physiological, and behavioral indicators (e.g., House, 1999). The triad of anxiety indicators is also typically viewed as response to either real or perceived threat (e.g., Barrios & O'Dell, 1998). T. J. Huberty (1997, p. 305) proposed a comprehensive definition of anxiety: "Anxiety is defined as apprehension, distress, or tension about real or anticipated internal or external threats that may be shown in cognitive, behavioral, or physiological patterns." Understanding possible manifestations of anxiety in each domain is important when undertaking psychodiagnostic evaluation of children and adolescents.

Cognitive/Subjective Manifestations

Cognitive symptoms of anxiety disorders include worry, rumination, and obsessive patterns of thinking, perhaps best epitomized by obsessive symptoms characteristic of Obsessive-Compulsive Disorder (OCD). In addition to thought content, other cognitive functions are disrupted in the presence of anxiety disorders, such as difficulties with focusing and sustaining attention, planning, and problem solving. Within the domain of cognitive functioning, children and adolescents may also demonstrate sufficient insight and judgment, verbalizing awareness that their anxiety is irrational or unrealistic. For example, an adolescent might explain that he knows that he has checked that the stove is off prior to sitting down to completing his homework; however, he cannot resist checking once more "just to be absolutely sure it's off." Authors have also identified the phenomenology of anxiety, that is, subjective cognitive symptoms, as an important domain to understand and assess. Thoughts of inadequacy, fear of negative appraisal of others, thoughts of going crazy and imagery of future harm or abandonment are examples of the subjective cognitive aspects of anxiety (Barrios & O'Dell, 1998).

In addition to the cognitive symptoms that characterize anxiety, there is evidence that cognitive processes are important in the development and maintenance of anxiety. Cognitive distortions and inaccurate attributions are two examples of faulty cognitive processes associated with anxiety. An example of a cognitive distortion is overestimation, which involves inaccurately assessing the likelihood that a feared event may occur. For instance, a child with separation anxiety may overestimate the odds that her parents may die in an automobile accident when returning from a business trip. The belief that her parents are at significant risk of death may initiate other symptoms of anxiety, such as physiological or behavioral symptoms. Cognitive attributions were introduced in the chapter on depressive disorders, mainly in relation to Beck's cognitive theory of depression, where faulty attributions are hypothesized to be important in the etiology of depression. Evidence for similar negative attributions has been found for individuals with anxiety disorders. For example, Panic Disorder has been conceptualized as a problem with the misinterpretation of bodily symptoms of fear, such as the sympathetic nervous system responses described earlier (A. T. Beck & Weishaar, 1989; Craske & Barlow, 1993). Using this conceptualization, Panic Disorder is treatable, in part, by retraining cognitions during exposure to bodily cues of fear, such as increased breathing rate. The process is known as interoceptive cue conditioning, whereby symptoms of panic are induced in a session and irrational cognitive thinking processes are identified, challenged, and restructured (Craske & Barlow, 1993).

For children and adolescents, there is also evidence to suggest that the presence of anxiety correlates with an increased bias to attend to potential threats in the environment (Foa et al., 2005). Humans demonstrate finite attentional resources; therefore, selective attention to threatening cues may correlate with anxiety, either as a predisposition toward anxiety or, perhaps, a consequence of anxiety. Experimental studies comparing children with anxiety disorders to control groups have documented biases toward processing threat information in anxious children.

Due to the links between anxiety and cognitive functioning, children and adolescents may be referred for nonspecific learning problems or attention-related concerns where anxiety presents as a causal or contributing factor. The presence of anxiety may legitimately explain academic difficulties, such as debilitating test anxiety which negatively impacts test performance and subsequent grades. In a similar manner, anxiety may serve as a contributor to academic problems, such as difficulty concentrating during classroom instruction or homework due to preoccupations with parents' safety. These examples provide practical justification for screening for symptoms of anxiety in the context of a comprehensive psycho-educational evaluation.

Physiological Manifestations

Physiological symptoms of anxiety include those associated with acute sympathetic response of the autonomic nervous system, such as increased respiration, tachycardia (i.e., increased heart rate), and galvanic skin response. Other physiological symptoms may be indirectly linked or sequelae of the sympathetic response, such as ongoing muscle tension, headaches, diarrhea, fatigue, and vomiting. As mentioned earlier, the sympathetic response serves to call the individual to action. There is some evidence that individuals with anxiety disorders have dysregulated physiological arousal systems.

The physiological manifestations of anxiety have been linked with inaccurate cognitive appraisal to provide a reasonable justification for including cognitive therapy techniques in the treatment of Panic Disorder. Physiological manifestations of anxiety and their biological mechanisms may directly cause behavioral symptoms of anxiety and serve as salient and powerful determinants of the individual's behavior.

Behavioral Symptoms

Barrios and O'Dell (1998) provide a list of behavioral symptoms associated with anxiety that includes nail biting, crying, thumb sucking, stuttering, and pacing. In addition to these behaviors, other behavioral manifestations of anxiety disorders take the form of escape or avoidant behaviors, such as those seen in phobias or trauma, or compulsive behaviors, such as checking, counting, or repeated hand washing. Behavioral symptoms may also give rise to physical manifestations of anxiety problems, such as skin irritation as a result of compulsive hand-washing behavior.

Avoidant behavior deserves special note. The importance of avoidant behavior in maintaining anxiety has been acknowledged for decades, first articulated in Mowrer's (1939) classical two-factor learning model of anxiety. The two-factor model proposes that anxiety is acquired due to pairing an anxiety response to a stimulus (i.e., classically conditioned or respondent conditioning; Barrios & O'Dell, 1998); however, anxiety is maintained due to avoidance of the stimulus paired with the initial anxiety response. Avoidant behavior results in reduction (or prevention) of the anxiety response, which is subsequently reinforced due to the removal of an aversive stimulus (i.e., avoidant behavior is negatively reinforced). Subsequent theoretical work has proposed a reinterpretation regarding which factors maintain avoidant behavior. Reformulations of avoidant behavior suggest that avoidance may not be maintained by fear reduction but rather understood as approach toward stimuli that cue a relaxation response. Regardless of the theoretical formulation, understanding the role of behavior in maintaining anxiety provides a useful heuristic in understanding, in part, why exposure and response prevention-based treatment models have been effective in treating various forms of anxiety (e.g., March & Mulle, 1998). Behavioral manifestations of anxiety are important to assess when evaluating for the presence of anxiety as well as avoidant behaviors that may serve to maintain symptoms of anxiety.

Comorbidities

Anxiety disorders co-occur with a range of other psychiatric disorders, such as depressive disorders, Attention-Deficit/Hyperactivity Disorder (ADHD), and disruptive behavior disorders (Angold et al., 1999). The highest risk for comorbidity is for the depressive disorders, and there appears to be roughly equal risk for comorbid attention-deficit or disruptive behavior disorders. In a clinic-referred sample, Verduin and Kendall (2003) found differential risk for comorbid depression among several anxiety disorders. Children with a primary diagnosis of Separation Anxiety Disorder were less likely to suffer from a comorbid depressive disorder when compared to children with a primary diagnosis of either Generalized Anxiety Disorder or Social Phobia, which did not dif-

fer. In the same clinic sample, comorbid risk for ADHD or Oppositional Defiant Disorder was equal across the three groups.

Anxiety disorders also co-occur with other anxiety disorders, a
phenomenon identified as homotypic comorbidity, which describes
the co-occurrence of disorders within the *same* diagnostic group
(Angold et al., 1999). The co-occurrence among anxiety disorders
appears to be fairly common, with almost 50% of children with
Generalized Anxiety Disorder also meeting criteria for a specific
phobia and almost 75% of children with Separation Anxiety Disorder also meeting criteria for Generalized Anxiety Disorder (Verduin
& Kendall, 2003). Data on comorbidity are summarized in Table 7.1.

The Tripartite Conceptualization of Depression and Anxiety Revisited

The tripartite model of depression and anxiety was introduced in
the chapter on depressive disorders (Chapter 6) and warrants brief
mention here. As a reminder, the tripartite model of anxiety and
depression was developed to account for the high rates of comorbidity found for anxiety and depression among both adults and
children. The physiological symptoms of anxiety (e.g., tachycardia,
increased respiration, sweaty palms) appear to be the most relevant when considering either a differential diagnosis between an
anxiety and depressive disorder or comorbid diagnoses of anxiety
and depression. Several measures, such as the Revised Children's
Manifest Anxiety Scale (RCMAS; C. R. Reynolds & Richmond,
2000), have been examined within the tripartite conceptualization
and shown to be somewhat useful in determining the presence
of physiological symptoms of anxiety separate from depression.
Other scales may also prove to be useful in assessing the presence
of physiological symptoms associated with anxiety, such as
the Somatization scale on the Behavior Assessment System for
Children—Second Edition (BASC-2; C. R. Reynolds & Kamphaus,
2004) and the Somatic Complaints Syndrome scale from the
Achenbach System of Empirically Based Assessment (ASEBA;
Achenbach & Rescorla, 2001).

Table 7.1 **Epidemiology and Comorbidity of Anxiety Disorders in Children and Adolescents**

EPIDEMIOLOGY ESTIMATES

	Prevalence (in %)	
	Childhood/Adolescence	Lifetime
Any diagnosed anxiety disorder	3.8–30.2	15–33
Separation Anxiety Disorder	1.2–12.9	5.2–12.9
Generalized Anxiety Disorder/ Overanxious Disorder	0.7–12.4	5–5.7
Specific Phobia	1.0–3.6	7.2–12.5
Social Phobia	0.3–1.1	3–13
Panic Disorder	0.1–4.4	1–4.7
Posttraumatic Stress Disorder	0.1–6.3	6.8–8
Obsessive-Compulsive Disorder	0.6–2.3	1.6–2.5

COMMON COMORBIDITIES

	Range for Children and Adolescents (%)	Median Odds Ratio*
Depressive disorders (all)	10–28	8.2
Conduct Disorder/Disruptive behavior	10	3.1
Attention-Deficit/Hyperactivity Disorder	10	3.0
Another anxiety disorder	19–63	—

*Odds ratios reported from Angold et al. (1999); odds ratios are interpreted as the likelihood of comorbid diagnosis (i.e., a diagnosis of a comorbid Conduct Disorder is about 3 times more likely when a child is diagnosed with an anxiety disorder versus undiagnosed with an anxiety disorder).

Sources: Data summarized from "Childhood Anxiety Disorders" (pp. 279–329), by A. M. Albano, B. F. Chorpita, and D. H. Barlow, in *Child Psychopathology,* second edition, E. J. Mash and R. A. Barkley (Eds.), 2003, New York: Guilford Press; "Comorbidity," by A. Angold, E. J. Costello, and A. Erkanli, 1999, *Journal of Child Psychology and Psychiatry, 40,* pp. 57–87; "Ten-Year Research Update Review: I. The Epidemiology of Child and Adolescent Psychiatric Disorders: Methods and Public Health Burden," by E. J. Costello, H. Egger, and Angold, A., 2005, *Journal of the American Academy of Child and Adolescent Psychiatry, 44,* pp. 972–986; "The British Child and Adolescent Mental Health Survey 1999: The Prevalence of *DSM-IV* Disorders," by T. Ford, R. Goodman, and H. Meltzer, 2003, *Journal of the American Academy of Child and Adolescent Psychiatry, 42,* pp. 1203–1211; and "Lifetime Prevalence and Age-of-Onset Distributions of *DSM-IV* Disorders in the National Comorbidity Survey Replication," by R. C. Kessler, P. Berglund, O. Demler, R. Jin, K. R. Merikangas, and E. E. Walters, 2005, *Archives of General Psychiatry, 62,* pp. 593–768.

Diagnostic Standards

The *Diagnostic and Statistical Manual of Mental Disorders, Fourth Edition, Text Revision* (*DSM-IV-TR*) defines multiple anxiety disorders for children and adolescents (Table 7.2). In addition, special education regulations as delineated in the Individuals with Disabilities Education Improvement Act (IDEIA) allow for special education services for children and adolescents diagnosed with anxiety disorders (Albano et al., 2003). In the following section, several of the most frequently diagnosed *DSM-IV-TR* anxiety disorders are briefly introduced as well as the IDEIA category of Emotional Disturbance.

Diagnostic and Statistical Manual of Mental Disorders, Fourth Edition, Text Revision

The current *DSM* classification system defines multiple anxiety disorders that may be diagnosed with children and adolescents: Panic Disorder, Social Phobia (also listed as Social Anxiety Disorder), Separation Anxiety Disorder, Obsessive-Compulsive Disorder, Posttraumatic Stress Disorder, Acute Stress Disorder, Generalized Anxiety Disorder (including Overanxious Disorder of Childhood), and Specific Phobia (American Psychiatric Association, 2000). As with other groups of *DSM* disorders, the anxiety disorders also feature a nonspecific category of Anxiety Disorder—Not Otherwise Specified (AD-NOS), which allows for description of anxiety or phobic symptoms that do not meet criteria for any of the other anxiety disorders. For example, a diagnosis of AD-NOS would be warranted if symptoms of anxiety are present but do not meet criteria in terms of duration or number (i.e., subthreshold symptomatology). A brief description of the *DSM-IV-TR*-defined anxiety disorders appears in Table 7.2. Two Adjustment Disorders in *DSM-IV-TR* include anxiety as a defining feature: Adjustment Disorder with Anxiety and Adjustment Disorder with Mixed Anxiety and Depressed Mood. Three of the most frequently diagnosed anxiety disorders in children and adolescents are highlighted in the next section: Generalized Anxiety

Table 7.2   Anxiety Disorders and Defining Features Defined in *DSM-IV-TR*

DSM Diagnostic Category	Core Features
Generalized Anxiety Disorder*	Persistent, excessive worry about a variety of events or activities (e.g., parents' health, the future), accompanied by additional symptoms (e.g., sleeping problems).
Panic Disorder	Unexpected and recurrent panic attacks followed by persistent worry of another panic attack occurring. Panic attacks are characterized by intense fear or discomfort occurring with a cluster of symptoms (e.g., tachycardia, trembling, choking sensations, feeling dizzy) that develop quickly and peak within a short period of time. May occur with or without Agoraphobia.
Posttraumatic Stress Disorder	Exposure to a traumatic event involving severe threat or actual harm where a person's response involved intense fear/helplessness/horror. Following the event, child or adolescent shows symptoms of (a) reexperiencing the event (e.g., recurrent nightmares), (b) avoiding stimuli that remind the person of the event or general numbing of responsiveness (e.g., avoiding those who remind person of the trauma, feeling detached), and (c) increased symptoms of arousal (e.g., outbursts of anger). Symptoms must last for at least 1 month.
Obsessive-Compulsive Disorder	Ruminative, obsessive thinking and/or compulsive behavior associated with affective distress, fear, and worry. Compulsive behavior tied to reduction of distress (e.g., counting, washing, checking) or to prevention of feared event occurring (e.g., tragedy). Obsessive thinking and/or compulsive behavior causes marked distress or occurs more than 1 hour daily.
Separation Anxiety Disorder	Excessive anxiety concerning separation from the home, caregivers, or attachment figures, defined by the presence of three or more symptoms. Examples of symptoms include persistent worry about future harm of attachment figures, reluctance to go to school or other places due to fear of separation, repeated nightmares about separation. Disturbance lasts at least 4 weeks.
Social Phobia/Social Anxiety Disorder	Excessive fear of social or performance situations where one is exposed to unfamiliar persons or possible negative evaluation from others. If most social situations are feared, social phobia may be described as generalized.
Specific Phobia	Excessive and persistent fear of an object/situation that is characterized by significant symptoms of anxiety in the presence of the feared object/situation. Fear and anxiety often lead to avoidance behavior. Subtypes of specific phobia include animal, natural environment (e.g., heights, storms, water), blood/injection/injury, situation (e.g., elevators, flying, bridges). Symptoms must occur for > 6 months for individuals under 18 years of age.

DSM-IV-TR = Diagnostic and Statistical Manual of Mental Disorders, Fourth Edition, Text Revision. Includes Overanxious Disorder of Childhood.

Disorder (GAD), Separation Anxiety Disorder (SAD), and Social Phobia (SP).

Generalized Anxiety Disorder: In the previous version of the *DSM*, Overanxious Disorder of Childhood was a separate diagnosable anxiety disorder for children, but is now subsumed within the GAD diagnostic category. Generalized Anxiety Disorder is characterized by excessive anxiety and worry about a number of activities or events, a state of anxiety that has been described as "free-floating" as opposed to being circumscribed to specific stimuli (e.g., Specific Phobia) or situations (e.g., Social Phobia). Feelings of anxiety and worry are accompanied by at least three of six symptoms: (1) feeling restless, "keyed up," or "on edge"; (2) easily fatigued; (3) difficulty concentrating; (4) feeling irritable; (5) muscle tension; and (6) sleeping difficulties (American Psychiatric Association, 2000). For a period of at least 6 months, worry and anxiety occur for more days than not; furthermore, the individual finds the worry difficult to control. Symptoms of anxiety must cause significant distress or impairment in social, occupational, academic, or other areas of functioning. The diagnostic criteria include one allowance for children such that only one of the six associated symptoms (e.g., irritability, sleeping problems) is needed for formal diagnosis.

Separation Anxiety Disorder: Separation Anxiety Disorder is the single anxiety disorder identified specifically among children and appears in the *DSM-IV-TR* section entitled "Disorders Usually First Diagnosed in Infancy, Childhood, or Adolescence." The defining feature of SAD is excessive worry regarding separation from home or separation from attachment figures, most typically parents. For diagnosis, anxiety exceeds developmental expectations. The anxiety must be characterized by at least three of eight specific symptoms, such as (a) recurring distress when separated from home or attachment figures; (b) persistent worry about losing or harm befalling attachment figures; (c) excessive worry that a negative event will lead to separation, such as being kidnapped or becoming lost; and (d) reluctance or refusal to go to school or other places due to separation-based fear. The examples provided reflect symptoms that are primarily cognitive/subjective and behavioral in nature; however, the SAD criteria also include physiological symptoms, such as repeated headaches and stomach aches, when separation from home or attachment figures occurs or is anticipated. For diagnosis, the cluster of symptoms must last at least 4 weeks, onset must be prior to the age of 18, and the symptoms must cause significant impairment in social, academic, or other areas of functioning (American Psychiatric Association, 2000). The SAD criteria also include the specifier "early onset" if onset occurs before 6 years of age.

Social Phobia or Social Anxiety Disorder: Social Phobia is characterized by marked and persistent fear of social or performance situations where the individual encounters unfamiliar persons or possible evaluation by others. For formal diagnosis, symptoms of anxiety are almost always invoked when the individual encounters the feared social situation. Situations that produce symptoms of anxiety are either endured with intense anxiety or distress or avoided altogether, and the individual recognizes that the fear is excessive to the situation or irrational. Anxious avoidance or distress significantly interferes with the individual's functioning in occupational, academic, or social arenas.

The diagnostic criteria include additional requirements and allowances for formal diagnosis of SP in children. For example, children must show capacity for age-appropriate social situations, and symptoms of anxiety must be present during peer interactions, not simply during interactions with adults. Children may express anxiety as crying, tantrumming, freezing, or shrinking from social interactions with unfamiliar persons. Additionally, symptoms must be present for at least 6 months for children (i.e., individuals under the age of 18).

Individuals with Disabilities Education Act

Although the presence of an anxiety disorder does not necessarily indicate the need for, or guarantee provision of, special education services, children and adolescents may be eligible for special education under the 1997 Individuals with Disabilities Education Act

(IDEA) and IDEIA (Public Law 108-446, 2004) federal guidelines. Similar to circumstances for children with depressive disorders, children with anxiety may be served under the disability category of Emotional Disturbance (ED), which is defined as a pervasive condition that adversely affects educational performance. Characteristics of ED particularly relevant to children with anxiety disorders are (a) the tendency to develop physical symptoms or fears associated with personal or school problems and (b) inability to maintain satisfactory interpersonal relationships with peers and teachers (House, 1999). When formal diagnosis of an anxiety disorder is rendered, the clinician should include information about possible eligibility for special education services with respect to symptoms of anxiety.

Assessment Methods and Procedures

A variety of self-report instruments exist to measure anxiety symptoms in children and adolescents (Table 7.3). Self-reports can be of significant value in assisting in the diagnosis of anxiety disorders

Table 7.3   **Description of Selected Self-Report Scales of Anxiety for Children and Adolescents**

	Proposed Clinical Uses	Ages (Years)	Number of Items	Subscales/Factors
BAI-Y	Identify ANX symptoms	7–14	20	Part of BYI, which includes measures of Depression, Anger, Disruptive Behavior, and Self-concept
MASC	Assess ANX symptoms	8–19	39	Physical Symptoms, Harm Avoidance, Social Anxiety, Separation/Panic, Total Anxiety, Inconsistency Index, Anxiety Disorders Index
RCMAS	Assess trait ANX	6–19	37	Physiological Anxiety, Worry/Oversensitivity, Social Concerns/Concentration, Lie Scale, Total Anxiety

Notes: ANX = Anxiety; BAI-Y = Beck Anxiety Inventory for Youth; BYI = Beck Youth Inventories of Emotional and Social Impairment; MASC = Multidimensional Anxiety Scale for Children; RCMAS = Reynolds Children's Manifest Anxiety Scale.

due to the subjective nature of some of the symptoms of anxiety. A smaller number of third-party ratings exist for detecting anxiety symptomatology, including caregiver-, teacher-, and clinician-rated scales. Finally, several diagnostic interviews exist that feature diagnostic algorithms tied to the *DSM-IV-TR* classification system.

Self-Report Instruments

Numerous self-report instruments are available for the assessment of anxiety disorders. A selected review of these instruments is offered in the next section.

Beck Anxiety Inventory for Youth: The Beck Youth Inventories of Emotional and Social Impairment (BYI) were introduced in the previous chapter on depressive disorders; therefore, the present discussion focuses on the Beck Anxiety Inventory for Youth (BAI-Y; J. S. Beck et al., 2001), a 20-item subscale focused on the assessment of symptoms of anxiety. Consistent with a multidimensional theory of anxiety, test authors explain that the BAI-Y was designed to assess (a) cognitive and emotional aspects of anxiety (e.g., scary thoughts, worry); (b) somatic symptoms of anxiety (e.g., shaky hands, heart pounding); (c) social components of anxiety (e.g., worry about teasing from others); and (d) specific fears (e.g., worry about school). Respondents are asked to indicate how well the items describe them over the past 2 weeks using a 4-item scale (0 = Never to 3 = Always).

The BAI-Y are designed for use with children ages 7 to 14 and were normed with a stratified standardization sample of 800 children representing 1999 U.S. Census data. Internal consistency reliability for the BAI-Y is generally adequate, with Cronbach α coefficients ranging from .89 to .91 for the standardization sample. Temporal stability, as measured by corrected reliability coefficients, ranged from .77 to .93 for a 1-week test-retest interval (J. S. Beck et al., 2001).

When all 100 BYI items (i.e., five scales with 20 items each) have been subjected to factor analysis, all 20 BAI-Y items load on the first unrotated factor, along with all of the items measuring depression and anger (J. S. Beck et al., 2001; Steer, Kumar, Beck, & Beck, 2005). Therefore, it is not clear if the BYI scales are measuring specific aspects of child psychopathology or if the bulk of the scales are measuring general affective distress (Bose-Deakins & Floyd, 2004). When the BAI-Y has been subjected to factor analysis apart from the remaining BYI scales, the scale yields a single factor (Steer et al., 2005). Test authors provide some evidence of convergent validity for the BAI-Y, as evidenced by a positive and significant relationship with the RCMAS Total Anxiety score ($r = .70$); however, both the BYI Depression and Anger scales also correlated strongly with the RCMAS Total (both $rs = .60$; J. S. Beck et al., 2001). For 12 children diagnosed with anxiety disorders, the BAI-Y did not yield clinically significant scores ($M = 50.44$; $SD = 6.54$), which suggests problems with the BAI-Y in detecting clinically significant symptoms of anxiety. Similar findings resulted in an outpatient clinic sample of 56 children diagnosed with anxiety disorders ($M = 50.02$; $SD = 8.60$; Steer et al., 2005).

Multidimensional Anxiety Scale for Children: The Multidimensional Anxiety Scale for Children (MASC; March, 1997) consists of 39 items designed to measure a wide range of anxiety symptoms in children and adolescents between the ages of 8 and 19. Respondents use a 4-point Likert scale (e.g., 0 = Never True about Me to 3 = Always True about Me) to rate each MASC item. The MASC yields a Total Anxiety score (39 items) and four factor scores: Physical Symptoms (12 items; e.g., feeling dizzy), Harm Avoidance (9 items; e.g., always obey), Social Anxiety (9 items; e.g., shy around others), and Separation/Panic (9 items; fear of being alone). The MASC also features an Inconsistency Index, an Anxiety Disorder Index, and a 10-item short form, the MASC-10 (March, 1997).

The MASC was normed on a sample of 2,698 children and adolescents (1,261 males, 1,437 females); however, the MASC does not adequately represent the Hispanic/Latino population in the United States according to recent census data (Caruso, 2001). Internal consistency reliability appears to be adequate for the Total Anxiety scale (Cronbach $\alpha = .90$) and factor scores (Cronbach $\alpha = .74$ to $.85$; March, Parker, Sullivan, Stallings, & Conners, 1997). Storch et al. (2005) reported good internal consistency reliability in a sample of 82 children diagnosed with Obsessive-Compulsive Disorder (Cronbach $\alpha = .92$ for the MASC Total score). Temporal stability reliability has been documented in two samples: a group of 142 students from a community sample (March, Sullivan, & Parker, 1999) and 24 children from a clinic sample (March et al., 1997). Total Anxiety score intraclass correlation coefficients (ICC) were .78 or higher for the clinic sample at two different test-retest intervals, while the Total Anxiety score ICC was .88 for the community sample. Temporal stability is lower for the MASC factor and subscale scores (ICCs range from .34 [Harm Avoidance in clinic sample] to .93 [Separation Anxiety in clinic sample]).

Test authors have provided a variety of validity evidence to support the use of the MASC. The MASC has shown an invariant factor structure across male and female samples and across age groups (March et al., 1997). The MASC has demonstrated convergent validity as evidenced by significant correlations between MASC Total Anxiety scores and RCMAS Total Anxiety scores ($r =$ .63; March et al., 1997). The MASC has also demonstrated divergent validity as evidenced by small to modest correlations ($rs = -.32$ to .34) between MASC scores and a self-report measure of depression.

Revised Children's Manifest Anxiety Scale: The RCMAS (C. R. Reynolds & Richmond, 2000) consists of 37 items designed to assess trait-based anxiety in children and adolescents ages 6 to 19. The RCMAS yields a Total Anxiety score (28 items) as well as four subscale scores to provide additional understanding of children's endorsement of anxiety symptoms. Children respond to items in yes/no format, and items are summed if endorsed in the problem direction. The RCMAS subscales are Physiological Anxiety (10 items; e.g., trouble catching breath), Worry/Oversensitivity (11 items; e.g., worry about future), Social Concerns/Concentration (7 items; e.g., hard to focus on schoolwork), and a Lie scale (9 items; e.g., always tell the truth; C. R. Reynolds & Richmond, 2000).

The RCMAS was normed with a sample of 4,972 children and adolescents from 13 states representing all geographic regions of the United States. Internal consistency reliability is generally acceptable (Cronbach's $\alpha > .79$) for the Total Anxiety score across all age groups, with the notable exception of Black females below the age of 12. For these subgroups, Cronbach α values ranged from .42 (6-

year-olds) to .76 (7-year-olds), and were significantly lower when compared to White female students at ages 6, 8, 10, and 11. Test authors caution the use of the scale with Black female students, suggesting special care in interpreting RCMAS test scores with these individuals. For the standardization sample, internal consistency reliability for the RCMAS clinical subscales ranges from .50s to .70s (α coefficients), with the Worry/Oversensitivity subscale demonstrating somewhat better reliability than the other clinical scales (C. R. Reynolds & Richmond, 2000). Internal consistency reliability for the Lie subscale was .77 for the entire standardization sample, with acceptable reliability for respondents ages 8 and older (C. R. Reynolds & Richmond, 2000). Test-retest reliability data are less available. Total Anxiety score temporal stability of .68 was found for a sample of elementary school students using a 9-month test-retest interval, and other studies have documented higher temporal stability using shorter intervals (Merrell, 2003).

Validity support for the RCMAS has come from factor analytic findings that generally support the presence of a general anxiety factor, three subordinate factors (i.e., Physiological Anxiety, Worry/Oversensitivity, Social Concerns/Concentration), and a Lie scale (C. R. Reynolds & Richmond, 2000). The RCMAS has shown concurrent and divergent validity as evidenced by a strong relationship with the State-Trait Anxiety Inventory for Children (STAIC) Trait scale ($rs = .65$ to .78) and minimal relationship with the STAIC State scale ($rs = -.10$ to .08). These findings support the interpretation of the RCMAS as a measure of stable, trait-based, and chronic anxiety.

In the context of the tripartite model, specific RCMAS items have been identified as potentially helpful in discriminating between anxiety and depression, particularly those from the Physiological Anxiety subscale. For example, RCMAS items 5 (trouble getting breath), 13 (sleeping problems), 17 (sick stomach), 19 (sweaty hands), and 21 (fatigue) have been identified as relevant to the measurement of physiological hyperarousal (PH) in the tripartite model (e.g., Joiner et al., 1996). Joiner et al. found that RCMAS items 5, 17, and 19 loaded on a PH factor as opposed to either positive or negative affect in a sample of 116 psychiatric inpatients diagnosed with a variety of depressive and anxiety disorders.

Third-Party Rating Instruments

Adult raters are popular for the assessment of numerous child disorders due to their practicality. They allow, for example, for the assessment of a large number of constructs in a relatively limited amount of clinician and informant time. This class of scales also provides an opportunity to compare the perceptions of different adults with those of children or adolescents themselves.

Behavior Assessment System for Children

The BASC was released in its revised form in 2004 with numerous improvements, additions, and options, including optionally derived content scales. The BASC-2 (C. R. Reynolds & Kamphaus, 2004) is a third-party rating scale of a range of behavioral difficulties in children and youth. With respect to symptoms associated with anxiety disorders, the BASC-2 features two clinical subscales of particular relevance, the Anxiety and Somatization scales (C. R. Reynolds & Kamphaus, 2004). For both the teacher and parent reports, the Anxiety subscale features items tapping cognitive/subjective and behavioral symptoms associated with anxiety, such as verbal reports of fearfulness (e.g., student says "I am afraid I will make a mistake") and symptoms of worry (e.g., students worries about what others think). The Somatization scale consists of items primarily tapping physiological features of anxiety, such as stomach aches, vomiting, shortness of breath, and verbal complaints of fears of becoming sick. Based on the multidimensional definition of anxiety proposed in this chapter, the BASC-2 seems to provide adequate coverage of the domains of anxiety.

Anxiety Subscale: When summarized across general and clinical normative samples, internal consistency coefficients (Cronbach's α) for the Anxiety subscale range from .75 to .87 for the Teacher Rating Scales (TRS). Similarly, Parent Rating Scales (PRS) internal consistency coefficients range from .77 to .87. The TRS temporal consistency coefficients range from .64 to .77 across samples for the Anxiety subscale. The PRS temporal consistency coefficients appear to be slightly stronger, as evidenced by a range from .73 to .84 for a general norm sample. Interrater reliability for the TRS form ranges from .23 (child form) to .52 (adolescent form), and interrater reliability for the PRS ranges from .57 (preschool form) to .80 (child form). The BASC-2 manual provides detailed evidence for the validity of the Anxiety subscale, as evidenced by its factor structure, relationships with similar measures of anxiety (e.g., ASEBA; Achenbach & Rescorla, 2001), and differences between general and clinical samples.

Somatization Subscale: Across general and clinical normative groups, internal consistency coefficients (Cronbach's α) for the TRS Somatization subscale range from .77 to .87, and PRS internal consistency coefficients range from .79 to .87. The TRS test-retest is .72 to .79, and the PRS test-retest is .65 to .84. Interrater reliability for the TRS is .19 (adolescent) to .74 (child); PRS interrater reliability is .53 (child) to .70 (preschool). Similar to the validity evidence presented for the Anxiety subscale, construct, concurrent, and criterion-related validity is also reported for the Somatization subscale.

Achenbach System of Empirically-Based Assessment

The venerable ASEBA provides an assessment of numerous constructs related to anxiety disorders.

Anxious/Depressed and Anxiety Disorders Scales: With respect to measurement of anxiety symptoms, the ASEBA (Achenbach & Rescorla, 2001) features a narrow-band empirically derived syndrome scale, Anxious/Depressed, for the Child Behavior Checklist (CBCL) and Teacher Report Form (TRF). Several items from the Anxious/Depressed scale are particularly relevant to the diagnosis of an anxiety disorder: nervous, fearful, worries, and dependent. The items included in the syndrome scale appear to be most relevant for assessment of cognitive/subjective and behavioral symptoms of anxiety. Due to the significant relationship that exists between symptoms of anxiety and those of depression across a range of empirical studies, it is not surprising that the ASEBA produced a syndrome scale that showed similar symptom overlap. The Anxious/Depressed scale shows adequate internal consistency reliability for the CBCL (Cronbach's $\alpha = .84$) and the TRF ($\alpha = .86$). The temporal stability of the Anxious/Depressed syndrome scale is also adequate, with r values of .82 for the CBCL (M test-retest interval = 8 days) and .89 for the TRF (M test-retest interval = 16 days).

To assist in diagnostic decision making, the ASEBA also features profile scores for several *DSM*-based diagnostic classes, including Anxiety Problems. The Anxiety Problems scale includes items tapping fearfulness of school, worry, and nervousness, among others, and yields a *T*-score (Achenbach & Rescorla, 2001). The items were selected by 22 child psychiatrists and psychologists with expertise in assessment of children's behavioral and emotional functioning. Test authors report slightly lower reliability coefficients for the Anxiety Problems scale when compared to the Anxious/Depressed syndrome scale. For the CBCL, Cronbach's $\alpha = .72$ and temporal stability = .80; for the TRF, $\alpha = .73$ and temporal stability = .73 (Achenbach & Rescorla, 2001). Validity data are presented for both the Anxiety/Depressed and Anxiety Problem scales in the ASEBA manuals. For example, both scales show adequate convergent validity with similar scales, such as the BASC Anxiety scale.

Somatic Complaints and Somatic Problems Subscales: Two additional ASEBA scales exist to measure physiological symptoms associated with anxiety: Somatic Complaints, an empirically based scale, and Somatic Problems, a *DSM*-oriented problem scale. The Somatic Complaints scale consists of 10 items, including dizziness, aches, headaches, nausea, and stomach aches. The expert-rated Somatic Problems scale features 8 of these items; therefore, reliability and validity data are almost identical for each scale. Internal consistency reliability ranges from .72 to .80 for the somatic scales across both parent and teacher rating forms. Temporal stability reliability coefficients range from .73 to .92. Validity evidence is also presented for the Somatic Complaints and Somatic Problems scales, such as convergent validity with the BASC Somatization scale.

Children's Yale-Brown Obsessive Compulsive Scale

The Children's Yale-Brown Obsessive Compulsive Scale (CY-BOCS) is a clinician-rated measure designed to assess obsessive-compulsive symptom severity in children and adolescents with a diagnosis of Obsessive-Compulsive Disorder (Scahill et al., 1997). The CY-BOCS typically involves interviewing child and parent together and relies on the clinician to integrate information gathered during the interview to yield information about the severity of symptoms. The CY-BOCS features checklists to indicate the presence of different types of obsessions (e.g., contamination) and compulsions (e.g., washing rituals). Severity for both obsessions and compulsions are rated by the clinician in five areas: (1) time occupied with symptoms, (2) interference from symptoms, (3) distress from symptoms, (4) resistance against symptoms, and (5) control over symptoms (Scahill et al., 1997). Severity ratings use a 0- to 4-point scale for each item, and severity ratings yield an Obsessions Severity score (range = 0 to 20), Compulsions Severity score (range = 0 to 20), and a CY-BOCS Total score (range = 0 to 40).

The CY-BOCS has shown adequate internal consistency reliability in samples of children diagnosed with Obsessive-Compulsive Disorder (Cronbach's α = .87 to .90 for the CY-BOCS Total score; Scahill et al., 1997; Storch et al., 2004). Both Obsessions Severity and Compulsions Severity subscales showed good internal consistency, as evidenced by strong mean item-subscale correlations and Cronbach's α = .80 and .82 for the Obsession and Compulsion Severity scores (Storch et al., 2004). Scahill et al. report good to excellent interrater reliability for the CY-BOCS, with ICC coefficients of .66 for the Compulsions Severity score, .91 for the Obsession Severity score, and .84 for the CY-BOCS Total. In contrast, item-by-item agreements ranged from poor to fair (α values ranged from .11 to .42). Temporal stability for the CY-BOCS has been reported to be good, with ICC values of .70, .76, and .79 for the Obsession,

Compulsion, and Total scores, respectively, over an average 41-day test-retest interval (Storch et al., 2004). The CY-BOCS has reliably shown a two-factor structure; however, it is not clear if items load on Obsessive and Compulsive factors or Severity and Impairment factors (Storch et al., 2005).

Structured and Semistructured Interviews

Anxiety Disorders Interview Schedule for DSM-IV: Child and Parent Versions: The Anxiety Disorders Interview Schedule for *DSM-IV:* Child and Parent Versions (ADIS:C/P; Silverman & Albano, 1996) consists of two semistructured interviews, the Child Interview Schedule and the Parent Interview Schedule, that are appropriate for use with children and adolescents between the ages of 6 and 18. The ADIS:C/P is organized to correspond directly to the anxiety disorder criteria sets delineated in the *DSM-IV* criteria (e.g., "Do you have bad dreams about being away from your parents?" for SAD). Child and parent responses are scored yes/no by the interviewer to indicate the presence or absence of symptoms; the number of symptoms are summed to yield a decision about the presence of anxiety disorders. The ADIS:C/P includes severity ratings whereby child and parent respondents rate anxiety interference and impairment on a 9-point scale that ranges from 0 (None) to 8 (Very severely disturbing/Disabling). For formal diagnosis on either form, the overall interference rating must equal or exceed 4 (Definitely Disturbing/Disabling). If child and parent results are discrepant for diagnosis (e.g., child interview yields diagnosis but parent interview does not), the presence of disorder from either respondent warrants formal diagnosis.

For both parent and child interviews, the interviewer uses a "Feeling Thermometer," a visual analogue scale that ranges from 0 to 8 to measure the degree of interference associated with different anxiety disorders. The ADIS:C/P also includes sections relevant for diagnosing depressive disorders, ADHD, and substance abuse disorders, as well as screening items for other disorders, such as eating disorders and Schizophrenia (Silverman & Albano, 1996).

In a clinic sample of 62 children (*M* age = 10.15 years), the ADIS:C/P has shown adequate short-term test-retest reliability (*M* test-retest interval = 11.7 days; Silverman, Saavedra, & Pina, 2001). Reliability of diagnosis was good to excellent for SAD, SP, Specific Phobia, and GAD for diagnoses using child-only, parent-only, and both child and parent information in rendering diagnostic decisions. The ADIS:C/P is also frequently used as an outcome for children and adolescents enrolled in anxiety treatment studies (Silverman & Ollendick, 2005).

Child and Adolescent Psychiatric Assessment: The Child and Adolescent Psychiatric Assessment (CAPA; Angold & Costello, 2000) is a structured diagnostic interview that has been developed for use with children and adolescents between the ages of 9 and 17. In addition to assessing for the presence of anxiety disorders, the CAPA also evaluates the presence of a range of disorders, such as disruptive behavior disorders and depressive disorders, both of which are frequently associated with anxiety. The CAPA has shown promising psychometric properties for diagnosing anxiety disorders. For example, test-retest reliabilities for GAD ($\alpha = .79$) and Overanxious Disorder ($\alpha = .74$) were excellent for a sample of 77 clinically referred children between the ages of 10 and 16 (Angold & Costello, 2000). The CAPA requires roughly 1 hour of interview time to complete with a child and requires training prior to using the instrument.

CASE STUDY

Identifying information, such as child and family name, has been removed or altered to protect confidentiality. A short interpretive description follows the report.

REFERRAL QUESTION AND BACKGROUND

Joshua was referred for psychological evaluation due to concerns with inattention, reading and writing achievement, and anxiety. Specifically, Joseph and Kelly Smith, Joshua's biological parents, reported that Joshua has difficulty sustaining attention during classroom instruction. Mr. and Mrs. Smith were also concerned with Joshua's variable reading comprehension and writing skills, especially while at school. Finally, Joshua's parents reported concerns regarding anxiety in eating, toileting, and separation from parents. Joshua's teacher, Mrs. Teach, reported that Joshua has difficulty staying focused in class and is often fidgety during instruction. Mrs. Teach also reported that Joshua seemed anxious throughout the day.

Joshua is an 8-year, 3-month-old second-grader at Pleasant Elementary School who currently lives with his biological mother and father. Mrs. Smith reported that Joshua is the product of a planned, uncomplicated pregnancy and met developmental milestones on time. Family history is significant for ADHD in a paternal uncle.

Mr. and Mrs. Smith reported some concerns about Joshua's eating habits, which began about 1 year ago. Joshua eats food prepared only by his mother and grandmother and *must* wash his hands immediately before touching any food. Joshua's routine for washing his hands includes scrubbing his hands with soap and holding his hands in front of him to allow them to air dry. He refuses to use any dryer device on his hands. When using a public bathroom, he will wait in the bathroom until someone else opens the door, so that he will not have to touch the door. If Joshua is unable to wash his hands, he will not eat the part of the food that his hands touched or he will use a food wrapper to hold the food. Mr. and Mrs. Smith report that this is an inconvenience when eating at restaurants and at home. In addition, Joshua will not eat or drink while visiting friends.

Mr. and Mrs. Smith also reported concerns about Joshua's sleeping. Joshua sleeps with his parents about 4 nights per week. He sometimes begins the night in his own bed, but will wake up after sleeping for 3 to 4 hours and will visit his parents' room. At this time, Joshua's mother usually takes him back to his room and sleeps in Joshua's room for the rest of the night. When asked, Joshua reported that he was often worried at night about someone breaking into his house and kidnapping him. He reported that he sometimes has problems catching his breath when he is worried at night. Overall, Joshua's ability to sleep alone is of concern to his family and disrupts family functioning.

Joshua's toileting habits are also of concern to Mr. and Mrs. Smith. Reportedly, Joshua prefers not to urinate or to defecate while at school. If he wakes up late for school and does not have the opportunity to use the bathroom before going to school, he will refuse to use the bathroom at school, instead waiting until he gets home.

Mr. and Mrs. Smith and Joshua report difficulties when Joshua is away from his parents. Joshua becomes quiet and agitated when he knows he will be separated from his parents. In addition, if Joshua is alone in a room in his house, he becomes extremely anxious and calls for his parents.

BEHAVIORAL OBSERVATIONS

Joshua required reassurance when separating from his parents and requested several breaks to check on the whereabouts of his mother and father. Otherwise, he was attentive and cooperative during testing. His hands were observed to be red and dry, which his parents attributed to excessive hand washing. Overall, test results are viewed as valid estimates of Joshua's cognitive abilities, academic achievement, and social-emotional functioning.

INTELLECTUAL FUNCTIONING

Joshua completed the Wechsler Intelligence Scale for Children—Fourth Edition as a measure of his overall intelligence. The Verbal Comprehension, Perceptual Reasoning, Working Memory, and Processing Speed Index scores combined to yield a Full-Scale IQ of 90 (25th percentile, Average). Joshua showed equally developed verbal and nonverbal reasoning abilities, and his overall Full-Scale IQ appears to be a valid reflection of his current cognitive functioning.

ACADEMIC ACHIEVEMENT

Joshua completed several measures of achievement, including the Woodcock-Johnson III Tests of Achievement; the Gray Oral Reading Tests—Fourth Edition; and the Test of Written Language—Third Edition. Overall, Joshua's academic achievement scores are age-appropriate with a Total Achievement score of 97 (42nd percentile, Average). Joshua showed age-appropriate reading comprehension skills during both silent and oral reading tasks. He also demonstrated adequate writing skills during contrived sentence writing and during spontaneous prose writing. His skills in the area of mathematics are also age-appropriate (Table 7.4).

BEHAVIORAL/SOCIAL-EMOTIONAL FUNCTIONING

Joshua's social and emotional functioning was assessed through parent, teacher, and self-report measures. In addition, examiners observed Joshua in the clinic setting and completed a child interview. The results across these sources yielded the following picture of Joshua's social and emotional functioning.

Two areas of concern emerged during the evaluation: (1) Joshua's considerable anxiety within the home and (2) his fear of germs. Joshua is unable to be alone in a room in the house, and he has difficulty falling sleep and staying asleep without a parent present. He reported fears about being contaminated by germs and will not eat food prepared by anyone other than his mother or grandmother. He feels that he *must* wash his hands immediately before eating anything.

Joshua's fears of being separated from his parents and of contamination from exposure to germs are associated with ruminating thoughts, worry, compulsive hand washing behaviors, avoidant behaviors, and physiological symptoms of anxiety. Joshua often worries about his parents' safety when away from them, and he is often quiet and sullen in anticipation of being separated from them. He must wash his hands before eating food, or he refuses to eat food that he touches. Joshua also worries about toileting while away from home and avoids public toilets due to concerns about being exposed to germs. He reported shortness of breath and difficulty falling asleep when he is worried.

SUMMARY

Joshua, an 8-year-old Caucasian male, was referred for psychoeducational evaluation of his current academic, behavioral, and emotional functioning. Joshua's parents raised specific concerns in the areas of inattention, academic achievement, and anxiety. They have

Table 7.4 **Psychometric Summary for Joshua**

WECHSLER INTELLIGENCE SCALE FOR CHILDREN— FOURTH EDITION (WISC-IV)

Scale/Index	Standard Score	Percentile
Verbal Comprehension	91	27
Perceptual Reasoning	96	39
Working Memory	94	35
Processing Speed	91	27
Full-Scale IQ	90	25

WOODCOCK-JOHNSON III TESTS OF ACHIEVEMENT (WJ III ACH)

Composite	Standard Score	Percentile
Broad Reading Composite	92	29
Broad Mathematics Composite	112	79
Broad Written Language	97	42
Total Achievement	97	42

GRAY ORAL READING TESTS—FOURTH EDITION (GORT-4)

Scale/Composite	Scaled/ Standard Score	Percentile
Fluency	8	25
Comprehension	9	37
Oral Reading Quotient	90	25

TEST OF WRITTEN LANGUAGE—THIRD EDITION (TOWL-3)

Scale/Composite	Scaled/ Standard Score	Percentile
Contextual Conventions	9	37
Contextual Language	9	37
Story Construction	11	63
Spontaneous Writing Composite	98	45

(continued)

Table 7.4   *Continued*

ACHENBACH CHILD BEHAVIOR CHECKLIST AND TEACHER REPORT FORM

Scale/Composite	T-Scores		
	Mother	Father	Teacher
Anxious/Depressed	68	65	63
Withdrawn/Depressed	54	54	50
Somatic Complaints	50	50	52
Social Problems	53	58	59
Thought Problems	61	67	72
Attention Problems	60	66	64
Rule-Breaking Behavior	57	57	58
Aggressive Behavior	57	53	52
Internalizing Composite	57	55	56
Externalizing Composite	58	54	60
Total Composite Score	58	58	64

BEHAVIOR ASSESSMENT SYSTEM FOR CHILDREN—PARENT RATING SCALES AND TEACHER RATING SCALES

Scale/Composite	T-Scores		
	Mother	Father	Teacher
Hyperactivity	44	52	63
Aggression	42	44	59
Conduct Problems	45	49	59
Anxiety	65	63	65
Depression	41	39	56
Somatization	41	41	46
Atypicality	38	55	64
Withdrawal	57	57	51
Attention Problems	60	61	63
Learning Problems	—	—	67
Externalizing Problems	43	48	62
Internalizing Problems	49	47	59
Behavior Symptoms Index	43	51	63
Adaptability	50	55	22
Social Skills	30	48	34
Leadership	35	43	33
Adaptive Skills Composite	37	48	29

Table 7.4   *Continued*

BEHAVIOR ASSESSMENT SYSTEM FOR CHILDREN—SELF-REPORT OF PERSONALITY (BASC-SRP)

Scale/Composite	T-Score
Attitude toward School	46
Attitude toward Teachers	53
Atypicality	66
Locus of Control	50
Social Stress	48
Anxiety	67
Depression	43
Sense of Inadequacy	47
Relationship with Parents	57
Interpersonal Relationships	53
Self-Esteem	57
Self-Reliance	58
School Maladjustment Composite	49
Clinical Maladjustment Composite	56
Emotional Symptoms Index	47
Personal Adjustment Composite	58

REVISED CHILDREN'S MANIFEST ANXIETY SCALE (RCMAS)

	Scaled Scores	T-Score	Percentiles
Physiological Anxiety	12		78
Worry/Oversensitivity	11		70
Social Concerns/Concentration	12		84
Lie	11		68
Total Anxiety Score		60	85

expressed concerns about Joshua's high level of anxiety related to food, toileting, and separation from parents. Joshua is functioning in the Average range of overall cognitive functioning, with equally developed verbal and nonverbal reasoning abilities. His academic attainment is also age-appropriate across all domains. He is performing on grade level in reading comprehension, written expression, and basic reading skills. His mathematics skills appear to be an area of relative strength. Joshua is excessively concerned about being away from his parents and being contaminated with germs. These concerns are associated with chronic feelings of worry and anxiety and are accompanied by behavioral avoidance and physical symptoms of anxiety, such as shortness of breath.

DIAGNOSTIC IMPRESSIONS

Joshua worries about germ contamination and engages in repetitive hand washing and rigid food handling behaviors and avoids public restrooms in response to his worries. His behaviors are disruptive to his family's functioning and disrupt his ability to interact with his friends and classmates on fields trips and during class activities involving eating meals and using public restrooms. Based on these reported symptoms, Joshua meets criteria for a formal diagnosis of Obsessive-Compulsive Disorder (*DSM-IV-TR* 300.3).

Joshua also reports significant symptoms of anxiety related to being separated from his parents. When he anticipates separation from his parents, he becomes withdrawn and quiet. In addition, he reported that he is worried that he might be taken from his home by an intruder. He displays a great deal of anxiety when he is left alone in a room in his house and will seek out a family member to sit in the room with him. Parents reported that the worries and behaviors have occurred for the past year and have caused significant distress to his family and to his ability to function socially. Based on these reported and observed symptoms, Joshua meets criteria for a diagnosis of Separation Anxiety Disorder (*DSM-IV-TR* 309.21).

RECOMMENDATIONS

1. Joshua would benefit from individual, cognitive-behavioral therapy (CBT) for treatment of his anxiety. In our opinion, CBT should consist of the following: (a) psychoeducational materials about anxiety, (b) guided exposure and response prevention, (c) relaxation exercises, (d) homework and practice outside of the therapy situation, and (e) parent coaching. We recommend

the manualized CBT treatment approach developed by Dr. John March and Karen Mulle (1998) for treatment of Joshua's OCD symptoms.

2. School professionals should consider Joshua eligible for special education services under the category of Emotional Disturbance. His contamination fears and anxieties about being separated from his parents are likely impacting his performance throughout the school day. For example, Joshua's preoccupying thoughts about exposure to germs and separation from his parents as well as his reticence to use the restrooms at school may yield inattention and fidgety behaviors observed during classroom instruction.

3. Joshua would benefit from contact with a mental health professional in the school setting, perhaps a school counselor or school psychologist, who could implement the therapy described here or support the efforts of an outpatient psychotherapist.

4. Mr. and Mrs. Smith should consult with a child psychiatrist to determine if Joshua is a good candidate for a trial of medication to treat symptoms of anxiety. We recommend implementation of CBT therapy initially; however, if Joshua does not respond to this treatment approach, additional consultation with a child psychiatrist is warranted.

Discussion of Case Study

Joshua's evaluation illustrates many of the concepts and assessment methods relevant to the assessment of anxiety symptoms in children. Joshua was referred due to concerns with inattention, academic functioning, and anxiety, which guided our selection of assessment instruments. Due to concerns about reading and written expression and the possibility of a learning disorder, we included measures of intellectual ability and academic achievement. In our opinion, the concerns about reading and writing warranted including additional measures of functioning in these areas. During formal cognitive and academic testing, Joshua showed age-appropriate intellectual functioning and academic attainment; therefore, we ruled out the presence of a specific learning disability in either reading or writing.

The parents' and teacher's concerns about inattention and activity level in the classroom raised diagnostic possibilities about the presence of an attention-deficit disorder, which we addressed in the battery with multiple measures of attentional functioning and hyperactivity. In addition to the third-party rating instruments, we also interviewed the parents and teacher regarding specific symptoms of ADHD. The results of these ratings and interviews revealed some elevation in the area of inattention, but little symptomatology associated with overactivity. We considered the difficulties with concentration to be symptomatic of Joshua's anxiety problems.

Interestingly, the parents' and teacher's concerns about Joshua's anxieties were identified almost as an aside in the initial intake interview. Once we began interviewing the parents and teacher, however, it became clear that Joshua was experiencing significant distress associated with contamination fears and separation from his parents. Although we did not use the ADIS:C/P during our parent or child interview, we systematically inquired about anxiety symptoms from each of the *DSM*-defined anxiety disorders. Our clinical interview resulted in Joshua's meeting formal diagnostic criteria for OCD and SAD. Joshua meets criteria for OCD due to the presence of compulsions, specifically repetitive hand washing that was applied rigidly around eating behaviors. Joshua's hand washing behavior was associated with the prevention of contamination from germs. His fear of germ contamination was associated with avoidance of public bathrooms, which caused significant distress during school. During our interview with Joshua, there was no recognition that the compulsive hand washing was unreasonable, which is a diagnostic allowance for OCD diagnosis in children.

We also rendered an additional diagnosis of SAD due to Joshua's excessive anxiety centered on separation from his parents, both outside and in the home. Parents reported that Joshua worried persistently about being separated from them due to kidnapping. He was also excessively fearful in his home and sought out his parents if he found himself alone in a room. He also refused to sleep alone, and if he woke during the nighttime without a parent, required the presence of a parent in order to sleep. Children's anxiety at bedtime that requires a parent to be present to reduce fear has been identified as a "cardinal symptom of separation anxiety" (Foa et al., 2005, p. 199). The anxiety had lasted for over 1 year according to Joshua's parents and had caused significant distress for Joshua and disrupted family functioning.

In response to the anxiety diagnoses, we recommended cognitive-behavior therapy (CBT), which has received empirical support as a therapy for OCD with children. In our recommendations, we outlined several of the active ingredients delineated in the March and Mulle (1998) treatment protocol for OCD in children, such as psychoeducation regarding the nature of anxiety and specific symptoms of OCD, cognitive training, relaxation training, graded exposure and response prevention, and involvement of parents. During the feedback session with Joshua's parents, we recommended March and Mulle's treatment manual as a resource guide and provided the parents with several cognitive-behaviorally oriented therapists in their community. We focused our recommendations on treating the OCD symptomatology first, as this seemed to be creating more distress for Joshua in the school setting.

As part of our report, we recommended that Joshua be considered eligible for special education services under the category of Emotional Disturbance due to the negative impact his anxiety symptoms seemed to have on his school performance. In the school setting, his teacher identified repetitive behaviors, difficulty concentrating, and problems with completing work assignments as difficulties for Joshua. In our opinion, Joshua's academic difficulties seemed to be associated with his anxiety, if not explained altogether by its presence. In our recommendations, we also identified the potential role of a school-based therapist, a school counselor or school psychologist, who might be employed as a contact person in the school setting to support Joshua's therapy. Of course, including multiple therapists in a child's treatment requires careful coordination and ongoing communication. Finally, we recommended consultation with a child psychiatrist regarding the possibility of a trial of psychotropic medication.

Conclusion

Anxiety is a normal aspect of human experience and has likely served an adaptive function for human beings. Fears and anxieties are also part of child and adolescent development; therefore, some degree of anxiety is to be expected in youth. Current definitions of anxiety are multidimensional and include cognitive/subjective, behavioral, and physiological constructs. Anxiety that is chronic and excessive and disrupts adaptive functioning may warrant diagnosis of a formal anxiety disorder.

The current psychiatric classification system identifies multiple anxiety disorders for children, with the most common being GAD, SAD, and SP. Anxiety disorders appear to be more common in females than males and are frequently comorbid with one another, as well as with depressive disorders, ADHD, and disruptive behavior disorders. Children and youth with anxiety disorders may be eligible for special education services under the category of Emotional Disturbance, but only if there is a reasonably clear link between symptoms of anxiety and educational performance.

A fairly large number of self-report instruments have been created specifically to measure anxiety symptoms in children and adolescents. Self-report instruments such as the RCMAS and MASC can assist in the detection and diagnosis of anxiety. Several broadband rating scales of children's behavioral adjustment include measures of anxiety and appear to provide reasonable coverage of the cognitive, behavioral, and physiological components of anxiety. Formal diagnostic interviews also exist for use with children and parents, such as the ADIS:C/P and CAPA, as well as specialized measures to detect and monitor anxiety symptoms, such as the CY-BOCS.

Traumatic Brain Injury

Juliana S. Bloom, Morris J. Cohen, and Jonathan M. Campbell

8

Chapter

Traumatic brain injury (TBI) is defined as acquired brain damage due to "an external physical force of sufficient magnitude to produce structural or physiological changes to nerve tissue and cause transient to permanent changes in behavior" (Rotto, 1998, p. 653). In the larger group of causes of acquired brain damage, TBIs are differentiated from nontraumatic brain injuries, which are conditions that result in brain damage that are not due to external physical force, such as brain tumors, infections, vascular accidents, and poisoning. Therefore, the essential difference between TBI and non-TBI is the presence versus absence of an external force impacting the skull and brain. Common etiologies of TBI include motor vehicle accidents, falls, gunshot wounds, and sports-related injuries (Arffa, 1998; Youse, Le, Cannizzaro, & Coelho, 2002). In addition, the incidence of TBI in infants has been increasing due to "shaken baby syndrome" (Hymel, 2002). Traumatic brain injury is the leading cause of death and disability in individuals under the age of 35 in the United States (Rotto, 1998; Semrud-Clikeman, 2001). More than 90% of these children and adolescents survive their injuries, but they, their families, and their communities bear the cognitive, emotional, and financial consequences (Rotto,

245

1998). The financial consequences can be significant; the average inpatient rehabilitation cost is $42,000 for a 32-day stay, and the cost for acute care is $98,000 for a 22-day stay (Youse et al., 2002). Over $48 billion is spent on the treatment and rehabilitation of individuals who have sustained TBI each year in the United States (Youse et al., 2002).

Constructs of Interest

Prior to considering the constructs related to TBI assessment, it is necessary to discuss the various types of injuries and issues, such as recovery of function and other phenomena, that warrant varied approaches to assessment.

Categories of Traumatic Brain Injury

In the group of TBIs, head injuries are defined as *open* or *closed*, depending on whether the meninges (i.e., three membranes consisting of connective tissue that enclose and protect the central nervous system) remain intact (Youse et al., 2002). In an open head injury, the brain injury is a result of a force that penetrates the skull and meninges (Youse et al., 2002), often a gunshot wound (Ewing-Cobbs & Bloom, 1999; Rotto, 1998). Damage as a result of an open head injury is usually restricted to the area of penetration, although diffuse injury due to shattered pieces of bone or bullets sometimes occurs (Ewing-Cobbs & Bloom, 1999). Open head injury tends to result in more specific cognitive or behavioral changes, depending on the location of the injury (Rotto, 1998). Closed head injuries, by contrast, result from a blow to the head that does not penetrate the meninges. Closed head injuries are more common than open head injuries and tend to result in global changes in emotions, cognitions, and behavior. Traumatic brain injurys have also been categorized into contact and noncontact injuries, with noncontact injuries arising when the brain accelerates and decelerates within the skull without contact by an external physical force (Ewing-Cobbs & Bloom, 2004).

Types of Traumatic Brain Injury

Insult from TBI occurs in two stages: primary injury and secondary injury (Arffa, 1998). Primary injuries result in damage of tissue and bleeding that is directly due to the impact, whereas secondary injuries are due to complications from the initial injury that result in further damage and also affect recovery (Rotto, 1998; Semrud-Clikeman, 2001).

Primary Injuries: Rotto (1998) identified three general types of primary injuries that result from closed head injuries: (1) skull fractures, (2) concussions, and (3) contusions. A skull fracture is a crack in the skull that can cause brain tissue damage, if depressed. A concussion is an injury that occurs when a force causes the brain to bounce around the inside of the skull, causing temporary loss of consciousness and a headache. A contusion arises if the injury causes bruising and bleeding of the brain vasculature. Extremely damaging contusions can form a clot of blood called an intracerebral hemorrhage (Arffa, 1998). Despite the fact that brain tissue is not penetrated during a closed head injury, primary injuries from closed head injuries can be quite severe.

In closed head injuries, the force of the injury causes the brain, which is suspended inside the skull in cerebrospinal fluid, to repeatedly bounce off the skull, damaging tissue with each impact (Rotto, 1998). Thus, damage to the brain occurs at the point of impact of the head on an object and at the brain area opposite the original point of impact (Semrud-Clikeman, 2001). The original blow is called the *coup,* and the rebounding impact is called the *contrecoup* (Semrud-Clikeman, 2001). Among other areas in the brain, brain damage frequently occurs at both the coup and contrecoup impact points.

Furthermore, during the impact of the brain against the inner surface of the skull, rough bones at the front of the skull preferentially damage the frontal and temporal lobes of the brain (Arffa, 1998; Rotto, 1998). Unique features of the skull explain why a blow to even the back of the head rarely results in damage to the occipital lobe but frequently results in damage to the frontal and temporal lobes (Arffa, 1998). The presence of rough bones at the front of the skull also helps explain how damage to the frontal and temporal lobes can occur in the case of motor vehicle accidents where the head does not strike an external object, such as a windshield (i.e., noncontact TBI).

The rapid and twisting movements of the brain that occur during impact can also result in stretching, shearing, and tearing of delicate blood vessels and nerve fibers (Youse et al., 2002). Because this movement causes the stretching and tearing of long white matter tracts, the damage is referred to as diffuse axonal injury (Semrud-Clikeman, 2001; Youse et al., 2002). Damaged axons undergo a series of cellular changes that eventually cause cellular death, even in neurons not damaged by the initial injury (Arffa, 1998). Furthermore, axons can also be damaged by excessive glutamate and aspartate, amino acid neurotransmitters that are released after an injury and can alter cellular functions (i.e., excitotoxic neurotransmission; Arffa, 1998). Diffuse axonal injury is thought to be related to the duration of loss of consciousness, with severe damage leading to long-lasting comas (Semrud-Clikeman, 2001). Furthermore, young children may be more susceptible to diffuse axonal injury because the process of myelination, which is thought to serve as a protective factor against axonal injury, has not yet been completed (Arffa, 1998). The greater risk of injury to nonmyelinated axons suggests that areas that myelinate later in development, such as the frontal lobes, are more susceptible to diffuse axonal injury. Diffuse axonal damage appears to occur more frequently with closed head injuries when compared to open head injuries (Rotto, 1998).

Secondary Injuries: Secondary injuries of TBI occur as a result of the physiological processes that occur after injury (Arffa, 1998). Intracranial secondary injuries include edema, hemorrhage, hematoma, infarction (i.e., the death of brain tissue due to insufficient blood flow), hydrocephalus, and seizures (e.g., Rotto, 1998; Semrud-Clikeman, 2001). Edema (i.e., swelling of the brain) occurs when there is a buildup of cerebrospinal fluid and blood due to a breakdown of the blood-brain barrier (Arffa, 1998). A hemorrhage is an escape of blood from the vascular system into the tissues of the brain, where it can cause tissue death. Hemorrhages are typically caused by vessels that are broken due to the initial injury. A hematoma (i.e., clotting of a mass of blood) also occurs due to broken blood vessels. Epidural hematomas (i.e., bleeding between the skull and outermost brain covering) are more common in children than adults who have sustained a TBI; hematomas can expand rapidly, requiring surgery (Arffa, 1998). Hydrocephalus (i.e., an excess of cerebrospinal fluid due to a blockage of the ventricular system) can be caused by scarring of brain tissue due to injury, but is rare in individuals who have sustained a TBI. If hydrocephalus is present, the excess cerebrospinal fluid may then create pressure on the brain, causing damage (Arffa, 1998). Seizures occur in 3% to 5% of children who have sustained a TBI (Semrud-Clikeman, 2001) and are unique to children (Arffa, 1998). Five percent of patients with sustained open head injuries develop epilepsy following TBI (Arffa, 1998).

Secondary injuries may also result from physiological problems due to the initial injury; for example, anoxia (i.e., a lack of oxygen) or hypoxia (i.e., insufficient oxygen) can arise if cardiovascular damage occurs due to the accident. Hyperthermia (i.e., excessive fever), electrolyte disturbance, hyperventilation, and damage to the hypothalamus and/or pituitary gland, which could cause later hormonal problems, can also occur after a TBI (Rotto, 1998).

Incidence and Epidemiology

Accurate epidemiological data is difficult to obtain due to the numerous criteria used for classification and methodological weaknesses in epidemiological studies. Typically, an underestimate of the true incidence rate is the result (Rotto, 1998). The incidence rate for TBI ranges from 180 to 295 per 100, 000 individuals (Arffa, 1998), and the mortality rate is 10 per 100,000 (Rotto, 1998), making it the leading cause of death for children in the United States (see Table 8.1). Furthermore, 100,000 to 170,000 children are hospitalized each year due to TBI, and six times that number visit the emergency room (Arffa, 1998). Overall, over 1 million children sustain traumatic brain injuries each year in the United States (Rotto, 1998), 300,000 of whom suffer permanent disability as a result of

Table 8.1 **Epidemiology, Types, and Causes of Traumatic Brain Injury (TBI)**

EPIDEMIOLOGY

U.S. incidence: 180–295/100,000 in children and adolescents.

Roughly one million U.S. children affected per annum.

Boys more likely than girls to sustain a TBI (2 to 4:1 male-to-female ratio).

CAUSES OF TBI (LEADING CAUSES DIFFER ACCORDING TO AGE)

Physical abuse (e.g., shaken baby syndrome)—leading cause of TBI in infants

Falls—General incidence: 35%; Under five years of age, falls account for 50% of TBIs.

Recreational activities: 29%

Motor vehicle accidents: 24%

TYPES OF TBI

Open head injury: Injury results from a penetrating wound from an external force (e.g., gunshot). Damage is frequently restricted to localized brain damage.

Closed head injury: Injury can involve contact or noncontact forces.

Contact forces: Injury results from head striking an object (e.g., dashboard).

Noncontact forces: Injury results from acceleration/deceleration of brain within skull without contacting an external force (e.g., shaken baby syndrome).

Primary injuries: Damage immediately following injury (e.g., tissue damage and hemorrhage).

Secondary injuries: Damage from TBI occurring after initial brain insult, includes:
–Edema (swelling); increased intracranial pressure, which may cause hypoxia or Ischemia; infarction (tissue death due to lack of blood flow), among others.

SEVERITY CLASSIFICATIONS OF TBI

Degree of consciousness

Degree of consciousness is most frequently assessed using the Glasgow Coma Scale (GCS; measured through motor response, verbal response, eye opening).

Severity	GCS Range	Frequency (%)	Examples of Functioning
Mild	13–15	75–95	Spontaneous eye opening; converses; obeys verbal commands
Moderate	9–12	18	Severity between Mild and Severe range
Severe	3–8	3–13	Eye opening absent, fails to follow one-stage commands or utter identifiable words

Table *8.1*   *Continued*

Degree of posttraumatic amnesia (PTA, i.e., loss of memory following injury)

Severity	Length of PTA
Very mild to mild	60 minutes or less
Moderate	1–24 hours
Severe to extremely severe	Over 24 hours to > 4 weeks

Sources: "Traumatic Brain Injury: Neuropsychological, Psychiatric, and Educational Issues" (pp. 313–331), by L. Ewing-Cobbs and D. R. Bloom, in *Handbook of Pediatric Psychology in School Settings,* R. T. Brown (Ed.), 2004, Mahwah, NJ: Erlbaum; and "Traumatic Brain Injury" (pp. 652–671), by P. C. Rotto, in *Health-Related Disorders in Children and Adolescents,* L. Phelps (Ed.), 1998, Washington, DC: American Psychological Association.

the injury (Patrick, Rice, & Hostler, 2002). With a mortality rate of 10 per 100,000 children, TBI kills five times as many children and adolescents each year as leukemia (Ewing-Cobbs & Bloom, 1999).

Gender: Males are at greater risk for sustaining a TBI when compared to females, with male to female ratios ranging between 2:1 and 4:1 (Rotto, 1998). Gender differences emerge after the age of five and peak during adolescence (Rotto, 1998). All told, males between the ages of 15 and 24 have the highest incidence rate of TBI across all demographic groups; injuries in this age group tend to be associated with motor vehicle accidents and have greater severity. In general, males also tend to sustain more severe injuries, with the death rate in males four times that in females (Arffa, 1998).

Age: The cause and severity of the injury sustained varies with age (Rotto, 1998). For example, shaken baby syndrome is the leading cause of brain injury among infants (Lord-Maes & Obrzut, 1996), and falls account for more than half of TBIs sustained by children under the age of five (Rotto, 1998). In the school-age years, pedestrian, bicycle, and motor vehicle accidents account for the majority of incidents (Rotto, 1998). The incidence rate increases each year from birth to age 14, then rises sharply beginning at age 15 (Arffa, 1998); motor vehicle accidents are thought to account for the majority of this increase.

Risk Factors: In addition to gender and age, poverty, single-parent households, congested living quarters, and a parental history of a psychiatric disorder, substance abuse, or physical illness place children at greater risk for TBI (Arffa, 1998). Children with cognitive problems, behavioral problems, and emotional problems are also at increased risk for TBI, specifically children who are hyperactive, impulsive, and aggressive (Arffa, 1998). In particular, children diagnosed with Attention-Deficit/Hyperactivity Disorder (ADHD) are at a higher risk for TBI (Teeter & Semrud-Clikeman, 1997). Finally, a past history of TBI places an individual at risk for a future TBI (Rotto, 1998). The increased risk following an injury is likely due to the continuation of circumstances that contributed to the first head injury compounded with the behavioral changes, such as an increase in impulsivity, which may have resulted from the initial TBI.

Recovery

Consensus has been reached in the TBI literature that recovery following a TBI progresses through a series of stages; however, varied stages are described in the literature (e.g., Youse et al., 2002). One common measure used to document recovery is the Rancho Los Amigos' Level of Cognitive Functioning Scale (LCFS; Hagen, Malkmus, & Durham, 1981). The LCFS is used to describe an individual's recovery in eight stages ranging from *Level I—No Response* (i.e., individual appears asleep and does not respond to external stimuli) to *Level VIII—Purposeful, Appropriate Response* (i.e., individual oriented and responsive to environment). The majority of recovery occurs in the first 6 to 12 months, although individuals recovering from TBI progress at varying rates (Rotto, 1998). Often, the full effect of an individual's TBI on their functioning is not realized for a year or more. Rate of recovery (and outcome) is complicated further in children, as injury and brain development interact (Lord-Maes & Obrzut, 1996). The rate and level of recovery has been shown to be related primarily to the degree of diffuse axonal injury (Arffa, 1998).

Outcomes

Outcomes for children and adolescents who have sustained a TBI are often conceptualized as multidimensional and include neurocognitive, behavioral, social, and family outcomes (see Table 8.2 for examples of each type of outcome).

Neurocognitive Outcomes: For children with TBI, neurocognitive disturbances are frequently present after initial recovery, such as difficulties with attention, memory, auditory processing, and executive functioning (Youse et al., 2002). In addition, poor performance during speeded tasks and difficulties in processing complex visual-spatial information has been frequently documented (e.g., Ewing-Cobbs & Bloom, 2004). Learning can be profoundly affected by slowed speed of processing, a subtle cognitive impairment, which may not appear until years later and is similar in presentation to learning disabilities and/or ADHD (Lord-Maes & Obrzut, 1996). Additional information about neurocognitive outcomes is provided later in the chapter; particularly, as such outcomes inform psychological assessment.

Social-Emotional and Behavioral Outcomes: In addition to problematic neurocognitive outcomes, behavioral and social-emotional changes have been documented after TBI (Andrews, Rose, & Johnson, 1998). Andrews et al. (1998) found that children who had sustained TBIs displayed significantly higher rates of aggression, antisocial behavior, maladaptive behavior, and loneliness. Children sustaining a TBI also displayed lower levels of self-esteem and adaptive behavior. In terms of formal psychiatric comorbidities, up to 44% of children with TBI show persistent problems with ADHD symptoms, up to 40% demonstrate significant changes in personality, 25% of children with TBI suffer from depressive disorders, and a sizeable group show problems with anxiety disorders (Ewing-Cobbs & Bloom, 2004). Neurological disruption may be largely at fault for changes in behavior and emotions, but changes may also be secondary reactions to the physical disabilities and/or cognitive problems that have occurred as a result of the injury (Andrews et al., 1998).

Table 8.2 **Frequently Reported Outcomes and Factors Associated with Outcomes**

NEUROPSYCHOLOGICAL OUTCOMES

Intelligence
Tends to stabilize one year post-injury
Performance IQ < Verbal IQ, on average

Executive functioning impairments (common in severe TBI)
Difficulties with organization, planning, disinhibition

Attention problems
Difficulties with sustaining, shifting and focusing

Memory and learning difficulties (slower rate of learning)
Presence of posttraumatic amnesia (loss of memory after injury)
Verbal memory affected more than visual memory

Slowed processing speed (robust finding)
May be due to focusing attention, fine motor skill problems, motor coordination problems

Speech and Language
Difficulties inferring meaning during communication
Problems with understanding social communication (receptive prosody)

PSYCHOLOGICAL AND BEHAVIORAL OUTCOMES

ADHD symptoms: up to 44% pre- and post-injury
Depressive disorders: 25% post-injury in severe TBI
Personality changes: up to 40% in severe TBI
Anxiety disorders
Aggressive behaviors

SOCIAL OUTCOMES

Difficulties with social problem solving
Difficulties managing social conflict
Difficulties coordinating play activities

FAMILY\FUNCTIONING

Increased parenting distress reported in 41% of families
Caregivers may report worry or guilt about the child's injury
Stress often due to increased dependence of child

Table 8.2   *Continued*

FACTORS ASSOCIATED WITH POORER OUTCOMES

Greater severity of injury

Younger age of child

Presence of family conflict

Presence of family psychiatric disorder

Presence of pre-injury child behavioral problems

Source: "Traumatic Brain Injury: Neuropsychological, Psychiatric, and Educational Issues" (pp. 313–331), by L. Ewing-Cobbs and D. R. Bloom, in *Handbook of Pediatric Psychology in School Settings*, R. T. Brown (Ed.), 2004, Mahwah, NJ: Erlbaum; "Traumatic Brain Injury" (pp. 652–671), by P. C. Rotto, in *Health-Related Disorders in Children and Adolescents*, L. Phelps (Ed.), 1998, Washington, DC: American Psychological Association; "Pediatric Neurological Conditions: Brain and Spinal Cord Injury and Muscular Dystrophy" (pp. 375–391), by S. Warchausky, D. G. Kewman, A. Bradley, and P. Dixon, in *Handbook of Pediatric Psychology*, M. C. Roberts (Ed.), 2003, New York: Guilford Press.

Family Outcomes: For children, TBI occurs in the context of a larger family unit; therefore, it is not surprising that TBIs have been shown to affect family functioning. Parents caring for a child with TBI report significant levels of burden and distress, up to one-third of caregivers reported significant levels of anxiety, depression, and social adjustment difficulties, particularly for children with severe TBI (Hawley, Ward, Magnay, & Long, 2003). For TBIs that require hospital admission, parents face worries about the child's survival and may experience feelings of guilt regarding the circumstances of the injury (Hawley et al., 2003). Forty-one percent of parents reported a significant increase in parenting stress due to their child's TBI (Hawley et al., 2003). Increased parenting stress is thought to be due, in part, to the increased dependency of the child with TBI.

Factors Related to Outcomes of TBI: Traumatic brain injury outcomes are related to the type and severity of damage to brain tissue and classification of severity (e.g., mild, moderate, or severe); severity of TBI injury is frequently reported to be the best predictor of outcome (E. Clark, Russman, & Orme, 1999). Often, neuroimaging devices do not reveal structural damage in individuals who have sustained a closed, *mild* TBI (Lord-Maes & Obrzut, 1996). The lack of observable neurobiological damage, however, does not mean that there have not been significant changes to the brain that can result in negative neuropsychological outcomes (Lord-Maes & Obrzut, 1996). Neurocognitive sequelae of TBI have also been shown to be related to the area of injury. As noted earlier, preferential damage to the frontal lobe in TBI is thought to account, in part, for the high percentage of children with TBI who show impaired attention and executive functioning. In addition, right-hemisphere injury appears to be associated with greater risk for overall intellectual impairment, whereas left-hemisphere injury has been shown to impact expressive language skills (Lord-Maes & Obrzut, 1996).

Although injury severity is strongly related to a variety of outcomes for TBI, pre- and postinjury child and family functioning have been shown to be predictive of outcome above and beyond TBI severity (see Table 8.2). Child preinjury behavioral adjustment, parenting stress, and parent psychopathology, among others, have been shown to predict TBI outcomes (Ewing-Cobbs & Bloom, 2004). Child age at TBI injury also predicts outcome, with younger children at risk for poorer outcomes. The interplay between brain injury, child adjustment, and family functioning illustrates the complexity of predicting future outcomes for children with TBI. As illustrated by the range of possible cognitive, behavioral, and psychological outcomes for children with TBI, assessment of the child's functioning across a variety of domains is important.

Diagnostic Standards

Traumatic brain injury classification has typically consisted of describing degree of impairment using general descriptors, such as mild, moderate, and severe. Classification is often based on: (a) degree and duration of loss of consciousness, (b) presence and length of posttraumatic anterograde amnesia (PTA; i.e., a period of time during which new memories cannot be stored; Youse et al., 2002), (c) neurocognitive dysfunction, and (d) severity of injury (Arffa, 1998; Rotto, 1998). The classifications reflect the consequences of the injury, not the severity of the injury itself; therefore, the descriptions have demonstrated some predictive value regarding the likelihood and severity of postinjury cognitive, emotional, and behavioral changes (Rotto, 1998). The general classification rules are not uniformly accepted, and other systems have incorporated variables such as the necessity for brain surgery, the presence of neuroradiological abnormalities, and length of hospitalization in describing impairment (Arffa, 1998). The lack of a universal classification system has been a significant confound in research on TBI (Arffa, 1998). In general, most professionals agree that the majority of pediatric TBIs are mild regardless of the classification system used to describe functioning (Ewing-Cobbs & Bloom, 1999).

Table 8.1 summarizes two common methods used to categorize brain injuries: (1) degree of consciousness and (2) PTA. Posttraumatic anterograde amnesia typically lasts four times as long as the loss of consciousness (Rotto, 1998). Assessment of PTA in children is complicated by the fact that memory in children is still progressing through developmental stages; therefore, clinicians often depend on parental information to determine the severity of PTA (Rotto, 1998).

Degree of Consciousness

The Glasgow Coma Scale (GCS; Teasdale & Jennett, 1976), which assesses TBI severity by rating motor responses, verbal responses, and degree of eye opening in the patient, is used widely in describing functioning shortly after the injury (Youse et al., 2002). Scores range from 3 to 15, with lower scores representing lower functioning and awareness; individuals in a coma typically receive scores of 8 or less (Rotto, 1998). The GCS was developed for and is typically used with adults; it is not considered to be reliable in infants or children (Rotto, 1998). The Children's Coma Scale (CCS; Raimondi & Hirschauer, 1984) has been developed to assess loss of consciousness in young children. The CCS assesses level of consciousness by rating eye movements, basic motor movements, and nonverbal reactions as opposed to rating response to commands and complex motor movements that are developmentally inappropriate for infants and small children (Semrud-Clikeman, 2001). The predictive validity of the CCS has not been sufficiently documented (Rotto, 1998).

Diagnostic and Statistical Manual of Mental Disorders, Fourth Edition (DSM-IV)

Traumatic brain injury is not listed as a mental disorder in the *DSM-IV* classification system (American Psychiatric Association, 2000); however, TBI can be coded as a general medical condition on Axis III, and if the TBI has caused a change or deterioration in cognitive functioning, personality, or behavior, these problems can be coded on Axis I in accordance with the symptoms (House, 1999; Patrick et al., 2002). For children with TBI, the most applicable diagnostic categories include Adjustment Disorders, Mood Disorders, Anxiety Disorders, and ADHD (Patrick et al., 2002). In addition, in cases in which a child or adolescent's personality has changed remarkably as a result of the TBI, a diagnosis of Personality Change Due to a General Medical Condition can be made (House, 1999). As House (1999) points out, personality change due to a medical condition marks the only occasion when a diagnosis relating to personality is rendered on Axis I.

Individuals with Disabilities Education Act

In 1990, TBI became a special education category under the Individuals with Disabilities in Education Act (IDEA, Public Law 101-476; House, 1999) and continues to be a category in the current revision (IDEIA, 2004; Public Law 108-446). Essentially, inclusion of TBI as an educationally related disability category requires public schools to provide children and adolescents with TBI a free and appropriate education if the TBI is impacting upon the student's ability to succeed educationally. Appropriate educational services may take the form of accommodations in general educational settings through the establishment of a Student Support Team, or via a special education inclusion model. More restrictive special education service models include placement in a resource classroom setting or within a self-contained special education placement, depending on the needs of the child or adolescent. Speech/language, occupational, and physical therapies may also be provided as related services. It is likely that children and adolescents with TBI will continue to require special education services, as one study showed that 80% of children and adolescents with severe TBI continued to require accommodations and extra assistance 2 years postinjury (Semrud-Clikeman, 2001).

General Approach to Assessment and Specific Assessment Methods

Comprehensive psychoeducational and/or neuropsychological evaluations are necessary in cases of TBI to document the child's functioning in cognitive, social-emotional, and behavioral domains (Lord-Maes & Obrzut, 1996) and to assist with transitioning the child with TBI from the hospital to home and school (Farmer, Clippard, Luehr-Wiemann, Wright, & Owings, 1996). Comprehensive psychological evaluations are also necessary to plan for effective education and identify appropriate accommodations. In cases of TBI, evaluation should be done as quickly as possible postinjury to provide a baseline for recovery, and reevaluations should be done to track progress (Semrud-Clikeman, 2001). Reevaluations should be conducted relatively frequently (i.e., every 6 months) in the first year or two after the injury, although evaluations can be less frequent as the child or adolescent's functioning stabilizes. Reevaluations are also useful in determining if a treatment or intervention is effective.

Evaluations of children and adolescents with TBI can be complex because of the variety and number of deficits observed (Semrud-Clikeman, 2001). Assessments should not only include evaluation of intelligence and academic achievement, but also executive functioning, attention and working memory, the ability to learn and remember new material, visual-perceptual and visual-motor/constructional skills, motor skills, sensory skills, social-emotional functioning, adaptive behavior, and behavioral adjustment. In many cases, a child clinical or school psychologist is not appropriately trained in assessing all of these domains and should rely on additional collaboration with neuropsychologists, neurologists, occupational therapists, physical therapists, and speech-language pathologists, to conduct a comprehensive multidisciplinary evaluation.

To determine the possible effects of the TBI on the child or adolescent's functioning, test data should be compared to preinjury functioning. In most instances, there is no pre-injury psychological evaluation; therefore, parent and teacher interview, report cards, and group administered end of year standardized achievement test data are useful in estimating pre-injury functioning. When available, information relevant to pre-injury functioning should be incorporated into the psychological report. It is important to approximate the child or adolescent's previous functioning to provide a framework of likely recovery and assist the school and family in setting realistic goals for the future (Semrud-Clikeman, 2001). Furthermore, research suggests that children who suffer head injuries have significantly higher rates of behavior problems *prior to injury* than noninjured matched controls (Light et al., 1998) as well as higher rates of socioeconomic deprivation (Demellweek, Baldwin, Appleton, & Al-Kharusi, 2002). When information is available, estimates of preinjury behavioral problems and socioeconomic disadvantage are factors that should be addressed during the evaluation and described in the final report.

Additional factors complicate the assessment of children and adolescents with TBI. For example, brain injuries in the same location may result in different symptoms in the developing brain depending upon when the TBI occurred in the course of development (Semrud-Clikeman, 2001). Therefore, the evaluation should emphasis the relationship between measures as opposed to the hypothesized relationship between the measures and brain damage (Semrud-Clikeman, 2001).

Previously, younger children were thought to be better able to recover from brain injury due to the plasticity of the developing brain; however, research now suggests that the immaturity of the brain should no longer be considered a protective factor (Benz, Ritz, & Kiesow, 1999). Rather, injury may disrupt new learning, causing a developmental lag over time, which was not present at the initial evaluation (Gil, 2003). Development lag may then result in later-emerging neuropsychological deficits, such as slower rates of learning (Benz et al., 1999). Thus, serial reevaluations are important in detecting changes in learning style and rate, and raw scores (as well as standard scores) should be compared across evaluations to see if and how much new learning is occurring (Semrud-Clikeman, 2001).

Further, it becomes imperative to make special education and other school personnel aware that even though on initial assessment following TBI the child earns scores on achievement testing (old learning) that are commensurate with intellectual expectancy this does not mean that the child can be reintegrated into a regular education classroom without special education services. The child's ability to sustain attention and learn new material will often times be significantly impacted resulting in progressive academic difficulty and frustration as the child is presented with new material that must be learned and recalled. In short, the child returning to school is a different learner than the child who attended school prior to the TBI.

In summary, there are many considerations to keep in mind when evaluating a child or adolescent with TBI. Evaluations should be conducted postinjury and at fixed intervals after the injury to document recovery, efficacy of intervention, and to plan appropriate educational interventions. Comparison of raw scores across evaluations is important in determining if new learning and skills are being acquired. Assessments need to include a wide variety of domains and may require a multidisciplinary approach. Test data should be placed in the framework of the child's or adolescent's previous functioning. Emphasis should be placed on the strengths and weaknesses in the child's or adolescent's profile rather than attempting to link the profile to brain damage, and the immaturity of the child's brain is not necessarily a protective factor after head injury.

Intelligence

Assessment of intelligence is essential for children and adolescents with TBI as broad cognitive deficits may be present due to the injury. Typically, deficits occur postinjury but improve until the 1st year postinjury, when IQ scores tend to stabilize (Ewing-Cobbs & Bloom, 1999). Research has shown that after 1 year of recovery, IQ scores tend to be in the average range with a relative deficit in Performance IQ (e.g., Benz et al., 1999; Ewing-Cobbs & Bloom, 2004). The relative deficit in Performance IQ is likely due to the increased need for speed and motor difficulty on nonverbal tasks. If lower nonverbal than verbal cognitive performance is documented with a measure of intelligence, it is essential to assess further to determine if difficulties with attention, motor skills, motor speed, visual-perceptual skills, planning, and/or problem solving contributed to the performance (Ewing-Cobbs & Bloom, 1999). Most children with TBI score in the average range in the verbal section of intelligence tests; however, as Semrud-Clikeman (2001) points out, Verbal IQ scores may overestimate verbal ability due to individualized and highly structured testing conditions. As many children with TBI have difficulties with attention and distractibility, results obtained during formal testing may not be ecologically valid and should always be compared to teacher and parent report.

Although intelligence tests are an important part of a thorough assessment, there are many potential problems that must be addressed when using intelligence tests with children and adolescents with TBI. First, children with TBI may perform poorly on nonverbal reasoning tasks that require speeded performance and motor coordination and produce a nonverbal IQ score that represents an underestimate of nonverbal reasoning potential. For example, initial findings using the Wechsler Intelligence Scale for Children—Fourth Edition (WISC-IV; Wechsler, 2003b) with children with open head and closed head TBI showed relative weaknesses on measures of processing speed relative to verbal comprehension and nonverbal reasoning abilities. Processing speed performance for each TBI group was low average (Open head TBI Processing Speed $M = 84.1$; Closed head TBI Processing Speed $M = 85.0$; Wechsler, 2003b). The WISC-IV findings are consistent with prior research indicating that the performance of children with TBI on measures of general cognitive ability may be confounded by impairments in psychomotor speed and fine motor coordination (Semrud-Clikeman, 2001). In general, it is not appropriate to use intelligence tests to predict future performance in children and adolescents with TBI; instead, a child's performance on intelligence tests should be used to document verbal skills and previously acquired knowledge (Semrud-Clikeman, 2001).

Academic Achievement

Problems in academic achievement and failure in school are often sequelae of TBI (Ewing-Cobbs & Bloom, 1999; Farmer et al., 1996;

Yeates, 2000). Academic problems seem to be largely restricted to individuals with moderate to severe TBI (Ewing-Cobbs & Bloom, 1999) and do not appear to occur with mild head injury (Light et al., 1998). Oftentimes, however, research studies have not shown significant differences on standardized measures of academic achievement between children and adolescents with TBI and matched controls (Ewing-Cobbs & Bloom, 1999; Yeates, 2000). It may be that problems in school performance are related to the neuropsychological deficits or changes in behavior these children and adolescents experience rather than a decline in skills developed prior to the TBI (e.g., retrograde amnesia for older learning; Yeates, 2000). Commonly used achievement batteries, such as the Woodcock-Johnson III Tests of Achievement—Third Edition (WJ III ACH; Woodcock, McGrew, & Mather, 2001), are useful in assessing a range of reading, writing, and math skills; however, achievement batteries may not provide enough floor to evaluate young children or children with severe TBI.

Language Skills

Although a loss of expressive language functioning is sometimes present after TBI, children and adolescents rarely experience persisting aphasia (Ewing-Cobbs & Bloom, 1999; Yeates, 2000). Subtle language problems are often present after TBI, particularly for children who sustain moderate to severe TBI (Ewing-Cobbs & Bloom, 1999). Long-term deficits have been found in confrontational naming, object description, language comprehension, sentence repetition, and verbal fluency (Yeates, 2000). In addition, deficits in discourse, or the pragmatic aspects of language, are sometimes found and may be a contributing factor to the poor social skills that are sometimes found in survivors of TBI (E. Clark et al., 1999).

Language assessment in TBI should include a thorough evaluation of the child or adolescent's expressive and receptive language skills. In light of problems that occur with social aspects of languages, discourse and pragmatic language skills should also be assessed in children with TBI. The Clinical Evaluation of Language Fundamentals—Third Edition (CELF-3; Semel, Wiig, & Secord, 1995), Peabody Picture Vocabulary Test—Third Edition (PPVT-III; Dunn & Dunn, 1997), Boston Naming Test—Second Edition (Kaplan,

Goodglass, & Weintraub, 2001) and selected language subtests from the Developmental Neuropsychological Assessment (NEPSY; Korkman, Kirk, & Kemp, 1998) are all useful tools in assessing receptive and expressive language skills. In addition, specialized measures of receptive prosody may be useful in cases in which the child is having difficulty understanding discourse or accurately interpreting pragmatic aspects of language (M. J. Cohen, Prather, Town, & Hynd, 1990).

Executive Functioning

Deficits in executive functioning, or the ability to solve problems and think flexibly, occur frequently after TBI (Yeates, 2000). The severity of executive function deficit has been found to correlate with the volume of frontal lobe lesion following injury (Yeates, 2000). Tests such as the Wisconsin Card Sort Task (Heaton, Chelune, Talley, Kay, & Curtiss, 1993) and the Tower subtest from the NEPSY (Korkman et al., 1998) are appropriate measures of executive functioning in children (Semrud-Clikeman, 2001). The NEPSY manual provides performance data on a small sample of children with TBI. When compared to a matched control group, children with TBI earned significantly lower NEPSY Attention/ Executive Functioning Domain scores (TBI $M = 72.13$, Control $M = 104.9$; Korkman et al., 1998). Additional insight into executive functioning can be obtained by having parents and teachers complete the Behavior Rating Inventory of Executive Function (BRIEF; Gioia, Isquith, Guy, & Kenworthy, 2000).

Attention

Problems with attention are frequently reported in children and adolescents with TBI, in part, due to the selective damage to the frontal lobes and underlying subcortical structures that occurs during head trauma (Ewing-Cobbs & Bloom, 1999). Results of research on the link between TBI and attention have varied depending on the aspect of attention measured, sample characteristics, time of recovery, and measures used (Ewing-Cobbs & Bloom, 1999). In studies using continuous performance tasks, attentional weaknesses have been documented for children with TBI in the form of decreased re-action time and increased distractibility. Impairments in attention were more pronounced for children with greater severity of injury and those who were younger at the time of the TBI (Yeates, 2000). Longitudinal studies have found deficits in psychomotor speed and dividing, focusing, shifting, and sustaining attention (Ewing-Cobbs & Bloom, 1999).

In terms of instrumentation, the NEPSY features measures of visual and auditory attention. Specific measures of sustained attention, such as the Conners' Continuous Performance Test-second edition (Conners & Multi-Health Systems Staff, 2000) and the Test of Variables of Attention (TOVA; L. Greenberg, 1996), may also be useful in supplementing short-term attention tasks, such as those included in the NEPSY Attention/Executive Functioning Domain. To supplement test findings from individually administered instruments, parent and teacher report of inattention and distractibility should be assessed with behavioral scales such as the Achenbach's Child Behavior Checklist (CBCL; Achenbach & Rescorla, 2001; the Behavior Assessment Scale for Children [BASC]; C. R. Reynolds & Kamphaus, 1998, and the Connors Behavior Rating Scales—Revised [CRS-R]; Conners, 1997). In addition, according to Semrud-Clikeman (2001), a classroom observation is crucial as the child's attention skills may be different in the classroom environment when compared to the testing environment.

Memory

Problems with memory are common in TBI, again thought to be due to preferential damage to frontal and meseal temporal lobes during head injury. Ewing-Cobbs and Bloom (1999), among others, consider memory problems to represent some of the most significant neuropsychological impairments that occur for children with TBI. Deficits have been found in many aspects of memory, but the verbal domain (Yeates, 2000) and deficits in delayed memory (Semrud-Clikeman, 2001) may be particularly severe. Memory deficits can be compounded by difficulties in attention; therefore, assessment of both attention and memory abilities is necessary for the child with TBI. A widely used and well-normed measure of attention in children is the Children's Memory Scale (CMS; M. J. Cohen, 1997). The CMS allows for comparison between the domains of attention/working memory, learning, verbal memory, visual memory, recall and recognition memory. When compared to control children, children with TBI showed impairments across a variety of memory domains, with verbal memory the most impaired (M. J. Cohen, 1997). The NEPSY battery also features measures of memory and learning, with evidence that children with TBI show greater impairments in verbal memory when compared to visual memory (Korkman et al., 1998).

Visual-Perceptual and Visual-Motor Skills

Approximately one third of children who suffer a TBI experience deficits in visual-motor and visual-perceptual skills (Semrud-Clikeman, 2001). The Bender-Gestalt Test (Bender, 1946) and Beery-Buktenica Developmental Test of Visual-Motor Integration (Beery & Beery, 2004) and the Clock Face Drawing Test (M. J. Cohen, Riccio, Kibby, & Edmonds, 2000) are examples of untimed measures of visual-motor integration skills. The Arrows subtest from the NEPSY and the Gestalt Closure subtest from the Kaufman Assessment Battery for Children—Second Edition (Kaufman & Kaufman, 2004) provide examples of measures of visual-perceptual skills *without* a motor component. When compared to the normative sample, children with TBI performed in the low average range on NEPSY measures of visual motor and visual perceptual skills (Korkman et al., 1998). Informal handwriting assessment may also be useful in evaluating a child's visual-motor and perceptual skills after suffering a TBI (Semrud-Clikeman, 2001).

Motor Skills

Another cognitive effect of TBI can be a decrease in fine motor skills, particularly timed motor skills (Yeates, 2000). Motor skills may be impaired as a result of motor planning, physical dexterity, or a combination of both in children with TBI. Research has shown that the ability to perform motor tasks quickly decreases corresponding to the severity of closed head injuries (Yeates, 2000). When assessing motor skills, it is important to use tests that do not have a visual-perceptual component so that poor visual-perceptual skills do not confound the results. The Halstead-Reitan Finger Oscillation Test (Reitan & Wolfson, 1993) is an example of a measure of fine motor skills without a visual-perceptual component. To parcel out the child's strengths and weaknesses, it is good practice to give one "pure" measure of visual-motor skills, motor skills, and visual-perceptual skills.

Social-Emotional and Behavioral Functioning

Many children and adolescents who suffer disability as a result of TBI experience depression and suicidal ideation (E. Clark et al., 1999). In addition, TBI is a risk factor in the development of many social-emotional psychiatric disorders, such as Major Depression Disorder, anxiety disorders, dysthymia, and Bipolar disorder (Patrick et al., 2002). The presence of psychiatric comorbidity is likely due to a number of factors, including adjustment to any impairments or disabilities that may have resulted from the TBI.

An increase in aggression, hyperactivity, and impulsivity is often found in children with TBI. For children with closed head injuries, behavioral changes occur in proportion to injury severity and the child's premorbid functioning (Yeates, 2000). Full understanding of behavioral outcomes in TBI has been hampered by findings that children and adolescents who sustain TBI often have behavioral problems prior to sustaining injuries (Light et al., 1998). Recent research on mild head injury suggests that the mildest degrees of head injury are not associated with *new* behavioral problems (Light et al., 1998), but more research is needed for children with moderate and severe head injury. The development of behavior problems and disorders following TBI, such as ADHD, cannot be fully ascribed to the injury due to the influence of the family and other variables (Max et al., 1998).

Regardless of the fact that the causal link between TBI and social, emotional, and behavioral problems is somewhat unclear, it is evident that children and adolescents who have suffered a TBI need to be carefully monitored in these domains. Behavioral scales such as the CBCL (Achenbach & Rescorla, 2001) and BASC-2 (C. R. Reynolds & Kamphaus, 2004) are useful assessment tools, but it is important to remember that they were not designed for use with children and adolescents with TBI (Yeates, 2000). Parent, teacher, and, if appropriate, child interviews should be conducted to screen for psychiatric disorders and decreased functioning in the social, emotional, and behavioral domains.

Interpretation and Communication of Findings

Due to the numerous factors affecting outcome, such as recovery over time and continuing development of the brain, it is not appropriate to make predictions about future outcomes for children with TBI based on assessment at a single point in time (Semrud-Clikeman, 2001). Assessment data is most appropriately used to document a child's current functioning and to plan intervention. Comprehensive evaluations provide data that should be used to document cognitive strengths that can inform the development of a useful Individualized Education Program (IEP).

Feedback to Family Members

The interpretive feedback session with parents should be approached with the understanding that family members are often profoundly affected by the TBI of a child (Lezak, 1988). Therefore, the clinician should remain cognizant of the effects of TBI on the family when communicating the results of the assessment and making educational and treatment recommendations. Results should be communicated in a clear and timely fashion, avoiding technical jargon and remaining open to questions from the family (Cullum, Kuck, & Ruff, 1990). If the individual with TBI is an adolescent and capable of participating in the feedback session, the clinician should consider either allowing the adolescent to attend the meeting or scheduling an additional meeting with the adolescent. Finally, grief counseling may be helpful to the parent to cope with their loss, and parent training may be helpful if the child or adolescent develops a behavior problem as a result of the injury.

Recommendations for the School

As the survival rate of children with TBI has increased to 90%, the number of children who return to school with cognitive, social-emotional, and behavioral problems has also risen (Rotto, 1998). In addition, because physical recovery frequently occurs before neurocognitive improvement, many children and adolescents who sustain TBI return to school with normal physical appearance and subtle cognitive problems (Lord-Maes & Obrzut, 1996). On discharge from the hospital or home, children may reenter the public school setting with mild to moderate impairments in memory, attention, and problem-solving skills, which may improve or may be lasting effects of the injury.

There are many factors that relate to the successful education of children who have suffered a TBI. The comprehensive evaluation, particularly the educational recommendations, should be reviewed by regular education teachers and school administrators as well as special education personnel to assist in determining eligibility for special education services and plan effective strategies and accommodations for the child's education. Evaluation results should also be used to develop an IEP. The family and educational professionals should be made aware that the child's IEP may require periodic modification during the first 2 years following the TBI as the child's brain undergoes physiological recovery. Strategies used to teach individuals who have learning disabilities and ADHD may prove valuable, although it should be recognized that TBI often requires unique strategies focused on enhancing recovery (Rotto, 1998). The behavioral plan may require the use of techniques such as relaxation training to reduce stress/anxiety, anger management training, and social skills training. School personnel and families should be educated regarding the effects and probable course of the injury, and the child's classmates should be provided adequate preparation to welcome the child into the classroom (Rotto, 1998). Counseling may be necessary for the child, family, and individuals at the child's school. Finally, it is essential that early and frequent communication takes place between the child or adolescent's family members, school, and rehabilitation specialists, which will result in improved long-term outcomes (Farmer et al., 1996).

Psychopharmacological Intervention

Often the behavior plan will not be effective in managing the cognitive, behavioral, and social-emotional problems associated with TBI. On these occasions the use of pharmacological agents may become a necessary component of the treatment program. The field of neuropharmacology is changing rapidly with the development of new medications; however, the use of pharmacological agents can be complicated by the numerous etiological factors contributing to problematic behaviors and the overlap between behaviors and common side effects arising from medications (Glenn, 2002; Hymel, 2002). Thus, it is essential that the treating physician prescribing medication take a broad look at the child with TBI and the context of the behaviors before prescribing medication (Hymel, 2002).

CASE STUDY

The following case study is based on a neuropsychological evaluation conducted at a children's hospital. Identifying information, such as child and family name, child sex, and other particulars has been removed, altered, or fictionalized to protect confidentiality.

REASON FOR REFERRAL

"Marvin" is a 7-year-old Causcasian male who was referred for an initial neuropsychological evaluation by his pediatrician and child neurologist, who were monitoring his functioning due to a traumatic brain injury (TBI) sustained from a motor vehicle accident at age 6. According to Marvin's mother, major changes in behavior and learning have taken place since the accident. Marvin is more easily distracted, has difficulty settling down to do school work, his reading ability has declined, and he seems to learn more slowly, particularly in phonics and language skills. Neuropsychological assessment was conducted in order to assess higher cortical functioning and make appropriate recommendations regarding school placement and the need for supportive therapies.

BACKGROUND INFORMATION

Marvin resides with his father, who completed college; his mother, who completed high school and some college; and his three older siblings, who are above average students. Family history is positive for one case of Alzheimer's disease, but is otherwise negative for neurological and psychiatric disorder including intellectual disability. Review of developmental and medical history with Marvin's mother indicates that Marvin is the product of a full-term pregnancy complicated by gestational diabetes. Following a planned C-section delivery, Marvin was born, weighing 7 pounds, 11 ounces. Developmental, motor, and language milestones were all obtained within normal limits.

Marvin's academic history was accelerated prior to the motor vehicle accident. Marvin attended a prekindergarten program at the age of 3. There were no concerns about his learning or behavior from his teacher. Marvin attended kindergarten at the age of 5, and was immediately placed in an advanced reading group due to his accelerated reading skills. At the end of kindergarten, Marvin completed the Iowa Test of Basic Skills. He earned a vocabulary score in the 96th percentile, reading at the 97th percentile, language at the 99th percentile, and math at the 98th percentile.

In the summer after kindergarten, Marvin was involved in the motor vehicle accident. Marvin was restrained in the left rear seat behind his mother, who was driving, when a head-on collision occurred. He was transported to the emergency room and received a Glasgow Coma Scale score of 5 (severe) due to his unresponsiveness. Marvin was intubated during transport due to his difficulty breathing. In the pediatric intensive care unit, Marvin experienced a left sided seizure and was administered Dilantin. One day after the accident, Marvin was extubated and 2 days later began to open his eyes and follow simple commands. A CT scan on the day of the accident showed small areas of increased density in the left posterior frontal lobe, and the junction of the thalamus and posterior limb of the internal capsule, which were consistent with external shear injury. A repeat scan 1 day later also showed evidence of intraventricular hemorrhage within the left occipital horn. Five days post injury, Marvin was transferred to rehabilitation service and seizure medication was discontinued after 10 days. His level of consciousness continued to improve; however, a mild left hemiplegia (due to contrecoup injury) was noted. Seventeen days after his TBI, Marvin was discharged from the hospital, although he continued to receive outpatient Physical Therapy, Occupational Therapy, and Speech-Language Therapy. Two months post injury, PT and OT were discontinued because Marvin no longer showed signs of left hemiplegia. Since that time Marvin has been home schooled by his mother.

GENERAL BEHAVIORAL OBSERVATIONS

Marvin presented himself for testing as a well-groomed young man who was in no apparent physical distress. He separated appropriately from his mother and cooperated well during the evaluation. Marvin made appropriate eye contact and exhibited good social skills throughout the evaluation, which consisted of two sessions over 2 days. Marvin's use of language was marked by word-finding difficulty and a slow rate of speech. His attention-span, activity level, and impulsivity within the context of this one-on-one assessment were age appropriate. However, he required frequent breaks due to fatigue. During challenging tasks, Marvin's initial response was "I don't know," although he provided an answer after encouragement from the examiner. He tended to make self-critical remarks during academic tasks. Lateral dominance is firmly established in the right hand. Vision and hearing were screened and found to be normal.

INTELLECTUAL FUNCTIONING

Intellectual functioning as measured by the Wechsler Intelligence Scale for Children—Third Edition (WISC-III) is found to be in the low average to average range. Specifically, Marvin earned a Full Scale IQ of 86 (Average Score = 100 ± 15; 95% confidence interval = 81 − 92), which was comprised of a Verbal IQ of 88 and a Performance IQ of 86. The 2 point verbal-performance discrepancy favoring verbal functioning is not significant and indicates that in general Marvin's verbal and nonverbal abilities are equally developed. It should be noted that these results are not consistent with premorbid achievement testing which was in the superior range. Individual subtest performance is as follows (Average Score = 10 ± 3):

Verbal Subtests	Scaled Score	Performance Subtests	Scaled Score
Information	10	Picture Completion	11
Similarities	7	Coding	8
Arithmetic	8	Picture Arrangement	9
Vocabulary	8	Block Design	5
Comprehension	6	Object Assembly	6
Digit Span	6	Symbol Search	7

Marvin was also administered the Leiter International Performance Scale—Revised (Leiter-R), a nonverbal measure of intelligence, in an attempt to minimize the linguistic requirements of intelligence testing. With language requirements minimized, Marvin was found to be functioning in the low average to average range of nonverbal ability/reasoning as evidenced by a Composite Score of 91. This result is consistent with Marvin's performance during the WISC-III.

Executive Functioning

To assess higher order executive functions, Marvin was administered the Tower subtest of the NEPSY. During this task, he was required to move three colored balls to target positions on three pegs in a prescribed number of moves. In addition, there were rules and time constraints that increased task difficulty and necessitated planning/forethought. Marvin scored within the borderline to low average range during this task. Similar to his performance during intelligence testing, the results are well below premorbid expectancy. Scoring is as follows:

NEPSY	Standard Score
Tower	80

Receptive and Expressive Language

Assessment of linguistic functioning was conducted in order to evaluate receptive and expressive language development. Analysis of Marvin's performance indicates that his receptive language is in the low average to average range. Specifically, his understanding of vocabulary words, repetition of sentences of increasing length, and understanding of complex multipart directions is in the low average to average range. Marvin's auditory discrimination and phonological processing abilities, skills necessary for reading, were found to be in the average range. Analysis of Marvin's expressive language development indicates that his vocabulary and sentence formulation skills are in the low average range. His ability to name pictured objects and rapidly name items belonging to a given category are in the deficient to borderline range. Scoring is as follows:

Receptive Language	Standard Score
Receptive Vocabulary—Third Edition (PPVT-III)	94
Auditory Discrimination (Wepman)	102
Phonological Processing (NEPSY)	90
Sentence Imitation (DTLA-3)	85
Concepts and Directions (CELF-3)	85
Comprehension of Instructions (NEPSY)	80

Expressive Language	Standard Score
Expressive Vocabulary (WISC-III)	90
Confrontational Picture Naming (Boston)	66
Verbal Fluency (NEPSY)	75
Formulated Sentences (CELF-3)	85

Dichotic Listening

The results of a Dichotic Listening Test for Consonant Vowel Syllables appears to indicate that language is lateralized in the left cerebral hemisphere as evidenced by a right ear advantage in Marvin's ability to perceive and report consonant-sound syllables presented simultaneously to each ear. Scoring is as follows:

Dichotic Listening	Number Correct
Left Ear	9/30
Right Ear	12/30

Visual-Perceptual Skills

To assess visual spatial perception/discrimination ability without a motor component, Marvin was administered the Visual Discrimination subtest of the Test of Visual Perceptual Skills (TVPS), the Gestalt Closure subtest of the Kaufman Assessment Battery for Children, and the Arrows Subtest of the NEPSY. Analysis of Marvin's performance indicates that his visual perceptual functioning is relatively spared as evidenced by average to above average performance, with the notable exception of low average performance during the Gestalt Closure subtest. This subtest required Marvin to name objects, which may have lowered his performance, given his difficulty with word-finding/retrieval. Scoring is as follows:

Visual Spatial Perception	Standard Score
TVPS	145
Gestalt Closure	85
Arrows (NEPSY)	95

Constructional Praxis

Constructional praxis, as measured by the Developmental Test of Visual Motor Integration (DTVMI) and a clock face drawing with the requested time of 3:00 is found to be in the average to high average range. Marvin had difficulty with number spacing and erasures during the clock face drawing indicative of poor motor planning. He demonstrated difficulty crossing the midline and was noted to perseverate. Scoring is as follows:

Constructional Praxis	Standard Score
DTVMI	94
Clock Face	
Form	113
Time	112

Fine Motor Skills

Fine motor finger oscillation as measured by a manual finger tapper is found to be within normal age level expectancy bilaterally. Scoring is as follows:

	Taps/10 Seconds
Right (dominant) Hand	24.66
Left (nondominant) Hand	23.00

Fine motor dexterity was measured by the Grooved Pegboard Test and is also found to be within normal age level expectancy in both hands. Taken together, the results indicate that Marvin is no longer exhibiting evidence of left hemiplegia. Scoring is as follows:

	Seconds to Completion
Right (dominant) Hand	36
Left (nondominant) Hand	55

Memory

To assess learning and memory, Marvin was administered the Children's Memory Scale (CMS). Analysis of Marvin's performance on the subtests comprising the Attention/Concentration Index indicates that Marvin is exhibiting low average focused attention/working memory skills, which are commensurate with current IQ, yet significantly below premorbid expectancy. Scoring is as follows:

	Standard Score
CMS Attention/Concentration Index	82
Numbers	75
Sequences	95
Picture Locations (supplemental)	90

Comparison of Marvin's above average General Memory Index (GMI = 116) with his best estimate of intellectual potential (FSIQ = 86) indicates that Marvin's ability to learn and remember new material is significantly above expectancy. However, a more detailed analysis of Marvin's performance indicates that he is demonstrating significant variability in his ability to learn and remember. Comparison of Marvin's auditory/verbal and visual/nonverbal index scores with his intellectual functioning as well as with each other indicates that Marvin's ability to learn and recall visual material is a significant strength and consistent with what would be expected, based on premorbid achievement testing. In contrast, Marvin demonstrated significant difficulty learning rote verbal material across three trials. However, once learned, Marvin was able to retain and retrieve this material 30 minutes later. Marvin earned the following CMS Index and subtest scores:

	Standard Score		Standard Score
Verbal Immediate Index	88	Visual Immediate Index	122
Stories	105	Dot Locations	125
Word Pairs	75	Faces	110
Verbal Delayed Index	115	Visual Delayed Index	115
Stories	105	Dot Locations	115
Word Pairs	120	Faces	110
Delayed Recognition Index	91		
Stories	85		
Word Pairs	100		
Learning Index	88		
Word Pairs	60		
Dot Locations	120		

Academic Achievement

To assess word recognition, spelling, and numerical calculation skills, Marvin was administered the Wide Range Achievement Test—Third Edition. Marvin demonstrated average word recognition, spelling and calculation skills. Scoring is as follows:

WRAT-3	Standard Score
Reading	103
Spelling	101
Arithmetic	99

Because this test measures reading recognition as opposed to reading fluency and comprehension, Marvin was also administered the Gray Oral Reading Test—Third Edition. On this instrument, Marvin was required to read stories aloud and then respond to multiple-choice questions related to the story content. The Passage score assesses both reading speed and accuracy while the Comprehension score assesses understanding of what is read. Marvin's reading was characterized by a slow rate but good accuracy and low average comprehension. Thus, it appears that Marvin's slow reading rate interferes with his ability to comprehend what he has read. Scoring is as follows:

GORT-3	Standard Score
Passage	90
Rate	<85
Accuracy	90
Comprehension	85

To assess written expression, Marvin was administered the Written Expression Test (WET), which required him to copy sentences from dictation and finish short passages with a single sentence. The story was then evaluated for punctuation and capitalization (style), spelling, and syntax. Scoring is as follows:

WET	Standard Score
Written Language Quotient	85

Thus, academically, Marvin demonstrates relative strengths in the areas of word recognition, spelling, and numerical calculation, contrasted by relative weaknesses in the areas of reading rate, reading comprehension, and written expression. It should be noted that Marvin is no longer developing academic skills at premorbid levels in that he has made only minimal academic gain in the 7 months since his head injury.

Adaptive Behavior

Adaptive behavior was measured using the Vineland Adaptive Behavior Scale—Interview Edition using his mother as the informant. Results indicate that Marvin's overall adaptive behavior falls within the borderline range as evidenced by a Composite score of 72 with significant variability noted. Specifically, Marvin is exhibiting deficient to borderline independent living and communication skills contrasted by low average to average socialization skills. Scoring is as follows:

Vineland	Standard Score
Communication Domain	77
Daily Living Skills	68
Socialization	89

Behavioral/Emotional Functioning

To assess behavioral/emotional functioning, the Conners' Behavior Rating Scales, the Behavior Assessment System for Children and a behavior rating scale, which reflects items related to the *DSM-IV* criteria for Attention Deficit/Hyperactivity Disorder, were completed by Marvin's father and mother. Analysis of the behavior rating scale data indicates that Marvin's father believes that Marvin has a significantly decreased attention span. Marvin's mother, who is also his homeschool teacher, endorsed a similar concern but to a milder degree. No other social, emotional, or behavioral concerns were reported.

Summary and Recommendations

The results of the neuropsychological evaluation indicate that Marvin is functioning within the low average range of intellectual ability. It should be noted that Marvin's intellectual ability is significantly below what would be expected of a child whose prior achievement testing was consistent with superior academic functioning. Neuropsychologically, Marvin demonstrates relative strengths in the areas of visual-spatial perception and his ability to learn and remember visual/nonverbal material. By contrast, Marvin shows relative weaknesses in expressive and receptive language, working memory, and his ability to learn verbal material. In general, Marvin processes information slowly, speaks slowly, and is quick to fatigue. Academically, when compared to premorbid achievement testing, results indicate that Marvin has made only minimal gain since his traumatic brain injury. Behaviorally, Marvin's parents endorsed a decreased attention span. Marvin's pattern of neuropsychological test performance is consistent with expressive and receptive aphasia, executive dysfunction, and inattention, all of which are secondary to severe traumatic brain injury.

As a result, it is recommended that Marvin receive special education services under the eligibility category of "Traumatic Brain Injury" should his parents elect to educate him within a public school setting. Marvin's Individualized Education Program (IEP) should include speech and language therapy, a behavioral plan focused on enhancing his attention, and accommodations that will minimize distractions in the classroom, such as preferential seating, instructions in small group settings, and efforts to redirect his attention. Given Marvin's superior visual learning and memory, it is recommended that reading/writing instruction emphasize visual approaches, along with continued training and phonetic word attack skills. In order to enhance Marvin's learning/retention, new material should be presented in an organized format, which is meaningful to him. Instruction should be supplemented with visual aides, demonstrations, and experiential learning given his strengths in visual learning and memory. Finally, Marvin should continue to receive neurological follow-up due to his TBI. In addition, Marvin's academic progress should be carefully monitored with neuropsychological re-evaluation carried out toward the end of the school year.

Discussion of Case Study

The case study illustrates the neuropsychological assessment approach described in the chapter. Marvin sustained a severe TBI as indicated by his Glasgow Coma Score of 5 and showed characteristic shear injuries and hemorrhage, primary injuries suffered from the automobile accident. CT scan documented injury in the left posterior frontal lobe, an area frequently injured in TBI. Marvin's neuropsychological assessment revealed average to low average general cognitive ability with several areas of difficulty commonly found in children with TBI, including: *attention/working memory* (CMS Attention/Concentration SS = 82, 12th percentile), *executive functioning* (NEPSY Tower SS = 80, 9th percentile), *auditory/verbal learning* (CMS Word Pairs SS = 75; 5th percentile), and *receptive and expressive language* (several measures of expressive language were SS ≤ 85, 15th percentile). Marvin's pattern of adaptive functioning also showed mild to moderate impairments in communication and daily living skills. Marvin showed a mild left hemiplegia (secondary to contrecoup injury), which required intervention during hospitalization and resolved after approximately 2 months of therapy. Although no formal psychological evaluation was available to document Marvin's preinjury academic functioning, group-administered standardized achievement scores were made available by the parents. Pre-injury data indicated that Marvin's academic skills were superior. Taken together, this evaluation provides information that documents Marvin's need for special education services under the eligibility category of Traumatic Brain Injury. The report also outlines educational strategies and accommodations that are based upon his neuropsychological profile of strengths and weaknesses. Finally, Marvin will continue to require careful follow-up throughout his academic career in order to make modifications in his special education program and develop transitional service programming to assist him as he hopefully moves from high school to vocational training and independent living.

Conclusion

Traumatic brain injury represents the most frequent cause of death in children and adolescents in the United States, and approximately 1 million children suffer TBIs per year in the United States. The frontal and temporal lobes are particularly susceptible to damage from a TBI due to the structural features of the skull. Children who suffer from TBI are at risk of demonstrating neuropsychological, physical, behavioral, emotional, and social difficulties postinjury. In the domain of neuropsychological functioning, children with TBI frequently show impairments in attention, executive functioning, learning and recall of new material, motor skills, and discourse. Impairment in these domains is thought to be associated with the increased susceptibility of frontal and temporal lobe damage in TBI. Families are also susceptible to significant increases in stress as a result of a child's TBI. Biological, psychological, and social factors all contribute to outcomes of children with TBI, with location and severity of brain injury acknowledged as the most important prognostic indicators of outcome. Above and beyond injury location and severity, however, psychosocial factors, such as parenting stress, also contribute significantly to the outcomes of children with TBI.

For children with TBI, psychological assessment is best approached from a neuropsychological conceptualization. A variety of domains require adequate assessment to appropriately document a child's functioning. Assessment domains should include: cognitive functioning, attention, executive functioning, visual spatial and visual-motor skills, learning and memory, academic achievement, language, adaptive functioning, and behavioral adjustment. Consultation with other professionals, such as child neurologists, speech pathologists, and occupational/physical therapists, is often required to render full description and documentation of the child's educational needs. Recommendations for education and behavior should be grounded in the assessment data collected from the comprehensive assessment.

Eating and Feeding Disorders

Kathryn F. Moon and Jonathan M. Campbell

9

Chapter

Eating and feeding problems are not uncommon for young children and adolescents, with the majority of the scientific literature focused on the two ends of the pediatric age range. Young children presenting with feeding problems are not unusual—between 1% to 5% of pediatric hospital admissions are due to concerns about a child's failure to thrive (American Psychiatric Association, 2000). Older children and adolescents may show evidence of disturbed eating manifested as Anorexia Nervosa (AN) or Bulimia Nervosa (BN). Lifetime prevalence rates of AN range from 0.2% to 0.9%, and average between 0.3% to 0.5% with approximately a 10:1 female to male ratio (American Psychiatric Association, 2000; Hoek & van Hoeken, 2003). The prevalence of BN is 1% to 3% with around a 30:1 female to male ratio (Gowers & Bryant-Waugh, 2004). Epidemiological data indicates a steady increase in AN incidence rates between the 1930s and 1970s, with relatively steady rates of incidence over the past 20 years (Currin, Schmidt, Treasure, & Jick, 2005; Hoek & van Hoeken, 2003). In contrast to AN, BN incidence rates appear to have increased between 1988 and 1996 (Currin et al., 2005).

Anorexia Nevosa and BN are most frequently diagnosed in adolescence, with the highest incidence rates reported between 14 and 19 years of age (Lewinsohn, Striegel-Moore, & Seeley, 2000); however, AN has been documented in children as young as age 8 (Gowers & Bryant-Waugh, 2004). Anorexia Nevosa and BN are chronic disorders that are characterized by frequent relapses and weight fluctuations. The outcome of eating disorders include premature death (e.g., due to self-imposed starvation in AN), lifelong medical problems (e.g., renal dysfunction; dental enamel erosion), and development of additional psychological problems (e.g., substance abuse). Mortality rates between 5% to 10% have been reported for both AN and BN, due to self-starvation, medical complications, or suicide (American Psychiatric Association, 2000; Rome et al., 2003). The rising prevalence rates and serious consequences for physical and mental health make the assessment of eating disorders particularly important for children and adolescents. With a particular focus on AN and BN, the goals of the chapter are to: (a) describe the eating and feeding disorders as delineated in the *Diagnostic and Statistical Manual of Mental Disorders, Fourth Edition, Text Revision* (*DSM-IV-TR*), (b) identify domains of psychological assessment relevant to the assessment of eating and feeding disorders, and (c) introduce instrumentation designed to assist in the diagnosis of eating and feeding disorders and comorbid psychological problems.

Constructs of Interest

Theoretical and research work has documented multiple domains of problematic functioning for children and youth with eating disorder psychopathology. The causal and contributing roles of self-perception, dysregulated eating behaviors, physical problems, and social-cultural variables are reviewed in the next section.

Self-Evaluation and Body Image

Kostanski and Gullone (1999) found that children as young as age 7 report concerns with body image. In a sample of 7- to 13-year-old children, Maloney, McGuire, Daniels, and Specker (1989) found that 45% wanted to be thinner and 37% had already tried to lose weight. Concerns about body weight and shape increase with the onset of puberty and increased body fat (Byely, Archibald, Graber, & Brooks-Gunn, 2000), and bodily changes associated with puberty coincide with the onset of eating disorders in early adolescence (Attie & Brooks-Gunn, 1989). A history of being overweight also often precedes the onset of BN (Marcus & Kalarchian, 2003). Cultural differences influence perceptions of the ideal body shape, a point illustrated by findings that industrialized nations with largely Western values yield consistently higher rates of AN and BN. The cultural differences are thought to be due, in part, to attractiveness being associated with thinness (Rome et al., 2003). Cultural influences are also apparent in the ideal body type reflected and promoted in mass media, particularly targeting adolescent girls. Grogan (1999) found that adolescent girls criticized the idealized body images portrayed in the media, yet often expressed a desire to portray the ideal as symbolized by "supermodels."

Binge Eating

Binge eating is present in BN, the binge-eating/purging subtype of AN, and Binge Eating Disorder (BED). The set of diagnostic criteria for BN in *DSM-IV-TR* provides the most often used definition of a binge eating episode. In the criteria, a binge eating episode is defined as: (a) eating, in a discrete period of time (e.g., within any 2-hour period), an amount of food that is definitely larger than most people would eat during a similar period of time and under similar circumstances, and (b) a sense of lack of control over eating during the episode (e.g., a feeling that one cannot stop eating or control what or how much one is eating). The *DSM-IV-TR* definition of binge eating was adapted from the Eating Disorder Examination (EDE; Fairburn & Cooper, 1993), a semi-structured interview considered to be the gold standard of diagnostic assessment for eating disorders (Wilson, Heffernan, & Black, 1996). The *DSM-IV-TR* does not provide a clear definition of the quantity of food required for a binge eating episode, leaving room for clinical judgment. Although lack of control is not explicitly defined in the criteria above, the research criteria for BED provide examples of the behavioral manifestations of lack of control (Pike, Loeb, & Walsh, 1995). The examples include eating rapidly, eating until uncomfortably full, eating large amounts of food without feeling hungry, eating alone due to embarrassment over the portion size, and feeling disgusted, depressed, or guilty following a binge eating episode (Pike et al., 1995).

Pike et al. (1995) point out that binge frequency is counted by episodes in BN, but it is counted by days in the criteria for BED. The reasoning behind the difference is due to the hypothesized absence of compensatory behaviors in BED, which may cause difficulty in determining distinct episodes of binge eating (Pike et al., 1995). Binge eating behavior must also be present for 6 months for a diagnosis of BED, but only 3 months for a diagnosis of BN. No criteria for size, frequency, or duration are provided for the binge-eating/purging subtype of AN. Therefore, the definition of binge eating may differ depending on diagnosis and clinician.

Compensatory Behaviors

Compensatory behaviors are activities to prevent weight gain after an episode of binge eating. The *DSM-IV-TR* differentiates between purging and nonpurging forms of compensatory behaviors. The type and frequency of compensatory behaviors often determine the appropriate diagnosis and subtype according to *DSM-IV-TR* criteria (Pike et al., 1995). Purging behaviors include self-induced vomiting, and the misuse of laxatives, diuretics, enemas, or other medications to prevent weight gain. Fasting and excessive exercise are considered nonpurging compensatory behaviors.

Developmental, Medical, and Nutritional Problems

Pediatric feeding disorders can be caused or maintained by oral-motor delays involving sucking, chewing, and swallowing, or the presence of medical problems, such as gastroesophageal reflex disease, which can cause pain during or after eating (Linscheid, Budd, & Rasnake, 2003). The medical complications associated with eating disorders are numerous, such as electrolyte imbalance, chronic dehydration, renal dysfunction, and death. For AN, there is a risk of growth retardation if onset occurs early, impaired calcification of bones, increased risk of osteoporosis later in life, and amenorrhea (Gowers & Bryant-Waugh, 2004). Medical complications arising from purging behaviors include erosion of dental enamel, hand calluses from self-induced vomiting, and trauma to the gastrointestinal tract (Wilson et al., 1996).

Comorbid Psychopathology

Similar to other psychological conditions, psychological disorders co-occur with AN and BN, such as depressive disorders, anxiety disorders, and substance abuse disorders; for example, Lewinsohn et al. (2000) reported comorbid psychopathology in 89.5% of adolescents diagnosed with eating disorders. Depressive disorders are consistently the most frequently comorbid problems for individuals with an eating disorder, with up to 84% meeting diagnostic criteria for a depressive disorder (Lewinsohn et al., 2000). Findings indicate that dysthymia may be more strongly associated with BN in adolescents than Major Depressive Disorder (Perez, Joiner, & Lewinsohn, 2004). The Perez et al. (2004) findings may be important for detection and treatment of depressive symptomatology in BN due to the generally less severe symptoms and more chronic course of dysthymia when compared to major depression. For individuals with eating disorders, lifetime prevalence of anxiety disorders has been estimated at over 60%; with obsessive-compulsive disorder prevalence reported to be 40%; social phobia, 20%; and specific phobia, 15% (Kaye, Bulik, Thorton, Barbarich, & Masters, 2004). The high comorbidity between eating disorders and both depressive and anxiety disorders suggests that eating disorders might best be conceptualized as a subset of internalizing behavior problems. Almost one third of adolescents and young adults with eating disorders also exhibit substance abuse disorders, which might suggest chronic difficulties with regulating impulses or attempts to reduce symptoms of anxiety and depression.

Comorbid Psychopathology and Subtypes of Eating Disorders: Several studies have focused on the behavioral differences between the restricting and binge-eating/purging subtypes of AN. In a study of adolescents with eating disorders, Geist, Davis, and Heinmaa (1998) found that the severity of Children's Depression Inventory (CDI) scores discriminated between subtypes of AN. Adolescents with the binge-eating/purging subtype of AN showed evidence of more depressive symptoms than adolescents who were diagnosed with the restricting subtype of AN. A similar result was found by Heebink, Sunday, and Halmi (1995) with the Beck Depression Inventory (BDI). Further, Wilson et al. (1996) noted behavioral differences between the subtypes of AN. Individuals with the restricting subtype were described as exhibiting obsessive behaviors and rigidity, whereas those with the binge-eating/purging subtype were described as more labile, exhibiting episodes of both rigidity and impulsivity. Wilson et al. (1996) also remarked that psychopathology and suicide attempts are more common for those with the binge-eating/purging subtype of AN than those with the restricting subtype of AN.

Biological, Psychological, and Social Risk Factors

Although eating disorders feature clear physical symptomatology, no biological abnormality has been identified as a clear cause for AN or BN (Rome et al., 2003). Among others, the neurotransmitter serotonin has been implicated in the etiology of eating disorders, largely due to the important role that serotonin plays in regulating appetite; however, pathological serotonin functioning is not found in all individuals with eating disorders. Twin studies consistently find higher rates of AN and BN in monozygotic twins as opposed to dizygotic twins, suggesting a genetic predisposition for the disorders (Wilson et al., 1996). Family history of depression or substance abuse is also associated with a diagnosis of BN (Wilson et al., 1996).

In a longitudinal study of temperament, G. C. Martin, Wertheim, et al. (2000) found that childhood temperamental characteristics were associated with later eating disorder psychopathology. In particular, adolescent girls with high scores on the Drive for Thinness subscale of the Eating Disorders Inventory (EDI) exhibited high levels of negative emotionality, such as crying or screaming, on three measures of childhood temperament from ages 3 to 4 onward. Girls with higher scores on the Bulimia subscale of the EDI demonstrated less task persistence from preschool onward and higher negative emotionality in early adolescence. Girls with the highest levels of body dissatisfaction also showed the highest levels of negative emotionality (G. C. Martin, Wertheim, et al., 2000). In general, negative emotionality preceded the onset of eating problems. Additionally, the finding of low task persistence may indicate impulsivity or poor self-regulation, both of which have been implicated in the diagnosis of BN (G. C. Martin, Wertheim, et al., 2000).

In addition to genetic, biological, and temperamental risk factors, significant childhood events, such as sexual abuse, have been shown to be associated with the onset of BN and the binge-eating/purging subtype of AN (Serpell & Troop, 2003). Several family variables have also been associated with an increased risk for eating disorders, such as parental discord, family dieting, parental obesity, and family concern about weight and shape (Shisslak & Crago, 2001). Further, Minuchin, Rosman, and Baker (1978) described the families of individuals with AN as being enmeshed, overprotective, rigid, avoiding conflict, and resolving conflict poorly. Familial interactions are also a risk factor in feeding disorders. Linscheid et al. (2003) reported that the caregiver responses to developmental changes in the child can affect feeding. The parent must be willing to gradually give control of the situation to the child for feeding to be effective. Further, the nature of the interaction between infant and feeder will become part of the social foundation for that relationship (Linscheid & Rasnake, 2001).

According to Byely et al. (2000), family and friends can also contribute to the risk of developing an eating disorder by unintentionally increasing sociocultural pressures to be thin by verbally communicating their own perceptions of body weight and shape. Extracurricular activities may also increase the risk of an eating disorder. Participation in athletic activities that emphasize weight control or size, such as wrestling, gymnastics, dancing, or horse racing, is associated with eating disturbances at a clinical or subclinical level (Wilson et al., 1996).

Gender and Socioeconomic Status Risk Factors

As introduced earlier in the chapter, it is well known that eating disorders occur more often in females than males, with evidence that children and adolescents from higher socioeconomic status (SES) face a higher risk. In contrast to the widely held notion that eating disorders occur in higher SES groups of adolescents, Pastore, Fisher, and Friedman (1996) also found alarming rates of eating problems in lower SES adolescents. In a sample of 1,001 high school students, Pastore et al. (1996) found that 25% of students were obese, 18% were overweight, and 5% were underweight. The authors also discovered that 6% of males and 15% of females reported abnormal attitudes toward eating behaviors as measured by the Eating Attitudes Test (EAT; Garner, Olmsted, Bohr, & Garfinkel, 1982). High EAT scores were correlated with low self-esteem and higher anxiety (Pastore et al., 1996). Table 9.1 includes an abbreviated listing of risk factors associated with eating disorders.

DSM-IV-TR and *International Classification of Disease, 10th Edition (ICD-10)*

For psychologists in the United States, the majority of eating disorder diagnoses are made using the *DSM-IV-TR* (American Psychiatric Association, 2000). The *DSM-IV-TR* delineates criteria for AN and BN as well as a general category for Eating Disorder—Not Otherwise Specified (ED-NOS). The *DSM-IV-TR* also outlines a set of research diagnostic criteria for BED, which is not recognized formally as a psychiatric diagnosis.

Anorexia Nervosa (AN):   The essential features of AN are a refusal to maintain a minimally age-appropriate body weight, which is accompanied by an irrational fear of weight gain and body image distortion. Formal diagnosis of AN occurs in the presence of an individual's *failure to gain weight or weight loss to below 85% of normal body weight for height and age* (Criterion A). Weight loss may occur via dieting, intense exercise, or purging behaviors, such as self-induced vomiting, diuretics, or laxatives. Weight loss or gain is viewed as a

Table 9.1   **Factors Associated with Increased Risk for Eating Disorders**

DEMOGRAPHIC VARIABLES

Adolescence/early adulthood age range
Female gender (10:1 female to male ratio for AN; 30:1 for BN)
Living in Western, industrialized society

FAMILY HISTORY AND OTHER RISK VARIABLES

Family history of eating disorder, depression, substance abuse, obesity
Parenting discord
High parenting expectations
Family dieting
Criticism of eating behaviors, shape, or body weight

ENVIRONMENTAL STRESSORS AND EVENTS

Sexual abuse
Pressure to be thin related to recreational or job activities (e.g., dance, modeling)
Onset of dieting regimen

PSYCHOLOGICAL AND PHYSICAL CHARACTERISTICS

Perfectionistic personality traits
Anxiety
Low self-esteem
Obesity (BN)
Early menarche (AN)

Note: AN = Anorexia Nervosa; BN = Bulimia Nervosa.

manifestation of self-control. Despite being underweight, individuals with AN maintain an *excessive fear of weight gain* (Criterion B) and have a *distorted body image* (Criterion C). The individual may feel generally overweight or feel that a specific body part is too large or "too fat." Self-esteem is strongly associated with body shape and body image. Anorexia Nervosa results in low levels of estrogen, which adversely affects regular menstrual cycles; therefore, the presence of *amenorrhea* (Criterion D) for at least three consecutive cycles is necessary for a diagnosis of AN in postmenarcheal females.

Unlike previous editions, *DSM-IV-TR* specifies two subtypes of AN. The *Restricting Type* is characterized by weight loss in the absence of binge eating and purging. Generally, individuals diagnosed with the Restricting Type of AN engage in diet restriction or excessive exercise. The *Binge-Eating/Purging Type* is characterized by periods of binge eating and purging through vomiting, laxatives, diuretics, or enemas.

The *International Classification of Disease,* 10th edition (*ICD-10;* World Health Organization, 1992) diagnostic criteria are similar to the *DSM-IV-TR* criteria for AN. *ICD-10* specifies that the hormonal changes that cause amenorrhea in females may cause loss of sexual interest and potency in males. *ICD-10* also includes a criterion of delayed pubertal onset for young individuals that is not present in *DSM-IV-TR.* The greatest difference between the two classification systems is the lack of subtypes of AN in *ICD-10.*

Bulimia Nervosa: Bulimia Nervosa is characterized by a pattern of *binge eating* (Criterion A) and *compensatory behaviors, such as purging* (Criterion B), *on average twice a week for 3 months* (Criterion C). There is an *overemphasis on body shape and weight* (Criterion D), particularly as bodily concerns relate to self-evaluation. Individuals with BN often feel depressed or guilty during and after an episode of binge eating. Such feelings lead to the use of compensatory methods to prevent weight gain. According to the *DSM-IV-TR,* the majority of individuals with BN employ self-induced vomiting to compensate for binge eating (American Psychiatric Association, 2000). Abuse of diuretics, laxatives, enemas, fasting, and excessive exercise constitute other forms of purging. Although individuals with BN may share the concerns of weight gain and body dissatisfaction found in individuals with AN, *a diagnosis of BN is not made if symptoms only occur during episodes of AN* (Criterion E).

The *DSM-IV-TR* specifies two subtypes of BN. Individuals with the *Purging Type* engage in compensatory methods, such as vomiting or abuse of laxatives, diuretics, or enemas, during the most recent episode of BN. The *Nonpurging Type* includes individuals who use fasting or excessive exercise rather than the methods described above to prevent weight gain, during the most recent episode of BN.

Wilson et al. (1996) argue that the *ICD-10* criteria for BN are inferior to those of *DSM-IV-TR.* Unlike *DSM-IV-TR, ICD-10* does not provide a definition of "binge eating," fails to mention loss of control, and places little emphasis on the importance of body weight and shape to the person's self-concept (Wilson et al., 1996).

Eating Disorder—Not Otherwise Specified: The ED-NOS category is used to describe individuals who exhibit disturbed eating patterns but do not meet criteria for AN (e.g., amenorrhea absent) or BN (e.g., lack of compensatory behaviors). One example of ED-NOS is *Binge-Eating Disorder* (BED). The *DSM-IV-TR* provides research criteria for BED. The features of BED include *recurrent episodes of binge eating (Criterion A)* as described in the diagnosis of BN. For BED, binge-eating episodes must be accompanied by *three additional symptoms, such as feelings of disgust or feeling uncomfortably full* (Criterion B). Binge-eating episodes occur on average *2 days per week for 6 months* (Criterion D) and are associated with *marked distress* (Criterion C). Individuals with BED *do not engage in compensatory behaviors* (Criterion E).

Feeding and Eating Disorders of Infancy or Early Childhood: In addition to the eating disorders above, *DSM-IV-TR* (American Psychiatric Association, 2000) includes three disorders specific to childhood. These include Pica, Rumination Disorder, and Feeding Disorder of Infancy or Early Childhood.

Pica: Pica is characterized by the repeated *consumption of nonnutritive substances for at least 1 month* (Criterion A). The behavior must be both *developmentally (Criterion B) and culturally inappropriate (Criterion C)* for a diagnosis to be warranted. If other psychological disorders are present, such as Mental Retardation, the symptoms must be sufficiently severe to warrant a separate diagnosis (Criterion D).

Rumination Disorder: Rumination disorder is defined by *recurrent regurgitation and rechewing of partially digested food for at least 1 month* (Criterion A). Food may be chewed and reswallowed or discharged from the mouth. To warrant a formal diagnosis, the behavior must *not be related to a general medical condition* (Criterion B), or *occur only during the course of AN, or BN* (Criterion C). If either Mental Retardation or a

Pervasive Developmental Disorder is present, the symptoms must be sufficiently severe to warrant a separate diagnosis.

Feeding Disorder of Infancy or Early Childhood: Feeding Disorder of Infancy or Early Childhood is the failure to eat adequately, marked by a significant weight loss or failure to gain weight over at least 1 month (Criterion A). The difficulties are not better accounted for by another mental disorder, general medical condition, or limited access to food (Criteria B and C). Onset must occur prior to 6 years of age (Criterion D). Failure to thrive is an example of this type of feeding disorder. The growth of children with failure to thrive is well below expectations, generally at or below the fifth percentile (Black, 2003).

Other Classification Systems

At least two additional classification/diagnostic systems require discussion when considering the assessment of eating disorders.

Great Ormond Street Diagnostic Checklist: The formal diagnostic criteria described previously present some problems for the diagnosis of eating disorders in children. For example, Netemeyer and Williamson (2001) noted the inappropriateness of the amenorrhea criterion for AN for young children. The authors also noted that *DSM-IV-TR* does not take into account the effects of poor nutrition on pubertal onset, making it difficult for practitioners to judge a child's expected height and weight. Finally, children may not be able to recognize or explain the abstract concepts of fear of gaining weight or body image distortion that are essential for diagnosis (Netemeyer & Williamson, 2001).

In response to the limitations of the *DSM* diagnostic criteria, R. Bryant-Waugh and Kaminski (1993) developed a diagnostic checklist designed to be developmentally appropriate for children. The Great Ormond Street Diagnostic checklist, which was developed for the identification of AN, includes (a) determined food avoidance, (b) weight loss or failure to gain weight appropriate to age, and (c) two or more of the following concerns: preoccupation with weight, preoccupation with caloric intake, distorted body image, fear of fatness, self-induced vomiting, extensive exercising, or laxative abuse.

Individuals with Disabilities Education Act

Although the presence of an eating disorder does not presume the presence of learning problems, children and adolescents with eating disorders may require special education services (Tate, 1993). Perfectionistic traits, mood lability, feelings of inadequacy, social skills deficits, and memory or concentration problems due to associated physical illness may impair the academic performance of these students (Garner, 1991). For the purposes of special education, individuals with eating disorders may be eligible for special education services under the Other Health Impairment (OHI) category under the Individuals with Disabilities Education Act (IDEA; 1999). To receive special education services, current medical and developmental or educational evaluations are required and must document the specific educational needs of the student with an eating disorder.

Due to the high co-occurrence of other psychopathology (e.g., Major Depressive Disorder, Obsessive-Compulsive Disorder) with eating disorders, children with eating disorders may also be eligible for special education services in other categories. As with OHI eligibility, receipt of special education services requires documentation of educational difficulties associated with the diagnosis.

Assessment Procedures

Due to the complex interplay between physical functioning, psychological factors, and social context, eating disturbances may cause a multitude of problems for a child or adolescent. Therefore, a comprehensive assessment approach is recommended and should include the following: (a) physical and medical examination, (b) nutritional assessment, and (c) thorough psychological evaluation consisting of interviews with the child/adolescent and family, self-report questionnaires, and behavioral assessment.

Physical Examination and Nutritional Assessment

Formal physical examination and nutritional assessment are outside the expertise of psychologists; however, the physical examination is necessary to rule out a medical condition or delayed oral-motor development, such as chewing, when rendering a diagnosis of an eating or feeding disorder (Kedesdy & Budd, 1998). Physical evaluation is also necessary to evaluate medical complications that arise secondary to eating disorders, such as cardiovascular abnormalities, endocrine dysfunction, and metabolic problems (Fairburn & Harrison, 2003). Similarly, the nutritional assessment is critical to determine current and past patterns of eating and caloric intake. Therefore, consultation with or referrals to physicians and dieticians should be included in a comprehensive assessment where eating disorders are suspected or confirmed.

Interviews

In the eating disorder literature, consensus exists regarding the superiority of interview-based methods versus self-report questionnaires for documenting eating disorder psychopathology. Interviews may take the form of an information-gathering session or a diagnostic interview format.

Informal Interviews: For a child who is suspected to have a *feeding* disorder, the parent interview should include detailed information about the child's history, such as developmental milestones, age of onset, routines, and current and past concerns (Linscheid et al., 2003). Information gathered during the interview will enable the clinician to determine the parents' expectations for their child, their attitudes toward food, and their understanding of feeding milestones (Linscheid et al., 2003).

The parent interview for an *eating* disorder should include the child's developmental and health history, and family history of eating or other psychological disorders, such as depression or substance abuse. Due to the secretive nature of bingeing and purging behaviors, parents may be unaware of the existence of these symptoms, much less their frequency or intensity; however, parents or caregivers should be asked to offer descriptions or perceptions of the problem and the effectiveness of any previous treatments. Due to comorbidities of eating disorders with internalizing disorders, such as depression and anxiety, families should be asked to describe the child's mood, friendships, stressors, stress tolerance, and personality traits. If the child is experiencing academic problems, the nature of such difficulties may be of relevance as well.

Although the child or adolescent may be present in the parent interview, he or she should also be interviewed alone. Some children or adolescents may be unwilling to share information in the presence of their parents or caregivers due to fears of criticism. In addition to the topics presented above, the child or adolescent should be asked specific questions about body image, bingeing, purging, exercise routines, patterns of eating, and general physical condition. Attitudes toward weight and puberty, self-esteem, perfectionistic traits, and fears of failure or weight gain will be important in determining the most appropriate diagnosis. Hobbies or activities of interest may also be relevant information, particularly if the activities involve valuation of body shape. Finally, menstrual history and possible negative sexual experiences should be addressed (Noordenbos, 2003).

Eating Disorders Examination and Children's Eating Disorders Examination: Although clinical interviews are helpful for gathering information, the Eating Disorders Examination (EDE) is considered the gold standard for the diagnosis of eating disorders (Wilson et al., 1996). In fact, the *DSM-IV-TR* definition of a binge-eating episode was adapted from the definition provided in the EDE (Wilson et al., 1996). The EDE is a semi-structured interview that yields an operationally defined diagnosis and measures the behavioral and cognitive features of eating disorder psychopathology over the previous 4 weeks. The EDE is conducted with the client and was designed to rectify problems encountered in self-report measures, such as the use of poorly defined terms (Kashubeck-West & Saunders, 2001).

The EDE includes four subscales: Eating Concern, Shape Concern, Restraint, and Weight Concern (Fairburn & Cooper, 1993). The EDE includes diagnostic items that assess bingeing and purging behavior that are essential for a diagnosis of an eating disorder. The

EDE also differentiates between objective bulimic episodes (*DSM-IV-TR* binge-eating episode) from subjective episodes (i.e., loss of control but insufficient quantity of food for a binge-eating episode). These episodes are also differentiated from objective overeating, which is not characterized by loss of control. Therefore, the EDE offers specific information on the nature of binge eating, which assists in diagnostic clarity.

The EDE was originally developed for adults; however, the interview has been adapted for use with children in the form of the Children's Eating Disorder Examination (ChEDE; R. J. Bryant-Waugh, Cooper, Taylor, & Lask, 1996). The ChEDE can be used to measure pathology associated with eating disorders in 8- to 14-year-old children (Tanofsky-Kraff et al., 2003). The ChEDE differs from the EDE in two aspects. First, the wording of many items was altered to match children's language abilities. Second, two items focused on the value of body shape and weight were augmented with a sort task (Tanofsky-Kraff et al., 2003). In addition to these modifications, Passi, Bryson, and Lock (2003) recommend the presentation of a calendar to aid the recall memory of respondents.

Interviews versus Self-Report Questionnaires

Despite the advantages of the EDE and ChEDE, such as their ability to ensure the child's understanding of key concepts, they require examiner training and approximately 60 minutes of examination time (Passi et al., 2003). Self-report measures have been studied as an attractive alternative to interviews due to their brevity and lack of interviewer bias; however, questionnaires may result in miscommunication, particularly for terms such as *binge eating* (Rosen, Vara, Wendt, & Leitenberg, 1990).

To combat ambiguity in rating scales, several researchers have made additional information available to children and adolescents. For example, Banasiak, Wertheim, Koerner, and Voudouris (2001) used a glossary to aid adolescent girls' interpretation of items. Passi et al. (2003) also found that providing adolescents with written information about difficult concepts before test administration improved the accuracy of their responses. Tanofsky-Kraff et al. (2003)

showed child participants photographs of meal portions to better determine the amount of food intake. These practices are thought to increase the reliability of children and adolescents' reports and are encouraged in clinical practice.

Self-Report Questionnaires for Eating Disorder Psychopathology

Several measures are available for assessing the perceptions of youth regarding symptoms of eating disorders.

Eating Disorders Inventory-2 and Eating Disorders Inventory—Children: One of the most frequently used measures of self-report eating disorder psychopathology is the Eating Disorders Inventory-2 (EDI-2; Garner, 1991). The EDI-2 contains 91 items and is designed for use with ages 12 or older. Available in either computer or paper-and-pencil format, the EDI-2 may be administered individually or in groups and requires approximately 20 minutes of test time (Garner, 1991). The EDI-2 includes norms for nonclinical high school boys and girls as well as norms for patients with bulimia nervosa and anorexia nervosa. Three subscales of the EDI-2 (Drive for Thinness, Bulimia, and Body Dissatisfaction) measure attitudes and behaviors associated with the core features of eating disorders, such as eating, weight, and shape (Garner & Barry, 2001). The remaining subscales (Ineffectiveness, Perfection, Interpersonal Distrust, Interoceptive Awareness, Maturity Fears, Asceticism, Impulse Regulation, and Social Insecurity) measure symptoms associated with eating disorders (Garner & Barry, 2001). The EDI-2 also includes a 4-page symptom checklist (EDI-SC) completed by the adolescent. Although the EDI-2 uses a 6-point Likert format, items are scored 0 to 3, with nonproblematic responses scored as 0. Garner (1991) explains that this is a rational-theoretical decision and only problem areas should contribute to the total subscale scores. Schoemaker, van Strien, and van der Staak (1994) challenged the EDI-2 scoring system, suggesting that a scoring system of 1 to 6 increases the sensitivity of the measure, particularly in nonclinical samples.

Although the EDI-2 was not designed as a screener, it has often been used to screen for eating disorder psychopathology (Kashubeck-West & Saunders, 2001). Schoemaker et al. (1994) hypothesized that the EDI-2 has been used as a screener because many thoughts and behaviors assessed by the EDI are thought to precede the onset of eating disorders (e.g., the EDI-2 Perfection subscale measuring perfectionistic personality traits).

Franko et al. (2004) developed and evaluated a children's version of the original EDI, the EDI-C. The EDI-C features 16 items that are identical to those on the EDI, 29 items with minor changes, and the remaining items significantly altered from the EDI. Franko et al. administered the EDI-C to a nonclinical sample of Black and White girls ages 11 and 12. Although the factor structure of the EDI-C was comparable across ethnic groups, with five of eight factors emerging, the structure differed from that of the EDI. In a comparison across racial groups, "perfectionism" emerged as a unique factor for White girls, whereas "body satisfaction" emerged as a unique factor for Black girls. In discussing their findings, Franko et al. (2004) stated that eating disorder psychopathology may differ between racial groups, which may lead to differential emphasis when assessing risk for eating disorders with Black and White adolescent girls. Overall, use and interpretation of the EDI-C should proceed cautiously until further validation has been completed.

Eating Attitudes Test and Children's Eating Attitudes Test: The Eating Attitudes Test (EAT) is a self-report measure of eating behaviors and attitudes present in AN (Engelsen & Hagtvet, 1999). There are three forms of the EAT: (1) the original 40-item version (Garner & Garfinkel, 1979), (2) a 26-item version (EAT-26; Garner et al., 1982), and (3) a 12-item version (EAT-12; Lavik, Clausen, & Pederson, 1991). The 40-item and 26-item versions of the EAT are highly correlated (Garner et al., 1982). Like the EDI-2, the EAT uses a 6-point Likert format, and the items are scored using the 0 to 3 system. The EAT has been determined to be an effective screener and is appropriate for use with adults and adolescents (Netemeyer & Williamson, 2001).

The EAT has been modified for children ages 8 to 13 in the form of the Children's Eating Attitudes Test (ChEAT; Maloney, McGuire, &

Daniels, 1988). The ChEAT consists of 26 items using a 6-point Likert format and assesses perceived body image, dieting practices, and obsessions/preoccupations with food. The scale requires approximately 30 minutes to complete and may be presented verbally or the child may complete the scale independently. According to Linscheid and Butz (2003), both the EAT and ChEAT tend to overestimate the prevalence of eating disordered behavior and should be interpreted with caution.

Eating Disorders Examination-Questionnaire (EDE-Q): The EDE is available in a self-report format, the Eating Disorders Examination-Questionnaire (EDE-Q; Fairburn & Beglin, 1994). The EDE-Q features 38-items derived from the EDE using a 7-point Likert scale response format (Passi et al., 2003). The scale requires approximately 15 minutes to complete, uses a 28-day time frame, and consists of the same four subscales as the EDE (Passi et al., 2003). Although the EDE-Q was created from the adult version of the EDE, it has been normed for adolescent girls between 12 and 14 years of age (J. C. Carter, Stewart, & Fairburn, 2001). Passi et al. (2003) compared the EDE and EDE-Q in a sample of adolescents with AN. Participants were asked to complete the EDE-Q, the EDE, and a second EDE-Q to determine whether explanations provided on the EDE would alter EDE-Q responses. Although the Weight Concern and Shape Concern subscale scores were highly correlated between the EDE and EDE-Q, the responses were significantly different, indicating that interviewer assistance may be required for accurate responses to questions posed in the EDE-Q (Passi et al., 2003).

Self-Report of Binge Eating

The Questionnaire of Eating and Weight Patterns—Adolescent Version (QEWP-A; W. G. Johnson, Grieve, Adams, & Sandy, 1999) consists of 12 questions focused on *DSM-IV-TR* criteria for BED, such as loss of control, frequency, and duration of binge-eating episodes (W. G. Johnson et al., 1999). The scale has been used with children between the ages 10 to 18 (W. G. Johnson et al., 1999). In a comparison of interview and multiple self-report measures of eating disorder psychopathology, the QEWP-A identified more episodes of problem eating and episodes of loss of control when compared to the ChEDE (Tanofsky-Kraff et al., 2003). Tanofsky-Kraff et al. (2003) hypothesized that the differences may be due to the lack of definition for the meal size required for an episode of problem eating on the QEWP-A. Alternatively, there is no operational definition of "loss of control" while eating on the QEWP-A; therefore, children may have used idiosyncratic definitions of the term *loss of control*. Tanofsky-Kraff et al. (2003) concluded that the QEWP-A is not as effective as the ChEDE or ChEAT at measuring psychopathology associated with eating disorders.

Self-Report of Body Image

A number of tests offer line drawings of human bodies ranging from thin to obese. The child or adolescent is asked to choose the figure that most closely resembles his or her current size and ideal size, and the difference score is thought to represent body dissatisfaction (R. M. Gardner, 2001). The Body Image Assessment—Child (BIA-C; Veron-Guidry & Williamson, 1996) and Body Image Assessment—Preadolescent (BIA-P; Veron-Guidry & Williamson, 1996) consist of four sets of nine body image silhouettes that resemble male and female children and adolescents. The BIA-C has been standardized for children aged 8 to 12, and the BIA-P was created for preadolescents aged 10 to 13. The Body Rating Scale (BRS; Sherman, Iacano, & Donnelly, 1995) offers a 9-item scale for preadolescent girls (BRS 11) and adolescent girls (BRS 17) but no scale for boys. These scales require little administration time; however, the facial characteristics on the drawings are Caucasian (R. M. Gardner, 2001). The usefulness of the body image scales in non-Caucasian populations is unknown.

Self-Report Measures of Depression, Personality, and Behavior

Due to the frequent co-occurrence between eating disorder psychopathology and internalizing disorders, such as depression and anxiety, it is important to include self-report measures of adjustment in the psychological assessment. Internalizing disorders feature cognitive and subjective symptoms that may be assessed, in part, via self report instruments.

Depression: Given the high comorbidity between depression and eating disorders, assessment of depressive symptomatology is important in comprehensive assessment. Two measures of depressive symptomatology have been used with children and adolescents with eating disorders. The Beck Depression Inventory—II (BDI-II) consists of 21 items constructed to correspond with *DSM-IV-TR* criteria. The BDI-II is appropriate for ages 13 and above, and administration requires 5 minutes (A. T. Beck, Steer, & Brown, 1996). The CDI is a 27-item self-report measure for the symptoms of depression; the measure is appropriate for ages 7 to 17 and requires 10 to 30 minutes of administration time (Kovacs, 1992).

Personality: The Minnesota Multiphasic Personality Inventory—Adolescent (MMPI-A) provides assessment of personal, social, and behavioral problems in adolescents. The MMPI-A consists of 478 items, requires 45 to 60 minutes, and is appropriate for ages 14 to 18 (Butcher et al., 1992). In a sample of 230 adolescent girls with eating disorders producing valid MMPI-A personality profiles, the highest Basic Scale elevations were reported for the Hypochondriasis (Hs), Depression (D), and Conversion Hysteria (Hy) subscales (Cumella, Wall, & Kerr-Almeida, 1999). Group differences between AN, BN, and ED-NOS diagnostic groups were found for the Psychopathic Deviate (Pd) and Mania (Ma) Basic Scales, with girls with BN scoring higher than other diagnostic groups on each scale. Analysis of the MMPI-A content scales revealed that girls with BN reported greater proneness to develop alcohol and drug use problems than girls with AN or ED-NOS. According to Cumella et al. (1999), the differences support conceptualizations of adolescents with BN as more impulsive and prone to alcohol and drug dependence than adolescents with AN (Cumella et al., 1999).

Self-Reported Behavioral Adjustment: The Behavior Assessment System for Children—Self-Report of Personality (BASC-SRP; C. R. Reynolds &

Kamphaus, 1998) is appropriate for children and adolescents aged 8 and older. It includes measures of Clinical Maladjustment (e.g., Sense of Inadequacy and Locus of Control), School Maladjustment (e.g., Attitude to School and Attitude to Teachers), Personal Adjustment (e.g., Interpersonal Relations and Self-Esteem), and a global Emotional Symptoms Index. The BASC also features a Parent Rating Scales (BASC-PRS) and Teacher Rating Scales (BASC-TRS), which are described in the following section.

Behavioral Assessment

Behavioral assessment includes structured and unstructured observational methods as well as caregiver reports. Although the psychological assessment measures described above are most appropriate for children and adolescents referred for possible *eating* disorders, the following behavioral assessments may also be used for children thought to have *feeding* disorders.

Food Diaries: Food diaries can offer detailed information regarding a child or adolescent's food intake and eating habits. Food diaries should be kept for 3 to 7 days, including at least 1 weekend day as eating patterns may differ between the week and weekend (Wolper, Heshka, & Heymsfield, 1995). A food diary may include date, time, location, people present, food eaten, estimated calories, and portion size (Linscheid et al., 2003; Wolper et al., 1995). Although food diaries offer a great deal of information in an organized manner, they also provide obstacles for assessment. Wolper et al. (1995) note that the accuracy of diaries is often acceptable initially but declines over time due to high demands of the diary recorder. A second concern is that the diary itself may alter food habits, offering a misleading picture of the individual's eating patterns (Wolper et al., 1995). Finally, parents must complete the food diaries for young children.

Observation of Mealtime: Linscheid et al. (2003) report that poor interaction patterns during mealtime may contribute to and sustain challenging behaviors observed in young children with feeding problems. Therefore, it is important for the clinician to observe the child and caregiver engaged in mealtime for the diagnosis of a feeding disorder. This observation may take place in the clinic, at home, or via videotape. In the clinic setting, parents should bring a variety of preferred and nonpreferred foods to the observation to approximate mealtime behaviors in the home. Linscheid et al. (2003) suggest that the child fast for 2 hours prior to the observation so that he or she is more likely to be hungry. Behaviors of interest may include likes and dislikes, means of communication, self-feeding skills, verbal encouragement, reactions, and ending the meal (Linscheid et al., 2003).

Structured Meal Observations: The Behavioral Eating Test (BET; Jeffrey et al., 1980) measures food and beverage consumption. The BET offers equal numbers of standard servings of nutritional foods and foods with little nutritional value (Netemeyer & Williamson, 2001). The child is instructed to taste the foods and consume as much as he or she likes. After an 8-minute observational period, the remaining food is weighed and its caloric content is determined. Another structured observation of meal consumption is Bob and Tom's Method of Assessing Nutrition (BATMAN; Klesges et al., 1983), which uses a time-sampling procedure to record the mealtime behaviors of the child and caregiver. The scale also includes environmental and social variables that may influence behavior during meals.

Third-Party Rating Scales: The Children's Eating Behavior Inventory (CEBI; L. A. Archer, Rosenbaum, & Streiner, 1991) is a 40-item questionnaire designed to measure eating and mealtime behavior. The test was designed to be completed by parents of children ages 2 to 12 and focuses on the child's likes and dislikes, parental stress, self-feeding skills, and mealtime compliance (Babbitt, Edlen-Nezin, Manikam, Summers, & Murphy, 1995). The items are divided into yes/no questions and a 5-point Likert section, and the scale has 2 domains: child and parent. The CEBI yields a total eating problem score and percentage of problem items. The scale can be completed in approximately 15 minutes.

Although the scales have not been evaluated explicitly with children and adolescents with eating or feeding disorders, the BASC-Parent (BASC-PRS) and Teacher Rating Scales (BASC-TRS;

C. R. Reynolds & Kamphaus, 1998) feature a number of subscales relevant to eating disorder psychopathology. The BASC yields composite scores for Internalizing Problems (e.g., Anxiety and Depression), Externalizing Problems (e.g., Aggression and Conduct Problems), and Adaptive Skills (e.g., Social Skills and Leadership). The BASC-TRS also includes a measure of School Problems (e.g., Study Skills and Learning Problems). Finally, the BASC includes a global index of functioning—the Behavioral Symptoms Index. The BASC-TRS and BASC-PRS are appropriate for parents and teachers of children ages 2.5- to 18-years-old.

Interpretation and Communication of Findings

Sattler (1998) outlined four general phases of an effective informing session that are applicable to parents with children with suspected or confirmed eating disorders. Initially, the clinician should seek to establish rapport with the parents. Rapport-building should include a review of the referral questions as well as the parents' hypotheses about the problems. The clinician should be sure to accentuate the child's and family's positive attributes as well as problem areas and diagnoses because individual and familial strengths are often critical to the child or adolescent's prognosis.

The second phase of the informing session is communication of the results (Sattler, 1998). While communicating results of the evaluation, clinicians should provide a clear, organized summary of the results and offer the parents multiple opportunities to ask questions. During the communicating of results, parents will likely find behavioral descriptions and anecdotal information more helpful in understanding eating disorder psychopathology as opposed to specific test scores. The parents should be informed of any diagnoses at the end of this phase, which parents may respond to with grief, denial, or embarrassment. The clinician should be prepared for these possibilities, such as responding with empathy, or outlining specific treatment options available to alleviate the parents' feelings of hopelessness.

In the third phase, the clinicians should present recommendations for intervention, if necessary (Sattler, 1998). It is important that the parents feel comfortable in their abilities to carry out the recommendations. Describing an initial treatment plan, referring for treatment, and providing information about support groups for individuals and families may be helpful during this phase of the informing session. The homepage of the National Eating Disorders Association (www.edap.org) offers an abundance of resources, program recommendations, and advocacy information. Book recommendations for families include *Eating Disorders—A Parent's Guide* by R. Bryant-Waugh and Lask (1999) as well as *Anorexia Nervosa: A Survival Guide for Families, Friends, and Sufferers* by Treasure (1998). These books are written for families and feature chapters written to improve collaboration between educators, therapists, and pediatricians. If inpatient treatment is required, the nature and duration of the treatment program should be explained to the family. If possible, the child or adolescent should have the opportunity to visit the hospital prior to admittance (Winston & Webster, 2003). The final phase of the informing session is termination (Sattler, 1998). During the termination phase, the clinician should assess the parents' reactions to the findings presented as well as their understanding of the actions required. The clinician should also welcome any additional questions and provide contact information to respond to future questions, if they arise.

Communicating Findings to Children and Adolescents

If the child or adolescent is able to understand the general findings, a separate informing session should be held with him or her (Sattler, 1998). Ideally, information provided to a child or adolescent about a diagnosis will improve understanding of current difficulties and dispel fears or misperceptions about assessment and treatment. In the case of eating disorders, the child or adolescent should be praised for having the courage to discuss difficulties during the evaluation (Noordenbos, 2003). According to Noordenbos (2003), some clients may be unwilling to participate in treatment because the eating disorder operates as a coping strategy. In these cases, it is important to offer clear indications of the goals and actions of therapy to increase motivation. The books and web site provided in the previous section are also appropriate for children and adolescents and can be recommended to them as well.

CASE STUDY

The following psychological report is from a private clinic. Identifying information, such as child and family name, child sex, and other particulars has been removed, altered, or fictionalized to protect confidentiality. An interpretation of findings follows the report.

REASON FOR REFERRAL AND BACKGROUND INFORMATION

Jamie is a 14-year-old female who was referred for psychological evaluation by her teacher Carol Alexander at Allen Academy. Mrs. Alexander requested the evaluation due to recent concerns about Jamie's poor academic performance, lethargy, and lack of motivation. The youngest of four siblings, Jamie lives in Shaw, Georgia with her parents. Jamie's father is a physician, and her mother is a beautician. Jamie was delivered via Caesarian-section approximately 3 weeks after the expected due date. During the first month, Jamie lost weight, and her parents described her as a fussy baby who was allergic to milk. Developmental milestones were met within normal limits; for example, Jamie sat without support at 7 months, spoke her first word at 10 months, and walked alone at approximately 13 months.

At the age of 8, Dr. Marie Askew conducted a psychoeducational evaluation with Jamie at the request of her tutors at Allen Academy. Dr. Askew noted symptoms of depressed mood, social withdrawal, feelings of hopelessness, and thoughts of suicide. As a result of that evaluation, Jamie was diagnosed with Major Depressive Disorder. Jamie participated in individual psychotherapy and was treated with Prozac for a short period of time following Dr. Askew's evaluation.

Throughout her school career, Jamie has been described by teachers as "glazed over" and withdrawn. Mrs. Hughes, Jamie's mother, also indicated that Jamie is shy around adults and new people. According to her mother, Jamie worries about being liked by peers and excelling at school. Outside of school, Jamie enjoys riding horses and dance; she is a dancer at Allen Academy and participates in local ballet and tap classes. Mrs. Hughes reported that Jamie spends much of her time dancing and often skips meals to save time for additional rehearsals. Ms. Hughes reported that in the past 12 months, Jamie has become increasingly isolated from her family, particularly at mealtime. Mrs. Hughes reported that she found empty laxative boxes in Jamie's garbage can 2 or 3 times during the last few months. At Mrs. Hughes' request, Jamie was evaluated by her pediatrician 2 months ago; no medical problems were noted and, despite concerns about mealtime behaviors and the use of laxatives, Jamie's weight was age-appropriate.

GENERAL OBSERVATIONS

Throughout the evaluation, Jamie exhibited an extremely flat emotional presentation with restricted range. She rarely showed any emotion, appeared tired, and demonstrated poor posture. Jamie appeared disinterested in the academic portions of the evaluation; however, she was compliant during formal testing. Upon interview, Jamie responded to questions in a forthright manner and expressed a greater range of emotion. In general, the evaluation results should be viewed as a valid reflection of Jamie's current functioning.

INTELLECTUAL FUNCTIONING AND ACADEMIC ACHIEVEMENT

To screen for the presence of a cognitive or academic disorder, Jamie completed the Wechsler Abbreviated Scale of Intelligence (WASI) and the Wide Range Achievement Test—Third Edition. Jamie's performance during the WASI indicated Superior range cognitive abilities with equally developed verbal and nonverbal reasoning skills. Similarly, Jamie academic achievement in the areas of single-word reading, math calculation, and spelling were Superior. Intellectual and academic screening results suggest the absence of cognitive or learning problems.

SOCIAL/EMOTIONAL FUNCTIONING AND EATING BEHAVIORS

To better understand Jamie's social and emotional functioning and behavioral adjustment, behavior rating scales were completed by her parents (Dr. and Mrs. Hughes), Jamie's teacher, Carol Alexander, and Jamie. In addition, the examiner completed interviews with Jamie, Mrs. Hughes, and Mrs. Alexander. Jamie's parents and teacher completed the Behavior Assessment System for Children (BASC-PRS and BASC-TRS). The following scores have a mean of 50 and a standard deviation of 10:

Clinical Scales	Mother	Father	Teacher
Hyperactivity	59	40	40
Aggression	63[a]	45	42
Conduct Problems	81[b]	55	51
Anxiety	93[b]	67[a]	35
Depression	88[b]	68[a]	42
Somatization	76[b]	55	59
Atypicality	58	54	59
Withdrawal	77[b]	64[a]	44
Attention Problems	84[b]	71[b]	66[a]
Learning Problems	—	—	55
Externalizing Problems Composite	77[b]	46	44
Internalizing Problems Composite	92[b]	62[a]	45
School Problems	—	—	61[a]
Behavior Symptoms Index	88[b]	60[a]	47

[a]At risk range. [b]Clinically significant score.

On the Adaptive Scales, scores below 30 are considered significantly low:

Adaptive Scales	Mother	Father	Teacher
Social Skills	32*	39*	38*
Leadership	41	45	42
Study Skills	—	—	33*
Adaptive Skills Composite	41	42	35*

*At risk range.

In describing Jamie's behavioral adjustment, Dr. and Mrs. Hughes noted significant behavioral problems in many areas, including inattention, depression, anxiety, social withdrawal, and social skills. Specifically, Dr. and Mrs. Hughes noted that Jamie cries frequently, becomes frustrated easily, worries, forgets things, and has trouble sleeping. Jamie's parents described her as shy around adults and that she sometimes has trouble making new friends.

Jamie's teacher, Mrs. Alexander, endorsed problems in the areas of inattention, social skills, and academic skills. Mrs. Alexander also noted that Jamie rarely studies with other students and does not appear confident during academic tasks. Upon interview, Mrs. Alexander noted that Jamie does not attend after-school tutorials despite teachers' beliefs that tutorials would help her improve her academic performance. Mrs. Alexander also noted problems in communicating the importance of completing school assignments to Dr. and Mrs. Hughes.

Jamie also completed the Behavior Assessment System for Children—Self-Report of Personality (BASC-SRP). The following scores have a mean of 50 and a standard deviation of 10:

Clinical Scales	*T*-Score
Attitude toward School	56
Attitude toward Teachers	59
Sensation Seeking	35
Atypicality	44
Locus of Control	67*
Somatization	39
Social Stress	58
Anxiety	45
Depression	64*
Sense of Inadequacy	62*
School Maladjustment Composite	55
Clinical Maladjustment Composite	59
Emotional Symptoms Index	58

Scores below 30 on the Personal Adjustment scales are considered significantly low.

Adaptive Scales	*T*-Score
Relations with Parents	35*
Interpersonal Relations	57
Self-Esteem	35*
Self-Reliance	46
Personal Adjustment Composite	42

*At risk range.

To better understand Jamie's personality, behavioral adjustment, and the presence of psychopathology, particularly symptoms indicative of an eating disorder, she completed three additional self-report measures: the Minnesota Multiphasic Personality Inventory—Adolescent (MMPI-A), Eating Disorder Inventory—Second Edition (EDI-2) and Eating Attitudes Test (EAT-26). Jamie produced a valid and interpretable MMPI-A personality profile (Modified Welsh Code: *'''23+14–7608/95: F/LK:). Consistent with other findings, Jamie endorsed symptoms of anxiety, depression, and somatic complaints, such as fatigue and physical exhaustion. Jamie's responses revealed that she is often unexcitable and shows little emotion; further, she reports feeling restless and tense. Results from the EDI-2 and EAT-26 revealed problems with feelings of ineffectiveness, preoccupations with food, bulimic behaviors, body dissatisfaction, and a stronger than average desire to be thin. Self-report findings indicate that Jamie is preoccupied with her weight and feels pressured to stay slender in order to stay on the dance team and to remain popular at school. Jamie reported being cautious about forming close relationships or sharing her thoughts and feelings with others. Although apparently liked by peers, Jamie is anxious and insecure about social relationships.

During clinical interview, Jamie reported binge-eating episodes and the use of compensatory behaviors in response to bingeing. Jamie stated that she has binged about 2 to 3 times per week over the past 6 months, most often binge eating between the five-block walk from ballet class to her home after school at either a fast food restaurant or ice cream shop. Similarly, Jamie reported using laxatives approximately 2 to 3 times per week over the past 6 months in order to "keep her weight down" due to the binge eating. Jamie reported that laxative use occurred prior to her parents arriving home from work. Jamie stated that she often feels hungry after dance classes, and "seeing how thin [her] classmates are" causes her to feel depressed about the shape of her body. Despite binge eating and laxative use, Jamie's weight has remained stable and within age-appropriate expectations. She denied missing menstrual periods.

In addition to eating problems, Jamie reported that her "feelings get hurt easily" and her friends are important to her. Jamie reported problems with the quality of her schoolwork and the amount of effort required to complete schoolwork. Jamie indicated self-esteem problems, particularly feelings of inadequacy. When questioned, Jamie stated that she also has a difficult relationship with her parents. Jamie reported that her parents expect her to excel academically, and she feels that she is not always able to meet their expectations.

SUMMARY AND CONCLUSION

Jamie is a 14-year-old girl who was referred for evaluation by her teacher, Carol Alexander. Mrs. Alexander requested an evaluation due to Jamie's lethargic behavior at school, poor academic performance during the semester, and apparent lack of motivation. Intelligence and academic screening revealed Superior range abilities and achievement, which were equally well-developed across all areas. Throughout the evaluation, Jamie appeared lethargic and demonstrated a restricted range of emotion. Overall, test findings are consistent with formal diagnoses of Bulimia Nervosa, Purging Type (*DSM-IV-TR* 307.51) and Major Depressive Disorder, Recurrent, Moderate (*DSM-IV-TR* 296.32).

Based on the diagnoses described earlier, the following are recommended:

1. Jamie should be examined by a pediatrician and nutritionist in order to evaluate her current physical status as well as to receive counseling regarding appropriate nutrition and health. Referral to a child psychiatrist is also recommended to determine the appropriateness of medical treatment for symptoms of depression.
2. Jamie should participate in individual cognitive-behavioral therapy (CBT) for symptoms of Bulimia Nervosa and depression. Cognitive-behavioral therapy has been shown to be an efficacious treatment for symptoms of both Bulimia Nervosa and depressive symptoms. For symptoms of Bulimia Nervosa, CBT should focus on modifying Jamie's abnormal eating behaviors and altering irrational weight- and shape-related cognitions. In our opinion, CBT targeting depressive symptoms should focus on challenging irrational beliefs informing her

self-worth and target increasing her self-efficacy. During the feedback session, the Hughes family was provided with a list of child psychotherapists with expertise in treating adolescents with eating disorders.

3. Due to the concerning degree of family distress, individual psychotherapy should be supplemented by family based intervention. Jamie needs a dependable support system, and Dr. and Mrs. Hughes need to be able to identify changes in Jamie's condition and assist her with the implementation of treatment. Additionally, Dr. and Mrs. Hughes may require therapeutic assistance with their own feelings about Jamie's diagnosis. Individual and family therapy should occur with separate therapists, who engage in close collaboration throughout intervention. Dr. and Mrs. Hughes were provided with referrals for family therapists in the area.

4. Jamie would likely benefit from being accompanied by a classmate during her walk from ballet class to her home. Based on the clinical interview, Jamie frequently engages in binge eating episodes during this period of time. With the presence of a supportive peer, we believe she would be much less likely to engage in binge eating during the transition from class to her house.

5. Based on consultation with Jamie's pediatrician, nutritionist, and individual therapist, Jamie should keep a food diary to determine her patterns of eating and caloric intake. Such a diary should include the foods eaten, time of meal, portion size, and estimated number of calories.

6. Treatment providers should collaborate closely in coordinating psychological and medical care for Jamie.

Discussion of Case Study

Jamie's psychological evaluation highlights the critical domains of interest and demonstrates the practical assessment methods described in the chapter. In particular, the evaluation made use of several self-reports of general behavioral adjustment and specific eating disorder psychopathology: the EDI-2, EAT-26, MMPI-A, and the BASC-SRP. Additionally, the clinician conducted interviews with Jamie and her mother to obtain information about Jamie's developmental and eating history as well as her current functioning. Jamie was diagnosed with Bulimia Nervosa, Purging Type due to repeated episodes of binge eating and laxative use over the past 6 months. Her symptoms met the *DSM-IV-TR* (American Psychiatric Association, 2000) criteria for severity and duration of the binging and purging episodes. During clinical interview and through self-report, Jamie provided evidence that her self-esteem was linked to the shape of her body and her weight. Jamie is not diagnosed with Anorexia Nervosa, Binge-eating/Purging Type because she does not exhibit severe weight loss or amenorrhea. Jamie is diagnosed with Bulimia Nervosa, Purging Type rather than Binge Eating Disorder (ED-NOS) because she engages in compensatory purging behaviors following a binge-eating episode.

Jamie also presented with clinically significant symptoms of Major Depressive Disorder as well as some symptoms of anxiety, both of which are not uncommon for individuals diagnosed with eating disorders. Depressive symptoms were observed by the assessment team during the examination and endorsed by Jamie's mother upon interview and questionnaire report. Jamie also indicated symptoms of depression in her interview and on self-report measures. Jamie reported feelings of ineffectiveness and low self-esteem, both of which are relevant to BN symptomatology. She also indicated conflict in the family over her academic performance and expectations.

The assessment services provided within the private clinic did not include other important professional disciplines; therefore, the recommendations emphasized the importance of follow-up evaluations with medical professionals, including a nutritionist. Although Jamie did not present with clear evidence of physical problems, such as emaciation, and her most recent physical examination revealed age-appropriate weight, a thorough physical examination is warranted due to the varied medical complications associated with BN. Recommendations for psychological treatment were based on outcome literature identifying CBT as an empirically supported therapy for BN (e.g., Fairburn & Harrison, 2003). Family therapy was also recommended due to family stress revealed during the interview. In our recommendations, we highlighted the importance of collaboration between treatment providers.

In terms of the risk factors and clinical features associated with BN, Jamie is an adolescent female being raised in an industrialized society. The onset of her eating disorder occurred in the most frequent age range for first diagnosis, between 14 and 19. Jamie was diagnosed with a depressive disorder prior to the present evaluation, suggesting that depression may have precipitated the onset of her eating disorder. Her depressive symptoms were marked by low self-esteem, which has been identified as a risk factor for eating disorders. Finally, Jamie was involved in ballet instruction, an activity that historically places importance on weight control.

Conclusion

With the rise in prevalence of eating and feeding disorders, particularly BN over the past 10 to 15 years, psychologists can expect referrals for children with eating disturbances. The chapter presented a summary of constructs of interest as well as recommended methods for assessment. Assessment of suspected eating or feeding disorders should include evaluation of multiple domains of functioning and ideally occur in the context of a multidisciplinary team. If multidisciplinary evaluation is not possible, referral to pediatricians is absolutely essential.

The EDE, a semi-structured interview closely aligned with *DSM-IV-TR* criteria, is considered the gold standard for diagnosis of eating disorders. Self-report measures such as the EDI-2, EAT, or EDE-Q offer possible alternatives to the EDE. Other methods such as the QEWP-A, BRS, and BIA measure specific behaviors in eating disorders. The high frequency of comorbid psychiatric disorders in the presence of eating disorders, particularly anxiety, depression, and substance abuse, make comprehensive assessment of social-emotional functioning important. Behavioral observation systems such as the BED, BATMAN, food diaries, or meal observations offer methods for functional analysis of problem behaviors. Parent report measures such as the BASC-PRS and CEBI are useful for delineating specific problem behaviors. When communicating findings of the evaluation with parents and the child or adolescent, clinicians should present findings in a clear, organized manner. Treatment plans, support groups, and printed materials should be made available to the family at the informing session.

Diagnosis of Attention-Deficit/ Hyperactivity Disorder and Its Subtypes

Mauricio A. García-Barrera and Randy W. Kamphaus

Constructs of Interest

Attention is a multidimensional construct that can refer to "alertness, arousal, selectivity, sustained attention, distractibility, or span of apprehension" (Barkley, 1998). According to accepted definitions of the disorder, individuals with Attention-Deficit/Hyperactivity Disorder (ADHD) have age-inappropriate difficulties with attention and tend to have most difficulty with sustained attention, particularly during uninteresting tasks, such as homework or independent class work. For these reasons, children with ADHD usually avoid difficult or uninteresting schoolwork or have difficulty concentrating on such schoolwork (Sanchez, Miller, Garcia, & Hynd, 2004).

Theoretically, ADHD is commonly associated with dysfunction in the frontal lobes, due to the association between the behavioral characteristics of ADHD and frontal lobe functions (Sanchez et al., 2004). Research has demonstrated that some neuropsychological measures associated with frontal lobe systems differentiate controls from children with ADHD, but some measures have failed in differentiating between individuals with ADHD and other clinical groups (Barkley, 1991b; Lazar & Frank, 1998; Matier-Sharma, Perachio, & Newcorn, 1995). Due to this inconsistent evidence the etiology of

319

ADHD remains controversial, although the search for neurological explanations for the disorder continues to be pursued with vigor.

Hynd and colleagues demonstrated that, although nondiagnosed children evidence bigger left than right anterior-width measurements of the frontal lobes, this normal anterior asymmetry is not found in children with ADHD. Moreover, children with ADHD have often shown significantly smaller right anterior width measurements than normal (Hynd, Semrud-Clikeman, Lorys, Novey, & Eliopulos, 1990). Alternatively, some MRI studies have supported the idea that a disturbed circuit underlies ADHD. The first area implicated is a dorsolateral circuit, which subserves executive function and includes the dorsolateral cortex, dorsal caudate nucleus head, internal globus pallidus, mediodorsal nucleus of the thalamus, and the dorsal cortex of areas 9 and 10 of the frontal lobes. A second area of interest is the orbitofrontal circuit, which has been associated with the control of behaviors and emotions. Another circuit that underlies motivation and inhibitory control is the anterior cingulate circuit (Sanchez et al., 2004).

According to neurochemical theories, neurotransmitters, specifically the catecholamines, dopamine, and norepinephrine, have been implicated in ADHD (Halperin et al., 1993, 1997; Zametkin & Rapoport, 1987). These neurotransmitters are thought to affect attention, inhibition, response of the motor system, and motivation. An imbalance in the formation of one of these neurotransmitters results in decreased stimulation of certain brain stem regions, such as the locus coeruleus, affecting arousal level and frontal lobe functioning. Several studies proving the efficacy of treatment with psychostimulants on ADHD have provided indirect support for the idea that altering the specific neurotransmitter's activity alleviates ADHD symptomatology (Pelham et al., 1990; Riccio, Hynd, & Cohen, 1996).

Although neurological and neuropsychological theory has held sway in the search for the principal etiology or etiologies of ADHD, these theories have not been sufficiently supported to be incorporated into accepted diagnostic criteria. Hence, the diagnosis of ADHD, like other disorders in this text, remains based on the assessment of behavioral indicators of the presence of the disorder, independent of presumed etiology. Assessment of etiology is important for the design of effective treatments for numerous disorders (Kamphaus & Frick, 2002).

Diagnostic Standards

One of the most controversial diagnoses in psychology and psychiatry has been the diagnosis of ADHD (National Institutes of Health, 2000; Paule et al., 2000). Two major parts of this controversy are discussed herein: (1) the difficulty in defining the core symptoms of this syndrome and (2) the concern about overdiagnosis.

First, the American Psychiatric Association has attempted, on several occasions, to create a collection of core symptoms that reflect the variety of expression of the disorder; in fact, the ADHD nomenclature has changed extensively. The second edition of the *DSM* (*DSM-II*), for example, prioritized the presence of motor overactivity as the core symptom for the syndrome. Attention-Deficit/Hyperactivity Disorder was then recognized as Hyperkinetic Reaction of Childhood (American Psychiatric Association, 1968).

In the *DSM-III*, two new ideas were included: (1) an emphasis on the core problems of attention deficit and (2) the recognition of the presence of attention problems without hyperactivity. This new conceptualization created the need for the distinction between two subtypes of the syndrome: (1) Attention-Deficit Disorder without Hyperactivity (ADD/WO) and Attention-Deficit Disorder with Hyperactivity (ADD/H), subtypes that differed in terms of the presence or absence of motor hyperactivity, but shared the necessary presence of inattention symptoms as primary for making the diagnosis (American Psychiatric Association, 1980). This dichotomous classification is consistent with recent research findings since factor analytic studies have demonstrated the existence of at least two core symptom dimensions: (1) inattention/disorganization and (2) impulsivity/hyperactivity (Lahey, Carlson, & Frick, 1997). Later, Barkley (1998) concluded that there was not empirical support for this two subtype conceptualization of ADHD. In contrast to what was suggested by research, the revision of the *DSM-III*, the *DSM-III-R*, tried to eliminate this dichotomy by removing the subtypes and by placing both hyperactivity and attention deficit at the same level of importance for making the diagnosis. The name "Attention-Deficit/Hyperactivity Disorder" was then established to indicate a unidimensional conceptualization of the syndrome (American Psychiatric Association, 1987).

The *DSM-IV* (American Psychiatric Association, 1994), and the most recent revision of the *DSM,* the *DSM-IV-TR* (American Psychiatric Association, 2000) attempted to diffuse the controversy between research findings and diagnostic criteria created by the *DSM-III-R.* This last revision rescued the subclassification of the syndrome and accepted the existence of three subtypes: (1) ADHD Predominantly Inattentive Type (ADHD-PI), to designate children with problems of inattention but without problems of impulsivity and hyperactivity; (2) ADHD Predominantly Hyperactive Type (ADHD-PHI), to designate children with problems of impulsivity and hyperactivity without problems of inattention; and finally (3) ADHD Combined Type (ADHD-C), to designate children with significant problems in both areas of behavior dysfunction.

Although this last version of the *DSM-IV* has been considered for years a better fit to research findings than previous editions, there is a group of researchers that disagree with the subtype classification (Kamphaus & Frick, 2002). They believe that ADHD-PI is not a subtype of ADHD and that this diagnosis may be applied to a subset of children that have qualitatively different disorders of attention and cognitive processing that should be separated from ADHD (Barkley, 1998, 2001, 2003a, 2003b; Milich, Balentine, & Lynam, 2001). There is also an argument that ADHD-PHI is not clearly separated from ADHD-C, and the latter could be just an early developmental stage of the former (Barkley, 2003a). These arguments are still under analysis and research, but these points have been discussed, criticized, and even considered unnecessary (Hinshaw, 2001; Lahey, 2001; Pelham, 2001).

Some of the findings from dimensional approaches to assessment of the core symptoms are also controversial, and challenge subtype classification. One study that investigated the categorization of ADHD using the *DSM-IV* criteria, and utilizing a latent class analytic approach, found three separate domains of symptoms: (1) a predominantly inattentive domain, (2) a hyperactive/impulsive domain, and (3) a combined domain, in agreement with the *DSM-IV* classification (Hudziak et al., 1998). However, the authors pointed out the inaccuracy of using a yes-no categorical approach to describe the symptomatology for the diagnosis of ADHD, due to the finding that the core symptoms appeared to be continuously distributed in the population (Hudziak et al., 1998).

Alternatively, Neuman et al. (1999), using a latent class approach as well but with the *DSM-III-R* criteria, identified two groups: (1) an inattentive group and (2) a group with combined hyperactive and impulsive symptoms. However, these data identified not only these two categories but also a number of additional classes, suggesting again the dimensional nature of the symptom distribution. These results raised a concern among clinicians about the possibility that children with significant attention problems are not being identified with the categorical model offered by the *DSM-IV* classification approach (Hudziak et al., 1998). Table 10.1 summarizes the major

Table 10.1   **Characteristics of Disorder and Dimension-Based Approaches to Diagnosis of ADHD**

Disorder Approach	Dimensional Approach
Focuses on qualitative diagnosis.	Considers quantitative variation throughout the distribution.
The emphasis is on the average differences between diagnosed extreme groups (in a normal curve) and the rest of the population	Considers continuous traits, normally distributed.
Methodologically, studies use relatively small selected samples, typically employing interviews.	Studies large unselected samples, generally using questionnaires.
Emphasizes clinical research.	Emphasizes non-clinical research
Statistically, this approach uses concordances.	Correlations are used. Even in genetic research, concordances are converted into liability (tetrachoric) correlations that assume a continuum of liability underlying a dichotomous disorder (liability-threshold model)

Source: "Dimensions and Disorders of Adolescent Adjustment: A Quantitative Genetic Analysis of Unselected Samples and Selected Extremes," by K. Deater-Deckard, D. Reiss, E. M. Hetherington, and R. Plomin, 1997, *Journal of Child Psychology and Psychiatry, 38*(5), pp. 515–525.

differences between what they call the dimensional and the disorder-oriented approaches (adapted from Deater-Deckard et al., 1997).

A second issue to consider regarding the controversy over ADHD diagnosis is the growing concern about misdiagnosis and even overdiagnosis of this syndrome. As a point of fact, there are reports of an increase of more than 500% in the amount of methylphenidate (e.g., Ritalin and Concerta) prescribed in the United States between 1991 and 1999. Prescriptions for amphetamines (e.g., Dexedrine and Adderall), another type of medication commonly used for ADHD, have been reported as having increased more than 2000% during the same interval (Sax & Kautz, 2003). There is also report of variation in the prescribing of stimulants among U.S. regions, since every State Board of Medical Examiners establishes different parameters (Burton, 2001; LeFever, Dawson, & Morrow, 1999). Furthermore, ADHD seems to be one of the most common referrals to school psychologists and child mental health providers (DuPaul & Stoner, 1994).

Regarding the increased amount of referrals for ADHD assessments, Sax and Kautz (2003) studied the referral source, or who first suggested the diagnosis of ADHD, surveying physicians in the metropolitan Washington, DC, area. Their study, although limited in its methodology, has been considered innovative and of clinical importance. The results showed that physicians perceived that teachers are most likely to be the first to suggest the diagnosis of ADHD (46.4%), followed by parents (30.2%) and primary care physicians (11.3%). The authors suggested that changes in the early elementary curriculum during the past 10 to 20 years, from a play-based curriculum to an emphasis on the early acquisition of literacy skills under a more academically oriented curriculum, could explain this increment in the referral of children from teacher to physician for suspected ADHD. They also recommended further research on the teacher's accuracy in suggesting the diagnosis (Sax & Kautz, 2003).

The *DSM-IV-TR* (American Psychiatric Association, 2000) included three major parameters that clinicians must systematically assess when making this diagnosis. The first parameter is the frequency and severity of the symptoms. This criterion establishes that at least six of nine symptoms must be present in any of the inattention-disorganization (Inattentive Type) or impulsivity-hyperactivity (Hyperactive Type) areas, or six of nine symptoms in both subtypes to classify a child as Combined Type. This criterion intends to certify the presence of a significant level of impairment to give a diagnosis of a *disorder*. Some researchers from a dimensional approach have criticized the use of these cutoff points as being arbitrary for determining who is affected if ADHD symptomatology is assumed to be on a continuum rather than categorical in nature (Hudziak et al., 1998, 1999; Neuman et al., 1999). This criterion has been also questioned when applied to preschoolers, because many young children exhibit these kinds of behavior and eventually outgrow them (Barkley, 2003a, 2003b; S. B. Campbell, 1990), and also when applied to adolescents or young adults as being too conservative for their age and normal developmental changes (Barkley, 1997, 2003b). Barkley (2003a, 2003b) suggests that the symptom cutoff score (of six over nine) may need to be adjusted for gender bias. He argues that girls display fewer *DSM-IV* items/symptoms and to a less severe degree than boys, in addition to the disproportional representation of males versus females in the *DSM* field trial, thus making the symptoms threshold more appropriate for males, resulting in a higher number of false negatives among the females. The threshold for diagnosis for both sexes may be set so low as to create overdiagnosis. Ostrander et al. (1998) studied the relationship between inattention scale *T*-scores on the BASC Parent Rating Scales and the Child Behavior Checklist for a larger sample of children diagnosed with ADHD. They found that the best concordance between the dimensional scales and the *DSM* criteria was a *T*-score of 61, thus suggesting that the *DSM* criteria may be selecting nearly 25% of the school age population for potential diagnosis with ADHD. This outcome is possible given the popularity of rating scales in school-based assessment programs (Hart & Lahey, 1999). These findings collectively call into question the diagnostic threshold of the *DSM* systems and argue for the use of cut scores or ranges of cut scores based on normative data for the population, a characteristic of dimensional rather than categorical approaches to diagnosis.

The second parameter is the onset and duration of the symptoms. The criterion here establishes two conditions: (1) the symptoms must be present and cause impairment before age 7 years; and (2) the symptoms must be present for at least 6 months. This latter parameter is consistent with the idea that ADHD is a lifelong pattern of maladaptive behavior and not a transient reaction to a stressor or to the demands of a particular developmental stage (Barkley, 1997). However, this criterion has been considered impractical in some cases, due to the common difficulty that clinicians experience when collecting accurate data about the past (Barkley, 1997), in addition to the fact that Inattentive Type symptoms are harder to detect in earlier elementary school years, which results in more diagnosis of the Hyperactive/Impulsive Type (Barkley, 1998, 2003b; Loeber, Green, Lahey, Christ, & Frick, 1992; Root II & Resnick, 2003). Barkley (2003a, 2003b) argues that the 6 months duration-criterion was chosen without research support; in addition, he considers that the 6-month period is too short and it should be a 12-month period at minimum.

The third and last parameter to consider when deciding if the levels of inattention and/or hyperactivity are abnormal is the specification of cross-situational consistency of symptoms. In other words, to meet this criterion the symptoms have to be observed and create impairment in two or more settings (e.g., home, school, or neighborhood). There are cases in which, given different conditions across settings (e.g., variety of demands, time of the day, or level of structure), it must be difficult to interpret this criterion; therefore, the clinician should observe and compare behaviors taking into account those differences in settings. Barkley (2003a, 2003b) argues that given the literature about the modest degree of agreement among parent and teacher ratings, the best detection of ADHD children might be achieved by blending the reports of both sources and to count the number of symptoms endorsed across them. There is not a consensus, however, about whether impairment in one setting is more important than another. It could very well be that impairment at home and in the community is less devastating than impairment in school, thus not warranting the diagnosis in out-of-school settings.

This syndrome has long been controversial also because comorbidities are omnipresent. Specifically, aggression and conduct problems are so commonly associated with ADHD-C that some researchers have wondered whether Conduct Disorder and Oppositional Defiant Disorder are separate syndromes from ADHD (Kamphaus & Frick, 2002). New theories of child classification, described in detail in the last chapter of this text, suggest that ADHD-C is an inherently complex disorder with diverse symptom presentation, more so than is acknowledged by the *DSM* system. Kamphaus et al. (1997), using teacher ratings, have shown that a cluster of children in the population may possess this complex form of the disorder that includes aggression, conduct, academic problems; sadness/depression; poorly developed social, study and interpersonal skills; and poor emotional self-control (see Figure 10.2). This cluster of child adjustment has been replicated in several samples using both parent and teacher ratings, and it is associated with significant behavioral and academic impairment at school (DiStefano et al., 2003). Findings such as these may influence changes in the *DSM* criteria of the future and, currently, may be useful for research purposes in anticipation of later clinical application. This complex form of the disorder, for example, suggests the need for a multipronged treatment regimen.

These cluster analytic results also reveal that typical forms of ADHD are characterized by significant deficits in the development of prosocial, proacademic, and self-regulatory skills. The assessment of these deficits, as opposed to behavioral excesses or symptoms, is necessary for adding important areas to the treatment plan.

Assessment Methods

When a child is referred as being suspected of having ADHD, it is necessary to design a multidimensional assessment plan—an evaluation process that should include multiple raters, multiple methods, and data from across multiple-settings. In other words, the evaluator should include all possible points of view and a variety of sources to collect enough data before making a diagnostic decision, keeping in mind that the ADHD diagnosis is controversial not only in the literature but also among the parents and teachers that refer for a consult (see Table 10.2 for a synthesis of major issues in the assessment process based on prior research). Furthermore, it is important to

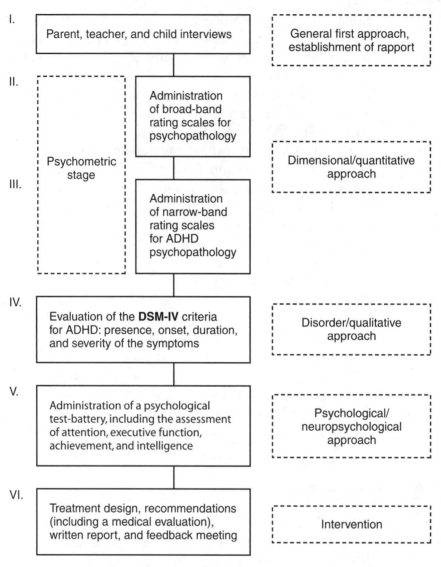

Figure 10.1

Assessment Process model.

address an evaluation process oriented toward intervention; for this reason, a consultative problem-solving model (Landau & Burcham, 1996) and functional analysis of behavior (Boyajian, DuPaul, Handler, Eckert, & McGoey, 2001; DuPaul & Ervin, 1996) are recommended as well.

Table 10.2   **Implications of Research findings for Assessment of ADHD**

Focus of Research	Implications for Assessment
Classification and presence of subtypes	Assess for presence of two core dimensions of behavior—inattention/disorganization and hyperactivity/impulsivity.
	Assess for subtypes based on presence of hyper-activity/impulsivity.
	Assess duration to determine if behaviors are chronic and stable.
	Assess situational variability of behaviors.
	Assess level of impairment associated with symptoms.
Presence of multiple comorbidities	Assess for presence of conduct problems/aggression.
	Assess for presence of learning problems.
	Assess for self-esteem problems.
	Assess social relationships and peer social status.
	Assess level of parent-child and teacher-child conflict.
Potential alternative causes	Obtain a developmental and medical history.
	Assess for intellectual and learning deficits.
	Assess for emotional difficulties.

Source: Clinical Assessment of Child and Adolescent Personality and Behavior (p. 384), second edition, by R. W. Kamphaus and P. J. Frick, 2002, Boston, MA: Allyn & Bacon. Copyright 2002, 1996, by Allyn & Bacon. Reprinted with permission.

This multimethod plan can be thought of as a series of steps. The first step is to determine to what extent the child presents symptomatology related to inattention and/or hyperactivity. The clinician must interview at least the parent(s), the teacher(s), and the child to obtain this information. The parent's interview is indispensable for obvious reasons; however, this vast source of information can be unreliable (Barkley, 1998). Wisely, Hinshaw (1994) stated that in the case of choosing just one assessment tool, among all the possible ones in diagnosing ADHD, a complete developmental and family history, taken from the parent interview, would be his choice. Alternatively, the teacher's interview provides invaluable data given their knowledge of how a child should behave according to his or her age and their access to observations of learning and social behavior. A child interview may not provide very reliable information, but it can be important for rapport, observation of behavior, social skills, adaptability, and for determining the presence of other psychopathology (Brock, 1997).

Different methods are used in this part of the process; structured, semi-structured, or unstructured models of interview can be helpful, always considering that this information will be the most important piece for the diagnosis because we are assessing behavior (Root II & Resnick, 2003). The advantages of a structured interview are that it intends to cover as much area of interest for diagnosis as possible; although it is considered to be sensitive and reliable in detecting ADHD, it should not be used alone (Hinshaw, 1994). If an unstructured interview is chosen, it must address a number of diagnostic questions including, for example, family history of ADHD, description of the symptoms/complaints, age of onset of the symptoms, how long the symptoms have been present, any developmental history that could be suggestive of ADHD, interpersonal-familial difficulties, learning difficulties, economic-social difficulties, and the environment at home and at school. The advantages of an unstructured interview are that it (a) provides opportunities to establish an adequate rapport with the clients, (b) is flexible, (c) focuses in the interviewer's concerns, and (d) provides a valuable source of psychosocial information. However, unstructured interviews have generally been found to be unreliable in diagnosing ADHD, with the lone exception of a modification of the Structured Developmental History of the Behavior Assessment System for Children (BASC; Johnson-Cramer, 1999), which is a semi-structured interview that combines elements of both methods: open questions and some fixed formats. Among its strengths, it (a) is reported to be a helpful method in assessing the child's developmental and school history, (b) is an excellent tool in documenting ADHD symptoms, (c) seems to be the friendliest to clinicians and clients, and (d) is also practical in terms of testing time (Barkley, 1991a, 1998; Brock, 1997; Hinshaw, 1994).

Rating scales are considered to be a very valuable tool in the assessment of ADHD because of their (a) suitability for documenting impairment in the two core symptom clusters, (b) use of a extensive normative data for comparison of the population at large, demonstrated reliability and validity, and (c) ease and reasonable cost of usage (Barkley, 1998; Brock, 1997; Demaray, Elting, & Schaefer, 2003; Hart & Lahey, 1999). There are two types of rating measures: (1) narrow-band and (2) broad-band. In the case of ADHD diagnosis, it is recommended to utilize broad-band measures first (e.g., Child Behavior Checklist; BASC). This type of scale allows the clinician to identify the behavioral traits and core constructs of the child's behavior. Broad-band measures provide normative data that can be utilized for differential diagnosis and assessment of comorbid features, facilitating the recollection of general information that helps with the detection of psychopathology when symptoms are significantly and clinically deviated from the norms. A narrow-band measure that assesses only the core symptoms of ADHD is recommended as a follow-up assessment if needed. This type of measurement will provide specific information concerning the assessment of ADHD symptomatology (Angello et al., 2003; Pliszka, Carlson, & Swanson, 1999; Volpe & DuPaul, 2001).

However, given the extensive array of rating scales currently available, several conditions must be analyzed when selecting an appropriate instrument: (a) age of the child, (b) cultural background, (c) purpose of the assessment (e.g., diagnosis, treatment, school placement), (d) psychometric properties of the instrument (validity evidence, reliability evidence), and (e) normative data. The clinician should also feel comfortable with its use, being informed about the strengths and limitations of the selected scale(s) (Angello et al., 2003; Demaray et al., 2003).

Some of the key factors regarding the selection of the scales that should be considered are discussed herein. First, pay close attention to item content. An ideal scale is one that provides the most valid measurement of the two core constructs of ADHD: hyperactivity/impulsivity and inattention/disorganization. Many measures include lists of behaviors that are similar to ADHD behaviors but are not exactly alike. Some are accurate, but some are distortions of what is currently viewed as a core symptom for this syndrome, and some are irrelevant. Unfortunately, some of these "junk" items are intermixed with core behaviors, and, as a result, some measures have no direct indicator of ADHD symptoms.

Second, some measures are not well designed to help the clinician with the identification of an ADHD subtype in the diagnostic process. Often measures provide overall composites or scales that include both types of behaviors, those indicative of inattention/disorganization and those indicative of impulsive/overactive behaviors. The problem arises when trying to distinguish between the ADHD-PI and ADHD-PHI because the items that ask for both types of behaviors are originally intermixed in the composite.

Third, as stated earlier, an ideal ADHD assessment battery must include multiple sources to obtain more reliable and accurate information. A clinician should have in hand at least one rating scale that provides a variety of forms that will help to determine the situational variability of behaviors. An ideal scale should have parent, teacher, and self-report versions. Therefore, we must choose a set of assessment instruments that provides a multi-informant and multimodal assessment of the core ADHD behaviors.

Fourth, a clinician should have information that allows comparison to age norms. Most of the scales' authors follow this rule, if the scales are validated and standardized properly. Although ADHD is still under continuous research, there is agreement across theories about the developmental change of the ADHD symptomatology throughout the life span. Therefore, an assessment must provide information that allows one to compare a child's behaviors to the behaviors of other children of a similar developmental level. However, it is important to recognize guidelines (e.g., *DSM*) when evaluating normative data. Indeed, in the case of ADHD, gender-specific norms are not recommended because definitions of ADHD do not make any restriction that the behaviors be inconsistent for a child gender, and there is even disagreement regarding ratio disproportion in the prevalence of ADHD between boys and girls. Table 10.3 summarizes general features of seven common rating scales for ADHD assessment (for an extended review of the most used rating scales in ADHD see Angello et al., 2003; Kamphaus & Frick, 2002; Demaray et al., 2003).

During the next assessment stage, review of data, clinicians should make an effort to review the child's complete school and health records, including previous intelligence, cognitive, or achievement

Table 10.3 **Descriptions of Measures of ADHD**

Rating Scale	Author(s)	Forms (Number of Items)	Age Range/ Grade Levels	Subscales
ADHD Rating Scale-IV (ADHD-IV)	DuPaul, Power, Anastopoulos, and Reid (1998)	Teacher (18) Parent (18)	5–18/K–12	Inattention, Hyperactivity/Impulsivity, Total
ADHD Symptom Checklist-4 (SC-4)	Gadow and Sprafkin (1997)	Teacher (50) Parent (50)	3–18/ PreK–12	Inattentive, Hyperactive/Impulsive, ODD, Peer Conflict, Stimulant Side Effects
ADD-H Comprehensive Teacher's Rating Scale (ACTeRS)	Ullmann, Sleator, and Sprague (1997)	Teacher (24) Parent (25)	5–14	Attention, Hyperactivity, Social Skills, Oppositional Behavior, Early Childhood (Parent only)
Attention Deficit Disorders Evaluation Scale—Second Edition (ADDES-2)	McCarney (1995a)	School (60) Home (46)	4–18 (School) 3–18 (Home)	Inattentive, Hyperactive/Impulsive
Early Childhood Attention Deficit Disorders Evaluation Scale (ECADDES)	McCarney (1995b)	Teacher (56) Parent (50)	2–6	Inattention, Hyperactive/Impulsive
BASC Monitor for ADHD (BASC-M)	Kamphaus and Reynolds (1998)	Teacher (47) Parent (46)	4–18	Attention problems, Hyperactivity, Internalizing Problems, Adaptive Skills
Conners' Parent and Teacher Rating Scales—Revised (CPRS-R, CTRS-R)	Conners (1997)	*Short Forms* Teacher (28) Parent (27) Student (27) *Long Forms* Teacher (59) Parent (80) Student (87)	3–17 (Parent/ Teacher)/PreK–12 12–17 (Student)	Oppositional, Cognitive Problems/Inattentive, Hyperactivity, ADHD Index Oppositional, Cognitive/Inattention, Hyperactivity, Anxious-Shy, Social Problems, Perfectionism, Psychosomatic (Parent only), Global Index, ADHD Index, DSM-IV Symptom Subscales (Inattentive, Hyperactive-Impulsive)

testing, report cards, and medical and psychological records. The goal here, when ADHD is suspected, is to determine the age of onset, severity, and duration of the symptoms, following the *DSM-IV* criteria.

Peer nominations and peer ratings have been very useful measures of behavior; however, it has become over time more difficult for clinicians to obtain the required authorizations that allow the collection of this type of data, due to its social impact among peers, although it remains a common tool for research purposes. Additionally, any behavioral observation of the child and of the parent-child interactions, informally collected during the interviews or during other tasks, becomes very useful later on the assessment process (Root II & Resnick, 2003). Self-reports of peer interactions are one tool that may be used to collect these data (C. R. Reynolds & Kamphaus, 2004), thereby approximating the need for direct data collection from peers (Kamphaus & Frick, 2002).

Psychological tests are also an important source of data for ruling out alternative causes or assessing comorbidities; however, there is not research or data that demonstrates a particular test as being the gold standard tool for ADHD diagnosis. Among all the possible psychological and neuropsychological types of tests, the Continuous Performance Test (CPT) seems to be the most common laboratory cognitive task used for ADHD diagnosis (Barkley, 1998; Brock, 1997; Goldstein & Goldstein, 1990; Rapport, Chung, Shore, Denney, & Isaacs, 2000; Riccio, Reynolds, & Lowe, 2001). Although the CPT and related measures possess evidence of sensitivity (Rapport et al., 2000); reviews of the literature have documented problems with specificity (Nichols & Waschbusch, 2004). In other words, these measures are able to detect inattention problems, but not their etiology. The inattention problems could be due to the effects of illness, medication, temporary difficulties, or any range of problems not associated with ADHD. The original paradigm of the CPT was developed by Rosvold, Mirsky, Sarason, Bransome, and Beck in 1956 to study vigilance in normal and in brain-damaged subjects. The paradigm consisted in two types of CPT tasks: The X-type in which the subjects were asked to respond by pressing a lever whenever they see the designated target letter appear (in this case, *X*), and the AX-type in which the target was the letter X only *after* the letter A was presented. Two types of errors are analyzed in the CPT: (1) *omission errors* (or misses), which are considered to be a measure of inattention, and (2) *commission errors* (or false alarms), which are considered to be a measure of impulsivity. Being the most common test in clinical and research-oriented literature, CPT has been modified since 1956 several times.

The most appropriate statement to make about the CPT and related measures is that they should not be used as the sole source of ADHD cognitive assessment or even diagnostic for ADHD as is sometimes the case in clinical practice (Swanson, 1992; for an extended review of the CPT and related measures, see Riccio et al., 2001).

There is an extensive list of direct measures and laboratory tasks that have been used and studied regarding ADHD assessment and diagnosis in both clinical and research settings (for an extended review of different laboratory measures typically used to assess characteristics associated with ADHD, see Rapport et al., 2000). Table 10.4 briefly summarizes some of the most widely used measures of attention, executive functions, and other cognitive abilities that can be related to or be affected by the ADHD symptomatology.

Finally, when the testing is completed, the clinician ends the assessment process with the report and a feedback session with the parents and the child. The written report should contain a synthesis of the developmental, medical, and academic history, and every test that was administered to the child. (For a detailed description of a report format see the case study.) A list of treatment recommendations must be included as well. One should start by suggesting a physical exam (if one has not yet been performed) to rule out medical problems that can produce symptomatology similar to or related to ADHD (American Academy of Pediatrics, 2000) and also to determine if there is any condition that can contraindicate the use of stimulants or other medications. The physician becomes, in this way, a member of the diagnostic team process, and this strategic alliance is especially recommended when the evaluation process is oriented toward a treatment plan. In many cases, there are physical conditions associated with ADHD symptoms that may require treatment in their own right, such as seizure disorders and asthma (Brock, 1997; Goldstein & Goldstein, 1990; Root II & Resnick,

Table 10.4 **Laboratory Cognitive Tasks for Assessing ADHD**

Test or Task	Task Description	Construct Measured or Cognitive Ability
Continuous Performance Test (CPT): Auditory or Verbal There are several versions (e.g. Rosvold, Mirsky, Sarason, Bransome, & Beck, 1956; M. Gordon, 1983; Conners, 1995)	The child is instructed to press a button each time a predetermined stimulus is presented.	*Attention:* Omission errors—number of times the designated stimulus is presented and the child fails to press the button. *Impulsivity:* Commission errors—number of times the child incorrectly presses the button when the designated stimulus is not presented. *Response inhibition:* From a variation of the original version in which the child is asked to respond when they detect a predetermined stimulus after seeing another predetermined letter.
Gordon Diagnostic System (M. Gordon, 1991)	Three tasks: 1. Standard Delay Task (delay responding for six seconds). 2. Standard Vigilance Task (respond to 1s followed by 9s). 3. Distractibility Task (ignore distracting stimuli).	*Attention:* Omission errors. –Inhibition of responding: Delay task –Sustained attention: Vigilance task –Selective attention: Distractibility task *Impulsivity:* Commission errors.
Stop Signal Task (SST): Go/No Go tasks (Logan, 1994)	The child is asked to respond as quickly as possible to visual stimuli and try to inhibit their responses when an auditory tone is heard (a forced-choice reaction time task).	*Behavioral inhibition/response time:* Ability to stop—suddenly and completely—a planned or ongoing thought or action. This ability is measured principally by the Stop Signal Reaction Time (SSRT), which is an estimation of the time the child needs to stop their usual behavior in response to a trained stop signal.
Tower of Hanoi, Porteus Mazes, WISC-Mazes, Rey-Osterreith Complex Figure Drawing Test	The child is asked to performed tasks were planning of motor responses is required to succeed (e.g., drawing, finding the way out from a maze, finding a sequence of movements in a goal-oriented task).	*Control of motor responses—Planning*

Table 10.4   *Continued*

Test or Task	Task Description	Construct Measured or Cognitive Ability
SST: Go/No Go, CPT, Match-to-Sample tests, Stroop Color-Word Test, Wisconsin Card Sorting Task.	Motor inhibition tests were the child is tested for errors of commission, decreased accuracy or shorter latency of response, interference effects from conflicting stimuli, and set-shifting difficulties.	*Control of motor responses—Execution and inhibition*
Backward digits span, self-ordered pointing, paced auditory serial addition, Simon Tone/Color Game and Dot Test of Visuospatial Working Memory	The child is asked to retain in a operational memory increasing amounts of information (letters, numbers, colors, tones, dots).	*Working memory*

2003). Figure 10.2 summarizes the recommended steps in the ADHD assessment process.

Attention-Deficit/Hyperactivity Disorder, Special Education, and Federal Law

Attention-Deficit/Hyperactivity Disorder (ADHD) has been fully recognized by both state and federal special education regulations, an important step toward ensuring that children with ADHD and academic deficits receive special school services based on need (Root II & Resnick, 2003). For example, Section 504 of the 1973 Rehabilitation Act prohibits schools from discriminating against people with disabilities; in other words, schools receiving any federal funds must provide an equal education for individuals with disabilities including ADHD. In addition, the Individuals with Disabilities Education Act (IDEA) provides for a free and appropriate public education for the child or adolescent with ADHD, it mandates a multidisciplinary evaluation process, and it requires the development of an individualized educational plan for each student diagnosed with ADHD. Finally, the Americans with Disabilities Act (ADA) mandates that reasonable accommodations be made for individuals who have a substantial limitation of a major life activity (such as learning, which can be

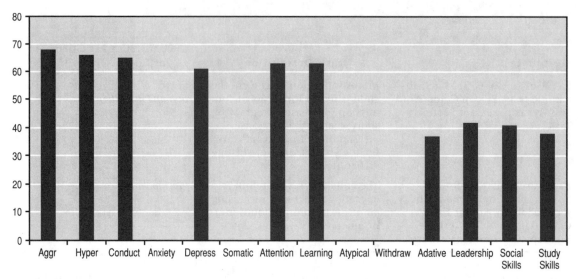

Figure 10.2

Cluster 3: Disruptive behavior problems. *Source:* "A Typology of Teacher Rated Child Behavior for a National U.S. Sample," by R. W. Kamphaus, C. J. Huberty, C. DiStefano, and M. D. Petoskey, 1997, *Journal of Abnormal Child Psychology, 25,* pp. 453–463.

impaired by ADHD) in areas such as schooling or the workplace. Thus, the more widespread diagnosis of ADHD has increased expenditures for special education program in the United States, making the disorder of greater concern and interest to policymakers.

CASE STUDY

The following psychological report is from a private clinic. Identifying information, such as child and family name, has been changed, disguised, or altered to protect confidentiality.

Name	Age	Education
Stephen	5 years	

ASSESSMENT PROCEDURES

A Developmental Neuropsychological Assessment (NEPSY)
Beery-Buktenica Developmental Test of Visual-Motor Integration (VMI)

Behavior Assessment System for Children (BASC)

   Parent Rating Scales (BASC-PRS)

   Structured Developmental History (BASC-SDH)

   Teacher Rating Scales (BASC-TRS)

Bracken Basic Concept Scale—Revised (BBCS-R)

Comprehensive Test of Phonological Processing (CTOPP)

Conners' Parent Rating Scales—Revised: Long Version (CPRS-R:L)

Conners' Teacher Rating Scales—Revised: Long Version (CTRS-R:L)

Kaufman Survey of Early Academic and Language Skills (K-SEALS)

Oral and Written Language Scales (OWLS)

Parent Interview

Wechsler Preschool and Primary Scale of Intelligence—Third Edition (WPPSI-III)

Woodcock-Johnson III Tests of Achievement (WJ III ACH)

REFERRAL QUESTION AND BACKGROUND

Stephen was referred for evaluation due to concerns about his learning difficulties. Stephen's parents noted that he appears to be learning at a slower rate in comparison to his classmates. Specifically, his parents reported problems with memory and reading.

Stephen's mother reported no problems during pregnancy or delivery. Developmental milestones were met on time with the exception of speech. Stephen began crawling at 7 months and walking alone at 14 months. Stephen received private speech therapy at the age of 2, but does not currently receive speech services. His parents did not report any significant childhood illnesses.

Stephen was placed in the 4-year-old kindergarten class last year and his teachers reported some difficulty on the playground with rough play, but reported no problems in the classroom. During this time, Stephen was evaluated for his overactivity and inattention but he did not meet criteria for a diagnosis of Attention-Deficit/Hyperactivity Disorder (ADHD). However, methylphenidate was prescribed, and Stephen began taking Ritalin, but due to severe emotional reactions, Adderall was prescribed and he is currently taking 10 mg once a day.

Stephen is currently in the 5-year-old kindergarten class. His parents characterize the class as very structured, ordered, and routine. His parents reported being concerned that Stephen is slower in most subjects than the other children in the class. For example, they noted that Stephen has difficulty putting small sentences together, but is good with phonics and can sound out most two-syllable words.

An interview was conducted with Stephen's current teacher. She reported that Stephen's work is inconsistent, in that one day he appears to know the material and the next he does not. She noted that Stephen's work has improved over the year, but he works at a slower pace and does not grasp concepts as quickly as other children in the class. She mentioned that Stephen's behavior has improved over the year and his listening skills have increased along with his attention span. In class, it is difficult to know how much Stephen comprehends while reading since he has to sound out every word, but he does well with phonics and is able to read one and two vowel words pretty well. She characterized Stephen as overactive, but cooperative, as having lots of friends, and being generally happy.

BEHAVIORAL OBSERVATIONS AND IMPRESSIONS

Stephen was evaluated over two sessions. Stephen appeared happy and very interested in working on different activities on the first day of testing. He engaged easily in conversation with the examiners and appeared to be working hard. Stephen appeared to be highly motivated by the stickers he received for completing activities and seemed very excited to receive a prize at the end of the day. On the second day of testing, Stephen was given his medication at the beginning of testing, but he appeared very inattentive for about the first hour of testing. He completed several identical subtests from the day before and he appeared to be more off task and easily distracted during these activities. He frequently asked when he could go home and did not appear motivated to complete some of the tasks. About mid-way through the morning on the second day, there was a notable change in his attention. He needed less re-direction and was able to focus his attention on the examiner as evidenced by his maintenance of eye contact.

INTELLIGENCE AND CONCEPTUAL REASONING

The Wechsler Preschool and Primary Scale of Intelligence—Third Edition (WPPSI-III) was given to assess Stephen's intellectual functioning. Stephen earned a Verbal IQ of 90 (25th percentile) and a Performance IQ of 108 (70th percentile), which fall in the Average range. There is a 90% chance that Stephen's "true" Verbal IQ falls in the range of 85 to 96 and his Performance IQ falls in the range of 102 to 113. Taken together, the Verbal and Performance scores yield an overall Full Scale IQ of 98 (45th percentile), which falls in the Average range. There is a 90% chance that Stephen's "true" Full Scale IQ falls in the range of 94 to 102. Stephen's nonverbal reasoning skills are slightly better developed than his verbal reasoning abilities; however, both fall in the Average range with no significant deficits. Stephen appeared to enjoy the nonverbal reasoning tasks that involved constructing designs with blocks and looking at pictures. The WPPSI-III also assesses processing speed and general language skills, such as naming simple objects in pictures. Again, Stephen's scores on both scales fall in the Average range.

ATTENTION AND EXECUTIVE PROCESSING

Stephen was given several subtests from a developmental neuropsychological assessment (NEPSY) to assess his auditory and visual attention, and executive processing skills such as planning and organization. The Tower subtest involves moving colored balls from one peg to another to construct a certain pattern within a limited number of moves and using one ball at a time. Stephen had difficulty moving one ball at a time and not holding more than one ball in his hand at a time. The auditory attention subtest involved Stephen listening to a series of words from the audiocassette recorder and following certain directions. The visual attention subtest involved Stephen looking over a page of several pictures of objects and marking particular objects.

These subtests were administered to compare Stephen's performance with and without medication. Overall, Stephen's scores fell in the Average range on both administrations. Stephen's scores on the visual attention subtest increased significantly on the second administration without his medication, but his auditory attention scores decreased slightly. Stephen appeared less focused while listening to the recorder and more intent on playing with the blocks; however, he seemed more focused on locating the pictures during the visual attention subtest. Overall, Stephen's attention and executive skills appear to be age appropriate when compared to other children his age.

MEMORY

Stephen's memory skills were assessed with the NEPSY, in particular his recognition and recall skills. Stephen appears to have equal strength in recognition and recall skills in terms of remembering faces and names, but showed a relative weakness, in comparison to these memory scores, in terms of remembering a story read to him. Overall, however, Stephen's scores on the memory domain fell in the Average range with a standard score of 109 (73rd percentile).

PERCEPTUAL AND MOTOR FUNCTIONING

Stephen's ability to integrate visual input with fine motor output was assessed with the Beery-Buktenica Developmental Test of Visual-Motor Integration (VMI) and the NEPSY. The VMI is a developmental sequence of geometric figures that requires the child to copy each design exactly as it appears. Stephen obtained an Average standard score of 106 (65th percentile). Results indicate slightly above age-level (6 years, 2 months age equivalent) visual-motor skills. Stephen obtained High Average scores on the Visuospatial domain on the NEPSY with a standard score of 118 (87th percentile). Stephen was asked to look at pictures of arrows and a bulls-eye and determine which arrows would go through the center of the bulls-eye if they were drawn completely and he was asked to copy more geometric figures similar to the VMI. It appears that Stephen shows strength with regard to visual perceptual functioning.

Stephen's scores on the motor subtests of the NEPSY fell in the Borderline to Above Average range. Stephen was asked to imitate finger tapping presented by the examiner, for example tapping his middle finger and thumb. He was also asked to imitate hand positions presented by the examiner, such as clinching a fist and putting the thumb between the middle and ring finger. Finally, Stephen was presented with a winding track about ½ inch in diameter on a piece of paper and was asked to trace a line along the track without going outside the lines. Stephen also traced the tracks on the second day of testing without his medication and his scores dropped significantly. He appeared to be quickly trying to finish without paying close attention to staying in the lines. In general, Stephen is functioning with age-appropriate skills in terms of motor development and perceptual abilities. During repetitive fingertip tapping, Stephen showed fatigue and a little bit of cramping in his hand that might have contributed to the Borderline scores.

ACADEMIC ACHIEVEMENT

Stephen completed several measures in order to assess his overall academic readiness and to determine his specific strengths and weaknesses within achievement domains. Stephen was given the Bracken Basic Concept Scale—Revised (BBCS-R) and the Kaufman Survey of Early Academic and Language Skills (K-SEALS) to assess his school readiness and early academic and language skills. The reading subtests of the Woodcock-Johnson III Tests of Achievement (WJ III ACH) were administered only. The Comprehensive Test of Phonological Processing (CTOPP) was given in order to evaluate Stephen's basic reading processing skills of phonological awareness, phonological memory, and naming speed. The Oral and Written Language Scales (OWLS) was administered to assess Stephen's listening comprehension and oral expressive language skills.

Basic Concepts and Early Academic Skills

The BBCS-R measures school readiness, along with particular concepts, such as direction/position, quantity, and time/sequence. Overall, Stephen's total test score and school readiness composite fell in the Average range with standard scores of 93 (32nd percentile) and 102 (55th percentile), respectively. All of Stephen's concept scores fell in the Average range, except quantity and time/sequence, which fell in the Low Average range.

Stephen's knowledge of early academic skills, such as vocabulary, numbers, letters, and words was assessed with the K-SEALS. Stephen was asked to point out certain numbers, letters, and whole words from lists of these items. At one point, Stephen said a "b" was a "d," but then corrected himself. Again, Stephen's scores fell in the Average range, with an overall early academic and language skills standard score composite of 100 (50th percentile). It appears Stephen displays age-appropriate early academic skills. Stephen shows weaknesses in speech articulation as evidenced by his Below Average score on the K-SEALS Articulation Survey. Stephen has difficulty making the /r/ sound in most of his words. For example, he would say "wabbit" for "rabbit," and "gween" for "green." He would also substitute the /w/ sound for "l," for example "wake" for "lake" and "swide" for "slide."

Reading Achievement

Word reading, psuedoword decoding, and reading comprehension were assessed by the Woodcock-Johnson III Tests of Achievement (WJ III ACH). Stephen's basic reading skills appear to be commensurate and in some areas higher than his intellectual functioning as measured by the WPPSI-III.

To assess his reading skills, Stephen was asked to identify single words, read one or two words and choose a picture that matched the phrase, read nonwords, and look at pictures and name the object. Stephen's single-word reading was assessed with the Letter Word Identification subtest of the WJ III ACH, and his scores fell in the High Average range. Stephen was able to correctly identify letters and say the following words: car, on, in, can, get, when, and must. He sounded out most of the words, but after a couple of tries he could say the word smoothly. However, Stephen had significant difficulty reading the sentences presented on the Reading Fluency subtest in which he was asked to read a sentence and tell if it were true or not (e.g., An apple is blue), thus the subtest was not completed. Stephen seemed to get upset when he had difficulty reading sentences. He immediately said he could not read it and his voice became soft and whiny.

Stephen's skills in reading comprehension were also assessed. On the Reading Comprehension subtest of the WJ III ACH, Stephen was asked to read one or two words and choose a picture that matched the phrase. His scores again fell in the Average range. Stephen was also asked to read words that were not real, such as "tiff" and "zoop" and say what sound "k" and "n" make. Stephen's scores fell in the Average range. Overall, Stephen's reading scores reflect that his skills are age appropriate.

Reading Processing Skills

Stephen's auditory processing skills were assessed to better understand the foundational skills that underlie his reading. Specifically, the basic reading processing skills of phonological awareness, phonological memory, and verbal fluency were assessed by the Comprehensive Test of Phonological Processing (CTOPP). Stephen demonstrated age-appropriate reading processing skills across all measures, with the exception of phonological memory.

Stephen's phonological awareness, or his ability to manipulate and blend sounds, was assessed with the CTOPP. Stephen's overall skills in phonological awareness fell in the Average range with a composite score of 96 (39th percentile). Stephen had some difficulty removing a letter sound or part from the middle of a word and blending the two remaining sounds together; however, he was able to listen to words in small parts and accurately blend the sounds together to make a word. For example "n-?p," he correctly said "nap." Stephen was also asked to determine which words were similar based on the beginning sound, which he did fairly well, but displayed some difficulty matching words based on ending sounds. Again, Stephen performed with appropriate age expectations.

Verbal fluency, or the ability to retrieve verbal information from memory quickly and effectively, was also measured by the CTOPP. Stephen was asked to name pictures of colors and objects as fast as he could. Stephen obtained a High Average standard score of 112 (79th percentile). Phonological memory, or the ability to remember and recall digits and nonwords, was also assessed with the CTOPP. Stephen obtained a Borderline standard score of 79 (8th percentile). Stephen had difficulty holding several pieces of information in his working memory at one time. He often could only remember three numbers from a four number set and he often left off the ending sound of the nonwords he was asked to repeat. Overall, the CTOPP results indicate that Stephen shows age-appropriate phonological processing skills, with variable auditory memory.

Stephen also completed subtests from the NEPSY to assess his phonological processing and speeded naming skills, but his scores were significantly below his scores on the CTOPP as evidenced by his Very Poor standard score of 69 (2nd percentile) on the language domain of the NEPSY. The phonological processing subtest of the NEPSY required Stephen to look at a series of pictures and choose the one that matched what the examiner was saying. However, the examiner only gave Stephen parts of words, for example "tele-" or "-indow" and Stephen was supposed to point to the picture of the telephone or window. Stephen appeared to have significant difficulty with this subtest. On the speeded naming subtest, Stephen was given pictures of circles and squares in different colors and sizes. Stephen was asked to name what the object was (circle or square), name the color (red, black, or yellow), and the size (big or little) as quickly as he could. He would often only give one or two features of the picture instead of all three. These activities seemed a little more complicated than those on the CTOPP, and overall it appears Stephen's scores on the CTOPP are a better indicator of his reading processing skills. His low scores on the NEPSY subtests could be indicators of difficulty with listening comprehension and oral expression due to the complexity of the tasks and the need to pay close attention to the directions.

Language Development

Stephen's listening comprehension and oral expression skills were assessed using the Oral and Written Language Scales (OWLS). It appears that Stephen shows weakness in oral expression as noted by his Borderline standard score of 76 (5th percentile). Stephen was given different scenarios in which he needed to express to the examiner what he would say in particular situations. Most often, Stephen's answers were given in incomplete sentences with the verb missing most of the time. Stephen performed in the Low Average range on the listening comprehension tasks as evidenced by his score of 87 (19th percentile). It appears that Stephen has some language difficulties in regards to more complicated and structured tasks, as evidenced by his low scores on the oral expression subtest.

BEHAVIORAL/SOCIAL-EMOTIONAL FUNCTIONING

His parents completed the Behavior Assessment System for Children—Parent Rating Scales (BASC-PRS) and the Conners' Parent Rating Scales—Revised: Long Version (CPRS-R:L) to provide information regarding Stephen's functioning across behavioral, social, and emotional domains. Stephen's teacher, Ms. J, also completed the Behavior Assessment System for Children—Teacher Rating Scales (BASC-TRS) and the Conners' Teacher Rating Scales—Revised: Long Version (CTRS-R:L) to assess school problems in addition to behavioral, social, and emotional areas.

Overall, his parents endorsed Clinically Significant scores in the areas of hyperactivity and attention, which is commensurate with Stephen's previous concerns about ADHD. His parents noted that Stephen has always been an active child even before he could walk he was tackling his brothers and wanting to play. His parents also endorsed At Risk scores in the area of aggression. They mentioned that Stephen can often become "hyper" when playing, but often does not mean it in an aggressive way, but just becomes overactive and does not think before he acts. His parents noted that Stephen gets along well with his peers, but they are concerned that his behavior might affect his friendships in the future if he cannot learn to control his impulsivity and hyperactivity.

Stephen's mother also endorsed Clinically Significant scores in the area of inattention, but she feels that his medication helps him focus his attention and she noted in the interview that Stephen's attention has improved during this school year. Her ratings also indicate that Stephen might be experiencing some anxiety and she reported that he sometimes appears anxious in class when he has trouble reading the work on the board, but raises his hands and asks questions when he needs to.

Tests of social-emotional functioning revealed that Stephen does display significant hyperactive and inattentive behavior.

SUMMARY

Stephen, a 5-year-old male, was referred for a psychoeducational evaluation due to concerns about possible learning difficulties. Specifically, his parents reported that Stephen is a slower learner than the other children in his class and he seems to have problems with memory and with reading. His parents want to know if Stephen has a learning disability and, if so, what kind of services would benefit him.

Stephen is functioning in the average range of overall intelligence with slightly better developed nonverbal versus verbal reasoning abilities. Stephen's overall academic readiness and early academic language scores are commensurate with his cognitive ability with scores in the average range. Stephen shows weakness in the areas of oral expression, articulation, and auditory memory. Stephen appears to perform better when visual prompts are used and when tasks do not require multiple steps for success. Overall, Stephen is achieving in the average range across academic areas; therefore, he does not show evidence of a specific learning disability in any area.

With regards to Stephen's social, emotional, and behavioral functioning, he appears to be experiencing significant difficulty with hyperactivity and inattention, which is currently being managed with psychostimulant medication. Stephen's teacher also noted minor difficulties with anxiety and perfectionism in the classroom.

DIAGNOSTIC IMPRESSIONS

Stephen does not meet diagnostic criteria for any type of learning disability; however, the present evaluation confirms prior suspicions of Attention-Deficit/Hyperactivity Disorder Combined Type (314.01).

The results of this evaluation and recommendations were shared with his parents during a feedback session (see Table 10.5).

Table 10.5   Psychometric Summary

WECHSLER PRESCHOOL AND PRIMARY SCALE OF INTELLIGENCE—
THIRD EDITION (WPPSI-III)

Composite	Standard Score
Verbal	90
Performance	108
Processing Speed	100
Full Scale	98
GL	91

Verbal Subtests	Scaled Score	Performance	Scaled Score
Information	7	Block Design	11
Vocabulary	9	Matrix Reasoning	11
Word Reasoning	9	Picture Concepts	12
Comprehension	(7)	Picture Completion	(14)
Similarities	(10)	Object Assembly	(11)

Processing Speed	Scaled Score	GL	Scaled Score
Symbol Search	10	Receptive Vocabulary	10
Coding	9	Picture Naming	7

WOODCOCK-JOHNSON III TESTS OF ACHIEVEMENT (WJ III ACH)

Subtests	Standard Scores	90% Confidence Intervals	GE
Letter-Word Identification	113	109–117	1.2
Reading Fluency	—	—	k.4
Passage Comprehension	92	84–101	1.0
Word Attack	109	94–123	>k.0
Picture Vocabulary	92	84–100	
Composites			
Basic Reading Skills	113	105–120	1.1

(continued)

Table 10.5   *Continued*

BRACKEN BASIC CONCEPT SCALE—REVISED (BBCS-R)

Subtests	Scaled Scores	Percentiles	Age Equivalent
School Readiness Cluster	10	50	5–11
Direction/Position	10	50	5–11
Self/Social Awareness	7	16	4–9
Texture/Material	9	37	5–6
Quantity	6	9	4–1
Time/Sequence	6	9	4–5

	Standard Scores	90% Confidence Intervals	Age
School Readiness Composite	102	97–107	5–4
Total Test	93	90–96	5–11

KAUFMAN SURVEY OF EARLY ACADEMIC AND LANGUAGE SKILLS (K-SEALS)

	Standard Score	Percentiles	Age Equivalent
Vocabulary	94	34	5–6
Numbers, Letters, & Words	106	66	6–5
Articulation Survey	—**Below Average		
Composite	100	50	
Expressive Skills	105	63	6–1
Receptive Skills	101	53	6–1
Number Skills	103	58	6–4
Letter & Word Sounds	108	70	6–6

A DEVELOPMENTAL NEUROPSYCHOLOGICAL ASSESSMENT (NEPSY)

	Standard/Scaled Scores		
	Medicated	Unmedicated	Percentiles
Tower	8	8	
Auditory Attention and Response Set	9	7	
Visual Attention	11	17	
Attention/Executive Domain	**95**	**104**	**37; 61**

Table 10.5   *Continued*

A Developmental Neuropsychological Assessment (NEPSY)

| | Standard/Scaled Scores | | |
	Medicated	Unmedicated	Percentiles
Phonological Processing	4		
Speeded Naming	3		
Comprehension of Instructions	7		
Language Domain	**69**		2
Fingertip Tapping	5		
Imitating Hand Positions	7		
Visuomotor Precision	14	7	
Sensorimotor Domain	**89**		23
Design Copying	15		
Arrows	11		
Visuospatial Domain	**118**		89
Memory for Faces	14		
Memory for Names	11		
Narrative Memory	9		
Memory Domain	**109**		73

The Beery-Buktenica Developmental Test of Visual-Motor Integration (VMI)

Standard Score	Percentile
106	65

Comprehensive Test of Phonological Processing (CTOPP)

Subtests	Scaled Scores	Grade Equivalent
Core		
Rapid Object Naming		
Elision	7	>K.0
Rapid Color Naming	11	1.4
Blending Words	12	1.7
Sound Matching	9	K.2
Rapid Object Naming	13	2.4
Memory for Digits	5	>K.0
Nonword Repetition	8	K.0

(continued)

Table 10.5   *Continued*

Subtests	Standard Scores	Percentiles
Composites		
Phonological Awareness	96	39
Phonological Memory	79	8
Rapid Naming	112	79

ORAL AND WRITTEN LANGUAGE SCALES (OWLS)

	Standard Scores	90% Confidence Intervals	Age Equivalent
Listening Comprehension	87	77–97	4–8
Oral Expression	76	67–85	3–11
Oral Composite	80	74–88	

BEHAVIOR ASSESSMENT SYSTEM FOR CHILDREN—PARENT RATING SCALES (BASC-PRS)

The BASC-PRS yields *T*-Scores with a mean of 50 and a standard deviation of 10. Scores above 70 are considered to be indicative of significant problems.

	T-Scores	
	Mother	Father
Hyperactivity	74	71
Aggression	66	68
Externalizing Problems Composite	72	71
Anxiety	55	50
Depression	49	47
Somatization	54	37
Internalizing Problems Composite	53	43
Atypicality	44	41
Withdrawal	33	42
Attention Problems	73	76
Behavior Symptoms Index	64	63

On the Adaptive Scales, scores below 30 are considered significantly low.

	Mother	Father
Adaptability	51	41
Social Skills	46	47
Adaptive Skills Composite	48	43

Table 10.5 *Continued*

CONNERS' PARENT RATING SCALE—REVISED: LONG VERSION (CPRS-R:L)

	T-Scores	
	Mother	Father
Oppositional	73	69
Cognitive Problems/Inattention	90	90
Hyperactivity	72	66
Anxious-Shy	48	50
Perfectionism	44	44
Social Problems	58	64
Psychosomatic	50	44
Conners' ADHD Index	76	76
Conners' Global Index: Restless-Impulsive	76	76
Conners' Global Index: Emotional Lability	72	63
Conners' Global Index: Total	77	74
DSM-IV Inattentive	75	80
DSM-IV Hyperactive-Impulsive	72	66
DSM-IV Total	75	75

CONNERS' TEACHER RATING SCALE—REVISED: LONG VERSION (CTRS-R:L)

	T-Scores
Oppositional	43
Cognitive Problems/Inattention	90
Hyperactivity	59
Anxious-Shy	56
Perfectionism	85
Social Problems	49
Conners' ADHD Index	61
Conners' Global Index: Restless-Impulsive	63
Conners' Global Index: Emotional Lability	43
Conners' Global Index: Total	57
DSM-IV Inattentive	73
DSM-IV Hyperactive-Impulsive	59
DSM-IV Total	66

(continued)

Table 10.5   *Continued*

BEHAVIOR ASSESSMENT SYSTEM FOR CHILDREN—TEACHER RATING SCALES (BASC-TRS)

Scores above 70 are considered to be indicative of significant problems.

	T-Scores
Hyperactivity	55
Aggression	47
Externalizing Problems Composite	51
Anxiety	69
Depression	55
Somatization	49
Internalizing Problems Composite	59
Attention Problems	61
Atypicality	53
Withdrawal	48
Behavior Symptoms Index	59

On the Adaptive Scales, scores below 30 are considered significantly low.

Adaptability	47
Social Skills	58
Adaptive Skills Composite	53

Conclusion

Attention-Deficit/Hyperactivity Disorder is one of the most studied syndromes in psychology, child psychiatry, and related disciplines; however, it remains controversial due to its prevalence, heterogeneity, increasing rates of psychostimulant prescriptions, etiology, and comorbidity; and, finally, because of its diagnostic reliance on clinical criteria after evaluation rather than on a specific diagnostic test or marker (Paule et al., 2000). Attention-Deficit/Hyperactivity Disorder diagnosis is a particularly challenging task for clinicians for two reasons: First, it is a high frequency referral problem; second, the diagnostic standards are not yet well developed enough to reach the same consensus level as is possible with "older" disorders such as Mental Retardation. The advised approach at this point is to assess the well-documented core symptoms of the disorder and to conduct a broad-based assessment; the latter being more important for documenting all areas of need for treatment planning. Regardless of the current diagnostic controversies, clinicians should be able to use existing psychometric technology to identify all needed areas of intervention. The clinician is also advised to keep an eye toward the future as new diagnostic rubrics for ADHD are likely to emerge.

Conduct Disorder and Oppositional Defiant Disorder

Carrah L. James and Jonathan M. Campbell

11

Chapter

The growing frequency of reports about youth violence has created an increase in public interest and concern regarding the disruptive behavior of children in school settings, particularly aggression. Less visibly reported is the important impact disruptive behaviors have on the educational outcomes and social lives of children. Children with severe conduct problems may disrupt classes and the learning of their peers, bully other children, and commit crimes at a cost to the community and population at large. According to the *DSM-IV-TR* (American Psychiatric Association, 2000), behaviors that characterize Oppositional Defiant Disorder (ODD) include hostility, negativity, and defiance directed at those in authority. For Conduct Disorder (CD), characteristic behaviors involve the violation of the basic rights of others and may include violence and criminal activity. Although there is no consensus, epidemiological studies document that between 5% and 10% of children between ages 8 and 16 demonstrate oppositional or disruptive behavior (Hill, 2002). For formal diagnoses, an aggregated estimate of the prevalence of ODD is 3.2% and 2% for CD (Lahey, Miller, Gordon, & Riley, 1999). Research about the developmental trajectories, poor outcomes, and high costs of CD suggests that the reliable and valid assessment of antisocial behavior in children and adolescents is a worthwhile goal. Considering the impact of disruptive behaviors on diagnosed children and their peers, accurate assessment and diagnosis of these problems is an essential step toward prevention and intervention of ODD and CD. Prior to discussing specific assessment strategies, the chapter briefly introduces constructs relevant to ODD and CD.

Constructs of Interest

The terminology associated with the assessment and diagnosis of ODD and CD is varied and somewhat confusing (see Table 11.1 for a list of terms associated with ODD and CD). Especially evasive are consistent operational definitions of aggression, hostility, antisocial behavior, psychopathy, and oppositional behavior. For example, different categories of aggression have been proposed in attempts to better predict outcomes for individuals diagnosed with CD; among these are: overt versus covert aggression, instrumental versus hostile aggression, proactive versus reactive aggression, socialized versus undersocialized aggression, and direct versus relational aggression, among others (Hinshaw & Lee, 2003; Loeber, Burke, Lahey, Winters, & Zera, 2000). Hinshaw and Lee (2003) identify several problematic issues with terminology used to characterize CD/ODD, such as: (a) different terminology and diagnoses being used for children and adults, for example, delinquent (ODD) versus criminal behavior (Antisocial Personality Disorder [APD]); (b) distinct categories of behaviors often co-occurring, such as internalizing and externalizing; (c) externalizing or disruptive behaviors including a wide range of possibilities, for example, inattentive symptoms associated with Attention-Deficit/Hyperactivity Disorder (ADHD) versus physical aggression; and (d) questionable extension of constructs formulated with adults being used with children, for example, psychopathy. Related to Hinshaw and Lee's (2003) critique of CD/ODD terminology, the distinction between APD and psychopathy bears brief mention here. Antisocial Personality Disorder is a current *DSM-IV* diagnostic category used to characterize the

Table 11.1   **Terminology Relevant to Diagnosis of Oppositional Defiant Disorder and Conduct Disorder in Children**

Antisocial Behaviors of Childhood or Adolescence: A V code of the *DSM-IV* that is characterized by antisocial behaviors of a transient nature and unrelated to mental disorder.

Antisocial Personality Disorder (APD): A diagnosis that must be preceded by evidence of conduct disorder (before age 15), and cannot be made before the age of 18. The hallmark characteristic of APD is a long-term pattern of violating laws and societal norms (American Psychiatric Association, 2000).

Callous-Unemotional Traits (CU): Lack of empathy, guilt, or remorse, and a flattened, feigned, or superficial affect (Barry, Frick, DeShazo, McCoy, Ellis, & Loney, 2000). CU traits are of interest to clinicians and researchers because they appear to be predictive of more negative outcomes for children with conduct problems when present versus absent (as noted by Lochman, Dane, Magee, Ellis, Pardini, & Clanton, 2001).

Conduct Disorder (CD): A *DSM-IV* diagnosis that is characterized by "a repetitive and persistent pattern of behavior in which the basic rights of others or major age-appropriate societal norms or rules are violated" (American Psychiatric Association, 2000, p. 93).

Disruptive Behavior Disorders: The *DSM-IV* heading under which ODD and CD fall.

Emotional Disturbance (also Severe Emotional Disturbance): An IDEA classification; a group that qualifies children for special education services. Children with CD or ODD who qualify for services would do so under the grouping of Emotional Disturbance. Psychotic disorders, mood disorders, and anxiety disorders severe enough to adversely affect a child's learning would also fall under this category.

Externalizing Behaviors: Conflict that occurs in the context of the child's interactions with the environment (Johnson, McCaskill, & Werba, 2001), as opposed to internal distress experienced by a child. Externalizing behaviors tend to be observable; they include aggression, hyperactivity, arguing, and criminal activities, among others.

Juvenile Delinquency: A legal term used to refer to criminal acts or rule violations committed by people under age 18.

Malingering: Intentional reporting of false or exaggerated symptoms of a disease to profit or achieve a goal, such as avoiding work or receiving financial compensation. This is represented as a V code in the *DSM-IV.*

Oppositional Defiant Disorder (ODD): A *DSM-IV* diagnosis that is characterized by negativistic and defiant behaviors that occur more frequently or severely than those exhibited by others of the same age group.

Psychopathy: The traditional two-factor model characterizes psychopathy as a pattern of behavior marked by social deviance and emotional void (Cooke & Michie, 2001); however, Cooke and Michie (2001) propose a three-factor construct characterized by affective (Deficient Affective Experience), behavioral (Impulsive and Irresponsible Behavioral Style), and social (Arrogant and Deceitful Interpersonal Style) components. Psychopathy is most closely associated with the *DSM-IV* diagnosis of APD.

display of patterns of *behaviors* such as aggression, lying, and disregard for the safety of others. *Psychopathy* is a term that emphasizes the *affective* characteristics of a person, often called callous-unemotional traits (Hinshaw & Lee, 2003), and may be described as lacking empathy, having no remorse, being exploitive, cold, and calculating. Although an in-depth discussion of all terms associated with antisocial behavior is beyond the scope of this chapter, it is important to point out that ideas and theories informing the assessment and diagnosis of ODD and CD are complex, multifaceted, and, at times, divergent.

When addressing and defining the constructs of ODD and CD for assessment and diagnostic classification, two important questions arise. First, are ODD and CD distinct disorders—are these disorders categorically different or do they differ only in severity? Second, for CD, do different symptoms predict different patterns and outcomes—is there evidence for further subtyping of CD, such as CD with callous-unemotional traits and CD with undersocialized aggression? The chapter focuses first on exploring these questions, then broader issues of risk factors, etiologies, and outcomes are discussed.

Although CD and ODD share considerable overlap in defining features and associated problems (Maughan, Rowe, Messer, Goodman, & Meltzer, 2004), Quay (1999) and Loeber, Burke, et al. (2000) offer reviews of the literature that support a distinction between ODD and CD. There are, however, many questions surrounding the degree of overlap between ODD and CD. Many sources strongly suggest a developmental relationship between the two disorders. For example, most people with persistent CD and/or adult APD will have been diagnosable with ODD at some point in their development (Loeber, Burke, & Lahey, 2002); however, most children diagnosed with ODD will not go on to develop CD (Hinshaw & Lee, 2003). Simple outcome predictions of diagnostic categories do not appear to be the best way to understand disruptive behavior disorders. A strong body of evidence suggests that certain behavior patterns, as opposed to categorical diagnoses, appear to be more predictive of outcomes.

Subgrouping strategies have been investigated to better understand individuals who present with disruptive and aggressive behavior, including (a) an individual's behavioral presentation, (b) the presence of comorbid psychological problems, and (c) age of onset of symptoms (Hill, 2002). Some have asserted that improved understanding of ODD and CD should include subtyping of an individual's behavioral presentation. For example, the presence of status offenses, such as truancy, versus violent crimes, such as rape, may suggest a more favorable outcome for an individual diagnosed with CD. Attempts to subtype behavioral presentations, however, have contributed to the growing number of aggression types that may or may not relate to each other in meaningful ways.

CD and ODD frequently co-occur with other diagnoses, particularly ADHD, depression, and anxiety (Angold et al., 1999). Studies have documented that the presence of several comorbid psychiatric conditions, such as ADHD or substance abuse, alongside CD/ODD results in a more problematic symptom profile, including greater academic problems, more problematic peer relationships, and worse outcomes than if either condition is diagnosed in isolation. It is unclear, however, whether the presence of comorbid psychiatric problems indicate greater severity of CD/ODD disorder or if individuals with additional diagnoses constitute a different diagnostic group altogether.

Age of onset has also been investigated with compelling evidence to suggest that the earlier the onset of disruptive behavior problems, the more chronic behavioral problems are in adulthood. Moffitt, Caspi, Harrington, and Milne (2002), for example, found differing outcomes among 26-year-old men who had been identified as exhibiting either childhood-onset or adolescent-onset antisocial behaviors. The childhood-onset group demonstrated more substance abuse, mental health diagnoses, violent crime, work and financial problems, and violence against women and children. The adolescent-onset group in general showed less severe outcomes, but demonstrated elevated problems when compared to other 26-year-olds. Age of onset has appeared as a subtyping feature in the current *DSM* diagnostic system for CD diagnosis, allowing for either childhood-onset or adolescent-onset specifiers. In addition to an earlier versus later onset of behavioral problems, other risk factors for negative outcomes have been identified in the literature.

Risk Factors and Etiological Considerations

Etiological explanations for CD and ODD are as vast and varied as the research literature (see Burke, Loeber, & Birmaher, 2002, for a thorough review of possible etiologies and risk factors in ODD and CD). Dodge and Pettit (2003) offer a model of the development of chronic conduct problems that proposes a transactional process between biological vulnerability and environmental variables such as parenting style, peers' influence, and social context, among others. Many sources suggest a multifaceted etiology that may be influenced by any combination of physiological factors (Bauer & Hesselbrock, 2003; Hill, 2002), neurocognitive variables (Blair, 2001), reading difficulties (Bennett, Brown, Boyle, Racine, & Offord, 2003), parenting variables (Hinshaw & Lee, 2003), and early peer interactions (Miller-Johnson, Coie, Maumary-Gremaud, Bierman, and the Conduct Problems Research Group, 2002) to name just a few. Hill (2002) offers four potential explanations for the outcome of CD, including (1) a final common pathway resulting from the cumulative effects of risk factors, (2) a final common pathway resulting from certain combinations of risk factors, (3) different conduct outcomes created by different types of influences, or (4) a diverse outcome resulting from one large influence such as an as yet unidentified/unnamed childhood personality disorder like APD.

In a review of the literature, Bassarath (2001) documents the following as the strongest risk factors for future delinquency: (a) prior engagement in antisocial behavior, (b) affiliation with antisocial peers, early rejection by peers, (c) substance use, (d) being male, and (e) being the child of an antisocial parent. Accounting for a variety of the risk factors identified, Dodge and Pettit (2003) proposed a biopsychosocial model to understand the etiology of CD and antisocial behavior. This model asserts that risk variables such as parenting, peers, biological predispositions, sociocultural contexts, and social-cognitive processes interact reciprocally to influence the development of chronic conduct problems. We introduce three broad areas of influence: (1) family, (2) gender, and (3) social/contextual factors. It is important to remember that risk factors are not causal and that many children with multiple risk factors do not develop antisocial behaviors. Relevant to the discussion of risk factors are protective factors such as the mastery of a skill, supportive relationships with adults, and family commitment to social values, among others, which result in less likelihood of a child demonstrating CD/ODD symptoms (Bassarath, 2001).

Family Variables: Although family associated risk factors are difficult to disentangle from each other and from genetic heritability, they are often cited as strong influences on the development of conduct problems. In a longitudinal study of 177 clinic-referred boys, Loeber, Green, Lahey, Frick, and McBurnett (2000) found that 40% of the children diagnosed with CD and 23% of the children diagnosed with ODD had a parent diagnosed with APD, compared to only 8% of those children in the clinic-referred control group who were not diagnosed with ODD or CD. Additionally, Shaw, Gilliom, Ingoldsby, and Nagin (2003) found that maternal depressive symptomatology and rejecting parenting style during the preschool developmental period were associated with persistence and severity of later conduct problems. Research findings documenting familial risk factor have been reported in the *DSM-IV-TR*, which now identifies several familial factors associated with ODD and CD in children. These include parental psychopathology, substance abuse, ADHD, severe marital discord, and neglectful parenting, among others (American Psychiatric Association, 2000).

Gender: Maughan et al. (2004) report that CD is much more prevalent among boys than girls (2.1% versus 0.8%) and that the rates of ODD among boys and girls seems to vary by informant, although boys seem to exhibit symptoms of ODD at higher rates than girls. The *DSM-IV-TR* (American Psychiatric Association, 2000) reports that, although childhood rates of ODD are higher for boys, girls and boys experience ODD symptoms at a similar rate in adolescence. R. Rowe, Maughan, Pickles, Costello, and Angold (2002) present evidence that suggests there may be a stronger developmental link between ODD and CD for boys than for girls. R. Rowe et al. (2002) found that ODD was a risk factor for CD in boys but not girls, although ODD in girls was a risk factor for continued ODD, depression, and anxiety. Additionally, in a review of the aggression literature, Loeber and Stouthamer-Loeber (1998) note that type and/or number of risk factors may differentially affect boys and girls.

Social and Contextual Factors: In a sample of 657 boys and girls, Miller-Johnson et al. (2002) found that rejection by peers in early childhood was a risk factor for early starting conduct problems. Also, friendship with deviant peers can influence a child's behavior, especially in adolescence, with a tendency toward delinquency facilitated by ongoing interactions with deviant peers (Coie & Miller-Johnson, 2001). In a comprehensive review of the literature, Burke, Loeber, and Birmaher (2002) summarized social and contextual risk factors that include living in an impoverished neighborhood, being exposed to life stressors in the presence of deficient coping skills, low socioeconomic status (SES), and other factors. Again, no single risk factor appears causative for conduct problems; it seems more likely that many risk factors act in concert with biological predispositions and situational variables to create an environment in which CD or ODD behaviors may develop.

Diagnostic Standards

As the chapter introduction suggests, assessment of disruptive behavior disorders is complex. Comorbidities, sex differences, nosological limitations, and cultural issues complicate the assessment and diagnostic process. Further, differences between the worlds of mental health and education exacerbate the issue. For example, a child might meet diagnostic criteria for ODD according to the *DSM-IV,* but that same child may *not* qualify for special education services, even if he or she might potentially benefit from such services. These circumstances can occur because the Individuals with Disabilities Education Act (IDEA), on which most special education qualifying criteria are based, is organized differently than *DSM* criteria. The IDEA does not use the same terminology as the *DSM* for classifying disruptive behavior problems. If a child with a diagnosis of ODD or CD were to receive special education services as a result of serious conduct problems or oppositional behaviors, he or she would fall under the IDEA classification of Emotional Disturbance, but only if the symptoms significantly impeded the child's education. Alternatively, children may qualify for services through special education but not have a medical/psychiatric diagnosis. A brief overview of *DSM* and IDEA criteria relevant to disruptive behavior problems follows.

Diagnostic and Statistical Manual of Mental Disorders

Some of the diagnostic challenges relevant to CD and ODD result from changing criteria over time. The symptom sets of CD and ODD have changed considerably over the past few revisions of the *DSM*. Diagnostic instruments are often based on *DSM* criteria, so that the measure will have significant diagnostic utility. When criteria are changed, new research is required to support the usefulness of a particular measure in assessing ODD or CD. The current *DSM* diagnostic criteria for ODD follow in a brief form:

Oppositional Defiant Disorder: Oppositional Defiant Disorder is characterized by "a pattern of negativistic, hostile, and defiant behavior lasting at least 6 months, during which four (or more) of the following are present" (American Psychiatric Association, 2000, p. 102) in a child who (a) loses his or her temper often; (b) argues with adults; (c) is noncompliant or defiant to the rules or requests of adults; (d) annoys people deliberately; (e) blames others for his or her own behavior; (f) is easily irritated by others; (g) is often angry, resentful, spiteful, or vindictive. These behaviors must occur more often than would be typical in others of similar age and development. The behaviors must cause "significant impairment in social, academic, or occupational functioning" (pp. 102) and must not be the result of a psychotic or mood disorder. Additionally, a diagnosis of CD supersedes a diagnosis of ODD. Symptoms of ODD are usually evident before 8 years of age; however, ODD can be diagnosed in adults if the criteria for APD or CD are not already met.

Conduct Disorder: Conduct Disorder is characterized by "a repetitive and persistent pattern of behavior in which the basic rights of others or major age-appropriate societal norms or rules are violated" (American Psychiatric Association, 2000, p. 98). Three criteria must have been present in the past 12 months, one of them in the past 6 months. Fifteen criteria are organized under the broad categories of: (a) aggression to people and animals (e.g., armed robbery), (b) destruction of property (e.g., vandalizing a car), (c) deceitfulness or theft (e.g., shoplifting), and (d) serious violations of rules (e.g., running away from home on multiple occasions). As with ODD, impairment caused by the behaviors must be significant. For adults who meet the criteria for APD, a diagnosis of APD supersedes a diagnosis of CD. With CD, subtype is specified based on age of onset, with Childhood-Onset Type diagnosed if at least one of the 15 behavioral criteria is met before age 10. Adolescent-Onset Type is diagnosed if there is an absence of any of the 15 behavioral criteria met before age 10. Additionally, three severity specifiers are offered: Mild, Moderate, and Severe; however, little guidance is provided for selecting a severity descriptor. For example, the Mild specifier is selected to describe CD where "few if any conduct problems in excess of those required to make the diagnosis [exist] *and* conduct problems cause only minor harm to others" (American Psychiatric Association, 2000, p. 99). The words *few* and *minor* are not defined.

Although the *DSM* offers much in the way of categorization, several issues regarding the diagnosis of disruptive behavior disorders should be noted. First, the diagnostic criteria focus solely on behaviors, whereas the text of the *DSM* asserts that the diagnosis of CD should be excluded if the behaviors are contextually based (Wakefield, Pottick, & Kirk, 2002). Although Wakefield et al. (2002) found that clinicians' judgments tended to support the text-based exclusion of behaviors caused by environmental variables as opposed to internal dysfunction, this type of inconsistent criteria is undesirable. As Wakefield and colleagues point out, this issue presents some interesting questions regarding the validity and generalizability of epidemiology, assessment, and treatment efficacy studies based on *DSM* diagnostic criteria. Second, the criteria for CD and ODD are extremely diverse. Lying to obtain favors carries the same weight as committing rape in rendering a diagnosis of CD; however, research suggests there are meaningful differences in outcome depending on which criteria are met (Burke, Loeber, Mutchka, & Lahey, 2002). Finally, as Quay (1999) points out, because so many of the CD criteria are law violations, any juvenile delinquent by virtue of his or her involvement in criminal activity is likely to meet the criteria for CD whether he or she exhibits any other defining features of CD, such as aggression.

Contextual Variables

Context is a relevant factor in interpreting test results and diagnosing disruptive behavior disorders. If a child is reared in an environment in which stealing or fighting, two of the behavioral criteria for CD, are normative or adaptive, a diagnosis of ODD or CD should only be made with extreme caution. Although harsh home environment and low SES are risk factors for disruptive behavior disorders, behaviors that are a product of context should not be considered pathological. For example, running away from home under conditions of abuse cannot qualify as meeting one of the three criteria for CD. Context for disruptive behaviors should be assessed during the interview process.

Gender Issues

Characteristics of ODD and CD may be differentially expressed by males and females. The growing literature on gender differences in ODD and CD symptom expression has also influenced text that appears in the *DSM-IV-TR*. The *DSM-IV-TR* (American Psychiatric Association, 2000) notes that, for example, "females with a diagnosis of Conduct Disorder are more likely to exhibit lying, truancy, running away, substance use, and prostitution," whereas "fighting, stealing, vandalism, and school discipline problems" (p. 97) are more characteristic for males.

Age

There are three major age-related issues associated with the assessment and diagnosis of disruptive behavior disorders. First, many of the criteria for ODD and some of the criteria for CD are common for children. Teenagers who break curfew, are irritable, and argue with adults would not be identified with CD or ODD, unless the frequency, duration, and severity of these behaviors exceed age-appropriate expectations and cause significant impairment. Second, the symptoms and disorders can present differently in childhood versus adolescence or adulthood. For example, aggressive behavior might exist as biting in young children versus fist fighting in adolescence. Third, behaviors characteristic of ODD and CD expressed by younger children may have other origins. For example, a child with social phobia may exhibit the "oppositional behavior" of school refusal, but the behavior is actually a function of anxiety and avoidance as opposed to defiance.

Comorbidity and Differential Diagnosis

ODD and CD show high rates of comorbidity with one another, ADHD (Lahey et al., 1999), and internalizing disorders (Lahey, Loeber, Burke, Rathouze, & McBurnett, 2002; Maughan et al., 2004). In one sample, 36% of girls and 46% of boys with ODD also had at least one other disorder according to *DSM-IV* criteria; this was 39% (girls) and 46% (boys) for those with CD (Maughan et al., 2004). Additionally, others have noted a connection between substance use problems and disruptive behavior disorders (Kuperman et al., 2001). Given the extensive comorbidities and high combordity rates, making differential diagnoses, or ruling out disorders that may mimic the symptoms of ODD or CD, can be especially challenging.

Individuals with Disabilities Education Act

Both the *DSM* and IDEA feature categories for identification of disruptive behavior problems. Although the purpose of the *DSM* is to classify disorder, this is not the purpose of IDEA. The IDEA's purpose, instead, is to identify disabilities that prevent children from fully benefiting from public education (House, 2002). Due to their discrepant purposes, *DSM* and IDEA categories do not directly correspond with each other (House, 2002). If qualifications are met, CD and ODD, as well as psychotic disorders, eating disorders, and mood disorders, would typically fall under the category of Emotional Disturbance. As with the *DSM,* there are problems with the IDEA classification system and its implementation. For example, the IDEA Emotional Disturbance category excludes children whose sole problem is social maladjustment; however, no definition of "Socially Maladjusted" is offered (House, 2002). Additionally, according to

House (2002), some states actually exclude CD and ODD from qualification for special education services under IDEA.

Assessment Methods

Instruments may assess ODD or CD using either categorical or dimensional approaches. In the former, a child either has the disorder or does not have the disorder, the essence of diagnostic classification using the *DSM*. In the latter, disruptive behaviors are hypothesized to lie on a continuum and measurement strategies built on the dimensional approach feature normative comparison data, such as that yielded by third-party rating scales. In the dimensional tradition, for example, all children are assumed to exhibit oppositional behavior, but a child who exhibits oppositional behaviors with a frequency, severity, and duration that significantly exceeds that of oppositional behaviors exhibited by his or her same age peers might be considered disordered. Although there are pros and cons to both types of assessment (Frauenglass & Routh, 1999), what is more important than choosing a categorical versus a dimensional approach is assessing behaviors in multiple ways, in multiple contexts, at multiple times, and by multiple raters. The aggregation of many types of data is said to reduce error variance (Merrell, 2003), increase reliability, and reduce the affects of rater bias (Frauenglass & Routh, 1999). Multiple methods exist for measuring disruptive behaviors, including third-party rating scales, interviews, observations, and self-reports. Raters may include parents, teachers, the child, or even peers; contexts at this age will almost always include school and home.

Although selecting specific measures and designing a comprehensive battery to assess disruptive behaviors is important, gaining information about the child's medical and developmental history, the family's structure, the economic and neighborhood conditions, among other factors, is a crucial step in the assessment process (Lochman et al., 2001). Such information provides a comprehensive picture of the variables potentially affecting the child's behavior. For example, it is important to know if a child has been severely abused in the past or has a strong family history of Bipolar Disorder when evaluating the child so that diagnostic possibilities such as Reactive Attachment Disorder and Bipolar Disorder can be properly assessed.

Third-Party Rating Scales

Third-party ratings are an important source of behavioral information regarding a child's functioning and should be utilized in the assessment of children's disruptive behavior. Parents and teachers represent the most typical informants, though other family members that may be in a position to rate the child's behavior may also be considered appropriate. Rating scales may range from broadband, such as the Child Behavior Checklist (CBCL; Achenbach, 1991a), the Behavior Assessment System for Children—Second Edition (BASC-2; C. R. Reynolds & Kamphaus, 2004), and the Conners Rating Scales—Revised (CRS-R; Conners, 1997), to more narrowly focused measures of behaviors associated with ODD and CD, such as the New York Teacher Rating Scale for Disruptive and Antisocial Behavior (NYTRS; Miller et al., 1995). Prior to discussing specific rating scales it is important to note that all measure some of the symptoms of CD and ODD, but they do not provide *DSM* diagnoses. Instead, rating scales provide information that may be useful in determining whether criteria for *DSM* diagnoses or IDEA eligibility criteria are met. Following is a very small sampling of the third-party rating scales available (see Collett, Ohan, & Myers, 2003, for a thorough review of narrow-band rating scales that assess disruptive behaviors and aggression). Floyd and Bose (2003) present a comprehensive review of behavior rating scales that are more closely tied with IDEA eligibility criteria and the classification of Emotional Disturbance (ED).

Behavioral Assessment System for Children: The BASC (C. R. Reynolds & Kamphaus, 1998), and its revision, the BASC-2 (C. R. Reynolds & Kamphaus, 2004) consist of an entire system of assessment that includes parent and teacher rating scales, a self-report, a structured interview, and an observation component. Although these are all important parts of the BASC, each can be administered individually, and for the purposes of this section, only the third-party rating scales are discussed. The BASC-PRS is the parent version of the rating scale and the BASC-TRS is the version given to teachers. The structure of the PRS and TRS is a series of statements about the child's behavior to which the rater responds by circling N, S, O, or A for never, sometimes, often, or almost always (respectively). Completion of the BASC should take between 10 and 20 minutes and is scored by computer.

The PRS and TRS produce five composite scores and a Behavioral Symptoms Index, as well as Clinical and Adaptive Scales. For purposes of assessing ODD and CD, elevated scores on the Externalizing Composite, the Clinical Scales of Aggression and Conduct Problems, and the Behavioral Symptoms Index will be of interest, although all of the scores may provide useful information. In the normative sample, children diagnosed with CD and ODD scored highest on the Conduct Problems scale, notably higher scores on the Aggression and Hyperactivity Scales, and very low scores on the Adaptability Scale (C. R. Reynolds & Kamphaus, 1998). Having multiple raters (e.g., both parents and multiple teachers) complete the rating scales can provide an even more comprehensive picture of the child's functioning. For example, by having more than one teacher complete the TRS, it may become apparent that problems are occurring in only one classroom. Discrepancies in third-party reports may provide guidance about the nature of the problems or inform intervention strategies.

Psychometrics of the BASC are quite good (Matazow & Kamphaus, 2001; Merrell, 2003; Schroder & Gordon, 2002), comparable in reliability and validity to the CBCL (Doyle, Ostrander, Skare, Crosby, & August, 1997). Another admirable quality of the BASC rating scales is that they also identify areas of strength for the child. Additionally, because raters may have biased interpretations of the child's behaviors, the BASC teacher and parent versions include F indexes, which may indicate an exaggeration of the symptoms on the part of the rater. Criticisms of the BASC are few, although Merrell (2003) notes that the PRS and TRS forms may be too long for frequent monitoring or routine screening of behavior.

Child Behavior Checklist: The CBCL (Achenbach, 1991a), a parent rating scale, and the corresponding teacher rating scale, the TRF, are among the most widely used and researched measures for assessing disruptive behavior (Merrell, 2003; Reitman, Hummel, Franz, & Gross, 1998). The CBCL and TRF are broadband rating scales and comprise parts of a comprehensive assessment system, known as the Achenbach System of Empirically Based Assessment (ASEBA; Achenbach & Rescorla, 2001). Like the BASC, the ASEBA has parent and teacher rating forms, direct observation forms, a self-report, and an interview schedule. The CBCL and TRF can be used for children ages 4 to 18 (as well as a recently developed preschool version). They each contain 113 items about the adaptive or problem behavior of the child and are endorsed as 0 (not true), 1 (sometimes true), or 2 (very or often true). There are also a number of open-ended questions. The CBCL and TRF should take about 20 minutes to complete.

The CBCL and TRF produce three broad scores—Internalizing, Externalizing, and Total Problems. Eight syndrome scores are also provided: Aggressive Behavior, Anxious/Depressed, Attention Problems, Delinquent Behavior, Social Problems, Somatic Complaints, Thought Problems, and Withdrawn. For the assessment of CD and ODD, the Aggressive Behavior and Delinquent Behavior subscales as well as Externalizing and Total Problems composites will be most salient. Although, as noted earlier, disruptive behavior disorders may have high comorbidity rates with internalizing disorders, so other scores should not be ignored.

Tackett, Krueger, Sawyer, and Graetz (2003) found the CBCL useful for distinguishing subtypes of CD, what the authors labeled overt-aggressive versus covert-delinquent, a distinction that may be of use in making treatment decisions. Although a well-researched measure with a long history, the CBCL is not without limitations. The CBCL may not be the best measure for assessing mild behavior problems due to its limited sensitivity below the clinical cutoff (Reitman et al., 1998). Schroeder and Gordon (2002) contend that, although psychometrics of the CBCL and TRF are generally good, "the normative sample excludes children who received mental health or special education services, so it is not representative of the general population" (p. 489, 494). Additionally, hand scoring is said to be cumbersome (Merrell, 2003; Schroeder & Gordon, 2002), although computer scoring software is available.

Conners Rating Scales—Revised: Among other domains, the CRS-R features assessment of conduct problems and symptomatology associated with ADHD. The CRS-R consists of both long and short versions for teachers and parents. Behaviors are rated from 0 to 3, with 0 being "not true, seldom, or never" and 3 being "very true or very frequently." The short forms take about 10 minutes to complete, and feature four subscales: Oppositional, Cognitive Problems, Hyperactivity, and an ADHD Index. The long forms should take about 20 minutes to complete and feature 14 subscales, although the subscales differ between the parent and teacher versions. For assessing ODD and CD symptoms, the most relevant CRS-R scales are Oppositional and *DSM-IV* Total Symptoms.

The CRS-R possesses sound reliability and validity data (Reitman et al., 1998). Although the CRS-R has a good normative sample (Reitman et al., 1998), children receiving special education services were not included and this exclusion tends to inflate scores and overidentify pathology (Ramsey, Reynolds, & Kaufman, 2002). Another potential downfall of the CRS-R is that the reading level required is considerably higher (9th or 10th grade level, depending on the form) than for the CBCL (5th grade level) or the BASC (2nd grade level; Ramsey et al., 2002).

New York Teacher Rating Scale for Disruptive and Antisocial Behavior: The NYTRS is a 92-item, narrowband, third-party rating scale designed to be completed by teachers to assess CD and ODD relevant behaviors that occur in the classroom. The NYTRS features Defiance, Peer Relations, Physical Violence, and Delinquent Aggression subscales and yields Antisocial Behavior and Disruptive Behavior composites. The psychometric properties of the NYTRS are good (Collett et al., 2003; Connor, 2002). A downside of the NYTRS is the lack of a nationally representative normative sample, as the current norms are based on a sample of 1,319 1st through 10th graders from New York.

Other notable broadband rating scales useful in assessing problem behaviors include the Revised Behavior Problem Checklist (RBPC; Quay & Peterson, 1996), the Eyberg Child Behavior Inventory (ECBI) and the Sutter-Eyberg Student Behavior Inventory— Revised (SESBI-R). Also, though narrowband rating scales are more typically used in research, the Children's Aggression Scale (Halperin, McKay, Grayson, & Newcorn, 2003; Halperin, McKay, & Newcorn, 2002) shows promising preliminary psychometric data as a narrowband, third-party rating scale for assessing externalizing behaviors.

For the purpose of evaluating externalizing behaviors associated with CD and ODD, Merrell (2003) suggests rating scales be used for early screening and to assess progress throughout the intervention process. Third-party rating scales allow a clinician to collect a large amount of data in a relatively short amount of time, particularly when compared to direct observation or interviewing multiple informants. Due to their completion and scoring times, they make quick work of initial screening for behavior problems. Although behavior ratings scales are probably the best choice for assessing disruptive behavior disorders, there are some drawbacks to their use. First, third-party ratings may be biased, conflicting, or inaccurate (Conner, 2002). These issues may pose difficulties for the examiner when it comes to interpreting scores. To combat this problem, clinicians are advised to obtain ratings from multiple sources, in multiple settings, at multiple times, and from multiple scales for a comprehensive picture of the child's behavioral functioning. Second, as discussed previously, children with ODD or CD may exhibit higher rates of internalizing disorders and, because internalizing behaviors may not be noticeable to informants, those qualities may be underreported. Third, Collett et al. (2003) noted that broadband behavior ratings scales like those detailed earlier do not provide extensive information about the precise nature of externalizing behavior, whereas narrowband measures, such as those that focus solely on aggression, might provide a better indication of clinical patterns. A final drawback is that rating scales rarely provide information about current, salient environmental variables that may be at work in a way that direct observation or interviewing might document.

Direct Observation and Interviewing

Due to the frequently observable symptoms of CD and ODD, direct observation represents a useful method of assessment for these disorders. Both the ASEBA and BASC systems have direct observation forms for use in a classroom or group setting, the Direct Observation Form (DOF) and the Student Observation System (SOS). These forms ask the rater to indicate the frequency with which certain behaviors occur in a specified time frame. Pertinent to assessment of CD and ODD, these scales provide documentation of aggression (e.g., gets in physical fights, physically attacks people, threatens people, or throws objects at others), oppositional behaviors (e.g., talking back to teacher, disobedient), and deceitful or delinquent behaviors (e.g., stealing, destroying property). Several other coding and observation procedures are available. The major drawback of direct observation is the time and expense involved. Even with the efficient DOF and SOS, time must be allocated for traveling to the observation site. Another limitation of direct observation is that the mere presence of the observer may alter the child's behavior such that it is not representative of the child's typical behavior. Direct observations will be most helpful when discrepant information is found on third-party rating scales, when there is a question of contextual influence or when planning an intensive intervention. Whether direct observations are possible, a thorough interview with both the child and caretaker(s) is essential.

There are several interview schedules available to assess symptoms of CD and ODD, which range in format from highly structured to semistructured. The Children's Interview for Psychiatric Syndromes (ChIPS) is a system of short, highly structured interviews that correspond directly to *DSM* diagnoses, including ODD and CD. The syndrome-specific interviews are preceded by a short interview on home, school, peers, and medication, and are designed to be completed with the child. There is a corresponding interview available for parents as well. Another structured interview that is available for parents and children is the Diagnostic Interview Schedule for Children—Version IV (DISC-IV; Shaffer, Fisher, Lucas, Dulcan, & Schwab-Stone, 2000) that asks specific questions about CD and ODD symptomatology, in addition to a range of other *DSM*-defined syndromes. An example of a semistructured interview is the Diagnostic Interview for Children and Adolescents (DICA; Reich, 2000), which is also available in child and parent formats. Each of these interviews can be administered to children as young as 6 years old, have normative data available (Connor, 2002), and appear useful for assessing externalizing problems such as ODD and CD (Merrell, 2003).

Outside the domain of structured interviews, clinical interview can be helpful. Clinical interviews may be even more loosely structured, providing increased flexibility, and enhancing rapport. If creating a clinical interview for assessing the presence of CD or ODD symptoms, Schroeder and Gordon (2002) suggest that developmental history, family characteristics, parenting styles, recent and ongoing stresses, and persistence of problem behaviors be addressed specifically. Other authors provide similar suggestions (Frauenglass & Routh, 1999; Lochman et al., 2001).

Interviews can provide a great deal of diagnostic information, and can be flexible so that the clinician is able to query areas of interest. Interviews provide implicit information as well, such as indicators of the family's attitudes toward the child, the child's behavior problems, and each other. Information gathered in interviews is, however, filtered through the informant's biases, so the clinician must keep in mind that these are subjective reports of the child's behaviors. Additionally, oppositional or aggressive children may be defensive or uncooperative with an interviewer, in which case the examiner must be skillful at communicating in a nonthreatening way; and in cases where the child refuses to cooperate, the clinician must rely solely on the report of the parents. A child's noncompliance with the assessment places the examiner at a disadvantage when assessing for the presence of internalizing symptoms. Although interviews are often the most time-consuming aspect of assessment for CD and ODD, they are vital and are not optional. When interviewing about symptoms of disruptive behavior disorders, clinicians should guard against neglecting to ask about areas of child competence, which might be utilized in intervention approaches. After talking for an extended period of time about disruptive behaviors, inquiring about areas of competence may also leave the parents and child with optimism about improving behavior.

Self-Reports

Self-reports of behavioral adjustment are important in the comprehensive assessment of children who present with concerns about disruptive behavior problems. Self-reports may be particularly useful in detecting the presence of internalizing symptomatology, such as depression, which frequently co-occurs with ODD and CD. Several self-report instruments are introduced in this section.

Minnesota Multiphasic Personality Inventory—Adolescent: The Minnesota Multiphasic Personality Inventory—Adolescent Version (MMPI-A) takes about an hour to complete, and is appropriate for teens aged 14 to 18 who read on at least a sixth grade level (Gumbiner, 2003). Gumbiner (2003) contends that one of the best uses of the MMPI-A is assessment of conduct disorders. The clinical scale most relevant to the assessment of ODD and CD on the MMPI-A is the Psychopathic Deviate (Pd) scale. Unfortunately, score elevations on this scale have been shown to relate to an array of clinical problems; therefore, it is impossible to conclude that Pd elevations equal a diagnosis of ODD or CD (Gumbiner, 2003). The MMPI-A also features Aggression and Conduct Problems content subscales that may complement the interpretation of clinical elevations. Elevated scores for girls tend to have different implications than elevated scores for boys. R. P. Archer and Krishnamurthy (2002) point out that, for example, boys who score high on the Conduct Problems content scale tend to present with issues of criminality, drug abuse, and violence, whereas girls with higher scores have a history of running away from home, skipping school, and being defiant.

Antisocial Process Screening Device: Due to the defining characteristics of ODD and CD discussed earlier, the self-report and measurement of child "psychopathy" is somewhat controversial. However, the Antisocial Process Screening Device (APSD; Frick & Hare, 2001) has received recent attention (Falkenbach, Poythress, & Heide, 2003; Lee, Vincent, Hart, & Corrado, 2003; Vitacco, Rogers, & Neuman, 2003). The APSD is a 20-item, self-report measure of antisocial behaviors backed by a three-factor model of Impulsiveness, Callous/Unemotional, and Narcissism (Frick, Bodin, & Barry, 2000; Vitacco et al., 2003). Initial results concerning its clinical utility are mixed. Falkenbach et al. (2003) suggest that the reliability of the APSD is satisfactory, although some scales demonstrated low internal consistency. Lee et al. (2003) found the APSD to be a poor measure of psychopathy among incarcerated adolescents when compared to a widely accepted gold standard of psychopathy assessment, the Psychopathy Checklist: Youth Version (PCL:YV; Frick & Hare, 2001), which is a semistructured interview and rating scale completed by a professional. The findings of Vitacco et al. (2003) also suggest mixed psychometric properties, although they contend that the APSD has the potential to be a useful screening device for the presence of psychopathy in incarcerated juveniles.

Although self-reports may be useful for measuring some of the unobservable, internalizing problems that often accompany ODD and CD, such as depression, there are problematic issues with using self-reports with this population. One of the unique challenges of using self-reports with children with suspected or confirmed symptoms of ODD or CD, involves the nature of the defining behaviors or symptoms, which may be illegal, aggressive, or deceitful. Children may be understandably reticent or unwilling to disclose these behaviors, or may "fake good." Alternatively, if children perceive that they have something to gain, such as sympathy or a less severe punishment by having a disorder, they may malinger, or "fake bad." Additionally, self-reports generally cannot be used with children under age 8, due to young children's limitations in self-awareness and conceptual understanding. The use of self-reports with children older than age 8 may also be problematic if cognitive or learning problems are present, and, even if comprehension is adequate, children may not be able or willing to accurately report on their behaviors or internal states. The self-report form of the BASC attempts to address some of these problems by including an L index, which indicates a tendency to report socially desirable responses, a V index designed to detect poor comprehension or uncooperativeness with testing (Matazow & Kamphaus, 2001) and an F index designed to detect "faking bad." The MMPI-A includes similar validity scales designed to detect social desirability, inconsistent responding, or attempts to exaggerate psychopathology (F scale; Gumbiner, 2003). Some recent research also indicates that self-report measures of antisocial behaviors may be useful for subtyping conduct problems in adolescents (Andershed, Gustafson, Kerr, & Stattin, 2002). In sum, although self-reports are certainly not stand-alone measures in the assessment of CD or ODD, they can provide helpful information about the child's internal states, self-perceptions, possible comorbid conditions, and personality characteristics (Merrell, 2003).

Preschool Assessment

Nagin and Tremblay (1999) and Shaw et al. (2003), among others, have shown that preschool-aged aggression is fairly common and it usually decreases over time; however, there is evidence to suggest the presence of a subgroup of highly persistent conduct problems beginning at preschool age. Keenan and Wakschlag (2002) contend that valid diagnoses of ODD and CD can be made in preschoolers. Although the presence of ODD and CD in preschoolers is controversial, the BASC-2 and the CRS-R have been normed on preschoolers and may be used to assess conduct problems in this population (Lidz, 2003). However, predictive accuracy improves with age (Bennett & Offord, 2001). Additionally, due to the age-related issues mentioned earlier and the lack of research on the validity of diagnosing disruptive behavior disorders in preschool children, results from these measures should be interpreted with great care.

CASE STUDY

The following psychological report is from a University-based clinic. Identifying information, such as child and family name, child sex, and other particulars has been removed, altered, or fictionalized to protect confidentiality. A short interpretive description follows the report.

REASON FOR REFERRAL

Joey Smith is a 7-year-old boy referred for evaluation by his mother due to concerns about disruptive behavior and academic difficulties. At the time of the evaluation, Ms. Smith reported that Joey was having difficulties with anger, pouting, and losing his temper. Additionally, she reported that Joey was behind in his academic classes and did not seem to be able to comprehend new information.

ASSESSMENT PROCEDURES

Behavior Assessment System for Children (BASC)
    Parent Rating Scales (BASC-PRS)
    Structured Developmental History (BASC-SDH)
    Teacher Rating Scales (BASC-TRS)
Bracken Basic Concept Scale—Revised (BBCS-R)
Child Interview
Conners' Parent Rating Scales—Revised: Long Version (CPRS-R:L)
Conners' Teacher Rating Scales—Revised: Long Version (CPRS-R:L)
Parent Interview
Peabody Picture Vocabulary Test—Third Edition, Form A (PPVT-III)
Woodcock-Johnson III Tests of Achievement (WJ III ACH)
Woodcock-Johnson III Tests of Cognitive Abilities (WJ III COG)

BACKGROUND INFORMATION

Joey was delivered via Caesarian section and weighed 7 pounds, following a full term, uneventful pregnancy. No problems were noted after delivery and Joey went home from the hospital with his mother on schedule. Developmental milestones were achieved within normal limits; results of a recent hearing and vision screening were normal. Mrs. Smith reported that Joey has not suffered from any major childhood illnesses or injuries; he is currently in good health and does not take medication. Joey attends first grade, is an only child, and lives with his mother, Ms. Smith. Joey's father has been largely uninvolved in rearing Joey due to verbal and physical abuse toward Ms. Smith when Joey was born, which resulted in divorce.

Ms. Smith reported that Joey "has always had temper tantrums" and exhibited concerning behaviors at home, specifically, kicking, slamming doors, and screaming when denied his way. She noted that Joey has temper tantrums at least twice a day while he is at home and consistently refuses to comply, specifically when she asks him to brush his teeth and do his homework. Ms. Smith reported that Joey has a difficult time following directions and often seems angry. She indicated that discipline techniques have not proven effective with Joey. She has tried spanking, removal of privileges, such as playing with toys, and time out, all of which have failed to result in significant behavior change.

Joey's educational history reveals a pattern of behavior, attention, and academic problems. Preschool and primary school teachers have reported the presence of disruptive behaviors at school. Over the past 3 years, Joey has engaged in the following behaviors at school: refusing to follow directions, throwing objects, and "talking-back" to his teachers. Attention problems, such as difficulty staying on-task and difficulty switching tasks were also noted by each of his teachers. Teachers also described learning difficulties and reported that Joey has always seemed to be behind his peers academically.

BEHAVIORAL OBSERVATIONS

Joey presented as an attractive and active youngster. He related well to the examiners and enjoyed playing with them during breaks from formal testing. Joey displayed emotional outbursts and often required redirection during testing. He flailed his arms and legs, cried, and refused to enter the testing room. Further, Joey pouted and threw his body on the ground when asked to clean up toys. Overall, Joey presented as an active child, exhibiting defiant behavior at times.

CLASSROOM OBSERVATION

Joey was observed in his classroom at Oakbend Elementary School. Joey appeared overactive and had difficulty staying in his seat, frequently walking around the room asking, "When are we going outside?" Further, he seemed inattentive, such as making humming noises during story time and asking the teacher to repeat directions. He required frequent redirection and one-on-one assistance throughout the morning. Additionally, he verbally insulted classmates, once stating, "You're so stupid!" when a child did not respond to a question correctly. In all, Joey appeared to be experiencing difficulties with hyperactivity, inattention, and peer difficulties in the classroom setting.

COGNITIVE AND ACADEMIC FUNCTIONING

To address concerns about academic functioning, the Woodcock-Johnson III Tests of Cognitive Abilities (WJ III COG) were used to evaluate Joey's cognitive functioning. Joey earned composite scores that fell within the Average range with equally developed verbal and nonverbal reasoning abilities. The Woodcock-Johnson III Tests of Achievement (WJ III ACH), Bracken Basic Concept Scale—Revised (BBCS-R), and Peabody Picture Vocabulary Test—Third Edition (PPVT-III) were used to assess Joey's academic attainment, mastery of basic relational concepts, and receptive language skills. Consistent with his performance during cognitive testing, Joey performed in the Average range across all academic and language tasks. Results indicate age-appropriate cognitive and academic functioning that is evenly developed across all areas.

SOCIAL-EMOTIONAL AND BEHAVIORAL FUNCTIONING

The Behavior Assessment System for Children—Parent (PRS) and Teacher Rating Scales (TRS) and the Conners' Parent (CPRS) and Teacher Rating Scales (CTRS) were used to assess Joey's social, emotional, and behavioral functioning across both home and school settings. The BASC scores are presented below for Ms. Smith and Joey's teachers:

	T-Scores		
BASC Clinical Scale/Composite	**Mother**	**Kindergarten**	**First Grade**
Hyperactivity	72	67	77
Aggression	64	61	74
Anxiety	39	55	50
Depression	54	53	58
Somatization	40	43	43
Attention Problems	80	78	78
Atypicality	41	53	61
Withdrawal	31	41	61
Externalizing Problems Composite	57	65	77
Internalizing Problems Composite	51	52	50
Behavior Symptoms Index	61	66	71
BASC Adaptive Scales/Composite			
Adaptability	58	53	45
Social Skills	43	37	26
Adaptive Skills Composite	51	37	36

Conners' scores are presented below for Ms. Smith and Joey's teacher:

	T-Scores	
Conners' Clinical Scale/Composite	**Mother**	**First Grade**
Oppositional	65	76
Cognitive Problems/Inattention	86	90
Hyperactivity	66	75
Anxious-Shy	38	56
Perfectionism	52	53
Social Problems	52	90
Psychosomatic	50	—
Conners' ADHD Index	76	80
Conners' Global Index: Restless-Impulsive	78	77
Conners' Global Index: Emotional Lability	77	68
Conners' Global Index: Total	80	77
DSM-IV Inattentive	80	85
DSM-IV Hyperactive-Impulsive	65	74
DSM-IV Total	74	81

Ms. Smith and Joey's teachers indicated that Joey demonstrates significant problems with hyperactivity, inattention, and defiant behaviors. In the area of hyperactivity, Ms. Smith noted that Joey is overly active, throws tantrums, cannot wait his turn, and acts without thinking. She indicated that Joey has a hard time staying in his seat during dinnertime and that he often climbs on things. Joey's teachers noted that he has a hard time waiting his turn and that he frequently bothers other children when they are working. During a teacher interview, Joey's first grade teacher indicated that he often wanders around the room and does not follow directions. Parent and teacher reports are consistent with Joey's behavior during the evaluation; he seems to be constantly "on the go" and has a difficult time sitting still.

In the area of inattention, Ms. Smith noted that Joey has a short attention span, is easily distracted, and has trouble concentrating. Ms. Smith noted that she has to redirect Joey continually while doing his homework and that he does not persist with tasks at hand. Joey's teachers also indicated that he has a difficult time sustaining concentration on academic work. Joey's first grade teacher also reported that Joey does not listen attentively to directions and is easily distracted by other children. During the evaluation, Joey had a difficult time concentrating on the task at hand and required frequent redirection.

Joey is also displaying a pattern of oppositional and defiant behavior. Ms. Smith described Joey as often losing his temper and actively refusing to comply with her requests. She indicated that Joey slams doors, stomps into his room, and hits things when he is denied his way. Joey's current teacher indicated that Joey threatens to hurt others and frequently bullies other children, such as hitting or teasing them. Additionally, Joey displayed defiant behavior during the evaluation, such as refusing to comply with requests and being uncooperative during testing procedures. Overall, Joey's attentional and behavioral difficulties are negatively impacting his performance at school and adjustment within the home.

SUMMARY AND DIAGNOSTIC IMPRESSIONS

Joey Smith, a 7-year-old boy, was referred for evaluation by his mother, Ms. Smith due to her concerns about his behavior and learning. Ms. Smith wanted to know more about Joey's behavioral adjustment and his difficulties comprehending new material. Ms. Smith was also concerned that Joey was academically "behind his peers."

Results of our evaluation reveal that Joey's intellectual abilities, academic skills, and receptive language are age-appropriate. He also demonstrates age-appropriate mastery of basic relational concepts that are important in order to benefit from formal instruction within the classroom. Behaviorally, Joey shows significant problems with inattention, hyperactivity, and impulsivity. Across classroom, home, and clinic environments, Joey exhibited difficulty sustaining attention, distractibility, and difficulty with tasks requiring sustained mental effort. He is overactive as evidenced by leaving his seat in the classroom and at the dinner table, squirming in his seat, and running around in inappropriate situations. Additionally, Joey has a difficult time waiting his turn, often interrupts others, and blurts out answers before questions have been completed. Joey's pattern of behavior is consistent with a diagnosis of Attention-Deficit/Hyperactivity Disorder-Combined Type (*DSM-IV-TR* 314.01).

Further, Joey's behavior is characterized by a pattern of defiant behavior in the home and school environments. Joey often argues with adults and refuses to comply with their requests or rules. At times, he is also verbally aggressive in both home and school situations. Joey's pattern of behavior is consistent with a diagnosis of Oppositional Defiant Disorder (*DSM-IV-TR* 313.81).

RECOMMENDATIONS

Based on the findings described previously, the following are recommended:

1. Joey and his mother would benefit from participation in Parent Child Interaction Therapy (PCIT), a behaviorally based intervention that has been shown to be effective in reducing oppositional and defiant behavior for young children. Within the context of PCIT, Ms. Smith will be instructed in methods to monitor targeted inappropriate behaviors, monitor and reward incompatible behaviors, and ignore inappropriate behavior. Parent Child Interaction Therapy will also focus on improving

the quality of the Smith's parent-child relationship, which is strained at the present time.

2. In order to reduce Joey's defiance within the home, he would benefit from increased structure at home. The home environment should be structured in terms of establishing rules that communicate Ms. Smith's expectations concerning academic performance and behavior; maintaining a schedule of required activities; and making reinforcement available for following rules. Consequences for appropriate and inappropriate behavior should be enforced on a consistent basis through positive reinforcement of appropriate behavior and ignoring inappropriate behavior. Ms. Smith is encouraged to increase Joey's responsibilities at home and to establish a realistic reinforcement strategy for his compliance.

3. Joey would benefit from having a more structured homework environment. Joey is experiencing difficulties working independently and would benefit from having specific times allotted and guidelines for completing his assignments. He would benefit from having someone check his progress periodically to answer any questions and to ensure that he is still on task.

4. Joey's symptoms of inattention make it more difficult for him to keep track of changing rules. We recommend that behavioral expectations and consequences at home and at school be as consistent as possible.

5. In light of Joey's difficulties with inattention, hyperactivity, impulsivity, and defiance it is recommended that school personnel review this report to determine the possible need for academic support and accommodations to facilitate Joey's success at school. Furthermore, the results may warrant review to determine the appropriateness of support and services in line with eligibility rules and guidelines. Interventions and modifications within the school setting might include:

   a. Conducting a functional behavioral assessment to better understand the functional properties of Joey's defiant behavior within the classroom. For example, it would help to know if Joey throws tantrums and is defiant within the classroom in order to avoid academic task demands or to gain social attention. A functional behavioral assessment should prove helpful in determining the antecedents, behaviors, and consequences of Joey's tantrums and defiant behavior and guide school professionals in modifying the environment to reduce both behaviors.

   b. Due to Joey's distractibility, accommodations within the classroom may help him attend to instruction, including preferential seating away from doorways, windows, or other students, as necessary, where stimuli might prove distracting.

6. Given the effectiveness of medication for improving symptoms of inattention, Joey would benefit from an evaluation by a child psychiatrist to determine if he would benefit from a trial of medication.

Discussion of Case Study

Joey's evaluation illustrates many of the concepts and practical assessment methods described in the chapter. Joey's behavioral adjustment was evaluated using interview, observation, and third-party rating scales. With respect to third-party rating scales, Joey's behavioral adjustment was evaluated using multiple informants (i.e., parent and teachers) and multiple measures (i.e., the BASC and CRS-R) across contexts (i.e., home and school) and time (i.e., prior and present school year). Results were remarkably consistent across raters, instruments, and contexts giving us increased confidence in our diagnosis of both ODD and ADHD. Joey's evaluation illustrates the frequent comorbidity observed between ODD and ADHD diagnoses. We did not detect the presence of significant internalizing problems, as ratings of anxiety and depressive symptoms were within normal limits for both the BASC and CRS-R, and internalizing symptoms were denied during the parent and child interviews.

Cognitive and language disorders were eliminated as explanations for Joey's defiance. For example, the receptive language screen indicated no significant impairments in understanding spoken directives. Furthermore, the BBCS-R revealed age-appropriate mastery of relational concepts commonly encountered during classroom instruction, such as, "Joey, mark letters that *begin* with the letter *r*"; or "Which number is *larger,* 5 or 7?" Ruling out cognitive and language problems are important because oppositional behaviors or defiance can be associated with difficulties understanding what is being asked. Despite the increased risk for comorbid learning disability for children with ODD and ADHD, Joey did not show evidence of a learning disorder in any area.

In the report, recommendations for interventions across home and school environments are behaviorally based and emphasize consistency across both contexts. Parent Child Interaction Therapy was selected as an appropriate treatment due to its empirical support in treating children with disruptive behavior disorders. The family was referred to a local child psychologist with expertise in PCIT intervention. Written to share with school professionals, the report also raises the possibility for special education eligibility due to the diagnoses rendered. Two eligibility options exist in Joey's situation, Other Health Impaired (OHI) or Emotional Disturbance (ED). Recommendations for classroom accommodations and behaviorally based interventions are outlined.

A final point of interest involves the social and familial context of the assessment. Although not formally diagnosed with a CD or ASPD, Joey's father may have exhibited behavioral symptoms that reached diagnostic thresholds for such problems. We learned that he was physically aggressive toward Ms. Smith, which resulted in separation and divorce. As described in the chapter, prevailing ideas of etiology for CD and ODD emphasize biopsychosocial interdependence. In Joey's case, he may be predisposed to exhibit aggressive behavior due to his father's genetic contribution; a social learning explanation seems inadequate as Joey's father was abusive right after Joey was born and Ms. Smith filed for divorced shortly thereafter. The divorce resulted in Joey being raised by one parent, which appears to have increased the stresses of parenting in the household. Therefore, biological and psychosocial variables appear important in understanding why Joey exhibits a pattern of oppositional and defiant behavior.

Conclusion

The serious consequences of the behaviors associated with ODD and CD make accurate diagnosis and intervention important. Crime, aggression, violence, and other symptoms of ODD and CD affect not only the individual but also the community at large. For example, Jones, Dodge, Foster, Nix, and the Conduct Problems Prevention Research Group (2002) note that preventing one child from developing severe conduct problems could save the public over $2 million. Another crucial issue in ODD/CD assessment and diagnosis involves the trajectory of the disorder. In the worst cases, this can be conceptualized as a move from ODD to CD to APD to psychopathy. Despite the apparent importance of detecting ODD and CD and a vast literature on measures relevant to diagnosis of these disorders, interpretation of assessment of ODD and CD remains challenging due to comorbidities, contextual variables, and issues of age, gender, and culture. Additionally, disruptive behavior disorders pose unique assessment challenges due to changes in symptom expression across time (e.g., aggression may look different in a 6-year-old than in a 16-year-old), disagreements about subtyping, and a motivation to actively hide or be unwilling to share symptoms (as these may include illegal, dangerous, or aggressive acts). Similar to other diagnostic questions, an assessment approach that utilizes multiple measures of behavior across multiple contexts is recommended when assessing for the presence of either ODD or CD. In the context of evaluating disruptive behavior problems, cognitive, academic, and language screening are recommended due to the increased rates of comorbid learning and language problems in groups of children diagnosed with ODD and CD.

Assessment and Diagnosis of Substance Use in Childhood and Adolescence

Meghan C. VanDeventer and Randy W. Kamphaus

12

Chapter

The adolescent period is viewed as the stage between childhood and adulthood. This developmental period between 14 and 22 years of age has been described as the greatest window of vulnerability for risk consequences across the life span (G. R. Adams, Cantwell, & Matheis, 2002). During this time, individuals are transitioning into adulthood and are therefore given more privileges and responsibilities. Sometimes this increase in freedom occurs earlier than an adolescent's ability to handle this freedom responsibly. In the search for independence and a separate identity from their parents, adolescents often experiment with a wide range of attitudes and behaviors. This experimentation may lead adolescents to partake in a number of risky behaviors such as sexual promiscuity, alcohol consumption, drug use, and reckless driving. With increased independence and opportunity, rates for heavy drinking increase and peak (Clark & Widanik, 1982, as cited in Bukstein, 1995).

Adolescent substance use and substance use disorders have become areas of major clinical and public health concern in the United States. Alcohol and drug use continue to be prevalent in epidemic proportions with more than 5 million adolescents (ages 12 to 17) admitting to drinking at least monthly (Johnston, O'Malley, & Bachman,

1998). The majority of teenagers use drugs and alcohol occasionally without negative consequences (71% of high school seniors drank alcohol in 2001) leading parents to assume that alcohol and drug use is normal; however, the reality of the situation is that half of these alcohol-using adolescents have had a binge episode (five or more drinks at one time) in the past month, and 3.6% drink daily (Jaffe & Solhkhah, 2004). These adolescents are the ones who are likely to engage in other risk-taking behaviors such as impaired driving, minor criminal activity, and unprotected sex. P. Rogers and Adger (1993) found that homicides, suicides, and injuries account for 80% of teenage deaths, and more than half of these are associated with alcohol (Jaffe & Solhkhah, 2004). Further, Garfinkel and Golombeck (1983) found that alcohol-related automobile accidents are the leading cause of injury and death among 15- to 24-year-olds, and substance involvement is a major risk factor for teen suicide (S. A. Brown, Aarons, & Abrantes, 2001). Frequent and continued consumption of substances among adolescents increases risk for developing substance use disorders as well as the possibility of emerging developmental competency and psychosocial functioning impairments (Chassin, Ritter, Trim, & King, 2003). Adolescent substance abuse has adverse social and economic ramifications, especially when its onset is early and the disorder does not remit in early adulthood (K. C. Winters, 2001).

Adolescent Epidemiologic Studies

Given the importance of studying adolescent substance use, several large-scale national epidemiological studies were launched in the 1970s to track adolescent substance use prevalence over time. The Monitoring the Future (MTF) studies are large annual surveys of nationally representative U.S. secondary school students that began in 1975 as a school-based survey of substance use among high school seniors. Since 1991, annual surveys have been administered to younger adolescents as well (8th and 10th graders). The most recent report on data that was collected in 2000 is based on over 45,000 students in 8th, 10th, and 12th grades in 435 schools nationwide (Johnston, O'Malley, & Bachman, 2001). Substance abuse is quite common by the end of the high school years. For example, 54% of 12th graders reported having used illegal drugs, with 24.9% using in the past month. The use of alcohol and tobacco was even more common.

The National Household Survey on Drug Abuse (NHSDA), directed by the Substance Abuse and Mental Health Services Administration (SAMHSA), has been conducted since 1971 and provides annual estimates of prevalence, incidence, demographic distribution, and correlates of use of illicit drugs, alcohol, and tobacco from over 70,000 U.S. residents aged 12 years and older. Data from the NHSDA and other epidemiological surveys of American youth suggest a steady developmental increase in use across adolescent years, with tobacco, alcohol, and marijuana use being relatively common. Gender differences in the prevalence of substance use do not appear to be substantial (Young et al., 2002). Adolescent surveys of substance use disorders are scarce, but suggest that dependence is most common with tobacco and marijuana and disorders are equally common for males and females (Young et al., 2002).

Diagnosis

Despite the growing concern that adolescent drug and alcohol abuse is becoming an epidemic, researchers and clinicians continue to struggle with the exact definition of adolescent substance use disorders. The distinction between adolescent substance use and misuse has been the subject of much debate among professionals. In American society, any alcohol use is illegal for adolescents and other drug use is illegal regardless of age. The term substance *use* has therefore been largely abandoned in favor of substance *abuse,* when referring to adolescents. This change reflects the ideology that any use among minors constitutes misuse because it is illegal (Jaffe & Solhkhah, 2004). This practice obscures the distinction necessary to classify substance abuse and dependence as health problems. The majority of adolescents experiment with substances; therefore, to define "abuse" as "use" implies that most adolescents require some sort of drug abuse intervention. To develop a valid diagnostic classification for adolescent substance use disorders, we must consider the basic purpose of diagnoses. A diagnosis must distinguish between individuals in a meaningful way. Diagnostic classifications are needed for clear communication among researchers and clinicians, referral to appropriate clinical interventions and treatments, and ensuring the accessibility of services that depend on third-party reimbursement (Harrison, Fulkerson, & Beebe, 1998). If diagnostic criteria are overly inclusive, the diagnosis is too heterogeneous to be meaningful.

Pandina (1986, as cited in Bukstein, 1995) offers several variables on which to operationally define adolescent substance abuse: (a) extreme levels of drug or alcohol use in quantity and/or frequency of use or intoxication, (b) criteria-based "symptomatic" use behaviors, and (c) negative consequences presumed to be due to substance use. Basing adolescent substance use disorder diagnoses on high levels of quantity and frequency does not appear to be of much use when considered by itself. Although information regarding the quantity of a substance consumed is useful, Giancola and Tarter (1999) have demonstrated that it does not give reliable information about substance abuse because adolescents vary both in the effects of various substances and in their reactions to them (G. R. Adams et al., 2002). Donovan and Jessor as cited in Bukstein (1995) showed that over 30% of high school seniors drank heavily at least once in a 2-week period. Assigning pathological status to a behavior with such a high prevalence is ambiguous. In the majority of these cases, we are likely observing a range of normal adolescent behavior and development in the context of our society (Bukstein, 1995).

The second option for diagnosing adolescent substance use disorders, criteria based on symptomatic use behaviors, is not practical at this time due to the fact that symptomatic behaviors of psychological dependence (e.g., impairment of control, craving, and preoccupation with use) are not well studied in adolescents (Bukstein, 1995).

The third option of defining adolescent substance use disorders by the presence of negative consequences of use has been adopted by the official nomenclature of the American Psychiatric Association, the *Diagnostic Statistical Manual* (*DSM*) as well as the *International Classification of Diseases* (*ICD*). Both of these diagnostic criteria were developed from research and clinical experiences with adults and their applicability to adolescents has not yet been ascertained. Age distinctions may be particularly important with respect to substance use disorders due to the incorporation of legal and social consequences into the criteria (Harrison et al., 1998). This issue is addressed more thoroughly later, but first let us look more closely at the *DSM* classification system.

The Evolution of the *Diagnostic and Statistical Manual of Mental Disorders*

Continued efforts to improve on the conceptualization of substance use disorders have resulted in numerous changes to the *DSM* classification system of substance use disorders throughout the years. The third edition of *Diagnostic and Statistical Manual of Mental Disorders* (DSM-III) was the first edition to change alcoholism from a unitary concept of dependence to a bipartite disorder consisting of abuse and dependence. Substance abuse was defined in terms of pathological use (e.g., inability to cut down or stop using, binges, blackouts, continued use despite physical problems) *and* impairment in social or occupational functioning due to use (e.g., violence while under the influence, legal problems, absence from work or school, or arguments with family or friends). Substance dependence was defined by the presence of tolerance or withdrawal in addition to either pathological use or impairment in social or occupational functioning due to use. Abuse could be diagnosed regardless of whether dependence was present. This taxonomy has been criticized on several bases, including the emphasis on physiological criteria and social impairment, lack of specific theoretical basis, and inclusion of two substance use disorders (G. R. Adams et al., 2002). *DSM-III* classification does not apply well to adolescents due to the rarity of significant withdrawal symptoms in adolescent substance misuse and the overemphasis of *DSM-III* on the physiologic symptoms of later stages of abuse and dependence (Bukstein, 1995). Affective and cognitive features, rather than physiological symptoms, predominate among adolescents during withdrawal from multiple substances. Therefore, clinicians should not rely on signs of physical dependence for classifying adolescent substance abuse or dependence (S. A. Brown et al., 2001).

Within a year of the release of *DSM-III* criteria, a work group was assembled to revise the substance use nomenclature. Specific problems that were to be addressed were the strong emphasis on social impairments, and the lack of a specific theoretical approach for conceptualizing abuse and dependence. The work group used a scientific, empirically driven approach to revision including collecting information from over 50 experts, a literature review on research addressing specific questions, reanalysis of existing data sets, and collection of new data to address issues that were not sufficiently studied previously (G. R. Adams et al., 2002).

In 1987, the *DSM-III-R* was released with criteria substantially changed from those of the *DSM-III*. The Edwards and Gross alcohol dependence syndrome (ADS; Edwards & Gross, 1976) was the theoretical basis for this edition of the *DSM*, as well as for the *DSM-IV* and the *ICD-10*. The ADS describes dependence rather broadly, including elements such as continued alcohol consumption in spite of knowledge that alcohol is the source of problems, tolerance to alcohol, withdrawal symptoms, seeking relief or avoiding withdrawal symptoms by further alcohol consumption, craving alcohol, a compulsion to drink, and returning to alcohol consumption. Edwards and Gross (1976) also acknowledged that the syndrome varies in levels of severity, illustrating the difficulty in specifying a critical threshold that distinguishes the ill from the well.

The *DSM-III-R* included nine criteria to be applied to all substances, de-emphasized the physical parameters of tolerance and withdrawal as defining features of dependence, and defined abuse as a residual category with a minimal threshold of one criterion among two for persons who did not meet dependence criteria but who nevertheless had problematic substance abuse (Cottler et al., 1995). The *DSM-III-R* defined abuse by either recurrent use in situations in which it is physically hazardous *or* continued substance use despite knowledge of a persistent or recurrent social, occupational, psychological, or physical problem caused or exacerbated by the use of a substance. Hasin and colleagues (as cited in Bukstein, 1995), however, found that, in a longitudinal study of male drinkers, alcohol abuse appeared to have a distinct course from alcohol dependence, calling into question the notion of abuse as a residual category. To meet criteria for dependence, an individual must have manifested at least three of nine symptoms within a 12-month period (American Psychiatric Association, 1987). These symptoms were: the substance abuse criteria, tolerance, withdrawal, drinking to avoid or relieve withdrawal, drinking in greater amounts or for a longer time than intended, unsuccessful attempts to quit or cut down on drinking, much time spent using alcohol, and important activities given up or reduced in favor of substance use. By including behaviors and cognitions and not requiring withdrawal and/or tolerance in the criteria for psychoactive substance dependence, the *DSM-III-R* probably included more adolescents as compared to the *DSM-III;* however, implicit in the concept of dependence in both the *DSM-III-R* and ADS are impaired control and craving, neither of which have received much research attention in adolescents (Bukstein, 1995). However, changes in the *DSM* systems occur at such a fast pace that revisions have occurred before extensive empirical knowledge can be drawn to guide these changes (K. C. Winters, Latimer, & Stinchfield, 1999).

The *DSM-IV* substance use work group was selected to represent varying clinical and research interests. The work group wanted the *DSM* criteria to be applicable across a broad range of substances and felt that any changes to be made would need to be supported by empirical data. Attempts were also made to eliminate discrepancies between *DSM* and *ICD-10* nomenclature to allow for comparisons to be made with international studies and facilitate communication. The *DSM-IV* work group went through a similar process as did the *DSM-III-R* group by consulting with 50 experts, conducting literature reviews, and analyzing existing data sets.

DSM-IV nomenclature differs from that of the *DSM-III-R* in several ways (Cottler et al., 1995), including (a) the abuse diagnosis was designed to be distinct from the dependence diagnosis rather than serve as a residual category for persons who do not meet dependence criteria, (b) the abuse diagnosis criteria were expanded from two to four, (c) the "duration" criterion for substance dependence found in the *DSM-III-R* was replaced with a "clustering" criterion that required at least three dependence criteria within a 12-month period, (d) dependence diagnoses were further specified as either physiological (tolerance or withdrawal were experienced) or non-physiological, and (e) it was required that the maladaptive pattern of substance use lead to clinically significant impairment or distress (Bukstein, 1995). Indeed, the *DSM-IV* appears to propose a broader definition of abuse and a narrower definition of dependence as compared to *DSM-III-R*. The negative social consequences and role impairment associated with substance use have been segregated under the diagnosis of abuse, whereas the cognitive, behavioral, and physiological adaptations have been placed under the diagnosis of dependence (Nelson, Rehm, Bedirhan Ustun, Grant, & Chatterji, 1999). Abuse represents problematic use without evidence of compulsive use and physiologic dependence, whereas dependence represents compulsive use, both with and without physiologic alterations (Cottler et al., 1995).

K. C. Winters and colleagues (1999) found that *DSM-IV* criteria for alcohol and cannabis produced relatively more abuse and fewer dependence cases in adolescents as compared to *DSM-III-R*. It appears as though the majority of *DSM-IV* new abuse recruits were judged by the *DSM-III-R* as noncases or "no diagnosis." This difference demonstrates a shift in the abuse threshold by virtue of a broader *DSM-IV* definition of abuse criteria. External validity data generally supported the current distinctions between *DSM-IV* abuse and dependence in adolescents but suggested that the current differences may not yet be optimal. The transference of the substance dependence criteria for frequent intoxication or withdrawal symptoms when expected to fulfill a major role obligation at work, home, or school to the diagnosis of substance abuse may have also influenced the reduction in dependence diagnoses (Bukstein, 1995). Halikas noted (as cited in Bukstein, 1995) that substance use at school and missing school due to use are behaviors that are commonly seen in adolescents with substance use problems. Mikulich, Hall, Whitmore, and Crowley (2001) found that rates of concordance between *DSM-III-R* and *DSM-IV* diagnoses varied across drug categories but were generally "good" to "excellent" for substance dependence while consistently lower for abuse diagnoses in adolescents.

Applying the *DSM-IV* to Adolescents

How appropriate is the *DSM-IV* substance use related diagnostic nomenclature for adolescents? Unfortunately, notwithstanding a few studies evaluating criteria in adolescents for limited substances, the absence of *DSM-III-R* substance use data on adolescents and the lack of *DSM-IV* field trial results pertaining to adolescent abusers make it very difficult to judge the validity or reliability of past and current nosologies for adolescents. It is not known whether the old criteria was adequate when applied to adolescents, and therefore no empirical context exists by which to judge whether the new criteria are a step forward or backward (K. C. Winters et al., 1999). It has been assumed that criteria for adult substance use disorders should apply to adolescents. This assumption is based on the belief that the substance use disorders in both adolescents and adults represent the same disorder or pathological process. Several studies have attempted to find chronological continuity in abuse from adolescence to adulthood to test this belief. A study by Donovan, Jessor, and Jessor (1983) supported the belief by suggesting that the adolescent "problem drinkers" form the core of those who develop adult alcohol abuse (as cited in Bukstein, 1995). Other studies, however, show evidence of discontinuity in drinker status between those labeled as problem drinkers in adolescence and problem drinkers in young adulthood (Jessor, 1984) and the lack of a predictive relationship between young adult drinking status and middle-age problem drinking (Cahalan & Cisin, 1976, as cited in Bukstein, 1995). Blane (1976) found that frequent heavy drinking in adolescents and the problems resulting from drinking appear to be self-limiting and are not highly predictive of alcoholism in adults (as cited in Bukstein, 1995).

In addition to the discontinuity between adolescent problem use and adult abuse/dependency demonstrated previously, several salient differences are evident between adolescent and adult substance use and abuse. These differences suggest that diagnostic criteria may perform quite differently for adolescents and adults (Pollock, Martin, & Langenbucher, 2000):

- Adolescents tend to use different substances and are more likely to be polysubstance users than adults (Chassin et al., 2003; Mikulich et al., 2001). Stewart and Brown (1995) report that, whereas 70% to 90% of adolescents in treatment for substance use are polysubstance users, polysubstance use in adult treatment samples ranges from 0% to 55% (as cited in Mikulich et al., 2001).

- Harford and Mills (1978) reported that adolescent drinking involves relatively higher quantity and lower frequency use compared to adults (as cited in Pollock et al., 2000). In *DSM-IV,* it was decided that a temporal overlap (clustering of symptoms) was more relevant than duration of symptoms. This clustering may produce lower rates of dependence in adolescents due to the greater temporal dispersion of symptoms in adolescents; however, Mikulich and colleagues (2001) found that the clustering criterion had little affect on prevalence rates of *DSM-IC* dependence diagnoses in a sample of 102 adolescents.

- Due to their younger age, adolescents are likely to have a shorter history of use than adults entering treatment, which may result in adolescents having different profiles of symptom patterns (e.g., less frequent and/or serious withdrawal and tolerance due to less time to develop those symptoms). K. C. Winters et al. (1999) state that withdrawal and alcohol-related medical problems have been found to have a very low prevalence even in clinical adolescent samples. Alternatively, Stewart and Brown (1995) examined 166 adolescents from inpatient substance treatment programs and found that withdrawal symptoms in their sample were in excess of those previously reported in adolescent substance abuse literature; however, they note that there is little empirical evidence assessing the applicability of *DSM-IV* withdrawal criteria to adolescents. Mikulich and colleagues (2001) also found that more than half of the adolescents in their sample dependent on cannabis, inhalants, or hallucinogens reported withdrawal symptoms. Although these studies have found evidence of withdrawal in adolescents, withdrawal is not a recognized symptom for cannabis, hallucinogens, inhalants, or PCP in *DSM-IV* (as cited in Mikulich, 2001; American Psychiatric Association, 1994). It also appears that in adolescents affective and cognitive features, rather than physiological symptoms, predominate during acute withdrawal from multiple symptoms (S. A. Brown et al., 2001).

- Symptoms such as tolerance and using more or longer than intended are actually quite common among adolescent users with and without substance abuse disorders, and thus have very low diagnostic specificity for adolescents (Stewart & Brown, 1995, as cited in Pollock et al., 2000). The development of tolerance for alcohol in particular is likely a normal developmental phenomenon that happens in the majority of adolescent drinkers (K. C. Winters, 2001).

- Social consequences for substance using adolescents differ from those experienced by adults. First, simply by virtue of their age and legal status, alcohol and drug use by adolescents is illegal; therefore, certain negative consequences may result from this legal issue rather than from the direct effects of substance use. Therefore, the same behavior that may elicit legal consequences for a minor is not subject to legal sanctions for an adult. Drinking may also cause problems with interpersonal relationships (with parents) for a minor simply because alcohol consumption is prohibited. Thus, one might expect the threshold for adverse consequences associated with alcohol to be lower for adolescents (Harrison et al., 1998). Adolescents also tend to report more social than physiological or psychological problems (Mikulich et al., 2001). By eliminating the "social" aspect of *DSM* dependence criteria and moving it to abuse criteria, adolescents appear to receive fewer *DSM-IV* dependence diagnoses and more abuse diagnoses for alcohol, cannabis, cocaine, and hallucinogens in comparison to adults (K. C. Winters et al., 1999).

Another problem that suggests limitations of *DSM-IV* criteria when applied to adolescents is that of *diagnostic orphans*. Haskin and Paykin (1998, as cited in K. C. Winters, 2001) use this term to describe individuals who reveal one or two dependence symptoms but no abuse symptoms and who therefore do not qualify for any diagnosis. Several investigations have found that diagnostic orphans are common among adolescent substance users, reporting rates that range from 10% to 30% (Kaczynski & Martin, 1995; Lewinsohn, Rohde, & Seeley, 1996). Kaczynski and Martin (1995) found that diagnostic orphans showed levels of drinking and drug use similar to adolescents diagnosed with alcohol abuse and significantly higher than those adolescent drinkers without any diagnosis. This suggests that these diagnostic orphans are falling through the cracks of the *DSM-IV* criteria or that the diagnostic criteria for abuse is overly exclusive (K. C. Winters, 2001).

Harrison and colleagues (1998) surveyed 79,398 public school students (grades 9 to 12) and found that, with respect to the *DSM-IV* criteria, the abuse/dependence diagnostic framework was not supported for adolescents. They suggest that an alternative diagnostic classification, such as a continuum of problem severity (one or two symptoms could be identified as abuse, three or four as serious abuse or risk of dependence, and five or more symptoms as probable dependence), may prove to be more useful as a true measure of problem severity. At least two other investigations (Fulkerson, Harrison, & Beebee, 1999; Pollock & Martin, 1999) have suggested combining *DSM-IV* abuse and dependence criteria into a single category for adolescents and differentiating abuse from dependence in terms of number of criteria experienced (as cited in Essau, 2002).

Alternatively, Lewinsohn et al. (1996) used principle components analysis to test the factorial structure of *DSM-IV* symptoms of alcohol abuse/dependence in a sample of 1,507 older (14- to 18-year-olds) community adolescents. Their findings supported the distinction between alcohol abuse and dependence in adolescence. Symptoms clustered on the two components along the lines of the abuse and dependence criteria, with the exception of the dependence symptom of reduced activities, which loaded on the abuse component. The results of other factor analytical studies have varied widely, with some supporting one dimension of alcohol misuse and other reporting multiple factors (Bryant, Rounsaville, & Babor, 1991; Cottler et al., 1995; Kosten, Rounsaville, Babor, Spitzer, & Williams, 1987; Morgenstern, Langenbucher, & Labouvie, 1994).

In general, more studies must be done to determine the applicability of *DSM-IV* diagnostic criteria to adolescents. Adolescent substance use and abuse does seem to differ markedly from adult substance use. Therefore, results from adult samples cannot simply be generalized to adolescents. Ultimately, substance use must be related to impairment or dysfunction in one or more life domains for it to be a disorder. Although a continuum of use patterns can be observed in adolescents, some kind of cutoff and label to describe an unacceptable level of substance use is necessary for identification of adolescents in need of intervention. Clinicians and researchers should be aware of both the strengths and weaknesses of current diagnostic systems to use diagnostic labels in a practical and appropriate manner (Bukstein, 1995).

Current Substance Use-Related Classification Systems

The two coexisting classification systems most widely used to diagnose substance use disorders today are the *Diagnostic and Statistical Manual of Mental Disorders, fourth edition* (*DSM-IV*; American Psychiatric Association, 1994), which remains the current dominant taxonomy in the United States, and the *International Classification of Diseases-10* (*ICD-10*; World Health Organization, 1993), which is used to guide mental health diagnoses outside of the United States. These systems serve to guide clinical practice, research, and education. Given our current level of knowledge about substance abuse in adolescents, the *DSM-IV* and *ICD-10* appear to be reasonable compromises for categorical diagnoses of substance abuse disorders on the way to a more valid and useful nosology for adolescents (Bukstein, 1995). As mentioned previously, attempts have been made to align *DSM-IV* and *ICD-10* diagnoses with each other; however, several small discrepancies still exist. Despite differences in details, both classifications share a common conceptual underpinning—Edward and Gross's (1976) concept of the ADS. Therefore, in the following, corresponding diagnoses from the two classification systems are presented side by side and their differences highlighted.

DSM-IV *and* **ICD-10** *Substance Dependence:*   The American Psychiatric Association (2000) defines substance dependence as "a cluster of cognitive, behavioral, and physiological symptoms indicating that the individual continues use of the substance despite significant substance-related problems" (p. 192). At least three criteria must be met within a 12-month period for an individual to qualify for either a *DSM-IV* or an *ICD-10* dependence diagnosis. An individual can qualify for substance dependence under *ICD-10* if criteria occur together over a 1-month period as well. Substance dependence is further specified by the presence or absence of physiological (tolerance or withdrawal) symptoms. Tolerance is defined as "the need for greatly increased amounts of the substance to achieve intoxication (or the desired effect) or a markedly diminished effect with continued use of the same amount of the substance" (American Psychiatric Association, 2000, p. 192). Tolerance is very common in adolescents and, although extreme levels of tolerance may be helpful in a diagnosis, tolerance at low or moderate levels of use may have limited utility as a diagnostic criterion to distinguish between substance use and abuse/dependence (Bukstein, 1995).

Substance withdrawal is defined in the *DSM-IV* as "the development of a substance-specific maladaptive behavioral change, with physiological and cognitive concomitants, that is due to the cessation of, or reduction in, heavy or prolonged substance use" (American Psychiatric Association, 2000, p. 201). The symptoms of withdrawal are substance-specific in both the *DSM-IV* and the *ICD-10*. The symptoms are very similar between the *DSM-IV* and the *ICD-10,* however, for the withdrawal diagnosis the *DSM-IV* additionally requires distress or impairment related to social, occupational, or other important activities (criterion B). Although significant withdrawal symptoms are rare in adolescents, the clinician should inquire about their presence (Bukstein, 1995).

Differences between the *ICD-10* and *DSM-IV* dependence, though subtle, could lead to disagreements in diagnostic decisions. Two differences are: (1) the inclusion of a craving symptom in the

ICD-10, and (2) *DSM-IV* criteria three and four are combined into one criterion in *ICD-10* (#2) and *DSM-IV* criteria five and six are combined into a single criterion in *ICD-10* (#5; Essau, 2002). Therefore, if an individual were to report craving as a symptom he or she could theoretically be diagnosed with substance dependence under the *ICD-10* but not the *DSM-IV.*

DSM-IV *Substance Abuse and* **ICD-10** *Harmful Use:* The abuse and harmful use diagnoses are viewed by some researchers as similar constructs because they are both residual categories to dependence in the sense that individuals can qualify for abuse or harmful use only if the dependence criteria are not fulfilled; however, there are differences between the abuse and harmful use criteria (Essau, 2002). Substance abuse is defined by the *DSM-IV* as "a maladaptive pattern of substance use manifested by recurrent and significant adverse consequences related to the repeated use of substances" (American Psychiatric Association, 2000, p. 198). "Impairment or distress" is shown through repeated experience of at least one of four criteria in a 12-month period: (1) recurrent use resulting in inability or failure to meet major role obligations at work, school, or home; (2) recurrent use in physically hazardous situations; (3) recurrent substance use-related legal problems; and (4) continued use despite continuing or recurrent social or interpersonal problems caused or worsened by the effects of the substance. It should also be noted that nicotine abuse does not exist. The *ICD-10* requirement of actual harm (criterion A) from substance use is vague in comparison to the substance abuse criteria of the *DSM-IV* (Essau, 2002).

Diagnostic Agreement between **DSM-IV** *and* **ICD-10:** One of the most comprehensive investigations of the agreement between *DSM-IV* and *ICD-10* diagnoses of substance use disorders worldwide was initiated in 1992 by the World Health Organization (WHO) in conjunction with the U.S. National Institute on Alcoholism and Alcohol Abuse (NIAAA) and the National Institute on Drug Abuse (NIDA). Few studies, previous to this one, had presented nosological comparisons of alcohol and drug use disorders that included both dependence and harmful use/abuse as separate categories (Hasin et al.,

1997). Hasin and colleagues (1997) collected data from 1,811 participants from psychiatric treatment, other medical, and community settings at twelve international sites. Agreement estimates between *DSM-IV* and *ICD-10* dependence diagnoses were excellent and consistent across instruments, drugs, and geographical settings. Due to these findings, Hasin and colleagues (1997) concluded that "further nosological comparisons do not appear warranted unless a future diagnostic system greatly changes the definition of dependence . . . the concept of the dependence syndrome, introduced 20 years ago, appears robust against many potential influences on its case identification properties under a wide variety of situations" (p. 224). In contrast, agreement estimates between abuse and harmful use diagnoses were poor to fair and less consistent between instruments. Hasin and colleagues (1997) concluded that this condition, as defined by all classification systems, suffers from a number of factors that lead to poor cross-system concordance: (a) poor reliability, (b) a hierarchical relationship to dependence that makes the abuse diagnosis conditional on the diagnosis of another condition—dependence that is measured well but not perfectly, (c) a variety of views on the proper definition and role of abuse in the nomenclatures, and (d) a prevalence that is often low because the dependence category is fairly broad and preempts the abuse diagnosis when both are present. Therefore, the harmful use/abuse category requires further conceptual as well as psychometric work, either to improve the category or to accumulate enough evidence to eliminate it from the nomenclature (Hasin et al., 1997).

Limited research has been done on the agreement between *DSM-IV* and *ICD-10* substance use disorder diagnoses in adolescents. Pollock and colleagues (2000) recruited a sample of adolescents from clinical settings and the community in Pittsburgh, Pennsylvania. All of the adolescents were regular drinkers. Only fair agreement was reported between the *DMS-IV* and the *ICD-10,* with the greatest discrepancy occurring between *ICD-10* harmful and use and *DSM-IV* abuse diagnosis. The rate of *ICD-10* harmful use diagnosis was much lower than abuse in the *DSM-IV.* The rate of dependence diagnoses was somewhat similar across systems. Martin and colleagues (1996;

as cited in Pollock et al., 2000) found that the harmful use symptom of physical or psychological harm tends to be a relatively late-stage symptom among adolescents. Therefore, adolescents who met this diagnostic criterion tended to meet the *ICD-10* criterion for dependence and did not qualify for harmful use diagnosis. In general, harmful use and abuse diagnoses should be interpreted with particular caution in adolescents (Essau, 2002).

Individuals with Disabilities Education Act Note: Substance Use Disorders are not included in the list of disability conditions identified as eligible for services under the Individuals with Disabilities Education Act (IDEA). However, it does appear that Substance Use Disorder can serve as the basis for qualification through the Other Health Impaired category, especially with documentation of how the Substance Use Disorder adversely affects educational adjustment and performance (House, 1999).

Risk Factors

"Why do adolescents begin to use psychoactive substances and why do some adolescents, and not others, progress to abuse of or dependence on specific substances?" (Bukstein, 1995). To answer this question, we must consider adolescent substance use in a developmental context. Although the diagnosis of substance use disorders usually does not occur until late adolescence, risk factors for substance abuse disorders are identifiable in childhood and early adolescence (Chassin & Ritter, 2001, as cited in Essau, 2002). By identifying these risk factors early on, interventions focused on decreasing exposure to risk factors or buffering their impact may help in preventing a disorder from developing.

Clayton (1992) defines a risk factor as "an individual attribute, individual characteristic, situational condition, or environmental context that increases the probability of drug use or abuse or a transition in level of involvement with drugs" (p. 15, as cited in Essau, 2002). Risk factors for substance abuse and dependence include a wide variety of variables spanning broad domains including biological, psychological, social, and environmental. Rarely, if ever, is a single risk factor sufficient to account for the progression from substance use to abuse. Rather, multiple risk factors combine and interact with each other and the environment to heighten an individual's likelihood of developing a substance use disorder (Bukstein, 1995). Predictive studies suggest that the number of risk factors predicts adolescent substance use better than any particular combination of risk factors (Bry, 1983, as cited in Bukstein, 1995). A comprehensive review of all substance use disorder risk factors would be beyond the scope of a single chapter. The following are examples of specific risk factors in each of the broader domains.

Substance Use

Substance use in itself can result in risk for continued and escalated use (Essau, 2002). Grant and Dawson (1997) identified onset of substance use prior to the age of 15 as a risk factor for later development of substance use disorders. Early initiation of substance use predicts not only increased frequency of substance use but also progression to more serious, illicit drugs (Essau, 2002). Farrell (1993) demonstrated the reciprocal relationship between escalated substance use and exposure to risk factors. Therefore, the earlier adolescents initiate substance use, the more time they have to be exposed to drugs and numerous other risk factors.

Genetic-Biological Factors

A family history of substance use disorders has been found to be a critical risk factor. In an attempt to establish a genetic mode of transmission for the disorder, researchers have used family aggregation studies as well as twin and adoption studies (Dinwiddie & Cloninger, 1991; Essau, 2002). Family aggregation studies have found significant relations between parental alcoholism and elevated levels of drug and alcohol use in adolescence. Milberger and colleagues (1999, as cited in Essau, 2002) found that adolescents who had at least one parent with a substance use disorder had significantly higher rates of drug and alcohol use disorders than controls. However, this evidence may also be due to social and environmental processes. Parental substance use disorders may result in family disruption, poor parenting, and increased environmental stress. Twin and adoption studies allow researchers to evaluate genetic influences independent of environmental influences. In twin studies, the agreement of substance use disorders among monozygotic twins who share genetic makeup is compared with concordance for substance use disorders among dizygotic twins who share only about half of their genes. Twin research has demonstrated higher concordance for substance use disorders in monozygotic twins, indicating a genetic influence (Bukstein, 1995). Adoption studies compare adoptees raised by nonbiologically related parents. More agreement between the adopted child and biological parents than between the adopted child and adoptive parents would support genetic factors. These types of studies have demonstrated that substance use disorders in a biological parent directly predict drug abuse and dependence in the adopted child (Cadoret, Yates, Troughton, Woodworth, & Stewart, 1995, as cited in Bukstein, 1995).

Psychological Factors

Psychological dimensions related to substance use disorders include temperamental and personality dimensions such as behavioral disinhibition, poor self-regulation, and sensation seeking (Chassin et al., 2003; Glantz, Weinberg, Miner, & Colliver, 1999). "Temperament refers to the core psychological characteristic present in infancy that provides the foundation for development of personality and other behavioral competencies" (Essau, 2002, p. 92). Temperament traits are based on genetic factors but are influenced by social and environmental factors as well. In two reviews, the personality characteristics most consistently associated with adolescent substance use included unconventionality, low ego control, sensation seeking, aggression, impulsivity, and an inability to delay gratification (Bates, 1993; Hawkins, Catalano, & Miller, 1992, as cited in Chassin et al., 2003).

Child Conduct Problems

Adolescent substance use disorders are related to the broader development of conduct problems and antisociality (Chassin et al., 2003). There is widespread empirical support that conduct problems and aggression predict adolescent substance use (Kellam, Brown, Rubin, & Ensminger, 1983, as cited in Chassin et al., 2003), escalation in use over time (Hussong, Curran, & Chassin, 1998), and later substance abuse and dependence diagnoses (Chassin, Pitts, DeLucia, & Todd, 1999). In addition, conduct disorder has been found to be a strong risk factor for adolescent substance use disorders for both boys and girls (Clark, Parke, & Lynch, 1999; Disney, Elkins, McGue, & Iacono, 1999, as cited in Chassin et al., 2003).

Peer-Related Factors

Being that peers play a central role in adolescent development, these influences also play a critical role in adolescent substance use, especially in the earliest stages of substance involvement. Farrell and colleagues (1993) have found peer influences such as models for substance use, attitudes toward substance use, and pressure to use substances to be among the strongest direct correlates and predictors of substance use and abuse in the literature.

Family-Related Factors

Parent-child attachment, parenting practices, family structure, and parent models for drug use have all been identified as risk factors for elevated levels of substance use and misuse. Several investigators have suggested that the effects of parents on adolescent substance use may be mediated through the effects of parenting on affiliations with deviant peer groups (Chassin, Curran, Hussong, & Colder, 1996; Dishion, Patterson, & Reid, 1988, as cited in Chassin et al., 2003) "Parent-child attachments provide a foundation for the socialization of children and for shaping their future attitudes, values, beliefs, and behaviors" (Essau, 2002, p. 95). Shedler and Block (1990) found that patterns of interactions between mothers and children reflecting insecure attachments in early childhood predicted frequent substance use in adolescents (as cited in Essau, 2002). Parenting practices such as inconsistent discipline, low levels of parental social support, and low levels of parental monitoring have been shown to prospectively predict the onset of substance use in adolescence (Colder & Chassin, 1999; Reifman, Barnes, Dintcheff, Farrell, & Uhteg, 1998, as cited in Chassin et al., 2003). Family structure and disruption have also been related to escalated substance use in adolescence. High levels of family conflict (Webb & Baer, 1995) and parental divorce and single-parent families (Duncan, Duncan, & Hops, 1998) have been associated with higher levels of substance use (as cited in Chassin et al., 2003). "Parental models for drug use have been found to have both direct and indirect influences on increased drug involvement in adolescence" (Essau, 2002, p. 96).

School- and Community-Related Factors

School factors including poor academic achievement, low educational aspirations, low interest in school, and low bonds to teachers have been found to predict increased levels of drug use (Newcomb & Felix-Ortiz, 1992, as cited in Essau, 2002). Many theories of substance use and deviant behavior suggest that estrangement from conventional mainstream social institutions, such as school, makes adolescents more vulnerable to engaging in problem behaviors, including drug use (Chassin et al., 2003). Felix-Ortiz and Newcomb (1992, 1999, as cited in Essau, 2002) found that community level risk factors, such as availability of drugs and perceived community support for drug use, are related to elevated levels of substance use. Certain community characteristics such as low socioeconomic status, high population density, low population mobility, physical deterioration, and high crime are also associated with greater substance use in adolescence (Brook, Whiteman, Gordan, & Brook, 1990, as cited in Bukstein, 1995).

Traumatic and Negative Life Events

Traumatic events such as physical and sexual abuse as well as other negative life events (e.g., serious illness of a family member, parental unemployment, or incarceration) have been associated with escalated substance use and abuse in adolescence (Essau, 2002). D. B. Clark, Lesnick, and Hegedus (1997) found that adolescents with alcohol use disorders reported significantly higher lifetime rates of physical and sexual abuse, violent victimization, and witnessing violence compared to controls.

Implications for Assessment

Clinicians must consider substance use and abuse by adolescents in a developmental context given the individual's unique biological and psychological characteristics, past experiences, and environmental context. Biological, social, parenting, and peer influences, as well as personality, coping style, and past experiences, can all contribute to the etiology, course, severity, and treatment of a substance use disorder. As stated previously, by identifying risk factors early on, we may also be able to prevent children from progressing into a substance use disorder.

Comorbid Psychiatric Disorders

Given the characteristics and risk factors associated with adolescent substance use disorders, it is not surprising that there are high rates of comorbidity between adolescent substance abuse/dependence and other disorders (Chassin et al., 2003). Consistent findings emerge across studies that link substance use disorders to other forms of child and adolescent psychopathology (Weinberg, Rahdert, Colliver, & Glantz, 1998). Two large scales studies indicated that 40% to 50% of nontreated individuals with a substance use disorder also meet criteria for a psychiatric disorder (L. N. Robins & Regier, 1991: Kessler et al., 1994). In adolescents, substance use and dependence appear to co-occur most often with Conduct Disorder (CD), Attention-Deficit/Hyperactivity Disorder (ADHD), and Major Depressive Disorder (MDD; Boyle & Offord, 1991; Stowell & Estroff, 1992, as cited in Whitmore et al., 1997). Winters (1990) estimates that, up to three quarters of clinical samples of drug-abusing teens have a coexisting disorder, most typically conduct disorder (50%), affective disorder (20%), or ADHD (20%; as cited in S. A. Brown et al., 2001). As Leshner (1997, p. 692, as cited in C. L. Rowe, Liddle, Greenbaum, & Henderson, 2004) stated, psychiatric comorbidity is "the usual, rather than the unusual, state of affairs" among substance abusers.

Meyer (1986) suggested that several specific relationships are possible between coexisting substance abuse and psychopathology: (a) psychiatric symptoms or disorders developing as a consequence of substance use or abuse; (b) psychiatric disorders altering the course of substance abuse; (c) substance abuse altering the course of psychiatric disorders; (d) psychopathology, both in the individuals and in their families, as a risk factor for the development of substance abuse; and (e) substance abuse and psychopathology originating from a common vulnerability (as cited in Bukstein, 1995). In truth, it appears that the direction of influence is often bidirectional with substance use/abuse and psychiatric disorders influencing each other (Bukstein, 1995). Studying these relationships is extremely important in that adolescent substance abusers with comorbid disorders appear to have earlier onset of substance use, greater frequency of use, and more chronic use than those without comorbid disorders (Clark & Neighbors, 1996; Horner & Scheibe, 1997; Rohde, Lewinsohn, & Seeley, 1996, as cited in C. L. Rowe et al., 2004).

Conduct Disorder and Attention-Deficit/Hyperactivity Disorder

The most consistent finding is that adolescent substance use disorders are commonly comorbid with ADHD and disruptive behavior disorders (ODD and CD), with Cohen and colleagues (1993, as cited in Chassin et al., 2003) finding that half of adolescents ages 10 to 20 with a substance use disorder were diagnosed with either ADHD, CD, or ODD. Conduct Disorder is the most common disorder associated with substance dependence in adolescence (Crowley & Riggs, 1995). Numerous investigators have observed that childhood antisocial behavior, including aggressiveness, predicts adult alcohol and drug problems (Kellam, Stevenson, & Rubin, 1993, as cited in Bukstein, 1995). Attention-Deficit/Hyperactivity Disorder also appears to be related to substance dependence (Windle, 1990, as cited in Whitmore et al., 1997), but several investigators have noted that ADHD alone, without comorbid CD, does not appear to increase the risk for later substance use (Barkley, Fischer, Edelbrock, & Smallish, 1990; Disney et al., 1999). C. S. Martin and colleagues (1994) analyzed the different dimensions of ADHD and CD and found that childhood aggression and impulsivity, but not hyperactivity, are associated with risk for later substance involvement.

Depression

In addition, depression symptoms are common among adolescents with CD (Puig-Antich, 1982, as cited in Whitmore et al., 1997) and may impact the severity and patterns of their substance involvement (Barkley et al., 1990). In 1995, Riggs and colleagues (as cited in Whitmore et al., 1997) found that depression in conduct-disordered adolescents contributed to earlier behavioral problems, more attentional deficits, and more substance dependence. Whitmore and colleagues (1997) found that symptoms of ADHD and MDD were common in adolescents with CD and were positively related to severity of substance dependence. Greenbaum and colleagues (1991, as cited in Whitmore et al., 1997) found that among adolescents referred for mental health services, those with both CD and depression had the highest rates of substance use disorders. Studies also suggest that associations between emotional disorders and substance use disorders are stronger for females than for males (Tarter, Kirisci, & Mezzich, 1997). Whitmore and colleagues (1997) found that severity of CD, MDD, and ADHD was jointly associated with severity of substance dependence in males, but MDD alone appeared to be the key factor related to substance dependence in females.

Anxiety Disorder

Data from the Epidemiologic Catchment Area study has shown a lifetime prevalence of substance use disorders in 23.7% of individuals reporting any anxiety disorder diagnosis, reflecting an increased risk of 1.7 times greater than those not having an anxiety disorder (L. N. Robins & Regier, 1991). Clarke and Jacob (1992, as cited in Bukstein, 1995) found that anxiety disorders were common among an adolescent treatment population with early onset alcoholism with 50% of the sample having at least one lifetime anxiety disorder diagnosis. Even substance-abusing adolescents without anxiety disorder diagnoses were found to have higher levels of anxiety than normal controls. The fact that many adolescents view substance use as a way to relieve tension and enhance social behavior may help to explain the possible role of anxiety in eventually leading to substance use disorders (Bukstein, 1995).

Eating Disorder

Several studies also point to high comorbidity between eating disorders (especially bulimia) and substance use disorders (Bulik, Sullivan, Epstein, Weltzin, & Kaye, 1992, as cited in Bukstein, 1995; Wilson, Becker, & Heffernan, 2003). Wilson (1991) found that normal-weight individuals with eating disorders consistently reveal significantly higher rates of past and present substance use problems than in the general population (as cited in Wilson et al., 2003). Some researchers suggest bulimia represents an alternative expression of a shared vulnerability or genetic predisposition; however, empirical support of this hypothesis is limited.

Implications for Assessment

Clinicians must recognize the importance of comorbid psychiatric disorders in the assessment of adolescents with substance abuse. Assessments of adolescent substance users cannot neglect evaluation of comorbid psychiatric disorders that may be contributing to or preventing improvement in substance use. Comorbid disorders influence the symptoms and behaviors displayed, the course of the component disorders, as well as the approach and response to treatment. "Clinicians should be aware of the possibility of multiple diagnoses in all referred adolescents, so that treatment can be integrated to address all of the adolescent's symptoms and behaviors" (Whitmore et al., 1997, p. 96).

"All adolescents presenting with mental health problems should be screened for substance abuse" (Jaffe & Solhkhah, 2004, p. 798). Substance abuse may be a major contributing factor to any change in mood, behavior, or cognitive functioning. S. A. Brown et al. (2001) outline common behavioral correlates of adolescent substance abuse. Unfortunately, these behaviors are typical of a variety of behavioral disorders of adolescence, and therefore cannot be assumed to be 100% due to a substance use disorder. Given the high rate of comorbidity found in substance abusing adolescents, it is often difficult to assess adolescent substance abuse and dependence separate from the functional impairment of coexisting disorders. S. A. Brown and colleagues (2001) offer several procedures that may enhance diagnostic accuracy with adolescents:

- Initiate assessment in areas in which the adolescent is most concerned or motivated rather than substance use specifically.
- Inquire about substance use separately from questions of problem behaviors and current difficulties.
- Determine onset of symptoms and problem behaviors in relation to drug involvement by constructing a time line (e.g., which behaviors or symptoms occurred before substance use or during periods of extended abstinence).
- Gather the same information from an outside informant, such as a parent, to confirm the sequence of difficulties, symptoms, and substance use.
- Utilize biochemical verification (e.g., using toxicology screen, urine samples, and hair samples).
- Assess symptoms on several occasions to ensure symptoms were not transient consequences of substance use.

Comprehensive Assessment: The Domain Model

"Given the multiple risk factors, frequent comorbidity, and multiple areas of possible dysfunction related to alcohol and other drug abuse, the comprehensive assessment of substance abuse and related problems in adolescents requires evaluation of many areas of functioning in the adolescent's life. Evidence overwhelmingly suggests that adolescent substance use is multidetermined with precursors and consequences encompassing a complex set of interconnected domains" (Meyers et al., 1999). Tarter's (1990) multilevel evaluation procedure for adolescents emphasizes the importance of exploring problems in all domains of the adolescent's life. He identifies six domains that should be thoroughly assessed using detailed questions or standardized instruments designed to assess that specific domain: (1) substance use behavior; (2) psychiatric and behavioral problems; (3) school and/or vocational functioning; (4) family functioning; (5) social competency and peer relations; (6) leisure and recreation. In terms of these domains, the severity of the substance use and the consequences for the adolescent must be defined.

Substance Use Behavior: In assessing substance use and related behaviors, questions should inquire about four major areas: (1) patterns of use, (2) negative consequences, (3) context of use, and (4) control of use. Detailed information about drug use behavior must be obtained. Patterns of use should include looking at age of onset and progression of use, quantity, frequency, variability, and types of substances used. Substances of abuse include alcohol, marijuana, sedative-hypnotics (such as barbiturates and most antianxiety drugs), cocaine, amphetamines, opiates, hallucinogens, PCP, inhalants, heroin, other narcotics, and tobacco. If a client endorses the use of a particular substance, detailed inquiry should follow about the consequences, context, and control of that particular substance. When looking at negative consequences, the clinician should ask about directly related effects of use in all areas of the client's life including school/vocational, social, family, psychological, and physical. Context of use should include time and place of use, peer use levels/attitudes/pressure, mood antecedents/consequences, expectancies, and overall attitudes and beliefs about drug use. When inquiring about control of use, the clinician may follow *DSM-IV* criteria for substance dependence.

Psychiatric and Behavioral Problems: Due to the prevalence of comorbidity in adolescent substance use disorders, screening as well as detailed assessment of coexisting psychopathology is an essential part of the assessment procedure. Inquiry should include an attempt to establish the chronology of symptoms and behaviors relative to the onset of specific substance use behaviors—are the symptoms or behaviors present during both substance use and abstinence? A family history of psychiatric disorders is also quite beneficial in untangling a confusing set of symptoms and behaviors.

School and/or Vocational Functioning: To succeed in the school environment, an adolescent must have adequate cognitive and interpersonal skills, behavioral controls, and at least a minimal level of achievement orientation. School failure can promote drug use behavior. The social environment of the school, such as the availability of drugs, degree of adult supervision, and opportunities for nonacademic recreational activity, may also significantly influence drug use in vulnerable individuals (Tarter, 1990). Academic failure and poor school behavior can also help to identify adolescent substance abusers (Bukstein, 1995).

Family Functioning: The organization, communication, social values, and cohesiveness of the family have been found to greatly influence the psychosocial adjustment and level of substance involvement in adolescents. The family is the primary avenue through which children establish socially normative behavior and values that guide adolescents as they become more independent. Clinicians should assess: (a) the family structure, (b) quality of family relationships, (c) parent management of adolescent behavior, (d) overt parent behaviors (including parental substance use), (e) parental attitudes and values, and (f) other stressors on the family (e.g., financial difficulties, or illness).

Social Competency and Peer Relations: "Social competency refers to the ability of the adolescent to function adequately with both peers and adults" (Bukstein, 1995, p. 106). Social competency should be evaluated across settings, including family, school, and peer competencies. During adolescence, peer relations are especially critical. Therefore, the clinician should specifically question the adolescent about these relations. In addition to normative measures, clinicians can also utilize direct observational assessment. Tarter (1990) suggests that the adolescent's interpersonal skills can be measured on 10 key dimensions: eye contact, smiles, duration of verbal responses, verbal elaboration or richness of language content, latency in responding in verbal interactions, affect, body gestures during interpersonal interaction, expression of regard for the welfare of others, spontaneous communications, and expression of appreciation.

Leisure and Recreation: An adolescent's engagement in deviant behavior and substance use may be influenced by the availability of leisure time and how it is used. The clinician should determine the adolescent's physical capacity to participate in activities and catalog the adolescent's past, present, and planned future activities to assess attitudes toward leisure.

Community and Social Context: The social context in which the adolescent functions is critical in assessment as well as intervention planning. The clinician must consider where the adolescent lives (e.g., economic status, gang involvement and violence, or prevalence of substance use). This social environment can greatly influence an adolescent's risk for, initiation to, and maintenance of substance use as well as the level of risk for relapse (Bukstein, 1995).

Process of Assessment

How do we go about assessing adolescents for substance use disorders, while taking into account these many influential domains? The recent development of assessment instruments tailored for adolescents has improved clinical and research measurement of adolescent substance use disorders; however, this sudden influx of a wide variety of instruments can make it quite overwhelming for clinicians to decide which instrument to use and when to use it. In selecting an assessment measure, clinicians must take several variables into account, including the level of assessment (e.g., screening versus diagnostic), method of assessment (e.g., interview, questionnaire, or biological measure), and the evidence available for the psychometric soundness of the measure.

Screening: Numerous clinicians and researchers recommend that all adolescents exhibiting mental health issues be screened for substance abuse (e.g., Bukstein, 1995; Center for Substance Abuse Treatment, 2003; Meyers et al., 1999). Screening is a preliminary step that determines whether a comprehensive assessment is needed. A screener should never be used to make a diagnostic decision. According to the Substance Abuse and Mental Health Services Administration (SAMHSA), a screening program should have the ability to be administered in about 10 to 15 minutes and should be applicable across diverse populations. It should focus on substance use severity as well as a core group of associated factors including legal problems, mental health status, educational functioning, and living situation (Center for Substance Abuse Treatment, 2003). A screening instrument should give the clinician the "big picture" without a lot of specific information; however, it should sufficiently cover the "red flag" areas of substance use disorders and psychosocial functioning (Center for Substance Abuse Treatment, 2003). Therefore, multidomain instruments, which assess a range of variables, would be most useful to both clinicians and researchers (Bukstein, 1995).

Comprehensive Assessment: The Center for Substance Abuse treatment (CSAT; 2003, p. 17) lists the purposes of the comprehensive assessment as:

- To document in more detail the presence, nature, and complexity of substance use reported during a screening, including whether the adolescent meets diagnostic criteria for abuse or dependence (based on *DSM-IV*).
- To determine the specific treatment needs of the client if substance abuse or substance dependence is confirmed so that limited resources are not misdirected.

- To permit the evaluator to learn more about the nature, correlates, and consequences of the youth's substance-using behavior.
- To ensure that related problems not flagged in the screening process (e.g., problems in medical status, psychological status, social functioning, family relations, educational performance, and delinquent behavior) are identified.
- To examine the extent to which the youth's family can be involved not only in comprehensive assessment but also in possible subsequent interventions.
- To identify specific strengths of the adolescent, family, and other social supports (e.g., coping skills) that can be used in developing an appropriate treatment plan.
- To develop a written report.

These more comprehensive assessment procedures usually score adolescents along a continuum or along several continua rather than dichotomously. The goals of these instruments may differ slightly from each other. Some measures focus on *DSM-IV* diagnosis, whereas others focus more on individualized assessment and treatment planning. Characteristics of substance use other than simply the diagnostic nomenclature (e.g., risk and protective factors, cognitive factors) should be included in comprehensive assessment to aide in treatment planning as well as provide insight into the etiology of the disorder (Essau, 2002).

Methods of Assessment

Interviews and Questionnaires: Structured and semistructured interviews are the most common and optimal methods both in screening and comprehensive/diagnostic assessment for substance use disorders. "Diagnostic interviews, in which clients are asked a set of predetermined questions, are considered by many researchers and clinicians to be the most comprehensive measures of substance use disorders" (C. S. Martin & Winters, 1998). Meyers and colleagues (1999) refer to clinical interviews as the "cornerstone" of the assessment and therapeutic process. They suggest that if self-report or computer-administered questionnaires are used to assess adolescents, these techniques should be supplemented with interview data. Although questionnaires can be useful, they lack the personal interaction of the interview. This personal interaction allows for rapport building as well as the opportunity to individualize assessment depending on the client. The clinician can make certain that the client understands the questions and make sure that he or she is paying attention and staying on task. Follow-up questions provide information that cannot always be obtained through the more rigid format of a questionnaire (C. S. Martin & Winters, 1998).

Structured and semistructured interviews differ in the degree of clinical judgment the interviewer must employ when administering the interview. Structured interviews have the interviewer read each question exactly as written and make decisions based on responses. The interviewer rates each symptom as either present or absence, based on detailed written symptom definitions. These types of interviews can be reliably administered by a trained layperson. Semistructured interviews are harder to administer being that they require the interviewer to elicit an initial response and then determine, through further probing, whether a symptom is present. These interviews allow the interviewer considerable freedom in adapting questions to the unique respondent. Semistructured interviews require a higher clinical skill level and more expertise than structured interviews.

Robins (1988), Cottler and Keating (1990), and Cottler and Compton (1993, as cited in Essau, 2002) have outlined 21 characteristics of a good diagnostic interview. Many of these characteristics refer to the reliability (variation in responses to the questions is due to change in substance use characteristics rather than factors such as time or person administering the instrument) and validity (the instrument measures the substance use characteristics that it intended to measure) of the interview. The reliability and validity of self-report instruments, such as interviews and questionnaires, depend on a variety of contextual and interpersonal factors (Carroll, 1995; Martin & Newman, 1988; Matarazzo, 1983; Prout & Chizik, 1988, as cited in Meyers et al., 1999). Meyers and colleagues (1999) suggest three domains that may contribute to measurement error: (1) characteristics of the measurement tool; (2) characteristics of the interviewer and respondent; and (3) conditions, confidentiality, and outcome of the assessment. Clinicians should be aware of these potential influences to minimize unreliable or invalid adolescent reporting. Unfortunately, many of the instruments developed to assess substance use disorders in adolescence still lack research on their psychometric properties.

Biological Measures: Screening instruments include biological measures as well as interview/self-report. Urinalysis is the most widely used biological measure due to its accuracy (Weinberg et al., 1998); however, mental health professionals must be aware of the uses and limitations of all biological measures. Meyers and colleagues (1999) suggest that despite the seeming objectivity of these measures, several problems exist in the use and interpretation of biological measures. These problems include:

- Because most biological measures detect only recent use, they are unable to identify or confirm historical or continuous use. The accuracy of the test is limited to the amount of time the specific drug stays in the body.
- Biological measures detect the occurrence of use but fail to provide information indicative of severity or chronicity.
- False negative findings can result from the deliberate tampering of samples by the individual under study unless strict collection procedures are implemented.
- False positive findings can be obtained unless tests are confirmed by expensive analytic methods (e.g., gas chromatography-mass spectrometry).
- Testing laboratories can yield accuracy inconsistencies contingent on the accountability procedures followed.

Therefore, biological measures, such as urinalysis, blood testing, or hair sampling, may be utilized during the screening phase; however, "the collection, analysis, and interpretation of their results requires prudent attention" (Meyers et al., 1999, p. 241).

Supplemental Sources of Information: Multiple sources of information (e.g., parents and teachers) can give additional important data beyond that which is provided by the adolescent. Sometimes adolescents are reluctant to tell the clinician everything about their behavior; therefore, supplemental sources can result in a fuller picture of the adolescent's functioning across settings. Unlike early childhood assessment however, where the interview with the parent is considered one of the most important pieces of the entire assessment, adolescents are considered reliable and valid informants of their own behaviors and feelings (Meyers et al., 1999). Research suggests that parents are not always reliable informants when it comes to behaviors of their children (Herjanic & Reich, 1982; Hill & Jones, 1997; as cited in Meyers et al., 1999; Wenar, 1961). This disparity between adolescent reports and their parents' reports may be due to increasing autonomy during adolescence. Therefore, parent reports should be valued but only as supplemental information and not the gold standard. Archival records, such as school grades and prior treatment charts, can help to provide the clinician with some initial information on the functioning of the adolescent.

The Present State of Adolescent Substance Use Assessment

Although many instruments have recently been developed to specifically screen or diagnose substance use disorders in adolescents, these instruments are still in the preliminary stages due to the lack of psychometric evidence as well as a lack of "true" screening instruments. In 1994, Leccese and Waldron stated, "What is striking at the moment is the nearly complete absence of peer-reviewed psychometric data for virtually all instruments in this area, including those in popular use" (p. 561). Screeners can be either unidomain (e.g., measuring a specific area, usually substance use) or multidomain (e.g., assessing a wider range of variables including behaviors, psychiatric symptoms, family and school functioning, and attitudes). Multidomain screeners are more useful to clinicians than unidomain screeners due to the many domains that influence adolescent substance use disorders (Bukstein, 1995). Many of the shorter unidomain screeners (e.g., DAP, ADI, CRAFFT) also lack psychometric support. Unfortunately, most of the multidomain adolescent substance use disorder screeners (e.g., Drug Use Screening Inventory—Revised [DUSI-R], Problem Oriented Screening Questionnaire [POSIT]) are much too long to be considered true screeners. These instruments are better suited for treatment planning rather than screening.

We suggest that, at the present time, clinicians should rely on the general child/adolescent diagnostic interview to screen and diagnose adolescent substance use disorders. The multidomain adolescent substance use disorder screeners and more comprehensive adolescent substance use disorder instruments can then be used to give more detailed information about the adolescent and aid in treatment planning. Several child/adolescent general diagnostic interviews, containing substance use disorders sections, are widely used in the United States and have certain strengths that cause us to come to this conclusion. First, these long-existing instruments have succeeded in accumulating adequate psychometric evidence. Second, these instruments are based on the *DSM-IV* and therefore allow clinicians to make *DSM-IV* diagnoses. Third, general interviews allow clinicians to assess multiple domains, comorbid psychiatric disorders, and substance use disorders simultaneously. Assessing for multiple domains and disorders is an important aspect of substance use disorder assessment due to the high rates of comorbidity and the many influential domains in adolescent substance use disorders. The following are only a subset of the many instruments available to assess adolescent substance use and misuse.

General Diagnostic Interviews

Structured Clinical Interview for the **DSM** *(SCID):* The SCID is a structured interview that has recently been adapted for assessment of *DSM-IV* and *ICD-10* alcohol and drug diagnoses for adolescents (C. S. Martin, Pollock, Bukstein, & Lynch, 2000). The SCID provides specific operational definitions for each symptom and exact questions that should be asked in a decision-tree format. Williams and colleagues (1992, as cited in Essau, 2002) examined a German and American sample of psychiatric patients and found that 1-week, test-retest kappa estimates of the reliability of SCID *DMS-III-R* substance abuse and dependence diagnoses were good to excellent. C. S. Martin and colleagues (2000) found that the interrater reliability of the SCID, *DSM-IV* version, diagnoses related to use of alcohol, cannabis, sedatives, hallucinogens, and inhalants were excellent in a sample (*N* = 79) of adolescents recruited from clinics and the general community of Pennsylvania, United States. Symptoms and diagnoses established with the *DSM-IV* version of the SCID have also shown good concurrent validity (e.g., are associated with measures of drinking and problem severity assessed at the same time; C. S. Martin & Winters, 1998).

Diagnostic Interview for Children and Adolescents: The Diagnostic Interview for Children and Adolescents (DICA) is a long-standing diagnostic interview of childhood and adolescent *DSM-IV* psychiatric disorders (see Reich, 2000). The DICA originally used a structured format, but has been revised to use a semistructured format and therefore requires extensive training (2 to 4 weeks) to administer. In 2001, Reich (as cited in Essau, 2002) conducted a 1-week test-retest study of the DICA using a small sample of adolescents recruited from community and clinical settings (*N* = 50). Kappa estimates of reliability of *DSM-IV* dependence diagnoses ranged from good to excellent (.86 for alcohol, .69 for cannabis, 1.0 for stimulants, .79 for cocaine, and .66 for hallucinogens). General findings on the DICA indicate that this instrument is reasonably reliable and valid for children and adolescents (C. S. Martin & Winters, 1998). Our understanding of the DICA's ability to assess adolescent substance use disorders will benefit from further investigation of the DICA's psychometric properties using larger samples.

Diagnostic Interview Survey for Children—Version IV: This structured interview has undergone several adaptations with the latest version Diagnostic Interview Survey for Children—Version IV (DISC-IV), published in 1997, being designed for diagnosis of *DSM-IV* and *ICD-10* childhood disorders. In addition to *DSM-IV* diagnoses, the DISC-IV assesses the degree of impairment that substance use disorders have on adolescents' distress, academic functioning, relations with parents, teachers, and so on, as well as participation in family and peer activities. Limited reliability and validity information exist for the DISC-IV, but earlier versions demonstrate generally favorable reliability and validity (Crowley, Mikulich, Ehlers, Whitmore, & MacDonald, 2001). Both the child and the parent versions of the DISC have shown good sensitivity in identifying youth who have received an independent medical diagnosis of an alcohol or drug use disorder (Fisher et al., 1993, as cited in C. S. Martin & Winters, 1998). Recent studies of the reliability of the DISC diagnoses in community samples have not included estimates for substance use disorders (Essau, 2002). In 1996, Ribera and colleagues (as cited in Essau, 2002) reported kappa estimated of the 1-week test-retest reliability to be .53 for alcohol abuse and .448 for drug abuse using the DISC 2.1. Roberts and colleagues (1996, as cited in C. S. Martin & Winters, 1998) showed only modest reliability for *DSM-III-R* substance use disorders.

Minnesota Multiphasic Personality Inventory—Adolescent: The Minnesota Multiphasic Personality Inventory—Adolescent (MMPI-A) is a self-report questionnaire developed, in 1992, for use with adolescents to assess a number of the major patterns of personality and emotional disorders. It is the adolescent version of the MMPI-2, which is one of the most widely used inventories for assessing adult psychopathology. The MMPI-A contains three scales designed to identify individuals who abuse substances. The MacAndrew Alcoholism Scale—Revised (MAC-R) is the revised form of the empirically derived 1965 MacAndrew Alcoholism Scale. This scale was developed to discriminate alcoholics from other psychiatric patients. The Alcohol/Drug Problem Proneness (PRO) scale was designed to empirically identify "personality and lifestyle patterns specifically associated with alcohol and drug use" (Weed, Butcher, & Ben-Porath, 1995; as cited in L. L. Murphy & Impara, 1996). The Alcohol/Drug Problem Acknowledgment Scale (ACK) was developed for the MMPI-A to assess an adolescent's willingness to acknowledge alcohol or drug use related symptoms, attitudes, or beliefs and is quite similar to the Addiction Admission Scale (AAS) of the MMPI-2.

Elevations on the ACK scale indicated the extent to which an adolescent acknowledged or admitted to substance problems in his or her MMPI-A self-description. Weed, Butcher, and Ben-Porath (1995, as cited in L. L. Murphy & Impara, 1996) found the AAS to be the strongest substance use scale in the MMPI-2. Validity studies of the MMPI-2 demonstrate the ability of the AAS to discriminate between those individuals who engage in substance abuse and those who do not; however, the MAC-R did not demonstrate this ability (L. L. Murphy & Impara, 1996). Ehrmann (1994, as cited in R. P. Archer, 1997) commented on the relative usefulness of the AAS as a direct measure of substance use as opposed to the more subtle measures of the MAC-R scale.

The MAC scale is the only MMPI special scale that has received empirical investigation with adolescents. Archer (1987, as cited in L. L. Murphy & Impara, 1996) showed MAC sale scores to be related to substance abuse among adolescents in public schools, hospitals, and residential psychiatric and drug treatment programs. High MAC scores also appear to be related to the abuse of a variety of drugs in addition to alcohol (Andrucci, Archer, Pancoast, & Gordon, 1989, as cited in L. L. Murphy & Impara, 1996). The validity of the MAC scales has also been questioned in adolescent populations. Elevated MAC scale scores have been found to be associated with a variety of personality characteristics including assertiveness, independence, and self-indulgence (Gordon, Anderson, & Gianetti, 1989, as cited in R. P. Archer, 1997), as well as delinquent behavior and conduct disorder diagnoses (Ortins, 1980; Gordon, Anderson, & Gianetti, 1989; Wisniewski, Glenwick, & Graham, 1985, as cited in R. P. Archer, 1997). Basham (1992) concluded that the MAC scale appears to measure a broad antisocial personality dimension in adolescents rather than the presence of a specific substance use problem (as cited in R. P. Archer, 1997).

Several studies have suggested that the MAC scale has the potential of being a useful screening device for substance abuse among adolescents, but they offer several cautions and limitations. R. P. Archer (1997) found that the MAC scale has little diagnostic utility among a non-White adult population. Greene (1991) cautioned that accuracy hit rates were too low to justify the use of the MAC as a screening device to detect substance abuse problems among patients in a medical treatment setting (as cited in R. P. Archer, 1997). Thus far, no studies have compared the MAC and MAC-R scales for the MMPI-A (R. P. Archer, 1997).

"Screening" Instruments

As mentioned previously, although these instruments are presented as screening devices in much of the literature, we feel that they are too detailed and lengthy to be regarded as true screeners. Therefore, we suggest that clinicians should use the general diagnostic interview to begin and then use the following longer "screening" instruments to aide in treatment planning:

Drug Use Screening Inventory—Revised: The Drug Use Screening Inventory—Revised (DUSI-R) is a 159-item yes/no self-report questionnaire, which may be administered as an interview, identifying specific problem areas in substance use, physical and mental health, and psychosocial adjustment in both adolescents and adults. It identifies specific problem areas in 10 domains of functioning and is estimated to take about 20 to 40 minutes to complete.

In 1992, Tarter, Laird, Bukstein, and Kaminer provided evidence of the content validity of the DUSI. They found that DUSI indexes correlated with the Kiddie Schedule for Affective Disorders and Schizophrenia (K-SADS) and *DSM-III-R* substance abuse criteria in a sample of adolescent substance abusers. One limitation of this study is the small sample size ($N = 25$). Tarter and colleagues (1994) evaluated the reliability of the DUSI in a study of 191 adolescents who met *DSM-III-R* criteria for a substance use disorder. They found that the DUSI could be useful in identifying and quantifying substance use and related problems (as cited in Dalla-Dea, De Micheli, & Souza Formigoni, 2003). Kirisci, Mezzich, and Tarter (1995) examined the discriminative power of the DUSI for identifying individuals who qualified for a *DSM-III-R* diagnosis of Psychoactive Substance Use Disorder (PSUD) in a sample of 846 adolescents. The subjects with PSUD had higher mean scores in each of the 10 domains. In the normal sample, the DUSI correctly classified 95% of the normal sample and 81% of the PSUD cases. De Micheli and Formigoni (2000, as cited in Dalla-Dea et al., 2003) separated a Brazilian adolescent sample of 213 into three substance dependence levels (nondependent, light/moderate dependent, and severe dependent) and found that the DUSI was able to distinguish between the groups not only in relation to drug use but also in relation to levels of associated behavior problems, leisure/recreation, and peer relationship areas.

Problem Oriented Screening Questionnaire: The Problem Oriented Screening Questionnaire (POSIT) is a self-report questionnaire, which may be administered as an interview, consisting of 139 true/false questions that measure functioning in 10 domains: (1) substance use, (2) physical health, (3) mental health, (4) family relationships, (5) peer relationships, (6) educational status, (7) vocational status, (8) social skills, (9) leisure and recreation, and (10) aggressive behavior/delinquency. Certain items are designated as "red flag" items, which, if endorsed, would indicate the need for further assessment. The POSIT is estimated to take 30 to 45 minutes to complete. Extensive validity and reliability testing has not been published on the POSIT (Leccese & Waldron, 1994). One study done by McLaney and Boca in 1994, evaluated the validity and reliability of the POSIT in a sample of 170 male and 64 female adolescents. They found that the pattern of correlations between the POSIT and the PEI scales demonstrated adequate convergent and divergent validity. Overall, the internal consistency reliability was less than what is considered acceptable; however, the most clinically relevant scales (e.g., substance use/abuse, mental health status, family relations, and aggressive behavior) demonstrated acceptable levels of reliability.

Substance Abuse Subtle Screening Inventory: The Substance Abuse Subtle Screening Inventory (SASSI-A) is an 81-item questionnaire that includes four subtle scales designed to identify abusers who are attempting to minimize their substance use. Of the 81 items, 55 of them are true/false indirect items, which lack an obvious relationship to substance use. The remaining 26 questions are face-valid items that ask the adolescent to report lifetime frequency of specific behaviors that assess negative consequences associated with substance misuse.

Despite its wide use, the psychometric properties of the SASSI-A have not been adequately examined (Gray, 2001, as cited in Sweet & Saules, 2003). Some researchers have questioned its psychometric properties (Gray, 2001; Clements, 2002; as cited in Sweet & Saules, 2003), whereas others describe it as a viable assessment instrument (Miller, 1990, as cited in Sweet & Saules, 2003). Rogers and colleagues (1997, as cited in Sweet & Saules, 2003) did a cross validation study of the SASSI-A and found that their results did not justify the use of the SASSI-A to classify adolescents who were not substance users and recommended further evaluation. Sweet and Saules (2003) examined the construct and convergent validity of the SASSI-A in a sample of 490 adolescent offenders from a suburban Circuit Court-Juvenile Division. They concluded that the SASSI-A face-valid scales have moderate utility for identifying substance dependence in this sample, while the subtle scales do not. No reliability statistics have been reported (Lecesse & Waldron, 1994).

Personal Experience Screening Questionnaire: The Personal Experience Screening Questionnaire (PESQ) is a 40-item questionnaire consisting of three subsections dealing with drug involvement, problem severity, psychosocial problems, and personal drug history. It takes approximately 10 minutes to complete. Winters et al. (2002) found that the problem severity portion of the PESQ has high internal reliability estimates (.92) and that the PESQ as a whole demonstrated satisfactory discriminant validity. The PESQ scores were found to be highly predictive of scores on a more comprehensive assessment instrument, the Personal Experience Inventory (PEI), which is described later (Leccese & Waldron, 1994). The content validity, construct validity, and criterion validity appear to be adequate for the PESQ (L. L. Murphy & Impara, 1996).

Specific Comprehensive Instruments

Although these comprehensive instruments allow for diagnoses as well as more detailed information regarding other domains, they fail to demonstrate why clinicians should utilize them rather than general diagnostic interviews that often give even more information on other domains and comorbid disorders as well as have better psychometric evidence. Therefore, the following specific comprehensive instruments should be used for treatment planning:

Adolescent Diagnostic Interview: The Adolescent Diagnostic Interview (ADI) is a structured interview, which covers *DSM-III-R* and *DSM-IV* diagnoses, using two to four questions for each abuse and dependence criterion and symptom (Essau, 2002). The interview explores the adolescent's drug use history and signs of abuse or dependence as well as school and interpersonal functioning, and psychosocial stresses. It also screens for several coexisting mental/behavioral disorders as well as memory and orientation problems; however, "the screening for other psychiatric disorders is very poorly developed, highly selective and inconsistent in the choice of screening questions, and frequently outright inaccurate" (L. L. Murphy & Impara, 1996, p. 2). The ADI can take from 30 to 90 minutes to administer.

Winters, Stinchfield, Fulkerson, and Henly (1993, as cited in Essau, 2002) indicated adequate interrater and test-retest reliability in a sample of 72 adolescents in a clinical setting. Kappas for diagnosis of dependence/abuse for all substances were quite high (ranging from .53 to 1.00 with the majority being greater than .75). High kappas were also reported for individual symptoms of alcohol/cannabis dependence (ranging from .66 to .97 with most being greater than .8). A 1-week test-retest assessment of reliability of alcohol/cannabis abuse and dependence, although lower, was marginally acceptable with value ranging from .52 to .83. Assessment of the validity of the ADI is very limited (L. L. Murphy & Impara, 1996).

Adolescent Drug Abuse Diagnosis: The Adolescent Drug Abuse Diagnosis (ADAD) is a 150-item structured interview, modeled after the adult measure (the Addiction Severity Index), which produces a comprehensive evaluation of the client and provides a 10-point severity rating for each of nine life problem areas: medical, school, employment, social, family, psychological, legal, alcohol, and drugs.

It takes approximately 45 to 60 minutes to complete. The ADAD was developed for use with adolescents in substance use disorder treatment settings; however, it has proven useful as a general assessment tool for adolescents in many settings (CSAT, 2003).

In 1989, Friedman and Utada (as cited in Leccese & Waldron, 1994) found support for many psychometric qualities of the instrument including interrater reliability (.84 to .95), test-retest reliability (.71 to .98), and concurrent, convergent, and discriminant validity. The CSAT (2003) remarked on the adequate psychometric properties of the ADAD. Adequate concurrent (external) validity (r between .43 and .67) was also established for all but two life problem areas (medical and social relations) by correlating with scores obtained on other previously validated instruments that measure the same life problem area.

Personal Experience Inventory: The Personal Experience Inventory (PEI) is a 276-item, self-administered questionnaire that takes approximately 45 to 60 minutes to complete. This instrument was developed, according to the authors (Winters & Henly, 1989, as cited in Leccese & Waldron, 1994), in response to the clinical need for a comprehensive and standardized self-report inventory to assist in the identification, referral, and treatment of adolescent substance abuse. It assesses multiple dimensions in two major domains of substance related dysfunction: (1) chemical involvement problem severity and (2) psychosocial and environmental risk factors. The chemical involvement section contains five "basic" and five "clinical" scales that evaluate the severity of substance involvement as well as the quantity and frequency of use of different drugs. The psychosocial section assesses eight personal risk factors for substance misuse (e.g., negative self-image, social isolation) and four environmental risk factors (e.g., peer chemical environment or family pathology). There are also six screens for other problems common among substance-involved youth (e.g., need for psychiatric referral, eating disorder signs/symptoms, sexual abuse, intrafamilial physical abuse, family chemical dependency history, and suicide potential; L. L. Murphy & Impala, 1996). In addition, the PEI has five validity indexes designed to estimate response bias and other sources of measurement error.

Test construction was meticulous and thorough with detailed descriptions of the standardization procedures as well as reliability and validity studies presented in the test manual as well as in a number of journal articles (Henly & Winters, 1988; Winters & Henly, 1989, as cited in Leccese & Waldron, 1994). The PEI was found to have good to excellent internal consistency (reliability). Test-retest reliability was generally adequate although less robust. The authors established construct validity by demonstrating that the PEI possesses: (a) convergent validity—correlations of several PEI scales were fairly high and significant with measures such as the Alcohol Dependence Scale and the Minnesota Multiphasic Personality Inventory; (b) criterion validity—the PEI scale scores differentiated those with and without a prior treatment history ($N = 348$) and those who received more intensive treatment referrals from less intensive referrals; and (c) discriminant validity—PEI scored differentiated clinical and nonclinical samples. Other validity studies have indicated that the PEI, especially the chemical severity section, effectively discriminates among subjects who varied by prior treatment history, treatment referral decisions, sample type, and intake diagnosis (L. L. Murphy & Impala, 1996). Winters, Stinchfield, and Henley (1993, as cited in Leccese & Waldron, 1994) investigated concurrent validity and found that the PEI basic problem-severity scales were significantly related to groupings made on the basis of *DSM-III-R* criteria and recommendations for treatment referral. In general, the PEI appears to be a valuable assessment tool, especially for treatment planning, with adequate psychometric properties.

Conclusion

The assessment and diagnosis of substance use disorders requires the acquisition of special expertise by child clinicians, due in part to the diverse nature of substances and use patterns, but also due to a lack of consensus regarding diagnostic criteria, and questionable psychometric properties of instruments developed for this purpose. Two key issues that need to be addressed by child clinicians are to (1) screen all children in late childhood and adolescence for the presence of substance use and (2) comprehensively assess use patterns when present.

Many children and adolescents are assessed routinely in schools for special education eligibility without sufficient screening for substance use, due in part to the fact that substance use disorders have not been incorporated into special education regulations and guidelines. If school psychologists alone would routinely screen for substance use, many children and adolescents would have a better chance of having substance use problems treated or deterred.

Erin T. Dowdy, Cheryl N. Hendry, and Randy W. Kamphaus

13

Chapter

The goals of research in the field of child behavioral classification are to (a) develop a classification system to organize behavioral expression, (b) evaluate the predictive value of the classification system, and (c) guide prevention/treatment options. To date, a number of studies have been conducted for the purpose of identifying behavioral typologies of adjustment in children.

A 1978 review by Achenbach and Edelbrock summarized early typological findings obtained via factor analysis (e.g., Peterson, 1961; Quay, 1964, 1966). Notably, these early works indicated the presence of broadband undercontrolled and overcontrolled syndromes, in addition to narrowband aggressive, delinquent, hyperactive, schizoid, anxious, depressed, somatic, and withdrawn syndromes across diverse samples of children and adolescents. Although these early results seemed promising, the authors asserted that "along with the need for greater uniformity of instrumentation and methods of analysis, there is a need for greater differentiation in the samples studied" (p. 1297).

Portions of this chapter are adapted from the dissertation studies of Drs. Erin T. Dowdy, and Cheryl N. Hendry.

Person-Oriented Methods of Classification

A blending of categorical and dimensional classifications might serve best the classification of child adjustment, ranging from optimal to pathological. As L. A. Clark, Livesley, and Morey (1997) suggested, "It is widely believed that categorical and dimensional models are inherently incompatible, and that one must choose between them. In actuality, however, it is more accurate to describe these models as existing in a hierarchical relation to one another, with dimensions being the blocks from which categories may be built" (as cited in Nathan & Langenbucher, 1999). Person-oriented, or multivariate, classification methods blend the aforementioned classification systems by producing a categorical classification through the use of dimensional scales as input. The resulting categorical classification uses many dimensional symptom measures and simultaneously accounts for behaviors along these dimensions while also accounting for severity of behaviors. The interaction among those variables is also accounted for to create a more meaningful classification system. Therefore, person-oriented approaches are seen as "complementary not competing" with single dimension or variable-oriented research (Magnusson & Bergman, 1990).

Person-oriented methods of classification differ from categorical and dimensional methods primarily in that they focus on the multiple characteristics of the individual, as opposed to one or a small number of variables (e.g., aggression + depression versus aggression in isolation). Variable-oriented approaches do not account for the significance of the variables to the individual, whereas person-oriented approaches consider the individual as a whole and not just as variables (Bergman, 2000; Bergman & Magnusson, 1997; Wangby, Bergman, & Magnusson, 1999). Individuals, as opposed to variables, are grouped into categories based on the similarities in their profile of available data (Magnusson & Cairns, 1996). Person-oriented methods capture quantitative differences in symptomatology, through dimensional scales, with the goal of creating a profile of constructs that underlie the disorder. These profiles can then be used as categorical classification tools.

Advantages of Person-Oriented Methods of Classification

Current psychiatric classification systems do not adequately consider individual development, whereas person-oriented systems focus on individuals (Bergman & Magnusson, 1997; Sroufe & Rutter, 1984). This focus on the individual fits well in theoretical models emphasizing holistic, dynamic, biopsychosocial, and biologically based systems of development. A common assumption of holistic, dynamic theoretical models is that individuals function as integrated organisms and are continuously interacting with their environment (Magnusson & Cairns, 1996). In a multivariate, or person-oriented model, all behaviors are assumed to interact with each other to generate the pattern of behavior that is observed, which is a basic premise of the dynamic systems point of view. Person-oriented research is also consistent with the biopsychosocial view of development, emphasizing the interactional and synergistic nature of systems on development (Waddington, 1971). Additionally, using multiple dimensions to classify behavior is in agreement with Gottlieb's biological-based theory that an individual's biological makeup and behavioral systems affect behavior (Gottlieb, 2000). This approach simultaneously accounts for behavior along several dimensions so that the interactions between the multiple variables and their interactions in their contexts of development can be accounted for (Kamphaus, DiStefano, & Lease, 2003).

Theoretically, person-oriented methods of classification are superior to categorical and dimensional methods, which fail to account for the interactional and additive nature among variables. Furthermore, multivariate methods have the ability to include information from a wide variety of sources. Parents, teachers, observations, and self-report measures can all contribute to a more accurate classification system. Children who might be healthy or below diagnostic thresholds can also be included in these classification systems, which allow for the use of large, representative samples to more adequately study the full range of child behavior (Kamphaus, Huberty, DiStefano, & Petoskey, 1997). Currently, person-oriented approaches appear to be closer than variable-oriented approaches to a realistic view of development

(Bergman & Magnusson, 1997) and allow for a more comprehensive understanding of the complexity and range of child behaviors (Meehl, 1995; Speece & Cooper, 1991).

Person-oriented methods of classification also account for, and provide greater sensitivity to, symptom severity and comorbidity to determine a suitable classification decision (LaCombe et al., 1991; Mash & Dozois, 1996). Initial research indicates that a multivariate approach to classification is superior to the *DSM* with regard to dealing with the issue of comorbidity. Van Lier, Verhulst, van der Ende, and Crijnen (2003) used a parent rating scale, the Child Behavior Checklist (CBCL) to determine whether patterns of disruptive disorders can be explained by a *DSM* diagnosis. Latent class analysis, a person-oriented method, was used to identify classes of children differing in patterns of disruptive behavior and results indicated that no classes were found in which children only had symptoms of a single *DSM* diagnosis. The researchers concluded that person-centered approaches, such as latent class analysis, should be employed rather than classification based on predetermined cut scores (van Lier et al., 2003). A person-oriented approach to examining correlates of early conduct problems was also found to be more valuable than variable-oriented analysis in a study conducted by M. T. Greenberg, Speltz, DeKlyen, and Jones (2001).

Statistical Methods for Person-Oriented Classification

The ability of person-oriented methods to deal with complex interactions and comorbidities and the focus on the individual has lead to an increased interest in the statistical methods that can classify individuals (Bergman & Magnusson, 1997). These statistical methods are consistent with theoretical approaches by seeking to capture the whole profile of variables that reflect the individual (Bergman, 2000). Cluster analytic methods were used in the 1960s and 1970s in an attempt to create new classification systems, but these methods were largely abandoned for this purpose due to statistical and practical issues (Blashfield, 1998). However, multivariate statistical techniques, such as cluster analysis and latent class analysis, have improved and are more widely used and understood. The construction of homogeneous groups, or clusters, of individuals is accomplished through cluster and latent class analysis (Bergman & Magnusson, 1997). The specific method chosen should depend on the specific case (Bergman, 2000).

Cluster analysis is a classification procedure that is used to group latent groups of people together from an underlying data set (Aldenderfer & Blashfield, 1984; Anderberg, 1973; Blashfield & Aldenderfer, 1988; Hartigan, 1975; Milligan & Cooper, 1987). The goal is to divide a heterogeneous sample of individuals into subgroups that are homogenous (Speece, 1995). Individuals are assigned to a cluster with which they are most similar to a "typical" member of the cluster (C. J. Huberty, DiStefano, & Kamphaus, 1997). Specifically, centroid information and cluster characteristics are examined for each cluster and then compared to the individual case. Through cluster analysis a set of descriptions, or typology, can be created by identifying typical patterns and then individuals can be classified according to this typology (Bergman, 2000; Wangby et al., 1999).

Latent class analysis is another classification procedure similar to cluster analysis in that they both seek to classify individuals into groups, or clusters, where individuals in a cluster are similar to each other and dissimilar to individuals in other clusters (Vermunt & Magidson, 2002). The primary goal of latent cluster analysis is to explain the relationships among variables using the smallest number of classes of individuals with similar patterns of behavior (van Lier et al., 2003). A primary difference between cluster analysis and latent cluster analysis is that latent cluster analysis identifies cases using a model-based method, wherein an underlying statistical model is used to identify similar classes of people (Muthen & Muthen, 2000). Latent cluster analysis also uses an iterative estimation function to assign individuals to classes and uses statistical indexes to determine the optimal number of classes (Vermunt & Magidson, 2002). Although there has been a strong resistance to using person-oriented analyses as opposed to traditional statistics, a change in methodology is needed to make scientific advances (Magnusson & Cairns, 1996).

Preliminary Support for Person-Oriented Profile Types

The stability and predictive validity of clusters, or classes of individuals, has been studied in several investigations using a variety of methods and measures. Mattison and Spitznagel (1999) studied the long-term stability of profile types as determined through the use of the CBCL, which is a parent rating scale. Profile types were created through cluster analysis in an attempt to represent the complete clinical presentation of the children. Children were originally classified into a profile type, or cluster, and were then reclustered 4.8 years later. Results indicated that the stability for profile types was good and similar to past results using CBCL and *DSM* diagnosis. By determining the individual's profile types, prediction of the child's diagnostic course could be made (Mattison & Spitznagel, 1999).

Flanagan, Bierman, and Kam (2003) found that cluster membership was predictive of later outcomes for first grade children. They found that strong evidence of sensitivity and specificity resulted from using a person-oriented approach to forming profiles. Toshiaki, Awaji, Nakazato, and Sumita (1995) found cluster membership to be predictive of outcomes in adults.

Although some studies suggest that multivariate approaches to classification allow for greater predictive validity (Fergusson & Horwood, 1995), others have shown prediction to be equally accurate using both cluster and variable approaches (Haapasalo, Tremblay, Boulerice, & Vitaro, 2000).

Although evidence exists that many latent traits are invariant in structure and quantity across cultures (Crijnen, Achenbach, & Verhulst, 1999), person-oriented methods of classification are not viable alternatives to traditional diagnostic categories because there is not yet a substantial accumulation of evidence suggesting that cluster types can be replicated across samples and instruments (Lessing, Williams, & Gil, 1982). Alternatively, a classification system utilizing teacher ratings for child behavior in schools is gaining wider acceptance in that cluster solutions can be replicated across samples. A seven-cluster solution was substantially replicated across: (a) samples in the U.S. population (Kamphaus et al., 1997), (b) a U.S. urban sample (DiStefano et al., 2003), (c) a U.S. rural sample (DiStefano et al., 2003), and (d) a sample in Medellin, Colombia (Kamphaus & DiStefano, 2001).

Evidence of instrument independent replication is more scarce, but holds promise, and suggests that some clusters of behavior, or profile types, are partially instrument independent (DiStefano et al., 2003; C. J. Huberty et al., 1997; Kamphaus et al., 1997, 1999, 2003). Studies by Caspi and Silva (1995), Flanagan et al. (2003), Curry and Thompson (1985), and Lessing et al. (1982) produced comparable clusters or classes of children with independent instruments, which also appear to overlap with the seven-cluster solution found by Kamphaus et al. (1997). This seven-cluster solution has been proposed to be adequate for classifying the behavioral adjustment of children in elementary school (DiStefano et al., 2003).

Disadvantages of Person-Oriented Methods of Classification

Although the advantages of person-oriented methods of classification appear to be promising, distinct disadvantages of this method remain. It has been suggested that the real-world applicability of clusters is limited because it involves a complex process to assign individuals to cluster membership. Additionally, classification systems derived from cluster analysis have not yet provided a substantial amount of information about their clinical and predictive value (Mattison & Spitznagel, 1999; Speece, 1995). The utility of clusters to inform clinicians about the future behavior of individuals is largely unknown (Blanchard, Morgenstern, Morgan, Labouvie, & Bux, 2003), suggesting the need for further studies on the predictive validity of clusters of individuals. Lessing et al. (1982) also suggested that cluster classification systems are just as vulnerable to reliability and validity problems as systems of psychiatric diagnosis. To summarize, person-oriented classification systems still lack the research base or wide acceptance necessary to transform or replace current diagnostic systems.

For the clinical utility of such a dimensional typology to be established, each cluster of behavior must be validated—not only replicated in independent samples of children, but also characterized and differentiated by marker variables of clinical importance.

To be optimally effective, classification systems should be reliable, valid, and consist of an integration of empirical methodology and clinical acumen. In this vein, Skinner (1981) has proposed a model for the endeavor of classification that encompasses theory formulation, internal validation, and external validation. To date, studies regarding the Behavior Assessment System for Children and Teacher Rating Scales—Child (BASC TRS-C) typology of child behavior have addressed, in part, the theory formulation and internal validation components of this model and characterization (see next section).

Investigators have utilized cluster analytic techniques for the purpose of identifying behavioral types in children and adolescents both with and without disabilities. Parents and teachers often complete behavior rating scales on given children and adolescents as a part of a comprehensive psychoeducational evaluation. In an ideal situation, multiple informants (e.g., one or more teachers and one or more parents/caregivers) will complete ratings. However, this is not always possible given time constraints and other impeding factors (Kamphaus & Frick, 2002). Parent ratings are advantageous in that parents tend to possess the most knowledge about their child for the longest period of time. However, parent ratings may also be limited due to biases and lack of knowledge regarding child development. Teachers, usually the second most important adult figures in children's lives, are viewed as being especially valuable in reporting child behavior. Although teachers are less likely than parents to voice concern about or rate internalizing behaviors as opposed to externalizing behaviors, they are nonetheless instrumental participants in special education and mental health assessments for children (Achenbach & McConaughy, 1992; DuPaul, Power, McGoey, Ikeda, & Anastopoulos, 1998; Kamphaus & Frick, 2002). It has been demonstrated that teachers' reports of child behavior predict poor outcomes (e.g., academic problems and school behavior problems) as well as or better than parents' ratings (Verhulst, Koot, & Van der Ende, 1994). Further, teachers have been shown to possess a high degree of accuracy in identifying children at risk for learning difficulties and attentional problems (Kamphaus & Frick, 2002).

Lessing et al. (1982) conducted a study to determine whether replicable types of children and adolescents could be identified by the cluster analysis of their scores on the Institute for Juvenile Research (IJR) Behavior Checklist Parent Form. Item scores range from 0 (behavior not observed) to 2 (behavior observed "often" or "very much so"), assessing socially competent, anxious, insecure, withdrawn, aggressive, distractible, unmotivated, depressed, paranoid, psychosomatic, incontinent, sexually maladjusted, and bizarre/autistic behaviors. Scores for three samples of children were submitted to cluster analysis, including one clinical sample ($N = 185$) and two mixed clinical and normal samples ($N = 358$ and $N = 373$). Seven replicable types across samples were identified: (1) high assets/flat symptom profile, (2) sociopathic/academic problems, (3) moderate assets/egocentric, (4) insecure/somaticizing, (5) aggressive/overreactive, and (6) diffuse, mixed pathology.

Curry and Thompson (1985) initiated a similar study, submitting scores of two matched samples of children referred for psychiatric services on the Missouri Children's Behavior Checklist (MCBC). Items were scored dichotomously, wherein the parent rates the child as having exhibited the behavior in the past 6 months (1 = yes, 0 = no). The items comprise six scales: (1) aggression, (2) inhibition, (3) activity level, (4) sleep disturbance, (5) somatization, and (6) sociability. For the two matched samples, each of which constituted 65 participants, the following seven clusters were identified: (1) Inhibited-nonaggressive, (2) low social skills, (3) behavior problem-free, (4) mildly aggressive, (5) aggressive-active, (6) aggressive-inhibited, and (7) undifferentiated disturbance. Classification rules for this cluster solution were applied to a sample of 44 nonreferred children and 65 developmentally disabled children. Notable differences in the frequency distributions among samples were noted, with significantly more "behavior problem-free" children in the nonreferred sample.

Continuing this line of research, R. J. Thompson, Kronenberger, and Curry (1989) cluster analyzed scores on the MCBC for three samples of children, including those referred for developmental disability evaluations ($N = 471$), children referred for psychiatric services ($N = 155$), and children with chronic illnesses ($N = 184$). Seven replicable behavior types were identified: (1) internal profile, (2) external profile, (3) mixed internal and external profile, (4) undifferentiated disturbance, (5) low social skills profile, (6) problem-free profile, and (7) sociable profile. Again, notable differences in the frequency distributions among samples were noted, with significantly more "behavior problem-free" children in the nonreferred sample, as well as the chronic illness sample.

Gdwoski, Lachar, and Kline (1985) investigated the value of the Personality Inventory for Children (PIC) in generating an empirically derived typology of child and adolescent psychopathology. The PIC consists of 600 dichotomously scored items, wherein the parent rates the child as having exhibited the characteristic or behavior (1 = true, 0 = false). The items comprise 12 substantive scales: (1) achievement, (2) intellectual screening, (3) development, (4) somatic concern, (5) depression, (6) family relations, (7) delinquency, (8) withdrawal, (9) anxiety, (10) psychosis, (11) hyperactivity, and (12) social skills. Personality Inventory for Children scores for 1,782 children and adolescents referred for multiple emotional and behavioral concerns were submitted to cluster analysis. The total sample was randomly split into two independent samples, 1 ($N = 889$) and 2 ($N = 893$) for the purpose of conducting replication analyses. Results yielded a total of 11 replicable behavioral types. These 11 types classified 82% of the total 1,782 cases analyzed. The first type represented a "within normal limits" group of children and adolescents. The score profiles of these individuals reflected the least severe symptomatology. Four groups, generally described as "cognitive dysfunction" types, were also identified. These four types were differentiated by degree of cognitive/learning impairment, social skills deficits, attention problems, and disruptive behaviors. In addition, six "emotional/behavioral/learning" types were identified. These groups were primarily differentiated according to levels of internalizing and externalizing emotional/behavioral indicators and school achievement.

LaCombe et al. (1991) furthered this investigation by identifying external correlates for each of the 11 behavioral types. Mental health case records of 327 of the original 1,782 individuals from the previous study were reviewed for the purpose of providing external validation for the profile types. Examination of case histories supported the general categories of types. For example, the "within normal limits" group was found to have the least severe presenting problems in addition to relatively typical development and healthy familial background. In contrast, the types categorized as having "cognitive dysfunction" were more likely to present with developmental difficulties, family histories of mental health problems, or diagnosable disorders. Those in the "emotional/behavioral/learning" type groups presented with higher incidences of reports of school achievement difficulties, attention problems, and familial conflict.

McDermott and Weiss (1995) submitted scores of a national sample of 1,400 children and adolescents on the Adjustment Scales for Children and Adolescents (ASCA) to cluster analytic procedures for the purpose of obtaining a normative typology of behavior. The sample was designed to reflect the population of all noninstitutionalized 5- to 17-year-old individuals in the United States. The ASCA is a rating scale completed by teachers that contains 97 "problem" and 26 "positive" behavioral indicators. The items form core syndrome scales, including Attention-Deficit Hyperactive, Solitary Aggressive-Provocative, Solitary Aggressive-Impulsive, Oppositional Defiant, Diffident, and Avoidant. Results were based on the score profiles across these six core syndromes and yielded 22 normative behavioral styles or types. Twelve of the types were generally grouped as "adjusted," accounting for 78.6% of all cases examined. One type was deemed as having "good" adjustment, thus reflecting normal symptom levels on all scales. Individuals having "adequate" adjustment were characterized into four types having mild problems related to both internalizing and/or externalizing difficulties. Those classified as having "marginal" adjustment were grouped into seven types having slightly higher levels of mixed internalizing and externalizing behavioral symptoms. Six "at-risk" types (16.2%) were identified, characterized by varying levels of oppositional, impulsive, and inattentive behaviors. Four "maladjusted" types (5.2%) also emerged, representing youth characterized by aggressive and schizoid behaviors.

Following on their recommendation to establish a more systematic method of examining child behavior profiles, Edelbrock and Achenbach (1980) investigated the utility of their own Child Behavior Profile (CBP; Achenbach & Edelbrock, 1978, 1979) for this purpose. The CBP is a rating scale designed to be completed by parents. It consists of 118 behavior problems and 20 social competence items. Separate editions of the CBP were developed to reflect each sex at ages 4 to 5, 6 to 11, and 12 to 16. In this study, a total of 2,683 score profiles were analyzed. All participants were clinically referred and included 1,050 boys aged 6 to 11, 633 boys aged 12 to 16, 500 girls aged 6 to 11, and 500 girls aged 12 to 16. Scores for each of the four groups were analyzed separately. Six reliable behavioral profiles were identified for boys aged 6 to 11, including Schizoid-Social Withdrawal, Depressed-Social Withdrawal-Aggressive, Schizoid, and Somatic Complaints, all of which were generally categorized as internalizing types (41.8% of the sample), and two externalizing types, Hyperactive and Delinquent (36.5% of the sample). For boys, 6.8% aged 6 to 11 remained unclassified. Six types were also identified for boys aged 12 to 16, including two internalizing types (28.9% of the sample), Schizoid and Uncommunicative, and four externalizing types (51.7% of the sample), including, Immature-Aggressive, Hyperactive, Uncommunicative-Delinquent, and Delinquent. Again, for boys, 3.9% aged 12 to 16 remained unclassified. Seven reliable behavioral profiles were identified for girls aged 6 to 11, including Depressed-Social Withdrawal, Somatic Complaints, and Schizoid-Obsessive, all of which were generally categorized as internalizing types (32.0% of the sample), one mixed type (10.1% of the sample), Sex Problems, and three externalizing types, including Hyperactive, Delinquent, and Aggressive-Cruel (38.9% of the sample). For girls, 2.7% aged 6 to 11 remained unclassified. Seven profiles were also identified for girls aged 12 to 16, including Anxious-Obsessive, Somatic Complaints, and Anxious-Obsessive-Aggressive, all of which were generally categorized as internalizing types (28.6% of the sample), one mixed type (12.9% of the sample), Hyperactive-Immature, and three externalizing types, including Delinquent, Depressed-Withdrawal-Delinquent, and Aggressive-Cruel (37.4% of the sample). Again, for girls, 2.2% aged 12 to 16 remained unclassified.

Additionally, this research group characterized these children via teacher behavior ratings, direct observations, cognitive measures, achievement tests, and personality inventories. Findings suggested that members of the internalizing behavioral types (Schizoid-Social Withdrawal, Depressed-Social Withdrawal-Aggressive, Schizoid, and Somatic Complaints) functioned better in terms of cognitive, academic, and social functioning than those belonging to the externalizing types (Hyperactive and Delinquent).

The first group ($N = 106$) consisted of boys clinically referred for behavior problems and general noncompliance. The second group ($N = 53$) represented boys who carried diagnoses of Attention-Deficit/Hyperactivity Disorder (ADHD), Oppositional Defiant Disorder (ODD), and/or Conduct Disorder (CD). The third group ($N = 69$) was comprised of boys who had not been referred for mental health services. Results of cluster analyses revealed the presence of four reliable profiles, including two "problem-free" groups, an externalizing group, and a mixed internalizing/externalizing group.

Typologies Derived from the Behavior Assessment System for Children

Several clustering studies utilizing the Behavior Assessment System for Children (BASC; C. R. Reynolds & Kamphaus, 1992) have been conducted to date. An investigation of child behavior ratings was conducted by Kamphaus et al. (1999) utilizing the Behavior Assessment System for Children (BASC; C. R. Reynolds & Kamphaus, 1992) Parent Rating Scales for Children (PRS-C) for a national normative sample of children 6 to 11 years of age ($N = 2,029$). Using the same methodology outlined by C. J. Huberty et al. (1997), a nine-cluster solution was identified. Likewise, the interpretation of the nine clusters was done on the basis of scale elevations with the following groups: (1) Adapted, (2) Physical Complaints/Worry, (3) Average, (4) Well Adapted, (5) Minimal Problems, (6) Attention Problems, (7) Internalizing, (8) General Psychopathology-Severe, and (9) Disruptive Behavior Problems. This cluster solution was quite similar to that obtained from scores on the TRS-C with two exceptions. Parent ratings yielded two additional clusters, Minimal Problems and Internalizing that were not present in the teacher rating cluster solution. The authors felt this to be reasonable in that parents would perhaps be more likely to identify internalizing problems and mild difficulties in their children than teachers, whose roles necessitate paying most attention to disruptive, externalizing behaviors in the classroom setting.

Additionally, a sample of 423 preschool children obtained from an "at-risk" public school system was used in this study for the purposes of replicating and cross-validating the obtained normative cluster solution. Using the cluster analytic methodology outlined by C. J. Huberty et al. (1997), a six-cluster solution was identified for the normative sample. The interpretation of the six clusters was done on the basis of scale elevations, with the following groups: (1) Well Adapted, (2) Average, (3) Physical Complaints/Worry, (4) Disruptive Behavior Problems, (5) Withdrawn, and (6) General Problems-Severe. The TRS-P normative cluster solution differed from the TRS-C solution only in that a seventh, mildly disruptive group did not emerge. Cluster analytic results using the independent sample of "at-risk" children yielded only a slightly different solution: (1) Well Adapted, (2) Average, (3) Internalizing, (4) Disruptive Behavior Problems, (5) Withdrawn, and (6) General Problems-Severe. In comparison to the Physical Complaints/Worry cluster identified in the normative sample, the Internalizing group that emerged from this sample appeared to have more impairment in that both the depression and anxiety scales were elevated. Results of cross-validation indicated considerable overlap, in that five of the six clusters had "hit rates" or levels of agreement of 50% or higher. Additionally, disciplinary referrals were utilized as external validation data and generally supported the cluster solution (e.g., children in the Disruptive Behavior Problems and General Problems-Severe clusters received the majority of disciplinary actions).

Scores from the Behavior Assessment System for Children (BASC; C. R. Reynolds & Kamphaus, 1992) Teacher Rating Scales—Child (TRS-C) for a national normative sample of children 6 to 11 years of age ($N = 1,227$) were subjected to cluster analytic techniques. From this, C. J. Huberty et al. (1997) developed a dimensional seven-cluster typology of child behavior. Per the recommendations of Blashfield and Aldenderfer (1988), clustering was completed using the Ward method followed by a K-means procedure. The seven BASC TRS-C clusters have been supported by evidence of internal validity via correlations between the corresponding structure r's for three pairs of half-samples of the normative sample, hit rates for cross-typology clustering of three pairs of half-samples, and examination of matched cluster centroid locations via linear discriminant function (LDF) plots (C. J. Huberty et al., 1997). Therefore, Kamphaus et al. (1997) offered substantive interpretation of the seven clusters on the basis of scale elevations, labeling them (1) Well Adapted, (2) Average, (3) Disruptive Behavior

Problems, (4) Learning Problems (since renamed "Academic Problems"), (5) Physical Complaints/Worry, (6) General Psychopathology-Severe, and (7) Mildly Disruptive (see Tables 13.1 and 13.2).

The original TRS-C study has been replicated in three different populations to date, including children in Medellin, Colombia (Kamphaus & DiStefano, 2001), and a rural as well as an urban sample of children in the United States (DiStefano et al., 2003). Kamphaus and DiStefano (2001) conducted a first test of cross-cultural generalizability of the BASC TRS-C typology using a sample of children from metropolitan Medellin, Colombia. Scores for a sample of 108 children ages 6 to 11 years were subjected to cluster analytic techniques. Overall, results showed that most of the U.S. teacher-rated types were

Table 13.1 **Mean *T*-Scores by Scale for the BASC TRS-C Normative Typology (*N* = 1,227)**

Scales	Cluster						
	1	**2**	**3**	**4**	**5**	**6**	**7**
Externalizing							
Aggression	44.00	**43.19**	**67.83**	49.25	49.63	**69.56**	57.74
Hyperactivity	43.48	44.56	**66.29**	52.34	49.60	**69.92**	57.52
Conduct Problems	45.26	45.60	**65.37**	51.32	47.60	**71.31**	52.66
Internalizing							
Anxiety	45.88	44.80	54.39	52.32	**58.40**	**70.62**	47.28
Depression	44.48	44.55	**61.05**	51.79	55.30	**76.35**	50.28
Somatization	46.58	45.25	53.64	48.87	**64.99**	**61.83**	47.39
School Problems							
Attention Problems	**40.99**	49.18	**63.43**	**60.77**	49.22	**68.34**	52.50
Learning Problems	**42.28**	49.30	**62.90**	**61.11**	50.56	**65.56**	49.70
Other Scales							
Atypicality	45.12	46.22	58.91	55.09	49.41	**80.83**	50.26
Withdrawal	45.11	47.24	54.96	**59.40**	53.79	**69.38**	45.16
Adaptive Skills							
Adaptability	**58.89**	50.10	**37.26**	**41.11**	48.19	**32.54**	46.64
Leadership	**59.02**	43.38	**41.85**	**38.83**	49.99	**41.60**	50.72
Social Skills	**58.81**	44.34	**41.16**	**39.70**	51.89	**42.33**	47.43
Study Skills	**59.98**	46.39	**37.97**	**38.35**	51.06	**38.52**	47.92

Notes: Values that differ from the *T*-Score mean of 50 by 7 points or more in either direction are in boldface. Cluster 1 = Well Adapted; Cluster 2 = Average; Cluster 3 = Disruptive Behavior Problems; Cluster 4 = Academic Problems; Cluster 5 = Physical Complaints/Worry; Cluster 6 = General Psychopathology-Severe; Cluster 7 = Mildly Disruptive.

Table 13.2   **Sample Sizes, Proportions, and Demographic Characteristics for the BASC TRS-C Normative Typology** (*N* = 1,227)

Cluster	N	%	M	F	Dx	C	AA	A	H	N	O
						Percentage					
1	417	34	39	61	4.2	77.9	12.7	1.7	7.2	0.2	0.2
2	228	19	48	52	4.8	48.7	43.4	0.4	6.1	0.4	0.9
3	103	8	78	22	19.6	57.3	30.1	0.0	10.7	1.0	1.0
4	149	12	60	40	13.4	63.1	32.9	0.0	2.0	1.3	0.7
5	134	11	40	60	5.8	73.1	17.2	0.0	8.2	0.0	1.5
6	51	4	67	33	17.6	73.1	19.2	0.0	7.7	0.0	0.0
7	145	12	70	30	8.5	65.5	24.8	1.4	6.9	0.7	0.7

Notes: The proportions that each cluster represents of the total sample do not total 100% due to the rounding of values to the nearest whole number. % = Percentage of total sample; M = Male; F = Female; Dx = Previously diagnosed with a behavioral; emotional; or academic problem; A = Asian-American; AA = African American; C = Caucasian; H = Hispanic; N = Native American; O = Other race/ethnicity. Cluster 1 = Well Adapted; Cluster 2 = Average; Cluster 3 = Disruptive Behavior Problems; Cluster 4 = Academic Problems; Cluster 5 = Physical Complaints/Worry; Cluster 6 = General Psychopathology-Severe; Cluster 7 = Mildly Disruptive.

identified in the Colombian sample (see Table 13.3). One exception was noted, in that the Mildly Disruptive cluster did not emerge.

A study by DiStefano et al. (2003) was conducted for the purpose of assessing the internal validity of the TRS-C typology. This was achieved by conducting cluster analyses with two large independent samples and cross classifying the existing and newly obtained teacher-rated typologies to compare cluster assignments among cluster solutions. Additionally, with one of the independent samples, the relationship between the behavioral typology and external indicators of adjustment in school was assessed by examining rates of referral for special education or prereferral intervention, disciplinary actions (i.e., major or minor disciplinary action, physical or verbal aggression, or sexual offense), and diagnosis such as ADHD referrals.

Data for two samples of children, 6- to 11-years-old, were collected. The first sample consisted of 537 children from a rural community in central Georgia with a history of significant poverty. Community demographics documented that 39.3% of the residents of the county had not completed high school and that 52.5% of school children were eligible for free or reduced lunch. The racial

Table 13.3   Mean *T*-Scores by Scale for the Medellin Cluster
Solution (*N* = 108)

Scales	Cluster					
	1	2	3	4	5	6
Aggression	45.00	46.77	**61.33**	44.23	47.69	**69.83**
Hyperactivity	**43.22**	47.88	**58.17**	48.54	46.77	**73.33**
Conduct Problems	43.81	47.77	56.61	47.93	49.31	**75.83**
Anxiety	**42.03**	48.81	55.78	54.00	50.69	**61.33**
Depression	43.88	46.42	**59.28**	47.15	49.62	**70.33**
Somatization	45.75	48.31	52.17	47.69	**58.13**	52.33
Attention Problems	40.72	**50.84**	57.56	58.69	43.15	67.33
Learning Problems	41.13	**49.23**	**55.11**	57.00	**46.69**	69.33
Atypicality	**42.59**	48.23	**58.56**	49.77	48.62	**69.33**
Withdrawal	**40.44**	**42.69**	53.22	**65.62**	**62.46**	**69.33**
Adaptability	**59.03**	48.96	**39.61**	47.92	**57.23**	**32.33**
Leadership	**58.34**	45.96	46.22	**40.15**	55.08	**42.67**
Social Skills	**59.34**	48.77	**42.56**	**42.92**	**57.92**	**38.67**
Study Skills	**58.63**	49.15	**43.22**	**38.00**	**60.23**	**36.00**
Cluster *N*	32	26	18	13	13	6
Medellin %	30	24	17	12	12	6
Normative %	34	19	8	12	11	4
Medellin % Male	34	50	89	62	31	67
Medellin % Low SES	34	46	50	62	62	67

Notes: Values that differ from the *T*-Score mean of 50 by 7 points or more in either direction are in boldface. Cluster 1 = Well Adapted; Cluster 2 = Average; Cluster 3 = Disruptive Behavior Problems; Cluster 4 = Academic Problems; Cluster 5 = Physical Complaints/Worry; Cluster 6 = General Psychopathology-Severe; Cluster 7 = Mildly Disruptive was not present in the Medellin sample. U.S. normative sample percentages by BASC TRS-C cluster provided for comparison.

and ethnic composition of the school system was 29.5% African American, 0.5% Hispanic, and 69.6% Caucasian. The second independent sample consisted of 1,076 children obtained from an urban community in the Southeastern U.S. through a research grant aimed at teacher professional development designed to improve the management of challenging behaviors in the regular education classroom. The county has been described as "at-risk" based on several educational factors. Approximately 23% of residents had not completed high school, and 58.2% of the school district population was eligible for free or reduced lunch. The racial and ethnic composition of these schools was 57.4% African American, 5.2% Hispanic, and

33.4% Caucasian. Because both these samples likely demonstrate more "at-risk" characteristics than the BASC normative data set, this study was able to better ascertain if the behavioral typology of children identified using the BASC normative sample could be reliably replicated.

The same clustering procedure used in prior BASC typological studies was employed to assure that differences in cluster solutions would not be the result of a different clustering algorithm or similarity indexes used to group the data. A seven-cluster solution was found with the rural sample. All seven of the clusters identified from the normative sample were present with results from the independent cluster analysis of the rural sample: (1) Well Adapted, (2) Average, (3) Disruptive Behavior Problems, (4) Academic Problems, (5) Physical Complaints/Worry, (6) General Problems-Severe, and (7) Mildly Disruptive (see Table 13.4). The interpretation of the seven rural sample clusters was determined to be similar to that of the normative data set. Cross-classification analysis revealed that both clustering methods had a relatively high degree of agreement, with cross validation hit rates reporting between 68.4 and 97.1% agreement between the two grouping methods. For cases that were not assigned to the same cluster, the majority of cases were assigned to a cluster with a comparable definition.

An eight-cluster solution was found with the urban sample. Again, all seven of the clusters from the normative sample were identified in this independent sample. An additional cluster, named Mildly Adapted, was also identified. This cluster was considered to represent a variation on the Well Adapted and Average clusters identified in the normative sample. The interpretation of the seven clusters found with the urban sample was similar to the solution found with the BASC norm data set (Table 13.5). For the purposes of cross-classification, the Mildly Adapted cluster was reordered between the Well Adapted and Average clusters as its profile resembled a middle ground between these two groups. Many children were classified into equivalent clusters based on the two clustering methods. Hit rates from the classification methods reported a high degree of agreement (at least 75%) for three clusters,

Table 13.4 **Mean *T*-Scores by Scale for the Rural Sample Cluster Solution (*N* = 537)**

Scales	1	Cluster 2	3	4	5	6	7
Externalizing							
Aggression	44.44	43.36	**77.79**	49.76	48.89	58.80	59.86
Hyperactivity	43.21	44.46	**74.18**	53.67	49.84	**61.29**	57.87
Conduct Problems	45.51	45.07	**70.27**	51.34	48.68	57.63	53.39
Internalizing							
Anxiety	44.10	43.49	52.45	53.67	**61.13**	**70.26**	44.52
Depression	43.11	43.14	58.45	48.67	51.47	**67.34**	48.84
Somatization	48.43	46.07	48.60	49.60	**81.76**	**64.77**	46.71
School Problems							
Attention Problems	**39.70**	48.09	**64.15**	**61.39**	50.94	**67.94**	52.01
Learning Problems	42.45	47.88	**63.06**	**63.33**	50.97	**69.37**	48.64
Other Scales							
Atypicality	45.05	46.12	**69.76**	53.82	52.37	**71.94**	48.43
Withdrawal	43.41	44.56	49.82	52.46	50.16	**66.74**	44.43
Adaptive Skills							
Adaptability	57.96	49.33	**32.90**	40.17	48.26	**35.03**	44.48
Leadership	57.01	41.65	**39.06**	36.48	46.00	**45.86**	45.86
Social Skills	59.29	45.22	**37.18**	39.60	50.92	**38.89**	43.16
Study Skills	**60.46**	45.31	**37.18**	**38.01**	50.08	**36.29**	45.49
Cluster *N*	110	162	33	82	38	35	77
Crawford Co. %	21	30	6	15	7	7	14
Normative %	34	19	8	12	11	4	12
Crawford % Male	31	54	91	67	37	63	56
U.S. Norm % Male	39	48	78	60	40	67	70

Notes: Values that differ from the *T*-Score mean of 50 by 7 points or more in either direction are in boldface. Cluster 1 = Well Adapted; Cluster 2 = Average; Cluster 3 = Disruptive Behavior Problems; Cluster 4 = Academic Problems; Cluster 5 = Physical Complaints/Worry; Cluster 6 = General Psychopathology-Severe; Cluster 7 = Mildly Disruptive. U.S. normative sample percentages by BASC TRS-C cluster provided for comparison.

Disruptive Behavior Problems, Physical Complaints/Worry, and Mildly Disruptive. The remaining clusters showed moderate levels of agreement between the two classification methods. Overall, hit rate values were generally lower for the urban sample than for the rural sample, possibly due to the more diverse population of students in the urban school system. However, results as a

Table 13.5   **Mean *T*-Scores by Scale for the Urban Sample Cluster Solution (*N* = 1,076)**

Scales	Cluster							
	1	**2**	**3**	**4**	**5**	**6**	**7**	**8**
Externalizing								
Aggression	**43.47**	44.03	**67.34**	48.83	50.33	**72.22**	**59.91**	44.26
Hyperactivity	**41.64**	**42.78**	**65.88**	49.16	51.25	**67.56**	**61.44**	43.44
Conduct Problems	43.99	45.43	**69.09**	52.17	50.39	**80.56**	53.31	44.87
Internalizing								
Anxiety	43.98	44.88	55.31	46.77	**58.30**	**86.94**	47.94	**42.24**
Depression	43.47	45.02	61.32	46.57	**54.83**	**84.50**	53.36	**42.96**
Somatization	45.76	43.92	**51.64**	44.36	67.93	**68.00**	46.67	**44.66**
School Problems								
Attention Problems	38.49	48.57	66.75	59.04	**53.06**	**66.12**	55.64	42.54
Learning Problems	40.32	49.63	65.13	61.96	52.69	67.50	51.43	43.06
Other Scales								
Atypicality	44.23	**45.68**	60.14	49.76	**53.81**	87.67	49.71	44.32
Withdrawal	43.70	47.46	**61.35**	53.55	55.58	**73.61**	46.56	43.56
Adaptive Skills								
Adaptability	**62.11**	52.06	**32.65**	45.25	**57.76**	**35.83**	**42.86**	57.76
Leadership	**65.38**	**42.77**	**39.61**	**36.99**	49.64	46.12	49.90	54.60
Social Skills	**65.45**	45.06	**39.68**	**39.70**	51.64	47.44	48.52	53.21
Study Skills	**63.90**	45.66	**38.56**	**38.02**	48.85	**40.33**	48.42	55.38
Cluster *N*	185	178	113	139	72	18	142	229
Clarke Co. %	17	17	11	13	8	2	13	21
Normative %	34	19	8	12	11	4	12	n/a
Clarke % Male	33	50	75	51	42	56	63	44
U.S. Norm % Male	39	48	78	60	40	67	70	n/a

Notes: Values that differ from the *T*-Score mean of 50 by 7 points or more in either direction are in boldface. Cluster 1 = Well Adapted; Cluster 2 = Average; Cluster 3 = Disruptive Behavior Problems; Cluster 4 = Academic Problems; Cluster 5 = Physical Complaints/Worry; cluster 6 = General Psychopathology-Severe; Cluster 7 = Mildly Disruptive; Cluster 8 = Mildly Adapted. U.S. normative sample percentages by BASC TRS-C cluster provided for comparison.

whole supported comparability among the two methods of classifying children into clusters.

External indicators of behavioral adjustment were also examined to provide support to the utility of this behavioral typology system. To this end, the frequencies of disciplinary infractions during the 1998 to 1999 school year were collected for each child in the urban sample. Eight actions were targeted: (1) referral for pre-referral interventions, (2) number of suspensions, (3) major disciplinary action (parents were called), (4) minor disciplinary action (parents were not called), (6) physical offense, (7) verbal offense, and (8) sexual offense. For each of the eight disciplinary actions, the numbers of infractions committed were calculated for each cluster. Results are displayed in Figure 13.1. Additionally, to determine the extent of differences among groups, one-way ANOVAs were conducted between clusters using each disciplinary action as the dependent variable. Significant differences among the clusters as to the number of disciplinary infractions committed were found. The majority of disciplinary actions were given to students in three clusters: (1) Disruptive Behavior Problems, (2) General Problems-Severe, and (3) Mildly Disruptive. For these clusters,

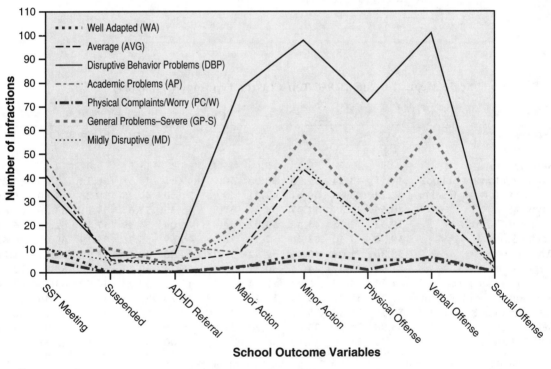

Figure 13.1

Number of occurrences of behavioral infractions by cluster for the Urban Sample Cluster Solution (*N* = 1,076).

major and minor disciplinary actions, physical offenses, and verbal offenses were most prevalent. Other clusters exhibited behavioral problems but with less intensity. Children in the Academic Problems group were most often referred for pre-referral intervention, perhaps due to their teachers' awareness of alternative instructional methods and programs designed to academically support these students in the classroom or identification for additional services. Children in the Average cluster had few disciplinary infractions, and infractions that were reported fell into the Minor Disciplinary Action or Verbal Offense category. Well Adapted and Physical Complaints/Worry children showed very few problems across the set of eight disciplinary actions. The disciplinary data provided initial but convincing evidence that the number of disciplinary offenses committed during a typical academic year helps support cluster differentiation.

Table 13.6   Scale Means for the SRP-C Ten-Cluster Typology (*N* = 4,981)

	Cluster									
Scales	1	2	3	4	5	6	7	8	9	10
Sample (%)	22.9	17.7	9.4	5.6	5.4	6.3	11.8	9.0	7.4	4.6
Attention toward School	**41.55**	**43.24**	**59.98**	**60.08**	50.91	49.15	46.58	**60.32**	55.09	**62.29**
Attention toward Teachers	**42.24**	43.88	50.61	**62.61**	48.93	51.50	47.28	**59.22**	54.60	**66.26**
Atypicality	**40.54**	46.89	44.37	54.47	52.57	45.35	**57.65**	54.11	**63.28**	**63.64**
Locus of Control	**39.52**	45.15	45.32	**59.02**	54.85	46.04	54.39	**57.12**	**62.44**	**66.18**
Social Stress	**39.32**	47.60	**43.00**	55.57	56.46	45.69	55.36	54.19	**65.05**	**66.62**
Anxiety	**38.80**	51.03	**42.06**	52.52	55.77	44.90	**58.19**	53.97	**62.77**	**61.26**
Depression	**41.94**	44.09	44.23	**60.52**	54.40	47.24	50.27	53.92	**65.96**	**72.81**
Sense of Inadequacy	**41.74**	44.89	46.04	**59.74**	51.15	47.85	50.23	**56.50**	**63.26**	**68.46**
Relationship with Parents	55.28	55.07	53.33	**31.38**	50.67	45.75	52.88	48.57	47.46	**30.65**
Interpersonal Relations	**56.57**	54.80	55.57	**42.79**	46.48	49.57	50.37	50.57	**37.27**	**26.58**
Self-Esteem	55.98	54.68	53.28	**39.70**	**31.90**	49.20	53.19	51.36	**43.06**	**29.72**
Self-Reliance	56.32	54.89	53.15	**36.66**	45.23	**37.00**	53.04	49.17	48.13	**33.83**

Notes: Boldfaced numbers represent either a 7-point increase or decrease from mean of 50. Cluster 1 = Well Adapted/Minimal Problems; Cluster 2 = Average; Cluster 3 = Attitude to School; Cluster 4 = Disruptive Behavior Problems; Cluster 5 = Low Self-Esteem; Cluster 6 = Low Self-Reliance; Cluster 7 = Physical Complaints/Worry; Cluster 8 = Attitude to Teacher and School; Cluster 9 = Internalizing; Cluster 10 = General Problems-Severe.

Meaningful clusters of child adjustment have also been identified for the BASC Self-Report of Personality—Child (SRP-C) for 8- to 11-year-olds by Kamphaus et al. (2003). This study of over 4,000 children from the national normative sample and approximately 500 cases from a local sample produced the 10-cluster solution shown in Table 13.6. The investigators used ratings by teachers and parents of these same children to assess the external validity of the clusters—a method that essentially failed in that the 10 clusters of adjustment could not be differentiated by parent or teacher BASC ratings. Alternatively, extensive peer ratings of these children could differentiate the clusters suggesting the validity of the cluster solution for describing the child's functioning in the context of peers.

Conclusion

The shortcomings of current classification systems are well documented in the research literature (Blashfield, 1998; Houts, 2002; Richters, 1997; Scotti and Morris, 2000) and significant dissatisfaction with these available clinical taxonomies remains (Malik & Beutler, 2002; Houts, 2002; Joiner & Schmidt, 2002). Despite these shortcomings, clinicians and researchers continue to classify and diagnose individuals for a variety of purposes, such as improved communication among professionals and ease of clinical description (Blashfield, 1998). Classification will continue and therefore it is imperative that classification systems advance along with empirical knowledge.

The most widely used method for classification, the *DSM*, involves categorical methods to classify behavior, whereas research suggests that behavior is distributed along a continuum, or dimensionally (Deater-Deckard et al., 1997; Fergusson & Horwood, 1995). These categorical methods have constrained research and scientific advancement (Sroufe, 1997), and it has been recommended that researchers use more quantitative, dimensional methods (Widiger, 1992). Dimensional methods improve on categorical methods but still make classification decisions based on the presence or absence of variables without accounting for the multiple characteristics of the individual.

Person-oriented, or multivariate, methods appear to be gaining support for classification purposes due to: (a) consistency with current theoretical models of psychological systems development (Gottlieb, 2000; Waddington, 1971), (b) the ability to more closely mirror empirical knowledge about symptomatology (van Lier et al., 2003), (c) advancements in test construction and validation (Kamphaus & Frick, 2002), (d) the availability of appropriate statistical techniques (Bergman & Magnusson, 1997), and (e) the potential ease of use due to the resulting categorical classification system (L. A. Clark, Livesley, et al., 1997; L. A. Clark et al., 1995).

Through a critique of the current classification methods, it is apparent that there is not yet a perfect system for classification. Both advantages and disadvantages of psychiatric, dimensional, and person-oriented methods of classification are evident in the literature. Research suggests that certain methods might be superior for classifying certain types of behavior while disadvantageous for other behaviors (Meehl, 1995). In the past, attempts have been made to develop a classification method useful for all psychopathology, against empirical knowledge suggesting the inadequacies of this singular approach. To date, research has not been undertaken with the idea of using separate classification methods for diverse symptomatology and circumstances. Future research programs must involve determining the optimal classification methods for specific circumstances.

With attention to the situations or conditions that could be advantageous to each method, the relative superiority of classification systems should be established through explicit comparisons (Achenbach, 1990). Research is needed to systematically compare methods of classification to discern which methods fit best with empirically supported knowledge of behavior, as well as which methods demonstrate adequate predictive validity, utility, and replicability (Blanchard et al., 2003; Fergusson & Horwood, 1995; Jablensky, 1999; Lessing et al., 1982; Mattison & Spitznagel, 1999). Although van Lier et al. (2003) examined whether patterns of behavior fit with the conceptualization of psychiatric disorders, a direct comparison between person-oriented and psychiatric methods of classification was not made. Specifically, psychiatric diagnoses were not compared to latent classes. Few studies have directly examined the relationship between categorical and dimensional approaches to classification (Arend et al., 1996). Final conclusions about the superiority of various methods of classification for specific circumstances await additional empirical research involving direct comparisons (Nathan & Langenbucher, 1999).

Classification systems that better account for etiology are needed. Evidence suggests that genetic factors make substantial contributions to a variety of mental disorders and etiological research could potentially provide the most convincing evidence for the validity of classification systems (Kendall, 2002). Research into the etiological basis of disorders should be conducted and classification methods that can account for etiology should be utilized.

There is now a corpus of cluster analytically derived knowledge that informs the classification of child behavior and psychopathology. First, the largest group of young children demonstrates optimal behavioral and emotional development, a pattern of development that is more than the mere absence of psychopathology. Well-adapted children, whether identified as such by parents, teachers, or children, possess greater social and related adaptive competencies than their peers. This cluster of children is noteworthy in that children of all races and ethnicity are represented, as well as all levels of socioeconomic status. Longitudinal studies are needed to test the hypothesis that these children are well inoculated against the development of significant behavioral or emotional problems, let alone some form of psychopathology.

There are two or more clusters of children with significant psychopathology, according to several raters, which are not identified consistently or given mental health, special education, or other necessary services. These findings echo those of studies that have classified community samples using the *DSM* (Romer & McIntosh, 2005). Better methods of screening and identifying young children are needed.

Comorbidity is the rule rather than the exception in child psychopathology. Cluster studies show that deviant types of adjustment are characterized by combinations of externalizing and internalizing symptomatology existing concurrently with poorly developed adaptive skills. Person-oriented methods appear ideally suited for classifying this wide range of symptom presentation.

Adaptive skills deficits are significant contributors to child maladjustment. Any comprehensive treatment and prevention efforts must aim to improve these competencies to enhance the development of children. The interplay of adaptive competencies and internalizing and externalizing symptomatology in the promotion of child adjustment is as yet unknown and worthy of further study.

Abela, J. R. Z., & Sullivan, C. (2003). A test of Beck's cognitive diathesis-stress theory of depression in early adolescents. *Journal of Early Adolescence, 23,* 384–404.

Achenbach, T. M. (1990). "Comorbidity" in child and adolescent psychiatry: Categorical and quantitative perspectives. *Journal of Child and Adolescent Psychopharmacology, 14,* 271–278.

Achenbach, T. M. (1991a). *Child Behavior Checklist for ages 4–18.* Burlington: University of Vermont.

Achenbach, T. M. (1991b). *Manual for the Child Behavior Checklist/4–18 and 1991 profile.* Burlington: University of Vermont, Department of Psychiatry.

Achenbach, T. M. (1995). Developmental issues in assessment, taxonomy, and diagnosis of child and adolescent psychopathology. In D. Cicchetti & D. Cohen (Eds.), *Developmental psychopathology: Vol. 2. Risk, disorder, and adaptation* (pp. 715–752). New York: Wiley.

Achenbach, T. M., & Edelbrock, C. S. (1978). The classification of child psychopathology: A review and analysis of empirical efforts. *Psychologial bulletin, 85,* 1275–1301.

Achenbach, T. M., & Edelbrock, C. S. (1979). The Child Behavior Profile: Pt. 2. Boys aged 12–16 and girls aged 6–11 and 12–16. *Journal of Consulting and Clinical Psychology, 47,* 223–233.

Achenbach, T. M., & McConaughy, S. H. (1992). Taxonomy of internalizing disorders of childhood and adolescence. In W. M. Reynolds (Ed.), *Internalizing disorders in children and adolescents* (pp. 19–60). New York: Wiley.

Achenbach, T. M., & Rescorla, L. A. (2001). *Manual for the ASEBA school-age forms and profiles.* Burlington: University of Vermont, Research Center for Children, Youth, and Families.

Adams, G. L. (1999). *Comprehensive Test of Adaptive Behavior* (Rev. ed.). Seattle, WA: Educational Achievement Systems.

Adams, G. R., Cantwell, A. M., & Matheis, S. (2002). Substance use in adolescence. In C. Essau (Ed.), *Substance abuse and dependence in adolescence.* Amsterdam: Harwood Academic.

Albano, A. M., Chorpita, B. F., & Barlow, D. H. (2003). Childhood anxiety disorders. In E. J. Mash & R. A. Barkley (Eds.), *Child psychopathology* (2nd ed., pp. 279–329). New York: Guilford Press.

Aldenderfer, M. S., & Blashfield, R. K. (1984). *Cluster analysis.* Beverly Hills, CA: Sage.

Aman, M. G., & Singh, N. N. (1986). *Manual for the Aberrant Behavior Checklist.* East Aurora, NY: Slosson Educational Publications.

Aman, M. G., & Singh, N. N. (1994). *Supplement to Aberrant Behavior Checklist manual.* East Aurora, NY: Slosson Educational Publications.

Aman, M. G., Singh, N. N., Stewart, A. W., & Field, C. J. (1985). The Aberrant Behavior Checklist: A behavior rating scale for the assessment of treatment effects. *American Journal of Mental Deficiency, 89,* 485–491.

463

Aman, M. G., Tasse, M. J., Rojahn, J., & Hammer, D. (1996). The Nisonger CBRF: A child behavior rating form for children with developmental disabilities. *Research in Developmental Disabilities, 17,* 41–57.

American Academy of Pediatrics. (2000). Clinical practice guideline: Diagnosis and evaluation of the child with attention-deficit/hyperactive disorder. *Pediatrics, 105*(5), 1158–1170.

American Association on Mental Retardation AD Hoc Committee on Terminology and Classification. (2002). *Mental retardation: Definition, classification, and systems of supports* (10th ed.). Washington, DC: American Association on Mental Retardation.

American Educational Research Association, American Psychological Association, & National Council on Measurement in Education. (1999). *Standards for educational and psychological testing.* Washington, DC: American Educational Research Association.

American Psychiatric Association. (1952). *Diagnostic and statistical manual of mental disorders.* Washington, DC: Author.

American Psychiatric Association. (1968). *Diagnostic and statistical manual of mental disorders* (2nd ed.). Washington, DC: Author.

American Psychiatric Association. (1980). *Diagnostic and statistical manual of mental disorders* (3rd ed.). Washington, DC: Author.

American Psychiatric Association. (1987). *Diagnostic and statistical manual of mental disorders* (3rd ed., rev.). Washington, DC: Author.

American Psychiatric Association. (1994). *Diagnostic and statistical manual of mental disorders* (4th ed.). Washington, DC: Author.

American Psychiatric Association. (2000). *Diagnostic and statistical manual of mental disorders* (4th ed., text rev.). Washington, DC: Author.

Anderberg, M. R. (1973). *Clutser analysis for applications.* New York: Academic Press.

Andershed, H., Gustafson, S. B., Kerr, M., & Stattin, H. (2002). The usefulness of self-reported psychopathy-like traits in the study of antisocial behavior among non-referred adolescents. *European Journal of Personality, 16,* 383–402.

Andrews, T. K., Rose, F. D., & Johnson, D. A. (1998). Social and behavioral effects of traumatic brain injury in children. *Brain Injury, 12,* 133–138.

Angello, L. M., Volpe, R. J., DiPerna, J. C., Gureasko-Moore, S. P., Gureasko-Moore, D. P., Nebrig, M. R., et al. (2003). Assessment of attention-deficit/hyperactivity disorder: An evaluation of six published rating scales. *School Psychology Review, 32*(2), 241–262.

Angold, A., & Costello, E. J. (2000). Child and Adolescent Psychiatric Assessment (CAPA). *Journal of the American Academy of Child and Adolescent Psychiatry, 39,* 39–48.

Angold, A., Costello, E. J., & Erkanli, A. (1999). Comorbidity. *Journal of Child Psychology and Psychiatry, 40,* 57–87.

Archer, L. A., Rosenbaum, P. L., & Streiner, D. L. (1991). The children's eating behavior inventory: Reliability and validity results. *Journal of Pediatric Psychology, 16,* 629–642.

Archer, R. P. (1997). *MMPI-A: Assessing adolescent psychopathology.* Mahwah, NJ: Erlbaum.

Archer, R. P., & Krishnamurthy, R. (2002). Essentials of MMPI-A assessment. In A. S. Kaufman & N. L. Kaufman (Series Eds.), *Essentials of psychological assessment series*. Hoboken, NJ: Wiley.

Arend, R., Lavigne, J. V., Rosenbaum, D., Binns, J. J., & Christoffel, K. K. (1996). Relation between taxonomic and quantitative diagnostic systems in preschool children: Emphasis on disruptive disorders. *Journal of Clinical Child Psychology, 25*(4), 388–397.

Arffa, S. (1998). Traumatic brain injury. In C. E. Coffey & R. A. Brumback (Eds.), *Textbook of pediatric neuropsychiatry* (pp. 1093–1140). Washington, DC: American Psychiatric Press.

Asperger, H. (1944). Die "autistischen psychopathen" im kindesalter. *Archiv für Psychiatrie und Nervenkrankheiten, 117*, 76–136.

Astley, S. J., & Clarren, S. K. (2001). Measuring the facial phenotype of individuals with prenatal alcohol exposures: Correlations with brain dysfunction [Electronic version]. *Alcohol and Alcoholism, 36*, 147–159.

Attie, I., & Brooks-Gunn, J. (1989). Development of eating problems in adolescent girls: A longitudinal study. *Developmental Psychology, 25*, 70–79.

Babbitt, R. L., Edlen-Nezin, L., Manikam, R., Summers, J. A., & Murphy, C. M. (1995). Assessment of eating and weight-related problems in children and special populations. In D. B. Allison (Ed.), *Handbook of assessment methods for eating behaviors and weight-related problems: Measures, theory, and research* (pp. 431–492). London: Sage.

Bailey, D. S. (2003). Who is learning disabled? *Monitor on Psychology, 34*, 58–60.

Banasiak, S. J., Wertheim, E. H., Koerner, J., & Voudouris, N. J. (2001). Test-retest reliability and internal consistency of a variety of measures of dietary restraint and body concerns in a sample of adolescent girls. *International Journal of Eating Disorders, 29*, 85–89.

Barkley, R. A. (1991a). Diagnosis and assessment of attention deficit-hyperactivity disorder. *Comprehensive Mental Health Care, 1*, 27–43.

Barkley, R. A. (1991b). The ecological validity of laboratory and analogue assessment methods of ADHD symptoms. *Journal of Abnormal Child Psychology, 19*, 149–178.

Barkley, R. A. (1996). Attention-deficit/hyperactivity disorder. In E. J. Mash & R. A. Barkley, R. A. (Eds.), *Child psychopathology* (pp. 63–112). New York: Guilford Press.

Barkley, R. A. (1997). Attention deficit hyperactivity disorder. In E. J. Mash & L. G. Terdel (Eds.), *Assessment of childhood disorders* (3rd ed., pp. 71–129). New York: Guilford Press.

Barkley, R. A. (1998). *Attention deficit hyperactivity disorder: A handbook for diagnosis and treatments* (2nd ed.). New York: Guilford Press.

Barkley, R. A. (2001). The inattentive type of ADHD as a distinct disorder: What remains to be done. *Clinical Psychology: Science and Practice, 8*(4), 489–493.

Barkley, R. A. (2003a). Attention-deficit/hyperactivity disorder. In E. J. Mash & R. A. Barkley (Eds.), *Child psychopathology* (2nd ed., pp. 75–143). New York: Guilford Press.

Barkley, R. A. (2003b). Issues in the diagnosis of attention-deficit/hyperactivity disorder in children. *Brain and Development, 25*, 77–83.

Barkley, R. A., Fischer, M., Edelbrock, C. S., & Smallish, L. (1990). The adolescent outcome of hyperactive children diagnosed by research criteria: Pt. 1. An 8-year prospective follow-up study. *Journal of American Academy of Child and Adolescent Psychiatry, 29*, 546–557.

Barnhill, G., Hagiwara, T., Myles, B. S., & Simpson, R. L. (2000). Asperger syndrome: A study of the cognitive profiles of 37 children and adolescents. *Focus on Autism and Developmental Disabilities, 15*, 146–453.

Baron-Cohen, S., Allen, C., & Gillberg, C. (1992). Can autism be diagnosed at 18 months? The needle, the haystack, and the CHAT. *British Journal of Psychiatry, 161*, 839–843.

Barrios, B. A., & O'Dell, S. L. (1998). Fears and anxieties. In E. J. Mash & R. A. Barkley (Eds.), *Treatment of childhood disorders* (2nd ed., pp. 249–337). New York: Guilford Press.

Barry, C. T., Frick, P. J., DeShazo, T. M., McCoy, M. G., Ellis, M., & Loney, B. R. (2000). The importance of callous-unemotional traits for extending the concept of psychopathy to children. *Journal of Abnormal Psychology, 109*, 335–340.

Bassarath, L. (2001). Conduct disorder: A biopsychosocial review. *Canadian Journal of Psychiatry, 46*, 609–616.

Bauer, L. O., & Hesselbrock, V. M. (2003). Brain maturation and subtypes of conduct disorder: Interactive effects on P300 amplitude topography in male adolescents. *Journal of the American Academy of Child and Adolescent Psychiatry, 42*, 106–115.

Beauchaine, T. P. (2003). Taxometrics and developmental psychopathology. *Development and Psychopathology, 15*, 501–527.

Beck, A. T., Steer, R. A., & Brown, G. K. (1996). *Beck Depression Inventory-II manual.* San Antonio, TX: Psychological Corporation.

Beck, A. T., & Weishaar, M. E. (1989). Cognitive therapy. In R. J. Corsini & D. Wedding (Eds.), *Current psychotherapies* (4th ed., pp. 285–320). Itasca, IL: Peacock Press.

Beck, J. S., Beck, A. T., & Jolly, J. B. (2001). *Beck youth inventories of social and emotional impairment.* San Antonio, TX: Psychological Corporation.

Beery, K. E., & Beery, N. A. (2004). *The Beery-Buktenica Developmental Test of Visual-Motor Integration: Administration, scoring and teaching manual* (5th ed.). Minneapolis, MN: NCS Pearson.

Belser, R. C., & Sudhalter, V. (2001). Conversational characteristics of children with Fragile X syndrome: Repetitive speech. *American Journal on Mental Retardation, 106*, 28–38.

Bender, L. (1946). *Instructions for the use of the Visual Motor Gestalt Test.* Alexandria, VA: American Orthopsychiatric Association.

Bennett, K. J., Brown, K. S., Boyle, M., Racine, Y., & Offord, D. (2003). Does low reading achievement at school ent

Bennett, K. J., & Offord, D. R. (2001). Screening for conduct problems: Does the predictive accuracy of conduct disorder symptoms improve with age? *Journal of the American Academy of Child and Adolescent Psychiatry, 40*, 1418–1425.

Benz, B., Ritz, A., & Kiesow, S. (1999). Influence of age-related factors on long-term outcome after traumatic brain injury (TBI) in children: A review of recent literature and some preliminary findings. *Restorative Neurology and Neuroscience, 14*, 135–141.

Bergman, L. R. (2000). The application of a person-oriented approach: Types and clusters. In L. R. Bergman, R. B. Cairns, L. G. Nilsson, & L. Nystedt (Eds.), *Developmental science and the holistic approach* (pp. 137–154). Mahwah, NJ: Erlbaum.

Bergman, L. R., & Magnusson, D. (1997). A person-oriented approach in research on developmental psychopathology. *Development and Psychopathology, 9*(2), 291–319.

Berringer, V. A. (2001). Understanding the "lexia" in dyslexia: A multidisciplinary team approach to learning disabilities. *Annals of Dyslexia, 51,* 23–48.

Beutler, L. E., & Malik, M. L. (2002). *Rethinking the* DSM: *A psychological perspective.* Washington, DC: American Psychological Association.

Bieberich, A., & Morgan, S. B. (1998). Affective expression in children with autism or Down syndrome. *Journal of Autism and Developmental Disorders, 28,* 333–338.

Bird, H. R. (1999). The assessment of functional impairment. In D. Shaffer, C. Lucas, & J. Richters (Eds.), *Diagnostic assessment of child and adolescent psychopathology* (pp. 209–229). New York: Guilford Press.

Bishop, D. V. M., & Baird, G. (2001). Parent and teacher report of pragmatic aspects of communication: Use of the Children's Communication Checklist in a clinical setting. *Developmental Medicine and Child Neurology, 43,* 809–818.

Black, M. M. (2003). Failure to thrive. In M. C. Roberts (Ed.), *Handbook of pediatric psychology* (pp. 499–509). New York: Guilford Press.

Blair, R. J. R. (2001). Neurocognitive models of aggression, the antisocial personality disorders, and psychopathy. *Journal of Neurology, Neurosurgery, and Psychiatry, 71,* 727–731.

Blanchard, K. A., Morgenstern, J., Morgan, T. J., Labouvie, E., & Bux, D. A. (2003). Motivational subtypes and continuous measures of readiness for change: Concurrent and predictive validity. *Psychology of Addictive Behaviors, 17*(1), 56–65.

Blashfield, R. K. (1998). Diagnostic models and systems. In A. S. Bellack, M. Hersen, & C. R. Reynolds (Eds.), *Comprehensive clinical psychology: Vol. 4. Assessment.* New York: Elsevier Science.

Blashfield, R. K., & Aldenderfer, M. S. (1988). The methods and problems of cluster analysis. In J. R. Nesselroade & R. B. Cattell (Eds.), *International handbook of multivariate experimental psychology* (2nd ed., pp. 447–473). New York: Plenum Press.

Block, A., & Hartsig, J. C. (2002). What families wish service providers knew. In R. L. Gabriels & D. E. Hill (Eds.), *Autism: From research to individualized practice* (pp. 255–271). Philadelphia: Jessica Kingsley.

Borthwick-Duffy, S. A. (1994). Epidemiology and prevalence of psychopathology in people with mental retardation. *Journal of Consulting and Clinical Psychology, 62,* 17–27.

Borthwick-Duffy, S. A., Lane, K. L., & Widaman, K. F. (1997). Measuring problem behaviors in children with mental retardation: Dimensions and predictors. *Research in Developmental Disabilities, 18,* 415–433.

Bose-Deakins, J. E., & Floyd, R. G. (2004). A review of the Beck Youth Inventories of Emotional and Social Impairment. *Journal of School Psychology, 42,* 333–340.

Bower, E. M. (1968). *Early identification of emotionally handicapped children in school.* Springfield, IL: Charles C. Thomas.

Boyajian, A. E., DuPaul, G. J., Handler, M. W., Eckert, T. L., & McGoey, K. E. (2001). The use of classroom-based brief functional analysis with preschoolers at risk for attention deficit hyperactivity disorder. *School Psychology Review, 30,* 278–293.

Brent, D. A. (1997). Practitioner review: The aftercare of adolescents with deliberate self-harm. *Journal of Child Psychology and Psychiatry and Allied Disciplines, 38,* 277–286.

Brent, D. A., Kolko, D. J., Birhamer, B., Baugher, M., Bridge, J., Roth, C., et al. (1998). Predictors of treatment efficacy in a clinical trial of three psychosocial treatments for adolescent depression. *Journal of the American Academy of Child and Adolescent Psychiatry, 37,* 906–914.

Brock, S. E. (1997). *Diagnosis of Attention-Deficit/Hyperactivity Disorder (ADHD) in childhood: A review of the literature.* Anaheim, CA: National Association of School Psychologist (ERIC Document Reproduction Service No. ED 410 512)

Brogan, C. A., & Knussen, C. (2003). The disclosure of a diagnosis of an autism spectrum disorder: Determinants of satisfaction in a sample of Scottish parents. *Autism, 7,* 31–46.

Brown, E. C., Aman, M. G., & Havercamp, S. M. (2002). Factor analysis and norms for parent ratings on the Aberrant Behavior Checklist-Community for young people in special education. *Research in Developmental Disabilities, 23,* 45–60.

Brown, S. A., Aarons, G. A., & Abrantes, A. M. (2001). Adolescent alcohol and drug abuse. In C. E. Walker & M. C. Roberts (Eds.), *Handbook of child clinical psychology* (3rd ed., pp. 757–775). New York: Wiley.

Bruininks, R. H., Thurlow, M., & Gilman, C. J. (1987). Adaptive behavior and mental retardation. *Journal of Special Education, 21,* 69–88.

Bruininks, R. H., Woodcock, R. W., Weatherman, R. F., & Hill, B. K. (1996). *Scales of Independent Behavior* (Rev. ed.). Chicago: Riverside.

Bryant, K. J., Rounsaville, B. J., & Babor, T. F. (1991). Coherence of the dependence syndrome in cocaine users. *British Journal of Addiction, 86,* 1299–1310.

Bryant-Waugh, R., & Kaminski, Z. (1993). Eating disorders in children: An overview. In B. Lask & R. Bryant-Waugh (Eds.), *Childhood onset anorexia nervosa and related eating disorders* (pp. 17–29). Hove, England: Erlbaum.

Bryant-Waugh, R., & Lask, B. (1999). *Eating disorders—A parent's guide.* Hammondsworth, England: Penguin Classics.

Bryant-Waugh, R. J., Cooper, P. J., Taylor, C. L., & Lask, B. D. (1996). The use of the Eating Disorder Examination with children: A pilot study. *International Journal of Eating Disorders, 19,* 391–397.

Bukstein, O. G. (1995). *Adolescent substance abuse: Assessment, prevention, and treatment.* New York: Wiley.

Burke, J. D., Loeber, R., & Birmaher, B. (2002). Oppositional defiant disorder and conduct disorder: Pt. 2. A review of the past 10 years. *Journal of the American Academy of Child and Adolescent Psychiatry, 41.*

Burke, J. D., Loeber, R., Mutchka, J. S., & Lahey, B. B. (2002). A question for *DSM-V:* Which better predicts persistent conduct disorder—Delinquent acts or conduct symptoms? *Criminal Behavior and Mental Health, 12,* 37–52.

Burton, T. M. (2001). Prescription drug use varies widely from state to state. *Wall Street Journal,* p. B4.

Butcher, J. N., Williams, C. L., Graham, J. R., Archer, R. P., Tellegen, A., Ben-Porath, Y. S., et al. (1992). *Minnesota Multiphasic Personality Inventory—Adolescent (MMPI-A) manual for scoring, administration, and interpretation.* Minneapolis: University of Minnesota Press.

Byely, L., Archibald, A. B., Graber, J., & Brooks-Gunn, J. (2000). A prospective study of familial and social influences on girls' body image and dieting. *International Journal of Eating Disorders, 28,* 155–164.

Campbell, J. M. (2003). Efficacy of behavioral interventions for reducing problem behavior in persons with autism: A quantitative synthesis of single-subject research. *Research in Developmental Disabilities, 24,* 120–138.

Campbell, J. M. (2005). Diagnostic assessment of Asperger's disorder: A review of five third-party rating scales. *Journal of Autism and Developmental Disorders, 35,* 25–35.

Campbell, J. M., & Morgan, S. B. (1998). Asperger's disorder. In L. Phelps (Ed.), *Health-related disorders in children and adolescents* (pp. 68–73). Washington, DC: American Psychological Association.

Campbell, S. B. (1990). *Behavior problems in preschoolers: Clinical and developmental issues.* New York: Guilford Press.

Cantwell, D. P. (1996). Classification of child and adolescent psychopathology. *Journal of Child Psychology and Psychiatry, 37,* 3–12.

Caron, C., & Rutter, M. (1991). Comorbidity in child psychopathology: Concepts, issues, and research strategies. *Journal of Child Psychology and Psychiatry and Allied Disciplines, 32,* 1063–1080.

Carpentieri, S. C., & Morgan, S. B. (1994). Brief report: A comparison of patterns of cognitive functioning of autistic and nonautistic retarded children on the Stanford-Binet (4th ed.). *Journal of Autism and Developmental Disorders, 24,* 215–223.

Carpentieri, S. C., & Morgan, S. B. (1996). Adaptive and intellectual functioning in autistic and non-autistic retarded children. *Journal of Autism and Developmental Disorders, 26,* 611–620.

Carroll, J. B. (1993). *Human cognitive abilities: A survey of factor-analytic studies.* New York: Cambridge University Press.

Carrow-Woolfolk, E. (1995). *Oral and Written Language Scales, Listening Comprehension, and Oral Expression Scales.* Circle Pines, MN: American Guidance Service.

Carter, A. S., Volkmar, F. R., Sparrow, S. S., Wang, J., Lord, C., Dawson, G., et al. (1998). The Vineland Adaptive Behavior Scales: Supplementary norms for individuals with autism. *Journal of Autism and Developmental Disorders, 28,* 287–302.

Carter, J. C., Stewart, D. A., & Fairburn, C. G. (2001). Eating disorder examination questionnaire: Norms for young adolescent girls. *Behavior Research and Therapy, 39,* 625–632.

Caruso, J. C. (2001). [Review of the Multidimensional Anxiety Scale for Children]. In B. S. Plake & J. C. Impara (Eds.), *Mental measurements yearbook* (14th ed., pp. 800–801). Lincoln, NE: Buros Institute of Mental Measurements.

Caspi, A., & Silva, P. S. (1995). Temperamental qualities at age three predict personality traits in young adulthood: Longitudinal evidence from a birth cohort. *Child Development, 66,* 486–498.

Center for Substance Abuse Treatment. (2003). *Screening and assessing adolescents for substance use disorders* (Treatment Improvement Protocol [TIP] Series 31). Rockville, MD: Substance Abuse Mental Health Services Administration.

Chapman, R. S., & Hesketh, L. J. (2000). Behavioral phenotype of individuals with Down syndrome. *Mental Retardation and Developmental Disabilities Research Reviews, 6,* 84–95.

Chassin, L., Pitts, S., DeLucia, C., & Todd, M. (1999). A longitudinal study of children of alcoholics: Predicting young adult substance use disorders, anxiety, and depression. *Journal of Abnormal Psychology, 108,* 106–119.

Chassin, L., Ritter, J., Trim, R. S., & King, K. M. (2003). Adolescent substance use disorders. In E. J. Mash & R. A. Barkley (Eds.), *Child Psychopathology* (2nd ed., pp. 199–230). New York: Guilford Press.

Chorpita, B. F., Albano, A. M., & Barlow, D. H. (1998). The structure of negative emotions in a clinical sample of children and adolescents. *Journal of Abnormal Psychology, 107,* 74–85.

Chorpita, B. F., Plummer, C. M., & Moffitt, C. E. (2000). Relations of tripartite dimensions of emotion childhood anxiety and mood disorders. *Journal of Abnormal Child Psychology, 29*(3), 299–310.

Clark, D. B., Lesnick, L., & Hegedus, A. M. (1997). Traumas and other adverse life events in adolescents with alcohol abuse and dependence. *Journal of the American Academy of Child and Adolescent Psychiatry, 36,* 1744–1751.

Clark, E., Russman, S., & Orme, S. (1999). Traumatic brain injury: Effects on school functioning and intervention. *School Psychology Review, 28,* 242–250.

Clark, L. A., Livesley, W. J., & Morey, L. (1997). Special feature: Personality disorder assessment—The challenge of construct validity. *Journal of Personality Assessment, 1,* 1205–1231.

Clark, L. A., & Watson, D. (1991). Tripartite model of depression: Psychometric evidence and taxonomic implications. *Journal of Abnormal Psychology, 100,* 316–336.

Clark, L. A., Watson, D., & Reynolds, W. S. (1995). Diagnosis and classification of psychopathology: Challenges to the current system and future directions. *Annual Review of Psychology, 46,* 121.

Cohen, M. J. (1997). *Children's Memory Scale manual.* San Antonio, TX: Psychological Corporation.

Cohen, M. J., Prather, A., Town, P., & Hynd, G. (1990). Neurodevelopmental differences in emotional prosody in normal children and children with left and right temporal lobe epilepsy. *Brain and Language, 38,* 122–134.

Cohen, M. J., Riccio, C., Kibby, M., & Edmonds, J. (2000). Developmental progression of clock face drawing in children. *Child Neuropsychology, 6,* 64–76.

Coie, J. D., & Miller-Johnson, S. (2001). Peer factors and interventions. In R. Loeber & D. P. Farrington (Eds.), *Child delinquents* (pp. 191–209). Thousand Oaks, CA: Sage.

Cole, D. A., Hoffman, K., Tram, J. M., & Maxwell, S. E. (2000). Structural differences in parent and child reports of children's symptoms of depression and anxiety. *Psychological Assessment, 12,* 174–185.

Collett, B. R., Ohan, J. L., & Myers, K. M. (2003). Ten-year review of rating scales VI: Scales assessing externalizing behaviors. *Journal of the American Academy of Child and Adolescent Psychiatry, 42,* 1143–1170.

Conners, C. K. (1995). *Conners' Continuous Performance Test.* Toronto, Ontario, Canada: Multi-Health Systems.

Conners, C. K. (1997). *Conners' Rating Scales—Revised Technical Manual.* North Tonawanda, NY: Multi-Health Systems.

Conners, C. K., & Multi-Health Systems Staff. (2000). *Conners' Continuous Performance Test II: Computer program for windows technical guide and software manual.* Toronto, Ontario, Canada: Multi-Health Systems.

Connor, D. F. (2002). *Aggression and antisocial behavior in children and adolescents: Research and treatment.* New York: Guilford Press.

Cooke, D. J., & Michie, C. (2001). Refining the construct of psychopathy: Towards a hierarchical model. *Psychological Assessment, 13,* 171–188.

Costello, E. J., Egger, H., & Angold, A. (2005). Ten-year research update review: I. The epidemiology of child and adolescent psychiatric disorders: Methods and public health burden. *Journal of the American Academy of Child and Adolescent Psychiatry, 44,* 972–986.

Cottler, L. B., Schuckit, M. A., Helzer, J. E., Crowley, T., Woody, G., Nathan, P., et al. (1995). The *DSM-IV* field trial for substance use disorders: Major results. *Drug and Alcohol Dependence, 38,* 59–69.

Courchesne, E. (1995). Infantile autism: Pt. 1. MR imaging abnormalities and their neurobehavioral correlates. *International Pediatrics, 10,* 141–154.

Craske, M. G., & Barlow, D. H. (1993). Panic disorder and agoraphobia. In D. H. Barlow (Ed.), *Clinical handbook of psychological disorders* (2nd ed., pp. 1–47). New York: Guilford Press.

Crick, N., & Dodge, K. A. (1994). A review and reformulation of social information-processing mechanisms in children's social adjustment. *Psychological Bulletin, 115,* 74–101.

Crijnen, A. A. M., Achenbach, T. M., & Verhulst, F. C. (1999). Problems reported by parents of children in multiple cultures: The Child Behavior Checklist syndrome constructs. *American Journal of Psychiatry, 156*(4), 569–574.

Crowley, T. J., Mikulich, S. K., Ehlers, K. M., Whitmore, E. A., & MacDonald, M. J. (2001). Validity of structured clinical evaluations in adolescents with conduct and substance problems. *Journal of the American Academy of Child and Adolescent Psychiatry, 40*(3), 265.

Crowley, T. J., & Riggs, P. D. (1995). Adolescent substance use disorder with conduct disorder and comorbid conditions. *NIDA Research Monograph, 156,* 49–111.

Cullum, C. M., Kuck, J., & Ruff, R. M. (1990). Neuropsychological assessment of traumatic brain injury in adults. In E. D. Bigler (Ed.), *Traumatic brain injury: Mechanisms of damage, assessment, intervention, and outcome* (pp. 129–163). Austin, TX: ProEd.

Cumella, E. J., Wall, A. D., & Kerr-Almeida, N. (1999). MMPI-A in the inpatient assessment of adolescents with eating disorders. *Journal of Personality Assessment, 73,* 31–44.

Currin, L., Schmidt, U., Treasure, J., & Jick, H. (2005). Time trends in eating disorder incidence. *British Journal of Psychiatry, 186,* 132–135.

Curry, J. F., & Thompson, R. J. (1985). Patterns of behavioral disturbance in developmentally disabled and categorically referred children: A cluster analytic approach. *Journal of Pediatric Psychology, 10,* 151–167.

Dalla-Dea, H. R. F., De Micheli, D., & Souza Formigoni, M. L. O. (2003). Effects of identification and usefulness of the lie scale of the drug use screening inventory (DUSI-R) in the assessment of adolescent drug use. *Drug and Alcohol Dependence, 72,* 215–223.

Das, J. P. (2004). Theories of intelligence: Issues and applications. In M. Hersen (Editor-in-Chief) & G. Goldstein & S. R. Beers (Vol. Eds.), *Comprehensive handbook of psychological assessment: Vol. 1. Intellectual and neuropsychological assessment* (pp. 5–23). Hoboken, NJ: Wiley.

Das, J. P., Naglieri, J. A., & Kirby, J. R. (1994). *Assessment of cognitive processes: The PASS theory of intelligence.* Boston: Allyn & Bacon.

Dawes, R. M., Faust, D., & Meehl, P. E. (1989). Clinical versus actuarial judgment. *Science, 243*(4899), 1668–1674.

Deater-Deckard, K., Reiss, D., Hetherington, E. M., & Plomin, R. (1997). Dimensions and disorders of adolescent adjustment: A quantitative genetic analysis of unselected samples and selected extremes. *Journal of Child Psychology and Psychiatry, 38*(5), 515–525.

Dekker, M. C., Nunn, R. J., Einfeld, S., Tonge, B. J., & Koot, H. M. (2002). Assessing emotional and behavioral problems in children with intellectual disability: Revisiting the factor structure of the Developmental Behavior Checklist. *Journal of Autism and Developmental Disorders, 32,* 601–610.

Demaray, M. K., Elting, J., & Schaefer, K. (2003). Assessment of attention-deficit hyperactivity disorder (ADHD): A comparative evaluation of five, commonly used, published rating scales. *Psychology in the Schools, 40*(4), 341–361.

Demellweek, C., Baldwin, T., Appleton, R., & Al-Kharusi, A. (2002). A prospective study and review of pre-morbid characteristics in children with traumatic brain injury. *Pediatric Rehabilitation, 5,* 81–89.

DeMyer, M. K., Barton, S., DeMyer, W. E., Morton, J. A., Allen, J., & Steele, R. (1973). Prognosis in autism: A follow-up study. *Journal of Autism and Childhood Schizophrenia, 5,* 109–128.

Dinwiddie, S. H., & Cloninger, C. R. (1991). Family and adoption studies in alcoholism and drug addiction. *Psychiatric Annals, 21,* 206–229.

Disney, E. R., Elkins, I. J., McGue, M., & Iacono, W. G. (1999). Effects of ADHD, conduct disorder, and gender on substance use and abuse in adolescence. *American Journal of Psychiatry, 156*(10), 1515–1521.

DiStefano, C., Kamphaus, R. W., Horne, A. M., & Winsor, A. P. (2003). Behavioral adjustment in the U.S. elementary school: Cross-validation of a person-oriented typology of risk. *Journal of Psychoeducational Assessment, 21,* 338–357.

Dodge, K. A., & Pettit, G. S. (2003). A biopsychosocial model of the development of chronic conduct problems in adolescence. *Developmental Psychology, 39,* 349–371.

Dombrowski, S. C., Kamphaus, R. W., & Reynolds, C. R. (2004). After the demise of the discrepancy: Proposed learning disability diagnostic criteria. *Professional Psychology: Research and Practice, 35,* 364–372.

Doyle, A., Ostrander, R., Skare, S., Crosby, R. D., & August, G. J. (1997). Convergent and criterion-related validity of the Behavior Assessment System for Children—Parent Rating Scale. *Journal of Clinical Child Psychology, 26,* 276–284.

Dunn, L. M., & Dunn, L. M. (1997). *Peabody Picture Vocabulary Test* (3rd ed.). Circle Pines, MN: American Guidance Service.

DuPaul, G. J., & Ervin, R. A. (1996). Functional assessment of behaviors related to attention-deficit/hyperactivity disorder: Linking assessment to intervention design. *Behavior Therapy, 27,* 601–622.

DuPaul, G. J., Power, T. J., McGoey, K. E., Ikeda, M. J., & Anastopoulos, A. D. (1998). Reliability and validity of parent and teacher ratings of attention-deficit/hyperactivity disorder symptoms. *Journal of Psychoeducational Assessment, 16,* 55–68.

DuPaul, G. J., & Stoner, G. (1994). *ADHD in the schools: Assessment and intervention strategies.* New York: Guilford Press.

Dykens, E. M. (2000). Annotation: Psychopathology in children with intellectual disability. *Journal of Child Psychology and Psychiatry and Allied Disciplines, 41,* 407–417.

Dykens, E. M., & Hodapp, R. M. (2001). Research in mental retardation: Toward an etiological approach. *Journal of Child Psychology and Psychiatry and Allied Disciplines, 42,* 49–71.

Edelbrock, C., & Achenbach, T. M. (1980). A typology of child behavior profile patterns: Distribution and correlates for disturbed children aged 6–16. *Journal of Abnormal Child Psychology, 8,* 441–470.

Edelbrock, C. S. (1985). Child behavior rating form. *Psychopharmacology Bulletin, 21,* 835–837.

Edwards, G., & Gross, M. (1976). Alcohol dependence: Provisional description of a clinical syndrome. *British Medical Journal, 1,* 1058–1061.

Ehlers, S., Gillberg, C., & Wing, L. (1999). A screening questionnaire for Asperger syndrome and other high-functioning autism spectrum disorders in school age children. *Journal of Autism and Developmental Disorders, 29,* 129–141.

Ehlers, S., Nyden, A., Gillberg, C., Sandberg, A. D., Dahlgren, S., Hjelmquist, E., et al. (1997). Asperger syndrome, autism, and attention deficit disorders: A comparative study of cognitive profiles of 120 children. *Journal of Child Psychology and Psychiatry and Allied Disciplines, 38,* 207–217.

Einfeld, S. L., & Tonge, B. J. (1995). The Developmental Behavior Checklist: The development and evaluation of an instrument for the assessment of behavioral and emotional disturbance in children and adolescents with mental retardation. *Journal of Autism and Developmental Disorders, 25,* 81–104.

Embregts, P. J. C. M. (2000). Reliability of the Child Behavior Checklist for the assessment of behavioral problems of children and youth with mild mental retardation. *Research in Developmental Disabilities, 21,* 31–41.

Emerson, E., Kiernan, C., Alborz, A., Reeves, D., Mason, H., Swarbrick, R., et al. (2001). The prevalence of challenging behaviors: A total population study. *Research in Developmental Disabilities, 22,* 77–93.

Engelsen, J. K., & Hagtvet, K. A. (1999). The dimensionality of the 12-item version of the Eating Attitudes Test: Confirmatory factor analyses. *Scandinavian Journal of Psychology, 40,* 293–300.

Essau, C. A. (Ed.). (2002). *Substance abuse and dependence in adolescence.* New York: Taylor & Francis.

Ewing-Cobbs, L., & Bloom, D. R. (1999). Traumatic brain injury. In R. T. Brown (Ed.), *Cognitive aspects of chronic illness in children* (pp. 262–289). New York: Guilford Press.

Ewing-Cobbs, L., & Bloom, D. R. (2004). Traumatic brain injury: Neuropsychological, psychiatric, and educational issues. In R. T. Brown (Ed.), *Handbook of pediatric psychology in school settings* (pp. 313–331). Mahwah, NJ: Erlbaum.

Fairburn, C. G., & Beglin, S. J. (1994). Assessment of eating disorders: Interview or self-report questionnaire? *International Journal of Eating Disorders, 16,* 363–370.

Fairburn, C. G., & Cooper, Z. (1993). The eating disorder examination (12th ed.). In C. G. Fairburn & G. T. Wilson (Eds.), *Binge eating: Nature, assessment, and treatment* (pp. 317–360). New York: Guilford Press.

Fairburn, C. G., & Harrison, P. J. (2003). Eating disorders. *Lancet, 361,* 407–416.

Falkenbach, D. M., Poythress, N. G., & Heide, K. M. (2003). Psychopathic features in a juvenile diversion population: Reliability and predictive validity of two self-report measures. *Behavioral Sciences and the Law, 21,* 787–805.

Farmer, J. E., Clippard, D. S., Luehr-Wiemann, Y., Wright, E., & Owings, S. (1996). Assessing children with traumatic brain injury during rehabilitation: Promoting school and community reentry. *Journal of Learning Disabilities, 29,* 532–548.

Farrell, A. D. (1993). Risk factors for drug use in urban adolescents: A three-wave longitudinal study. *Journal of Drug Issues, 23,* 443–462.

Farrell, A. D., Danish, S. J., & Howard, C. W. (1992). Risk factors for drug use in urban adolescents: Identification and cross validation. *American Journal of Community Psychology, 20,* 236–286.

Federal Register. (1999, March 12). *Assistance to states for the education of children with disabilities and the Early Intervention Program for infants and toddlers with disabilities* (Final Regulations, 34 CFR Parts 300 and 303).

Fergusson, D. M., & Horwood, J. (1995). Predictive validity of categorically and dimensionally scored measures of disruptive childhood behaviors. *Journal of the American Academy of Child and Adolescent Psychiatry, 34,* 477–487.

Filipek, P. A., Accardo, P. J., Ashwal, S., Baranek, G. T., Cook, E. H., Dawson, G., et al. (2000). Practice parameter: Screening and diagnosis of autism. *Neurology, 55,* 468–479.

Flanagan, K. S., Bierman, K. L., & Kam, C. M. (2003). Identifying at-risk children at school entry: The usefulness of multibehavioral problem profiles. *Journal of Clinical Child and Adolescent Psychology, 32,* 396–407.

Fletcher, J. M. (1985). External validation of learning disability typologies. In B. P. Rourke (Ed.), *Neuropsychology of learning disabilities: Essentials of subtype analysis* (pp. 187–211). New York: Guilford Press.

Fletcher, J. M., Francis, D. J., Rourke, B. P., Shaywitz, S. E., & Shaywitz, B. A. (1992). The validity of discrepancy-based definitions of reading disabilities. *Journal of Learning Disabilities, 25,* 555–561.

Fletcher, J. M., Lyon, G. R., Barnes, M., Stuebing, K. K., Francis, D. J., Olson, R. K., et al. (2002). Classification of learning disabilities: An evidence based evaluation. In R. Bradley, L. Danielson, & D. Hallahan (Eds.), *Identification of learning disabilities: Research to practice* (pp. 185–250). Mahwah, NJ: Erlbaum.

Flint, J., & Wilkie, A. O. M. (1996). The genetics of mental retardation. *British Medical Bulletin, 52,* 453–464.

Floyd, R. G., & Bose, J. E. (2003). Behavior rating scales for assessment of emotional disturbance: A critical review of measurement characteristics. *Journal of Psychoeducational Assessment, 21,* 43–78.

Foa, E. B., Costello, E. J., Franklin, M., Kagan, J., Kendall, P., Klein, R., et al. (2005). Part III: Anxiety disorders. In D. L. Evans, E. B. Foa, R. E. Gur, H. Hendin, C. P. O'Brien, M. E. P., Seligman, et al. (Eds.), *Treating and preventing adolescent mental health disorders* (pp. 162–253). New York: Oxford University Press.

Ford, T., Goodman, R., & Meltzer, H. (2003). The British Child and Adolescent Mental Health Survey 1999: The prevalence of *DSM-IV* disorders. *Journal of the American Academy of Child and Adolescent Psychiatry, 42,* 1203–1211.

Franko, D. L., Striegel-Moore, R. H., Barton, B. A., Schumann, B. C., Garner, D. M., Daniels, S. R., et al. (2004). Measuring eating concerns in Black and White adolescent girls. *International Journal of Eating Disorders, 35,* 179–189.

Frauenglass, S., & Routh, D. K. (1999). Assessment of the disruptive behavior disorder: Dimensional and categorical approaches. In H. C. Quay & A. E. Hogan (Eds.), *Handbook of disruptive behavior disorders* (pp. 49–74). New York: Kluwer/Plenum Press.

Freund, L. S., & Reiss, A. L. (1991). Rating problem behaviors in outpatients with mental retardation: Use of the Aberrant Behavior Checklist. *Research in Developmental Disabilities, 12,* 435–451.

Frick, P. J., Bodin, S. D., & Barry, C. T. (2000). Psychopathic traits and conduct problems in community and clinic-referred samples of children: Further development of the Psychopathy Screening Device. *Psychological Assessment, 12,* 382–393.

Frick, P. J., & Hare, R. D. (2001). *The Antisocial Process Screening Device.* Toronto, Ontario, Canada: Multi-Health Systems.

Gardner, H. (1993). *Multiple intelligences: The theory in practice.* New York: Basic Books.

Gardner, R. M. (2001). Assessment of body image disturbance. In J. K. Thompson & L. Smolak (Eds.), *Body image, eating disorders, and obesity in youth: Assessment, prevention, and treatment* (pp. 193–213). Washington, DC: American Psychological Association.

Garfinkel, B. D., & Golombek, H. (1983). Suicidal behavior in adolescence. In B. D. Garfinkel & G. H. Golombek (Eds.), *The adolescent and mood disturbance* (pp. 189–217). New York: International Unversities Press.

Garner, D. M. (1991). *Eating Disorder Inventory-2 manual.* Odessa, FL: Psychological Assessment Resources.

Garner, D. M., & Barry, D. (2001). Treatment of eating disorders in adolescents. In C. E. Walker & M. C. Roberts (Eds.), *Handbook of clinical child psychology* (pp. 692–713). New York: Wiley.

Garner, D. M., & Garfinkel, P. E. (1979). The Eating Attitudes Test: An index of the symptoms of anorexia nervosa. *Psychological Medicine, 9,* 273–279.

Garner, D. M., Olmsted, M. P., Bohr, Y., & Garfinkel, P. E. (1982). The Eating Attitudes Test: Psychometric features and clinical correlates. *Psychological Medicine, 12,* 871–878.

Gdowski, C. L., Lachar, D., & Kline, R. B. (1985). A PIC profile typology of children and adolescents: Empiricially derived alternative to traditional diagnosis. *Journal of Abnormal Psychology, 94,* 346–361.

Geist, R., Davis, R., & Heinmaa, M. (1998). Binge/purge symptoms and comorbidity in adolescents with eating disorders. *Canadian Journal of Psychiatry, 43,* 507–512.

Giancola, P. R., & Tarter, R. E. (1999). What constitutes a substance of abuse? In R. T. Ammerman, P. J. Ott, & R. E. Tarter (Eds.), *Prevention and societal impact of drug and alcohol abuse* (pp. 21–28). Mahwah, NJ: Erlbaum.

Gil, A. M. (2003). Neurocognitive outcomes following pediatric brain injury: A developmental approach. *Journal of School Psychology, 41,* 337–353.

Gillberg, C., & Billstedt, E. (2000). Autism and Asperger syndrome: Coexistence with other clinical disorders. *Acta Psychiatrica Scandinavica, 102,* 321–330.

Gillham, J. E., Carter, A. S., Volkmar, F. R., & Sparrow, S. S. (2000). Toward a developmental operational definition of autism. *Journal of Autism and Developmental Disorders, 30,* 269–278.

Gilliam, J. E. (1995). *Gilliam Autism Rating Scale.* Austin, TX: ProEd.

Gilliam, J. E. (2001). *Gilliam Asperger's Disorder Scale.* Austin, TX: ProEd.

Gioia, G., Isquith, P., Guy, S., & Kenworthy, L. (2000). *Behavior rating inventory of executive function.* Odessa, FL: Psychological Assessment Resources.

Gladstone, T. R. G., & Kaslow, N. J. (1995). Depression and attributions in children and adolescents: A meta-analytic review. *Journal of Abnormal Child Psychology, 23,* 597–606.

Gladstone, T. R. G., Kaslow, N. J., Seeley, J. R., & Lewinsohn, P. M. (1997). Sex differences, attributional style, and depressive symptoms among adolescents. *Journal of Abnormal Child Psychology, 25,* 297–306.

Glantz, M. D., Weinberg, N. Z., Miner, L. L., & Colliver, J. D. (1999). The etiology of drug abuse: Mapping the paths. In M. D. Glantz & C. R. Hartel (Eds.), *Drug abuse: Origins and interventions* (pp. 3–45). Washington, DC: American Psychological Association.

Glenn, M. B. (2002). A differential diagnostic approach to the pharmacological treatment of cognitive, behavioral, and affective disorders after traumatic brain injury. *Journal of Head Trauma Rehabilitation, 17,* 273–283.

Goldstein, S., & Goldstein, M. (1990). *Managing attention disorders in children: A guide for practitioners.* New York: Wiley.

Gordon, M. (1983). *The Gordon Diagnostic System.* DeWitt, NY: Gordon Systems.

Gordon, M., Lewandowski, L., & Keiser, S. (1999). The LD label for relatively well-functioning students: A critical analysis. *Journal of Learning Disabilities, 32,* 485–490.

Gottlieb, G. (2000). Understanding genetic activity within a holistic framework. In L. R. Bergman, R. B. Cairns, L. G. Nilsson, & L. Nested (Eds.), *Developmental science and the holistic approach* (pp. 180–201). Mahwah, NJ: Erlbaum.

Gowers, S., & Bryant-Waugh, R. (2004). Management of child and adolescent eating disorders: The current evidence base and future directions. *Journal of Child Psychology and Psychiatry, 45,* 63–83.

Grant, B. F., & Dawson, D. (1997). Age of onset of alcohol use and its association with *DSM-IV* alcohol abuse and dependence: Results from the national longitudinal alcohol epidemiological survey. *Journal of Substance Abuse, 9,* 103–110.

Greenberg, L. (1996). *Test of variables of attention.* Los Alamitos, CA: Universal Attention Disorders.

Greenberg, M. T., Speltz, M. L., DeKlyen, M., & Jones, K. (2001). Correlates of clinic referral for early conduct problems: Variable- and person-oriented approaches. *Development and Psychopathology, 13,* 255–276.

Greenspan, S. (1981). Defining childhood social competence: A proposed working model. In B. K. Keogh (Ed.), *Advances in special education* (Vol. 3, pp. 1–39). Greenwich, CT: JAI Press.

Greenspan, S. (1999). A contextualist perspective on adaptive behavior. In R. L. Schalock (Ed.), *Adaptive behavior and its measurement: Implications for the field of mental retardation* (pp. 61–80). Washington, DC: American Association on Mental Retardation.

Grogan, S. (1999). *Body image: Understanding body dissatisfaction in men, women, and children.* London: Routledge.

Grossman, H. J. (Ed.). (1983). *Classification in mental retardation* (Rev. ed.). Washington, DC: American Association on Mental Deficiency.

Grove, W. M., & Meehl, P. E. (1996). Comparative efficiency of informal (subjective, impressionistic) and formal (mechanical, algorithmic) prediction procedures: The clinical-statistical controversy. *Psychology, Public Policy, and Law, 2,* 293–323.

Gumbiner, J. (2003). *Adolescent assessment.* Hoboken, NJ: Wiley.

Haapasalo, J., Tremblay, R. E., Boulerice, B., & Vitaro, F. (2000). Relative advantages of person- and variable-based approaches for predicting problem behaviors from kindergarten assessments. *Journal of Quantitative Criminology, 16*(2), 145–168.

Hagen, C., Malkmus, D., & Durham, P. (1981). *Rancho Los Amigos: Levels of cognitive functioning.* Downey, CA: Professional Staff Association of Rancho Los Amigos Hospital.

Hagerman, R. J. (1999). Psychopharmacological interventions in fragile X syndrome, fetal alcohol syndrome, Prader-Willi syndrome, Angelman syndrome, Smith-Magenis syndrome, and velocariofacial syndrome. *Mental Retardation and Developmental Disabilities Research Reviews, 5,* 305–313.

Halperin, J. M., McKay, K. E., Grayson, R. H., & Newcorn, J. H. (2003). Reliability, validity, and preliminary normative data for the Children's Aggression Scale—Teacher Version. *Journal of the American Academy of Child and Adolescent Psychiatry, 42,* 965–971.

Halperin, J. M., McKay, K. E., & Newcorn, J. H. (2002). Development, reliability, and validity of the Children's Aggression Scale—Parent Version. *Journal of the American Academy of Child and Adolescent Psychiatry, 41,* 245–252.

Halperin, J. M., Newcorn, J. H., Koda, V. H., Pick, L., McKay, K. E., & Knott, P. (1997). Noradrenergic mechanisms in ADHD children with and without reading disabilities: A replication and extension. *Journal of the American Academy of Child and Adolescent Psychiatry, 36*(12), 1688–1697.

Halperin, J. M., Newcorn, J. H., Schwartz, S. T., McKay, K. E., Bedi, G., & Sharma, V. (1993). Plasma catecholamine metabolite levels in ADHD boys with and without reading disabilities. *Journal of Clinical Child Psychology, 22,* 219–225.

Hammen, C., & Rudolph, K. D. (1996). Childhood depression. In E. J. Mash & R. A. Barkley (Eds.), *Child psychopathology* (pp. 153–195). New York: Guilford Press.

Hammen, C., & Rudolph, K. D. (2003). Childhood mood disorders. In E. J. Mash & R. A. Barkley (Eds.), *Child psychopathology* (2nd ed., pp. 233–278). New York: Guilford Press.

Harrison, P. A., Fulkerson, J. A., & Beebe, T. J. (1998). *DSM-IV* substance use disorder criteria for adolescents: A critical examination based on a statewide school survey. *American Journal of Psychiatry, 155*(4), 486–492.

Hart, E. L., & Lahey, B. B. (1999). General child behavior rating scales. In D. Shaffer & C. P. Lucas (Eds.), *Diagnostic assessment in child and adolescent psychopathology* (pp. 65–87). New York: Guilford Press.

Hartigan, J. A. (1975). *Clustering algorithms.* New York: Wiley.

Hasin, D., Grant, B. F., Cottler, L., Blain, J., Towle, L., Ustun, B., et al. (1997). Nosological comparisons of alcohol and drug diagnoses: A multisite, multi-instrument international study. *Drug and Alcohol Dependence, 47,* 217–266.

Hastings, R. P., Brown, T., Mount, R. H., & Cormack, K. F. M. (2001). Exploration of psychometric properties of the Developmental Behavior Checklist. *Journal of Autism and Developmental Disorders, 31,* 423–431.

Hawley, C. A., Ward, A. B., Magnay, A. R., & Long, J. (2003). Parental stress and burden following traumatic brain injury amongst children and adolescents. *Brain Injury, 17,* 1–23.

Haynes, S. N., & O'Brien, W. H. (1988). The Gordian knot of *DSM-III-R* use: Integrating principles of behavior classification and complex causal models. *Behavioral Assessment, 10,* 95–105.

Heaton, R. K., Chelune, G. J., Talley, J. L., Kay, G. G., & Curtiss, G. (1993). *Wisconsin Card Sorting Test manual: Revised and expanded.* Odessa, FL: Psychological Assessment Resources.

Heebink, D. M., Sunday, S. R., & Halmi, K. A. (1995). Anorexia nervosa and bulimia nervosa in adolescence: Effects of age and menstrual status on psychological variables. *Journal of the American Academy of Child and Adolescent Psychiatry, 34,* 378–382.

Helzer, J. E., & Hudziak, J. J. (2000). *Defining psychopathology in the twenty-first century: DSM-V and beyond.* Washington, DC: American Psychiatric Association.

Hill, J. (2002). Biological, psychological and social processes in the conduct disorders. *Journal of Child Psychology and Psychiatry, 43,* 133–164.

Hinshaw, S. P. (1994). *Attention deficits and hyperactivity in children.* Thousand Oaks, CA: Sage.

Hinshaw, S. P. (2001). Is the Inattentive type of ADHD a separate Disorder? *Clinical Psychology: Science and Practice, 8*(4), 498–501.

Hinshaw, S. P., & Anderson, C. A. (1996). Conduct and oppositional defiant disorders. In E. J. Mash & R. A. Barkley (Eds.), *Child psychopathology* (pp. 113–149). New York: Guilford Press.

Hinshaw, S. P., & Lee, S. S. (2003). Conduct and oppositional defiant disorders. In E. J. Mash & R. A. Barkley (Eds.), *Child psychopathology* (2nd ed., pp. 144–198). New York: Guilford Press.

Hoek, H. W., & van Hoeken, D. (2003). Review of the prevalence and incidence of eating disorders. *International Journal of Eating Disorders, 34,* 383–396.

Hoskyn, M., & Swanson, H. L. (2000). Cognitive processing of low achievers and children with reading disabilities: A selective meta-analytic review of the published literature. *School Psychology Review, 29,* 102–119.

House, A. E. (1999). DSM-IV *diagnosis in the schools.* New York: Guilford Press.

House, A. E. (2002). DSM-IV *diagnosis in the schools.* New York: Guilford Press.

Houts, A. C. (2002). Discovery, invention, and the expansion of the modern diagnostic and statistical manuals of mental disorders. In J. E. Helzer & J. J. Hudziak (Eds.), *Defining psychopathology in the twenty-first century: DSM-V and beyond.* Washington, DC: American Psychiatric Association.

Howlin, P., & Asgharian, A. (1999). The diagnosis of autism and Asperger syndrome: Findings from a survey of 770 families. *Developmental Medicine and Child Neurology, 41,* 834–839.

Huberty, C. J., DiStefano, C., & Kamphaus, R. W. (1997). Behavioral clustering of school children. *Multivariate Behavioral Research, 32,* 105–134.

Huberty, T. J. (1997). Anxiety. In G. G. Bear, K. M. Minke, & A. Thomas (Eds.), *Children's needs: Vol. 2. Development, problems, and alternatives* (pp. 305–314). Bethesda, MD: National Association of School Psychologists.

Hudziak, J. J., Heath, A. C., Madden, P. F., Reich, W., Bucholz, K. K., Slutske, W., et al. (1998). Latent class and factor analysis of *DSM-IV* ADHD: A twin study of female adolescents. *Journal of the American Academy of Child and Adolescent Psychiatry, 37,* 848–857.

Hudziak, J. J., Wadsworth, M. E., Heath, A. C., & Achenbach, T. M. (1999). Latent class analysis of child behavior checklist attention problems [In Process Citation]. *Journal of the American Academy of Child and Adolescent Psychiatry, 38*(8), 985–991.

Hussong, A., Curran, P., & Chassin, L. (1998). Pathways of risk for accelerated heavy alcohol use among adolescent children of alcoholic parents. *Journal of Abnormal Child Psychology, 26,* 453–466.

Hymel, K. P. (2002). Inflicted traumatic brain injury in infants and young children. *Infants and Young Children, 15,* 57–65.

Hynd, G. W., Semrud-Clikeman, M., Lorys, A. R., Novey, E. S., & Eliopulos, D. (1990). Brain morphology in developmental dyslexia and attention deficit disorder/hyperactivity. *Archives of Neurology, 47,* 919–926.

Individuals with Disabilities Education Act Amendments of 1997, Pub. L. No. 105-17, 20 U.S.C. Chap. 33, § 1415 *et seq.* (EDLAW, 1997).

Individuals with Disabilities Education Improvement Act of 2004, Pub. L. No. 108-446.

Ittenbach, R. F., Spiegel, A. N., McGrew, K. S., & Bruininks, R. H. (1992). Confirmatory factor analysis of early childhood ability measures within a model of personal competence. *Journal of School Psychology, 30,* 307–323.

Iwata, B. A., Dorsey, M. F., Slifer, K. J., Bauman, K. E., & Richman, G. S. (1994). Toward a functional analysis of self-injury. *Journal of Applied Behavior Analysis, 27,* 197–207. (Reprinted from *Analysis and Intervention in Developmental Disabilities, 2,* 3–20, 1982).

Jablensky, A. (1999). The nature of psychiatric classification: Issues beyond ICD-10 and DSM-IV. *Australian and New Zealand Journal of Psychiatry, 33,* 137–144.

Jacques, H. A. K., & Mash, E. (2004). A test of the tripartite model of anxiety and depression in elementary and high school boys and girls. *Journal of Abnormal Child Psychology, 32,* 13–25.

Jaffe, S. L., & Solhkhah, R. (2004). Substance abuse disorders. In J. M. Wiener & M. K. Dulcan (Eds.), *Textbook of child and adolescent psychiatry* (3rd ed., pp. 795–812). Washington, DC: American Psychiatric Publishing.

Jeffrey, D. B., Lemnitzer, N. B., Hickey, J. S., Hess, M. S., McLellarn, R. W., & Stroud, J. M. (1980). The development of a behavioral eating test and its relationship to a self-report food attitude scale in young children. *Behavioral Assessment, 2,* 87–89.

Jensen, P. S., Koretz, D., Locke, B. Z., Schneider, S., Radke-Yarrow, M., Richters, J. E., et al. (1993). Child and adolescent psychopathology research: Problems and prospects for the 1990s. *Journal of Abnormal Child Psychology, 21*, 551–580.

Jensen, P. S., Rubio-Stipec, M., Canino, G., Bird, H., Dulcan, M., Schwab-Stone, M. E., et al. (1999). Parent and child contributions to diagnosis of mental disorder: Are both informants always necessary? *Journal of the American Academy of Child and Adolescent Psychiatry, 38*, 1569–1579.

Jensen, P. S., Watanabe, H. K., Richters, J. E., & Roper, M. (1996). Practitioner questions about research. *Journal of the American Academy of Child and Adolescent Psychiatry, 35*(6), 698–699.

Jessor, R. (1984). Adolescent development and behavioral health. In J. D. Matarazzo, S. M. Weiss, J. A. Herd, N. E. Miller, & S. M. Weiss (Eds.), *Behavioral health: A handbook of health enhancement and disease prevention* (pp. 69–90). New York: Wiley.

Johnson, J. H., McCaskill, J. W., IV, Werba, B. E. (2001). Aggressive, antisocial, and delinquent behavior in childhood and adolescence. In C. E. Walker & M. C. Roberts (Eds.), *Handbook of clinical child psychology* (3rd ed., pp. 393–413). New York: Wiley.

Johnson, W. G., Grieve, F. G., Adams, C. D., & Sandy, J. (1999). Measuring binge eating in adolescents: Adolescent and parent versions of the questionnaire of eating and weight patterns. *International Journal of Eating Disorders, 26*, 301–314.

Johnson-Cramer, N. L. (1999). Assessment of school-aged children with comorbidity of attention deficit disorder and low birth weight classifications. *Dissertation Abstracts International, 59*(7), 2344A.

Johnston, C., & Murray, C. (2003). Incremental validity in the psychological assessment of children and adolescents. *Psychological Assessment, 15*, 496–507.

Johnston, L. D., O'Malley, P. M., & Bachman, J. G. (1998). *National survey results on drug use from the Monitoring the Future Study, 1975–1997: Vol. 1. Secondary school students* (NIH Publication No. ADM 98-4345). Rockville, MD: National Institute on Drug Abuse.

Johnston, L. D., O'Malley, P. M., & Bachman, J. G. (2001). *Monitoring the future: National results on adolescent drug use—Overview of key findings, 2000* (NIH Publication No. 01-4923). Bethesda, MD: National Institute on Drug Abuse.

Joiner, T. E., Catanzaro, S. J., & Laurent, J. (1996). Tripartite structure of positive and negative affect, depression, and anxiety in child and adolescent psychiatric inpatients. *Journal of Abnormal Psychology, 105*, 401–409.

Joiner, T. E., Katz, J., & Lew, A. S. (1997). Self-verification and depression among youth psychiatric inpatients. *Journal of Abnormal Psychology, 106*, 608–618.

Joiner, T. E., & Lonigan, C. J. (2000). Tripartite model of depression and anxiety in youth psychiatry inpatients: Relations with diagnostic status and future symptoms. *Journal of Clinical Child Psychology, 29*, 372–382.

Joiner, T. E., & Schmidt, N. B. (2002). Taximetrics can "do diagnostics right" (and isn't quite as hard as you think). In L. E. Beutler & M. L. Malik (Eds.), *Rethinking the* DSM: *A psychological perspective—Decade of behavior* (pp. 107–120). Washington, DC: American Psychological Association.

Jones, D., Dodge, K. A., Foster, E. M., Nix, R., & Conduct Problems Prevention Research Group. (2002). Early identification of children at risk for costly mental health service use. *Prevention Science, 3,* 247–256.

Jopp, D. A., & Keys, C. B. (2001). Diagnostic overshadowing reviewed and reconsidered. *American Journal on Mental Retardation, 106,* 416–433.

Kaczynski, N. A., & Martin, C. S. (1995, June). *Diagnostic orphans: Adolescents with clinical alcohol symptomatology who do not qualify for* DSM-IV *abuse or dependence diagnosis.* Paper presented at the annual meeting of the Research Society on Alcoholism, Steamboat Springs, CO.

Kamphaus, R. W. (2001). *Clinical assessment of child and adolescent intelligence* (2nd ed.). New York: Springer.

Kamphaus, R. W., & DiStefano, C. (2001). Evaluación multidimensional de la psicopatología infantíl. *Revista de Neuropsicología, Neuropsyqiatría y Neurociencias, 3*(1), 85–98.

Kamphaus, R. W., DiStefano, C., & Lease, A. M. (2003). A self-report typology of behavioral adjustment for young children. *Psychological Assessment.*

Kamphaus, R. W., & Frick, P. J. (2002). *Clinical assessment of child and adolescent personality and behavior* (2nd ed.). Boston: Allyn & Bacon.

Kamphaus, R. W., Huberty, C. J., DiStefano, C., & Petoskey, M. D. (1997). A typology of teacher rated child behavior for a national U.S. sample. *Journal of Abnormal Child Psychology, 25,* 453–463.

Kamphaus, R. W., Petoskey, M. D., Cody, A. H., Rowe, E. W., Huberty, C. J., & Reynolds, C. R. (1999). A typology of parent rated child behavior for a national U.S. sample. *Journal of Child Psychology and Psychiatry and Allied Disciplines, 40,* 1–10.

Kanner, L. (1943). Autistic disturbances of affective contact. *Nervous Child, 2,* 217–250.

Kanner, L., Rodriguez, A., & Ashenden, B. (1972). How far can autistic children go in matters of social adaptation? *Journal of Autism and Childhood Schizophrenia, 2,* 9–33.

Kaplan, E., Goodglass, H., & Weintraub, S. (2001). *Boston Naming Test* (2nd ed.). Baltimore: Lippincott, Williams, & Wilkins.

Kashubeck-West, S., & Saunders, K. (2001). Body image. In J. J. Robert-McComb (Ed.), *Eating disorders in women and children: Prevention, stress management, and treatment* (pp. 185–200). Boca Raton, FL: CRC Press.

Kaufman, A. S., & Kaufman, N. L. (2004). *Kaufman Assessment Battery for Children* (2nd ed.). Circle Pines, MN: American Guidance Service.

Kaye, W. H., Bulik, C. M., Thorton, L., Barbarich, N., & Masters, K. (2004). Comorbidity of anxiety disorders with anorexia and bulimia nervosa. *American Journal of Psychiatry, 161,* 2215–2221.

Kedesdy, J. H., & Budd, K. S. (1998). *Childhood feeding disorders: Biobehavioral assessment and intervention.* Baltimore: Paul H. Brookes.

Keenan, K., & Wakschlag, L. S. (2002). Can a valid diagnosis of disruptive behavior disorder be made in preschool children? *American Journal of Psychiatry, 159,* 351–358.

Kendall, R. E. (2002). Five criteria for an improved taxonomy of mental disorders. In J. E. Helzer & J. J. Hudziak (Eds.), *Defining psychopathology in the twenty-first century:* DSM-V *and beyond.* Washington, DC: American Psychiatric Association.

Kessler, R. C., Berglund, P., Demler, O., Jin, R., Merikangas, K. R., & Walters, E. E. (2005). Lifetime prevalence and age-of-onset distributions of *DSM-IV* disorders in the National Comorbidity Survey Replication. *Archives of General Psychiatry, 62,* 593–768.

Kessler, R. C., McGonagle, K. A., Zhao, S., Nelson, C. B., Hughes, M., Eshelman, S., et al. (1994). Lifetime and 12-month prevalence of *DSM-III-R* psychiatric disorders in the United States: Results from the National Comorbidity Study. *Archives of General Psychiatry, 51,* 8–19.

Kim, J. A., Szatmari, P., Bryson, S. E., Streiner, D. L., & Wilson, F. J. (2000). The prevalence of anxiety and mood problems among children with autism and Asperger syndrome. *Autism, 4,* 117–132.

Kirisci, L., Mezzich, A., & Tarter, R. (1995). Norms and sensitivity of the adolescent version of the Drug Use Screening Inventory. *Addictive Behaviors, 20*(2), 149–157.

Klaiman, R. S., & Phelps, L. (1998). Fragile X syndrome. In L. Phelps (Ed.), *Health-related disorders in children and adolescents* (pp. 299–308). Washington, DC: American Psychological Association.

Klein, D. N., Dougherty, L. R., & Olino, T. M. (2005). Toward guidelines for evidence-based assessment of depression in children and adolescents. *Journal of Clinical Child and Adolescent Psychology, 34,* 412–432.

Klesges, R. C., Coates, T. J., Brown, G., Sturgeon-Tillisch, J., Moldenhauer-Klesges, L. M., Holzer, B., et al. (1983). Parental influences on children's eating behavior and relative weight. *Journal of Applied Behavior Analysis, 16,* 371–378.

Klin, A., Carter, A., Volkmar, F. R., Cohen, D. J., Marans, W. D., & Sparrow, S. S. (1997). Developmentally based assessments. In D. J. Cohen & F. R. Volkmar (Eds.), *Handbook of autism and pervasive developmental disorders* (2nd ed., pp. 411–447). New York: Wiley.

Klin, A., Volkmar, F. R., & Sparrow, S. S. (Eds.). (2000). *Asperger syndrome.* New York: Guilford Press.

Klin, A., Volkmar, F. R., Sparrow, S. S., Cicchetti, D. V., & Rourke, B. P. (1995). Validity and neuropsychological characterization of Asperger syndrome: Convergence with nonverbal learning disabilities syndrome. *Journal of Child Psychology and Psychiatry and Allied Disciplines, 36,* 1127–1140.

Korkman, M., Kirk, U., & Kemp, S. (1998). *NEPSY: A developmental neuropsychological assessment.* San Antonio, TX: Psychological Corporation.

Kostanski, M., & Gullone, E. (1999). Dieting and body image in the child's world: Conceptualization and behavior. *Journal of Genetic Psychology, 160,* 488–499.

Kosten, T. R., Rounsaville, J., Babor, T. F., Spitzer, R. L., & Williams, J. B. W. (1987). Substance-use disorders in *DSM-III-R. British Journal of Psychiatry, 151,* 834–843.

Kovacs, M. (1992). *Children's Depression Inventory Manual.* North Tonawanda, NY: Multi-Health Systems.

Krug, D. A., & Arick, J. R. (2003). *Krug Asperger's Disorder Index.* Austin, TX: Pro-Ed.

Kuperman, S., Schlosser, S. S., Kramer, J. R., Bucholz, K., Hesselbrock, V., Reich, T., et al. (2001). Developmental sequence from disruptive behavior diagnosis to adolescent alcohol dependence. *American Journal of Psychiatry, 158,* 2022–2026.

LaCombe, J. A., Kline, R. B., Lachar, D., Butkus, M., & Hillman, S. B. (1991). Case history correlates of a Personality Inventory for Children (PIC) profile typology. *Psychological Assessment, 3,* 678–687.

Lahey, B. B. (2001). Should the combined and predominantly inattentive types of ADHD be considered distinct and unrelated disorders? Not now, at least. *Clinical Psychology: Science and Practice, 8*(4), 494–497.

Lahey, B. B., Carlson, C. L., & Frick, P. J. (1997). Attention-deficit disorders: A review of research relevant to diagnostic classification. In T. A. Widiger, A. J. Frances, H. A. Pincus, R. Ross, M. B. First, & W. Davis (Eds.), DSM-IV *sourcebook* (Vol. 3, pp. 163–188). Washington, DC: American Psychiatric Association.

Lahey, B. B., Loeber, R., Burke, J., Rathouz, P. J., & McBurnett, K. (2002). Waxing and waning in concert: Dynamic comorbidity of conduct disorder with other disruptive and emotional problems over 7 years among clinic-referred boys. *Journal of Abnormal Psychology, 111,* 556–567.

Lahey, B. B., Miller, T. L., Gordon, R. A., & Riley, A. W. (1999). Developmental epidemiology of the disruptive behavior disorders. In H. C. Quay & A. E. Hogan (Eds.), *Handbook of disruptive behavior disorders* (pp. 23–48). New York: Kluwer/Plenum Press.

Lambert, S. F., McCreary, B. T., Joiner, T. E., Schmidt, N. B., & Ialongo, N. S. (2004). Structure of anxiety and depression in urban youth: An examination of the tripartite model. *Journal of Consulting and Clinical Psychology, 72,* 904–908.

Landau, S., & Burcham, B. G. (1996). Best practices in the assessment of children with attention disorders. In A. Thomas & J. Grimes (Eds.), *Best practices in school psychology III* (pp. 817–829). Bethesda, MD: National Association of School Psychologists.

Laurent, J., Catanzaro, S. J., & Joiner, T. E. (2004). Development and preliminary validation of the Physiological Hyperarousal Scale for Children. *Psychological Assessment, 16,* 373–380.

Laurent, J., Catanzaro, S. J., Joiner, T. E., Rudolph, K. D., Potter, K. I., Lambert, S., et al. (1999). A measure of positive and negative affect for children: Scale development and preliminary validation. *Psychological Assessment, 11,* 326–338.

Lavik, N. J., Clausen, S. P., & Pedersen, W. (1991). Eating behavior, drug use, psychopathology, and parental bonding in adolescents in Norway. *Acta Psychiatrica Scandinavica, 84,* 387–390.

Lazar, J. W., & Frank, Y. (1998). Frontal systems dysfunction in children with attention deficit/hyperactivity disorder and learning disabilities. *Journal of Neuropsychiatry and Clinical Neurosciences, 10*(2), 160–167.

Leccese, M., & Waldron, H. B. (1994). Assessing adolescent substance use: A critique of current measurement instruments. *Journal of Substance Abuse Treatment, 11*(6), 553–563.

Lee, Z., Vincent, G. M., Hart, S. D., & Corrado, R. R. (2003). The validity of the antisocial process screening device as a self-report measure of psychopathy in adolescent offenders. *Behavioral Sciences and the Law, 21,* 771–786.

LeFever, G. B., Dawson, K. V., & Morrow, A. L. (1999). The extent of drug therapy for attention deficit hyperactivity disorder among children in public schools. *American Journal of Public Health, 89,* 1359–1364.

Lessing, E. E., Williams, V., & Gil, E. (1982). A cluster-analytically derived typology: Feasible alternative to clinical diagnostic classification of children? *Journal of Abnormal Child Psychology, 10,* 451–482.

Lewczky, C. M., Garland, A. F., Hurlburt, M. S., Gearity, J., & Hough, R. L. (2003). Comparing DISC-IV and clinician diagnosis among youths receiving public mental health services. *Journal of the American Academy of Child and Adolescent Psychiatry, 42,* 3, 349.

Lewinsohn, P. M., Gotlib, I. H., Lewinsohn, M., Seeley, J. R., & Allen, N. B. (1998). Gender differences in anxiety disorders and anxiety symptoms in adolescents. *Journal of Abnormal Psychology, 107,* 109–117.

Lewinsohn, P. M., Pettit, J. W., Joiner, T. E., & Seeley, J. R. (2003). The symptomatic expression of major depressive disorder in adolescents and young adults. *Journal of Abnormal Psychology, 112,* 244–252.

Lewinsohn, P. M., Rohde, P., & Seeley, J. R. (1996). Alcohol consumption in high school adolescents: Frequency of use and dimensional structure of associated problems. *Addiction, 91,* 375–390.

Lewinsohn, P. M., Streigel-Moore, R. H., & Seeley, J. R. (2000). Epidemiology and natural course of eating disorders in young women from adolescence to young adulthood. *Journal of the American Academy of Child and Adolescent Psychiatry, 39,* 1284–1292.

Lezak, M. D. (1988). Brain damage is a family affair. *Journal of Clinical and Experimental Neuropsychology, 10,* 111–123.

Lidz, C. S. (2003). *Early childhood assessment.* Hoboken, NJ: Wiley.

Light, R., Asarnow, R., Satz, P., Zaucha, K., McCleary, C., & Lewis, R. (1998). Mild closed-head injury in children and adolescents: Behavior problems and academic outcomes. *Journal of Consulting and Clinical Psychology, 66,* 1023–1029.

Linscheid, T. R., Budd, K. S., & Rasnake, L. K. (2003). Pediatric feeding problems. In M. C. Roberts (Ed.), *Handbook of pediatric psychology* (pp. 481–498). New York: Guilford Press.

Linscheid, T. R., & Butz, C. (2003). Anorexia nervosa and bulimia nervosa. In M. C. Roberts (Ed.), *Handbook of pediatric psychology* (pp. 636–651). New York: Guilford Press.

Linscheid, T. R., & Rasnake, L. K. (2001). Eating problems in children. In C. E. Walker & M. C. Roberts (Eds.), *Handbook of clinical psychology* (pp. 523–541). New York: Wiley.

Liss, M., Harel, B., Fein, D., Allen, D., Dunn, M., Feinstein, C., et al. (2001). Predictors and correlates of adaptive functioning in children with developmental disorders. *Journal of Autism and Developmental Disorders, 31,* 219–230.

Lochman, J. E., Dane, H. E., Magee, T. N., Ellis, M., Pardini, D. A., & Clanton, N. R. (2001). Disruptive behavior disorders: Assessment and intervention. In H. B. Vance & A. Pumariega (Eds.), *Clinical assessment of child and adolescent behavior* (pp. 231–262). New York: Wiley.

Loeber, R., Burke, J. D., & Lahey, B. B. (2002). What are adolescent antecedents to antisocial personality disorder? *Criminal Behavior and Mental Health, 12,* 24–36.

Loeber, R., Burke, J. D., Lahey, B. B., Winters, A., & Zera, M. (2000). Oppositional defiant and conduct disorder: Pt. I. A review of the past 10 years. *Journal of the American Academy of Child and Adolescent Psychiatry, 39,* 1468–1484.

Loeber, R., Green, S. M., Lahey, B. B., Christ, M. A. G., & Frick, P. J. (1992). Developmental sequences in the age of onset of disruptive child behaviors. *Journal of Child and Family Studies, 1,* 21–41.

Loeber, R., Green, S. M., Lahey, B. B., Frick, P. J., & McBurnett, K. (2000). Findings on disruptive behavior disorders from the first decade of the Developmental Trends Study. *Clinical Child and Family Psychology Review, 3*(1), 37–60.

Loeber, R., & Stouthamer-Loeber, M. (1998). Development of juvenile aggression and violence: Some common misconceptions and controversies. *American Psychologist, 53,* 242–259.

Logan, G. D. (1994). On the ability to inhibit thought and action: A user's guide to the stop signal paradigm. In D. Dagenbach & T. H. Carr (Eds.), *Inhibitory processes in attention, memory, and language* (pp. 189–239). San Diego, CA: Academy Press.

Lord, C. (1997). Diagnostic instruments in autism spectrum disorders. In D. J. Cohen & F. R. Volkmar (Eds.), *Handbook of autism and pervasive developmental disorders* (2nd ed., pp. 460–483). New York: Wiley.

Lord, C., & Risi, S. (1998). Frameworks and methods in diagnosing autism spectrum disorders. *Mental Retardation and Developmental Disabilities Research Reviews, 4,* 90–96.

Lord, C., Risi, S., Lambrecht, L., Cook, E. H., Leventhal, B. L., DiLavore, P. C., et al. (2000). The Autism Diagnostic Observation Schedule—Generic: A standard measure of social and communication deficits associated with the spectrum of autism. *Journal of Autism and Developmental Disorders, 30,* 205–223.

Lord, C., Rutter, M., DiLavore, P. C., & Risi, S. (2001). *Autism Diagnostic Observation Schedule Manual.* Los Angeles: Western Psychological Services.

Lord, C., Rutter, M., & Le Couteur, A. (1994). Autism Diagnostic Interview—Revised: A revised version of a diagnostic interview for caregivers of individuals with possible pervasive developmental disorders. *Journal of Autism and Developmental Disorders, 24,* 659–685.

Lord-Maes, J., & Obrzut, J. E. (1996). Neuropsychological consequences of traumatic brain injury in children and adolescents. *Journal of Learning Disabilities, 29,* 609–617.

Lovaas, O. I., Schreibman, L., Koegel, R., & Rehm, R. (1971). Selective responding by autistic children to multiple sensory input. *Journal of Abnormal Psychology, 77,* 211–222.

Luckasson, R., Borthwick-Duffy, S., Buntinx, W. H. E., Coulter, D. L., Craig, E. M., Polloway, E. A., et al. (2002). *Mental retardation: Definition, classification, and systems of supports* (10th ed.). Washington, DC: American Association on Mental Retardation.

Luckasson, R., Coulter, D. L., Polloway, E. A., Reiss, S., Schalock, R. L., Snell, M. E., et al. (1992). *Mental retardation: Definition, classification, and systems of supports* (9th ed.). Washington, DC: American Association on Mental Retardation.

Luiselli, J. K., Campbell, S., Cannon, B., DiPietro, E., Ellis, J. T., Taras, M., et al. (2001). Assessment instruments used in the education and treatment of persons with autism: Brief report of a survey of national service centers. *Research in Developmental Disabilities, 22,* 389–398.

Lyon, G. R., Fletcher, J. M., & Barnes, M. (2002). Learning disabilities. In E. J. Marsh & R. A. Barkley (Eds.), *Child psychopathology* (2nd ed., pp. 520–588). New York: Guilford Press.

Lyon, G. R., Fletcher, J. M., Shaywitz, S. E., Shaywitz, B. A., Torgesen, J. K., Wood, F. B., et al. (2001). Rethinking learning disabilities. In C. E. Finn, R. Rotherham, & C. R. Hokanson (Eds.), *Rethinking special education for a new century* (pp. 259–287). Washington, DC: Thomas B. Fordham Foundation and Progressive Policy Institute.

Magnusson, D., & Bergman, L. R. (1990). A pattern approach to the study of pathways from childhood to adulthood. In L. N. Robins & M. Rutter (Eds.), *Straight and devious pathways from childhood to adulthood* (pp. 101–115). New York: Cambridge University Press.

Magnusson, D., & Cairns, R. B. (1996). Developmental science: Toward a unified framework. In R. B. Cairns, G. H. Elder, & E. J. Costello (Eds.), *Developmental science* (pp. 7–30). Cambridge: Cambridge University Press.

Malik, M. L., & Beutler, L. E. (2002). The emergence of dissatisfaction with the *DSM.* In J. E. Helzer & J. J. Hudziak (Eds.), *Defining psychopathology in the twenty-first century: DSM-V and beyond.* Washington, DC: American Psychiatric Association.

Maloney, M. J., McGuire, J. B., & Daniels, S. R. (1988). Reliability testing of a children's version of the Eating Attitudes Test. *Journal of the American Academy of Child and Adolescent Psychiatry, 29,* 541–543.

Maloney, M. J., McGuire, J. B., Daniels, S. R., & Specker, B. (1989). Dieting behavior and eating attitudes in children. *Pediatrics, 84,* 482–489.

Manjiviona, J., & Prior, M. (1995). Comparison of Asperger syndrome and high-functioning autistic children on a test of motor impairment. *Journal of Autism and Developmental Disorders, 25,* 23–39.

Manjiviona, J., & Prior, M. (1999). Neuropsychological profiles of children with Asperger syndrome and autism. *Autism, 3,* 327–356.

March, J. S. (1997). *Multidimensional Anxiety Scale for Children.* North Tonawanda, NY: Multi-Health Systems.

March, J. S., & Mulle, K. (1998). *OCD in children and adolescents: A cognitive-behavioral treatment manual.* New York: Guilford Press.

March, J. S., Parker, J., Sullivan, K., Stallings, P., & Conners, C. K. (1997). The Multidimensional Anxiety Scale for Children: Factor structure, reliability, and validity. *Journal of the American Academy of Child and Adolescent Psychiatry, 36,* 554–565.

March, J. S., Sullivan, K., & Parker, J. (1999). Test-retest reliability of the Multidimensional Anxiety Scale for Children. *Journal of Anxiety Disorders, 13,* 349–358.

Marcus, M. D., & Kalarchian, M. A. (2003). Binge eating in children and adolescents. *International Journal of Eating Disorders, 34,* S47–S57.

Martin, C. S., Earleywine, M., Blackson, T. C., Vanyukov, M. M. Moss, H. B., & Tarter, R. E. (1994). Aggressivity, inattention, hyperactivity, and impulsivity in boys at high and low risk for substance abuse. *Journal of Abnormal Child Psychology, 22,* 177–203.

Martin, C. S., Pollock, N. K., Bukstein, O. G., & Lynch, K. G. (2000). Interrater reliability of the SCID alcohol and substance use disorders sections among adolescents. *Drug and Alcohol Dependence, 59,* 173–176.

Martin, C. S., & Winters, K. C. (1998). Diagnosis and assessment of alcohol use disorders among adolescents. *Alcohol Health and Research, 22,* 95–105.

Martin, G. C., Wertheim, E. H., Prior, M., Smart, D., Sanson, A., & Oberklaid, F. (2000). A longitudinal study of the role of childhood temperament in the later development of eating concerns. *International Journal of Eating Disorders, 27,* 150–162.

Mash, E. J., & Dozois, D. J. (1996). Child psychopathology: A developmental systems perspective. In E. J. Mash & R. A. Barkley (Eds.), *Child psychopathology* (pp. 3–60). New York: Guilford Press.

Matazow, G. S., & Kamphaus, R. W. (2001). Behavior Assessment System for Children (BASC): Toward accurate diagnosis and effective treatment. In J. W. Andrews, D. H. Saklofske, & H. L. Janzen (Eds.), *Handbook of psychoeducational assessment: Ability, achievement, and behavior in children* (pp. 257–289). San Diego, CA: Academic Press.

Mather, N., & Woodcock, R. W. (2001a). Application of the Woodcock-Johnson Tests of Cognitive Ability—Revised to the diagnosis of learning disabilities. In A. S. Kaufman & N. L. Kaufman (Eds.), *Specific learning disabilities and difficulties in children and adolescents: Psychological assessment and evaluation* (pp. 55–96). New York: Cambridge University Press.

Mather, N., & Woodcock, R. W. (2001b). *Examiner's manual: Woodcock-Johnson III Tests of Cognitive Abilities.* Itasca, IL: Riverside.

Matier-Sharma, K., Perachio, N., & Newcorn, J. (1995). Differential diagnosis of ADHD: Are objective measures of attention, impulsivity and activity level helpful? *Child Neuropsychology, 1,* 118–127.

Matson, J. L., Mayville, E. A., Lott, J. D., Bielecki, J., & Logan, R. (2003). A comparison of social and adaptive functioning in persons with psychosis, autism, and severe or profound mental retardation. *Journal of Developmental and Physical Disabilities, 15,* 57–65.

Matson, J. L., & Sevin, J. A. (1994). Theories of dual diagnosis in mental retardation. *Journal of Consulting and Clinical Psychology, 62,* 6–16.

Mattison, R. E., & Spitznagel, E. L. (1999). Long-term stability of child behavior checklist profile types in a child psychiatric clinic population. *Journal of the American Academy of Child and Adolescent Psychiatry, 38,* 700–707.

Maughan, B., Rowe, R., Messer, J., Goodman, R., & Meltzer, H. (2004). Conduct disorder and oppositional defiant disorder in a national sample: Developmental epidemiology. *Journal of Child Psychology and Psychiatry, 45,* 609–621.

Max, J. E., Lindgren, S. D., Knutson, C., Pearson, C. S., Ihrig, D., & Welborn, A. (1998). Child and adolescent traumatic brain injury: Correlates of disruptive behaviour disorders. *Brain Injury, 12,* 41–52.

Mayes, S. D., & Calhoun, S. L. (2003). Analysis of WISC-III, Stanford-Binet: IV, and academic achievement test scores in children with autism. *Journal of Autism and Developmental Disorders, 33,* 236–271.

Mayes, S. D., Calhoun, S. L., & Crites, D. L. (2001). Does *DSM-IV* Asperger's disorder exist? *Journal of Abnormal Child Psychology, 29,* 236–271.

Mazzocco, M. M. (2000). Advances in research on the fragile X syndrome. *Mental Retardation and Developmental Disabilities Research Reviews, 6,* 96–106.

McDaniel, W. F., Passmore, C. E., & Sewell, H. M. (2003). The MMPI-168(L) and ADD in assessing psychopathology in individuals with mental retardation: Between and within instrument associations. *Research in Developmental Disabilities, 24,* 19–32.

McDermott, P. A., & Weiss, R. V. (1995). A normative typology of healthy, subclinical, and clinical behavior styles among American children and adolescents. *Psychological Assessment, 7,* 162–170.

McEvoy, R. E., Rogers, S. J., & Pennington, B. F. (1993). Executive function and social communication deficits in young autistic children. *Journal of Child Psychology and Psychiatry, 34,* 563–578.

McGrew, K. S., & Bruininks, R. H. (1990). Defining adaptive and maladaptive behavior within a model of personal competence. *School Psychology Review, 19,* 53–73.

McGrew, K. S., & Woodcock, R. W. (2001). *Technical manual: Woodcock-Johnson III.* Itasca, IL: Riverside.

McLaney, M. A., & Boca, F. D. (1994). A validation study of the Problem-Oriented Screening Instrument for Teenagers (POSIT). *Journal of Mental Health, 3*(3), 363–377.

Meehl, P. E. (1995). Bootstraps taximetrics: Solving the classification problem in psychopathology. *American Psychologist, 50,* 266–275.

Merrell, K. W. (2003). *Behavioral, social, and emotional assessment of children and adolescents* (2nd ed.). Mahwah, NJ: Erlbaum.

Mesibov, G. B., Adams, L. W., & Klinger, L. G. (1997). *Autism: Understanding the disorder.* New York: Plenum Press.

Mesibov, G. B., Shea, V., & Adams, L. W. (2001). *Understanding Asperger syndrome and high functioning autism.* New York: Plenum Press.

Meyers, K., Hagan, T. A., Zanis, D., Webb, A., Frantz, J., Ring-Kurtz, S., et al. (1999). Critical issues in adolescent substance use assessment. *Drug and Alcohol Dependence, 55,* 235–246.

Mikulich, S. K., Hall, S. K., Whitmore, E. A., & Crowley, T. J. (2001). Concordance between *DSM-III-R* and *DSM-IV* diagnoses of substance use disorders in adolescents. *Drug and Alcohol Dependence, 61,* 237–248.

Milich, R., Balentine, A. C., & Lynam, D. R. (2001). ADHD combined type and ADHD predominantly inattentive type are distinct and unrelated disorders. *Clinical Psychology: Science and Practice, 8*(4), 463–488.

Miller, L. S., Klein, R. G., Piacentini, J., Abikoff, H., Manoj, R. H., Samoilov, A., et al. (1995). The New York Teacher Rating Scale for Disruptive and Antisocial Behavior. *Journal of the American Academy of Child and Adolescent Psychiatry, 34,* 359–370.

Miller-Johnson, S., Coie, J. D., Maumary-Gramaud, A., Bierman, K., & the Conduct Problems Research Group. (2002). Peer rejection and aggression and early starter models of conduct disorder. *Journal of Abnormal Child Psychology, 30,* 217–230.

Milligan, G. W., & Cooper, M. C . (1987). Methodology review: Clustering methods. *Applied Psychological Measurement, 11,* 329–354.

Millon, T. (1991). Classification in psychopathology: Rationale, alternatives, and standards. *Journal of Abnormal Psychology, 100,* 245–261.

Minshew, N. J., Goldstein, G., & Siegel, D. J. (1997). Neuropsychologic functioning in autism: Profile of a complex information processing disorder. *Journal of the International Neuropsychological Society, 3,* 303–316.

Minuchin, S., Rosman, B. L., & Baker, L. (1978). *Psychosomatic families: Anorexia nervosa in context.* Cambridge, MA: Harvard University Press.

Moffitt, T. E., Caspi, A., Harrington, H., & Milne, B. J. (2002). Males on the life-course-persistent and adolescence-limited antisocial pathways: Follow-up at age 26 years. *Development and Psychopathology, 14,* 179–207.

Moldavsky, M., Lev, D., & Lerman-Sagie, T. (2001). Behavioral phenotypes of genetic syndromes: A reference guide for psychiatrists. *Journal of the American Academy of Child and Adolescent Psychiatry, 40,* 749–761.

Molina, B. S. G., & Pelham, W. E. (2003). Childhood predictors of adolescent substance use in a longitudinal study of children wtih ADHD. *Journal of Abnormal Child Psychology, 112,* 497–507.

Morgan, S. (1988). Diagnostic assessment of autism: A review of objective scales. *Journal of Psychoeducational Assessment, 6,* 139–151.

Morgan, S. B. (1984). Helping parents understand the diagnosis of autism. *Journal of Developmental and Behavioral Pediatrics, 5,* 78–85.

Morgenstern, J., Langenbucher, J., & Labouvie, E. W. (1994). The generalizability of the dependence syndrome across substances: An examination of some properties of the proposed *DSM-IV* dependence criteria. *Addiction, 89,* 1105–1113.

Mowrer, O. H. (1939). A stimulus-response analysis of anxiety and its role as a reinforcing agent. *Psychological Review, 46,* 533–565.

Murphy, C. C., Boyle, C., Schendel, D., Decoufle, P., & Yeargin-Allsopp, M. (1998). Epidemiology of mental retardation in children. *Mental Retardation and Developmental Disabilities Research Reviews, 4,* 6–13.

Murphy, D. A., Marelich, W. D., & Hoffman, D. (2000). Assessment of anxiety and depression in young children: Support for two separate constructs. *Journal of Clinical Child Psychology, 29,* 383–391.

Murphy, L. L., & Impara, J. C. (Eds.). (1996). *Assessment of substance abuse.* Lincoln: University of Nebraska Press.

Muthen, B., & Muthen, L. K. (2000). Integrating person-centered and variable-centered analyses: Growth mixture modeling with latent trajectory classes. *Alcoholism: Clinical and Experimental Research, 24*(6), 882–891.

Myers, K., & Winters, N. C. (2002). Ten-year review of rating scales: Pt. II. Scales for internalizing disorders. *Journal of the American Academy of Child and Adolescent Psychiatry, 41,* 634–659.

Myles, B. S., Bock, S. J., & Simpson, R. L. (2001). *Asperger Syndrome Diagnostic Scale.* Los Angeles: Western Psychological Services.

Nagin, D., & Tremblay, R. E. (1999). Trajectories of boys' physical aggression, opposition, and hyperactivity on the path to physically violent and nonviolent juvenile delinquency. *Child Development, 70,* 1181–1196.

Nathan, P. E., & Langenbucher, J. W. (1999). Psychopathology: Description and classification. *Annual Review of Psychology,* 79–107.

National Institutes of Health. (2000). National Institutes of Health Consensus Development Conference Statement: Diagnosis and treatment of Attention Deficit/Hyperactivity Disorder (ADHD). *Journal of the American Academy of Child and Adolescent Psychiatry, 39*(2), 182–193.

National Research Council. (2001). *Educating children with autism* (C. Lord & J. P. McGee, Eds.), Committee on Educational Interventions for Children with Autism, Division of Behavioral and Social Sciences and Education. Washington, DC: National Academy Press.

Nease, D. E., Volk, R. J., & Cass, A. R. (1999). Investigation of a severity-based classification of mood and anxiety symptoms in primary care patients. *Journal of the American Board of Family Practice, 12*(1), 21–31.

Nelson, C. B., Rehm, J., Bedirhan Ustun, T., Grant, B., & Chatterji, S. (1999). Factor structures for *DSM-IV* substance disorder criteria endorsed by alcohol, cannabis, cocaine, and opiate users: Results from the WHO reliability and validity study. *Addiction, 94*(6), 843–855.

Netemeyer, S. B., & Williamson, D. A. (2001). Assessment of eating disturbance in children and adolescents with eating disorders and obesity. In J. K. Thompson & L. Smolak (Eds.), *Body image, eating disorders, and obesity in youth: Assessment, prevention, and treatment* (pp. 215–233). Washington, DC: American Psychological Association.

Neuman, R. J., Todd, R. D., Heath, A. C., Reich, W., Hudziak, J. J., Bucholz, K. K., et al. (1999). Evaluation of ADHD typology in three contrasting samples: A latent class approach. *Journal of the American Academy of Child and Adolescent Psychiatry, 38,* 25–33.

Nichols, S. L., & Waschbusch, D. A. (2004). A review of the validity of laboratory cognitive tasks used to assess symptoms of ADHD. *Child Psychiatry and Human Development, 34*(4), 297–315.

Nihira, K. (1999). Adaptive behavior: A historical overview. In R. L. Schalock (Ed.), *Adaptive behavior and its measurement: Implications for the field of mental retardation* (pp. 7–14). Washington, DC: American Association on Mental Retardation.

Nihira, K., Leland, H., & Lambert, N. (1993). *AAMR Adaptive Behavior Scale, Residential and Community* (2nd ed.). Austin, TX: ProEd.

Noordenbos, G. (2003). Early identification. In J. Treasure, U. Schmidt, & E. V. Furth (Eds.), *Handbook of eating disorders* (2nd ed., pp. 455–466). Chichester, West Sussex, England: Wiley.

Osterling, J., Dawson, G., & McPartland, J. (2001). Autism. In C. E. Walker & M. C. Roberts (Eds.), *Handbook of clinical child psychology* (3rd ed., pp. 432–452). New York: Wiley.

Osterling, J. A., Dawson, G., & Munson, J. A. (2002). Early recognition of 1-year-old infants with autism spectrum disorder versus mental retardation. *Development and Psychopathology, 14,* 239–251.

Ostrander, R., Weinfurt, K. P., Yarnold, P. R., & August, G. J. (1998). Diagnosing attention deficit disorders with the Behavioral Assessment System for Children and the Child Behavior Checklist: Test and construct validity analyses using optimal discriminant classification trees. *Journal of Consulting and Clinical Psychology, 66,* 660–672.

Parker, J. G., & Asher, S. R. (1987). Peer relations and later personal adjustment: Are low-accepted children at risk? *Psychological Bulletin, 102,* 357–398.

Passi, V. A., Bryson, S. W., & Lock, J. (2003). Assessment of eating disorders in adolescents with anorexia nervosa: Self-report questionnaire versus interview. *International Journal of Eating Disorders, 33,* 45–54.

Pastore, D. R., Fisher, M., & Friedman, S. B. (1996). Abnormalities in weight status, eating attitudes, and eating behaviors among urban high school students: Correlations with self-esteem and anxiety. *Journal of Adolescent Health, 18,* 312–319.

Patrick, P. D., Rice, S., & Hostler, S. L. (2002). *DSM-IV:* Diagnosis of children with traumatic brain injury. *NeuroRehabilitation, 17,* 123–129.

Paule, M. G., Rowland, A. S., Ferguson, S. A., Chelonis, J. J., Tannock, R., Swanson, J. M., et al. (2000). Symposium overview: Attention deficit/hyperactivity disorder—Characteristics, intervention, and models. *Neurotoxicology and Teratology, 22,* 631–651.

Pelham, W. E. (2001). Are ADHD/I and ADHD/C the same or different? Does it matter? *Clinical Psychology: Science and Practice, 8*(4), 502–506.

Pelham, W. E., Jr., Greenslade, K. E., Vodde-Hamilton, M., Murphy, D. A., Greenstein, J. J., Gnagy, E. M., et al. (1990). Relative efficacy of long-acting stimulants on children with attention-deficit-hyperactivity-disorder: A comparison of standard methylphenidate, sustained-release dextroamphetamine, and pemoline. *Pediatrics, 86,* 226–237.

Perez, M., Joiner, T. E., & Lewinsohn, P. M. (2004). Is major depressive disorder or dysthymia more strongly associated with bulimia nervosa? *International Journal of Eating Disorders, 36,* 55–61.

Peterson, D. R. (1961). Behavior problems of middle childhood. *Journal of Consulting Psychology, 25,* 205–209.

Phelps-Terasaki, D., & Phelps-Gunn, T. (1992). *Test of Pragmatic Language Examiner's Manual.* San Antonio, TX: Psychological Corporation.

Pike, K. M., Loeb, K., & Walsh, B. T. (1995). Binge eating and purging. In D. B. Allison (Ed.), *Handbook of assessment methods for eating behaviors and weight-related problems: Measures, theory, and research* (pp. 303–346). London: Sage.

Pliszka, S. R., Carlson, C. L., & Swanson, J. M. (1999). *ADHD with comorbid disorders: Clinical Assessment and Management.* New York: Guilford Press.

Pollock, N. K., Martin, C. S., & Langenbucher, J. W. (2000). Diagnostic concordance of DSM-III, DSM-III-R, DSM-IV, and ICD-10 alcohol diagnoses in adolescents. *Journal of Studies on Alcohol, 61,* 439–446.

Poznanski, E. O., & Mokros, H. B. (1995). *Children's Depression Rating Scale* (Rev. ed.). Los Angeles: Western Psychological Services.

Public Law 108-446. (2004). Individuals with Disabilities Education Improvement Act of 2004. *Federal Register,* Vol. 69, 2647–2808.

Puig-Antich, J., & Chambers, W. (1978). *The schedule for affective disorders and schizophrenia for school-age children (Kiddie-SADS).* New York: New York State Psychiatric Institute.

Purves, D., Augustine, G. J., Fitzpatrick, D., Katz, L. C., LaMantia, A., & McNamara, J. O. (1997). *Neuroscience.* Sunderland, MA: Sinauer Associates.

Quay, H. C. (1964). Personality dimensions in delinquent males as inferred from the factor analysis of behavior ratings. *Journal of Research in Crime and Delinquency, 1,* 33–37.

Quay, H. C. (1966). Personality patterns in pre-adolescent delinquent boys. *Educational and Psychological Measurement, 26,* 99–110.

Quay, H. C. (1999). Classification of the disruptive behavior disorders. In H. C. Quay & A. E. Hogan (Eds.), *Handbook of disruptive behavior disorders* (pp. 3–21). New York: Kluwer/Plenum Press.

Quay, H. C., & Peterson, D. R. (1996). *Manual for the Revised Behavior Problem Checklist—PAR version.* Odessa, FL: Psychological Assessment Resources.

Raimondi, A. J., & Hirschauer, J. (1984). Head injury in the infant and toddler: Coma scoring and outcome scale. *Child's Brain, 11,* 12–35.

Ramirez, S. Z., & Morgan, V. (1998). Down syndrome. In L. Phelps (Ed.), *Health-related disorders in children and adolescents* (pp. 68–73). Washington, DC: American Psychological Association.

Ramsey, M. C., Reynolds, C. R., & Kaufman, R. W. (2002). Essentials of behavioral assessment. In A. S. Kaufman & N. L. Kaufman (Series Eds.), *Essentials of psychological assessment series*. Hoboken, NJ: Wiley.

Rapport, M. D., Chung, K., Shore, G., Denney, C. B., & Isaacs, P. (2000). Upgrading the science and technology of assessment and diagnosis: Laboratory and clinic-based assessment of Children with ADHD. *Journal of Clinical Child Psychology, 29*(4), 555–568.

Regier, D. A., Kaelber, C. T., Roper, M. T., Rae, D. S., & Sartorius, N. (1994). The ICD-10 clinical field trial for mental and behavioral disorders: Results in Canada and the United States. *American Journal of Psychiatry, 151,* 1340–1350.

Reich, W. (2000). Diagnostic Interview for Children and Adolescents (DICA). *Journal of the American Academy of Child and Adolescent Psychiatry, 35,* 193–203.

Reitan, R. M., & Wolfson, D. (1993). *The Halstead-Reitan Neuropsychological Test Battery: Theory and clinical interpretation* (2nd ed.). Tuscon, AZ: Neuropsychological Press.

Reitman, D., Hummel, R., Franz, D. Z., & Gross, A. M. (1998). A review of methods and instruments for assessing externalizing disorders: Theoretical and practical considerations in rendering a diagnosis. *Clinical Psychology Review, 18,* 555–584.

Rescorla, L. (1989). The Language Development Survey: A screening tool for delayed language development in toddlers. *Journal of Speech and Hearing Disorders, 54,* 587–599.

Reynolds, C. R., & Kamphaus, R. W. (1992). *Behavior Assessment System for Children*. Circle Pines, MN: American Guidance Service.

Reynolds, C. R., & Kamphaus, R. W. (1998). *Behavior Assessment System for Children: Manual*. Circle Pines, MN: American Guidance Service.

Reynolds, C. R., & Kamphaus, R. W. (2004). *Behavior Assessment System for Children—Second Edition (BASC-2)*. Circle Pines, MN: American Guidance Service.

Reynolds, C. R., & Richmond, B. (1985). *Revised Children's Manifest Anxiety Scale: Manual*. Los Angeles: Western Psychological Services.

Reynolds, C. R., & Richmond, B. O. (2000). *Revised Children's Manifest Anxiety Scale: Manual*. Los Angeles: Western Psychological Services.

Reynolds, W. M. (1987). *Suicidal Ideation Questionnaire (SIQ): Professional manual*. Odessa, FL: Psychological Assessment Resources.

Reynolds, W. M. (1989). *Reynolds Child Depression Scale: Professional manual*. Odessa, FL: Psychological Assessment Resources.

Reynolds, W. M. (2002). *Reynolds Adolescent Depression Scale: Professional manual* (2nd ed.). Lutz, FL: Psychological Assessment Resources.

Riccio, C. A., Hynd, G. W., & Cohen, M. J. (1996). Etiology and neurobiology of ADHD. In W. M. Bender (Ed.), *Understanding ADHD* (pp. 23–44). Upper Saddle River, NY: Merrill.

Riccio, C. A., Reynolds, C. R., & Lowe, P. A. (2001). *Clinical applications of continuous performance tests: Measuring attention and impulsive responding in children and adults*. New York: Wiley.

Richters, J. E. (1997). The Hubble hypothesis and the developmentalists' dilemma. *Development and Psychopathology, 9*(2), 193–229.

Ritvo, E. R., & Freeman, B. J. (1977). National Society for Autistic Children definition of the syndrome of autism. *Journal of Pediatric Psychology, 2,* 146–148.

Roberts, R. E., Lewinsohn, P. M., & Seeley, J. R. (1995). Symptoms of *DSM-III-R* major depression in adolescence: Evidence from an epidemiological survey. *Journal of the American Academy of Child and Adolescent Psychiatry, 34,* 1608–1617.

Robins, D. L., Fein, D., Barton, M. L., & Green, J. A. (2001). The Modified Checklist for Autism in Toddlers: An initial study investigating the early detection of autism and pervasive developmental disorders. *Journal of Autism and Developmental Disorders, 31,* 131–144.

Robins, L. N., & D. A., Regier (Eds.). (1991). *Psychiatric disorders in America: The Epidemiologic Catchment Area study.* New York: Free Press.

Roelveld, N., Zielhuis, G. A., & Gabreëls, F. (1997). The prevalence of mental retardation: A critical review of recent literature. *Developmental Medicine and Child Neurology, 39,* 125–132.

Rogers, P., & Adger, H. (1993). Alcohol and adolescence. *Adolescent Medicine: State of the Art Reviews, 4,* 295–304.

Rogers, S. J. (1998). Empirically supported comprehensive treatments for young children with autism. *Journal of Clinical Child Psychology, 27,* 168–179.

Roid, G. H. (2003a). *Stanford-Binet Intelligence Scales: Examiner's manual* (5th ed.). Itasca, IL Riverside.

Roid, G. H. (2003b). *Stanford-Binet Intelligence Scales: Technical manual* (5th ed.). Itasca, IL Riverside.

Roid, G. H., & Miller, L. (1997). *Leiter International Performance Scale—Revised.* Wood Dale, IL: Stoelting.

Rome, E. S., Ammerman, S., Rosen, D. S., Keller, R. J., Lock, J., Mammel, K. A., et al. (2003). Children and adolescents with eating disorders: The state of the art. *Pediatrics, 111,* 98–108.

Romer, D., & McIntosh, M. (2005). The roles and perspectives of school mental health professionals in promoting adolescent mental health. In D. L. Evans, E. B. Foa, R. E. Gur, H. Hendin, C. P. O'Brien, M. E. P. Seligman, et al. (Eds.), *Treating and preventing adolescent mental health disorders: What we know and what we don't know* (pp. 598–615). New York: Oxford University Press.

Root R. W., II, & Resnick, R. J. (2003). An update on the diagnosis and treatment of attention-deficit/hyperactivity disorder in children. *Professional Psychology: Research and Practice, 34*(1), 34–41.

Rosen, J. C., Vara, L., Wendt, S., & Leitenberg, H. (1990). Validity studies of the Eating Disorders Examination. *International Journal of Eating Disorders, 9,* 519–528.

Rosvold, H. E., Mirsky, A. F., Sarason, I., Bransome, E. D., & Beck, L. H. (1956). A continuous performance test of brain damage. *Journal of Consulting Psychology, 20,* 343–350.

Rotto, P. C. (1998). Traumatic brain injury. In L. Phelps (Ed.), *Health-related disorders in children and adolescents* (pp. 652–671). Washington, DC: American Psychological Association.

Rowe, C. L., Liddle, H. A., Greenbaum, P. E., & Henderson, C. E. (2004). Impact of psychiatric comorbidity on treatment of adolescent drug abusers. *Journal of Substance Abuse Treatment, 26,* 129–140.

Rowe, R., Maughan, B., Pickles, A., Costello, E. J., & Angold, A. (2002). The relationship between *DSM-IV* oppositional defiant disorder and conduct disorder: Findings from the Great Smoky Mountains Study. *Journal of Child Psychology and Psychiatry, 23,* 365–373.

Rutter, M. (1978). Diagnosis and definition of childhood autism. *Journal of Autism and Developmental Disorders, 8,* 139–161.

Rutter, M., & Sroufe, L. A. (2000). Developmental psychopathology: Concepts and challenges. *Development and Psychopathology, 12*(3), 265–296.

Sanchez, J., Miller, C. J., Garcia, M. A., & Hynd, G. W. (2004). Reading disabilities in children with attention-deficit hyperactivity disorder: Ecological factors as related to IQ of children. *Psycho-Lingua, 31*(2), 89–92.

Sattler, J. (1998). *Clinical and forensic interviewing of children and families: Guidelines for the mental health, education, pediatric, and child maltreatment fields.* San Diego, CA: Author.

Sax, L., & Kautz, K. J. (2003). Who first suggests the diagnosis of attention deficit/hyperactivity disorder? *Annals of Family Medicine, 1*(3), 171–174.

Scahill, L., Riddle, M. A., McSwiggin-Hardin, M., Ort, S. I., King, R. A., Goodman, W. K., et al. (1997). Children's Yale-Brown Obsessive Compulsive Scale: Reliability and validity. *Journal of the American Academy of Child and Adolescent Psychiatry, 36,* 844–852.

Scahill, L., Schwab-Stone, M., Merikangas, K. R., Leckman, J. F., Zhang, H., & Kasl, S. (1999). Psychosocial and clinical correlates of ADHD in a community sample of school-age children. *Journal of the American Academy of Child and Adolescent Psychiatry, 38,* 976–984.

Schoemaker, C., van Strien, T., & van der Staak, C. (1994). Validation of the Eating Disorders Inventory in a nonclinical population using transformed and untransformed responses. *International Journal of Eating Disorders, 15,* 387–393.

Schopler, E., Mesibov, G., & Kunce, L. J. (Eds.). (1998). *Asperger syndrome or high-functioning autism?* New York: Plenum Press.

Schopler, E., Reichler, R. J., & Renner, B. R. (1988). *The Childhood Autism Rating Scale (CARS).* Los Angeles: Western Psychological Services.

Schrank, F. A., & Woodcock, R. W. (2001). *Woodcock-Johnson III Compuscore and Profiles Program* [Computer software]. Itasca, IL: Riverside.

Schroeder, C. S., & Gordon, B. N. (2002). *Assessment and treatment of childhood problems: A clinician's guide* (2nd ed.). New York: Guilford Press.

Scott, F. J., Baron-Cohen, S., Bolton, P., & Brayne, C. (2002). The CAST (Childhood Asperger Syndrome Test): Preliminary development of a UK screen for mainstream primary-school age children. *Autism, 6,* 9–31.

Scotti, J. R., & Morris, T. L. (2000). Diagnosis and classification. In M. Hersen & R. T. Ammerman (Eds.), *Advanced abnormal child psychology* (2nd ed., pp. 15–32). Mahwah, NJ: Erlbaum.

Semel, E., Wiig, E. H., & Secord, W. A. (1995). *Clinical evaluation of language fundamentals* (3rd ed.). San Antonio, TX: Harcourt Assessment.

Semrud-Clikeman, M. (2001). *Traumatic brain injury in children and adolescents: Assessment and intervention.* New York: Guilford Press.

Serpell, L., & Troop, N. (2003). Psychological factors. In J. Treasure, U. Schmidt, & E. V. Furth (Eds.), *Handbook of eating disorders* (2nd ed., pp. 151–167). Chichester, West Sussex, England: Wiley.

Shaffer, D., Fisher, P., Lucas, C. P., Dulcan, M. K., & Schwab-Stone, M. E. (2000). NIMH Diagnostic Interview Schedule for Children Version IV (NIMH DISC-IV): Description of the differences from previous versions, and reliability of some common diagnoses. *Journal of the American Academy of Child and Adolescent Psychiatry, 39,* 28–38.

Shaffer, D., Pfeffer, C. R., & Work Group on Quality Issues. (2001). Practice parameter for the assessment and treatment of children and adolescents with suicidal behavior. *Journal of the American Academy of Child and Adolescent Psychiatry, 40*(Suppl.), S24–S51.

Shaw, D. S., Gilliom, M., Ingoldsby, E. M., & Nagin, D. S. (2003). Trajectories leading to school-age conduct problems. *Developmental Psychology, 39,* 189–200.

Shea, V. (1993). Interpreting results to parents of preschool children. In E. Schopler, M. E. VanBourgondien, & M. M. Bristol (Eds.), *Preschool issues in autism* (pp. 185–198). New York: Plenum Press.

Shepard, L. A. (1989). Identification of mild handicaps. In R. L. Linn (Ed.), *Educational measurement* (3rd ed.). New York: Macmillan.

Sherman, D. K., Iacono, W. G., & Donnelly, J. M. (1995). Development and validation of Body Rating Scales for adolescent females. *International Journal of Eating Disorders, 18,* 327–333.

Shisslak, C. M., & Crago, M. (2001). Risk and protective factors in the development of eating disorders. In J. K. Thompson & L. Smolak (Eds.), *Body image, eating disorders, and obesity in youth: Assessment, prevention, and treatment* (pp. 103–125). Washington, DC: American Psychological Association.

Siegel, L. S. (1999). Issues in the definition and diagnosis of learning disabilities: A perspective on *Guckenberger v. Boston University. Journal of Learning Disabilities, 32*(4), 304–319.

Silverman, W. K., & Albano, A. M. (1996). *Anxiety Disorders Interview Schedule for Children for* DSM-IV: *Child and Parent Versions.* San Antonio, TX: Psychological Corporation/Graywind Publications Incorporated.

Silverman, W. K., & Ollendick, T. H. (2005). Evidence-based assessment of anxiety and its disorders in children and adolescents. *Journal of Clinical Child and Adolescent Psychology, 34,* 380–411.

Silverman, W. K., Saavedra, L. M., & Pina, A. A. (2001). Test-retest reliability of anxiety symptoms and diagnoses with the Anxiety Disorders Interview Schedule for *DSM-IV:* Child and Parent Versions. *Journal of the American Academy of Child and Adolescent Psychiatry, 40,* 937–944.

Simpson, J. A., & Weiner, E. S. C. (Eds.). (1989). *The Oxford English dictionary* (2nd ed.). New York: Oxford University Press.

Skinner, H. A. (1981). Toward the integration of classification theory and methods. *Journal of Abnormal Psychology, 90,* 68–87.

Smith, J. J., & Graden, J. L. (1998). Fetal alcohol syndrome. In L. Phelps (Ed.), *Health-related disorders in children and adolescents* (pp. 68–73). Washington, DC: American Psychological Association.

South, M., Williams, B. J., McMahon, W. M., Owley, T., Filipek, P. A., Shernoff, E., et. al. (2002). Utility of the Gilliam Autism Rating Scale in research and clinical populations. *Journal of Autism and Developmental Disorders, 32,* 593–599.

Sparrow, S. S., Balla, D. A., & Cicchetti, D. V. (1984). *Vineland Adaptive Behavior Scales* (Interview ed., survey form manual). Circle Pines, MN: American Guidance Service.

Speece, D. L. (1995). Cluster analysis in perspective. *Exceptionality, 5*(1), 31–44.

Speece, D. L., & Cooper, D. H. (1991). Retreat, regroup, or advance? An agenda for empirical classification research in learning disabilities. In L. V. Feagans, E. J. Short, & L. J. Meltzer (Eds.), *Subtypes of learning disabilities: Theoretical perspectives and research* (pp. 33–52). Hillsdale, NJ: Erlbaum.

Spruill, J., & Black, S. (2001). Assessment of children's intelligence. In C. E. Walker & M. C. Roberts (Eds.), *Handbook of clinical child psychology* (pp. 111–123). New York: Wiley.

Sroufe, L. A. (1997). Psychopathology as an outcome of development. *Developmental Psychopathology, 9*(2), 251–268.

Sroufe, L. A., & Rutter, M. (1984). The domain of developmental psychopathology. *Child Development, 55,* 17–29.

Stanovich, K. (1999). The sociopsychometrics of learning disabilities. *Journal of Learning Disabilities, 32*(4), 304–319.

Stanovich, K. (2005). The future of a mistake: Will discrepancy measurement continue to make the learning disabilities field a pseudoscience? *Learning Disability Quarterly, 28*(2), 103–106.

Stanovich, K., & Siegel, L. S. (1994). Phenotypic performance profile of children with reading disabilities: A regression-based test of the phonological-core variable-difference model. *Journal of Educational Psychology, 86,* 24–53.

Stark, K. D., & Laurent, J. (2001). Joint factor analysis of the Children's Depression Inventory and the Revised Children's Manifest Anxiety Scale. *Journal of Clinical Child Psychology, 30,* 552–567.

Steer, R. A., Kumar, G., Beck, A. T., & Beck, J. S. (2005). Dimensionality of the Beck Youth Inventories with child psychiatric outpatients. *Journal of Psychopathology and Behavioral Assessment, 27,* 123–131.

Sternberg, R. J. (1988). *The triarchic theory of mind: A new theory of human intelligence.* New York: Penguin.

Steubing, K. K., Fletcher, J. M., LeDoux, J. M., Lyon, G. R., Shaywitz, S. E., & Shaywitz, B. A. (2002). Validity of IQ/discrepancy classifications of reading disabilities: A meta-analysis. *American Educational Research Journal, 39,* 469–518.

Stone, W. L., Coonrod, E. E., & Ousley, O. Y. (2000). Brief report: Screening tool for autism in 2-year-olds (STAT): Development and preliminary data. *Journal of Autism and Developmental Disorders, 30,* 607–612.

Stone, W. L., & Hogan, K. L. (1993). A structured parent interview for identifying young children with autism. *Journal of Autism and Developmental Disorders, 23,* 639–652.

Storch, E. A., Murphy, T. K., Geffken, G. R., Bagner, D. M., Soto, O., Sajid, M., et al. (2005). Factor analytic study of the Children's Yale-Brown Obsessive-Compulsive Scale. *Journal of Clinical Child and Adolescent Psychology, 34,* 312–319.

Storch, E. A., Murphy, T. K., Geffken, G. R., Soto, O., Sajid, M., Allen, P., et al. (2004). Psychometric evaluation of the Children's Yale-Brown Obsessive-Compulsive Scale. *Psychiatry Research, 129,* 91–98.

Stovall, D. L. (2001). Review of the Children's Depression Rating Scale (Rev. ed.). In B. S. Plake & J. C. Impara (Eds.), *The fourteenth mental measurements yearbook* (pp. 253–255). Lincoln, NE: Buros Institute of Mental Measurements.

Sudhalter, V., & Belser, R. C. (2001). Conversational characteristics of children with Fragile X syndrome: Tangential language. *American Journal on Mental Retardation, 106,* 389–400.

Swanson, J. M. (1992). *School-based assessments and interventions for ADD students.* Irvine, CA: K.C. Publications.

Sweet, R., & Saules, K. K. (2003). Validity of the Substance Abuse Subtle Screening Inventory—Adolescent Version (SASSI-A). *Journal of Substance Abuse Treatment, 24,* 331–340.

Szatmari, P., Archer, L., Fishman, S., Streiner, D. L., & Wilson, F. (1995). Asperger's syndrome and autism: Differences in behavior, cognition, and adaptive functioning. *Journal of the American Academy of Child and Adolescent Psychiatry, 42,* 1662–1671.

Szymanski, L., & King, B. H. (1999). Practice parameters for the assessment and treatment of children, adolescents, and adults with mental retardation and comorbid mental disorders. *Journal of the American Academy of Child and Adolescent Psychiatry, 38*(Suppl.), S5–S31.

Tackett, J. L., Krueger, R. F., Sawyer, M. G., & Graetz, B. W. (2003). Subfactors of *DSM-IV* conduct disorder: Evidence and connections with syndromes from the Child Behavior Checklist. *Journal of Abnormal Child Psychology, 31,* 647–654.

Tallent, N. (1999). *Psychological report writing* (4th ed.). Englewood Cliffs, NJ: Prentice Hall.

Tanofsky-Kraff, M., Morgan, C. M., Yanovski, S. Z., Marmarosh, C., Wilfley, D. E., & Yanovski, J. A. (2003). Comparison of assessments of children's eating-disordered behaviors by interview and questionnaire. *International Journal of Eating Disorders, 33,* 213–224.

Tarter, R. E. (1990). Evaluation and treatment of adolescent substance abuse: A decision tree method. *American Journal of Drug and Alcohol Abuse, 16,* 1–46.

Tarter, R. E., Kirisci, L., & Mezzich, A. (1997). Multivariate typology of adolescents with alcohol use disorder. *American Journal on Addictions, 6,* 150–158.

Tarter, R. E., Laird, S. B., Bukstein, O., & Kaminer, Y. (1992). Validation of the Adolescent Drug Use Screening Inventory: Preliminary findings. *Psychology of Addictive Behaviors, 6*(4), 233–236.

Tate, A. (1993). Schooling. In B. Lask & R. Bryant-Waugh (Eds.), *Childhood onset anorexia nervosa and related eating disorders* (pp. 233–248). Hove, England: Erlbaum.

Teasdale, G., & Jennett, B. (1976). Assessment and prognosis of coma after head injury. *Acta Neurochirurgica, 34,* 45–55.

Teeter, P. A., & Semrud-Clikeman, M. (1997). *Child neuropsychology: Assessment and interventions for neurodevelopmental disorders.* Needham Heights, MA: Allyn & Bacon.

Thompson, J. R., McGrew, K. S., & Bruininks, R. H. (1999). Adaptive and maladaptive behavior: Structural and functional characteristics. In R. L. Schalock (Ed.), *Adaptive behavior and its measurement: Implications for the field of mental retardation* (pp. 15–42). Washington, DC: American Association on Mental Retardation.

Thompson, R. J., Kronenberger, W., & Curry, J. F. (1989). Behavior classification system for children with developmental, psychiatric, and chronic medical problems. *Journal of Pediatric Psychology, 14,* 559–575.

Thorndike, R. L., Hagen, E. P., & Sattler, J. M. (1986). *Technical manual for the Stanford-Binet Intelligence Scales* (4th ed.). Chicago: Riverside.

Toshiaki, F., Awaji, R., Nakazato, H., & Sumita, Y. (1995). Predictive validity of subtypes of chronic affective disorders derived by cluster analysis. *Acta Psychiatrica Scandinavica, 91,* 379–385.

Towbin, K. F. (1997). Pervasive developmental disorder not otherwise specified. In D. J. Cohen & F. R. Volkmar (Eds.), *Handbook of autism and pervasive developmental disorders* (2nd ed., pp. 123–147). New York: Wiley.

Treasure, J. (1998). *Anorexia nervosa: A survival guide for families, friends, and sufferers.* Hove, England: Psychology Press.

Treffert, D. A. (1988). The idiot savant: A review of the syndrome. *American Journal of Psychiatry, 145,* 563–572.

van Lier, P. A. C., Verhulst, F. C., van der Ende, J., & Crijnen, A. A. M. (2003). Classes of disruptive behaviour in a sample of young elementary school children. *Journal of Child Psychology and Psychiatry and Applied Disciplines, 44,* 377–387.

Vellutino, F., Fletcher, J., Snowling, M., & Scanlon, D. (2004). Specific reading disability (dyslexia): What have we learned in the past 4 decades? *Journal of Child Psychology and Psychiatry, 45,* 2–40.

Vellutino, F., Scanlon, D., & Lyon, G. (2000). Differentiating between difficult to remediate and readily remediated poor readers. *Journal of Learning Disabilities, 33,* 223–238.

Vellutino, F., Scanlon, D., Sipay, E., Small, S., Pratt, A., Chen, R., et al. (1996). Cognitive profiles of difficult-to-remediate and readily remediated poor readers: Early interventions as a vehicle for distinguishing between cognitive and experiential deficits as basic causes of specific reading disability. *Journal of Educational Psychology, 88,* 601–638.

Verduin, T. L., & Kendall, P. C. (2003). Differential occurrence of comorbidity within childhood anxiety disorders. *Journal of Clinical Child and Adolescent Psychology, 32,* 290–295.

Verhulst, F. C., Koot, H. M., & Van der Ende, J. (1994). Differential predictive value of parents' and teachers' reports of children's problem behaviors: A longitudinal study. *Journal of Abnormal Child Psychology, 22,* 531–546.

Vermunt, J. K & Magidson, J. (2002). Latent class cluster analysis. In J. A. Hagenaars & A. L. McCutcheon (Eds.), *Applied latent class models* (pp. 89–106). Cambridge, England: Cambridge University Press.

Veron-Guidry, S., & Williamson, D. A. (1996). Development of a body image assessment procedure for children and preadolescents. *International Journal of Eating Disorders, 20,* 287–293.

Vitacco, M. J., Rogers, R., & Neumann, C. S. (2003). The antisocial process screening device: An examination of its construct and criterion-related validity. *Assessment, 10,* 143–150.

Volkmar, F. R., Carter, A., Sparrow, S. S., & Cicchetti, D. V. (1993). Quantifying social development in autism. *Journal of the American Academy of Child and Adolescent Psychiatry, 32,* 627–632.

Volkmar, F. R., Cook, E. H., Pomeroy, J., Realmuto, G., & Tanguay, P. (1999). Practice parameters for the assessment and treatment of children, adolescents, and adults with autism and other pervasive developmental disorders. *Journal of the American Academy of Child and Adolescent Psychiatry, 38*(Suppl.), 32S–54S.

Volpe, R. J., & DuPaul, G. J. (2001). Assessment with brief behavior rating scales. In J. W. Andrews & D. H. Saklofske (Eds.), *Handbook of psychoeducational assessment: Ability, achievement, and behavior in children* (pp. 357–387). San Diego, CA: Academic Press.

Waddington, C. H. (1971). Concepts of development. In L. R. Aronson, E. Shaw, & E. Tobach (Eds.), *Biopsychology of development* (pp. 17–23). New York: Academic Press.

Wakefield, J. C., Pottick, K. J., & Kirk, S. A. (2002). Should the *DSM-IV* diagnostic criteria for conduct disorder consider social context? *American Journal of Psychiatry, 159,* 380–386.

Wallander, J. L., Dekker, M. C., & Koot, H. M. (2003). Psychopathology in children and adolescents with intellectual disability: Measurement, prevalence, course, and risk. In L. M. Glidden (Ed.), *International review of research in mental retardation* (Vol. 26, pp. 93–134). New York: Academic Press.

Wangby, M., Bergman, L. R., & Magnusson, D. (1999). Development of adjustment problems in girls: What syndromes emerge? *Child Development, 70*(3), 678–699.

Warchausky, S., Kewman, D. G., Bradley, A., & Dixon, P. (2003). Pediatric neurological conditions: Brain and spinal cord injury and muscular dystrophy. In M. C. Roberts (Ed.), *Handbook of pediatric psychology* (pp. 375–391). New York: Guilford Press.

Wechsler, D. (1939). *Wechsler-Bellevue Intelligence Scale.* New York: Psychological Corporation.

Wechsler, D. (1958). *The measurement and appraisal of adult intelligence* (4th ed.). Baltimore: Williams & Wilkins.

Wechsler, D. (1981). *Manual for the Wechsler Adult Intelligence Scale* (Rev. ed.). San Antonio, TX: Psychological Corporation.

Wechsler, D. (1991). *Manual for the Wechsler Intelligence Scale for Children* (3rd ed.). San Antonio, TX: Psychological Corporation.

Wechsler, D. (1997a). *Administration and scoring manual for the Wechsler Adult Intelligence Scale* (3rd ed.). San Antonio, TX: Psychological Corporation.

Wechsler, D. (1997b). *Technical manual for the Wechsler Adult Intelligence Scale* (3rd ed.) and the *Wechsler Memory Scale* (3rd ed.). San Antonio, TX: Psychological Corporation.

Wechsler, D. (1999). *Manual for the Wechsler Abbreviated Scale of Intelligence.* San Antonio, TX: Psychological Corporation.

Wechsler, D. (2002a). *Administration and scoring manual for the Wechsler Preschool and Primary Scale of Intelligence* (3rd ed.). San Antonio, TX: Psychological Corporation.

Wechsler, D. (2002b). *Technical and interpretive manual for the Wechsler Preschool and Primary Scale of Intelligence* (3rd ed.). San Antonio, TX: Psychological Corporation.

Wechsler, D. (2003a). *Administration and scoring manual for the Wechsler Intelligence Scale for Children* (4th ed.). San Antonio, TX: Psychological Corporation.

Wechsler, D. (2003b). *Technical and interpretive manual for the Wechsler Intelligence Scale for Children* (4th ed.). San Antonio, TX: Psychological Corporation.

Weinberg, M. Z., Rahdert, E., Colliver, J. D., & Glantz, M. D. (1998). Adolescent substance abuse: A review of the past 10 years. *Journal of the American Academy of Child and Adolescent Psychiatry, 37*(3), 252–261.

Weiss, B., & Garber, J. (2003). Developmental differences in the phenomenology of depression. *Development and Psychopathology, 15,* 403–430.

Wenar, C. (1961). The reliability of mothers' histories. *Child Development, 32,* 491–500.

Westen, D., Heim, A. K., Morrison, K., Patterson, M., & Campbell, L. (2002). Simplifying diagnosis using a prototype-matching approach: Implications for the next edition of the *DSM.* In L. Beutler & M. Malik (Eds.), *Rethinking the DSM: Psychological perspectives* (pp. 221–250). Washington, DC: American Psychological Association.

Whitmore, E. A., Mikulich, S. K., Thompson, L. L., Riggs, P. D., Aarons, G. A., & Crowley, T. J. (1997). Influences on adolescent substance dependence: Conduct disorder, depression, attention deficit hyperactivity disorder, and gender. *Drug and Alcohol Dependence, 47,* 87–97.

Widiger, T. A. (1992). Categorical versus dimensional classification: Implications from and for research. *Journal of Personality Disorders, 6*(4), 287–300.

Wilson, G. T., Becker, C. B., & Heffernan, K. (2003). Eating disorders. In E. J. Mash & R. A. Barkley (Eds.), *Child psychopathology* (2nd ed., pp. 687–715). New York: Oxford University Press.

Wilson, G. T., Heffernan, K., & Black, C. M. D. (1996). Eating disorders. In E. J. Mash & R. A. Barkley (Eds.), *Child psychopathology* (pp. 541–571). New York: Guilford Press.

Winston, A., & Webster, P. (2003). Inpatient treatment. In J. Treasure, U. Schmidt, & E. V. Furth (Eds.), *Handbook of eating disorders* (2nd ed., pp. 349–367). Chichester, West Sussex, England: Wiley.

Winters, K. C. (2001). Assessing adolescent substance use problems ad other areas of functioning: State of the art. In P. M. Monti, S. M. Colby, & T. A. O'Leary (Eds.), *Adolescents, alcohol, and substance abuse: Reaching teens through brief intervention* (pp. 80–108). New York: Guilford Press.

Winters, K. C., Latimer, W., & Stinchfield, R. D. (1999). The *DSM-IV* criteria for adolescent alcohol and cannabis use disorders. *Journal of Studies on Alcohol, 60,* 337–344.

Winters, N. C., Myers, K., & Proud, L. (2002). Ten-year review of rating scales: Pt. III. Scales assessing suicidality, cognitive style, and self-esteem. *Journal of the American Academy of Child and Adolescent Psychiatry, 41,* 1150–1181.

Wittchen, H. U. (1996). What is comorbidity: Fact or artefact? *British Journal of Psychiatry, 168,* 7–8.

Wolper, C., Heshka, S., & Heymsfield, S. B. (1995). Measuring food intake: An overview. In D. B. Allison (Ed.), *Handbook of assessment methods for eating behaviors and weight-related problems: Measures, theory, and research* (pp. 215–240). London: Sage.

Woodcock, R. W., McGrew, K. S., & Mather, N. (2001). *Woodcock-Johnson III.* Itasca, IL: Riverside.

World Health Organization. (1992). *International classification of diseases and related health problems* (10th ed.). Geneva, Switzerland: Author.

World Health Organization. (1993). *The ICD-10 classification of mental and behavioural disorders: Diagnostic criteria for research.* Geneva, Switzerland: Author.

Yeates, K. O. (2000). Closed-head injury. In K. O. Yeates, M. D. Ris, & H. G. Taylor (Eds.), *Pediatric neuropsychology: Research, theory, and practice* (pp. 93–115). New York: Guilford Press.

Young, S. E., Corley, R. P., Stallings, M. C., Rhee, S. H., Crowley, T. J., & Hewitt, J. K. (2002). Substance abuse and dependence in adolescence: Prevalence, symptom profiles and correlates. *Drug and Alcohol Dependence, 68,* 309–322.

Youse, K. M., Le, K. N., Cannizzaro, M. S., & Coelho, C. A. (2002, June 25). Traumatic brain injury: A primer for professionals. *ASHA Leader.*

Zametkin, A. J., & Rapoport, J. L. (1987). Neurobiology of attention-deficit disorder with hyperactivity: Where have we come in 50 years? *Journal of the American Academy of Child and Adolescent Psychiatry, 26,* 676–686.

Author Index

Subject Index